31st Pacific Asia Conference on Language, Information and Computation 2017 (PACLIC 31)

Cebu City, Philippines
16 – 18 November 2017

Editor:

Rachel Edita Roxas

ISBN: 978-1-5108-6725-3

PACLIC 31

Proceedings of the 31st Pacific Asia Conference on Language, Information and Computation

November 16-18, 2017
University of the Philippines Cebu
Cebu City, Philippines

Rachel Edita Roxas
Editor

Foreword

It is with great pride that the Philippines hosted the 31st Pacific Asia Conference on Language, Information and Communication (or PACLIC) from November 16 to 18, 2017 held at the University of the Philippines Cebu.

A warm welcome to all the participants from over the world who came to exchange knowledge and ideas on language. Following the long tradition of PACLIC conferences, PACLIC 31 (2017) emphasizes the synergy of theoretical frameworks and processing of natural language, providing a forum for researchers from different fields to share and discuss progress in scientific studies, development and application of the topics related to the study of languages. Included in the proceedings are 2 keynote speeches, 3 invited talks, 26 oral papers, and 22 poster papers.

Thank you to our organizers. Our local organizer, University of the Philippines Cebu headed by Chancellor Atty Liza D. Corro and her able team. And our other organizers namely: National University (Philippines), the Computing Society of the Philippines – Special Interest Group on Natural Language Processing, and the Linguistic Society of the Philippines.

Gratitude is also expressed to our conference co-chairs who have labored towards the successful implementation of this conference: Robert Roxas of University of the Philippines Cebu, Nathaniel Oco of National University, and Shirley Dita of De La Salle University. We express our thanks to the members of our Program Committee who reviewed the many papers that were submitted to us.

Warm gratitude is also extended to our sponsors who willingly gave their support to this event.

To those who worked behind the scenes to make this conference possible, I would also like to extend my heartfelt thanks and until we host PACLIC in the Philippines again.

Rachel Edita Roxas
Conference Chair, PACLIC 31 (2017)

Steering Committee

Hee-Rahk Chae, Hankuk University of Foreign Studies
Chu-Ren Huang, Hong Kong Polytechnic University
Rachel Edita O. Roxas, National University (Philippines)
Maosong Sun, Tsinghua University
Benjamin T'sou, City University of Hong Kong
Kei Yoshimoto, Tohoku University
Min Zhang, Soochow University

Conference Chair

Rachel Edita Roxas, National University (Philippines)

Co-Chairs

Robert Roxas, University of the Philippines Cebu
Nathaniel Oco, National University (Philippines)
Shirley Dita, De La Salle University

Local Organizing Committee

Dhong Fhel Gom-os, University of the Philippines Cebu
Rubelito Abella, University of the Philippines Cebu
Maricris Camatang, University of the Philippines Cebu
Michelle Rodriguez, University of the Philippines Cebu

Program Committee

Shirley Dita, De La Salle University (co-chair)
Qin Lu, Hong Kong Polytechnic University (co-chair)
Alice Mae Arbon, Silliman University
Aireen Arnuco, De La Salle University
Stephane Bressan, National University of Singapore
Hee-Rahk Chae, Hankuk University of Foreign Studies
Kuang-Hua Chen, National Taiwan University
Hsin-Hsi Chen, National Taiwan University
Jin-Woo Chung, Korea Advanced Institute of Science and Technology
Siaw-Fong Chung, National Chengchi University
Guohong Fu, Heilongjiang University
Helena Hong Gao, Nanyang Technological University
Wei Gao, Qatar Computing Research Institute
Yasunari Harada, Waseda University
Choochart Haruechaiyasak, National Electronics and Computer Technology Center
Munpyo Hong, Sungkyunkwan University
Jong-Bok Kim, Kyung Hee University
Mac Kim, Commonwealth Scientific and Industrial Research Organisation's Data61
Oi Yee Kwong, Chinese University of Hong Kong
Yong-Hun Lee, Chungnam National University
Dongsik Lim, Hongik University
Erlyn Manguilimotan, Weathernews, Inc.
Miren Morales, De La Salle University
Yoshiki Mori, Universiy of Tokyo
Natchanan Natpratan, Kasetsart University
Ponrudee Netisopakul, King Mongkut's Institute of Technology Ladkrabang
Robertus Nugroho, Commonwealth Scientific and Industrial Research Organisation's Data61
Nathaniel Oco, National University (Philippines)
Chutamanee Onsuwan, Thammasat University
Ryo Otoguro, Waseda University
Cecile Paris, Commonwealth Scientific and Industrial Research Organisation
Jong Park, Korea Advanced Institute of Science and Technology
Rodolfo Raga, Jose Rizal University
Robert Roxas, University of the Philippines Cebu
Rachel Edita Roxas, National University (Philippines)
Samira Shaikh, University of North Carolina at Charlotte
Virach Sornlertlamvanich, Thammasat University
Keh-Yih Su, Academia Sinica
Michael Tanangkingsing, National Taiwan University
Aline Villavicencio, Federal University of Rio Grande do Sul
Chang Xu, Commonwealth Scientific and Industrial Research Organisation's Data61
Cheng-Zen Yang, Yuan Ze University
Satoru Yokoyama, Chiba Institute of Science
Liang-Chih Yu, Yuan Ze University

Jiajun Zhang, Institute of Automation Chinese Academy of Sciences
Hai Zhao, Shanghai Jiao Tong University
Michael Zock, Centre Nationnal de la Recherche Scientifique

Table of Contents

Keynote and Invited Speakers

Modeling Answering Strategies for the Polar Questions across Languages

Jong-Bok Kim
Kyung Hee University, Seoul
jongbok@khu.ac.kr

Abstract

This paper provides a discourse-based account of polar questions and answering particles. Arguing against syntax-based ellipsis analyses, the paper suggests that polarity particles are anaphoric in nature and their interpretation is determined by the antecedent evoked by the context. It also suggests that the parametric differences between the polarity-based (e.g., English, Swedish, German) and the truth-based answering system (e.g., Korean, Chinese, Japanese) have to do with the tight interactions between the anaphoric nature of answering particles and discourse.

1 Introduction

Polar questions and responses by answering particles like *yes* and *no* are everyday interactions between interlocutors in daily language uses (see, among others, Jones 1999, Holmberg 2016, Krifka 2013, Fretheim 2017):

(1) A: Are we invited?

  B: Yes. (=You are invited.)

  B′: No. (=You are not invited.)

(2) A: Aren't you tired today?

  B: (#)Yes. (=I am tired today.)

  B′: No. (=I am not tired today.)

The answering particle *yes* or *no* here serves as a proper response to the polar questions, assigning proposition-like meanings as given in the parentheses.

In addition to this analytic question of how a single particle induces a sentential interpretation, an ensuing question arises from language differences in the responses to negative questions. Consider the exchanges in (2) and corresponding Korean examples in the following (see Kim 2017):

(3) A: ne onul an phikonhay?
   you today not tired?
   'Aren't you tired today?'

  B: Ung. 'yes' (=I am not tired.)

  B′: Ani. 'no' (=I am tired today.)

As seen from the contrast between English and Korean, the meaning of *yes* differs. In English, the response *yes* confirms the positive proposition of the question while the corresponding *yes* in Korean confirms the negative proposition denoted by the question. Such a difference distinguishes the polarity-based answering system from the truth-based answering system (Jones 1999).

This paper tries to offer a discourse-based approach to account for these two as well as related questions. The paper argues that the propositional meaning of the answering particles is not derived from syntactic operations like movement-and-deletion. It rather has to do with the anaphoric nature of the answering particles (Ginzburg and Sag 2000, Farkas and Bruce 2010, Krifka 2013, Roelofsen and Farkas 2015). It also shows that the parametric differences between the two different types of answering system, the polarity-based system (e.g., English, Swedish, German) and the truth-based system (e.g., Korean, Chinese, Japanese), are due to tight interactions between the anaphoric nature of answer particles and discourse. The paper then shows how this

31st Pacific Asia Conference on Language, Information and Computation (PACLIC 31), pages 2–9
Cebu City, Philippines, November 16-18, 2017

intuitive idea can be modeled within the grammar of HPSG (Head-driven Phrase Structure Grammar).

2 Some key features in polar questions and responses

2.1 Parametric differences and language variations in polar questions

As noted in the beginning, there are four main ways of polar questions with responses. Each of the positive and negative polar questions can employ *yes* or *no* as their responses. These particles can be followed by an elliptical or full sentence, as seen from the following examples:

(4) Q: Belgian ba si Paul? (Tagalog)
          Belgian is   Paul
          'Is Paul Belgian?

    A: Oo, Belgian siya. 'Yes, he's Belgian.'

    A′:   Hindi', hindi' siya Belgian. 'No, he isn't Belgian.'

As seen earlier, parametric variations among languages come from responses to negative questions. Consider Swedish and Japanese examples (data from Holmberg 2016):

(5) Q: Är du inte troött? (Swedish)
          are you not tired
          'Are you not tired?'

    A: Nej (jag är inte trött)
          no I   am not tired
          'No (I'm not tired)'

(6) Q: kimi tukarete nai (Japanese)
          you tired   not
          'Are you not tired?'

    A: hai/un 'yes' (=I am not tired.)

As illustrated here, the key difference between the two languages is that in languages with the polarity system (e.g., Swedish), the negative particle *no* means the speaker's agreement with the negative proposition. However, in languages with the truth-based system (e.g., Japanese), it is the positive particle *yes* that is employed for the agreement with the negative proposition denoted by the negative question.

A complication arises in languages that allow three-valued responses to polar questions. Languages like Swedish, Danish, Norwegian, French, German, and Old English allow one negative response word and two affirmative particles. For instance, in Swedish, there are two positive answer particles, *ja* and *jo*, and one negative answer particle *nei*. The key difference between *ja* and *jo* lies in the presupposition of the polar question. Observe the following Swedish examples (data from Fretheim 2017):

(7) A: drack du inte upp ditt kaffe?
          drank you not up   your coffee
          'Did you not drink up your coffee?'

    B: nej. 'No. (I didn't.)

    B′   #ja.

    B″   jo. 'Yes. (I did.)

The polar question is negative, *ja* is not natural since it requires the antecedent to presuppose a positive polarity preposition, while *jo* is a proper one which intends to deny A's negative proposition.

In addition, note that answers to polar questions can vary. In particular, in languages like Korean and Finnish, polar questions can be answered by echoing the verb in the polar question:

(8) Q: ku chinkwu hakhoy-ey
          the friend   conference-to
          o-ass-e?
          come-PST-QUE
          'Did the friend come to the conference?'

    A: ung. o-ass-e.
          yes. come-PST-DECL
          'Yes. (They) came.'

    A′:   an o-ass-e.
          not come-PST-DECL
          '(They) didn't come.'

When the answer is a negative proposition, the prefix negator *an* is employed.

3 Syntax-based Analyses

3.1 Arguments for syntax-based analysis

The first key question in the analysis of answering systems to polar questions concerns how answering particles like *yes* and *no* can have sentential interpretations. Kramer and Rawlins (2011) and Holmberg (2013, 2016) suggest that the particles *yes* and *no* contain clausal structure that undergoes PF-deletion, assimilating them to elliptical constructions such as fragment answers. In particular, Holmberg (2016), adopting the movement-deletion approaches for elliptical constructions suggested by Merchant (2001, 2004) and subsequent work, suggests that the stand-alone answer particle as well as echoed verb are derived from clausal ellipsis as represented in the following:

(9) Q: Did the student come?

A: Yes. [~~The student came.~~]

A′: o-ass-e   [~~ku~~ haksayng
come-PST-DECL the student
~~t~~].(Korean)

'Yes. The student came.'

To insure answering particles to get the proper interpretations, Holmberg suggests that polar questions all introduce a polarity variable functioning as the head of PolP as given in (10):

(10) $[_{CP}$ Did$[\pm Pol]$ $[_{PolP}$ the student $[\pm Pol]$ $[_{VP}$ come]]]

Accepting Hamblin's (1973) view that polar questions are propositional abstracts (having the set of alternative propositions p and $\neg p$), Holmberg (2016) suggests that polar questions like (10) evoke the variable Pol with two possible values: (10) in turn then means 'What is the value of $[\pm pol]$ such that the student came?' The answer particle functions as binding the polarity variable:

(11) $[_{FocP}$ yes$[+Pol]$ $[_{PolP}$ ~~the student $[+Pol]$ $[_{VP}$ came]~~]]

The answer particle positioning in the Spec of Focus in the CP domain assigns either affirmative (for *yes*) or negative value (for *no*) to the polarity variable of the head Pol. The PolP then undergoes ellipsis, subject to the LF-identity condition between the antecedent and the elided part.

Holmberg's analysis offers a simple account for the examples including the one in (8) where the polarity value of the answering particles matches that of the polar question. Consider another matching example where a negative polar question is answered with the negative particle:

(12) Q: Isn't Alfonso coming to the party?

A: No. (= he isn't coming to the party?)

In Holmberg's analysis, the answer *no* carries the negative polarity value and thus assigns negative value to the head PolP. This yields a desired sentential interpretation.

3.2 Issues in syntax-based analyses

As just have earlier, the interplay of the syntactic constraints and ellipsis seems to work well for such cases, but one immediate question arises with respect to instances where the polarity value of the answer particle does not match with that of the putative antecedent linked to the polar question.

(13) Q: Does he drink coffee?

A: No (Nope). (=He doesn't drink coffee.)

(14) Q: Doesn't he drink coffee?

A: Yes, (he does).

For instance, the condition with the antecedent in (13) assigns a 'positive' value to the head of PolP because of the positive statement, but then there is a feature clash with the 'negative' value of the particle *no*. The escape hatch Holmberg (2016) adopts is that the negative feature of the negative particle is interpretable while the one in the putative clause is uninterpretable (because of its antecedent). In examples like (14), *yes* functions as an affirmative focus operator which has no variable to bind since the antecedent is already marked negative. The deletion of PolP would then give an unwanted interpretation. The suggested solution is to alternatively allow TP ellipsis under identity with TP of the antecedent.

Another issue arises from languages with three-valued response systems. As noted earlier, the Scandinavian languages (Swedish, Norwegian) as well as Indo-European languages like French and German have one negative answering particle and two positive ones. This three-valued system undermines the two-valued, syntactic analysis (e.g., Kramer and Rawlins 2011, Holmberg 2013, 2016) in which the deletion relies on the LF-identity between the antecedent of the polar question and the elided part. Consider the following French data (Ginzburg and Sag 2000):

(15) Q: est ce que Mimi est sérieuse?
'Is Mimi diligent?'

A: oui/non

(16) a.   est ce que Mimi n'est pas sérieuse
           'Isn't Mimi diligent?'

      A: *oui/si/non

As seen from the data, French has three answering particles: one negative particle *non* and two positive answering particles *oui* and *si*. The particle *oui* requires a positive discourse antecedent while *si* presupposes a negative one (see Ginzberg and Sag 2000 also). This indicates that the answering system needs to refer to discourse information.

Within this type of syntax-based ellipsis analysis, it is crucial to identify the linguistic antecedent linked to the answer. However, note examples like (17) where particle is used with exophoric antecedent (Tian and Ginzburg 2016):

(17)   (Context: A child is about to touch the
          socket.) Adult: No!

There is no syntactic identity condition that we can refer to here. It is not possible to identify any overt antecedent at syntax.

3.3 Language variations: polarity and truth-based systems

As we have seen earlier, with respect to answering negative polar questions, there are two different answering systems, polarity-based and truth-based ones. Holmberg (2013, 2016) attributes the difference of these two systems to different positions of negation in each language. Homlberg's key suggestion is three different types of negation across languages: high, middle, and low negation.

(18) $[_{CP}$ Foc not $[_{PolP}$ [±Pol] $[_{TP}$ ... $[_{NegP}$ not
        $[_{VP}$ not ...]]]]]

Holmberg suggests that in languages like Cantonese or Korean, the negation is assumed to be within a VP so that it does not affect the Pol value. That is, the particle answer *yes* with the interpretation of *yes, she is not diligent* would not cause any feature clash in the polarity value. Holmberg claims that with this low negation, negation is "distance enough from the unvalued sentential polarity head not to assign value to it'. However, in English, the negation in such a case is in high position, and *yes* cannot be linked

to the negative proposition: it must be linked to the positive proposition such that *yes she is diligent*.

Holmberg's system thus suggests that the language with the truth-based system has only low negation. However, in languages like Cantonese, Japanese, and Korean, there are surely examples where the negation is in high position, but still induces the truth-based system (Kim 2016). For instance, the negative copula *ani-ta* 'not-DECL' in Korean is clearly in the high position with respect to the main proposition in question:

(19) a.   Mimi-ka   pwucilenha-n kes   ani-ci?
           Mimi-NOM diligent-MOD thing not-QUE
           'Is it not the case that Mimi is diligent?'

      b.   Ung. 'Yes' (=Mimi is not diligent)

In this example, the negative copula combines with the clause of Mimi's being diligent. The clause introducer *kes* ensures the copula negation in the high position, but the affirmative answer just affirms the negative proposition.[1] Holmberg (2016: 199), recognizing such a problem for a similar example in Japanese, suggests that such an example involves the high negation as in English.

As the nature of the two answering systems tells us, in the polarity-based system, when the English speaker answers a polar question, the affirmative particle is linked to the truth of the situation under discussion (not the denotation of the polar question) while the negative one is linked to the falsity of the proposition denoted by the situation. Meanwhile, within the truth-based system, the affirmative particle affirms the denotation of the polar question (true or false situation) while the negative particle denies this denotation. This means that what matters is the anaphoric nature of answering particles in each language (mainly two types), not the position of the negation.

4 Modeling a discourse-based interactive approach

4.1 Base-generation and interpretation

The starting point of our analysis is to assume that polar questions and answers particles as response

---

[1] The expression *kes* in such an example is often taken to be a sentential nominalizer or complementizer. See Kim (2016).

involve no ellipsis but are generated 'as is'.[2] The stand-alone response particles obtain their interpretations on the basis of the surrounding context. In terms of semantics, polar questions are traditionally taken to introduce two propositions, one and the negation of the other (p and $\neg p$). The response particles *yes* and *no* confirm the truth of these two values (Hamblin 1973, Farkas and Bruce 2010, Krifka 2013, among others).

Different from the traditional view, we, following the idea of Ginzburg and Sag (2000), accept the view that questions are taken as propositional abstracts and polar questions are 0-ary proposition abstracts in which the set of abstracted elements is the empty set as given in (20a) (Ginzburg and Sag 2000, Kim 2016). The semantic content of polar questions can also be represented in terms of lambda calculus and simplified feature structures for the question *Is Mimi diligent?*:[3]

(20) a. Is Mimi diligent?

b. $\lambda \{\ \}[\text{diligent(m)}]$

c.
$$\left[\text{SEM} \begin{bmatrix} question \\ \text{PARAMS} \quad \{\ \} \\ \text{PROP} \begin{bmatrix} \text{QUANTS} \quad \langle\ \rangle \\ \text{NUCL} \quad [diligent(m)] \end{bmatrix} \end{bmatrix} \right]$$

Polar questions are thus treated uniformly in terms of an empty PARAMS (parameter) value, but asking the truth value of the propositional (PROP) meaning.[4]

As for the syntax of the isolated answer particle functioning as a response to the polar question, we follow the analyses of Ginzburg and Sag (2000) and take the particle as well as other short answers to be

a complete, non-sentential constituent. Expressions like *yes, maybe, probably, sure, right*, and so forth, can have stand-alone uses with a complete propositional meaning. These expressions behave like adverbials, but have a propositional semantic content, constructed from a polar question. An appropriate response will function as the propositional abstract, yielding the value p or its negation $\neg p$ (e.g., $\{r|\ \text{SimpleAns}(r, \lambda\{\ \}p)\}\ \{p, \neg p\}$). For example, the answer particle *yes* will have the following semantic contents:

(21)
$$\begin{bmatrix} \text{SYN} \quad \text{S} \\ \text{SEM} \quad [\text{ASSERT} \quad \boxed{1}] \\ \text{MAX-QUD} \begin{bmatrix} \text{PARAMS} \quad \{\ \} \\ \text{PROP}\,|\,\text{NUCL} \quad \boxed{1}[diligent(m)] \end{bmatrix} \end{bmatrix}$$

AdvP
$$\begin{bmatrix} \text{SYN} \quad [\text{POS} \quad adv] \\ \text{SEM} \quad [\text{ASSERT} \quad \boxed{1}] \end{bmatrix}$$

yes

As given here, the answering particle *yes*, functioning as an adverbial expression in the independent clause, represents a complete meaning identified with the propositional meaning of MAX-QUD (maximal question-under-discussion). The contextual information contains the attribute MAX-QUD, whose value is of type question and represents the question currently under discussion. The stand alone *no* will have the similar structure and semantic composition. The only difference lies in the semantics:

(22)
$$\begin{bmatrix} \text{SEM}[\text{ASSERT} \quad \neg\,\boxed{1}] \\ \text{DGB} \begin{bmatrix} \text{MAX-QUD} \begin{bmatrix} \text{PARAMS} \quad \{\ \} \\ \text{PROP}\,|\,\text{NUCL} \quad \boxed{1}[diligent(m)] \end{bmatrix} \end{bmatrix} \end{bmatrix}$$

The meaning of *yes*, as given in (21), is asserting the value $\boxed{1}$ which is identical with the propositional of the MAX-QUD, which is constructed from a polar question in the context. That

---

[2]Much of the analysis here is developed from Kim (2017).

[3]The message or an utterance denotes a *proposition, outcome, fact*, or *question*. For example, the content of the sentence *Mimi is diligent* is a proposition whose truth or falsity directly involves the real world. And the content of *whether Mimi is diligent* is a question which is resolved according to whether the proposition is true or false. By contrast, the meaning of an imperative sentence like *Leave on time!* makes reference to future outcomes involving the hearer's leaving while exclamative sentences like *What a nice hat you have!* denote a fact. See Ginzburg and Sag (2000) for details.

[4]The feature QUANTS take a list of quantifiers as value while the feature NUCL takes an element of type relation as its value.

is, the particle picks up the nucleus of the propositional meaning from the MAX-QUD and asserts it.
The particle *no* differs from *yes* in that its semantic
content is asserting the negative value of the propositional nucleus meaning that has no quantification
information.

4.2 Answering a negative question in the polarity-based system

The analysis for answering a negative question is not
different from the one for answering a positive question we have just seen. For instance, the semantic
content for *Isn't he gentle?* would be something like
the following:

(23) a. $\quad \lambda\{\quad\}[\neg gentle(i)]$

b.
$$\left[\text{SEM} \left[\begin{array}{l} question \\ \text{PARAMS} \quad \{\quad\} \\ \text{PROP} \left[\begin{array}{l} \text{QUANTS} \quad \langle \, not\text{-}rel \, \rangle \\ \text{NUCL} \quad [\, gentle(i)\,] \end{array} \right] \end{array} \right] \right]$$

Uttering such a negative question would evoke the
MAX-QUD to include a propositional meaning with
the quantification information. We have noted that
the semantic content of *yes* and *no* as a response to a
positive proposition is to confirm or disconfirm not
the propositional meaning, but the nucleus meaning
of the proposition, not referring to the quantification
information.

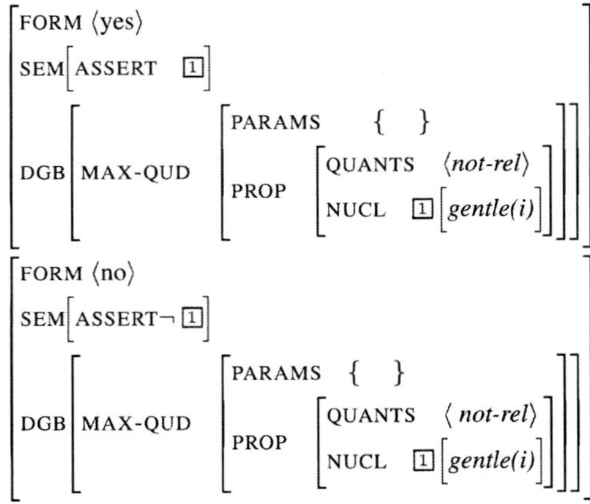

Figure 1: Semantic content of *yes* and *no*

As illustrated in Figure 1, the particle *yes* response
to the question affirms not the negative proposition

but just the truth value of the nucleus meaning [*gen-
tle(i)*]. Meanwhile, *no* in (20) disaffirms the nucleus meaning of [*gentle(i)*], eventually gives us the
propositional meaning such that he is not gentle.

4.3 Answering a negative question in the truth-based system

The head-final language Korean also uses answering
particles like *ung* 'yes' and *ani* 'no' as a response to
the polar question. As we have seen, a key difference from English arises from answers to a negative
question:

(24) A: i mwuncey elyep-ci anh-ci?
         this problem difficult-CONN not-QUE?
         'Isn't this problem difficult?'

    B: Ung. 'yes' (=It is not difficult.)

    B′: Ani. 'no' (=It is difficult.)

Different from English, the affirmative particle *ung*
'yes' confirms the negative proposition, not the positive proposition. That is, in the Korean system the
answer to a negative question confirms or discon-
firms the truth of the negative proposition, one key
property of the truth-based system.

The key claim of our proposal is that in the truth-
based system, answering particles refer to the propositional meaning including the QUANT information
while in the polarity-based system, answering particles refer to the nucleus meaning (equal to the
propositional meaning minus the quantification information). The answering particle *ung* 'yes' and
ani 'no' will thus have the information as given in
Figure 2.

As illustrated in Figure 2, the answering particle
ung 'yes' to the negative question asserts not the
value of the NUCL but the value of the proposition
(PROP) including the quantification value. This is
why the answer particle *yes* in Korean to the negative proposition means not 'This problem is difficult'
but affirms the proposition 'This problem is not difficult'. Meanwhile, the answer *ani* 'no' means discon-
firming the *not-rel* of the proposition 'The problem
is difficult'.

(25)   [ASSERT $\neg[\neg(\text{difficult}(m))]$]]

This means Korean, different from English, may allow a double negation interpretation. Of course, because of a heavy processing load, such an instance

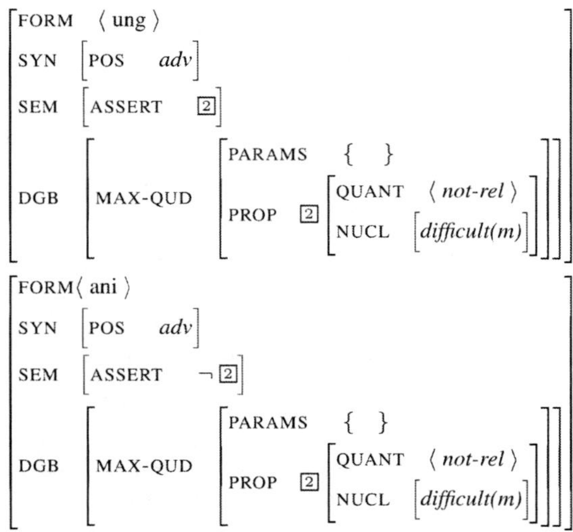

Figure 2: Semantic content of *ung* and *ani*

is not often used in authentic data (Roelofsen and Farkas 2015).

4.4 Some consequences

The present system is discourse-based since the information recorded in the QUD plays a key role. This implies that the propositional meaning of answering particles is constructed from a polar question in the context. The analysis then would have no difficulties in picking up a proper meaning of the answering particle in exophoric cases like (26), repeated here.

(26)   (Context: A child is about to touch the socket.) Adult: No!

There is no syntactic identity condition that we can refer to here. It is not possible to identify any overt antecedent at syntax. However, in our semantic/pragmatic-based system, the negative particle can mean that the speaker does affirm the negative value of the proposition such that the child touches the socket.

As noted earlier, in languages like Korean, an echoed verb can be a reply to a polar question:

(28) Q: ne cemsim mek-ess-ni?
           you lunch-PL eat-PST-QUE
           'Did you have lunch?'

     A: (ung) mek-ess-e.
           yes eat-PST-DECL
           'Yes, I had lunch.'

Holmberg (2016) suggests two different groups of the verb-echo system, one generated by the pro-drop plus VP ellipsis after the focus movement of the echoed-verb and the other by the so-called 'big ellipsis' which deletes a big constituent including the subject.

The first option would have a structure like the following for (28) (see Holmberg 2016: 75 for Thai)

(29)   [[IP ~~cemsim~~ [mek-ess-e$_i$ [VP ~~ne t$_i$~~]]]]

The verb *mek-ess-e* 'eat-PST-DECL' moves and adjoins to I, and the VP is deleted under identity the VP of the question with the pro-drop of the subject *ne* 'you'. This analysis is quite problematic for languages like Korean. For example, in Korean the echoed-verb answer is possible with the subject or object arguments being indefinite, which cannot be then pro-dropped:

(30) Q: haksayng yelye myeong
           student   several CL
           manna-ss-e?
           meet-PST-DECL
           'Did you meet several students?'

     A: manna-ss-e 'meet-PST-DECL'

It is prevalent that the subject of the polar question is indefinite with the echoed-verb reply.

Note that the DI approach we pursue here avoids such a problem since there is no derivational processes or invisible elements. Uttering the polar question in (27) would evoke the following MAX-QUD information:

As represented here, the question under discussion is whether the hearer ate lunch or not, and the answer here also represents this proposition. The response *mek-ess-e* 'eat-PST-DECL' confirms this proposition with the context providing the arguments for the predicate.

5 Conclusion

We have shown that stand-alone answer particles are just nonsentential utterances with anaphoric nature and their interpretations refer to the context in question. We have also seen that the main difference between the polarity-based and truth-based answering concerns whether the propositional anaphoric expressions refer to the propositional meaning including the negative quantification or to its nucleus meaning minus the quantification meaning. The former is the truth-based system (e.g., Korean) whereas the latter is the polarity-based system (e.g., English). Thus what matters in polarity answers is the 'anaphoric potential' of the polarity particle and the 'polarity sensitivity' of the question-under-discussion (QUD).

Acknowledgements

For helpful comments and discussion, I thank the conference participants including Hiroya Fujisaki, David Oshima, and Rachael Roxas. I also thank Incheol Choi, Jungsoo Kim, Okgi Kim, Joanna Nykiel, and Rok Sim for helpful comments. This work was supported by Global Research Network Program through the Ministry of Education of the Republic of Korea and the National Research Foundation of Korea (NRF-2017S1A2A2041092).

References

Farkas, Donka F., & Kim B. Bruce. 2010. On reacting to assertions and polar questions. *Journal of Semantics* 27: 81-118.

Fretheim, Thorstein. 2017. The pragmatics of 'yes' and 'no'. In Assimakopoulos, Stavros (ed.), *Pragmatics at its interfaces*, 175–200. Mouton: De Gruyter.

Ginzburg, Jonathan and Raquel Fernandez. 2010. Computational models of dialogue. In Clark, Alexander, Chris Fox, and Shalom Lappin (eds.), *Handbook of computational linguistics and natural language processing*, 429-481. Chichester, UK: Wiley-Blackwell.

Ginzburg, Jonathan and Ivan A. Sag. 2000. *Interrogative Investigations*. CSLI Publications, Stanford, CA.

Hamblin, Charles. 1973. Questions in Montague English. *Foundations of Language* 10(1): 41-53.

Holmberg, Anders. 2013. The syntax of answers to polar questions in English and Swedish. *Lingua* 128: 31-50.

Holmberg, Anders. 2016. *The syntax of Yes and No.* Oxford University Press.

Jones, Bob Morris. 1999. *The Welsh Answering System.* Berlin: Mouton de Gruyter.

Kim, Jong-Bok. 2016. *The Syntactic Structures of Korean: A Construction Grammar Perspective.* Cambridge University Press.

Kim, Jong-Bok. 2017. On the Anaphoric Nature of Particle Responses to the Polar Questions in English and Korean. *Korean Journal of Linguistics* 42(2): 153-177.

Kramer, Ruth and Kyle Rawlins. 2011. Polarity particles: An ellipsis account. In Proceedings of *the 39th Annual Meeting of the North East Linguistic Society*, 479-492.

Krifka, Manfred. 2013. Response particles as propositional anaphors. In Proceedings of *the 23rd Semantics and Linguistic Theory Conference.*

Merchant, Jason. 2004. Fragments and ellipsis. *Linguistics and Philosophy* 27: 661-738.

Roelofsen, Floris and Donka Farkas. 2015. Polarity particle responses as a window onto the interpretation of questions and assertions. *Language* 91, 359-414.

Tian, Ye, and Ginzburg, Jonathan. 2016. "No, I AM": What are you saying no to? In *Sinn und Bedeutung* 21.

International Speech Communication Association Distinguished Lecture: Principles and Design of a System for Academic Information Retrieval based on Human-Machine Dialogue

Hiroya Fujisaki
University of Tokyo
`fujisaki@alum.mit.edu`

Abstract

With the rapid progress of computer technology and world-wide development of information networks, a vast amount of information is now being generated, published, and stored at a number of sites distributed all over the world. Such an affluence of information, however, is useless or may even become harmful unless one has a means for rapidly retrieving the information that it truly necessary and appropriate. Conventional systems for information retrieval, however, are not always easy to use for inexperienced users, and are neither efficient nor accurate. In many cases, it is difficult for the user to identify and express his/her intention precisely, and it is difficult also for the system to infer the user's intention correctly. These difficulties can be alleviated by introducing spoken dialogue between the user and the system. Furthermore, in conventional systems using keywords, the accuracy of retrieval is reduced by the existence of synonymy, polysemy and homonymy, as well as of unknown words. Still another shortcoming of conventional systems is the lack of ability for properly estimating the degree of relevance of a document to the user's query, as well as the lack of a proper viewpoint on the cost/performance of retrieval.

This talk describes the outcome of a successful Japanese national project conducted under the "Research-for-the-Future" program and led by the speaker as the principal investigator. The system is based on the following three original principles: (a) Dialogue Management based on both User and System Modeling (by introducing a novel type of interacting automaton), (b) Use of "Key Concepts" in information retrieval (including processing of polysemy, homonymy, and unknown words), and (c) Optimization of Retrieval Performance through Relevance Score Estimation (by introducing a measure of relevance of search results based on users' judgments. The advantages of these novel principles have been demonstrated by a pilot system.

31st Pacific Asia Conference on Language, Information and Computation (PACLIC 31), page 10
Cebu City, Philippines, November 16-18, 2017

Assessing Authenticity in Media Englishes and the Englishes of Popular Culture

Andrew Moody
University of Macau, Macau
amoody@umac.mo

Abstract

'Authenticity' has long been a primary concern of sociolinguistic analyses. Early sociolinguistic work insisted that data collected should be 'spontaneous and naturally occurring', a methodological dictum that was, in large part, borrowed from dialectology's search for 'authentic' Englishes that were thought to be endangered by modernization and, later, urbanization. In many ways, authentic Englishes are imagined to represent both literally and imaginatively 'authentic identities' of the speakers of those languages. The emphasis on 'authentic' Englishes significantly coincides with the development across a number of English-speaking communities of a 'Standard Language Ideology', which promotes myths of 'purity' and 'timelessness' of the standard language. As standardized Englishes are usually adopted as media languages -- and frequently named after the media that use them, such as 'BBC English' or 'American Broadcast Standard' -- these media languages risk losing features that may signal 'authentic' language or identities. And the pursuit if authenticity in media Englishes is amplified in Englishes of pop culture, where authenticity must be manufactured as part of the process of creation. This essay will explore the historical basis for the processes that manufacture authenticity in English varieties as normal recurring process of standardization in a pluricentric model of world Englishes.

31st Pacific Asia Conference on Language, Information and Computation (PACLIC 31), page 11
Cebu City, Philippines, November 16-18, 2017

Corpus Linguistic Analysis for Language Planning

Joel Ilao
De La Salle University
`joel.ilao@dlsu.edu.ph`

Abstract

The Filipino language, the Philippines' national language, is based on the lingua franca of Manila, the nation's capital. It has shown rapid and significant changes in its vocabulary, orthography and grammar, thanks to the Philippines' rich colonial history and the conscious efforts in the national and institutional levels to standardize the grammar and orthography of the language. This fact is proof that the socio-political landscape of the times shapes the language of its people. In this talk, I will describe my forays in the analysis and processing of text corpora largely written in the Filipino language. Through corpus linguistic analysis of a historical text collected from various publication domains and genres, and covering approximately one century, I will illustrate some observable long-term and short-term trends in Filipino writers' writing styles, and conduct correlational analysis with some notable Philippine Socio-linguistic trends. Acknowledging that language plays a vital role in the formation of a national identity, and hence, should be cultivated towards intellectualization, I propose that ICT could effectively be used to monitor language usage and provide added insights for language planners, in understanding the interplay between language and socio-political developments. Thus, for this talk, I will also describe various ways by which corpora could automatically be harnessed and analyzed, and used to identify areas of language use that could be highlighted or further improved. Practical insights in large scale text analysis would also be provided; the depictions would all be drawn from my experiences as a corpus linguistic researcher.

31st Pacific Asia Conference on Language, Information and Computation (PACLIC 31), page 12
Cebu City, Philippines, November 16-18, 2017

Modality Markers in Cebuano and Tagalog

Michael Tanangkingsing
National Taipei University of Technology
`miguelntut@gmail.com`

Abstract

Philippine languages, which are predicate-initial, have "defective" verbs (coined by Pigafetta, n.d.) that are formal particles that occur at clause-initial position (like a predicate), lack inflection, and take a complement clause and that generally convey an epistemic stance. At the same time, there are also second-position modal enclitics that attach to the clause-initial predicate expressing epistemic attitude. Both topics, epistemic enclitics and "defective" verbs, have not been properly examined and investigated in Philippine languages primarily due to their peripheral and polysemous nature. Aside from enclitics and verbs, modality may occur in other forms too. In this talk, I shall present the forms and functions of the modal markers in two Philippine languages, Cebuano and Tagalog, as well as how they interact with each other, with pronominal enclitics and other particles, and with negation. In the process of such an investigation, a typology of Philippine languages will be developed in terms of modality features, such as those listed above. Furthermore, I will show current progress in the study of modality in Formosan languages and discuss how these efforts can inform and complement modality studies in Philippine languages. These will hopefully enable us to gain enough understanding of the issues and write up a grammar of modality in Philippine (and, hopefully, Formosan) languages.

31st Pacific Asia Conference on Language, Information and Computation (PACLIC 31), page 13
Cebu City, Philippines, November 16-18, 2017

Oral Papers

Between Reading Time and Information Structure

Masayuki Asahara
National Institute for Japanese Language and Linguistics,
National Institutes for the Humanities, Japan
`masayu-a@ninjal.ac.jp`

Abstract

This paper presents a contrastive analysis between the reading time and information structure in Japanese. We overlaid the reading time annotation BCCWJ-EyeTrack and an information structure annotation on the Balanced Corpus of Contemporary Written Japanese. Statistical analysis based on a mixed linear model showed that the "specificity," "sentience," and "commonness" of the Japanese information structure affect the reading time. These three characteristics produce different patterns of delay in the reading time. Especially, the reading time patterns differ depending on the commonness such as new information or bridging. The results suggest that new information and bridging can be classified by the reading time pattern.

1 Introduction

Information structures[1] such as definiteness and specificity affect the selection of articles. However, some languages such as Japanese and Russian do not have articles for noun phrases (NPs). The definiteness and specificity in such languages are not overtly marked in their surface form.

Nagata et al. (Nagata et al., 2005) proposed a statistical model to detect article errors made by English learners. They constructed the model by using an enormous text produced by English native speakers. However, when we consider the choice of articles in some languages by native speakers of a language with no articles, careful attention must be paid

___
[1]We focus on the information status which is a fundamental notion to define the *theme* and *rheme* in the information structure.

to the information structures in their NPs. Moreover, when texts in language without articles are translated by humans or machine translation systems into a target language with articles, we should consider the information structure of the source language.

Other aspects of information structures are the information status and commonness. The information status indicates whether the co-referred mention appears in the preceding discourse (`discourse-old`) or not (`discourse-new`). Commonness is defined as whether the speaker assumes that the hearer already knows the information (`hearer-old`), can estimate the information (`bridging`), or does not know the information `hearer-new`. Bridging reference cannot be resolved purely from the surface forms of written texts. Previous research (Hou et al., 2013) tried to resolve bridging references by using annotated corpora and world knowledge. However, bridging is an information structure for the language recipient (hearer). It should incorporate recipient features such as the reading time to estimate whether an NP is `bridging` or not (i.e., `hearer-new`). Moreover, identifying if readers can resolve a bridging reference with their own knowledge is important for user-oriented information extraction and document summarization.

These information structures are correlated with animacy, sentience, and agentivity. The features of information structures may affect the reading time; there are various ways to monitor the reading time, such as eye tracking to obtain gaze information.

This paper presents a contrastive analysis between the reading time and information structures in Japanese in order to classify information structures according to the gaze information. We over-

31st Pacific Asia Conference on Language, Information and Computation (PACLIC 31), pages 15–24
Cebu City, Philippines, November 16-18, 2017

laid the reading time annotation BCCWJ-EyeTrack (Asahara et al., 2016) and information structure annotation on the Balanced Corpus of Contemporary Written Japanese (BCCWJ) (Maekawa et al., 2014). We performed statistical analysis on the overlaid data. The results showed that different patterns of reading time can be observed to determine variations in the information structure.

2 Related Work

First, we present related work on eye tracking. The Dundee Eyetracking Corpus (Kennedy and Pynte, 2005) contains reading times for English and French newspaper editorials from 10 native speakers of each language that were recorded by using eye-tracking equipment. The corpus does not target a specific set of linguistic phenomena but instead provides naturally occurring texts for testing diverse hypotheses. For example, Demberg and Keller (Demberg and Keller, 2008) used the corpus to test Gibson's dependency locality theory (DLT) (Gibson, 2008) and Hale's surprisal theory (Hale, 2001). The corpus also allows for replications to be conducted; for example, Roland et al. (Roland et al., 2012) concluded that previous analyses (Demberg and Keller, 2007) had been distorted by the presence of a few outlier data points.

Second, we present related work on information structure annotation. Götze et al. (Götze et al., 2007) devised criteria for annotating the information status (given/accessible/new), topic (aboutness/frame setting), and focus (new-information focus/contrastive focus) independently of languages and linguistic theories. Prasad et al. (Prasad et al., 2015) discussed the bridging annotation standard of the Penn Discourse Treebank (Miltsakaki et al., 2004) and PropBank (Palmer et al., 2005).

Third, we present language analyses or models with reading time or eye tracking gaze information. Barret et al. (Barrett et al., 2016) presented a POS tagging model with gaze patterns. Klerke et al. (Klerke et al., 2015) presented a grammaticality detection model for machine processed sentences. Iida et al. (Iida et al., 2013) presented an analysis of eye-tracking data for the annotation of predicate–argument relations.

Our paper is slightly different from these preceding papers. We present corpus-based psycholinguistic research on the relationship between the information structure and reading time, including gaze information, of the language recipient.

3 Data and Method

We used the overlaid data of BCCWJ-EyeTrack and information structure annotations, as given in Table 1. We present the data below in detail.

3.1 Reading Time Data: BCCWJ-EyeTrack

We now explain the two measurement methods for estimating the reading time: eye tracking and self-paced reading. The order of tasks was fixed with eye tracking in the first session and a self-paced reading method in the second session. Each participant saw each text once with the task and segmentation of the texts counterbalanced across participants.

Eye tracking was recorded with a tower-mounted EyeLink 1000 (SR Research Ltd). The view was binocular, but data were collected from each participant's right eye at a resolution of 1000 Hz. Partic-

Table 1: Data format

Column Name	Type	Description
surface	factor	Word surface form
time	int	Reading-time
logtime	num	Reading-time (log)
measure	factor	Reading time type
sample	factor	Sample Name
article	factor	Article information
metadata_orig	factor	Document structure tag
metadata	factor	Metadata
length	int	Number of characters
space	factor	Boundary with space or not
subj	factor	Participant ID
setorder	factor	Segmentation type order
rspan	num	Result of reading span test
voc	num	Result of vocabulary test
dependent	int	Number of Dependents
sessionN	int	Session order
articleN	int	Article display order
screenN	int	Screen display order
lineN	int	Line display order
segmentN	int	Segment display order
is_first	factor	The leftmost segment
is_last	factor	The rightmost segment
is_second_last	factor	The second rightmost segment
infostatus	factor	Information status
definiteness	factor	Definiteness
specificity	factor	Specificity
animacy	factor	Animacy
sentience	factor	Sentience
agentivity	factor	Agentivity
commonness	factor	Commonness

ipants looked at the display by using a half-mirror; their heads were fixed with their chins on a chin rest. Unlike self-paced reading, during eye tracking all segments were shown Simultaneously. This allowed more natural reading because each participant could freely return and reread earlier parts of the text on the same screen However, participants were not allowed to return to previous screens. Stimulus texts were shown in a fixed full-width font (MS Mincho 24 point) and displayed horizontally as is customary with computer displays for Japanese; there were five lines per screen on a 21.5-in display.[2] Under the segmented condition, a half-width space was used to indicate the boundary between segments. In order to improve the vertical tracking accuracy, three empty lines were placed between lines of text. A line break was inserted at the end of a sentence or when the maximum 53 full-width characters per line was reached. Moreover, line breaks were inserted at the same points in the segmented and unsegmented conditions to guarantee that the same number of non-space characters were shown under both conditions. Figure 1 shows the screen dump of the eye tracking results.

The same procedure was adopted for the self-paced reading presentation except that the chin rest was not used, and participants could move their heads freely while looking directly at the display. Doug Rohde's Linger program Version 2.94[3] was used to record keyboard-press latencies while sentences were shown by using a non-cumulative self-paced moving-window presentation. This had the best correlation with eye-tracking data when different styles of presentation were compared for English (Just et al., 1982). Sentence segments were initially shown masked with dashes. Participants pressed the space key of the keyboard to reveal each subsequent segment of the sentence, while all other segments reverted to dashes. Participants were not allowed to return to reread earlier segments.

Twenty-four native Japanese speakers who were 18 years of age or older at the time participated in the experiment for financial compensation. The experiments were conducted from September to December 2015. The collected profile data included the

age (in 5-year brackets), gender, educational background, eyesight (all participants had uncorrected vision or vision corrected with soft contact lenses or prescription glasses), geographical linguistic background (i.e., the prefecture within Japan where they lived until the age of 15), and parents' place of birth. Table 2 shows the profile data for the participants. The vocabulary size of the participants was measured by using a Japanese language vocabulary evaluation test (Amano and Kondo, 1998). Participants indicated words they knew from a list of 50 words, and scores were calculated by taking word-familiarity estimates into consideration. As a measure of the working memory capacity, the Japanese version of the reading span test was conducted (Osaka and Osaka, 1994). Each participant read sentences aloud, each of which contained an underlined content word. Table 3 shows the results of the tests. After each set of sentences, the participant recalled the underlined words. If all words were successfully recalled, the set size was increased by one sentence (sets of two to five sentences were used). The final score was the largest set for which all words were correctly recalled; a half point was added if half of the words were recalled in the last trial.

Reading times were collected for a subset of the core data of the BCCWJ (Maekawa et al., 2014), which consisted of newspaper articles (PN: published newspaper) samples. Articles were chosen if they were annotated with information such as syntactic dependencies, predicative clausal structures, co-references, focus of negation, and similar details following the list of articles that were given annotation priority in the BCCWJ.

The 21 newspaper articles[4] chosen were divided into four datasets containing five articles each: A, B, C, and D. Table 4 presents the numbers of words, sentences, and screens (i.e., pages) for each dataset. Each article was presented as starting on a new screen.

Articles were shown segmented or unsegmented (i.e., with or without a half-width space to mark the boundary between segments). Segments con-

---

[2]EIZO FlexScan EV2116W (resolution: 1920 × 1080 pixels) set 50 cm from the chin rest.

[3]http://tedlab.mit.edu/~dr/Linger/

[4]The original BCCWJ-EyeTrack paper (Asahara et al., 2016) presented 20 articles. However, there were two consecutive articles in dataset C. These two articles were presented on separate screens. Thus, we split them into two for statistical analysis.

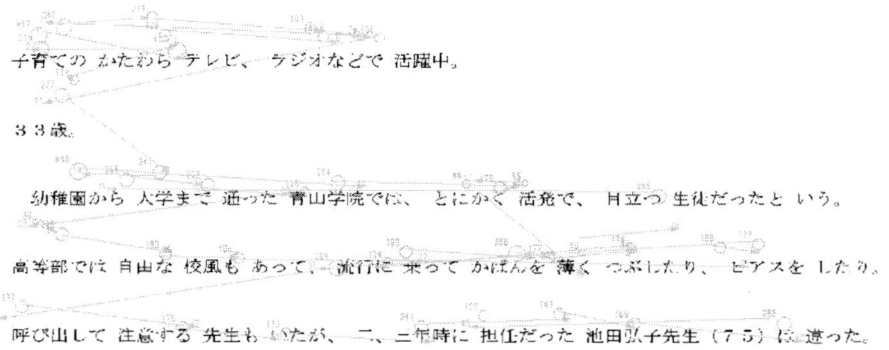

Figure 1: Screen Dump of the Eye Tracking Results

Table 2: Profile data for the participants

Age range (years)	Females	Males	Gender not given	Total
-20	1	1		2
21-25		2		2
26-30	2			2
31-35	3			3
36-40	9		1	10
41-45	3			3
46-50	1			1
51-		1		1
total	19	4	1	24

Table 3: Results for reading span test and vocabulary-size test

Vocab. size	Reading span test score								Total
	1.5	2.0	2.5	3.0	3.5	4.0	4.5	5.0	
36,000 -		1	1						2
38,000 -		4		1					5
40,000 -	1	1							2
42,000 -		1							1
44,000 -						1			1
46,000 -									0
48,000 -			1						1
50,000 -			4	1	1		1		7
52,000 -			1					1	2
54,000 -	1								1
56,000 -									0
58,000 -			1						1
60,000 -		1							1
Total	2	8	8	2	1	1	1	1	24

formed to the definition for *bunsetsu* units (a content word followed by functional morphology, e.g., a noun with a case marker) in the BCCWJ as prescribed by the National Institute for Japanese Language and Linguistics. Each participant was assigned to one of eight groups of three participants each. Each group was subjected to one of the eight experimental conditions with varying combinations of measurement methods and boundary marking for different datasets presented in different orders.

During the self-paced reading session, each segment was displayed separately, and participants could not return to reread earlier parts of the text. Therefore, the latencies for the button presses are straightforward measures of the time spent on each segment.

For the eye-tracking data, five types of measure-

Table 4: Data set sizes

Data set	Segments	Sentences	Screens
A	470	66	19
B	455	67	21
C	355	44	16
D	363	41	15

ments were used: first fixation time (FFT), first pass time (FPT), regression path time (RPT), second pass time (SPT), and total time (TOTAL). These are explained in Figure 2.

The FFT is the fixation duration measured when the gaze first enters the area of interest. In the figure, the FFT for "the first fiscal year settling of accounts also" (hereafter "the area of interest") is the duration of fixation 5.

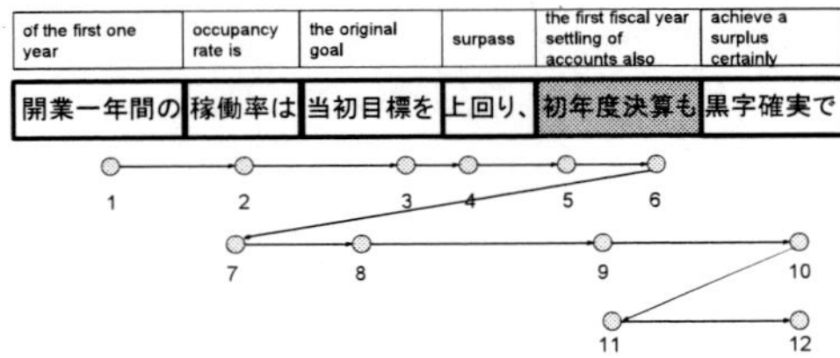

Figure 2: Example of fixations

Table 5: Basic statistics of information structure labels

infostatus	discourse-new		discourse-old	
	1345		678	
definiteness	definite	indefinite	either	-
	1122	899	2	-
specificity	specific	unspecific	either	neither
	1157	749	116	1
animacy	animate	inanimate	either	-
	342	1680	1	-
sentience	sentient	insentient	either	-
	337	1678	8	-
agentivity	agent	patient	both	neither
	192	338	2	1491
commonness	hearer-new	hearer-old	bridging	neither
	494	1036	489	4

The FPT is the total duration of fixation from the moment the gaze first stops within the area of interest until it leaves the focus area by moving to the right or left of this area. In the figure, the FPT is the sum of the durations of fixations 5 and 6.

The RPT is the total span of from the moment the gaze enters the area of interest until it crosses the right boundary of this area for the first time. In the figure, the RPT is the sum of the durations for fixations 5–9. The RPT can includes fixations to the left of the left boundary (e.g., 7 and 8) and durations of fixations when the gaze returns to the area of interest (e.g., 9).

The SPT is the total span of time the gaze spends in the area of interest excluding the FPT. In the figure, the SPT is the sum of the durations of fixations 9 and 11.

The TOTAL is the total duration that the gaze spends within the area of interest. In other words, it is the sum of the SPT and FPT. In the figure, TOTAL is the sum of the durations of fixations 5, 6, 9, and 11.

Table 1 presents the data. `surface` is the surface form of the word. The reading time (i.e., `time`) is converted into log scale (i.e., `logtime`). `measure` is the reading type {SELF, FFT, FPT, RPT, SPT, TOTAL}. `sample`, `article`, `metadata_orig`, `metadata` are information related to the article. `length` is the number of characters in the surface form. `space` is whether spaces are present between segments. `subj` is the participant ID, which is used as a random effect for the statistical analysis. `setorder` is the presentation order of the space. `rspan`, `voc` are features of the participants. `dependent` is the number of dependents for the segments. The dependency relation is annotated by humans

Table 6: Parameters of the linear mixed model for the self paced reading time (SELF) (`logtime`)

	Estimate	Std. Error	t value
(Intercept)	2.893	0.062	46.51
length	0.102	0.002	**42.31**
space=T	0.003	0.004	0.86
dependent	-0.005	0.003	-1.61
sessionN	-0.021	0.022	-0.94
articleN	-0.023	0.007	**-3.23**
screenN	-0.032	0.002	**-11.19**
lineN	-0.014	0.002	**-6.10**
segmentN	-0.005	0.001	**-4.83**
is_first=T	0.047	0.006	**7.19**
is_last=T	0.040	0.008	**4.71**
is_second_last=T	-0.011	0.005	**-2.11**
space=T:sessionN	-0.019	0.044	-0.43
is=discourse-old	-0.005	0.005	-0.98
def=indefinite	0.004	0.015	0.30
spec=specific	0.044	0.016	**2.78**
spec=unspecific	0.001	0.010	0.16
ani=inanimate	-0.000	0.050	-0.02
sent=insentient	-0.105	0.067	-1.56
sent=sentient	-0.098	0.050	-1.94
ag=both	-0.058	0.049	-1.18
ag=neither	-0.004	0.007	-0.69
ag=patient	-0.013	0.008	-1.63
com=hearer-new	0.025	0.007	**3.59**
com=hearer-old	-0.020	0.009	**-2.11**
com=neither	0.000	0.025	0.01

45 data points (0.69%) were excluded in the 3-SD trimming.

(Asahara and Matsumoto, 2016). `sessionN`, `articleN`, `screenN`, `lineN`, `segmentN` are the display order of the elements. `is_first`, `is_last`, `is_second_first` are the layout features on the screen.

Table 7: Parameters of the linear mixed model for the first pass time (FPT) (`logtime`) (only information structure related)

	Estimate	Std. Error	t value
(Intercept)	2.303	0.102	22.53
is=discourse-old	0.005	0.010	0.50
def=indefinite	0.024	0.026	0.90
spec=specific	0.064	0.028	**2.26**
spec=unspecific	0.031	0.018	1.70
ani=inanimate	0.210	0.104	**2.01**
sent=insentient	-0.001	0.129	-0.01
sent=sentient	0.194	0.086	**2.25**
ag=both	-0.050	0.087	-0.57
ag=neither	0.014	0.012	1.19
ag=patient	-0.006	0.015	-0.43
com=hearer-new	0.024	0.012	1.95
com=hearer-old	0.000	0.017	-0.03
com=neither	0.002	0.043	0.05

13 data points (0.24%) were excluded in the 3-SD trimming.

Table 8: Parameters of the linear mixed model for the regression path time (RPT) (`logtime`) (only information structure related)

	Estimate	Std. Error	t value
(Intercept)	2.188	0.118	18.48
is=discourse-old	-0.003	0.011	-0.30
def=indefinite	0.041	0.030	1.34
spec=specific	0.095	0.032	**2.95**
spec=unspecific	0.038	0.020	1.82
ani=inanimate	0.112	0.119	0.94
sent=insentient	0.248	0.150	1.65
sent=sentient	0.345	0.102	**3.37**
ag=both	-0.054	0.100	-0.54
ag=neither	0.013	0.014	0.91
ag=patient	-0.000	0.017	-0.01
com=hearer-new	0.001	0.014	0.09
com=hearer-old	-0.018	0.019	-0.94
com=neither	0.042	0.049	0.86

43 data points (0.81%) were excluded in the 3-SD trimming.

Table 9: Parameters of the linear mixed model for the total time (TOTAL) (`logtime`) (only information structure related)

	Estimate	Std. Error	t value
(Intercept)	2.500	0.105	23.69
is=discourse-old	0.009	0.010	0.89
def=indefinite	0.036	0.027	1.32
spec=specific	0.070	0.029	**2.39**
spec=unspecific	0.016	0.019	0.88
ani=inanimate	0.177	0.108	1.63
sent=insentient	-0.027	0.133	-0.20
sent=sentient	0.130	0.089	1.46
ag=both	-0.025	0.091	-0.28
ag=neither	0.006	0.013	0.50
ag=patient	-0.011	0.015	-0.70
com=hearer-new	0.030	0.013	**2.34**
com=hearer-old	-0.000	0.017	-0.02
com=neither	0.033	0.045	0.74

5 data points (0.09%) were excluded in the 3-SD trimming.

3.2 Information Structure Annotation

This subsection presents information structure annotation. The detailed explanation is in (Miyauchi et al., 2017) We set the following seven labelset for the NP segments:

- information status (`infostatus:is`)
- definiteness (`definiteness:is`)
- specificity (`specificity:spec`)
- animacy (`animacy:ani`)
- sentience (`sentience:sent`)
- agentivity (`agentivity:ag`)
- commonness (`commonnness:com`)

The information status is the distinction between new and old/given information. In some discourses, the information that the speaker wants to convey to the hearer is `discourse-new`, and the information that the hearer already knows is `discourse-old`.

The definiteness is a semantic category about whether it is possible for hearers to identify referents (Lyons, 1999) and (Heim, 2011). An NP referent that a speaker considers to be identifiable for the hearer is `definite`, and an NP referent that the speaker does not consider to be identifiable is `indefinite`. In this research, the scope of definiteness was set to be the range before and after three sentences.

The specificity is a semantic category about whether speakers think of specific referents or not (von Heusinger, 2011). An NP is `specific` when its referent is either regarded to be unique or is specified by speakers. An NP is `unspecific` when its referent is not. Similar to the definiteness, the scope of specificity is set to be the range before and after three sentences for the annotation.

The animacy is a category about whether referents are alive. Living creatures (e.g., human beings, animals) are `animate`, and nonliving objects (including plants) are `inanimate`. In our research, the tags of animacy were annotated judging solely from the NP in question. The sentience may be addressed as a concept of animacy. This parameter expresses whether referents have emotion. An NP is `sentient` when its referent moves of its own free will and `insentient` when its referent does not.

For example, the choice of verbs *aru / iru* (i.e., "exist") is based not so much on a distinction between animate and inanimate but between sentient and insentient. Thus, we needed to set the parameter of sentience. Because there are cases in which the presence or absence of sentience cannot be determined, the tags of sentience were annotated judging from not only the NP but the predicate of the sentence in question.

The agentivity show the roles played in a situation by those related to the situation. An NP whose referent intentionally performs an act is an `agent`, and an NP whose referent undergoes a change from an act is a `patient`. The tags of agentivity were annotated judging from both the main and subordinate clauses, including the NP in question. Furthermore, we introduced the `both` and `neither` tags.

The commonness is a parameter expressing whether the speaker assumes that the hearer already knows the information. Information that the speaker thinks the hearer already knows is `hearer-old`, and information that the speaker does not think the hearer already knows is `hearer-new`. In other words, `hearer-old` information is common ground for both the speaker and hearer, and `hearer-new` information is not. In addition to these two labels, we introduced the label `bridging` for when the NP is a bridging anaphora. Note that, when annotators judge commonness, they may use their worldly knowledge.

Table 5 presents the basic statistics of information structure labels. We introduced `either` for the definiteness, specificity, animacy, sentience, and agentivity when the annotator cannot judge the label from the limited contextual information. We also introduced `neither` for the specificity, agentivity, and commonness when the concept is not appropriate for the NP.

3.3 Statistical Analysis

We investigated the reading time (`logtime`) of NPs that were annotated with the information structure labels. During the preprocessing, we excluded data {`authorsData`, `caption`, `listItem`, `profile`, `titleBlock`} of `metadata`. We also excluded zero-millisecond data points from the eye tracking data. The number of data points were 6444 for SELF; 5268 for FFT, FPT, RPT, and TO-TAL; and 2081 for SPT. After model-based trimming was used to eliminate points beyond three standard deviations, the model was rebuilt (Baayen, 2008). `subj` and `article` were considered as random effects, as expressed in the following formula:

```
logtime ~ space * sessionN + length + dependent
+ is_first + is_last + is_second_last + articleN
+ screenN + lineN + segmentN + infostatus
+ definiteness + specificity + animacy
+ sentience + agentivity + commonness
+ (1 | subj) + (1 | article)
```

4   Results

Tables 6, 7, 8, and 9 present the results for the reading time types of SELF, FPT, RPT, and TOTAL, respectively. The fixed effects other than the information structure labels are omitted in the FPT, RPT, and TOTAL.

When the absolute *t*-value of an effect was larger than 1.96, we regarded the factor as statistically significant and put the sign of the estimate. Otherwise, we placed a value of 0 to indicate nonsignificant factors. The results were very similar to those of the previous report (Asahara et al., 2016). [5] However, *anti-locality* phenomena (Konieczny, 2000) in which a head is read faster if it is preceded by more dependents were not observed for the eye-tracking method with the NPs.

5   Discussion

Table 10 presents the result for the fixed effects of the labels related to the information structure.

The information status `discourse-new, old` did not affect the reading time. Whereas the definiteness affected only TOTAL of the eye-tracking data, the specificity affected SELF, FPT, RPT, and TOTAL. Thus, the specificity has a stronger effect than the definiteness for the reading time of Japanese. The animacy (`animate/inanimate`) affected only FPT. However, the sentience (`sentient/insentient`) affected FPT and RPT. These two did not affect the self-paced reading. The agentivitiy showed no significant effect. Finally, the commonness, which is a feature for the hearer, affected SELF and TOTAL. The most important result is that the

---

[5] Whereas Asahara et al.'s paper was based on `time`, ours was based on `logtime` to reduce the outliers in the model.

Table 10: Summary: reading time and information structures

Fixed Effect		SELF	FFT	FPT	SPT	RPT	TOTAL
`infostatus=discourse-old`	(vs. `discourse-new`)	0	0	0	0	0	0
`definiteness=indefinite`	(vs. `definite`)	0	0	0	0	0	+
`specificity=specific`	(vs. `either`)	+	0	+	0	+	+
`specificity=unspecific`	(vs. `either`)	0	0	0	0	0	0
`animacy=inanimate`	(vs. `animate`)	0	0	+	0	0	0
`sentience=insentient`	(vs. `either`)	0	0	0	0	0	0
`sentience=sentient`	(vs. `either`)	0	0	+	0	+	0
`agentivity=both`	(vs. `agent`)	0	0	0	0	0	0
`agentivity=neither`	(vs. `agent`)	0	0	0	0	0	0
`agentivity=patient`	(vs. `agent`)	0	0	0	0	0	0
`commonness=hearer-new`	(vs. `bridging`)	+	0	0	0	0	+
`commonness=hearer-old`	(vs. `bridging`)	-	0	0	0	0	0
`commonness=neither`	(vs. `bridging`)	0	0	0	0	0	0

reading times of SELF and TOTAL may split for `hearer-new` and `bridging`.

In sum, the reading time showed that different patterns of reading time to determine the `specificity`, `sentience` and `commonness` in the information structure.

6 Conclusions

This paper presents a contrastive analysis between the reading time and information structure. The results showed the different patterns of promotion or interference of the reading time for the information structure of the NPs. They may lead to the possibility of classifying information structures by the reading time pattern.

The previous co-reference resolution methods addressed the issue of the information status based on whether or not an NP is mentioned in the previous discourse. However, these methods cannot identify the information structure for a recipient, such as the commonness (`hearer-new`, `-old` or `bridging`). It is necessary to introduce a recipient reaction feature to identify the commonness. The results in this paper showed that the reading time is a potential feature that can be used to solve bridging.

Our future work will involve building a classifier to split `bridging` and `hearer-new` based on the reading time for each subject participant. The classifier will be able to detect bridging that cannot be resolved by the subject participant's knowledge. This will enable us to develop user-oriented information extraction or document summarization models that incorporate present `hearer-new` Information.[6]

Acknowledgement

The work reported in this article was supported by the NINJAL research project of the Center for Corpus Development. This work was also supported by JSPS KAKENHI Grant Number JP25284083 and JP17H00917.

---

[6]The subject participants of BCCWJ-EyeTrack wrote a summary of the presented text (BCCWJ-SUMM).

References

Shigeaki Amano and Tadahisa Kondo. 1998. Estimation of mental lexicon size with word familiarity database. In *Proceedings of International Conference on Spoken Language Processing*, volume 5, pages 2119–2122.

Masayuki Asahara and Yuji Matsumoto. 2016. BCCWJ-DepPara: A Syntactic Annotation Treebank on the 'Balanced Corpus of Contemporary Written Japanese'. In *Proceedings of the 12th Workshop on Asian Langauge Resources (ALR12)*, pages 49–58.

Masayuki Asahara, Hajime Ono, and Edson T. Miyamoto. 2016. Reading-Time Annotations for 'Balanced Corpus of Contemporary Written Japanese'. In *Proceedings of COLING 2016, the 26th International Conference on Computational Linguistics: Technical Papers*, pages 684–694.

R. H. Baayen. 2008. *Analyzing Linguistic Data: A practical Introduction to Statistics using R*. Cambridge University Press.

Maria Barrett, Joachim Bingel, Frank Keller, and Anders Søgaard. 2016. Weakly supervised part-of-speech tagging using eye-tracking data. In *Proceedings of the 54th Annual Meeting of the Association for Computational Linguistics (Volume 2: Short Papers)*, pages 579–584.

Vera Demberg and Frank Keller. 2007. Eye-tracking evidence for integration cost effects in corpus data. In *Proceedings of the 29th meeting of the cognitive science society (CogSci-07)*, pages 947–952.

Vera Demberg and Frank Keller. 2008. Data from eye-tracking corpora as evidence for theories of syntactic processing complexity. *Cognition*, 109(2):193–210.

Edward Gibson. 2008. Linguistic complexity: Locality of syntactic dependencies. *Cognition*, 68:1–76.

Michael Götze, Thomas Weskott, Cornelia Endriss, Ines Fiedler, Stefan Hinterwimmer, Svetlana Petrova, Anne Schwarz, Stavros Skopeteas, and Ruben Stoel. 2007. Information structure. In Stefanie Dipper, Michael Götze, and Stavros Skopeteas, editors, *Information structure in cross-linguistic corpora: annotation guidelines for phonology, morphology, syntax, semantics and information structure*, volume 7, pages 147–187. Universitätsverlag Potsdam.

John Hale. 2001. A Probabilistic Earley Parser as a Psycholinguistic Model. In *Proceedings of the second conference of the North American chapter of the association for computational linguistics*, volume 2, pages 159–166.

Irene Heim. 2011. Definiteness and indefiniteness. In Klaus von Heusinger, Claudia Maienborn, and Paul Portner, editors, *Semantics: An International Handbook of Natural Language Meaning*, volume 2, pages 996–1025. Mouton de Gruyter.

Yufang Hou, Katja Markert, and Michael Strube. 2013. Global inference for bridging anaphora resolution. In *Proceedings of the 2013 Conference of the North American Chapter of the Association for Computational Linguistics: Human Language Technologies*, pages 907–917, Atlanta, Georgia, June. Association for Computational Linguistics.

Ryu Iida, Koh Mitsuda, and Takenobu Tokunaga. 2013. Investigation of annotator's behaviour using eye-tracking data. In *Proceedings of the 7th Linguistic Annotation Workshop and Interoperability with Discourse*, pages 214–222.

Marcel A. Just, Patricia A. Carpenter, and Jacqueline D. Woolley. 1982. Paradigms and Processes in Reading Comprehension. *Journal of Experimental Psychology: General*, 3:228–238.

Alan Kennedy and Joël Pynte. 2005. Parafoveal-on-foveal effects in normal reading. *Vision Research*, 45:153–168.

Sigrid Klerke, Héctor Martínez Alonso, and Anders Søgaard. 2015. Looking hard: Eye tracking for detecting grammaticality of automatically compressed sentences. In *Proceedings of the 20th Nordic Conference of Computational Linguistics (NODALIDA 2015)*, pages 97–105.

Lars Konieczny. 2000. Locality and parsing complexity. *Journal of Psycholinguistic Research*, 29(6).

Christopher Lyons. 1999. *Definiteness*. Cambridge University Press, Cambridge.

Kikuo Maekawa, Makoto Yamazaki, Toshinobu Ogiso, Takehiko Maruyama, Hideki Ogura, Wakako Kashino, Hanae Koiso, Masaya Yamaguchi, Makiro Tanaka, and Yasuharu Den. 2014. Balanced Corpus of Contemporary Written Japanese. *Language Resources and Evaluation*, 48:345–371.

Eleni Miltsakaki, Rashmi Prasad, Aravind K Joshi, and Bonnie L Webber. 2004. The penn discourse treebank. In *LREC*.

Takuya Miyauchi, Masayuki Asahara, Natsuko Nakagawa, and Sachi Kato. 2017. Annotation of Information Structure on "The Balanced Corpus of Contemporary Written Japanese. In *Proceedings of 2017 Conference of the Pacific Association for Computational Linguistics*.

Ryo Nagata, Tatsuya Iguchi, Fumito Masui, Atsuo Kawai, and Isu Naoki. 2005. A statistical model based on the three head words for detecting article errors. *IEICE TRANSACTIONS on Information ans Systems*, E88-D(7):1700–1706.

Mariko. Osaka and Naoyuki Osaka. 1994. [Working memory capacity related to reading: measurement with the Japanese version of reading span test] (in Japanese). *Shinrigaku Kenkyu: The Japanese Journal of Psychology*, 65(5):339–345.

Martha Palmer, Daniel Gildea, and Paul Kingsbury. 2005. The proposition bank: An annotated corpus of semantic roles. *Conputational Linguistics*, 31(1):71–105.

Rashmi Prasad, Bonnie Webber, Alan Lee, Sameer Pradhan, and Aravind Joshi. 2015. Bridging sentential and discourse-level semantics through clausal adjuncts. In *Proceedings of the First Workshop on Linking Computational Models of Lexical, Sentential and Discourse-level Semantics*, pages 64–69.

Douglas Roland, Gail Mauner, Carolyn O'Meara, and Hongoak Yun. 2012. Discourse expectations and relative clause processing. *Journal of Memory and Language*, 66(3):479–508.

Klaus von Heusinger. 2011. Specificity. In Klaus von Heusinger, Claudia Maienborn, and Paul Portner, editors, *Semantics: An International Handbook of Natural Language Meaning*, volume 2, pages 1058–1087. Mouton de Gruyter.

Doubt, incredulity, and particles in Japanese falling interrogatives

Lukas Rieser
Kyoto University
Kyoto, Japan
lukasjrieser@gmail.com

Abstract

I propose an analysis of the particles *no*, *ka*, *yo*, and *ne* as speech act modifiers, accounting for the readings of falling interrogatives with and without particles by predicting what they convey about the speaker's belief revision and formation process. The analysis is set in a CCP-framework formalizing utterance felicity in terms of belief and evidence conditions in which speech act felicity is compositionally derived from illocutionary force, sentence final intonation, and modification by particles.

1 Japanese sentence final particles

Sentence final particles (SFPs) are a highly productive class of expressives[1] in Japanese. The empirical scope of this paper are the interrogative marker *ka* and the particles *no*, *yo*, and *ne* . While there is only a consensus to classify *yo* and *ne* as SPFs, I analyze all four particles as SFPs in the sense of speech act modifiers occurring in the sentential periphery.

SFPs in the Japanese clause   Japanese is a strictly left-branching language, hence elements further right in linear order generally scope syntactically higher and enter the semantic derivation later than such further left. Therefore, layered clause models have been proposed in descriptive Japanese grammar.[2] Minami (1974), for instance, locates SFPs in the outermost layer of the clause, which encodes meta-information on the transmission of information

by the utterance. Minami's next inner layer hosts the interrogative particle *ka* and the speech act modal[3] *daroo*, which encode information on the speaker's judgment of the truth of the prejacent. The position of *daroo* is immediately preceded by that of *no*[4] in linear order, which in turn is preceded by tense morphology, as (1) below illustrates.

(1)   V-T-*no*-(*daroo*)-*ka*-*yo*-*ne*

SFPs as speech-act modifiers   In line with the intuitions and observations motivating layered clause models, I propose that *no*, *daroo* and *ka* modify utterance felicity conditions w.r.t. speaker belief and available evidence (subjective, related to speaker judgment), *yo* and *ne* w.r.t. speaker assumptions on addressee belief (intersubjective, related to information sharing/transmission). On my analysis, all thus modify utterance meaning on the speech act level where felicity is computed. As analyzing speech act felicity is independently necessary to account for bare (particle-less) utterances, this is a relatively parsimonious way of accounting for the contribution of Japanese sentence final expressives.

2 Japanese falling interrogatives

Falling interrogatives (FIs) occur frequently in Japanese and have uses clearly distinct form canonical, information-seeking questions. In the remainder of this section, I introduce the observations to be accounted for in the analysis.

---

[1] In the sense of not contributing truth-conditional meaning.

[2] *cf.* Narrog (2009) for extensive discussion of various layered models, Davis (2011) for discussion pertaining to SFPs.

[3] *cf.* Hara and Davis (2013), Rieser (2017c) for analysis as a speech act modifier operating on a Gricean quality threshold.

[4] *cf.* Rieser (2017a) for discussion on the structural and functional distinction with the homophonous complementizer *no*.

31st Pacific Asia Conference on Language, Information and Computation (PACLIC 31), pages 25–33
Cebu City, Philippines, November 16-18, 2017

2.1 Two readings of FIs and *no*

Davis (2011) observes a contrast in felicity between (2) with and wihtout *no* under the scenarios in (3).

(2) Tori-ga   konna tokoro-ni sum-eru (no) ka.
     birds-NOM   such_a place-in   live-POT *no* *ka*
     "Can birds live in a place like this!?"/
     "Birds can live in a place like this after all!"

(3) a. Scenario 1: S assumes birds cannot live here, but looking out the window is surprised to discover that in fact they do. She utters (2) to indicate her surprise.
     b. Scenario 2: S believes that birds cannot live here. Her friend says something that suggests they do. She utters (2) to indicate that her friend is mistaken.

In Scenario 1, the *no*-FI is preferred; in Scenario 2, only the bare FI is felicitous. Davis labels the salient reading under Scenario 2 the rhetorical question reading, similar to English rhetorical polar questions as the first translation indicates. He argues that such a reading is incompatible with *no* due to its evidential properties (which I also assume in my analysis).

I label the salient interpretation under Scenario 1 the **incredulity reading**,[5] that under Scenario 2 the **doubt reading**. In Scenario 1, the speaker revises a previous belief in light of new evidence supporting the prejacent, while in Scenario 2 the speaker rejects the prejacent as it is incompatible with a previous belief. The incredulity reading thus indicates that evidence-based belief revision is underway and the previous belief is to be discarded, the prejacent representing the *revised belief* to replace the previous belief. The doubt reading, on the other hand, indicates no belief revision takes place and the previous belief is to be retained, the prejacent representing an *unaccepted belief*.[6]

In this way, (*no*-)FIs convey information about the speaker's belief revision and formation process, *i.e.* judgment process w.r.t. the prejacent. I propose that this encoded in utterance felicity conditions characterizing admissible utterance contexts.

---

[5]Thus labeled as it intuitively conveys that the speaker finds the prejacent "hard to believe" or "unbelievable".

[6]It should be noted that in many cases, in particular soliloquous uses, the doubt reading conveys suspension of judgment rather than outright rejection of the prejacent.

2.2 Incredulity, doubt and *yo* in FIs

Davis further observes that *yo*-FIs disallow what I label doubt readings and must be interpreted as assertions (note that I defend distinguishing assertions as falling declaratives from FIs). Consider (4) showing a *yo*-FI with and without *no*, adapted from Davis' data by Taniguchi (2016).

(4) Sonna mono taberu (no) ka yo.
     such thing eat   *no* *ka yo*
     "What the hell! He isn't going to eat that!"/
     "Holy shit! He's going to eat that!"

Taniguchi observes that (4) conveys "negative bias" (the speaker tends not to believe the preajcent) without *no*, but "positive bias" (the speaker tends to believe the preajcent) with *no*, as the translations suggest. While (4) without *no* conveys stronger doubt, both versions of the *yo*-FI are incredulity readings in my terminology as they indicate that the speaker at least considers revising a previous belief, in contrast to the bare FI in (2) which receives a doubt reading. Taniguchi proposes analyzing *ka-yo* utterances as update with a self-addressed question (*ka*) followed by self-corrective update (*yo*) to derive the communicative effect of *yo*-FIs.

I propose an alternative, compositional derivation of what FIs with particles mean from the effects that *ka*, *yo*, and *no* have on speech act felicity. This accounts for Davis's observation that *yo*-FIs are assertion-like as *yo* introduces (addressee) commitment like (rising) declaratives, and for Taniguchi's observations on bias, as *no* requires evidence in principle sufficient for felicitous assertion, indicating that belief revision is well underway.

2.3 Reluctant acceptance and *ne*

FIs with *ne* convey speaker doubt and seek an evaluation of the prejacent from the addressee, as in (5).

(5) Sonna mono taberu (no) ka ne.
     such   thing eat   *no* *ka ne*
     "So is he actually going to eat this?"/
     "So he is actually going to eat this..."

The salient reading of the *ne*-FI in (5) without *no* is a doubt reading, in contrast to the *yo*-FI in (4), which even without *no* receives an incredulity reading. Adding *no* to (5) makes an incredulity reading available which in contrast with the mirative nuance of (4) conveys what I label "reluctant acceptance" — that the speaker is at least considering to *also* accept the preajcent. Crucially, as suggested by the translations with "so" referring to a previous utterance of the addressee, *ne*-FIs convey a speaker assumption that the addressee believes the prejacent to be true.

I propose a compositional account of *ne*-FIs on which *ka* conveys speaker doubt, *ne* the assumption that the addressee believe the prejacent, which predicts that they occur in situations where there is a discrepancy between speaker and addressee belief.

3 Framework for speech act felicity

While the framework sketched below also covers handling rising interrogatives (canonical questions) and rising declaratives,[7] I focus on FIs to account for the observations above. The framework builds on the following assumptions: (i) Speaker commitment from assertion can be derived from satisfaction of Gricean quality maxims; (ii) in interrogatives, quality requires the speaker to *not* believe the prejacent to be true; (iii) FIs convey that the speaker *forgoes* commitment to the prejacent. In the remainder of this section, I define belief and evidence propositions as the basis to formalize felicity conditions, provide definitions for the CCP model, and implement the assumptions in (i) through (iii) above.

3.1 Belief and evidence in speech acts

Felicity conditions are captured in form of belief and evidence propositions. First, **belief propositions** of the form $B_x^w \varphi$ are defined by doxastic accessibility:[8]

(6) a. $B_x^w \varphi \quad \rightarrow \forall w'.wR_x^{dox}w' : w' \in W^\varphi$
  b. $\neg B_x^w \varphi \quad \rightarrow \exists w'.wR_x^{dox}w' : w' \notin W^\varphi$
  c. $B_x^w \neg\varphi \rightarrow \forall w'.wR_x^{dox}w' : w' \notin W^\varphi$

Thus, "x believes φ to be true at w" ($B_x^w \varphi$) means that *at all worlds* compatible with x's beliefs at w, φ is *true* ; "x does not believe φ to be true at w" ($\neg B_x^w \varphi$) means that *at least at one world* compatible with x's beliefs at w, φ is *false*, and "x believes φ to be false at w" ($B_x^w \neg\varphi$) means that *at no worlds* compatible with x's beliefs at w at which φ is *true* (φ is false at all worlds compatible with x's beliefs at w).

Additional assumptions such as circumstantial and stereotypical conversational backgrounds are taken to be encoded in R^{dox} for simplicity, as this issue is not central to the analysis.

Second, **evidence propositions** are defined in terms of evidence required to back up speaker commitment arising from felicitous assertion. The question of what constitutes evidence in natural language is very complex[9] and I set it aside here. Focusing on evidence-related felicity condition on assertion, I define evidence propositions of the form $EV_x^w \varphi$ relative to belief propositions in the following defeasible entailment relation.[10]

(7) a. $EV_x^w \varphi > B_x^w \varphi$
  b. $(EV_x^w \varphi > B_x^w \varphi) \wedge EV_x^w \varphi \vdash B_x^w \varphi$
  c. $(EV_x^w \varphi > B_x^w \varphi) \wedge B_x^w \neg\varphi \nvdash B_x^w \varphi$

Thus, from the premise that x has evidence supporting φ at w one can infer by (7-a) that x believes φ at w as in (7-b), unless there is an additional premise that x believes φ to be false at w as shown in (7-c).

Finally, I define the notion of **public belief** as in (8-a) to capture commitment that arises from assertion. Gunlogson (2003) and Davis (2011) employ the similar notion of public commitment, which differs in that I take public belief to be independent of private belief, *i.e.* an agent can publicly believe φ, but privately not believe φ. Furthermore, public belief is recursive as defined in (8-b).

(8) a. $PB_x^w \varphi \rightarrow B_y^w B_x^w \varphi$
  b. $PB_x^w \varphi \rightarrow PB_y^w B_x^w \varphi$

Thus, when φ is a public belief of x, all other participants (here: only y, as I assume two participants x and y for simplicity) thus believe that x believes φ. The additional stipulation in (8-b) states that other participants' beliefs as of (8-a) are also public beliefs. This is to distinguish cases of incidental shared belief from those of public belief arising from observable linguistic (or other) behavior, *i.e.* from "manifest events" in the sense of Stalnaker (2002).[11]

---

[7]For details, in particular regarding *no*, see Rieser (2017a).

[8]The notation for accessibility relations follows Kaufman *et al.* (2006). W^φ is the set of worlds at which φ is true, $W^{\neg\varphi}$ the set of worlds at which φ is false, and $w \notin W^\varphi \rightarrow w \in W^{\neg\varphi}$.

[9]*cf.* McCready (2014) for discussion pertinent to Japanese.

[10]As defined by Asher and Lascarides (2003).

[11]In parallel to (8-b), I define *mutual introspection* in Rieser (2017b), to account for the publicity-sensitivity of the German particles *doch* and *ja* wich *e.g.* not felicitous in assertions that function to publicly announce the prejacent.

3.2 CCPs, input and output conditions

I use the following definitions in the CCP-model:

$\mathcal{U}$...utterance (DEC or INT with $\downarrow$ or $\uparrow$)

c...input context (world before utterance)

c'...output context (world after utterance)

$\mathcal{B}^{\mathcal{U}}$...set of belief conditions $\mathcal{U}$ imposes on c

$\mathcal{E}^{\mathcal{U}}$...set of evidence conditions $\mathcal{U}$ imposes on c

$\mathcal{PB}^{\mathcal{U}}$...set of public beliefs that arise from $\mathcal{U}$ (*i.e.* set of belief propositions added in c')

(9) shows the CCP of an utterance $\mathcal{U}(\varphi)$.[12]

(9) $\quad [\![\mathcal{U}(\varphi)]\!] = \{\langle c, c'\rangle \mid$
$$\mathcal{B}^{\mathcal{U}} \subseteq c \wedge \mathcal{E}^{\mathcal{U}} \subseteq c \wedge c' = c \cup \mathcal{PB}^{\mathcal{U}}\}$$

An utterance $\mathcal{U}$ is thus a set of pairs of admissible input and output contexts, and is felicitous iff for the world w at utterance time (the set of true propositions) $\exists c \in \langle c, c'\rangle \in \mathcal{U} : c \subset w$ holds, *i.e.* all belief and evidence propositions in an admissible input context c are true at utterance time (thus w itself is an admissible context). Admissible input contexts c must contain the members of $\mathcal{B}^{\mathcal{U}}$ and $\mathcal{E}^{\mathcal{U}}$, output contexts c' those and the members of $\mathcal{PB}^{\mathcal{U}}$.

To represent conditions on input contexts (felicity conditions) and on output contexts (commitments) in a more compact notation for ease of exposition, I henceforth also write $B_x^c\varphi$ for $B_x\varphi \in \mathcal{B}^{\mathcal{U}}$, $EV_x^c\varphi$ for $EV_x\varphi \in \mathcal{E}^{\mathcal{U}}$, and $PB_x^{c'}\varphi$ for $PB_x \in \mathcal{PB}^{\mathcal{U}}$.

3.3 Felicity conditions of assertions and FIs

I derive input conditions on falling declaratives from the two Gricean maxims of quality (Grice, 1975).

QI Do not say anything you believe to be false.

QII Do not say anything for which you lack
adequate evidence.

QI states that the speaker may not believe $\neg\varphi$ in c, that is $\neg B_S^c\neg\varphi$, and must have evidence sufficient to assert φ in c, that is $EV_S^c\varphi$.

(i) Commitment from assertion The evidence rule connects the two maxims of quality by the inference shown in (10) repeated from (7-b).

---

[12]I build on Davis' (2011) relational CCPs as sets of input / output context pairs, with the difference that I assume that there is a unique output context for each admissible input context.

(10) $\quad (EV_x^w\varphi > B_x^w\varphi) \wedge EV_x^w\varphi \vdash B_x^w\varphi$

Satisfaction of $EV_S^c\varphi$ (**QI**) ensures that the premise $EV_S^w\varphi$ is met, and satisfaction of $\neg B_S^c\neg\varphi$ (**QII**) rules out that the blocking condition $B_S^w\neg\varphi$ applies — thus, the inference in (10) goes through if an an assertion of φ by S is observed and judged felicitous, and the observer must assume that $B_S^w\varphi$ holds. Thus, commitment from assertion arises as $PB_S^{c'}\varphi$. (11) shows an according falling declarative CCP.

(11) $\quad [\![\text{DEC}(\varphi)\downarrow]\!] = \{\langle c, c'\rangle \mid$
$$\neg B_S^c\neg\varphi \wedge EV_S^c\varphi \wedge PB_S^{c'}\varphi\}$$

Assertion thus changes the context successfully if for utterance time w, $\neg B_S^w\neg\varphi$ and $EV_S^w\varphi$ hold, *i.e.* w is an admissible input context c. The assertion then gives rise to a public belief $PB_S^{w'}\varphi$, w' being the output context c' paired with c in $\text{DEC}(\varphi)\downarrow$.

(ii) Quality in interrogatives While Gricean maxims only cover assertions, (falling) interrogatives also come with belief conditions, *cf.* for instance Searle (1969). Inspired by Gricean quality, I propose a maxim **Q int** for interrogative utterances.

Q int Do not doubt what you believe to be true.

"Doubting" in **Q int** means "use in an interrogative utterance", reflecting the intuition that it is infelicitous to convey doubt over (in an FI) or ask about (in a question) something that one actually believes to be true — thus, $\neg B_S^c\varphi$ holds for interrogatives.

Recall that even when there is evidence for φ, the inference that the speaker believes φ does not go through for the if the blocking condition $B_x^w\neg\varphi$ holds, as blocked inference on the evidence rule repeated from (7-c) as (12) shows.

(12) $\quad (EV_x^w\varphi > B_x^w\varphi) \wedge B_x^w\neg\varphi \nvdash B_x^w\varphi$

FIs do not require $B_S^w\neg\varphi$ to hold, but tolerate it in contrast to assertions. I propose that adding *no* to FIs introduces a condition requiring evidence for the prejacent in the input context, compatible with an utterance world w at which $B_S^w\neg\varphi$ and $EV_S^w\varphi$ both hold, giving rise to a belief revision reading.

(iii) Forgone commitment from FIs While FIs can thus indicate that belief revision is underway, no speaker commitment arises from them by default. Furthermore, as assertion is an alternative to FIs,

28

they can give rise to a Q-implicature[13] in the form negated public belief $\neg PB_S^{c'}\varphi$ as in the CCP below, conveying that the speaker *forgoes commitment* to the prejacent.

(13) $[\![\text{INT}(\varphi)\!\downarrow]\!] = \{\langle c, c'\rangle \mid \neg B_S^c\varphi \wedge \neg PB_S^{c'}\varphi\}$

Negated public belief is defined in (14).

(14) a. $\neg PB_x^w\varphi \rightarrow B_y^w\neg B_x^w\varphi$
      b. $\neg PB_x^w\varphi \rightarrow PB_y^w\neg B_x^w\varphi$

As $\neg PB_x^{c'}\varphi$ is a conversational implicature, it can be canceled, so that $\neg B_S^c\varphi$ remains the only necessary condition on FIs. For instance, *no*-FIs indicate belief revision and $\neg PB_x^{c'}\varphi$ is canceled when the observer assumes revision is complete.

4 What particles do

I propose to analyze SFPs as paraphrased below.

no adds an input condition requiring evidence supporting φ available to both S and A.

ka marks interrogative force in Japanese utterances (with final falling intonation).[14]

yo adds an input condition $B_S^c\neg B_A\varphi$, and commits the speaker to $PB_A^{c'}\varphi$ in the output context.

ne adds an input condition $B_S^c B_A\varphi$.

That is, *ka* changes force from DEC to INT, introducing the felicity condition $\neg B_S^c\varphi$. The effects of *no*, *yo*, and *ne* on CCPs of FIs and, as a consequence, speech act felicity conditions are shown below.

4.1 *No*

As shown in (15), *no* adds a condition $EV_{\mathcal{X}}^c\varphi$ requiring evidence for the prejacent in in the input context.

(15) $[\![\mathcal{U}(no(\varphi))]\!] = \{\langle c, c'\rangle \mid \mathcal{B}^{\mathcal{U}} \subseteq c \wedge$
      $[\mathcal{E}^{\mathcal{U}} \cup EV_{\mathcal{X}}\varphi] \subseteq c \wedge c' = c \cup \mathcal{PB}^{\mathcal{U}}\}$

With *no*, evidence for φ must be accessible to not only the speaker but *all participants*, written as $\mathcal{X}$. That *no* has an evidential meaning has been proposed before, also by Davis (2011), who takes *no* to introduce an evidence presupposition. On my analysis, the evidence condition that *no* introduces as a

speech act modifier is of the same type as that required by **QII**, so that *no* makes a relatively small difference in assertions, only changing the extant evidence condition $EV_S^c\varphi$ to $EV_{\mathcal{X}}^c\varphi$.[15]

In the case of (falling) interrogatives, however, *no* has a more pronounced effect as they do not have and evidence condition of their own. In combination with the belief condition $\neg B_S^c\varphi$ (which tolerates $B^w\neg\varphi$ in the input context), $EV_{\mathcal{X}}^c$ characterizes an utterance situation where the speaker does not believe φ, but there is mutually accessible evidence for φ, giving rise to the incredulity reading.

4.2 *Yo*

Next, I propose *yo* modifies both input conditions and commitment in the CCP as shown in (16).

(16) $[\![\mathcal{U}(yo(\varphi))]\!] = \{\langle c, c'\rangle \mid [\mathcal{B}^{\mathcal{U}} \cup B_S\neg B_A\varphi] \subseteq c \wedge$
      $\mathcal{E}^{\mathcal{U}} \subseteq c \wedge c' = c \cup [\mathcal{PB}^{\mathcal{U}} \cup PB_S B_A\varphi]\}$

Yo introduces two changes: first, it adds an input condition $B_S^c\neg B_A\varphi$, *i.e.* that the speaker believe the addressee not to believe φ to be true. Second, it adds an output condition $PB_S^{c'}B_A\varphi$, *i.e.* speaker commitment to a belief that the addressee believe the prejacent to be true. This analysis also accounts for the "corrective" character of *yo*-assertions in a similar way as the update function STRONGASSERT (which forces addition of φ to a context set that already contains $\neg\varphi$ by non-monotonic update) proposed for *yo* by McCready (2005), who also suggests an input condition on the lines of $B_S^c\neg B_A\varphi$ independently.[16]

In FIs, this condition is added on top of $\neg B_S^c\varphi$ from *ka* (*i.e.* from INT), which conveys a speaker assumption that neither participant believes the prejacent to be true in the input context. Taken together with commitment arising from *yo*, this makes a belief revision reading (discussed in more detail in the next section) and thus an incredulity reading salient.

While the analysis of *yo* in Davis (2011) is similar in spirit, my proposal differs in two main points. First, I do not assume *yo* gives rise to $PB_S^{c'}\varphi$, *i.e.* does not commit the speaker, accounting for neg-

---

[13]*i.e.* a Quantity implicature in the sense of Geurts (2010).

[14]Final rising utterances without politeness morphology are ambiguous between declaratives and interrogatives in Japanese.

[15]Uses of *no*-assertions are highly varied and differ rather subtly from plain assertions, *cf.* Noda (1997) and Najima (2007) for extensive discussion. For discussion of how the present analysis accounts for some properties of *no*-assertions such as mirative overtones see Rieser (2017a).

[16]McCready (2009) modifies this aspect of the analysis.

atively biased readings of *yo*-FIs. Second, I do not take *yo* to occupy the same spot as final falling intonation, which I take to enter the derivation before the addition of particles. This is indirectly supported by the observation that German modal particles have similar functions as Japanese SFPs[17] but do not occur sentence-finally, which speaks against a shared position of speech act modifiers and intonation.

4.3 *Ne*

Finally, I propose *ne* modifies the CCP by adding a belief condition to the input context, as (17) shows.

(17) $\llbracket \mathcal{U}(ne(\varphi)) \rrbracket = \{\langle c, c' \rangle \mid [\mathcal{B}^{\mathcal{U}} \cup B_S B_A \varphi] \subseteq c \wedge$
$\mathcal{E}^{\mathcal{U}} \subseteq c \wedge c' = c \cup \mathcal{P}\mathcal{B}^{\mathcal{U}}\}$

Ne adds only $B_S^c B_A \varphi$, *i.e.* the speaker is required to assume that the addressee believe the prejacent to be true. This accounts for the observation frequently encountered in the descriptive literature that *ne* is a consensus-seeking or confirming particle, as this is predicted in the case of assertion, which also give rise to speaker commitment. It also straightforwardly accounts for the markedly different effect of *ne* in FIs by the combination of $B_S^c B_A \varphi$ with $\neg B_S^c \varphi$ from *ka*, indicating discrepant beliefs of speaker and addressee in the utterance situation (discussed in more detail in the next section).

It should be noted that there is a compositionality issue with regard to *yo-ne* utterances, as assuming that *yo* and *ne* both modify the basic utterance's felicity conditions at the same time leads to contradictory belief conditions. One way out is to assume, as for instance Takubo and Kinsui (1997) do, that modification is sequential. This can be paraphrased as *yo* imposing φ on the addressee and *ne* reinforcing this. As *yo* adds a commitment $PB_S^{c'} B_A \varphi$, it changes the context much like a (rising) declarative does. This makes it plausible that *yo* performs an update of its own right, which can then be confirmed with *ne*. The present framework is not capable of modeling such incremental context change and I leave this point for further research, also as I am not concerned with combination of *yo* and *ne* here. Alternatively, the observations in Oshima (2014) suggest that *yone* might be best analyzed as an independent lexical item.

5   Belief revisions and particles in FIs

The doubt and incredulity readings of bare FIs as well as versions with particles can be located within a belief revision process. To illustrate this, I define DOX$_x$, the doxastic state of agent x, as the set of worlds compatible with x's beliefs at a world:

(18)   DOX$_x(w) = \{w' \mid wR_x^{dox}w'\}$

Next, I define three types of doxastic states (DOX$^\alpha$, DOX$^\beta$, DOX$^\gamma$) by their relation to W^φ and $W^{\neg\varphi}$.[18]

(19)   a.   DOX$^\alpha \subseteq W^{\neg\varphi}$
      b.   DOX$^\beta \not\subseteq W^{\neg\varphi} \wedge$ DOX$^\beta \not\subseteq W^\varphi$
      c.   DOX$^\gamma \not\subseteq W^\varphi$

An agent in a state of type α thus believes φ to be false, an agent in a state of type γ believes φ to be true. In a state of type β, neither holds — the speaker considers both φ and $\neg\varphi$ possible. The sequence of doxastic states follows the stages of the belief revision process illustrated below.

5.1   Schema of belief revision under evidence

The schema below shows revision of $B_x \neg\varphi$ to $B_x \varphi$, *i.e.* x believes φ to be false and revises this belief.

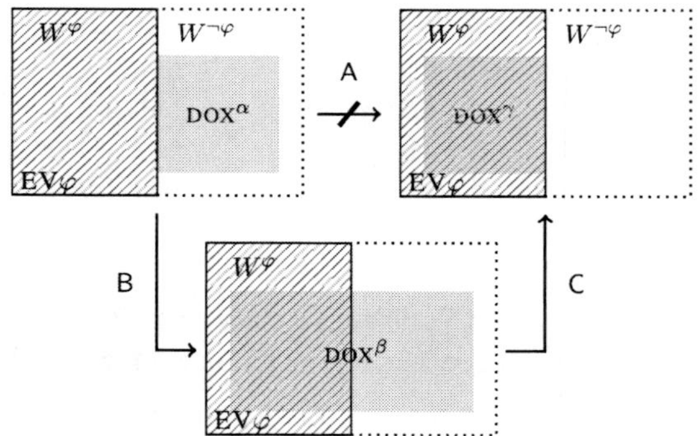

The shaded area represents evidence for φ, which can motivate belief revision from DOX$^\alpha$. Monotonic belief update, *i.e.* narrowing of DOX$^\alpha$ to DOX$^\gamma$ is not possible, as represented by the crossed-out arrow A, as there are no accessible φ-worlds in DOX$^\alpha$. Therefore, revision requires two steps — first, the DOX$^\alpha$ needs to be widened to DOX$^\beta$, represented by arrow

---

[17]As demonstrated in Rieser (2017b), where I analyze *doch* and *ja* as speech-act modifiers in a similar framework.

[18]Note that the subset notation is but a more compact variant, as for instance DOX$^\alpha$ can equivalently be defined as a doxastic state DOX such that $\forall w'.wR^{dox}w' : w' \in W^{\neg\varphi}$ etc.

B.[19] From the widened DOX$^\beta$, narrowing to DOX$^\gamma$ is possible, as represented by arrow C.

In the remainder of this section, I discuss how the proposed analysis accounts for the observations on particles in FIs, making reference to the belief revision schema where appropriate.

5.2 Doubt and incredulity: *no*

(20) Tori-ga   konna tokoro-ni sum-eru (no) ka.
      birds-NOM such_a place-in live-POT *no* *ka*
      "Can birds live in a place like this!?"/
      "Birds can live in a place like this after all!"

The addition of *no* in (20), repeated from (2), has the effect of making evidence in support of the prejacent mandatory in the input context. The bare FI without *no*, on the other hand, merely indicates that in the input context, the speaker does not believe prejacent φ to be true (which corresponds to a doubt reading).

Recall that *no* marks evidence in principle strong enough for assertion of φ. Thus, only the bare FI can be used to reject φ, while the *no*-FI typically receives a belief revision, or incredulity reading.

Bare FIs and doubt In Davis's doubt scenario, the speaker rejects accepting a claim by the addressee. Recall that, according to the analysis proposed above, the following holds for a bare FI.

(21) context before INT$(\varphi)\!\downarrow$: $\neg B^c_S\varphi$

In the belief revision schema, this only excludes doxastic states of type γ, so that speaker can either be in a state of type α or type β, *i.e.* either believe φ to be false be neutral. On the doubt reading as in Davis's example, the speaker is in a state of type α, *i.e.* believes φ to be false so that $B^w_S\neg\varphi$ holds in the utterance situation, and either does not consider belief revision at all as in (non-)step A, or suspends judgment by widening a state of type α to type β as in step B. In such cases, the implicature $\neg PB^{c'}\varphi$ (forgone commitment) arises and the utterance conveys that the speaker does not believe φ to be true.

Another reading of plain FIs should be mentioned here. It frequently occurs in soliloquy and conveys that the speaker is in a process of belief formation

from a doxastic state of type β based on observed evidence, corresponding to step C in the schema. In such cases, no negative bias arises.

Summing up, bare FIs can not convey full belief revision with both widening and narrowing (steps B and C), but can convey either individually. Bare FIs thus do not have belief revision readings like *no*-FIs.

***No*-FIs and incredulity** In Davis's incredulity scenario, the speaker reacts to evidence that has just come to the her attention, but is in conflict with a previously held belief. Recall that, according to my analysis, the following holds for a felicitous *no*-FI.

(22) context before INT$(\varphi)\!\downarrow$: $\neg B^c_S\varphi \wedge EV^c_\chi\varphi$

The *no*-FI thus conveys that the speaker's doxastic state is of type α or β, and that there is evidence for φ in principle strong enough for assertion of φ. In such an utterance situation, the speaker must take either step B, step C, or both. Note that if the speaker is in a state of type β, belief *formation* rather than *revision* happens as no widening needs to take place, as in soliloquous bare FIs mentioned above.

The crucial point to make w.r.t. the bias conveyed by *no* in FIs is that bare FIs tend to be negatively biased as they give rise to $\neg PB^{c'}_S\varphi$, while *no*-FIs are positively biased as they indicate that belief revision is underway, potentially canceling $\neg PB^{c'}_S\varphi$. This contrast comes out even more sharply with *yo*, as it directly adds commitment.

5.3 Shared doubt and incredulity: *yo*

Yo adds strong addressee orientation, as it conveys a speaker assumption that the addressee does not believe the prejacent to be true, but commits the addressee to it from the speaker's perspective.

(23) Sonna mono taberu (no) ka yo.
      such thing eat   *no* *ka* *yo*
      "What the hell! He isn't going to eat that!"/
      "Holy shit! He's going to eat that!"

In (23), repeated from (4), *yo* minimally indicates that the speaker is revising her assumptions about addressee belief, while the speaker doubts φ in the input context. The utterance thus either conveys that the speaker is learning that rather than both the speaker and the addressee doubting φ, the addressee actually believes it to be true, or that a shared belief

---

[19]I gloss over the question of how exactly widening, *i.e.* non-monotonic belief update works, seeking only to predict what FIs and particles convey w.r.t. stages in the schema, but *cf.* Gärdenfors (1985) and references therein for discussion.

that φ is true is in the process of formation, and both participants share doubt and incredulity. While this reading is salient in (23), changing the agent of 'eat' in (23) to the addressee ("You are going to...") foregrounds the reading on which the speaker revises an assumption about addressee belief.

For an account in the formal framework, consider belief conditions on and commitments from *yo*-FIs.

(24)   a. before $\text{INT}(yo(\varphi))\downarrow$: $B_S^c \neg B_A \varphi \wedge \neg B_S^c \varphi$
        b. after $\text{INT}(yo(\varphi))\downarrow$: $PB_S^{c'} B_A \varphi$

Revision of the speaker assumption w.r.t. addressee belief is reflected in the transition from $B_S^c \neg B_A \varphi$ to $PB_S^{c'} B_A \varphi$. The second input condition $\neg B_S^c \varphi$ indicates that the speaker assumes *both* participants doubt the prejacent. On the purely addressee-oriented reading, the speaker continues not believing φ, but learns that the addressee believes it. This is the negatively biased reading of *yo*-FIs.

When *no* is added to the *yo*-FI, evidence supporting the prejacent is required in the input context. In the belief revision schema, this means that step B and potentially C are taken (*i.e.* belief revision is underway) if the speaker believes φ to be false in the utterance situation, and that step C is taken (*i.e.* belief formation is underway) if the speaker is neutral in the input context. In either case, adding *no* gives rise to a positively biased reading on which the speaker accepts, or tends to accept, φ, and the speaker's belief revision or formation process is mirrored by what is assumed regarding addressee belief.

The mirative overtones in the form of surprise over the prejacent (or the addressee's belief that the prejacent holds) are readily explained by the input conditions, requiring the speaker to assume that neither participant believes the prejacent to be true. Also note that where the utterance is interpreted as indicating full belief revision, the forgone commitment implicature $\neg PB_S^{c'} \varphi$ is canceled.

5.4 Doubt and discrepant belief: *ne*

Utterances with *ne* are addressee-oriented like those with *yo*, but do not indicate any change in speaker assumptions regarding addressee belief. In assertions, *ne* signals or seeks agreement, while in FIs is indicates discrepant belief. The *ne*-FI (25), repeated here from (5), is an expression of doubt without, and one of reluctant acceptance with *no*.

(25)   Sonna mono taberu (no) ka ne.
        such   thing eat   *no* *ka ne*
        "So is he actually going to eat this?"/
        "So he is actually going to eat this..."

The present analysis predicts the following conditions on and commitments from a *ne*-FI.

(26)   a. before $\text{INT}(ne(\varphi))\downarrow$: $B_S^c B_A \varphi \wedge \neg B_S^c \varphi$
        b. after $\text{INT}(ne(\varphi))\downarrow$: $PB_S^{c'} B_A \varphi$.

In contrast to *yo*, *ne* only indirectly gives rise to $PB_S^{c'} B_A \varphi$ by carrying over the input condition $B_S^c B_A \varphi$. *Ne* in assertions thus indicates the speaker is confirming an assumption about addressee belief rather than attempting to convince the addressee as with *yo*. Assertions with *ne* are consensus seeking as they give rise to $PB_S^{c'} \varphi$, so that adding *ne* indicating that $B_S^c \varphi B_A \varphi$ holds indicates that φ is a shared belief. FIs, on the contrary, not only presuppose $\neg B_S^c \varphi$, but also give rise to the forgone commitment implicature $\neg PB_S^{c'} \varphi$. Thus, when *ne* occurs in FIs, it indicates a persistent discrepancy between speaker and addressee belief rather than consensus.

The salient reading of *ne*-FIs without *no* is intersubjective in that the speaker, as in assertions, seeks to confirm the status of the prejacent as a shared belief with the addressee, but carries strong negative bias — the goal is to convince the addressee of the prejacents' falsity, in sharp contrast with assertions.

Adding *no* gives rise to a reading on which the speaker, however reluctantly, considers joining the addressee in forming a shared belief based on the available evidence, that is taking step B, step C, or both. A surprise reading is unlikely as $B_S^c B_A \varphi$ makes it implausible that evidence for φ and thus the possibility that φ might be true just came up.

According to the proposed analysis, *ne*-FIs thus indicate a discrepancy between speaker and addressee belief, in stark contrast with assertions. This is compatible with the perception reported by informants that *ne*-FIs have a somewhat arrogant feel, casting doubt on the correctness of addressee belief, while *ne*-assertions, on the contrary, feel friendly. This is in line with the present proposal, but would be difficult to capture by encoding either shared belief or a status as old information in terms of hearer-newness directly into *ne*'s meaning, as would be indicated by generalizations based on assertions only.

References

Nicholas Asher and Alex Lascarides. 2003. *Logics of Conversation*. Cambridge University Press.

Christopher Davis. 2011. *Constraining Interpretation: Sentence Final Particles in Japanese*. Ph.D. thesis, University of Massachusets - Amherst.

Peter Gärdenfors. 1985. *Knowledge in flux. Modeling the dynamics of epistemic states*. MIT Press.

Bart Geurts. 2010. *Quantity implicatures*. Cambridge University Press.

Herbert P Grice. 1975. Logic and conversation. In Peter Cole and Jerry L. Morgan, editors, *Syntax and Semantics, Vol. 3, Speech Acts*, pages 41–58. Academic Press, New York.

Christine Gunlogson. 2003. *True to form: Rising and falling declaratives as questions in English*. Ph.D. thesis, UCSC.

Yurie Hara and Christopher Davis. 2013. Darou as a deictic context shifter. *Proceedings of Formal Approaches to Japanese Linguistics (FAJL)*, 6:41–56.

Stefan Kaufmann, Cleo Condoravdi, and Valentina Harizanov. 2006. Formal approaches to modality. In William Frawley, editor, *The expression of modality*, pages 71–106. Mouton de Gruyter.

Eric Scott Jr. McCready. 2005. *The Dynamics of Particles*. Ph.D. thesis, University of Texas at Austin.

Eric McCready. 2009. Particles: Dynamics vs. utility. *Japanese/Korean Linguistics*, 16(6).

Eric McCready. 2014. What is evidence in natural language? In Eric McCready, Katsuhiko Yabushita, and Kei Yoshimoto, editors, *Formal Approaches to Semantics and Pragmatics*, pages 155–180. Springer.

Fujio Minami. 1974. *Gendai nihongo no koozoo*. Taishukan Publishing.

Yoshinao Najima. 2007. *Noda no imi, kinoo: kanren-seiriron no kanten kara*. Kurishio.

Heiko Narrog. 2009. *Modality in Japanese: The layered structure of the clause and hierarchies of functional categories*. John Benjamins Publishing.

Harumi Noda. 1997. *"No(da)" no kinoo*. Kuroshio Publishers.

David Yoshikazu Oshima. 2014. On the functional differences between the discourse particles ne and yone in japanese. In *Proceedings of PACLIC 28*.

Lukas Rieser. 2017a. *Belief States and Evidence in Speech Acts: The Japanese Sentence Final Particle no*. Ph.D. thesis, Kyoto University.

Lukas Rieser. 2017b. Discourse particles as CCP-modifiers: German *doch* and *ja* as context filters. In M Otake, S Kurahashi, Y Ota, K Satoh, and D Bekki, editors, *New Frontiers in Artificial Intelligence, JSAI-isAI 2015 Workshops*, volume 10091 of *LNAI*, pages 93–108. Springer.

Lukas Rieser. 2017c. Quality of commitment: Japanese *daroo* as a speech act operator. *Investigationes Linguisticae*, 27. To appear.

John R. Searle. 1969. *Speech Acts*. Cambridge University Press.

Robert C. Stalnaker. 2002. Common ground. *Linguistics and Philosophy*, 25:701–721.

Yukinori Takubo and Satoshi Kinsui. 1997. Discourse management in terms of mental spaces. *Journal of Pragmatics*, 28(6):741–758.

Ai Taniguchi. 2016. Setnece-final *ka-yo* in Japanese: A compositional account. *Proceedings of FAJL 8: Formal Approaches to Japanese Linguistics*, pages 165–176. (MITWPL 79).

The Phrasal-Prepositional Verbs in Philippine English: A Corpus-based Analysis

Jennibelle R. Ella
De La Salle University Manila
jennibelle.ella@gmail.com

Shirley N. Dita
De La Salle University Manila
shirley.dita@gmail.com

Abstract

The study determines the most common forms of phrasal-prepositional verbs (PPVs) in Philippine English using the ICE-PHI and describes their syntactic and semantic features, following Quirk et al.'s (1985) framework. Thirty nine out of the forty-eight words from the list of Quirk et al. (1985) and Biber et al. (1999) were found in the corpus using AntConc 3.4. Results show that *come up with, get out of, look forward to, come out with, hold on to*, and *catch up with* are the most frequently used PPVs by Filipinos. These PPVs occur in active voice. They are intransitive verbs and are also inseparable. Findings further reveal that the meanings of the PPVs are the same as the single-word verb meanings provided by the online dictionaries of phrasal verbs, and those single-word verb meanings can replace the PPVs. Hence, they are idiomatic. The study implies that Filipinos use minimal number of PPVs. They appear to be conservative in their choice of PPV structure, but generally show proficiency in using PPVs in their utterances.

1 Introduction

Multi-word verbs (henceforth MWVs) are word combinations often used by native speakers in conversation because of their colloquial tone (Biber, Johansson, Leech, Conrad, & Finegan, 1999). To distinguish MWVs from other complex verb forms, Quirk, Greenbaum, Leech, and Svartvik (1985) classified MWVs into phrasal verb, prepositional verb, and phrasal-prepositional verbs. A phrasal verb consists of a verb and a particle and is either intransitive or transitive. An intransitive phrasal verb functions like a predication adjunct inseparable from its lexical verb (e.g. *The plane has now taken off.*)

while a transitive phrasal verb requires a direct object (e.g. *Victoria will set up the equipment.*). Moreover, a prepositional verb has a lexical verb and a preposition with which it is semantically and/or syntactically associated (e.g. *Look at the billboards.*). And finally, a phrasal-prepositional verb (henceforth PPV) takes a verb, an adverb, and a preposition, with two main structural patterns: verb+ particle + preposition +NP (e.g. *Jason had to keep away from salty snacks.*) and verb + NP + particle + preposition + NP (e.g. *They fobbed her off with a cheap perfume.*). According to Quirk et al. (1985), "many of them have idiomatic metaphorical meanings which are difficult or impossible to paraphrase" (p. 1179).

Interestingly, corpora-based studies have made it relatively easier to determine the typical behavior of the MWV expressions in both spoken and written discourse (Gardner & Davies, 2007; Ryoo, 2013; Biber et al., 1999). More so, a shift of approach on phrasal verbs, from the traditional to the cognitive, has greatly helped non-native speakers in understanding how productive the particles are (Cubillo, 2002; Kiativutikul and Phoocharoensil, 2014; Garcia-Vega, 2011). For instance, the particle *up* can have five meaning extensions ranging from literal to figurative ones (Rosca and Baicchi, 2016). Lindner (1981 in Lu Zhi and Sun Juan, 2015) clarified that "all the items of phrasal verbs sharing the same particles, literal or metaphoric, are correlated with one image schema, influencing the whole meaning of phrasal verbs" (p. 3). Understandably, the entire phrase, not its individual units, provides the primary meaning (Sinclair, 2008 in Garnier & Schmitt, 2015).

31st Pacific Asia Conference on Language, Information and Computation (PACLIC 31), pages 34–41
Cebu City, Philippines, November 16-18, 2017

Second language and foreign language learners nonetheless find MWVs ambiguous because of their notoriously difficult nature. Most of these MWVs do not have the equivalent expressions in the native language or they are non-existent at all in the mother tongue (Bensal, 2012). Viewed relevant in learning a second or foreign language to attain fluency, most students memorize the list of MWVs in their textbook. But according to Lu Zhi and Sun Juan (2015), learning about the multiple senses of MWVs can actually be systematic.

As a major category of MWVs, PPVs have not been extensively studied (Biber et al., 1999). To date, corpus-based studies on PPVs utilizing ICE-Philippines have yet to be reported. It is therefore the aim of this study to fill this gap and offer significant contributions to the existing literature in Philippine English. This study attempts to determine the most common forms of PPVs in Philippine English and describe their syntactic and semantic features.

2 Methodology

The data used for this study were drawn from the Philippine component of the International Corpus of English (ICE). Following the ICE standards as outlined by Nelson (1996), these four components included spoken and written texts in the form of public and private dialogue, scripted and unscripted monologue, student writing, letters, academic papers, popular papers, reportage, and instructional materials among others.

The PPVs were taken from the list presented in *A Comprehensive Grammar of the English Language* (Quirk et al., 1985, pp. 1179) and *Longman Spoken and Written English Corpus* (Biber et al., 1999, pp. 426-427). The PPVs are *break in on, catch up on, catch up with, check up on, come down with, cut down on, do away with, face up to, get away with, get down to, keep away from, keep up with, look down on, look forward to, look out for, look up to, put up with, run away with, stand up for, turn out for, get out of, come out of, get back to, go up to, get on with, get away with, get off at, get off with, go out for, get away from, go over to, hold on to, turn away from, turn back to, come in for, get back into, go along with, hand over to, keep up with,*

look out for, come out with, bring up in, come up with, give in to, come down to, end up with, go on to, and move on to. These 48 PPVs were searched in ICE-PHI using AntConc 3.4. The top five most frequent PPVs were considered for syntactic and semantic analysis.

For syntactic features, each of the five PPVs was analyzed in terms of type (I or II), transitivity and intransitivity, separability and inseparability, and voice. For semantic features, the meanings of the PPVs were determined based on the binary contrasts – idiomatic and non-idiomatic (Quirk et al., 1985). The online version of Oxford Dictionaries, MacMillan Dictionary, and Cambridge Dictionary of phrasal verbs were consulted for the single-word verb meanings of the PPVs.

3 Results

3.1 The Most Common Forms of Phrasal-Prepositional Verbs in Philippine English

Out of the 48 PPVs that were searched, 39 PPVs in the present, present participle, past, and past participle forms were found in the corpus, and they appeared more frequently in the spoken registers. Table 1 presents the most frequent PPVs in Philippine English. These are *come up with, get out of, look forward to, come out with, hold on to,* and *catch up with.* The last two PPVs share the fifth position, having the same number of instances.

In contrast, the least used PPVs in Philippine English are *check up on, look away from, look down on, run away with, go up to, catch up on, go out for, face up to, get down to, keep up with,* and *come down with,* occurring with only one hit each.

Phrasal-Prepositional Verbs	frequency		Total
	Spoken	Written	
come up with	49	24	73
get out of	29	15	44
look forward to	20	23	43
come out with	20	2	22
hold on to	8	4	12
catch up with	2	10	12

Table 1. Most common forms of PPVs

3.2 Syntactic Features of Phrasal-Prepositional Verbs

Occurring generally in the medial position (1 & 2) and rarely in the final position (3), *come up with* typically followed the type 1 pattern. With the absence of a direct object (henceforth DO) after the verb, this PPV is thus considered intransitive and inseparable, as illustrated in the sentences that follow:

(1) Okay so what he did was he grouped the workers into smaller groups asked them to *come up with* what they thought was a reasonable quota reasonable working hours. <ICE-PHI:S1B-006#17:1:A>

(2) Although maybe your organization Math Circle may *come up with* an arrangement with Computer Services Center wherein maybe they can *come up with* uh simple mainframe <.> fami </.> <.> familiariza </.> familiarization seminars okay for you people somewhere in your third or fourth year okay. <ICE-PHI:S2A-049#115:1:A>

(3) Then and then you integrate it with the visuals and I want to see you know I wanna hear my voice and then I wanna see what kind of visuals you *come up with*. <ICE-PHI:S1A-085#147:1:A>

Come up with appears in most of the sentences after the infinitival *to* in (1), forming an infinitival phrase and suggesting a purpose. Other usage is evident after the modals *can* and *may* in (2), and the personal pronoun *you* in (3). While most of the sentences with *come up with* take a complex noun phrase (henceforth NP) (2, 3), there is also a rare instance that *come up* with appears with a noun clause (1). The NP and the noun clause following the MWVs are therefore recognized as the object(s) of the PPVs and not as objects of the preposition *with*. Another pattern becomes evident in (3), where the PPV did not take an object.

In the case of *get out of*, both type 1 and type 2 syntactical patterns are observed; that means, it can be used as either intransitive in (4) or transitive in (5 & 6). Examples are provided below:

(4) *Get out of* that bed because we need it for somebody who's really sick okay <ICE-PHI:S2A-032#74:1:A>

(5) In a loyalty check conducted today the President is said to still be confident of having the support to *get him out of* the impeachment process <ICE-PHI:S2B-004#114:1:C>

(6) President Estrada's decision to *get the government out of* gambling appears to have been made without the necessary legal study. <ICE-PHI:S2B-003#56:1:A>

In the absence of the subject, *get out of* takes the initial position in (4) while in (5), it appears in the medial position after the infinitival *to*, thereby forming the infinitival phrase to modify *support*. The verb *get* and the particles *out of* are inseparable in (4) as the role of the verb is intransitive. In contrast, in (5), the verb and the particles are separable because of the presence of the pronoun *him* that takes the action of the verb *get*, giving a transitive role to the verb mentioned. The pronoun *him* understandably shares a central role in the expression as it becomes the DO. PPV as a lexical unit may appear discontinuous because of the pronoun *him*, being the DO, but it must be emphasized that *him* effectively intervenes between the elements *get* and *out of*, which in this case is a single semantic unit. Notably, *him* must intervene; it is then obligatory as a pronoun that its placement must be after the verb and not after the preposition. If the sentence is structured in this manner **… President is said to still be confident of having the support to get out of him the impeachment process*, there is obviously no syntactic relationship between the PPV and the pronoun, and the pronoun and the object. The NP *the impeachment process* is also acceptable since it behaves syntactically as a prepositional object and shows less tendency to passivize.

In (6), the expression *get the government out of* becomes part of the infinitival phrase that is a postmodifier to the main subject *decision*. This falls also under the type 2 pattern because the NP *the government* serves as its DO. Of the 44 times it appeared in the data, *get out of* generally collocates with a noun or a NP in (7) and occasionally with a pronoun in (8) or an adverb in (9).

(7) A new hegemon or a rogue nation may rise to challenge the predominance of the United States and *get out of* its sphere of influence. <ICE-PHI:S2B-035#57:1:A>

(8) What do you *get out of* it <&> inaudible answer </&>. <ICE-PHI:S1B-005#128:1:A>

(9) I wanna </[> </{> get out of here as fast as I can. <ICE-PHI:S1A-018#158:1:B>

Apparently used as active voice, *look forward to* is seen more popularly in the written than in spoken discourse. It generally appears in the medial position, acting as the main verb in (10) and forming the infinitival phrase in (11).

(10) He 's been *looking forward to* this all year round. <ICE-PHI:W1B-008#31:1>

(11) There's something to *look forward to*. <ICE-PHI:S2A-038#37:1:A>

Moreover, it follows the type 1 pattern as it will be cumbersome to insert a NP or a pronoun in the expression (**I look something forward to; *I look the party forward to; *I look her forward to.*). The verb and the particles are inseparable as the verb has an intransitive role and implies a syntactic function with other elements. It usually takes a prepositional object as exemplified in (10) with pronoun *this*. In (11), *look forward to* does not take a prepositional object and thus shows divergence from what is typical in the corpus.

The PPV *come out with* is intransitive, and it restricts the movement of the elements as it can make the expression troublesome. In (12), *come out with* occurs as part of the infinitival phrase that serves as the complement to the verb *planning*.

(12) Philippine P.E.N. is planning to *come out with* an anthology of works by members published in the 1990s. <ICE-PHI:W1B-016#145:8>

Moreover, *hold on to* follows the type 1 pattern (13 & 14) that suggests the intransitivity of the verb. The particles cannot be disjoined from its verb as they always must be written right next to the verb, so an attempt to put NP in between the elements may result in grammar error. Examples of these are shown below:

(13) Reach forward as far as you can just forward and *hold on to* your toes. <ICE-PHI:S2A-052#94:2:B>

(14) The illegitimate daughter, Maria Rosa, would later turn out to be the single reason why her mother held on to life and sanity. <ICE-PHI:W2E-006#6:1>

In (13), *hold on to* is written after the conjunction *and* as part of the compound verb of a simple sentence while in (14), it is positioned as part of the relative clause. In both instances, the prepositional object is evident.

Finally, *catch up with* in the past form functions as the main verb of the independent clause in a complex sentence in (15). It also shows that an attempt to cut the string of words into single units may invite questions in terms of its acceptability. The pronoun *us* follows the PPV, which takes the role of the prepositional object as shown below:

(15) The work bug *caught up with* us as we saw a McDonald 's store with a new burger that they launched. <ICE-PHI:W1B-011#133:2>

3.3 Semantic Features of Phrasal-Prepositional Verbs

The word *come* is defined by the online Oxford English Dictionary as *to move or travel towards or into a place thought of as near or familiar to the speaker*. It also means *to arrive/occur/happen/take place*. Linking the verb to its preposition, the particle *up* commonly appears with a motion verb like *come* to suggest direction or movement. It is considered the most productive because it can be used together with different classes of verbs but still retains its directionality. The preposition *with* means *accompanied by or having/possessing something*. When the three elements are combined, *come up with* becomes a PPV, which means *to produce/create/devise/think up*. For instance, if in (16 & 17) as shown below, *come up with* is replaced by a single-word verb *produce* and the thought remains the same, then the phrase possesses an idiomatic meaning.

(16) And hopefully with a very sincere effort with the President and with the support of both

houses of Congress to _come up with_ (**produce**) an amnesty program for the rebels. <ICE-PHI:S2A-001#117:1:B>

(17) Pardo directed the GETB and Trade Undersecretary Nelly Villafuerte to review the system and _come up with_ (**produce**) the recommendations on the issue. </p> <ICE-PHI:W2C-006#98:5

Interestingly, in (16 & 17) the word _produce(d)_ fits the intention of the speakers and does not give room for the listener/ reader to doubt about the kind of message being conveyed. The utterances use the appropriate PPV to make sense and to intensify its semantic content by emphasizing the object of the PPV. Remarkably in (17), the PPV provides the successive action, but the writer could have opted to use a single-word verb as the proposition suggests a level of formality because of the topic discussed. It may be inferred then that the writer chose the "less formal" expression to build a better writer-reader relationship.

Get out of means _to evade/avoid/escape/cut_ in Oxford Dictionaries. In MacMillan Dictionary, this PVV has the following meanings: _get out of something means to avoid doing something; get something out of something means to get pleasure or benefit from something; get out of something is to take off clothes so that one can put on more comfortable clothes; get something out of someone is to persuade someone or give information or money; and get out of here means to tell someone to leave._ The multiple meanings generated from the expression would necessitate different scenarios to make their usage appropriate and acceptable. Examples are given below:

(18) Now it is a sad fact though that students _get out of_ (**leave**) the university with having the barest knowledge of polymers. <ICE-PHI:S2A-035#14:1:A>

(19) Then _get out of it_ (**leave/cut**), of that relationship.<ICE-PHI:S1A 7#76:1:B>

(20) Let 's say for example you _get six out of_ ten sixty percent. <ICE-PHI:S1B-020#2:1:A>

* Let 's say for example you **leave** six ten sixty percent.

(21) In a loyalty check conducted today the President is said to still be confident of having the support to _get him out of_ the impeachment process. <ICE-PHI:S2B-004#114:1:C>

*In a loyalty check conducted today the President is said to still be confident of having the support to **leave him** the impeachment process.

(22) The second type are the dishonest cab drivers because they are tampering the cab meter just to _get enough out of_ you. <ICE-PHI:W1A-012#98:5>

*The second type are the dishonest cab drivers because they are tampering the cab meter just to **benefit** from you.

In (18), the speaker gives his/her observation about the students who get out of the university but still lack knowledge of polymers. The PPV is replaced by _leave_, and the sentence still makes sense, giving a hint that it is a verbal idiom. In (19), the speaker gives an order to _get out of_ the relationship, which presupposes that the listener is in a relationship that is no longer healthy or beneficial to him/her. The single verb _leave_ or _cut_ is deemed appropriate to replace the PPV as it provides the same intended meaning. In (20), the attempt to replace the PPV with _leave_ brings semantic constraint. The expression _get six out of ten_ indicates transparency and should be taken in its literal sense.

In (21), the PPV has a direct object _him_ referring to the President, properly positioned after the verb and effectively intervenes between the verb and the particle. To test whether the expression is idiomatic or non-idiomatic, PPV can again be tried to be substituted by a single verb. In this case, however, the intent to replace _get him out of_ with _leave him_ should not be pursued since doing so may create ambiguity in making meaning. Its semantic content probably entails a closer examination of its context. Further, _get enough out of you_ as an expression in (22) can be taken in its literal sense since there is no single-word verb that can be used to capture what must be conveyed. Replacement can only be made possible by considering a prepositional verb in *benefit from*, which violates the single-word verb rule but still makes the expression a verbal idiom. However, what comes after the verb is an adjective, which cannot function as a DO. Syntactically, the expression is acceptable as it has become popular in informal spoken discourse, but it cannot be labeled as DO because only the noun or pronoun can perform the role. Hence, the construction of the expression is atypical.

MacMillan Dictionary notes the meaning of *look forward to* as *to feel happy and excited about something that is going to happen*. In another online dictionary, it means *to await eagerly*. This PPV is found to be more popular in the written than in spoken discourse. Its meaning is reflected in the way it is used in the succeeding sentences:

(23) I *look forward to* (**await (eagerly)/ feel happy and excited about**) working with you and contributing to research in the area of linguistics where my interest lies. <ICE-PHI:W1B-024#89:5>

In (23), *look forward to* is used at the end of a formal letter to express that the writer is hopeful that something will happen. These samples provide evidence that Filipinos are aware of its idiomatic status and in fact practice its correct usage. Labeling a PPV like this as informal and colloquial can already be challenged since its use extends to formal letters.

Further, *come out with* means *to say something suddenly and unexpectedly* in Cambridge Dictionary. The use of *come out with* in (24) seems to be redundant since the word *statement* comes after the PPV. The speaker may have opted to say *"will give a statement…"* rather than *"come out with the statement"* to make the message clear. In (25), *come out with* is incorrectly used, causing the change of meaning when the standard meaning (dictionary) is applied. *Produce/introduce/launch* can give better meaning sense.

(24) But uh I feel and I believe that uh the group uh of uh the the this corporation that wanted to get the franchise will *come out with* (**say /**

declare) the statement that there was no pay off. <ICE-PHI:S1B-034#131:1:D>

(25) Because if ever they *come out with* (**say / declare**) a big proposal they might beassured of a business that would yield profit to the company that they are working for. <ICE-PHI:S1A-089#104:1:B>

Cambridge Dictionary states that *hold on to* means *to keep something you have*. This PPV can be replaced in (26 & 27) by the word *keep* and can still retain its meaning. The change of PPV to a single-word verb in (26) makes *keep* become parallel with *seek* in the second clause. In (27), the insertion of *keep* in the place of *hold on to* makes the meaning more transparent as it becomes formal. In both instances, the word *keep* was able to give the same meaning in a clear and concise manner and thereby considered idiomatic.

(26) There was no job he would *hold on to* (**keep**), no other job he would seek. <ICE-PHI:W2F-009#117:1>

(27) You know what I call imperial Manila want to *hold on to* (**keep**) those powers and to that money as if their dear lives depended on it. <ICE-PHI:S2A-028#98:1:A>

(28) *Hold on to* your toe. <ICE-PHI:S2A-052#172:2:B>

**Keep* your toe.

In contrast, the PPV in (28) if it is to be replaced with a one-word standard meaning from the dictionary, the sentence will accommodate *keep* and will result in **keep your toe*. Syntactically, it follows the correct order, but semantically, the sentence may sound cumbersome since *your toe* is a body part, which a person does not normally lose. Because the verb *hold* can act as transitive or intransitive, the meaning of the combination should be taken separately. In this particular instance, *hold on to* is non-idiomatic because the individual meanings of the components in the sentence are apparent (Quirk et al., 1985).

The final PPV is *catch up with*, which in MacMillan Dictionary means *to affect, apprehend, influence, etc*. In (29), *affected* can replace the PPV and still make the sentence sound meaningful, thereby proving the idiomatic characteristic of the PPV.

(29) I wasn't able to continue with the last part of this paragraph because time *caught up with* (**affected**) me. <ICE-PHI:W1B- 001#18:1>

Another distinct finding is the overuse of PPV in one sentence. In (30 & 31), *come up with* was repeatedly used. In (30) where *come up with* was mentioned three times, there is an assumption that the speaker is an instructor who requires a class project, and the repetition occurs because he wants to emphasize that there can be variety (e.g. lamp, wall decoration, electrical project). In (31), the speaker tries to suggest an arrangement or a mainframe in which he/she used the expression twice.

(30) They have to *come up with* a lamp or they may have to *come up with* a wall decoration or they should *come up with* an electrical project anything that has something to do with reports and this may be the application of all the things that they learned in <mention> Technical Writing </mention> <ICE-PHI:S1A-089#78:1:A>

(31) Although maybe your organization Math Circle may *come up with* an arrangement with Computer Services Center wherein maybe they can *come up with* uh simple mainframe <.> fami </.> <.> familiariza </.> familiarization seminars okay for you people somewhere in your third or fourth year okay. <ICE-PHI:S2A-049#115:1:A>

4 Discussion

Based on the results, Filipinos show minimal usage of PPVs, although this is quite expected. Biber et al. (1999) pointed out that the occurrences of PPVs are common in conversation and fiction, but rare when compared to phrasal verbs and prepositional verbs. It clearly implies that Filipinos, as non-native speakers, are conservative in using PPVs in their utterances. As it has become the

convention, English as a subject is taught as a formal language where proper usage of words and expressions are emphasized. Furthermore, many Filipino students who are not required by social contexts to speak in English will tend to have a lesser fluency in English. Another possible explanation is the fact that MWVs do not exist in Tagalog or Filipino, the mother tongue. Speakers' difficulties may arise from their tendency to translate an expression or find an equivalent in order for them to keep up with the conversation (Bensal, 2012). And in truth, the complexity of constructing PPVs can also be contributing to the infrequent use of PPVs.

The PPVs in the present study typically occur in the active voice. Bensal (2012) noted that active voice is more preferred than the passive voice, for it allows the speaker to express himself/herself in a more direct and emphatic manner. Moreover, the PPVs are hardly passivized as their construction can be awkward and barely acceptable. For example, *His own version has been *come up with*; *Your toes are *held on to*.

Except for *get out of*, PPVs fall under Type 1 with intransitive role and behave like all other intransitive phrasal verbs. Because they only have one semantic role, DO is not necessary in the expression since it can create discontinuity in the expected order of elements. Additionally, Filipinos conveniently use PPVs that are typically inseparable, and as such, they do not show any movement of particles.

According to Quirk et al. (1985), "the semantic unity of phrasal verbs can often be manifested in single-word verb" (p. 1162). The six PPVs are proven to have an idiomatic status. Their meanings are not predictable, and the fact that there could be many verb and particle combinations that can occur during substitution, the meaning assigned to a particular verb or to a particle does not remain constant (as in the case of *come up with* and *come out with*). Each PPV has only one meaning sense upon examining the sentence and comparing the meaning of the PPV and the meaning taken from the online dictionary.

The misuse of PPV (in *come up with* and *come out with*) in a few utterances may have only occurred due to confusion in the use of particle. Nonetheless, it does not seem to be problematic, and it cannot be considered errors as the number may be insignificant in the first place. However, repetition (*come up with)* makes the utterance uninteresting to listen to. According to Dixon (1991), "it is infelicitous to repeat the same word several times in a sentence" (p. 91). This may have been avoided if only the speakers were able to clarify their semantic motivation in using such expressions in one sentence.

5 Conclusion

The study aimed to determine the most common forms of PPVs and describe the syntactic and semantic features of the most frequent PPVs. The six most common PPVs found in the corpus were mostly used in the present tense. Although there were 39 PPVs out of 48 PPVs in the corpus, these occurrences can still be considered low compared to the volume of existing PPVs in the English language. The study suggests that Filipinos, being second language learners, are conservative in using PPVs. The few instances of PPVs in both the spoken and written discourse may stem from the assumption that they just rely on the PPVs they previously know. Syntactically, the lack of variation in the expression indicates that they show the tendency to adopt only one structure, which may also have something to do with unfamiliarity with other expressions, complexity of structure, or limited vocabulary. However, it is significant to point out that, generally, knowledge and proficiency in the use of PPVs are evident, suggesting that the speakers are confident in using the PPVs they know in spoken and written discourse.

References

Cambridge Dictionary. Retrieved April 2, 2017 from http://www.dictionary.cambridge.org/us/.

Choorit Kiativutikul and Supakorn Phoocharoensil. 2014. A corpus-based study of phrasal verbs: carry out, find out, and point out. International Journal of Research Studies in Language Learning, 3 (7), 73-88.

Dee Gardner and Mark Davies. 2007. Pointing out frequent phrasal verbs: A corpus-based analysis. TESOL Quarterly: A Journal for Teachers of English to Speakers of Other Languages and of Standard English as a Second Dialect, 41 (2), 339-359.

Douglas Biber, Geoffrey Leech, Stig Johansson, Susan Conrad, and Edward Finegan. 1999. Longman grammar of spoken and written English. Pearson Education Limited, Harlow, England.

Edwina Bensal. 2012. The prepositional verbs in Asian Englishes: A corpus-based analysis. Unpublished Master's Thesis, De La Salle University Manila.

Lu Zhi and Sun Juan (2015). A view of research on English polysemous phrasal verbs. Journal of Literature and Art Studies, 5 (8), 649-659.

MacMillan Dictionary. Retrieved April 2, 2017 from http://www.macmillandictionary.com/us.

Mari Carmen Campoy-Cubillo. 2002. Phrasal and prepositional verbs in specialized texts. IBERICA 4, 95-111.

Melodie Garnier and Norbert Schmitt. 2015. The PHave list: The pedagogical list of phrasal verbs and their most frequent meaning senses. Language Teaching Research, 19 (6), 645-666.

Michelle Garcia-Vega. 2011. Transitive phrasal verbs with the particle out: A lexicon grammar analysis. Southern Journal of Linguistics, 35 (1), 75-110.

Randolph Quirk, Sidney Greenbaum, Geoffrey Leech and Jan Svartvik. 1985.A comprehensive grammar of the English language. Longman, London:

Robert M. W. Dixon. 1991. A new approach to English grammar on semantic principles. Calendon Press, Oxford.

A Type-Logical Approach to Japanese Potential Constructions

Hiroaki Nakamura
Institute for Promotion of Higher Education
Hirosaki University
1, Bunkyo-cho, Hirosaki, Aomori Prefecture
036-8560, JAPAN
hiroaki@hirosaki-u.ac.jp

Abstract

Potential constructions have long attracted much attention in Japanese Linguistics, mainly focusing on the case alternation of object NPs. I will point out some important characteristics of the constructions they have missed and propose a completely new analysis from a view point of logical grammar. First, we show significant differences between potential and passive sentences which have been assumed to been projected from one and the same suffix –*rare* 'can'. I suggest that these two uses must be distinguished at least in contemporary Japanese. Our type-logical approach to unbounded dependencies has an empirical coverage broader than traditional and generative grammatical approaches and can explain the fact that various arguments including adjuncts can be marked with nominative. We also examine interesting interactions of case alternation with scope alternation.

1   Introduction

Potential constructions have long attracted much attention in Japanese Linguistics, mainly focusing on their meanings and case-alternation phenomena. I argue in this paper that the past studies have failed to describe their important characteristics in significant ways and propose a completely new analysis from a formal grammar view point. To show what is wrong with the past analyses, let us observe the points Japanese traditional linguistics have assumed, and show why the potential suffix *rare* must be distinguished from the passive *rare*, and then propose an analysis which can properly deal with a broad empirical coverage. Observe the standard active and passive pair in Japanese in (1).

(1) a. Hitobito-wa   sakuban takusan-no
  People-Top   last-night a lot of
        banana-o   tabeta.
      bananas-Acc   ate.
 'People ate a lot of bananas last night.'
   b.   Takusan-no   banana-ga sakuban
        A lot of   bananas last night
 hitobito-niyotte   taber-are-ta.
        people by   eat-Pass-Past
        'A lot of bananas were eaten by people last
        night.'

Sentences in (1) show a typical active-passive correspondence where the passive suffix -*rare* is used to form the passive complex verb *taber-are-ta* 'were eaten,' the theme argument *banana* is subjectivized and the agent argument is demoted to the adjunct marked with oblique case. In Japanese linguistics, it has been assumed that the same suffix -*rare* is also used to form the potential verbs and that the distinction in interpretation between passives and potentials is dependent on contexts. It is also suggested that complex potential verbs project active or passive potential sentences and the distinctions were made depending on surface case markings of arguments, as exemplified in (2) (see Teramura 1982 for discussion on this dichotomy):

(2) a. Kodomo-ga   kono banana-o   taber-are-u.
   Children-Nom this banana-Acc eat-can-Pres

'The child can eat this banana.' (active)
b.   Kono banana-ga   mou   taber-are-ru.
    This banana-Nom already eat-Can-Pres
'This banana can be eaten now.' (passive)

Teramura (1982) and his followers call sentences like (2a) 'active potentials' and those like (2b) passive potentials. This dichotomy has led to the analyses dealing with the contrast in (2) in terms of active/passive voice alternation. It seems, however, that this kind of analysis is completely wrong. We will show several pieces of evidence which are clearly inconsistent with the voice-based account of potential constructions.

First, let us consider the difference in the subject status of the two constructions. In Japanese linguistics, it has been assumed that the discontinuous honorific form *o ... ni-nar* triggers agreement with the subjects. In the literature, the behaviors of prefix *o* and the suffix (light verb) (-*ni*)-*nar*- are sometimes accounted for independently and given separate positions and functions, but I simply take it as a kind of discontinuous morpheme which 'sandwiches' a verb stem and mark its external argument as a person to whom the speaker shows his or her deference.

Subject honorification has been assumed to target subjects, referring to people worthy of respect and generative grammarians have suggested the head of honorific form *o ... ni-nar* agree with the subjects which have moved to the spec, TP or Spec, vP position (see Kishimoto 2012, Hasegawa 2006, among others). We argue that the discontinuous morpheme *o .. ni-nar* does NOT, in fact, trigger honorific agreement with the sentential subjects. Consider (I attach the negative predicate just to make sentences sound natural):

(3) a. Sensei-ga   gakusei-o   o-sikari-ni-nar-e-nai.
     Prof-Nom   student-Acc Hon-blame-Hon-
                               Can-NOT-Pres
     'The professor[+honorific] cannot scold students.'
b. Sensei-ni   gakusei-ga   o-sikari-ni-nar-e-nai.
     Prof-Dat   student-Nom Hon-blame-Hon-
                               Can-NOT-Pres
c. Sensei-ga   gakusei-ni   o-sikar-are-ni-natta.
     Prof-Nom   student-BY   Hon-blame-Pass-
                               Hon-Past.
     'The professor[+honorific] was blamed by students.'

It should be noticed here that the derived form *sikar-rare* comprising the base verb and the passive suffix in (3c) is wrapped by the honorific form *O ... ni-nar*, whereas the discontinuous honorific form first combines with the base verb, and then is followed by the potential suffix in potential (3a) and (3b). In (3a), the nominative *sensei* 'teacher' is marked as the person worthy of respect, so the honorific *o ....ninar-* targets the subject which is the agent of the base verb *sikar-*, as predicted from the past work. In (3b), the target of honorification is not nominative object, but the dative subject, which should be taken to agree with the honorific form. In passive (3c), though the derived subject is the target of honorification, it is the theme argument of the base verb. We will show that the subject honorification can and must target the external argument (i.e., the agent of base verbs because the potential suffix combines only with action verbs), regardless of their case markings, in potential sentences, whereas only the derived subject (i.e., the theme argument) can be marked as a person to respect in passive sentences. We will also discuss phenomena regarding quantification and anaphora resolution to propose a new, proper analysis of the potential constructions.

2   Difference between Passive and Potential Uses of the Suffix *Rare*

Though it is widely assumed that one and the same suffix *rare* is used in both passive and potential constructions, we will argue that the two uses must be clearly distinguished at least in contemporary Japanese. Besides, though many researchers like Teramura (1982) have argued that potential constructions are divided into active and passive ones, we believe this dichotomy, as well as the notion of 'nominative object' in generative grammar (we will come back to this shortly) is simply wrong, and claim that there be only one analysis of potential sentences regardless of the surface case markings of their (non-)arguments. In addition to (apparent) active-passive pairs like (2a) and (2b), any argument or its possessor argument can actually become subjects in potential sentences, whereas only theme arguments can and must be subjects in passive constructions.

(4) a. Kono naifu-ga/-de   katai kami-o/kami-ga
     this knife-Nom/-With   hard paper-Acc/- Nom
     yoku kir-(ar)e-ru. (potential)
     well cut-Can-Pres
     'They can cut papers well with this knife.'
b.*Kono naifu-ga   kami-o   yoku kiru.
                             (active)

c. *Kono naifu-ga   (kami-o)   yoku kir(are)-ta.
                                              (passive)

(5) a. Kono michi-ga/-kara   tyozyo-made   nobor-e-ru
      This path-Nom/-From   top-up-to   climb-Can-
                                                    Pres
      'This path enables you to climb up to the top of
      the mountain.'
   b. Kono-michi-ga   cyozyo-made   nobor-u.
                                              (active)
   c. *Kono-michi-ga   cyo-zyo-made   nobor-are-ta.
                                              (passive)

In potential (4a) and (5a), potential sentences with
the instrument and locative arguments   marked
with nominative as well as their original oblique
cases,   whereas   their   active   and   passive
counterparts   are   completely   ungrammatical.
Therefore, the notion of active/passive potentials is
simply wrong. It should be noticed in passing that
honorification can be applied even to (4a)(*kono
naifu-ga   kami-o   joozuni o-kir-ini-nar-eru*
'Pro[+respect] can cut hard paper well with this
knife' and (5a)(*Kono michi-ga tyozyo-made o-
nobor-ininar-e-ru* 'This path enables you[+respect]
to climb up to the top' to mark the pro subjects as
persons to be worthy of respect'), while it cannot
apply to the active and passive counterparts. We
argume, therefore, that the characterization of
subject   honorification   as   a   diagnosis   of
subjecthood seems also wrong at least in the
examples we have seen so far. In potential
constructions, the honorific form wrapping the
base verbs indicates that the speakers show respect
to the persons referred by the outermost arguments
of the base verbs, not of the derived complex
predicates.

Another   fact   showing   the   difference
between the passive and potential verbs is
observed in sentences with the subject-oriented
anaphor *zibun* 'self'. While *zibun* can show up in
all potential constructions and construed as picking
out the same individuals with explicit or implicit
agent arguments of base verbs, the coreferential
readings   are   possible   only   with   the   derived
subjects in passives.
(6) a. Oisii karee-ga   jibuni-no daidokoro-de
      delicious curry-Nom self-Pos   kitchen-In
      tsukur-(rar)e-ru.   (potential)
      make-can-Press
   b.*[?]Oisii karee-ga   jibuni-no daidokoro-de
      tsukur-(rar)e-ru.   (passive)

In (6b), *karee* 'curry' cannot be construed as an
antecedent of the anaphora for pragmatic reasons
(i.e., it is not [+Human]).

The properties of potential constructions that
any argument of base verbs can be the subject of a
matrix   sentence   and   that   subject   oriented
honorification and anaphora agree with the agent
argument of a base verb regardless of its surface
case   marking   shows   a   sharp   contrast   with   the
properties of passives though the two constructions
have been assumed to be projected from the same
suffix. From now on, let us focus on the derivation
and interpretation of potential constructions in the
next section.

3   Type-Logical   Account   of   Potential Constructions

In this paper, I assume that the readers are familiar
with some version of logical grammars (especially,
type-logical and/or categorial grammars) and omit
basic explanations except for a few basic rules. In
addition   to   the   normal   elimination/introduction
rules, we need to posit the infixation or extraction
operators to insert a constituent into or extract it
from a bigger constituent. Let us assume that a
linguistic expression is a triple <prosodic form,
meaning, syntactic category>. Here, s_1, ..., s_n stand
for prosodic forms with + as concatenation
operator, A/B or B\A stands for a functional
category looking for an expression of category B
(on the right in the former and on the left in the
latter) to form an expression of category A.

(7) Elimination and Introduction

Elimination

$$
\frac{s_1 \quad s_2 \\ \alpha{:}A/B \quad \beta{:}B}{s_1{+}s_2{:}\alpha(\beta){:}A} \; /E
\qquad
\frac{s_2 \quad s_1 \\ \beta{:}B \quad \alpha{:}B\backslash A}{s_2{+}s_1{:}\alpha(\beta){:}A} \; \backslash E
$$

Introduction

$$
\frac{\dfrac{[x{:}B]^n}{s_1{:}\alpha{:}A}}{s_1{:}\lambda x.\alpha{:}A/B} \; /I^n
\qquad
\frac{\dfrac{[x{:}B]^n}{s_1{:}\alpha{:}A}}{s1{:}\lambda x.\alpha{:}A\backslash B} \; \backslash I^n
$$

The elimination rules /E and \E are often called
modus ponens. These rules derive an expression of

category A as a conclusion from expressions of categories B and A/B or B\A as premises. The introduction rules correspond to lambda-abstraction in semantics. Assuming some arbitrary x of category B, we suppose that an expression of category A can be derived. Then we discharge the assumption x:B (linguistically, phonologically null elements of category B) to abstract over *x* and create a function of category A\B or A/B as a conclusion, depending on where the discharged assumption is located. The assumption and the step at which it is discharged are coindexed with an integer *n*, and the discharged assumption is shown in square brackets.

In addition to the standard elimination and introduction rules, we need the special elimination (infixation/wrapping) and introduction (extraction) operators to deal with discontinuity (See Morrill 1994, 2011, Carpenter 1997 for discussion).

(8) Infixation and Extraction Constructor

    a. If a, b $\in$ Cat, then B $\downarrow$ A $\in$ Cat.

       Type(B $\downarrow$ A) = Typ(B)$\rightarrow$Type(A)

    b. If a, b $\in$ Cat, then A $\uparrow$ B $\in$ Cat.

       Type(A $\uparrow$ B) = Typ(B)$\rightarrow$Type(A)

The category A $\downarrow$ B stands for a function that wraps an argument of category B with discontinuous expressions and form the expression of category A. The idea of (8b) is that an expression of category A has an expression of category B missing somewhere within it.

(9) $\downarrow$ Elimination (Infixation)

$$\frac{\begin{array}{cc} \vdots & \vdots \\ s_3 & s_1{+}s_2 \\ \beta{:}B & \alpha{:}A \downarrow B \end{array}}{s_1{+}s_3{+}s_2{:}\alpha(\beta){:}A} \downarrow E$$

(10) $\uparrow$ Introduction (Extraction)

$$\frac{\dfrac{\begin{array}{ccc} s_1 & [x{:}B]^n & s_3 \\ \vdots & & \vdots \end{array}}{s1{+}s3{:}\alpha{:}A}}{s1{+}s3{:} \lambda x.\ \alpha{:}B \uparrow A} \uparrow I^n$$

First we assume an arbitrary expression of category B within the discontinuous expressions s^1 and s^3 which are taken to be a single constituent of category A. Where *x*:B is extracted, we discharge

this assumption, which is represented as in [*x*:B]^n (as in standard implication introduction rules, the assumption and the stage where the introduction rules applies must be co-indexed with integer *n*), and get the discontinuous constituent with an expression of category B missing anywhere inside it, to which category A $\uparrow$ B is assigned. As an example of infixation, we show the derivation of a potential predicate wrapped by the discontinuous honorific form.

(11)   tabe   o-ni-nar   -e   ru

$$\frac{\dfrac{\text{eat}'(x,y){:}V \quad V\downarrow V \quad \Diamond{:}V\backslash V \quad \text{PRES}}{\text{o-tabe-ni-nar}{:}\text{eat}'(x_{[+respect]},y){:}V}\,\downarrow E}{\text{o-tabe-ninar-e-}\Diamond V{:}\text{eat}'(x_{[+respect]},y)}$$

Note here that the $\uparrow$ introduction rules must have been involved here implicitly to allow for delay of the concatenation of the base verb and its arguments until the derived complex predicate combines nominative NPs.

Given the standard and additional elimination and introduction rules above, we can show the derivation of potential constructions. In the same spirit as many current lexicalist approaches, we assume passive predicates in Japanese are lexically formed accompanied by changes in their argument structures, as we have seen from the passive examples, so let us focus on the derivations of potential sentences, where we will argue the potential predicates are NOT formed in the lexicon, but derived in syntax via the $\uparrow$ introduction rule. Let us take (3a) and (3b) as examples, where the object NP is assigned nominative or accusative case. When it is marked with accusative case, we don't need any new device to explain the derivation. The verb stem *sikar* 'scold' combines with the object, then the derived passive form is wrapped by the honorific form. We use the introduction rule to postpone the concatenation of the base verb and direct object. Here let us assume that the potential verb takes an experiencer argument in its own argument structure, and looks for the base verb with a gap and a pro agent (this is the target of honorification), which is construed as an anaphora if the experiencer of the potential verb is phonologically realized (see Steedman 1996 for a lexicalist approach to control). The derivation of a part of (3b) can be shown in (12).

(12)   gakusei-ga $[x:n_{th}]^2$ o-sikar-i-nar   -e-ru
                                         scold':$s\backslash n_{pro}\backslash n$ $\diamondsuit$:$((s\backslash n)\uparrow n)\backslash(s\backslash n)$
                    ----
                    scold'($pro_{[+respect]}$,x): $s\backslash n_{pro}$

                         $\diamondsuit$scold($pro_{ana[+respect]}$,x)(y_{Exp}):$(s\backslash n_{pro})\backslash n_{Exp}$
                         --$\uparrow I^2$
$(s\backslash n)/(s\uparrow(n...n)\uparrow n)$ $\diamondsuit$(scold($pro_{ana[+respect]}$,x):$((s\backslash n_{pro}))\backslash n_{Exp})\uparrow n)$

                    $\diamondsuit$(scold($pro_{ana[+respect]}$,student')(y):$(s\backslash n_{Exp})$

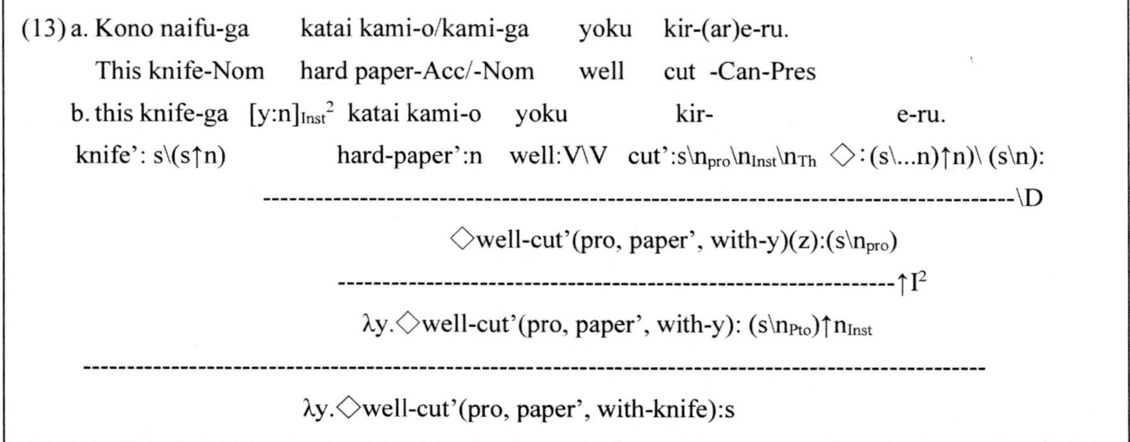

(13) a. Kono naifu-ga   katai kami-o/kami-ga   yoku   kir-(ar)e-ru.
        This knife-Nom   hard paper-Acc/-Nom   well   cut -Can-Pres
     b. this knife-ga $[y:n]_{Inst}^2$ katai kami-o   yoku   kir-   e-ru.
        knife': $s\backslash(s\uparrow n)$ hard-paper':n   well:V\V   cut':$s\backslash n_{pro}\backslash n_{Inst}\backslash n_{Th}$ $\diamondsuit$:$(s\backslash...n)\uparrow n)\backslash (s\backslash n)$:
                         --\D
                    $\diamondsuit$well-cut'(pro, paper', with-y)(z):$(s\backslash n_{pro})$
                         ---$\uparrow I^2$
                    $\lambda y.\diamondsuit$well-cut'(pro, paper', with-y): $(s\backslash n_{Pto})\uparrow n_{Inst}$

                    $\lambda y.\diamondsuit$well-cut'(pro, paper', with-knife):s

In Japanese, it is well-known that nominative case is licensed by a tensed verb. We also assume that a nominative NP is able to combine an open proposition (and/or ab open predicate) in a stative sentence, which means a nominative noun phrase can combine with a proposition (or predicate) with a missing argument somewhere inside it if the latter can be construed as a property of the former. This assumption can be proved by the derivation of (13) above, where the instrument argument of the base verb appears as the major subject.

In (13), we assume that optional arguments like the instrument argument here can be added (inserted) into argument structures of base verbs anytime. The base verb *kir-* 'cut' combines with the direct object first, and then consumes the optional instrument premise y:n_{Inst} via the standard elimination rule. After the base verb combines with *rare*, this assumption is discharged to form an open proposition with an instrument gap missing (the discharged assumption is shown in brackets in (13b)). The nominative instrument must be raised to be the special category which looks for an open proposition on its right. In (13b), the derived predicate correctly denotes a property of the subject (it has a property to make it possible for anyone to cut hard paper with it). Notice here that an arbitrary number of nominative noun phrases can occur in potential constructions because there is no limit on the number of application of the $\uparrow$ introduction rule. Observe (14) as an example containing multiple nominative phrases.

(14) Kono naifu-ga   sentan-ga   katai kami-ga
     this knife-Nom   edge-Nom   hard-paper-Nom
     yoku kir-(ar)e-ru.
     well cut-Can-Pres

where the subject corresponds to the possessor of the instrument NP *sentan-de*, so the remaining predicate means a set of sets of entities which enables anyone to cut hard paper with its edge.' Since the argument structure is not changed in a potential sentence, subject honorification can be applied to (14), marking the agent of the base verb as a person worthy of respect.

4 Quantification in Potential Constructions

In Japanese generative linguistics, many authors tried to explain the case-alternation phenomena we have seen so far in terms of Case-checking, but they have made the same mistakes as traditional grammarians did. Object noun phrases marked with nominative in potential (and other stative) sentences are called 'nominative object', which is quite misleading and clearly excludes the possibilities that oblique and possessor arguments become subjects of potential predicates. They have tried to explain the case alternation in terms of A-movement, not A'-movement which might allow a wide variety of arguments to be the major subjects as in the tough constructions. In addition to the fact that our analysis of subjectivization in potential sentences covers a much wider variety of data, we will show that our approach can easily deal with the phenomenon of quantifier-scope alternation between noun phrases with different case markings and the modal verb *rare*. Tada (1992) pointed out a very interesting phenomenon concerning quantified objects, as in:

(15) a. Taroo-ga   migime-dake-o   tsumu-re-ru.
      Taroo-Nom right-eye-only-Acc   close-CAN-
                                      Pres
      'Taroo can close only his right eye.'
                  (only>can, can>only)
    b. Taroo-ga   migime-dake-ga tsumur-e-ru.
                  (only>can, *can>only)

(15a) means that Taroo can wink (*rare* scopes over *migime-dake*) or Taroo cannot close his left eye (*migime-dake* scopes over *rare*). On the other hand, (15b) with its object marked with nominative case does not mean Taroo can wink. Tada explained this scope difference in terms of NP-movement, which cannot apply to the wide range of subjectivization possibilities we have seen in potential constructions here. The oblique argument cannot be (at least directly) moved to the position where its nominative case is licensed. On the other hand, our explanation using the extraction constructor can easily account for all potential case alternations while giving appropriate meanings to the sentences. I just show the derivation of the potential sentence including the oblique argument modified by only subjectivized.

(16) a. Kono naifu-dake-de   enpitsu-ga   kezur-e-ru.
       this knife-Only-With pencil-Nom   sharpen-
                                        Can-Pres
      (CAN > ONLY, *ONLY > CAN)
    b. Kono naifu-dake-ga enpitsu-ga   kezur-e-ru.
          (ONLY > CAN, *CAN>ONLY)

Regardless of word order, the oblique noun phrase (instrument argument, etc.) must take the narrow scope with respect to the suffix *rare* here, whereas the instrument argument marked with nominative case must outscope the suffix *rare*. The former interpretation can be easily derived only with the elimination rule, so let us see the derivation of the wide scope reading of the instrument subject.

We suppose the empty instrument argument $[n{:}x]$ as an optional assumption, which is discharged after the formation of the complex verb phrase of category n ↑ s (whose type is a function from individuals to sets, as with the standard slash categories), as shown by the square brackets. The instrument subject is a standard generalized quantifier which takes the whole predicate as an argument and return the truth value, and has a similar meaning with the universal quantifier,

---

(17)   Kono naifu-dake-ga $[x{:}n]^1$ enpitu-ga $[y{:}n]^2$ kezur-(rar)e-ru.
       this knife-ONLY-Nom   pencil-Nom   sharpen-CAN-Pres
       s/(s↑n): $\lambda P. \forall x(Px \rightarrow knife(x))$ (s\n)/(n ↑ (n\s))   n\(n\s): $\Diamond sharpen(pro,y,x)$
       ---------------------------------   --\E
                                 n\s: $\Diamond sharpen'(pro, y, x)$
                         ------------------------------------↑I²
                        n ↑ (n\s)): $\lambda y. \Diamond sharpen(pro,y, x)$
                   --/E
                   s\n: $\Diamond sharpen(pro, pencil', x)$
            -- ↑ I¹
                  n ↑ s: $\lambda x \Diamond sharpen(pro, pencil,x)$

        --/E
           s: $\forall x(\Diamond sharpen(pro, pencil,x) \rightarrow Knife(x))$

---

though its necessary and sufficient conditions should be reversed. The derived predicate phrase denotes the set of entities which enables arbitrary persons to cut hard paper with them.

Our approach can easily deal with sentences with an arbitrary number of nominative NPs (and corresponding missing arguments of base verbs) because the multiple applications of the ↑ introduction rule are allowed. We have argued that the subject in Japanese stative sentence is licensed when it can combine with an open proposition, so we can NOT predict the semantic role of the subject when we process it. We reconstruct the whole meaning of the potential sentence, using the logic we introduced above. To construct a predicate phrase with a missing argument (or adjunct) in it, a base verb combines with the assumption x:np first. Then we discharge it via the ↑ introduction operation, which corresponds to lambda-abstraction to bind the variable. Note here that the category s ↑ n is simply assigned to open propositions with a gap inside it. In (17), the subject (corresponding to the instrument argument of the base verb) takes the open proposition projected from the tensed potential predicate as an argument, and scope over the whole predicate including the suffix CAN. We assume here that the meaning of *dake* 'only' is a kind of universal quantifier with its antecedent and precedent of the standard universal quantifier reversed. So we can correctly derive the meaning of sentence (17) as shown below:

(18) $\forall x[\Diamond cut'(pro, hard\ paper, with\text{-}x) \rightarrow knife'(x)]$

(18) means that no knives other than this knife enable any person to cut hard paper with it.

3.1   Conclusion

We argue that the potential and passive constructions should be dealt with in a completely different way from the approaches Japanese traditional and generative grammar have pursued so far. Passive and potential uses of rare must be distinguished and treated separately even though they are projected from the (etymologically) same suffix. We also suggest that passives are derived in the lexicon accompanied by changes in their argument structures while potential predicates are constructed in syntax with proper semantic analysis in which any argument of base verbs can become the subjects, which combine with open propositions of the discontinuous category derived by the ↑ introduction and lambda abstraction. The derived complex potential predicates are built up in a compositional manner, and eventually denote the complex properties of the subjects. We also suggested subject honorification should be treated to target external arguments of verbs, instead of subjects. In potential constructions, the argument structures of base verbs are NOT changed, so, whether their external arguments are realized explicitly or implicitly, the agent NPs (assuming that the verb stems in potential predicates are action verbs) must be the targets of honorification. We explained the important phenomena concerning quantified arguments of base verbs with a wide variety of case alternations.

References

Carpenter, Bob. 1997. Type-Logical Semantics. MIT Press, Massachusetts.

Chomsky, Noam. 1977. On wh-movement. In Peter Culicover, Thomas Wasow, and Adrian Akmajian (eds.), Formal syntax. 77-132. Academic Press, New York.

Chomsky, Noam. 1981. Lectures on Government and Binding. Foris, Dordrecht.

Hicks, Glyn. 2009. Tough-Constructions and their Derivation. Linguistic Inquiry 40:535-566.

Hasegawa, N. 2006. Honorifics. In Martin Everaert and Henk van Riemsdijk, eds., The Blackwell Companion to Syntax., 493-543. Blackwell, Oxford.

Inoue, Kazuko 2006. Case (With Special Reference to Japanese). In Martin Everaert and Henk van Riemsdijk, eds., The Blackwell Companion to Syntax. Vol III. pp. 295-373. Blackwell, Oxford.

Kishimoto, Hideki. 2012. Subject Honorification and the Position of Subjects in Japanese. Journal of East Asian Linguistics 21:1-41.

Morrill, Glyn. 1994. Type-Logical Grammar. Springer, Dordrecht.

Morrill, Glyn. 1995. Discontinuity in Categorial Grammar. Linguistics and Philosophy 18:175-219.

Morrill, Glyn. 2011. Categorial Grammar - Logical Syntax, Semantics, and Processing. Oxford University Press, London.

Steedman, M. 1996. Surface Structure and Interpretation. MIT Press, Massachusetts.

Szablcsi, Anna. 2010. Quantification. Cambridge University Press, Edinburgh.

Tada, Hiroaki. 1992. Nominative Objects. Japanese. Journal of Japanese Linguistics 14:91-108.

Takano, Yuji. 2003. Nominative Objects in Japanese and Complex Predicate Constructions: A Prolepsis Analysis. Natural Language & Linguistic Theory 21: 779-834.

Teremura, Hideo. 1982. Nihongo-no Sinakusu-to Imi. Kuroshio Publishers, Tokyo.

Standard and Nonstandard Lexicon in Aviation English: A Corpus Linguistic Study

Ramsey S. Ferrer
Philippine State College of Aeronautics
Piccio Garden, Villamor, Pasay City,
Philippines
ramsey_ferrer@dlsu.edu.ph

Jollene G. Empinado
Philippine State College of Aeronautics
Piccio Garden, Villamor, Pasay City,
Philippines
empinado34@gmail.com

Eloisa Marie N. Calico
Philippine State College of Aeronautics
Piccio Garden, Villamor, Pasay City,
Philippines
calicoeloisamarie@yahoo.com

Jan Yharie T. Floro
Philippine State College of Aeronautics
Piccio Garden, Villamor, Pasay City,
Philippines
janyhariefolor@gmail.com

Abstract

This study aims at investigating the lexical items in Aviation Phraseology that has both standard and nonstandard meanings when Pilot and Air Traffic Controller (ATC) use them in radiotelephony. A collection of Cockpit Voice Recorder or Quick Access Recorder transcripts with 26,421 words from the Civil Aviation Authority of the Philippines (CAAP) and from International Airlines' accessible transcripts has been the primary data for scrutiny. Through a corpus-based analysis and a survey research, the present study reveals that the lexical items *go ahead, hold short, priority,* and *affirm* are used sporadically in nonstandard ways that might lead to ambiguity, and thus posing potential errors. In the survey conducted for Pilots and ATCs, both affirm the occurrence of nonstandard use in Aviation Phraseology. ATCs assert that the nonstandard use of such lexical items frequently occur during Route or En-route Clearance while Pilots confirm that these transpire during Takeoff Clearance, Altitude Clearance, Approach Clearance, and Landing Clearance. Precisely, the nonstandard use of Aviation Phraseology in this study shows nonconformity in the efforts of the International Civil Aviation Organization to provide "maximum clarity, brevity, and unambiguity". Furthermore, awareness of this phenomenon must be heightened among aviation students who are future aeronautical professionals in the field.

1   Introduction

English started as the official language of the International Civil Aviation Organization (ICAO) in 1951, and only in 2011 has the ICAO implemented language requirements on aviation personnel including the usage of standard phraseology in all radio communication. In recent years, the majority of aviation disasters have been caused by human errors, and one of the most common forms is miscommunication, which can potentially lead to catastrophic repercussions. One contributing factor to the occurrence of miscommunication is the wrong interpretation of instructions. For instance, the controller may use a certain word with standard definition to command, but the pilot may interpret the word in non-standard way. Consequently, a single miscommunication may result in a bigger problem due to wrong interpretation.

In June 2014, the Transportation Safety Board of Canada (TSB) reported a runway incursion at Ottawa International airport between a Medevac helicopter and A300 cargo plane. The airport controller amended LF 4 Medevac's IFR clearance by stating: "LF 4 Medevac Roger, *while we wait* amend your Ottawa 3 for a right turn heading 290° balance unchanged". The tower controller observed that AW139 was taxiing across the hold short line while FDX 152 Heavy (A3OO) was landing on runway 25. According to the findings, Medevac helicopter was given an amendment to its instrument flight rules clearance. The airport controller's first transmission to LF4 Medevac began with non-standard phraseology "*while we wait*", which can be confused with "*line up and wait*". As a result, the Medevac pilot expected that a clearance to take off would follow the amendment to the instrument flight rules clearance. Another factor is that the Medevac pilot did not check if runway was clear before taxiing across the hold short line, leading to the runway incursion with FDX 152 Heavy (A300) approaching to land.

In March 2013, another case occurred when the non-standard phraseology *"actually standby ah"* was used in Boeing 727. The freighter was cleared to takeoff on a runway occupied by two snow clearance vehicles. The cancellation of take-off clearance was not received, but a successful high speed rejected takeoff was accomplished on sight of the vehicles before their position was reached. The controller's failure to 'notice' the runway blocked indicator on his display and to his non-standard use of Radio-Transmission communications, i.e. *"actually standby ah"* when he cleared B727 for takeoff and saw the vehicles on the runway, added to the occurrence. The right phraseology should be *"takeoff clearance cancelled"*, and any such cancellation issued after the aircraft has started to roll should take the form *"abort takeoff"*. It was found out that the controller had never been required to use either of these phrases since qualifying.

In the light of these cases, it is vital to analyze the discourse between pilots and ATCs, who may be native or non-native English speakers, and to recognize the standard phraseology used in non-standard ways, which may probably lead to ambiguity and thus posing potential errors to communication.

The ICAO puts a great emphasis on non-native English speakers in acquiring a certain level of ATC proficiency, whereas native speakers of English are not prompted by ICAO to adhere to the standard phraseology. According to Hyejeong and Elder (2009), the ICAO considers the level of English proficiency of non-native aviation personnel before implementing the ICAO language policies. The article emphasizes that the responsibilities for miscommunication in aviation where English is used as a *lingua franca*, are distributed across native and non-native English speaking ATCs and pilots.

Tewtrakul and Fletcher (2010, cited in Swinehart, 2013) conducted a study in Bangkok International Airport with 312 flight recorded citing for common error among three groups: Thai ATC-Thai pilot, Thai ATC-native English speaking pilot, and Thai ATC-foreign pilot who is a non-native English speaker and does not speak Thai. The study revealed that radiotelephony misunderstandings arise most often among non-native English speakers. Indeed, it is worth noting that the responsibilities shared by pilots and ATCs must adhere to the use of standard phraseology. However, some lexical items (e.g. hold short, priority, etc.) in aviation phraseology could be used in non-standard ways. Mendez-Naya (2006) investigated the evolution of the term *right* over time. While the word *right* has a standard use as an adjunct of direction, other definition has also been espoused as "correct" and "exactly". Furthermore, it also functions as a discourse marker, locative or time expressions, adverbs, prepositional phrases, or clauses modifier, making the term more ambiguous. More recently, Swinehart (2013), who expanded Mendez-Naya's study, examined a particular lexical item *right* and examined its usage in standard and non-standard ways through a corpus of Cockpit Voice Recording (CVR) transcripts from National Transportation Safety Board (NTSB). Surprisingly, only 18.2% of occurrences of *"right"* in CVR transcripts were used in standard ways. This is a very alarming since almost 80% are generally used in various nonstandard ways. It can be concluded that this is an apparent deviation from the ICAO's efforts to provide "maximum clarity, brevity, and unambiguity" (p. 3-2), creating ambiguity in a field of discourse where clarity of communication is vital. Although Swinehart's (2013) corpus-based study looked into how the lexical item *right* was used in non-standard ways, the present study broadly investigates other lexical items irrespective of their typologies (Bratanić & Ostroški Anić, 2009). In addition, Swinehart's (2013) study still needs theoretical underpinnings as regards the nonstandard use of such lexical items. This occurrence can be explicated by the emergence of the world Englishes across the globe where pilots and ATCs who may be native or non-native English speakers use English in their own right.

The pioneering model of World Englishes formulated by Braj Kachru in early 1980s, also known as the Kachru's Concentric model, allocates the presence of English: the inner circle, where language functions as a native language (ENL); the outer circle, where English functions as a secondary language (ESL); and lastly, the expanding circle where English serves as foreign language (EFL). This model may politically show the nativeness and non-nativeness of English speaking ATCs and pilots in different nations. However, Rosenberger (2009:23) argued that, "while some nations may never have been easy to classify in this tripartite system, the world-wide use of English has produced increasingly overlapping areas of the three circles." Although there is a need to revisit Kachru's three-circle model in this regard, it is still vital to be taken into account since pilots and ATCs either native or non-native speakers of English coming from different nations speak different varieties of English. Precisely, there is a need to understand the World Englishes paradigm and use it as a theoretical underpinning in describing the lexical items in standard phraseology having non-standard definition. These alarming problems led the researchers to investigate the most common lexicon in standard phraseology with nonstandard definition in aviation discourse that may pose potential problems in communication. Despite the importance of communication for aviation safety, there is a lack of research that would systematically examine the language of pilots and ATCs.

2   Methodology

This study primarily used corpus linguistic approach in order to answer the questions and to yield findings that are implicative for improving the radiotelephony communication of ATCs and pilots in the Philippines. The corpus is a collection of CVR or QAR transcripts from the CAAP (2016), and transcripts from international airlines' accessible transcripts. It is worth noting that all of these transcripts were obtained on the basis of availability due to high confidentiality. While the Air Traffic Services (ATS) of the CAAP agreed to accommodate interviews with the pilots and ATCS, it could not provide or release copies of the conversation transcripts. However, due to strong requisition of the study, the ATS released only three transcripts, ensuring that the airline companies remained anonymous.

In addition, the study adapted the survey of Said (2011) from the International Air Transportation Association (IATA). Through convenience sampling, the survey was launched for the ATCs and pilots who provided necessary information as regards the use of standard phraseology with nonstandard definition and the situations in which this phraseology typically occurs.

3   Results and Discussion

The study investigated lexical items used in Aviation Phraseology that has both standard and nonstandard meanings.

3.1   Lexical Items Utilized in Standard and Nonstandard Ways

The lexical item *go ahead* with standard definition predominantly appeared in the corpus, having only one occurrence of its nonstandard counterpart. On the other hand, the lexical item *hold short* with standard definition also predominantly occurred in the corpus, having only one occurrence of its nonstandard counterpart. The lexical items *priority* and *affirm* were both used in nonstandard ways

Lexical Items	Standard Use	Non-standard Use
Go ahead	87.50% (7)	12.50% (1)
Hold short	85.71% (6)	14.29% (1)
Priority	0%	100% (1)
Affirm	0%	100% (1)

Table 1: Identified Lexical Items

3.2 Standard and Nonstandard Definitions of Identified Lexical Items

The lexical items *go ahead, hold short, priority* and *affirm* were identified in the corpus with standard and nonstandard definitions. The standard definitions were based on Radiotelephony Manual ICAO's Standard Phraseology while the nonstandard definitions of the identified lexical items were based on the analyses in the ATCs Air Traffic Controllers' and Pilots' surveys and on the ICAO Phraseology Reference Guide.

Lexical Items	Standard Use	Nonstandard Use
Go Ahead	to give permission to state a request	to move forward
Hold Short	to not cross or enter the mentioned runway	to proceed or to continue
Priority	to state emergency situation that is often mentioned together with the terms "MAYDAY" or "PAN-PAN"	considered nonstandard if it does not state the kind of emergency
Affirm	used to define "yes"	should be "affirmative" which is often misheard as "negative"

Table 2: Standard and Nonstandard Definitions of the Identified Lexical Items

3.2.1 Go ahead

An example of lexical item *go ahead* in nonstandard use appeared in the recorded conversation from the Air Traffic Controller and flight crew between Asiania 222 and Etihad 513.

Listing 1

Asiana 222: hold short at Juliet, Asiana 222
ATC: ETD 513 follow Oceania on holding short Juliet Runway
ETD 513: I\x92II make a report
ATC: Go ahead
ETD 513: Echo tango delta 513 at hoel give us regional chart from your left.
ATC: \x85Regional chart from left T523
ATC: Asiana 222, there ah.. call the ramp and see hold\x85
Asiana 222: Repeat\x85 Asiana 222

In the transcript, the pilot of Asiana 222 misunderstood the instruction when the Air Traffic Controlled said the phraseology *go ahead*. The pilot of Asiana 222 assumed it was their aircraft that was instructed to proceed in the mentioned runway using the phraseology *go ahead*, not knowing that the instruction to go ahead and make a report was for ETD 213.

3.2.2 Hold short

The nonstandard use of *hold short* also appeared in the conversation between the Air Traffic Controller and the pilot of Asiana 222. The pilot of Asiana 222 was instructed to hold short at Juliet. However, the aircraft was seen to have kept moving because the pilot misinterpreted the phraseology *go ahead* as *to proceed* or *to continue*.

Listing 2

ATC: Asiana 222, you are supposed to hold short at Juliet, sir.
ATC: Asiana 222\x85
Asiana 222: (unreadable)
ATC: I can make a report, so hold short of Juliet, you're already passing\x85
Asiana 222: Ah.. I though you made some alignment on empire\x85
ATC: The empire is not moving. I told you to hold short and call the ramp
Asiana 222: \x85Copy
ATC: Echo tango delta 513 what\x92s the ramp on you?

ETD 513: Okay\x85 that\92s a\x85 hotel\x85 523
ATC: Okay. Will it be open sir.
ETD 513: (unreadable)

3.2.3 Priority

The lexical item *priority* appeared in the corpus once .In this situation, the pilot used the word *priority* to state his concern where ICAO highly advised that when stating an emergency, the pilot and air traffic controllers must use the standard phraseology, i.e. in any instances that need an immediate assistance, *MAYDAY* is used while *PAN-PAN* can be used in situations that do not require an immediate assistance but can be considered as an urgency message

Listing 3

> **27 TWR:** Blue Jay Six-Zero-Four-Four, hold short Fox-one
> **30 SRQ6044:** Hold short Fox-one
> **33 RP-C1432:** Tower, One-Four-Three-two we requested **priority** because of a losing oil pressure you made go around
> **44 TWR:** RP-C One-Four-Three-Two climb four thousand runway heading contact one-two-one-one say again last

3.2.4 Affirm

Another phraseology that may lead into misunderstanding on the Radio telecommunication between pilot and air traffic controllers is the use of the phrase *affirmative*. In ICAO Standard Phraseology, the use of *affirm* phraseology is defined as *yes*. Some nations use the word *affirmative* which can be considered as a non-standard phraseology because of the fact that *affirmative* can be heard as *negative*.

Listing 4

> **UA224:** it\x92s UA224, do you have weather at Manchester and Bradley?
> **BOS APP:** **Affirmative**, stand by.

3.3 Situations where Nonstandard Use Occurs: Air Traffic Controller Survey

28.57% of the respondents picked Route or En-route Clearance where nonstandard phraseology is most commonly used in the corpus. However, it is during Taxi Clearances, Landing Clearances, and Approach Clearances where nonstandard phraseology is seldom used with 3.57%

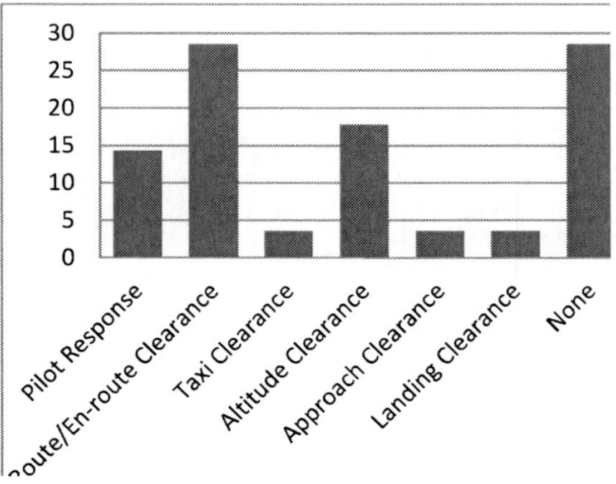

Figure 1: Air Traffic Controllers Survey

3.4 Situations where Nonstandard Use Occurs: Pilot Survey

It is during Takeoff Clearances, Altitude Clearances, Approach Clearances, and Landing Clearances where nonstandard phraseology is commonly used with 15.79% in the corpus. However, the pilot agreed that it is during Route or En-route Clearances and Taxi Clearances where nonstandard phraseology is seldom used.

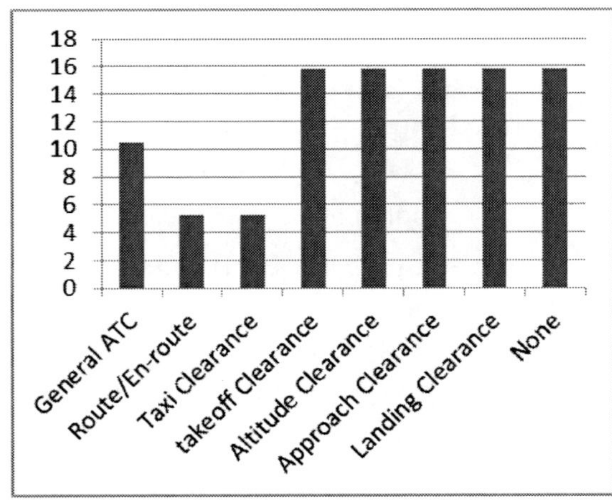

Figure 2: Pilots Survey

4   Conclusion and Recommendation

This study investigated lexical items in aviation phraseology with standard and nonstandard definitions as used by ATCs and pilots. As revealed in the corpus, these are *hold short, go ahead, affirm* and *priority*. According to the surveys conducted with ATCs and pilots in the Philippines, it is during Route Clearances or En-route Clearance where nonstandard phraseology is mostly encountered while the least used occurs during clearances for General ATC.

According to the Air Traffic Controllers and Pilots and on the ICAO radiotelephony manual, Air Traffic controllers, pilots and aviation students should be aware that there are existing lexical items with standard and non-standard definition or use. In using the lexical item *go ahead,* the air traffic controller and the pilot must state the aircraft call sign to avoid the confusion in radio telephony communication. In using the lexical item *hold short,* the pilot should read back the last message transmitted by the air traffic controller to clarify that the message is fully understood. In using the lexical item *priority,* the pilot should state the reason of requesting a priority. Using the word *priority* may lead into a confusion with the phraseology *Mayday. Mayday. Mayday.* and *Pan-Pan. Pan-Pan. Pan-Pan,* which can also be used to request an urgent message. In using the lexical item *affirm,* the pilot and air traffic controller should avoid the use of *affirmative* to avoid instances where it can be misheard as "negative".

Air traffic controllers, pilots and aviation students should also know that the nonstandard definition of a lexical item can create confusion and should know the proper phraseology for each situation during flight operation, so that there will be a pellucid communication in giving clearances to prevent confusion.

Acknowledgments
We thank the Civil Aviation Authority of the Philippines (CAAP) for providing us the necessary data for this study. We also thank the Pilots and Air Traffic Controllers who responded scrupulously to our queries in order to make this study possible.

References

Braj Kachru (1986). The Alchemy of English: The Spread, Functions, and Models of Nonnative Englishes. Oxford & New York: Pergamon Institute of English

Brett R.C. Molesworth and Dominique Estival. (2014). Miscommunication in General Aviation: The Influence of External Factors on Communication.

Hanada Said. (2011). Pilots/Air Traffic Controllers Phraseology Study. International Air Transport Association.

International Civil Aviation Organization 2004: Manual on the Implementation of ICAO Language Proficiency Requirements. Retrieved from http://caa.gateway.bg/upload/docs/9835_1_ed.pdf

Kim Hyejeong and Catherine Elder. (2009). Understanding Aviation English as a Lingua Franca: Perceptions of Korean Aviation Personnel. Australian Review of Applied Linguistics, 32(3):23.1-23.17.

Maja Bratanić and Ana Ostroški Anić. (2009). Aviation English Terms and Collocations. Zagreb: Fakultet Prometnih Znanosti

Nicholas Swinehart. (2013). Aviation English Corpus Linguistics: Using the Right Phraseology?. Aviation English Corpus Linguistics, 2-5.

Stylometric Studies based on Tone and Word Length Motifs

Hou Renkui
The Hong Kong Polytechnic University,
Hong Kong

hourk0917@163.com

Huang Chu−Ren
The Hong Kong Polytechnic University,
Hong Kong;

churen.huang@polyu.edu.hk

Abstract: We propose a new approach to stylometric analysis combining lexical and textual information, but without annotation or other pre-processing. In particular, our study makes use Chinese tones motifs and word length motifs automatically extracted from unannotated texts. The proposed approach is based on linked data in nature as tone and word-length information is extracted from a lexicon and mapped to the text. Support vector machine and random forest were used to establish the classification models for author differentiation. Based on comparative study of classification results of different models, we conclude that the combination of word-final tones motifs, segment-final motifs and word length motifs provides the best outcome and hence is the best model.

Keywords: Stylometric analysis, Tones motifs, Word length motif, Chinese prose

1 Introduction

Style refers to linguistic choices made by an author that distinguish his/her writing from those of other authors (Herdan 1966). Stylometric analysis, can distinguish texts written by different authors by measuring some stylistic features in text. It is assumed that quantitative authorship attribution is that the anonymous author of a text can be selected from a set of possible authors by comparing the values of textual measures in that text to their corresponding values in each possible author's writing samples (Grieve 2007). In fact, textual measurements are assumed to include conscious and unconscious aspects of the author's style. It would then be an asset to find the features of the unconscious aspect, since they can not be consciously manipulated by the author (García & Martin 2006). Stylometric analysis involves extracting style markers, i.e. stylometric features, and classifying the texts represented by those features according to authors (Stamatatos et al. 2000). These models can be seen as the text classification according to their authors.

The most effective features to discriminate between different authors, i.e. style markers, should be determined at first. A great variety of measures, including sentence length, word length, word frequencies, character frequencies and vocabulary richness had been proposed. Savoy (2012) compared the performance obtained when using word types or lemmas as text representations.

Koppel et al. (2009) compared the performances of several representative learning methods for authorship attribution and showed that the choice of the learning algorithm is no more important than the choice of the features by which the texts are to be represented.

This paper examines whether lexical information, such as tones motifs and word length motifs, can serve as effective stylometric features in authorship attribution. The motivation of such a study is both to find an effective model of stylometric study without annotation and processing, as well as to test the effectiveness of the linked data approach to stylometric studies.

31st Pacific Asia Conference on Language, Information and Computation (PACLIC 31), pages 56–63
Cebu City, Philippines, November 16-18, 2017

1.1 Literature review

Mosteller and Wallace's (1964) influential work in authorship attribution was based on Bayesian statistical analysis of the frequencies of a small set of common and topic-independent words (e.g., "and", "to", etc.) achieved productive and significant discrimination results between the candidate authors. Since then and until the late 1990s, research in stylometry was dominated by attempts to define features for quantifying writing style (Homes 1994, 1998), and to explore the new modeling methods.

Since the late 1990s, the study of authorship attribution have changed because of the vast amount of electronic texts available through Internet media. Koppel & Argamon (2009) considered a number of feature types that have been, or might be, used for the attribution problems. A number of earlier works that have surveyed and compared various types of feature sets, include Love (2002), Zheng et al. (2006), Abbasi and Chen (2008), and Juola (2008).

Most stylometric studies are lexically based, especially because it is the level of language where repetitions may be reliably used as a basis for measurement (Holmes 1994).

Grieve (2007) compared thirty-nine different types of textual measurements commonly used in attribution studies, in order to determine which are the best indicator of authorship. Stamatatos (2009) summarized the text representation features, style markers, and the computational requirements for measuring them. The most common words (articles, prepositions, pronouns, etc.) are found to be among the best features to discriminate between authors (Argamon & Levitan, 2005). Savoy (2015) found that some simple selection strategies (based on occurrence frequency or document frequency) may produce similar, and some times better, results compared with more complex ones. For example, García & Martin (2006) proposed that the function words prove to be more reliable identifiers of authorship attributions because of their higher frequencies.

There are also many researches for Chinese authorship attribution. Most of the researches focused on the distribution of character, word, lexical, syntax and semantic in the stylometric analysis. Wei (2002) examined the authorship attribution of the Chinese classical literary masterpiece, "The Dream of Red Mansion", using the distribution of common words. Ho (2015) thought Chinese auxiliary words, namely "的、地、得", can represent the writing style of different authors; Hence can be used as measurement to judge the author of literary texts. Xiao & Liu (2015) examined the stylistic difference between the literatures of Jinyong and Gulong using text clustering. He & Liu (2014) examined the difference of usage of rimes of a Chinese syllable in the prose of different Chinese authors based on text clustering. Other than this study, there were very few stylometric studies making use of the lexico-phonological characteristics of Chinese, and certainly not the unique tonal features.

1.2 Research question and methodology

The information of character features is easily available for any natural languages and corpus, and they have been proven to be quite useful to quantify the writing style (Grieve 2007). The tones are the important and essential components and play an important role in Chinese language to determine the meaning of different words and characters. While there are few studies to examine whether tones can be used as stylometric in authorship attribution in Chinese language.

There are four tones which are high and level tones (阴平 *YinPing*), rising tones (阳平 *YangPing*), falling-rising tones (上声 *ShangSheng*), falling tones (去声 *QuSheng*). Except these four tones, there is also a light tone.

This study hypothesizes that different authors tend to have different characteristic pattern of tone motifs and word length motifs usage. We selected the tone motifs and word length motifs in the different specific positions in the sentences as the characteristics to classify the texts according to their authors.

Support vector machine (SVM) algorithm and Random Forest were selected to establish the classification model. 5-fold cross-validation was used to measure the generalization accuracy. In order to avoid the contingency, the 5-fold cross-validation was run 30 times repeatedly. The average value of identification error rate (Stamatatos & Fakotakis 2000, Tan et al. 2006), i.e., erroneously classified texts/total texts, was used to validate the classification result.

We use the open source programming language and environment R (R Core Team 2016) to realize the classification experiments. The function of *ksvm* in R package *kernlab* and the function *randomForest* of R package *randomForest* were used to classify the texts from different authors.

2 Corpus

In the studies of stylometric analysis, an important problem is that the distribution of the training corpus over the different authors is uneven. For example, it is not unusual to have multiple training texts for some authors and very few training texts for other authors.

Another important question is the size of one text sample per authors. The text samples should be long enough to adequately extract the style of them which can be used as text representation features. Different from the existing researches of authorship attribution, this study focuses on the stylometric analysis of Chinese literary texts of different authors and explores whether the tones motifs and word length moitfs of Chinese language can be used as stylometric properties. It isn't rigorous than the authorship attribution in the data collection of this study. So we selected the similar number of texts of different authors and the similar size of every texts to establish the corpus for this study.

In this study, the proses of four Chinese writers were selected to build the corpus, as shown in Table 1. They are Congwen Shen, Zengqi Wang, Qiuyu Yu and Ziqing Zhu.

Table 1: Corpus scale using this study

	Text number	Word type	Word token
Congwen Shen	40	11551	101670
Zengqi Wang	38	14289	111589
Qiuyu Yu	38	11294	90132
Ziqing Zhu	38	13011	123674

Chinese language texts are written Chinese character by character. We try to resolve the question of multi-sound characters by segmenting the texts from character sequences to word sequences using the Chinese lexical analysis system created by Institute of Computing Technology of Chinese Academy of Science (ICTCLAS). Most of multi-sound characters have one pronunciation in a word.

Then we establish a system for extracting the tones of the characters based on the grammatical knowledge-base of contemporary Chinese.

3 Experiments results

Firstly, Chinese sentence should be defined in this study because the sentence-initial and sentence-final characters will be considered. A sentence in Chinese text, however, is not easily defined for the lack of reliable convention to mark end-of-sentence, and because of frequent omission of sentential components including subjects and predicates (Huang and Shi 2016). Consequently, Chinese sentences are often defined in terms of characteristics of speech, rather than text (Lu 1993; Huang & Shi, 2016). Chao (1968) and Zhu (1982) offer similar definitions that rely on pauses and intonation changes at the boundaries of sentences.

According to the approach of many Chinese Treebank (e.g. Chen et al. 1996 for Sinica TreeBank, Huang and Chen 2017) and the analysis of sentence length distribution in quantitative linguistics (Hou et al. 2017) all segments between commas, semicolons, colon, periods, exclamation marks, and question marks expressing pauses in utterances are marked as sentences. Actually, the sentences by this definition are the clauses and conform to the sentence definitions relying on pauses and intonation changes in the utterances. In Wang & Qin (2013) and Chen (1994), the sentence by this operational definition is called sentence segment (hereinafter segment). Wang & Qin (2013) considered that sentence segment length is more relevant to language use in Chinese. So the sentence segments are used as the unit for extracting the sentence-initial and sentence-final characters.

There are often unique rhythms when the different proses are read. This unique rhythm is an inherent characteristic of a prose. Wang et al. (2011) proposed that there are different rhythms between the texts from different authors whilst there are similar rhythms between the texts of an author.

The motif was inspired by the F-motiv for musical "texts" (Boroda 1982) and continued in linguistics by Köhler (2006, 2008) who used the concept of L-motifs, i.e. length motifs. Boroda defined the "F-Motiv" with respect to the duration of the notes of a musical piece because units common in musicology were not usable for his purpose.

According to Köhler & Naumann (2010) and Köhler (2015), linguistic motif is defined as:

The longest continuous sequence of equal or increasing values representing a quantitative property of a linguistic unit. Thus a L-motif is a continuous series of equal or increasing length values.

Following the definition, any text or discourse can be segmented in an objective, unambiguous, and exhaustive way, i.e. it guaranties that no rest will remain (Köhler 2008).

In addition, motifs can be defined for any linguistic unit and for any linguistic property.

And motifs have an appropriate granularity, with respect to which motifs are scalable.

Word length is an important indicator for stylometric analysis and has significances in prosodic linguistics. L-Motif of word was defined as a maximal sequence of monotonically equal and increasing numbers which represent the length of the adjacent words in a sentence segment. According to this definition, a given text can be segmented some paragraphs which are represented by an uninterrupted sequence of L-segments of word. For example, in the following paper, the word L-moitf is (2), (1, 2), (1, 2, 2), (1, 1, 1, 1, 2), (1, 2, 2), (1, 2).

白河 到 沅陵 与 沅水 汇流 后 ， 便 略 显 浑浊 ， 有 出山 泉水 的 意思 。

Tone is the category variable, we defined the tone-motif as the longest continuous sequence of equal tones.

This part will examine whether tone motifs, word length motifs and their combination can be used as stylistic characteristics of the different authors. The segment-initial and segment-final tone motif, the word-final tone motif were considered. The paragraph was considered as a unit to compute the segment-initial and segment-final tone motif. The segment was considered as a unit to compute the word-final tone motif and word length motif.

Table 2: The classification results using the tone motif, word length motif and their combination as characteristics

	Stylometric markers	Identification error rate	
		SVM	RF
1	word-final tone motifs	27.77%	26.01%
2	segment-final tone motifs	47.85%	50.91%
3	word-final tone motifs + segment-final tone motifs	24.15%	20.7%
4	bigrams of word-final tone motifs	34.35%	36.1%
5	word-final tone motifs + their bigrams	30.75%	26.85%
6	word length motifs	35.16%	33.83%
7	word-final tone motifs + word length motifs	20.07%	19.07%
8	word-final tone motifs + segment-final tone motifs + word length motifs	14.02%	14.62%

The texts from different authors were represented by the motifs and classified according to their authors. SVM and random forest were used to establish the classification model and the 5-fold cross validation was used to validate the classification results, as shown in Table 2 and Figure 1.

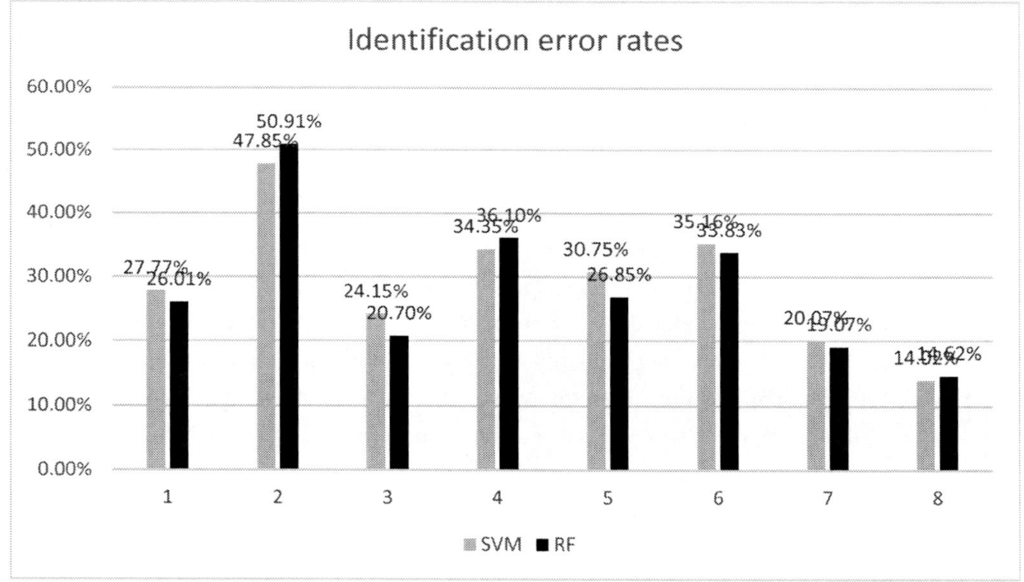

Figure 1: Classification results using the tone motif, word length motif and their combination as characteristics (1-8 on the horizon level represent the characteristics as shown in table 2)

From textural characteristics 1 and 5 in Table 2, we can see that the bigrams of word-final tone motif can't improve the classification result when they combines word-final tone motifs. So we can say that the bigrams of word-final tone motifs can't help to differ different authors and influence the classification results. Maybe this is because the bigrams of word-final motif are sparse.

Although, the identification error rate of classification result is very high when only the segment-final tone motifs were used as the textual measurement, the combination of them and word-final tone motifs can reduce the identification error rate. This is the unexpected and interesting result. Compared with SVM, the classification model established using random forest can obtain the good classification result.

Combination of word length motifs and word-final tone motifs can make a relative low identification error rate.

From Table 2 and Figure 1, we can see that the classification result is well when the combination of segment-final and word-final tone motifs and word-length motifs is selected to represent the different texts from different authors.

Classification And Regression Trees (CART) was selected to establish a classification tree, as shown in Figure 2, using combination of word-final tone motifs and segment-final tone motifs and word length motifs as text characteristics. The tree outlines a decision procedure for determining the author of the texts.

In Figure 2, the leaf nodes specify a partition of the data, i.e. a division of the data set into a series of non-overlapping subsets that jointly comprise the full data set (Baayen 2008). For any node, the most useful predictor was selected to split it, for example word length motif (1-2-2, represented by $x47$). From the classification tree, we can see that the few predictors can roughly determine the authors of the texts. This conforms to the classification results using SVM and random forest establish the classification model.

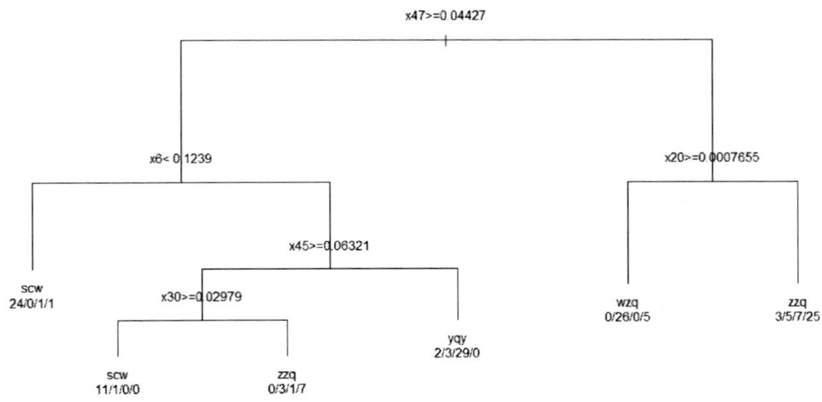

Figure 2: CART tree for the identification of authors

4 Conclusion

Chinese is a tonal language where tones, just like other lexical features, differentiate meanings. Most of previous studies in the Chinese stylometric analysis selected features at the words level or higher level as the textual measurement to identify the authors of the texts. Some examples of the selected features included words and syntactic information of the texts. Very few studies select the sub-lexical features mark the writing style of an author. In this study, we examine whether the Chinese tones motifs and word length motifs can be used as the stylometric characteristics. The tone motifs and word length motifs are both lexical feature that can be linked from other lexical resources and do not required annotated texts.

After comparing the classification results when using all the mentioned linguistic characteristics represent texts respectively, the experiments show that the combination of word-final tones motifs and segment-final tones motifs and word length motifs can effectively differentiate texts from these selected four authors.

The most important feature of our proposed methodology is the linked data approach without any dependence on annotated data or complex text processing, such as PoS tagging or parsing. Note complex processing introduces errors that can be propagated and that requirement of annotated data often lead to data sparseness problems. Our proposed methodology can apply to any plain text, as long as a link to existing lexicon for tonal and word-length information. The tonal and word-length information are inherent information carried by the word, the basic textual elements; hence the methodology is applicable to unannotated big data and will have wide applications in nearly all forms of big data as well as literary texts.

Funding

Reference

Baayen, R. H. (2008). Analyzing linguistic data: A practical introduction to statistics using R. New York: Cambridge University Press.

Boroda, Moisei (1982): Häufigkeitsstrukturen musikalischer Texte. In: Orlov, Jurij K./Boroda, Moisei G./Nadarejšvili, Isabela Š.[eds.]: Sprache, Text, Kunst. Quantitative Analysen. Bochum: Brockmeyer, 231-262.

Chao, Yuen Ren. (1968). A Grammar of Spoken Chinese. Berkeley and Los Angeles: University of California Press.

Chen, H. H. (1994). The contextual analysis of Chinese sentences with punctuation marks. Literary and linguistic computing, 9(4), 281-289

Chen, Keh-jiann, Chu-Ren Huang, Li-ping Chang, and Hui-Li Hsu. 1996. Sinica Corpus: Design Methodology for Balanced Corpora. In. B.-S. Park and J.B. Kim. Eds. Proceedings of the 11th Pacific Asia Conference on Language, Information and Computation. Seoul:Kyung Hee University. pp. 167-176.

García, A. M., & Martin, J. C. (2006). Function words in authorship attribution studies. Literary and Linguistic Computing. Vol. 22, No. 1, 49-66.

Grieve, J. (2007). Quantitative authorship attribution: An evaluation of techniques. Literary and linguistic computing, 22(3), 251-270.

Herdan, G. (1966). The advanced theory of language as choice and chance. New York: Springer-Verlag.

Ho, James. (2015). From the Use of Three Functional Words "的, 地, 得" Examining Author's Unique Writing Style – And on Dream of Red Chamber Author Issues. BIBLID. 120:1, 119-150.

Holmes, D. I. (1994). Authorship attribution. Computers and the Humanities, 28(2): 87-106.

Holmes, D. I. (1998). The evolution of stylometry in humanities scholarship. Literary and Linguistic Computing. 13(3), 111-117.

Hou, R., Huang, C. & Liu, H. (2017). A study on Chinese register characteristics based on regression analysis and text clustering. Corpus Linguistics and Linguistic Theory, 0(0), https://doi:10.1515/cllt-2016-0062.

Huang, Chu-Ren and Dingxu Shi. 2016. A Reference Grammar of Chinese. Cambridge: Cambridge University Press.

Huang, C.-R. & K.-J. Chen. (2017). Sinica Treebank. In N. Ide and J. Pustejovsky (eds), Handbook of Linguistic Annotation. Berlin & Heidelberg: Springer.

Juola, P. (2008). Author attribution, Foundations and Trends in Information Retrieval, 1(3), 233–334.

Koppel, M., Schler, J., & Argamon, S. (2009). Computational methods in authorship attribution. Journal of the American Society for information Science and Technology, 60(1), 9-26.

Köhler, R. (2006). The frequency distribution of the lengths of length sequences. In: J. Genzor and M. Bucková [Eds.]: Favete linguis. Studies in honour of Victor Krupa. Slovak Academic Press, Bratislava, 145-152.

Köhler, R. and S. Naumann (2008). Quantitative text analysis using L-, F- and T-segments. In: Preisach, Burkhardt, Schmidt-Thieme, Decker [Hrsg.]: Data Analysis, Machine Learning and Applications. Berlin, Heidelberg: Springer, S. 637-646.

Köhler, Reinhard; Naumann, Sven (2010). A syntagmatic approach to automatic text clas sification. Statistical properties of F- and L-motifs as text characteristics. In: Grzybek, Peter; Kelih, Emmerich; Mačutek, Ján (eds.), Text and Language: 81-89. Wien: Prae sens.

Köhler, R. (2015). Linguistic Motifs. Sequences in Language and Text, 69, 89

Love, H. (2002). Attributing authorship: An introduction. Cambridge University Press.

Lu, Jianming. (1993). The features of Chinese sentences. Chinese Language Learning. No.1, 1-6.

Mosteller, F., and D.L. Wallace. Inference and Disputed Authorship: The Federalist. Reading. Reading, Mass: Addison Wesley, 1964.

R Core Team (2016). R: A language and environment for statistical computing. R Foundation for Statistical Computing. Vienna. Austria. https://www.R-project.org

Stamatatos, E., Fakotakis, N., & Kokkinakis, G. (2000). Automatic text categorization in terms of genre and author. Computational linguistics, 26(4), 471-495.

Stamatatos, E. (2009). A survey of modern authorship attribution methods. Journal of the American Society for information Science and Technology. 60(3), 538-556.

Tan, Pang-Ning, Michael Steinbach & Vipin Kumar (Translated by Ming Fan & Hongjian Fan). (2006). Introduction to Data Mining. P115. Beijing, China: Posts & Telecom Press

Wang, K., & Qin, H. (2014). What is peculiar to translational Mandarin Chinese? A corpus-based study of Chinese constructions' load capacity. Corpus Linguistics and Linguistic Theory, 10(1), 57-77.

Wang, Shao-kang, Dong Ke-jun & Yan Bao-ping. (2011). Research on Authorship Identification Based on Sentence Rhythm Feature. Computer Engineering. Vol.37, No.9. 4-5 +8.

Wei, Peiquan. (2002). From the distribution of common words examining the author issue of Dream of Red Chamber Author. Memorial Li Fanggui's 100th Anniversary International Symposium on Chinese History. Seattle: University of Washington.

Xiao, Tianjiu & Liu, Ying. (2015). A stylistic analysis of Jin Yong's and Gu Long's fictions based on text clustering and classification. No. 5: 167-177.

Zhu, Dexi. (1982). Lectures on Grammar. Beijing, China: Commercial Press.

Ensemble Technique Utilization for Indonesian Dependency Parser

Arief Rahman
Institut Teknologi Bandung
Indonesia
23516008@std.stei.itb.ac.id

Ayu Purwarianti
Institut Teknologi Bandung
Indonesia
ayu@stei.itb.ac.id

Abstract

Two of the main problems in creating an Indonesian parser with high accuracy are the lack of sentence diversity in treebank used for training and suboptimal uses of parsing techniques. To resolve these problems, we build an Indonesian dependency treebank of 2098 sentences (simple and complex sentences) and use ensemble techniques to maximize the usage of available dependency parsers. We compare the combination of seven parsing algorithms provided by MaltParser and MSTParser, which provides both transition-based and graph-based models. From our experiments, we found that the graph-based model performs better than the transition-based model for Indonesian sentences. We also found no significant accuracy difference in models between several simple ensemble models and reparsing algorithms.

1   Introduction

Text parsing is one of the major tasks in natural language text processing (NLP). Text parsing is the process of determining the syntactic structure of a sentence. The result of text parsing is a syntactical tree, which is mostly used for higher-level NLP tasks, like sentiment analysis (Di Caro and Grella, 2013) and semantic role labeling (Johansson and Nugues. 2008).

There are two kinds of text parsing to date: constituent parsing and dependency parsing. Constituent parsing parses a sentence by determining the constituent phrases of the sentence hierarchically, usually by using a grammar (Aho, 2003). Dependency parsing, on the other hand, parses a sentence by determining a dependency relation for each word in a sentence. In this research, we use dependency parsing, because it is suited for analyzing languages with free word order, such as Indonesian (Nivre, 2007). Figure 1 shows an example of a parsed Indonesian sentence using dependency structure.

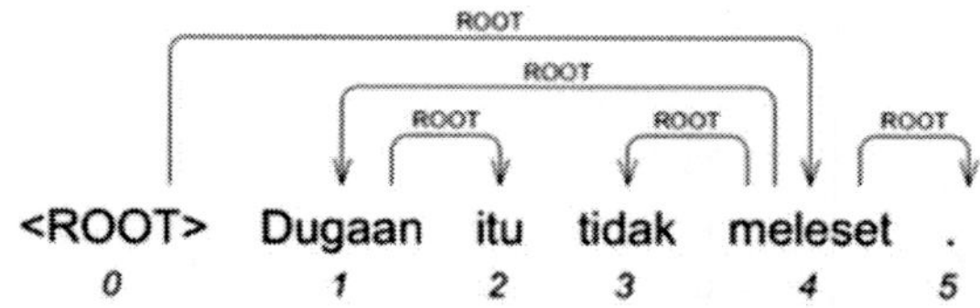

Figure 1. Example of a parsed Indonesian sentence
(TL: *That allegation does not miss*) with
dependency structure

Up until now, there have been only a few studies regarding Indonesian dependency parsing (Sulaeman, 2012; Green et.al, 2012). Most of the previous researches focused on rule-based parsing (Purwarianti et.al, 2013), which yielded quite a low accuracy, compared to other languages. Based on these researches, we use ensemble parsing techniques (Surdeanu and Manning, 2010) in our works. We also built a dependency Treebank corpus used for the model training with 2098 sentences.

In the following sections, we describe the relevant studies and some basic concepts about dependency parsing and its models. We then describe the corpus used in this research, our experiment settings, and finally the results and analysis.

2 Related Works

There are two studies that are related to ensemble dependency parsing, which is Surdeanu & Manning's work for English (Attardi and Dell'Orletta, 2009), and Green et al.'s work for Indonesian (Green et.al, 2012). Surdeanu & Manning created an ensemble dependency parser using parsing algorithms from both MaltParser and MSTParser for English. This research used CoNLL 2008 shared task corpus as the treebank for training and testing. There are two types of ensemble models used in this research: ensemble model at learning (using stacking) and ensemble model at runtime (using voting mechanism). The ensemble system at runtime used both weighted and unweighted voting scheme. The system also used a reparsing algorithm (Attardi and Dell'Orletta, 2009) to ensure the resulting dependency graphs always form a tree. The employed reparsing algorithms are Eisner's algorithm (Eisner, 1996) and Attardi's algorithm (Attardi and Dell'Orletta, 2009).

There are three conclusions that can be inferred from this research. First, an ensemble model that combines several base parsers at runtime performs significantly better than an ensemble model that combines two parsers at learning time. Second, well-formed dependency trees can be guaranteed without significant performance loss by linear-time approximate reparsing algorithms. Lastly, unweighted voting performs as well as weighted voting for the re-parsing of candidate dependencies.

Green et al.'s (2012) research consists of making treebank for Indonesian and analyzing ensemble technique effectivity on Indonesian dependency parser using self-training. This research used four out of five parsing algorithms provided by MaltParser (Nivre, Stack, Planar, and 2-Planar) as its base parsers. This research used 100 Indonesian sentences from IDENTIC (Larasati, 2012) as the treebank. The treebank was split into three parts: one for training, one for self-training tuning, and one for testing. The ensemble techniques used was Chu-Liu Edmonds reparsing algorithm with the unweighted voting scheme.

From this research, Green et al. (2012) concluded that self-training and ensemble parsing can be used to increase overall accuracy for Indonesian dependency parsing. Our work differs from Green et al.'s work by using base parsers from two different parsing models (transition-based and graph-based model), where Green et al.'s and only use one parsing model (transition-based model); and also the treebank size which is 20 times larger than Green et al.'s. Our experiment scheme is also different since we conducted a cross validation scheme in calculating the accuracy.

3 MaltParser and MSTParser

Both MaltParser and MSTParser are data-driven dependency parsers, which use treebank as training data for making parsing models. Both of these parsers are language-independent, which allows any language to be used in the parser without any compromise in accuracy. However, these parsers have different ways to parse sentences. Both of these parsers will be explained in the next sections.

3.1 MaltParser

MaltParser was introduced by Nivre et al. (2007). It is a data-driven and language-independent dependency parser. MaltParser uses transition-based model during parsing. This model uses transition machine, which contains four main components: a set of parsing states, a set of parsing transitions, the initial parsing state, and a set of terminating parsing states. The parsing result of a transition-based model is a transition sequence that can be used to transform the initial parsing state into a terminating parsing state. The learning problem comes from determining the best action to make at each state. This can be achieved learning an "oracle" function.

There are five parsing algorithms available in MaltParser, which can be seen in Table 1. Each of these algorithms differs on the data structures used to represent the parsing states and the set of transitions available for every parsing state.

Algorithm	Parsing Mode	Data Structure	Complexity	Projective?
Nivre	Arc-eager	Stack	$O(n)$	Yes
	Arc-standard	Stack	$O(n)$	Yes
Covington	Projective	Two lists	$O(n^2)$	Yes
	Non-projective	Two lists	$O(n^2)$	No
Stack	Projective	Stack	$O(n)$	Yes
	Non-projective lazy	Stack	$O(n)$	No
	Non-projective eager	Stack	$O(n)$	No
Planar		Stack	$O(n)$	Yes
2-Planar		Two stacks	$O(n)$	Yes

Table 1. Transition-based Algorithm Used by MaltParser

3.2 MSTParser

MSTParser is a data-driven and language-independent dependency parser that uses graph-based model. The graph-based model adds a weight to each directed edge in a dependency graph, which is determined by the dot product of the feature weight vector and the score vector based on the current dependency relation. The overall graph is scored, which equals to the product of all weights of all directed edges. The graph-based model will be able to determine the best dependency tree for a sentence by finding the spanning tree of the dependency graph created with maximum score.

There are two parsing algorithms available in MSTParser: Eisner and Chu-Liu Edmonds algorithm. The first one is Eisner algorithm, which uses dynamic programming (memoization) to find the maximum spanning trees. It has a complexity of $O(n^3)$ and can only build projective trees. The second one is Chu-Liu Edmonds algorithm, which uses recursive greedy selection to find the maximum spanning tree. It has a complexity of $O(n^2)$ and can build both projective and non-projective trees.

4 Ensemble Technique

In NLP, ensemble technique is a parsing technique that uses a collaboration of several unique parsing models to parse sentences better than individually. Ensemble technique can be applied during learning and during parsing. Ensemble technique can be applied during learning by having a parsing model parse a test data, and then uses another parsing model to repair the mistakes made by the previous parser. These steps are repeated until all parsers are used. Several examples of ensemble during learning are stacked parsing and guided model (Fan et.al, 2008; Nivre and McDonald, 2008).

Ensemble technique can also be applied during training by having several base parsers parse the same test data. The base parsers are trained using the same training data. After that, the result from each base parser will be used to determine one final dependency graph that considers all of the base parsers' results. There are three kinds of ensemble during parsing to date: meta-classifier, voting system, and reparsing algorithm. We will only discuss the voting system and the reparsing algorithm in this paper.

In voting system, every token in a sentence will have a dependency relation that was determined by majority voting. Every dependency relation from all of the base parsers will be tallied according to a voting scheme (weighted or unweighted). After that, the best dependency relation for each token will be used for the final dependency graph. In practice, voting scheme is simpler than meta-classifier and performs at the same level as meta-classifier.

There two types of voting that can be used for voting system: weighted and unweighted. Unweighted voting makes all base parsers give the same score for all dependency relations. On the other hand, weighted voting makes base parsers with better accuracy give bigger score for particular dependency relations. When using voting system, the dependency relation with the biggest score for a particular token will be used by the ensemble parser to create the final dependency graph. Voting is done until every token has a dependency relation.

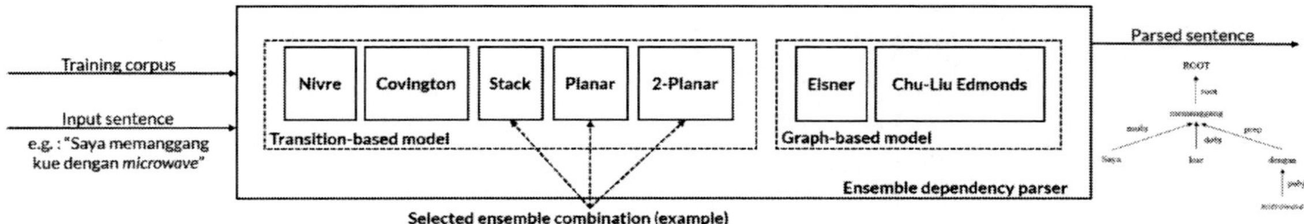

Figure 2. Overall ensemble parsing process

Sometimes, the dependency graphs that are created by the voting system does not make a dependency tree. To resolve this, a reparsing algorithm can be used to parse the dependency graph by finding the maximum spanning tree of the graph. The weight of each directed edge is calculated by tallying the dependency relations from all of the base parsers using a weighting scheme (weighted or unweighted). Three of the most used reparsing algorithms are Eisner algorithm, Chu-Liu Edmonds algorithm, and Attardi algorithm. Our work uses voting system with unweighted voting scheme and all of the reparsing algorithms (all with unweighted weighting scheme).

There are three main steps on doing ensemble parsing. The first step is training all of the base parsers with parsing algorithms and learning algorithm provided by MaltParser and MSTParser. The base parsers are trained using the treebanks that will be listed in the next section. The second step is parsing the test sentences using a particular base parsers combination. The parsing result is in CoNLL. The last step is using a particular ensemble technique to create an ensemble tree. The whole process of ensemble parsing can be seen in Figure 2.

5 Experiments

5.1 Experimental Settings

Our treebank statistic is shown in Table 2. We performed the experiments using our treebank that contains 2098 sentences. We used Kuncoro's treebank (2013), which contains 2018 sentences, and added 80 sentences, which we manually parsed from news sites like Kompas and Tempo to include in our treebank.

There are three main scenarios in our research. In the first scenario, we compared the performances of the base parsers in parsing Indonesian sentences. There were eleven single parsers that were compared: Nivre eager, Nivre standard, Covington projective, Covington non-projective, Stack projective, Stack eager, Stack lazy, Planar, 2-Planar, Eisner, and Chu-Liu Edmonds. The parsers were tested using 10-fold cross validation and used the same learning algorithm (SVM).

In the second scenario, we compared the performances of four ensemble techniques: voting system with unweighted scheme, Eisner reparsing algorithm, Chu-Liu Edmonds reparsing algorithm, and Attardi reparsing algorithm. All of the reparsing algorithms used unweighted weighting scheme. The ensemble combination used is 2-Planar, Eisner, and Chu-Liu Edmonds parsing algorithms. The parsers were tested using 10-fold cross validation and used the same learning algorithm (SVM).

In the third scenario, we compared the performances of ensemble parsers that use different algorithm combination. There were six ensemble combinations that were compared: all parsing algorithms (both from MaltParser and MSTParser), all algorithms from MaltParser, all algorithms from MSTParser, all projective parsing algorithms, all non-projective algorithms, and three algorithms with the highest accuracy (according to the first scenario). The parsers used Eisner reparsing algorithm with unweighted weighting scheme and were tested using 10-fold cross validation and used the same learning algorithm (SVM).

5.2 Results and Analysis

The results of the four experiments are shown in Table 3, Table 4, and Table 5. The metric used in this work is UAS (unlabeled attachment score). We don't use LAS (labeled attachment score) since we have no dependency label in our treebank yet.

Sentence Type		Number of Sentences (Percentage)	
Number of clauses	Simple sentence	1067	(50.86%)
	Compound sentences	349	(16.63%)
	Complex sentence	527	(25.12%)
	Complex-compound sentence	155	(7.39%)
Presence of gerund	Present	50	(2.38%)
	Not present	2048	(97.62%)
POS tag of central dependency	Transitive verb	1017	(48.47%)
	Intransitive verb	989	(47.14%)
	Adjective	69	(3.29%)
	Noun	8	(0.38%)
	Others	15	(0.71%)
Deletion type	None	1630	(77.69%)
	Anaphoric	312	(14.87%)
	Cataphoric	89	(4.24%)
	Structural	67	(3.19%)

Table 2. Indonesian Treebank Statistic

The result from Table 4 shows that Chu-Liu Edmonds algorithm is the best parsing algorithm to be used for Indonesian sentences. One of the main factors that contribute to Chu-Liu Edmonds' high accuracy is the fact that graph-based model can handle long distance dependency well, which most Indonesian sentences have. We can see from the results that Chu-Liu Edmonds dominated both the accuracy on parsing the long sentences and the short sentences. Theoretically, transition-based models should have been able to parse short sentences better than graph-based model. However, the results showed the opposite. This could be caused by Indonesian sentences tendency to use long distance dependencies, even in short sentences.

Another interesting thing that can be inferred from these results is the fact that transition-based models generally performed better when parsing sentences with outlier predicates (like adjectives and nouns). This is most likely because of the rich feature representations that transition-based model has, which depends on the data structures used to represent the parsing state. Figure 3 and 4 shows the example of this occurrence.

The result from Table 5 shows that there is no significant accuracy difference on the ensemble technique used. However, voting system with unweighted scheme has a little higher accuracy than others (0.01%), because the resulting graphs are not reparsed, which make the individual dependency accuracy better than those that use reparsing algorithm. The accuracy indifference may be caused by the fact that all of the reparsing algorithms used unweighted voting scheme, which would make the weight of many dependency relations to be the same, regardless of the algorithm.

The result from Table 6 shows that the parser that uses the combination of the top three base parsers (2-Planar, Eisner, and Chu-Liu Edmonds) has the highest accuracy. This is because of the ensemble property itself. Most of the correct majority decisions (from the best parsers) were able to repair the best parser's mistakes. We can also see that parsers combining all algorithms have lower accuracy than others. This is because of the fact that most of the parsing algorithms created the same dependency trees, especially for the same variants (like Nivre's standard and eager mode). This resulted in most majority decisions to come from the algorithms with several variants.

Parsing Algorithm	Accuracy			
	Overall	Outlier Predicates	Sentence with > 15 tokens	Sentence with ≤ 15 tokens
Nivre-eager (Malt)	83.5%	**60.00%**	77.16%	85.81%
Nivre-standard (Malt)	82.9%	55.71%	75.51%	85.54%
Covington projective (Malt)	82.4%	51.43%	75.25%	85.01%
Covington non-projective (Malt)	82.6%	50.00%	75.40%	85.29%
Stack projective (Malt)	83.3%	55.71%	76.23%	85.81%
Stack eager (Malt)	83.7%	57.14%	77.58%	85.86%
Stack lazy (Malt)	83.9%	57.14%	78.17%	85.90%
Planar (Malt)	84.1%	57.14%	77.85%	86.30%
2-Planar (Malt)	84.7%	54.29%	78.79%	86.82%
Eisner (MST)	85.8%	54.29%	80.68%	87.51%
Chu-Liu-Edmonds (MST)	**86.1%**	52.86%	**80.89%**	**87.86%**

Table 3. Accuracy of Single Dependency Parsers

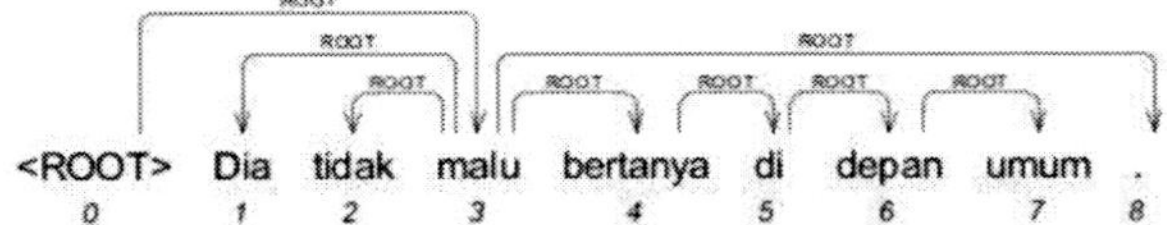

Figure 3. Correct dependency tree for sentence *Dia tidak malu bertanya di depan umum* (He is not ashamed of asking questions in public)

Figure 4. Parsing result for sentence *Dia tidak malu bertanya di depan umum* (He is not ashamed of asking questions in public) using 2-Planar, Eisner, and Chu-Liu Edmonds parsing algorithm respectively

Ensemble Technique	Accuracy
Unweighted majority	**86.6%**
Eisner	86.5%
Chu-Liu-Edmonds	86.5%
Attardi	86.5%

Table 4. Accuracy of Parsers with Different Ensemble Technique

Ensemble Technique	Accuracy
All parsing algorithms (MaltParser + MSTParser)	85.5%
All parsing algorithms from MaltParser	85.1%
All parsing algorithms from MSTParser	86.0%
All projective parsing algorithms	85.6%
All non-projective parsing algorithms	85.3%
Top three parsers (2-Planar, Eisner, and Chu-Liu Edmonds)	**86.5%**

Table 5. Accuracy of Parsers with Different Ensemble Combination

6 Problems While Creating Indonesian Treebank

During the making of our Indonesian Treebank, we encountered several problems that should be solved in the future works. Most of the problems revolve around labeling standards. The first problem is the POS-tags standards. Our current treebank uses proprietary standards for both the coarse-grained and fine-grained POS-tags. While our standards are adequate to cover most word types, the lack of standards for POS-tags makes it difficult to merge several treebanks to create a larger data set for future studies. INACL has issued a POS-tags standard for Indonesian[1], however, there is still a matter of mapping the old POS-tags standards to the new POS-tags standards.

The second problem is the lack of dependency labels for Indonesian. At the time this research is concluded, there were no dependency label standards that can be used to label each dependency relation in a treebank. This would drastically reduce the usefulness of the parser results for most semantic-related NLP tasks since the dependency label is one of the main features in those tasks. One possible solution is to use the dependency label standards from Universal Dependencies (Nivre et al., 2016), which has a universal dependency labeling scheme.

7 Conclusions and Future Works

From our experiments, we concluded that the graph-based model is better than transition-based models for the Indonesian language. We also concluded that different simple ensemble techniques and ensemble combinations do not give significant accuracy difference between models.

Potential future works lie in using more intricate ensemble techniques (e.g. weighting models by its proficiency in creating dependencies for different POS-tags) or better base parsers (using deep learning or word embedding as features during parsing). Other major future works lie in creating a big and complete dependency treebank, which can be done by merging several treebanks from several studies using one labeling standards for both its POS-tags and dependency labels.

References

Aho, A. V. (2003). Compilers: Principles, Techniques, and Tools (for Anna University), 2nd Edition, Pearson Addison Wesley.

---

[1] http://inacl.id/inacl/wp-content/uploads/2017/06/INACL-POS-Tagging-Convention-26-Mei.pdf

Attardi, G., and Dell'Orletta, F. (2009). Reverse Revision and Linear Tree Combination for Dependency Parsing. Proceedings of Human Language Technologies: The 2009 Annual Conference of the North American Chapter of the Association for Computational Linguistics, Companion Volume: Short Papers, pp. 261-264.

Chang, C.-C., and Lin, C.-J. (2011). LIBSVM: A Library for Support Vector Machines. ACM Transactions on Intelligent Systems and Technology (TIST), Volume 2 Issue 3, April 2011, Article Number 27.

Di Caro, L., and Grella, M. (2013). Sentiment Analysis via Dependency Parsing. Computer Standards & Interfaces, Elsevier. Volume 35, Issue 5, September 2013, pp 442-453.

Eisner, J. M. (1996). Three New Probabilistic Models for Dependency Parsing: An Exploration. Proceedings of the 16th Conference on Computational Linguistics - Volume 1, pp. 340-345.

Fan, R.-E., Chang, K.-W., Hsieh, C.-J., Wang, X.-R., & Lin, C.-J. (2008). LIBLINEAR: A Library for Large Linear Classification. The Journal of Machine Learning Research, pp. 1871-1874.

Green, N., Larasati, S. D., and Zabokrtsky, Z. (2012). Indonesian Dependency Treebank: Annotation and Parsing. 26th Pacific Asia Conference on Language, Information, and Computation, pp. 137-145.

Johansson, R., and Nugues, P. (2008). Dependency-Based Syntactic-Semantic Analysis with PropBank and NomBank. Proceedings of the Twelfth Conference on Computational Natural Language Learning, CoNLL '08, (pp. 183-187).

Jurafsky, D., and Martin, J. (2009). Speech and Language Processing: An Introduction to Natural Language Processing, Computational Linguistics, and Speech Recognition. Pearson Prentice Hall.

Jurafsky, Adhiguna. (2013). *Pemanfaatan Pengurai Ensemble dan Teknik Self-Learning untuk Meningkatkan Akurasi Pengurai Bahasa Indonesia* [Ensemble Parsers and Self-Learning Technique Utilization to Increase Indonesian Parser Accuracy]. Institut Teknologi Bandung.

Larasati, S. D. (2012). IDENTIC Corpus: Morphologically Enriched Indonesian-English Parallel Corpus. LREC, pp. 902-906.

Nivre et al. (2007). MaltParser: A Language-Independent System for Data-Driven Dependency Parsing. Natural Language Engineering. 13, pp. 95-135.

Nivre, J., & McDonald, R. T. (2008). Integrating Graph-Based and Transition-Based Dependency Parsers. Proceedings of ACL-08: HLT, pp. 950–958, Columbus, Ohio

Nivre, J., de Marneffe, M. C., Ginter, F., Goldberg, Y., Hajic, J., Manning, C. D., ... & Tsarfaty, R. (2016, May). Universal Dependencies v1: A Multilingual Treebank Collection. In *LREC*.

Purwarianti, A., Saelan, A., Afif, I., Ferdian, F., Wicaksono, A.F. (2013). Natural Language Understanding Tools with Low Language Resource in Building Automatic Indonesian Mind Map Generator. International Journal on Electrical Engineering and Informatics, Vol 5, No. 3, September 2013.

Sulaeman, M. K., and Purwarianti, A. (2012). "Dependency Parsing for Indonesian with GULP". Proceeding of ICEEI (International Conference of Electrical Engineering and Informatics) 2011. July 2011. Bandung, Indonesia

Surdeanu, M., and Manning, C. D. (2010). Ensemble Models for Dependency Parsing: Cheap and Good? Human Language Technologies: The 2010 Annual Conference of the North American Chapter of the Association for Computational Linguistics, pp. 649-652.

Raising to Object in Japanese: An HPSG Analysis

Akira Ohtani

Faculty of Informatics, Osaka Gakuin University

2-36-1 Kishibe-minami, Suita, Osaka 564-8511, Japan

`ohtani@ogu.ac.jp`

Abstract

This paper discusses the so-called raising to object (RTO), which provides interesting problems with respect to the syntactic/semantic status of an accusative-marked NP. We argue that two types of matrix verb, control and raising, must be recognized in the construction. The linearization approach can capture the possibility of word order variation, especially, the distribution of accusative-marked NP in the construction. Moreover, we suggest that RTO involves a non-thematic NP related to the embedded predicate via predication.

1 Introduction

In some languages, an argument that belongs semantically to an embedded clause is realized syntactically as an object of a matrix clause, this "raising to object" (RTO) is schematized as follows:

(1) $[_{matrix}$ subject ... object$_i$ $[_{embedded}$ Δ_i ...] ...]

The term "raising" has its origin in the transformational analysis of such constructions in which the subject of the lower clause is "raised" to become the object of the matrix verb (Postal, 1974; Lasnik and Saito, 1991; among others).

In Japanese, it has been noted in the literature on transformational syntax that examples such as (2) share syntactic properties with English counterparts:

(2) a. Yamada-wa Tanaka-o$_i$ [t_i baka da]
       Yamada-TOP Tanaka-ACC   fool COP
       to   omotta.
       COMP thought
       'Yamada thought Tanaka [to be a fool.]'

b. Yamada-wa   [Tanaka-ga   baka da]
   Yamada-TOP Tanaka-NOM   fool COP
   to   omotta.
   COMP thought
   'Yamada thought [that Tanaka was a fool.]'
   (Kuno (1976): pp. 23-24, Slightly altered.)

As those glosses indicate, (2a) and (2b) show the same case alternation patterns that English exhibits.

There are a number of conditions which must be satisfied in order to form a grammatical RTO construction, but in this paper, we focus on the predicational relation between the accusative-marked NP and the complement predicate. More specifically, we argue that RTO involves a non-thematic NP related to the embedded predicate via predication.

2 Word Order and Embedded Predicate

While there can be no doubt that Kuno's (1976) RTO phenomenon exists in Japanese (Tanaka, 2002), there are at least two questions that cannot be accounted for by his analysis.

One of the problems is concerned with the word order of an accusative-marked NP, which can be generally scrambled. Consider (3):

(3) a. Yamada-wa   Tanaka(-no   koto)-o
       Yamada-TOP   Tanaka-GEN   matter-ACC
       baka da to omotta.
       fool is that thought
       'Yamada thought Tanaka to be a fool.'
                            (Kuno 1976: 24)

b. Yamada-wa baka da to Tanaka*(-no koto)-o
   omotta.   (Kuno 1976: 35)

31st Pacific Asia Conference on Language, Information and Computation (PACLIC 31), pages 72–80
Cebu City, Philippines, November 16-18, 2017

Kuno's observation indicates that *Tanaka-o* 'Tanaka -ACC' can not be located to the right of the complement clause, while *Tanaka-no koto-o* 'Tanaka-GEN matter-ACC' can. The question arising from this contrast is: How can we derive the difference between *Tanaka-o* and *Tanaka-no koto-o* to account for their scramblability?

Another question comes from the restriction of embedded predicates. Kuno suggests that this is limited to 'either adjectives or nominal + copula *da*' (Kuno 1976, p. 33). Consider (4):

(4) a.*Ken-wa Naomi-o Tokyo-ni kita to
     K-TOP N-ACC Tokyo-DAT came that
     omotta.
     thought
     'Ken thought that Naomi came to Tokyo.'

    b. Ken-wa Naomi-o futot-teiru to
       K-TOP N-ACC fattened-PROG that
       omotta.
       thought
       '(Lit.) Ken thought that Naomi was being fattened.'

As Kuno's restriction predicts, RTO is not licensed in (4a) with *kita* 'came'. However, it is licensed in (4b) with *futot-teiru* 'being fattened', though the predicate is neither the adjectives or nominal + copula *da* form. The question arising immediately from this contrast is: How can we define the nature of the embedded predicates allowing RTO?

In the rest of this paper, we will seek the answer to these questions, examining how RTO can be dealt with within the framework of HPSG (Pollard and Sag, 1987; Pollard and Sag, 1994; Sag, Wasow and Bender, 2003).

3 Two Types of Matrix Verb

In this section, we will argue that there are two types of *omow* 'think', and account for the scramblability in (3), based on their lexical entries.

3.1 NP-*no koto* Sentence and Control Verb

Kuno extensively discusses that control (equi) constructions like (5) have a number of properties which are not found in raising constructions.

One of his tests comes from the scramblability of the complement clause. Compare (5) with (3):

(5) a. Yamada-wa Tanaka-ni sore-o suru
       Yamada-TOP Tanaka-DAT it-ACC do
       koto-o meijita
       that-ACC ordered
       'Yamada ordered Tanaka to do it.'
                              (Kuno 1976: 34)

    b. Yamada-wa sore-o suru koto-o Tanaka-ni
       meiji-ta.   (Kuno 1976: 35)

Tanaka-ni 'Tanaka-DAT' in (5b) and *Tanaka-no koto-o* 'Tanaka-GEN matter-ACC' in (3b) can be located to the right of the complement clause, while *Tanaka-o* 'Tanaka-ACC' in (3b) can not. It is noteworthy that the dative-marked NP and the NP-*no koto-o* behave in the same manner.

Another test is concerned with the equi-NP. Kuno points out that equi-NP deletion is not obligatory process, although (6) is less natural than (5a).

(6)?Yamada-wa Tanaka$_i$-ni kare$_i$-ga sore-o
     Yamada-TOP Tanaka-DAT he-NOM it-ACC
     suru koto-o meijita
     do that-ACC ordered
     '(Lit.) Yamada ordered Tanaka that he do it.'
                              (Kuno 1976: 35)

Now consider a raising construction with a resumptive pronoun *kare-ga* 'he-NOM':

(7) Yamada-wa Tanaka?(?)(-no koto)-o
     Yamada-TOP Tanaka-GEN matter-ACC
     kare$_i$-ga baka da to omotta.
     he-NOM fool is that thought
     '(Lit.) Yamada thought Tanaka that he was a fool.'

It is interesting that *kare-ga* 'he-NOM' co-occurs with NP-*no koto-o*. Though we will not be concerned with the problem of how resumptive pronouns are licensed, the crucial point here is that *Tanaka-ni* 'Tanaka-DAT' in (6) and *Tanaka-no koto-o* 'Tanaka-GEN matter-ACC' in (7) share certain characteristics.

Kuno indicates that when the object of raising verbs is human, *no koto* appears optionally after NP for the human (Kuno 1976, p.41). However, the above discussion shows that the sentence with *no koto* is a control construction and that there are two types of *omow* 'think'. Thus, we propose the following lexical entries for two types of *omow* 'think':

(8) a. *Raising Verb:*

$$
\left[\begin{array}{l}
\text{SYN}\left[\begin{array}{l}
\text{HEAD } verb \\
\text{VAL}\left[\begin{array}{l}
\text{SUBJ}\langle\text{NP}[nom]_i\rangle \\
\text{COMPS}\left\langle\begin{array}{l}
\boxed{2}\text{NP}[acc], \\
\text{XP}[\text{SUBJ}\langle\boxed{2}\rangle]{:}\boxed{1}
\end{array}\right\rangle
\end{array}\right]
\end{array}\right] \\
\text{SEM}\left[\begin{array}{ll}
\text{RELN} & \text{think} \\
\text{THINKER} & i \\
\text{ARG} & \boxed{1}
\end{array}\right]
\end{array}\right]
$$

b. *Control Verb:*

$$
\left[\begin{array}{l}
\text{SYN}\left[\begin{array}{l}
\text{HEAD } verb \\
\text{VAL}\left[\begin{array}{l}
\text{SUBJ}\langle\text{NP}[nom]_i\rangle \\
\text{COMPS}\left\langle\begin{array}{l}
\text{NP}[acc]_j, \\
\text{XP}[\text{SUBJ}\langle\text{NP}_j\rangle]{:}\boxed{1}
\end{array}\right\rangle
\end{array}\right]
\end{array}\right] \\
\text{SEM}\left[\begin{array}{ll}
\text{RELN} & \text{think} \\
\text{THINKER} & i \\
\text{THINK\_OF} & j \\
\text{ARG} & \boxed{1}
\end{array}\right]
\end{array}\right]
$$

It should be noted that in a raising verb (8a), an accusative-marked NP is located outside XP against the Exceptional Case-marking (ECM) analysis (Kaneko, 1988; Ueda, 1988; Hiraiwa, 2001; Taguchi, 2009) in which such an NP is located inside XP as shown in (9a):

(9) a. Ken-wa
   Ken-TOP

   [$_{XP}$ Naomi-(ga/o)   kawaii to] omotta.
   Naomi-NOM/ACC pretty that thought
   'Ken thought Naomi (was pretty / to be pretty).'

   b. Ken-ga   omotteiru nowa
   Ken-NOM thinking is

   [$_{XP}$ Naomi-(ga/*o)   kawaii] toiukoto da.
   Naomi-NOM/ACC pretty   that   is
   'What Ken thinks is that Naomi is pretty.'

In (9b), when *Naomi* is marked with *ga*, the complement clause XP containing it can be clefted. On the other hand, when *Naomi* is marked with *o*, the clause can not be clefted although the accusative-marked NP is expected to be occupied within XP. This test suggests that an accusative-marked NP is not a constituent of XP. Therefore, we regard RTO construction without *no koto* as having the feature structure as (8a), and propose two types of lexical entry of *omow* 'think' as shown in (8).

3.2 Scrambling as Domain Union

Let us now turn to the scramblability illustrated in (3), and repeated in (10) with some modification:

(10) a. Yamada-wa   Tanaka(-no   koto)-o
   Yamada-TOP Tanaka-GEN   matter-ACC
   baka da to   omotta.
   fool is that thought
   'Yamada thought Tanaka to be a fool.'

   b.*Yamada-wa baka da to Tanaka-o omotta.

   c. Yamada-wa baka da to Tanaka-no koto-o omotta.

To explain the difference in (10b) and (10c), we adopt Reape's (1996) linearization approach:

(11) a. Word order is determined within the *word order domain*.

   b. The *word order domain* is encoded by the feature DOM.

   c. The *word order domain* of a daughter may be the same as a subpart of the domain of its mother.

   d. The value of DOM is a list of elements of type NODE, which consists of the features PHON and SYNSEM
   (Pollard, Kasper and Levine, 1993).

(11c) is described by the *sequence union* relation:

(12) a. union($\langle\rangle$, $\langle\rangle$, $\langle\rangle$)

   b. union($\langle A|X\rangle$, $\langle Y\rangle$, $\langle A|Z\rangle$) if union(X, Y, Z)

   c. union($\langle X\rangle$, $\langle A|Y\rangle$, $\langle A|Z\rangle$) if union(X, Y, Z)

That is, Z is a list obtained by merging X and Y with the condition that the relative order of elements in X and Y is preserved in Z. For example, let $A = \langle a, b\rangle$ and $B = \langle c, d\rangle$, then union(A, B, C) iff C is one of the sequences in $\{\langle a, b, c, d\rangle, \langle a, c, b, d\rangle, \langle a, c, d, b\rangle, \langle c, d, a, b\rangle, \langle c, a, d, b\rangle, \langle c, a, b, d\rangle\}$.

Returning to the word order of (10a), the following feature structure (14a) and (14b) can be applied. Though N(O)D(E) features of the complement and the head daughter, $\boxed{3}$ and $\boxed{4}$, are permutable in principle, we also assume the following linear precedence rule (13), which is needed to explain the head-final property of Japanese.

(13) X < head

(14) a. *Raising Construction:*

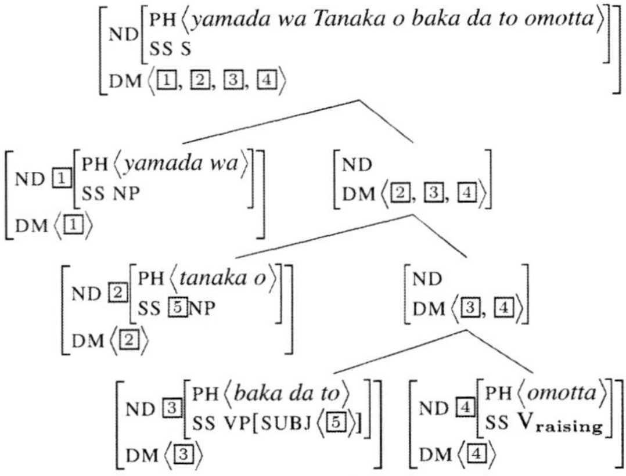

b. *Control Construction:*

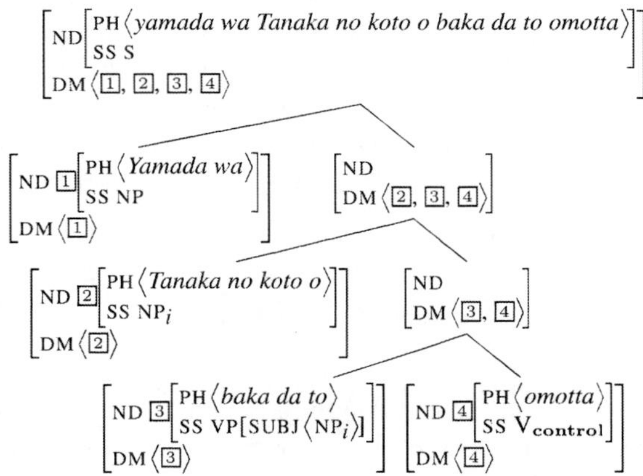

Since four elements in the D(O)M are permutable with each other as long as (13) is preserved, a total of six DM is derived as follows:

(15) a. DM ⟨1, 2, 3, 4⟩

    Yamada-wa Tanaka-o baka da to omotta.

    Yamada-wa Tanaka-no koto o baka da to omotta.

  b. DM ⟨1, 3, 2, 4⟩

    ?(?) Yamada-wa baka da to Tanaka-o omotta.

    Yamada-wa baka da to Tanaka-no koto o omotta.

  c. DM ⟨2, 1, 3, 4⟩

    Tanaka-o Yamada-wa baka da to omotta.

    Tanaka-no koto o Yamada-wa baka da to omotta.

  d. DM ⟨2, 3, 1, 4⟩

    Tanaka-o baka da to Yamada-wa omotta.

    Tanaka-no koto o baka da to Yamada-wa omotta.

  e. DM ⟨3, 1, 2, 4⟩

    ?(?) baka da to Yamada-wa Tanaka-o omotta.

    baka da to Yamada-wa Tanaka-no koto o omotta.

  f. DM ⟨3, 2, 1, 4⟩

    ?(?) baka da to Tanaka-o Yamada-wa omotta.

    baka da to Tanaka-no koto o Yamada-wa omotta.

Notice that not only (15b), with the word order of (10b) originally pointed out by Kuno (1976), but also (15e) and (15f) for raising verb are highly marginal. Moreover, notice that these DM include the linear precedence 3 < 2, which is clearly rejected by a rule like (16):

(16) 2 < 3

However, we cannot assume (16) as a linear precedence rule, because it fails to limit the freedom of order between NP and VP complement daughters of a control construction as shown in (15). The question arising here is: How can we derive the effect of the application of rule (16) only to (14a)?

To solve this problem, we also assume the following linear precedence rule:

(17) $\boxed{n}$ NP < [VAL … ⟨$\boxed{n}$⟩]

Though we assume (17) without going into any detail about it here for the lack of space, it properly eliminates the illegitimate word order in Korean/Japanese small clause and other constructions which includes raising (Yoo, 1993).

Let us turn to (16). There is a structure-sharing relation between the NP in ND 2 and that in ND 3 as shown in (14a). Now, applying (17) to these NPs, 2 and 3 are not permutable indirectly:

(18) $\left[\text{ND} \boxed{2} \begin{bmatrix} \text{PH} ⟨\textit{Yamada-o}⟩ \\ \text{SS} \boxed{5}\text{NP} \end{bmatrix} \right] < \left[\text{ND} \boxed{3} \begin{bmatrix} \text{PH} ⟨\textit{baka da to}⟩ \\ \text{SS} [\text{SUBJ} ⟨\boxed{5}⟩] \end{bmatrix} \right]$

Note that the control construction is not relevant to (17) since a VP complement's subject is only coindexed with an NP complement, not structure-shared. Therefore, the difference in scramblability between *Tanaka-o* 'Tanaka-ACC' with a raising verb and *Tanaka-no koto-o* 'Tanaka-GEN matter-ACC' with a control verb arises.

4 Restriction of Embedded Predicate

In this section, we will argue the restriction of an embedded predicate allowing RTO, and note on the predicational relation between an accusative-marked NP and the embedded predicate.

4.1 Form of Embedded Predicate

Kuno (1976) suggests that the embedded predicate of RTO construction is limited to 'either adjectives or nominal + copula *da*.' This generalization predicts the unacceptability of the accusative-marked NP in (19), because the complement is a verb:

(19) Ken-wa Naomi-(ga/*o)   kuru to omotta.
     Ken-TOP Naomi-NOM/ACC come that thought
     'Ken thought Naomi came.'

Kuno (1976) and Oshima (1979) also point out that when the past tense form of predicate appears, RTO is not licensed or only marginally licensed.

However, some of the speakers we polled judged *baka-dat-ta* 'was a fool' case not so bad:

(20) Ken-wa   Naomi-o   (baka da / (?)? baka
     Ken-TOP Naomi-ACC fool is   fool
     datta) to omotta.
     was   that thought
     'Ken thought that Naomi was a fool.'

Oshima (1979) and Ueda (1988) indicate that the complement clause of RTO is infinitive, but there is no implication for Kuno's and this account of RTO.

The problem here is not so simple. Sakai (1996) points out the fact that the embedded predicate is not regulated by its form. Consider (21):

(21) a. Takashi-wa   ooame-(ga/*o)   furi
        Takashi-TOP   heavy rain-NOM/ACC rain
        soo   da to omotta.
        is going to is that thought
        'Takashi thought that it was going to rain heavily any minute now.'

     b. Takashi-wa   kono   okashi-(ga/o)
        Takashi-TOP   this   cake-NOM/ACC
        oishi   soo   da to omotta.
        delicious looks like is that thought
        'Takashi thought this cake was appetizing.'
        (Sakai 1996: 7, English translation, Ohtani)

The grammaticality of the accusative-marked NP in (21b) is clearly problematic for Kuno's analysis, because (21b) does not involve either the adjectives or nominal + copula *da* form. Moreover, the following sentence, involving gerundive form *teiru* 'being' also sounds good:

(22) Ken-wa Naomi-(ga/o)   futot-teiru   to
     K-TOP Naomi-NOM/ACC fattened-PROG that
     omotta.
     thought
     'Ken thought that Naomi was being fattened.'

Examples (21b) and (22) show that RTO is not regulated by form and tensedness of the predicate, and it is also unexpected on the case alternation-motivated account of RTO.

To explain (21), Sakai (1996) proposes that the essential nature of embedded predicate of RTO construction is the type of predication for the predicate, which is originally suggested in Borkin (1984):

(23) The predication in complements is a characteristics or an attribute of the entity represented by the raised NP.   (Cited from Sakai 1996: 6)

We accept this intuition that the embedded predicate and its subject must reflect the relation '*has a property X*,' and that there is stage/individual-level predicate (Carlson, 1977) asymmetry for licensing RTO. This approach also accounts for various judgements in (20) and the following examples because such a distinction highly depends on speakers.

Now compare the embedded predicate of (19)–(21), repeated as (24a)–(24d):

(24) a. Naomi-ga   kuru.
        Naomi-NOM come
        'Naomi comes.'

     b. Naomi-wa baka da.
        Naomi-TOP fool is
        'Naomi is a fool.'

     c. Ooame-ga   furi soo   da.
        heavy rain-NOM rain is going to is
        'It is going to rain heavily.'

     d. Kono okashi-wa oishi   soo   da.
        kono cake-TOP delicious look like is
        'This cake is appetizing.'

Only (24b) and (24d), which are the embedded predicate part of grammatical sentence, mean that the subject has a property described by its predicate. We point out here for later discussion that this distinction is also reflected on the marker of a subject, i.e., *ga* and *wa*.

Next, consider (25). The case alternation reflects the interpretation of the embedded complements, if the assumption here is correct.

(25) a. *Stage-level Predicate Interpretation:*
 Ken-wa Naomi-(ga/??o) *saikin*
 Ken-TOP Naomi-NOM/ACC recently

 futottekita to omotta.
 has gained weight that thought

 'Ken thought that Naomi had gained weight
 recently.'

 b. *Individual-level Predicate Interpretation:*
 Ken-wa Naomi-(??ga/o) *umaretsuki*
 Ken-TOP Naomi-NOM/ACC by nature

 futotteiru to omotta.
 stout that thought

 'Ken thought that Naomi was stout by nature.'

By putting some modifiers forcing a stage/individ-
ual-level interpretation, nominative/accusative case
alternation is observed.[1]

4.2 RTO as Structure-Sharing

The next questions are: How is accusative case-
marking allowed to take place in individual-level
predicate and why is it disallowed in stage-level
predicate?

In section 4.1, we pointed out the relation between
semantic property of the predicate and the marker of
its subject. It is summarized as follows:

(26) a. The subject of a stage-level predicate is
 marked with a marker *ga*.

 b. The subject of an individual-level predicate
 is marked with a marker *wa*.

---

[1]If a stage-level predicate has some lexical property to license nominative marker as in (25a), it is also predicted that
a small clause with such a predicate also allows a *ga*-marked
argument. Consider (i):

   (i) a.??Watashi-wa bukka-(ga/o)   takaku omou.
         I-TOP   price-NOM/ACC high   think

      b. Watashi-wa *saikin* bukka-ga takaku omou.
        I-TOP   recently price-NOM high   think

      '(Lit.) I think that prices are recently high.'

It is sometimes assumed that the realization of nominative
marker is associated with tense (Takezawa, 1987). In (i) the
small clause predicate lacks overt tense morpheme and the subject of the embedded predicate is unable to be marked with
nominative as in (i)a. However, by putting modifier forcing
a stage-level interpretation, a nominative marker is allowed in
(i)b. This also suggests that a stage-level predicate licenses a
nominative case.

Based on the summary in (26), we propose that the
embedded predicate (24a) and (24b), repeated as
(27a) and (27b), has the following feature specification:

(27) a. Naomi-ga kuru.
 Naomi-NOM come

 'Naomi comes.'

$$\text{S}$$

 $\boxed{1}$ NP[*nom*] V$\begin{bmatrix} \text{SUBJ} \langle \boxed{1} \rangle \\ \text{ARG-ST} \langle \boxed{1} \rangle \end{bmatrix}$

 b. Naomi-wa baka da.
 Naomi-TOP fool is

 'Naomi is a fool.'

$$\text{S}$$

 $\boxed{1}$ NP[*top*]$_i$ VP$\begin{bmatrix} \text{SUBJ} \langle \boxed{1} \rangle \\ \text{RESTR} \langle \dots i \dots \rangle \end{bmatrix}$

In (27b), NP[*top*] is the the following abbreviation
for an explanatory purpose:

(28) NP[*top*]$_i$ $\begin{bmatrix} \text{HEAD} & [\text{CASE} & unspecified] \\ \text{SEM} & [\text{INDEX} & i] \\ \text{CONX} & [\text{TOPIC} & i] \end{bmatrix}$

These feature structures capture that both *ga* and *wa*-
marked NP in (27a) and (27b) are equally syntactic subject, but that they reflect the different semantic interpretations, concerning to generic, existential,
topic, and so on (Kubo, 1992; Endo, 1994).

We claim that RTO asymmetry discussed in section 4.1 arises from the interaction between the case
feature specification shown in (27) and the possibility of structure-sharing. Consider (29).

In (29a) the matrix object is specified as NP[*acc*].
On the other hand, the embedded subject is specified
as NP[*nom*] because the nominative case is specified
by some lexical property of the stage-level predicate.
Thus, structure-sharing between them with $\boxed{1}$ is not
possible, consequently RTO is not licensed.

In (29b) the matrix object is specified as NP[*acc*]
and at this point there is no difference between (29a)
and (29b). However, the embedded subject is specified as NP[*top*] and the case feature is not specified
by the embedded predicate. As shown in (28), topic
represents semantic information rather than grammatical relation as case, thus *top* and *nom* are not
treated as the same sort and the structure-sharing of
$\boxed{1}$ in (29b) is possible.

(29) a. *Stage-level Predicate:

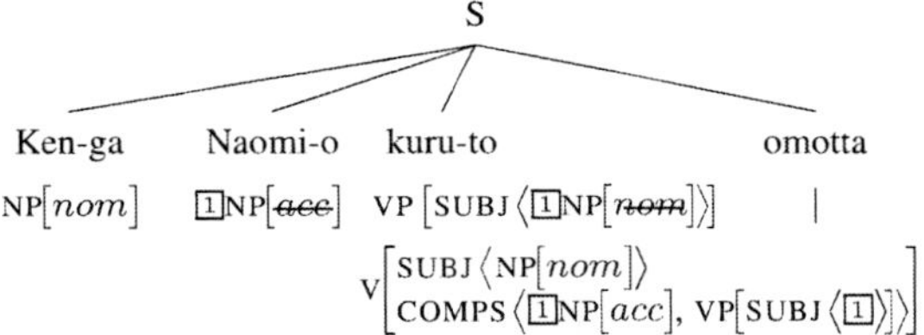

b. Individual-level Predicate:

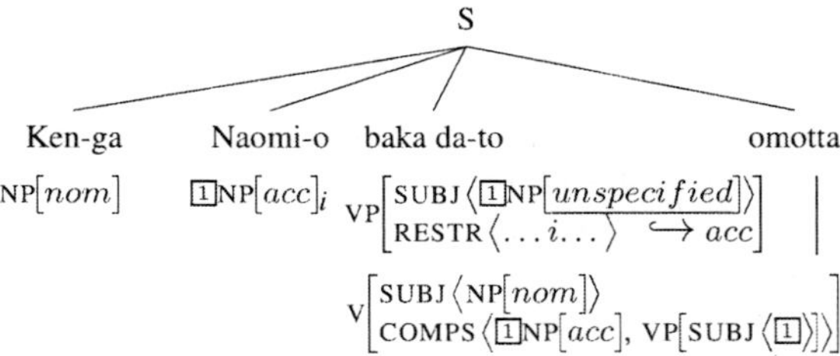

5 Some Constructions for licensing RTO

In the previous section, we discussed the crucial role that the stage/individual-level distinction of the embedded predicates plays in licensing RTO. In this section, we argue more specifically that the construction which involves a non-thematic NP related to the embedded predicate via predication allows RTO.

5.1 Multiple Subject Construction

Multiple Subject Construction where two or more nominative-marked noun phrases occur in a single sentence as shown in (30a), have long been a central object of theoretical and empirical studies (Kuno, 1973; among others).

(30) a. Tokyo-ga   bukka-ga   takai.
    Tokyo-NOM price-NOM high

    'It is Tokyo where prices are high.'

   b. Tokyo-wa   bukka-ga   takai.
    Tokyo-TOP price-NOM high

    'As for Tokyo, prices are high.'

A Japanese sentence is restricted to at most one *wa*-marked topic phrase, which, if present, appears in sentence-initial position as shown in (30b). Interestingly, (30b) licenses RTO as shown in (31).

(31) Ken-ga   Tokyo-o   bukka-ga   takai to
    Ken-NOM Tokyo-ACC price-NOM high that
    omotta.
    thought

    'As for Tokyo, Ken thought prices were high.'

The stage/individual-level distinction also predicts this state of affairs, because the predicate part of multiple subject construction also attributes an essential property to a person or an entity (Kuno, 1973) like individual-level predicate which allows RTO. Thus we can give the feature specification of the sentence in (31) as (32).

(32)

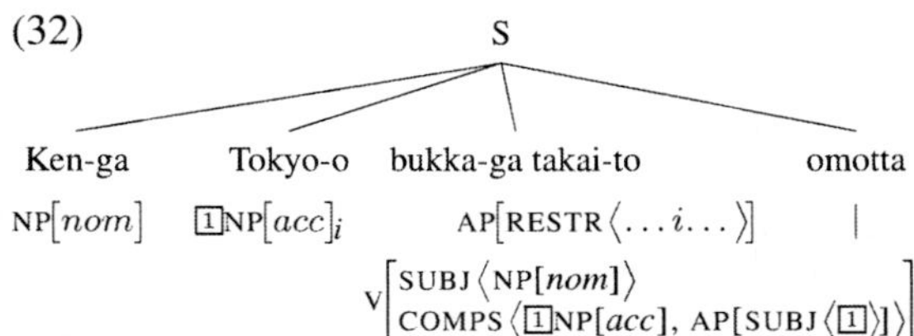

5.2 Bare Topic Construction

Bare topicalization, a kind of topicalization with a non-*wa*-marked topic in Japanese, is also accounted for if RTO involves a non-thematic NP related to the embedded predicate via predication. See (33).

(33) a. Sono hito-wa
    that   person-TOP
    kinoo-no   jiken-no   hannin da.
    yesterday-GEN incident-GEN culprit is

   b. Sono hito,
    that   person
    kinoo-no   jiken-no   hannin da.
    yesterday-GEN incident-GEN culprit is

    '(Lit.) That person, is the culprit of yesterday's incident. '   (Taguchi 2009: 415)

Ordinary topicalization in (33a) and bare topicalization in (33b) pattern in the same way with respect to a number of properties. Taguchi (2009) points out that they differ in that the former can apply in embedded clauses, while the latter cannot, as shown in (34a) and (34b), respectively.

(34) a. Watashi-wa [sono hito-wa,
    I-TOP   that   person-TOP
    kinoo-no   jiken-no   hannin da
    yesterday-GEN incident-GEN culprit is
    to] omot-teiru.
    that think-PROG

    '(Lit.) I am believing that that person, is the culprit of yesterday's incident.'

b.*Watashi-wa [sono hito,
   I-TOP   that person

   kinoo-no   jiken-no   hannin da
   yesterday-GEN incident-GEN culprit is

   to] omot-teiru.
   that think-PROG   (Taguchi 2009: 415)

Taguchi argues that the apparent matrix/embedded asymmetry regarding bare topicalization actually does not exist and embedded bare topicalization has been treated as ECM construction.

(35) Watashi-wa [sono hito-o
   I-TOP   that person-ACC

   kinoo-no   jiken-no   hannin da
   yesterday-GEN incident-GEN culprit is

   to] omot-teiru.
   that think-PROG

   '(Lit.) I am believing that that person to be the culprit of yesterday's incident.'

Putting aside the theoretical matters in the literature on transformational syntax, here we accept this observation that the embedded bare topic construction is allowed. Under our framework, the feature structure of the sentence (35) is shown in (36):

(36)

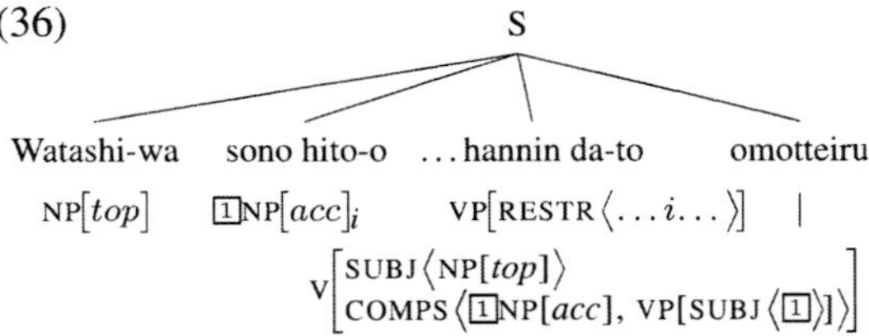

It should be noted that our analysis also allows the ordinary topic construction as (33a) to license RTO because the subject of embedded predicate is not thematic and any case is not specified.

Topicalization in Japanese does not involve movement since it is free of island effects (Kuno, 1973).

(37) a. Sono hito-wa$_i$ [$_{adjunct}$ pro_i
   that person-TOP

   shin-de mo   ] daremo naka-nai.
   die-INF even.if anyone cry-NEG

   'No one cries even if that person dies.'

  b. Sono hito-wa$_i$ [$_{complex\ NP}$ pro_i
   that person-TOP

   taberu mono]-ga nai.
   eat   thing -NOM absent

   'He doesn't have anything to eat.'

Like the topic NPs in (37), the accusative-marked NPs of RTO in (38) is free from island effects.

(38) a. Watashi-wa [sono hito-o$_i$ [$_{adjunct}$ pro_i
   I-TOP   that person-ACC

   shin-de mo   ] daremo naka-nai
   die-INF even.if anyone cry-NEG

   to] omot-teiru.
   that think-PROG

   '(Lit.) I am believing no one will cry even if he died.'

  b. Watashi-wa [sono hito-o$_i$ [$_{complex\ NP}$ pro_i
   I-TOP   that person-ACC

   taberu mono]-ga nai   to] omot-teiru.
   eat   thing-NOM absent that think-PROG

   '(Lit.) I am believing him not to have anything to eat.'

This also suggests that an accusative-marked NP of RTO relates to the predicate part via predication.

There are a number of conditions which must be satisfied in order to form a grammatical RTO. This section shows some of the constructions and its conditions of predicational relation between the accusative-marked NP and the embedded predicate.

6 Conclusion

This paper discussed RTO, which provides interesting problems with respect to the syntactic/semantic status of an accusative-marked NP in the construction. We proposed that two types matrix verb, control and raising, must be recognized. We also suggested that the stage/individual-level distinction of the embedded predicates, more specifically, a non-thematic NP related to the embedded predicate via predication plays a crucial role for licensing RTO.

The conclusions outlined here are shown to account for problems illustrated by the possibility of word order changing and the restriction of the embedded predicate, which are not explained in Kuno (1976).

Acknowledgments

We are indebted to two anonymous reviewers and Robert Logie for their invaluable comments. This research is partially supported by the Grant-in-Aid for Scientific Research (C), 16K00313 of the Japan Society for the Promotion of Science (JSPS).

References

Borkin, A. 1984. *Problems in Form and Function.* Ablex Publishing Corporation.

Carlson, N. G. 1977. Reference to Kinds in English. Ph.D. thesis, University of Massachusetts. Ph. D. dissertation, University of Massachusetts, Amhrest, MA.

Endo, Y. 1994. *Stage/Individual-level Nouns. MIT Working Papers in Linguistics,* 24:83–99.

Hiraiwa, K. 2001. *Multiple Agree and the Defective Intervention Constraint in Japanese. Proceedings of the 1st HUMT Student Conference in Language Research (MIT Working Paper in Linguistics),* 40:67–80.

Kaneko, Y. 1988. On Exceptional Case-Marking in Japanese and English. *English Linguistics,* 5:271–294.

Kubo, M. 1992. *Japanese Syntactic Structure and Their Constructional Meanings.* Ph. D. dissertation, Massachusetts Institute of Technology, Cambridge, MA.

Kuno, S. 1973. *The Structure of the Japanese Language.* The MIT Press, Cambridge, MA.

Kuno, S. 1976. Subject Raising. In M. Shibatani ed., *Syntax and Semantics 5: Japanese Generative Grammar,* 17–49. Academic Press, NY.

Lasnik, H. and Saito, M. 1991. *On the Subject of Infinitives. Proceedings the Cicago Linguistic Society,* 27:324–343.

Oshima, S. 1979. Conditions on Rules: Anaphora in Japanese. In G. Bedell, E., Kobayashi and Muraki, M. eds., *Explorations in Linguistics: Papers in Honor of Kazuko Inoue,* 423–448. Kenkyusya, Tokyo.

Pollard, C., Kasper, R. and Levine, B. 1993. *Studies in Constituent Ordering: Toward a Theory of Linearization in Head-Driven Phrase Structure Grammar* Grant Proposal to the National Science Foundation (NSF), Ohio State University, Columbus.

Pollard, C. and Sag, A. I. 1987. Information-Based Syntax and Semantics Vol. 1: Fundamentals. CSLI Publications. Stanford, CA.

Pollard, C. and Sag, A. I. 1994. Head-driven Phrase Structure Grammar. Chicago University Press, Chicago.

Postal, P. 1974. On Raising: One Rule of English Grammar and Its Theoretical Implication. The MIT Press, Cambridge, MA.

Sag, A. I., Wasow, T., Bender, M. E. 2003. Syntactic Theory: A Formal Introduction. CSLI Publications. Stanford, CA.

Reape, M. 1996. *Getting Things in Order.* In Bunt, H. et al. eds., *Discontinuous Constituency (Natural Language Processing),* 6:209–253, Mouton de Gruyter, New York.

Sakai, H. 1996. Raising Asymmetry and Derivational Uniformity [Kuriagebun no Hitaisyousei to Hasei no Tooitusei]. *Kansai Linguistics Society,* 16:1–11.

Taguchi, S. 2009. *Japanese ECM as Embedded Bare Topicalization. Proceedings the North East Linguistic Society,* 38:415–426.

Takezawa, K. 1987. *A Configurational Approach to Case-marking in Japanese.* Ph. D. dissertation, University of Washington, Seattle.

Tanaka, H. 2002. Raising to Object Out of CP. *Linguistic Inquiry,* 33(4):637–652.

Ueda, M. 1988. Exceptional Case-Marking in Japanese. *Sophia Linguistica,* 22/23:39–46.

Yoo, E. J. 1993. *Subcategorization and Case-Marking in Korean. Papers in Syntax (Ohio State Working Paper in Linguistics),* 42:178–198.

Using Stanford Part-of-Speech Tagger for the Morphologically-rich Filipino Language

Matthew Phillip V. Go
De la Salle University
Manila, Philippines
matthew.go123@gmail.com

Nicco Nocon
De la Salle University
Manila, Philippines
noconoccin@gmail.com

Abstract

This research focuses on the implementation of a Maximum Entropy-based Part-of-Speech (POS) tagger for Filipino. It uses the Stanford POS tagger – a trainable POS tagger that has been trained on English, Chinese, Arabic, and other languages and producing one of the highest results in each language. The tagger was trained for Filipino using a 406k token corpus and considering unique Filipino linguistic phenomena such as high morphology and intra-sentential code-switches. The Filipino POS tagger resulted to 96.15% tagging accuracy which currently presents the highest accuracy and with a large lead among existing POS taggers for Filipino.

1 Introduction

A Part-of-Speech (POS) tagger is a software that classifies words into its word classes or lexical categories (Bird et al., 2009). POS tags and taggers have proven its importance in Natural Language Processing (NLP) when used in advanced NLP researches such as grammar checkers (Go and Borra, 2016), information extraction (Surdeanu et al., 2011), and word-sense disambiguation (Chen et al., 2009). In a pipeline architecture of an advanced research such as an information extraction system, POS taggers are usually found in the first section producing POS tags or tag sequences. These POS tags may be used as basic features or to produce more advanced features such as syntactic structures using a constituency parser and dependencies between words using a dependency parser (Surdeanu et al., 2011; Chen and Manning, 2014).

Despite being a fundamental NLP tool towards advanced NLP researches, there seems to be few researches made towards the development of a high-performing POS tagger for Filipino, the national language of the Philippines – a Southeast Asian country with a population of 101 million people[1].

The following are the list of POS taggers developed for Tagalog, the dialect from where Filipino was based on: TPOST (Rabo and Cheng, 2006), MBPOST (Raga and Trogo, 2006), PTPOST4.1 (Go, 2006), Tag-Alog (Fontanilla and Wu, 2006), and SVPOST (Reyes et al., 2011); Adding to the list is the recently published POS tagger designed for Filipino named SMTPOST (Nocon and Borra, 2016). The key difference between Tagalog and Filipino is the presence of accepted English words such as 'cellphone', 'laptop', 'professor', 'polo shirt' as part of the Filipino language leading to nonce borrowings (single word code switching) and even intra-word code switching such as *nag-conduct* 'conducted' (added prefix *nag-*) and *tinetext* 'texting (someone)' (added infix *-in-*).

Looking into the design of the taggers, TPOST and MBPOST are closely similar because both systems utilize a lexicon list, surrounding words, capitalization, and affix features using a stemmer; where tagging rules are extracted from the training to be used during testing. PTPOST4.1 uses Hidden Markov Model (HMM), Viterbi algorithm, lexicon list, stemmer, and the previous (left) tag before the word. SVPOST makes use of Support Vector Machines (SVM) with predefined features for its training and tagging. SMTPOST presents a novel

---

[1]Based on Philippine Census of Population 2015

31st Pacific Asia Conference on Language, Information and Computation (PACLIC 31), pages 81–88
Cebu City, Philippines, November 16-18, 2017

approach of using Statistical Machine Translation (SMT) in tagging by 'translating' feature representation of words to POS tags. For example, the verb *kumakain* 'eating' will be represented as @*um$ka* highlighting the infix *-um-* and the partial reduplication *ka* which is then paralleled to its respective POS tag VBTR_VBAF (imperfective actor-focus verb) during training.

In terms of evaluation, an independent experiment was conducted to test the performance of the early POS taggers: TPOST, MBPOST, PTPOST4.1 and Tag-Alog using 120,000 words as data, 4% of which were used as testing data (Miguel and Roxas, 2007). The taggers scored 70%, 77%, 78.3%, and 72.5%, respectively, with PTPOST4.1 as the highest among the four. SVPOST on the other hand, conducted its own experiment on 122,318 words producing an 81% accuracy score. SMTPOST, being the most recent development among all Filipino POS taggers, produced 84.75% accuracy in its own 70,312 word dataset. These results however are relatively low compared to the state-of-the-art POS taggers for English (97.64%), French (97.8%), German (96.9%), Arabic (96.26%), and Chinese (93.46%) (Choi, 2016; Denis and Sagot, 2009; Toutanova et al. , 2003).

These low POS tagging results also hinders the progress of advanced NLP researches in the Filipino language. For instance, named entity recognition for Filipino is considered to be still in its infancy stage due to the limitation of researchers to either manually or semi-automatically tag their Filipino datasets which still requires a very tedious and time-consuming tagging or cleaning process (Lim et al., 2007).

Analysis show that works for Filipino and the other languages differ in two major factors: features and algorithms used. All of the POS taggers for Filipino uses few features: capitalization, presence of affixes, and partial/full reduplication which is produced during a pre-processing stage by hand-crafted rules and a stemmer (Rabo and Cheng, 2006; Nocon and Borra, 2016). Incorrect stemming by the stemmer also cascaded as tagging errors as seen in TPOST which accounted for 25% of the tagging errors in the mentioned work. Algorithms used for Filipino which mostly relied on sentence template rules, affix features, feature-value(tag) pairs

vary significantly than what algorithms the state-of-the-art POS taggers for the other languages are using: Conditional Random Fields, Maximum Entropy Cyclic Dependency Network, Maximum Entropy Markov Model, and others.

Due to significant developments in POS tagging, researches show that existing algorithms applied for these high-performing POS taggers are also usable for other languages, up to a certain extent. The Stanford POS Tagger[2], which uses maximum entropy cyclic dependency network as its core algorithm, has been applied in several languages and achieved decent tagging accuracy results: English (97.28%), Chinese (93.99%), Arabic (96.26%), French (not specified), and German (96.9%) with minimal tweaks such as character length of prefix and suffix to consider, unicode shapes for non-alphabetic languages, distributional similarity, and context window. The Stanford Part-of-Speech (POS) tagger has also been packaged in such a way that it is easy to use for training and testing custom models of different languages.

This research explores the usage of the Stanford POS tagger for the Filipino language taking into consideration the unique Filipino linguistic phenomena such as free word order structure, and a large vocabulary of root, derived, and borrowed words. This paper is organized as follows: in the next section, we discuss the Stanford POS Tagger, followed by the Filipino linguistic phenomena in Section 3; in Section 4, we describe the experiments conducted in creating a Filipino model for the Stanford POS Tagger; analysis of results are then shown in Section 5, ending the paper with the conclusion and future works in Section 6.

2 Stanford POS Tagger

The Stanford POS Tagger (SPOST), originally written by Kristina Toutanova in 2003 and maintained by the Stanford NLP Group since then, is one of the highest-performing POS tagger usable for multiple languages. It has been applied in at least four languages: English (97.28%), Chinese (93.99%), Arabic (96.26%), and German (96.9%) achieving top results for each language. The group has also released

---

[2]http://nlp.stanford.edu/software/tagger.shtml

the software publicly with extensive documentation written in Java discussing how fellow researchers can use the POS tagger for advanced researches or create tagging models for their target languages. The Stanford NLP community has also released packages of the POS tagger and making them usable in other programming languages (i.e. Python, PHP, Javascript, and others)[2].

The POS tagger uses maximum entropy cyclic dependency network as its core algorithm. It has been designed such that researchers can train models using different features called Extractor-Frames. Among these ExtractorFrames are tags, word shapes, unicode shapes, prefix, suffix, distributional similarity, which have shown impressive improvements when used/combined properly (Charniak et al., 1993).

3 Filipino Linguistic Phenomena

Understanding the linguistic phenomena of the Filipino language is important in determining the necessary features to be included when training a tagger model for Filipino. This section discusses the following linguistic phenomena: free-word order structure, high degree of morphology, code switches, and ambiguity of some Filipino words.

A sentence in Filipino can be written in multiple ways. For instance, the English sentence 'Juan went to the market.' can be translated as *Si Juan ay nagpunta sa palengke.* word-per-word translated as 'Juan [ay] went to market.' which follows the subject (focus)-predicate format. It can also be written in predicate-subject format *Nagpunta si Juan sa palengke.* In many cases, phrases can be re-ordered such as *Nagpunta sa palengke si Juan.* without any confusion / loss of information (Ramos, 1971).

The Filipino language has a high degree of morphology having at least 50 affix combinations, partial and full reduplication, and compound words. These morphologies are categorized into three: *inflectional*, a change in word form to represent case, gender, number, tense, person, mood, or voice such as the word *nagsisitakbuhan* 'running (present, actor focus, plural)' from the root word *takbo* 'run'; *derivational*, a change in word form that changes a word's part-of-speech (e.g. *nagsuot* 'wore (past, object focus, singular' from the root word *suot* 'clothes

worn by a person'; and *compounding*, where independent words are concatenated together to form a new word (e.g. *anak* 'child' + *pawis* 'persipiration' = *anak-pawis* 'poor (noun)' (Bonus, 2003). Verb morphologies in Filipino are also complex with the different affix combinations that changes a verb's meaning, aspect (perfective, imperfective, contemplative), and focus (actor, object/goal, benefactive, locative, instrumental, and referential)[3].

Caused by past colonizations or settlements by countries such as Spain and America, the Filipino language has been greatly influenced by their languages having loanwords or Filipinized words (i.e. *bintana* 'window' from Spanish word *ventana*, *Keyk* from English word 'cake'), and having Filipinos naturally speaking English words (Americans were the last colonizers) as part of their Filipino sentences (e.g. *Computer Science ang course niya* 'His course is in Computer Science'). Additionally, rapid technology also led to more borrowed words such as 'cellphone', 'print', 'picture'. It is also common in the Filipino language to affixate English words to change its part-of-speech, for example *Phinophotoshop niya yung picture sa kanyang laptop.* 'He is editing his pictures on his laptop using Photoshop.' wherein the word 'photoshop' is affixated with a reduplication of the first syllable *Pho* and the infix *in* to denote an imperfective actor-focus verb.

Similar with English and other languages, Filipino also has its own sets of ambiguous words. Some words are ambiguous that they can be used as adjectives [JJD] or as common nouns [NNC] (i.e *balanse* 'balance' as [JJD] *balanse na buhay* 'balanced life' and as [NNC] *balanse sa buhay* 'balance in life'). Other examples include *indibidwal* 'individual' as single [JJD] or a particular person [NNC].

4 Filipino Model for Stanford POS Tagger

In creating a maximum entropy POS tagger for Filipino using the Stanford POS tagger (SPOST), features, or ExtractorFrames as Stanford calls it, that will capture unique Filipino linguistic phenomena were carefully considered and included along with the features that were commonly used in creating the other languages' tagger models: *left3words* (word and tag contexts), *naacl2003unknowns* (suffix and

---

[3]MGNN Tagset: `http://goo.gl/dY0qFe`

word shape feature extractors), and word shapes. Post-tagging processes were also included to augment and improve the tags provided by the Filipino tagger model and the SPOST.

For this tagger, the MGNN tagset originally presented in SMTPOST is used (Nocon and Borra, 2016)[3]. The tagset provides 230 tags consisting of 161 compound tags and 69 basic tags, revised and updated based from its predecessor, the Rabo tagset (Rabo and Cheng, 2006). The compound tags clearly present the features of the Filipino word such as: an adjective *magandang* 'beautiful' which has the ligature *-ng* with POS tag [CCP] attached to it, is denoted by [JJD_CCP] 'adjective with ligature' as compared to Rabo's tag [JJD]; and verbs' multidimensional features, where the word *kumakain* being an imperfective [VBTR] and actor-focused verb [VBAF] is denoted as [VBTR_VBAF] than Rabo's tagset that is only capable of tagging one or the other, that is either as [VBTR] or [VBAF].

To cover the high degree of morphology in the Filipino language in which prefixes, infixes, suffixes, and combination of them are evident, features extracting prefixes of length one to six for prefixes ranging from *i-* (*i-* + *tayo* 'stand up' = *itayo* 'put up') to *pinaka-* (*pinaka-* + *matalino* 'smart' = *pinakamatalino* 'smartest') and infixes with length of two for the infixes *-in-* (*-in-* + *bati* 'greet' = *binati* 'greeted') and *-um-* (*-um-* + *takbo* 'run' = *tumakbo* 'ran') were included in some tests.

A post-tagging process of overwriting POS tags of English common nouns[4] such as 'ability', 'locker', 'structure' from [NNC] 'common noun' to [FW] 'foreign word' were also included in some tests. This is done after consulting with two Filipino linguists that such words should be tagged as [FW] and not left as [NNC].

In the SPOST training tagger properties files, a number of tags from the MGNN tagset were also defined as closed class, or tag groups that have a limited number of words / symbols as its members namely: [PRS], [PRP], [PRSP], [PRO], [PRQ], [PRL], [DTC], [DTCP], [DTP], [DTPP], [LM], [CCA], [PMP], and [PMC]. Other configuration in the tagger properties file were kept similar to the configurations used in most tagger properties files of other languages trained using SPOST.

5 Results & Analysis

For this research, we used a Filipino corpus containing 15,166 sentences with a total of 406,509 tokens (54,583 of which are unique). The corpus consists of English Wikipedia sentences that were manually translated to Filipino and tagged with part-of-speech tags by Filipino linguists. The corpus has been divided into two parts: training and testing data following the 80/20 split.

For comparison of results, the Filipino tagger model in SPOST was compared with SMTPOST (Nocon and Borra, 2016) and HPOST, which is an upgraded version of SMTPOST with additional post-tagging rule-based processes. As recalled, SMTPOST is the highest-performing POS tagger for Filipino at this time of writing. All three taggers: SMTPOST, HPOST, and SPOST were trained and tested on the same corpus. Table 1 clearly shows the significant lead of the maximum entropy-based SPOST achieving 96.15% accuracy compared to the statistical machine translation-based SMTPOST's 89.11% and SMT with rule-based post-tagging HPOST's 91.63%.

POS Tagger	Accuracy
SMTPOST	89.11%
HPOST	91.63%
SPOST (best model)	96.15%

Table 1: Comparative Results of Existing POS Taggers

5.1 Finding the Best Feature Set

The best model[5] mentioned in Table 1 uses the *left5words* macro extractor frame which uses two words before, two words after, and two tags before the word to be tagged; *naacl2003unknowns* extractor frame which extracts word shape features and suffixes of the word; *word shapes(-1,1)* or the word shapes of the word before, word to be tagged, and the word after; and distributional similarity of words, which are the same set of extractor frames found in most tagger models of other languages created on SPOST. The distributional similarity was

---

[4] http://www.desiquintans.com/nounlist

[5] Filipino model for SPOST: https://github.com/matthewgo/FilipinoStanfordPOSTagger

trained on a Filipino Wikipedia corpus containing 17.18 million tokens. Extractor frames extracting *prefixes* of lengths one to six and *infixes* of lengths two are also included in this tagger model. These set of features allow SPOST to understand Filipino morphology and use it for tagging. Furthermore, this model uses a post-tagging process of overwriting English common nouns that were tagged as [NNC] to [FW] instead. For example, the word 'forum' if tagged as [NNC] but is in the English dictionary, the tag will be replaced into [FW].

Before achieving the best model, Table 2 shows the different models created and their corresponding accuracies sorted by the sequence of updates performed on the tagger model. Note that all the models discussed in Table 2 uses *naacl2003unknowns* and *wordshapes(-1,1)* configurations.

To begin with, it is noteworthy to discuss that the initial model using the default features: *left3words*, *naacl2003unknowns, wordshapes(-1,1)* and the conjugate gradient search method *(cg)* alone already scored 95.67% which is 4.04% higher than the state-of-the-art for Filipino on the same train and test data. All succeeding models however were trained using the quasi-newton search method *(owlqn2)* because of its faster training time, relatively higher accuracy, and that it is the search method used in training models of other languages for SPOST.

As seen in Table 2, series of experiments on tagger models and the improvements after inclusion or change of features are shown. The first experiment started with comparing two search methods: *cg* and *owlqn2*. After discovering that *owlqn2* performs explicitly better in terms of training speed and accuracy, the next comparison was to choose which context features to use: either *left3words* which looks at word features of the words x_{-1}, x_0, and x_1 — wherein x_0 is the word to be tagged, and x_{-1} and x_1 are its left and right adjacent words, respectively, and tags t_{-2} and t_{-1} as features; or extending it to *left5words* which uses the features of x_{-2}, x_{-1}, x_0, x_1 and x_2, and the same tags. The experimentation was followed by using *pref(6)* as feature and distributional similarity *(distsim)* learned from a 17.18 million word corpus. Another testing captured both prefixes *pref6* and infixes *inf2* such as *-um-* and *-in-*. Next, combined distributional similarity, prefixes, and infixes which showed higher results than

Feature Set	Accuracy
cg-left3words	95.67%
left3words	95.80%
left5words	95.81%
left3words-pref6	95.80%
left5words-pref6	95.83%
left3words-distsim	95.89%
left5words-distsim	95.89%
left3words-pref6-inf2	95.84%
left5words-pref6-inf2	95.84%
left3words-distsim-pref6 -inf2	95.90%
left5words-distsim-pref6 -inf2	95.92%
left3words-pref6-inf2 -engNNCasFW	96.08%
left5words-pref6-inf2 -engNNCasFW	96.12%
left3words-distsim-pref6 -inf2-engNNCasFW	96.13%
left5words-distsim-pref6 -inf2-engNNCasFW	96.15%

Table 2: Results of Tagger Models

the previous experimentations. Lastly, to account for the intra-sentential code switches in Filipino, an overwrite process was performed for which English common nouns[4] tagged as [NNC] into [FW]. The tagger model using *left5words, distsim, pref6, inf2*, and with the post-tagging process of overwriting English common nouns [NNC] as [FW] showed the highest performance among all models, achieving 96.15% accuracy – that is 78,469 out of 81,610 words were correctly tagged. With this in mind, its high accuracy shows that the tagger is significantly closer to the human's tagging reliability whose estimated error rate is at 3% (Manning, 2011).

5.2 Breakdown of Errors

Adding to the results, top 10 POS tags with the highest frequency and distribution in the gold test data is shown at Table 3. The Common Noun [NNC] tag is the highest in terms of frequency and distribution with 11,015 and 13.5%, respectively; while Determiner for Common Noun (Plural) [DTCP] tag is the lowest, with 2,546 counts and 3.12% distribution.

POS Tag	Frequency	Dist. %
NNC	11,015	13.5%
NNP	7,834	9.6%
CCB	5,104	6.25%
CCT	4,952	6.07%
CCP	4,075	4.99%
DTC	3,959	4.85%
PMC	3,921	4.8%
FW	3,188	3.91%
PMP	3,039	3.72%
DTCP	2,546	3.12%

Table 3: Tags Distribution

Gold Tag	Mistagged	Recall %
NNC	366 / 11,015	96.68%
JJD	265 / 2,037	86.99%
VBW	219 / 810	72.96%
FW	167 / 3,188	94.76%
RBD	160 / 282	39.72%
JJD_CCP	155 / 1,430	89.38%
VBOF	128 / 795	71.32%
VBTS_VBOF	108 / 123	12.2%
RBW	106 / 723	85.34%
VBTS	103 / 1,730	94.05%
VBTR	103 / 1301	92.08%
RBD_CCP	95 / 230	58.7%
VBTS_VBAF	55 /59	6.78%

Table 4: Tagging Errors Breakdown

Table 4 shows the tagging errors from the test using the best tagger model, namely those POS tags that have been mistagged, the number of mistagged words and their respective recall rate – analyzed to understand the current limitations of the Filipino SPOST, and the linguistic phenomena or other reasons causing the errors. Among the list, [NNC] or common nouns have the highest number of mistagged words in terms of frequency, accounting 366 out of the total 3,141 tagging errors in the test data (11.65%). Words that should have [NNC] were mistagged as [VBW] (141), [JJD] (110), [FW] (57), and others. Interestingly, 137 out of 141 [NNC]s that were incorrectly tagged as infinitive verbs [VBW] had the prefix *pag* or *pag-* such as *pag-angkat* 'import', *pagbabago* 'change', and *pagbaha* 'flooding'.

This is mainly because there are some [VBW]s that actually uses the same prefixes such as *pagbigay ng ligtas..* 'to give a safe..', and *pagkatapos* 'after finishing..' leading to confusion once detecting the prefix feature *pag* or *pag-*. On the other hand, 140 out of the 219 mistaggings of [VBW] were tagged as [NNC] and 105 of these also uses the prefix *pag* and *pag-* such as *paglalahad* 'access/approach' and *pagsabi* 'telling'.

Mistaggings [NNC] into [JJD] and vice-versa are seen in the results having 110 and 125 instances, respectively. This shows that there are Filipino words that are ambiguous and can possibly be tagged with either of the POS tags. For instance, the word *opisyal* 'official' can act as a noun such as *ang opisyal ng bayan* 'the town official' or as an adjective such as *ang opisyal na bilang* 'the official count'. The same applies to the word *bilog* 'circle' which can act as a noun or an adjective 'circular' with the same Filipino spelling.

Common nouns or [NNC]s were also mistagged as [FW]s 57 times according to the gold standard. However, results show that 27 of these 'errors' are actually English words that should be tagged with [FW], showing tagging inconsistencies by linguists whom have created the gold standard. With this in mind, tagging errors by SPOST exhibits the amount of difficulty to distinguish between [NNC] and [FW] as they are used in the same context, just that [FW] tags are borrowed English common nouns used in Filipino sentences. On the other hand, 125 out of the 167 misclassified [FW] were tagged as [NNC]; this is mainly attributed to the fact that the English nouns list used in this research only used 4,401 English common nouns, which has missed out many other English [NNC]s that can be overwritten as [FW]s. In this case, increasing the English nouns list may reduce these tagging errors.

'How' adverbs [RBD] (160) and 'how' adverbs with ligature *-ng* as suffix [RBD_CCP] (106) accounts for 8.47% (266 / 3,141) of the mistaggings in the test data. 89 of [RBD]s were mistagged as adjectives [JJD]s and 51 of [RBD_CCP] were mistagged as adjectives with ligature *-ng* [JJD_CCP]. In the English language, majority of the adverbs can be distinguished apart from adjectives by having the suffix '-ly' such as 'happily', and 'safely'. Whereas for the Filipino language, the distinction does not apply as instances such as *galit na lumabas* 'angrily exited' and *galit na lalaki* 'angry man' uses the same word *galit* 'angry' as an adverb and adjective. But it must be noted that one can distinguish the proper POS tag by looking at t_2 – that if it is a verb or an adjective, t_0 should be [RBD], and if it is a noun, then [JJD] should be the tag. However, this research did not use the feature *bidirectional5words* which uses t_1 and t_2 instead of *left5words* due to its high memory usage requirement.

In the experiments conducted, the verb group, denoted by the POS tag prefix [VB-], accounts for 36.29% (1,140 / 3,141) of all the mistaggings in the test dataset and 832 of these are *specific* errors wherein verbs are incorrectly assigned with other verb POS tags. An important reason why such mistaggings happen is the push for the use of two dimensions in verb POS tags. In Filipino, affixes changes a verb's aspect (perfective, imperfective, and contemplative) and its focus (actor, object, locative). Combinations of certain affixes will then immediately provide a verb's aspect and focus.

One type of verb tagging error concerns with distinguishing between perfective [VBTS] and imperfective [VBTR] verbs. SPOST incorrectly tagged [VBTS] as [VBTR] 41 times and the opposite 59 times. The two tags uses almost the same set of affix sets except that [VBTR] uses a partial reduplication to denote that the action is still ongoing, as seen in the example *nagbabahagi* 'sharing' [VBTR] vs *nagbahagi* 'shared' [VBTS] from the root *bahagi* 'share', and *kinukulang* 'lacking' vs *kinulang* 'lacked' from the root *kulang* 'lack'. As part of the analysis, the partial reduplication phenomena was not included as a feature for the Filipino SPOST, which may have caused the tagging errors between the two.

Another type of verb tagging errors is about tagging verbs with two dimensions such as [VBTS_VBOF] and [VBTS_VBAF] with low recall rates at 12.2% (15 / 123) and 6.78% (4 / 59), respectively. For the case of [VBTS_VBOF], it was mistagged as [VBTS] 67 times and as [VBOF] 29 times. As for [VBTS_VBAF], it was mistagged as [VBAF] 54 times and as [VBTS] 1 time.

According to a linguist who has participated in creating the gold standard tagged data, the Filipino verb phenomena is challenging to tag. Significantly

in the case of the sentence *Tumunog ang orasan ng cellphone.* 'The cellphone's alarm clock has rang.', wherein the word *tumunog* 'rang' has the infix *-um-* is usually used in a perfective actor-focus verb such as *kumain ang bata ng avocado* 'The kid ate an avocado'. As the first verb's / sentence's focus is clearly the 'alarm clock' (an object), should the verb be tagged as object-focus or as actor-focus because of the infix *-um-*? Another example are the words *tinanggihan* 'rejected' and *pinuntahan* 'went to', where both words have the same set of affixes – the infix *-in-* and suffix *-han* but they have different focuses in the examples *tinanggihan niya ang offer* 'He rejected the offer' and *pinuntahan niya ang bayan* 'He went to the city', having object and locative focus, respectively because the focus word 'offer' is an object and the word *bayan* 'town' is a location, respectively. Note that the other words in the sample sentences have the same respective set of POS tags. These examples show the difficulties in Filipino verbs which requires understanding of the semantic meaning of the nouns, root verb in tagging the focus of a verb.

Lastly, for the case of [VBTS_VBAF], it has been mistagged as VBAF 54 times out of all its 59 instances. Upon observation, the training data shows that it contains 2,352 [VBAF] tagged words and only 137 [VBTS_VBAF] words affecting the tagging results on the test data. This simply shows that the gold standard data still has room for improvement as verbs' aspect should be easy to identify.

6 Conclusion & Future Works

This research presents an implementation of a trained Filipino POS tagger using the Stanford POS tagger, which uses Maximum Entropy Cyclic Dependency Network as its core algorithm. By using built-in features such as *left5words, naacl2003unknown* which also captures suffixes, *wordshapes*, distributional similarity (*distsim*), adding *prefix(6)* and *prefix(2,1)* features to capture Filipino prefixes and infixes, and adding a simple POS tag overwrite function to replace English common nouns' POS tags [NNC] with foreign word [FW], the Filipino Stanford POS tagger scored 96.15% accuracy – beating other existing POS taggers even on the same train and test dataset.

Future works for improving the tagging accuracy of the developed POS tagger include experimentations on using *bidirectional5words* as feature, further cleaning of the train and test dataset, and experiments on solving the tagging difficulties on adjectives vs adverbs, verb groups, English words as [FW], and others.

Acknowledgments

This work was supported by the Department of Science and Technology (DOST) – ERDT, DOST-SEI, and Philippine Commission on Higher Education (CHED). Thanks to Nathaniel Oco and Joey Chua who have assisted us in this research.

References

Steven Bird, Ewan Klein, and Edward Loper. 2009. *Natural Language Processing with Python*. O'Reilly Media Inc.

Don Erick Bonus. 2003. The Tagalog Stemming Algorithm. Master's Thesis. De la Salle University.

Eugene Charniak, Curtis Hendrickson, Neil Jacobson, and Mike Perkowitz. 1993. Equations for Part-of-Speech Tagging. *AAAI 11*, pages 784-789.

Danqi Chen and Christopher Manning. 2014. A Fast and Accurate Dependency Parser Using Neural Networks. *Proceedings of EMNLP 2014*.

Ping Chen, Wei Ding, Chris Bowes, and David Brown. 2009. A Fully Unsupervised Word Sense Disambiguation Method Using Dependency Knowledge. *Proceedings of the Human Language Technologies: The 2009 Annual Conference of the North American Chapter of the ACL*, pages 28-36.

Jinho Choi. 2016. Dynamic Feature Induction: The Last Gist to the State-of-the-Art. *Proceedings of the NAACL-HLT 2016*, pages 271-281.

Shirley Chu. 2009. Language Resource Development at DLSU-NLP Lab. The School of Asian Applied Natural Language Processing for Linguistics Diversity and Language Resource Development ADD-4: Language Resource Technology.

A. Cortez, D.J. Navarro, R. Tan, and A. Victor. 2005. PTPOST: Probabilistic Tagalog Part-of-Speech Tagger. De la Salle University.

Pascal Denis and Benot Sagot. 2009. Coupling an annotated corpus and a morphosyntactic lexicon for state-of-the-art POS tagging with less human effort. *Proceedings of the 23rd Pacific Asia Conference on Language, Information, and Computation*.

G.K. Fontanilla, and H.w. Wu. 2006. Tag-Alog: A Rule-based Part-of-Speech Tagger For Tagalog. De la Salle University-Manila.

K. Go 2006. PTPOST 4.1: Probabilistic Tagalog Part-of-Speech Tagger. De la Salle University-Manila.

Matthew Phillip Go and Allan Borra. 2016. Developing an Unsupervised Grammar Checker for Filipino Using Hybrid N-grams as Grammar Rules. *Proceedings of the 30th Pacific Asia Conference on Language, Information, and Computation (PACLIC30)*, 105-113.

L.E. Lim, J.C. New, M.A. Ngo, M.C. Sy, and N.R. Lim. 2007. A Named-Entity Recognizer for Filipino Texts. *Proceedings of the 4th National Natural Language Processing Research Symposium*.

Christopher D. Manning. 2011. Part-of-speech tagging from 97% to 100%: Is it time for some linguistics?. *Proceedings of the 12th International Conference on Computational Linguistics and Intelligent Text Processing*.

Dalos D. Miguel and Rachel Edita O. Roxas. 2007. Comparative Evaluation of Tagalog Part-of-Speech Taggers. *Proceedings of the 4th National Natural Language Processing 2007*.

Nicco Nocon and Allan Borra. 2016. SMTPOST: Using Statistical Machine Translation Approach in Filipino Part-of-Speech Tagging. *Proceedings of the 30th Pacific Asia Conference on Language, Information, and Computation (PACLIC30)*, 391-396.

Vladimir Rabo and Charibeth Cheng. 2006. TPOST: A Template-based Part-of-Speech Tagger for Tagalog. *Journal of Research in Science, Computing and Engineering*, 3(1).

Rodolfo Raga Jr. and Rhia Trogo. 2006. Memory-based Part-of-Speech Tagger. De la Salle University-Manila

Teresita V. Ramos. 1971. *Makabagong Bararila ng Pilipino*. Rex Book Store.

C. D. E. Reyes, K. R. S. Suba, A. R. Razon, and P. C. Naval Jr.. 2011. SVPOST: A Part-of-Speech Tagger for Tagalog Using Support Vector Machines. *Proceedings of the 11th Philippine Computing Science Congress*

Mihai Surdeanu, David McClosky, Mason R. Smith, Andrey Gusev, and Christopher D.Manning. 2011. Customizing an Information Extraction System to a New Domain. *Proceedings of the ACL 2011 Workshop on Relational Models of Semantics (RELMS 2011)*, pp. 2-10.

Kristina Toutanova, Dan Klein, Christopher Manning, and Yoram Singer. 2003. Feature-Rich Part-of-Speech Tagging with a Cyclic Dependency Network. *Proceedings of HLT-NAACL 2003*, pp. 252-259.

Unsupervised Bilingual Segmentation using MDL for Machine Translation

Bin Shan, Hao Wang, Yves Lepage
Graduate School of Information, Production and Systems
Waseda University
2-7 Hibikino, Wakamatsu-ku, Kitakyushu, Fukuoka, 808-0135, Japan
{reynolds@fuji., oko_ips@ruri., yves.lepage@}waseda.jp

Abstract

In statistical machine translation systems, a problem arises from the weak performance in alignment due to differences in word form or granularity across different languages. To address this problem, in this paper, we propose a unsupervised bilingual segmentation method using the minimum description length (MDL) principle. Our work aims at improving translation quality using a proper segmentation model (lexicon). For generating bilingual lexica, we implement a heuristic and iterative algorithm. Each entry in this bilingual lexicon is required to hold a proper length and the ability to fit the data well. The results show that this bilingual segmentation significantly improved the translation quality on the Chinese–Japanese and Japanese–Chinese subtasks.

1 Introduction

Words are generally the smallest processing units in varieties of NLP tasks. However, there is no guarantee that such smallest processing units can fit any NLP tasks. Especially in bilingual tasks (e.g. statistical machine translation), different languages have different writing systems or segmentation granularity. Such problem should be considered as a critical factor of performance in translation quality. For instance, in machine translation experiments on 11 Europarl corpora (Koehn, 2005), Finnish has the lowest translation accuracy as evaluated by BLEU scores when translated into English. French–Spanish has the highest BLEU scores. Finnish is a non-Indo-European and agglutinative language. French and Spanish have very similar grammar. Thus, the problem arising from different grammatical structure could lead a poor generalization when training SMT system uses such data. This is one aspect. Another aspect, there still exists some problem even segmenting language to generate similar vocabulary. In our view, we suppose that similar units should have a proper size. If similar units are too general, it will cause that size of model become too large and a over-fitting problem in model itself. Namely, too general similar units could not solve this problem indeed. Too general similar units problem also appears in (Virpioja et al., 2007) where they perform monolingual segmentation at the morphological level for Finnish-English translation and put the segmented data to a phrase-based statistical machine translation system. That paper indicates the segmented corpus has lower out-of-vocabulary rates and generates more refined phrases with better generalization ability. However, the results of experiment show that they could not improve translation accuracy. In their method, the sentences already had similar units by morphological level segmentation. However, as we mentioned earlier, over-general similar units also go against on improving the translation quality.

On account of those problem, we suppose that data should be segmented through more proper method which could generate similar units holding proper size and goodness-to-fitting data. Fortunately, minimum description length (MDL) principle as an important principle in information theory has shown a good performance in finding units which could hold a trade-off on that aspect. More details about this

89

31st Pacific Asia Conference on Language, Information and Computation (PACLIC 31), pages 89–96
Cebu City, Philippines, November 16-18, 2017

technology are discussed in section 2.1.

In this paper, we firstly introduce the main technology. Then we propose a bilingual model and an iterative search algorithm to generate the best model. To evaluate our approach, we put the segmented corpus by our method into Moses (Koehn et al., 2007) and use BLEU score and NIST score as an evaluated measure.

2 MDL-based segmentation

2.1 Minimum description length

The Minimum Description Length was first introduced by (Rissanen, 1978). In our method, we suppose to use Crude MDL (Grünwald, 2005), which has two parts.

$$\begin{aligned} M' &= \arg\min_M \mathrm{DL}(D, M) \\ &= \arg\min_M \mathrm{DL}(M) + \mathrm{DL}(D|M) \end{aligned} \tag{1}$$

Where $\mathrm{DL}(.)$ denotes the description length. The $\mathrm{DL}(D|M)$ represents the description length of data given by model or data cost. $\mathrm{DL}(M)$ is the description length of the model or model cost. The principle requires a minimum model, which can produce a lowest description length of two parts. The $\mathrm{DL}(D|M)$ requires that the model has better ability to fit the data. The $\mathrm{DL}(M)$ requires that the model has simpler structure. As González-Rubio and Casacuberta (2015) said, the MDL provides a joint estimation of the structure and parameters (probability distribution) of the model. It naturally provides a mechanism against over-fitting or being too general by implementing two parts in this principle.

2.2 Related works

MDL has been used in common inductive inference tasks (Grünwald, 2005). In this section, we mainly introduce applications. De Marcken (1996) tries to infer the monolingual grammar structure using MDL. Yu (2000) introduce unsupervised monolingual word induction approach using MDL. Approximately, Hewlett and Cohen (2011) implement a heuristic search algorithm and use MDL as criterion to produce the best monolingual segmentation scheme. Zhikov et al. (2010) also employ an MDL-based as criterion with a more efficient greedy algorithm. Chen (2013) proposes a compression-based method using MDL and improve the performance of monolingual segmentation. Argamon et al. (2004) use an efficient recursive method on morphological segmentation using MDL. Those early works focus on exploiting MDL to achieve monolingual segmentation, and indicate that MDL-based method has an excellent performance on unsupervised monolingual segmentation. For bilingual NLP tasks using MDL, Saers et al. (2013) try to build an inversion transduction grammars with MDL. González-Rubio and Casacuberta (2015) try to improve the translation quality by inferring a phrase-based model using MDL. Actually, those works focus on achieving different NLP tasks using MDL.

Our work employs the same technologies as previous works. However, we extend MDL-based monolingual model to bilingual. In addition, previous works using MDL on bilingual tasks did not give the bilingual segmentation method. However, we focus on simultaneously segmenting bilingual data.

3 Methodology

3.1 Bilingual model

Our method builds a bilingual word segmentation scheme. Comparing with the monolingual models, we propose the bilingual model. The bilingual model M can be represented as a bilingual lexicon (a set of unit pairs).

$$M = \{a_i \mid a_i = (s_i, t_i), s_i \in S, t_i \in T\}$$

(s_i, t_i) is the ith unit pair in M, and S and T respectively belongs to source and target types sets. s_i and t_i are source units and target units. Moreover, a single symbol is a basic unit in the monolingual setting. For the bilingual setting, we could extend to choose single symbol pairs as basic units. Thus, if the set only consisting of basic units, we call it basic set M_{basic}. Figure 1 illustrates the similarities and differences between units in the monolingual and bilingual. there are varieties of interpretations to MDL-model using different technologies. Our formula mainly is derived from Zhikov et al. (2010) and Yu (2000).

Generally, the description length of data given by

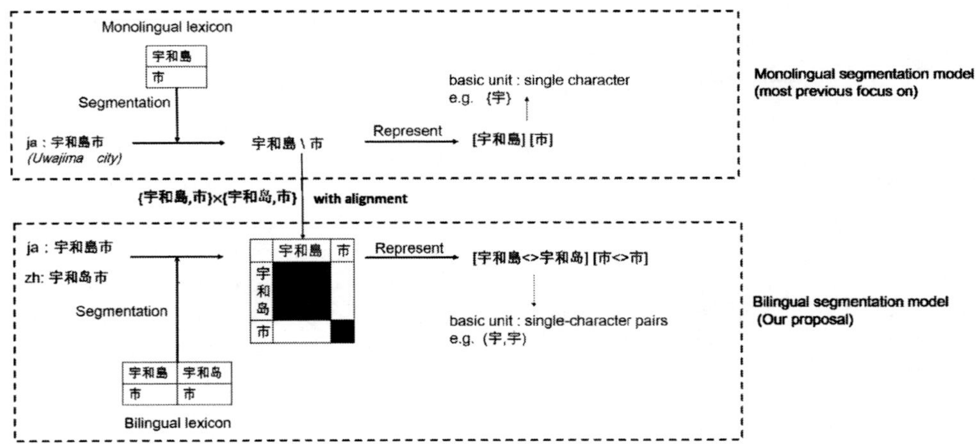

Figure 1: Monolingual and Bilingual

1. The essence of bilingual model is treated **the Cartesian product** as the set of source and target types **with alignment**.

2. A basic unit in a monolingual sentence is a single character / letter, which in a bilingual sentence should be a single character/letter pair.

3. Any sentences can be represented as several units following the order according to the monolingual / bilingual lexicon. For representation, " [...] " represents a unit. "... <> ..." represents an alignment which is used to connect the source and target word.

model $\mathrm{DL}(D|M)$ is calculated using Shannon-Fano code. For the data cost,

$$\mathrm{DL}(D|M) = \sum_i^M -C(a_i)\log P(a_i) \qquad (2)$$

Where $P(a_i) = -\log\frac{C(a_i)}{N}$ is the *self-information* of a_i. a_i represents an alignment unit (s_i, t_i). $C(a_i)$ is a frequency of a_i in data D. Equation 2 gives the total information contained in the data given by the model M.

For the description length of model $\mathrm{DL}(M)$, different work pieces introduce different calculations. The common point in the calculation is the product of the length in character of units and an estimate of per-character entropy (Zhikov et al., 2010) (in the bilingual setting, "character" should be replaced with "character pairs" or "basic unit pairs"). The estimate of every basic unit pairs entropy is not easy, Yu (2000) suggests to use average entropy as estimation. Using average entropy as estimation will improve the speed of implementing our following algorithm a lot. Namely, the calculation of model cost generally covert to count the size of model. However, with this estimation, we could not capture the

probability distribution of basic units. Thus, at the precision perspective, we ignore the effects of sub-structure. So we calculate model cost using

$$\mathrm{DL}(M) = \sum_i^{|M|} b \times len(a_i) \qquad (3)$$

Where $len(a_i)$ is the number of basic alignment units in a_i. $b = -\log_2 |M_{ini}|$ and which represents binary code length of initial model. Where M_{ini} is the simplest bilingual lexicon (model) which has the lowest model cost and just includes basic unit pairs. $len(M_{ini})$ is the basic lexicon size. Thus, b is constant when the data given.

For the basic model M_{ini}, it should have the lowest description length of the model. Besides, it is an initial model in our method. However, the description length of data given by the initial model in most cases will be very large. So we need to merge some smaller unit pairs into some bigger ones in order to decrease the description length of data. Likewise, the description length of the model will increase if we merge some unit pairs. Therefore, there exists a trade-off in two parts and the best model we excepted is such a trade-off model.

91

Basic unit: （宇, 宇）（和, 和）（島, 島）（市, 市）（で, 在）（は,在）

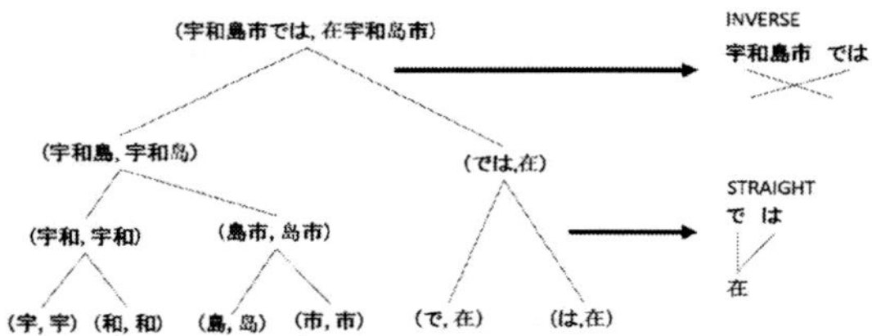

Figure 2: A efficient searching path by ΔDL

1. In this binary tree, the leaves are the basic unit. Every node is an alignment unit. Every father node can be represented by the child node.

2. Input the candidates can be represented as two child nodes.

3. Two child nodes should be combined into a father node with two ways: INVERSE and STRAIGHT.

3.2 Bilingual segmentation

As De Marcken (1996) showed, every sentence has a hierarchical structure and he calls the Viterbi representation for a sentence. He tries to search the best model by inputting possible candidates with two operations (add and delete). They represent candidates as a binary combination of two units which could be found in the current model. Likewise, Lardilleux et al. (2012) shows how to segment bilingual sentences by building the bilingual binary tree structure with a recursive binary splitting method. The same place in previous works, they all choose a binary combination or split way to search the best model. Actually, this measure is a common way to search the best model by using MDL principle. The binary representation brings an efficient path to search the best model. We just evaluate the changes in description length, when possible candidates are applied to the current model.

So our problems can be converted to evaluate the changes in description length after a new alignment unit is accepted by model. Every accepted candidate will bring a ΔDL, it can search the best model by evaluating the changes (Figure 3.2). Another important point, from those structures we can find that there exist two direction search algorithms. Those are bottom-to-top search method with binary combination and top-to-bottom with binary split.

3.3 Quantifying changes in description length

The MDL-based method provide an evidence to define the best model with the sum of data and model cost. Our method employs a heuristic algorithm to iteratively generate a new model from the current model. Due to our model is bilingual lexicon, we generate new model through adding possible candidates to current lexicon. For giving the evidence of possible candidates, every candidate should be evaluated to a change ΔDL in description length. When the ΔDL can decrease the DL(D, M), the candidates will be applied to the current model. For example, when we apply a candidate $a_1 a_2$, it can be represented as a_1 and a_2 in current model M.

Considering the MDL-based methods generally consist of model and data cost, the changes are evaluated as:

$$\Delta\text{DL}(D, M) = \Delta\text{DL}(M) + \Delta\text{DL}(D|M)$$

For a candidate $a_1 a_2$ to be feed into the model, we just evaluate the changes of two parts.

For the ΔDL$(D|M)$ with four parts:

$$\Delta DL(D|M) = \delta_1 + \delta_2 - \delta_3 + \delta_4$$

$\delta_1 = (C(a_1) - C(a_1 a_2)) \log \frac{C(a_1) - C(a_1 a_2)}{N - C(a_1 a_2)}$ is difference on a_1,

$\delta_2 = (C(a_2) - C(a_1 a_2)) \log \frac{C(a_2) - C(a_1 a_2)}{N - C(a_1 a_2)}$ is difference on a_2,

$\delta_3 = C(a_1 a_2) \log \frac{C(a_1 a_2)}{N - C(a_1 a_2)}$ is difference on new input $a_1 a_2$,

$\delta_4 = K \log \frac{N'}{N}$ are changes on other alignment units, actually we can find the changes on other alignment units just are about the total number. K is the number of other alignment units.

For the ΔDL(M),

$$\Delta\text{DL}(M) = b \log \frac{len(a_1) + len(a_2)}{len(a_1 a_2)} = b\delta_m$$

As shown in the above formula, b is a constant and we just need to focus on changes of the total model length. As for changes on length of model, we just need to care about whether any inputs change the counts of old units in model to 0. Due to the counts change into 0, it should be removed from the model. We assign $\frac{len(a_1) + len(a_2)}{len(a_1 a_2)}$ as the difference value δ_m. So we have:

1. When frequency of a_1 or a_2 changes to 0 after input operation, the $\delta_m = 1$

2. When frequency of a_1 and a_2 changes to 0 after input operation, the $\delta_m = 0$

3. When frequency of a_1 and a_2 does not change in 0 after input operation, the $\delta_m = 2$

By calculating the sum of changes on two parts, we can give the inputs an evidence about accepting or not.

3.4 Search Algorithm

The previous section introduced that we use the ΔDL to evaluate changes of possible candidates on description length. However, the order of applying a new alignment unit is also very important. González-Rubio and Casacuberta (2015) introduced that the order of inputting candidates should be sorted by the ascending of $\Delta\mathrm{DL}(D|M)$. In our method, we take the following strategy:

1. Segment corpus to characters and use word alignment tools to get a character alignment result as basic model.

2. Collect all the possible binary combination candidates from the data and model.

3. Run an iterative procedure to generate models.

4. Repeat the 2 to 3 until the description length will not reduce.

Algorithm 1 describes the processing of iterative generating model in step 3. First, we collect all possible candidates (line 2 to 3). Then we estimate the variation in description length when those candidates are applied to model (line 4 to 9). Then we evaluate the changes in total description length and use those candidates to update the model (line 11 to 15). Finally, the whole loop will end until the description length of the model could not reduce any more (line 17).

4 Experiment

Our method are evaluated through building Chinese–Japanese SMT experiments. For getting initial bilingual model, the extra alignment tool

---

Algorithm 1 Iterative Generate Model

Input: M : Initial model consist of basic units
Output: M' : Generated model

1: **while** $\Delta > 0$ **do**
2:     $\Phi \leftarrow collect(D, M)$
3:     $candidates \leftarrow ascending\_sort(\Phi)$
4:     **for** $s \in candidates$ **do**
5:         $delta = eval\_DL\_data(s)$
6:         **if** $delta > 0$ **then**
7:             $true\_candidates.append(s)$
8:         **end if**
9:     **end for**
10:    $C \leftarrow ascending\_sort(true\_candidates)$
11:    **for** $s \in C$ **do**
12:        $true\_delta \leftarrow eval\_total\_DL(s)$
13:        **if** $true\_delta > 0$ **then**
14:            $M' \leftarrow update(M, s)$
15:        **end if**
16:    **end for**
17: **end while**

---

is used. The results obtained with the proposed method are compared the results obtained using *Kytea*[1] as segmentation technologies.

4.1 Setup

In our experiment, we use ASPEC [2] as experiment corpus. Due to the low performance of the current word alignment tools for character alignment on Latin languages, we cannot perform our method with the letter to letter alignment on Latin languages. However, it works well for Chinese and Japanese. So we select the Chinese and Japanese as our experiment corpus. For word alignment tools, we use *MGiza++*[3] to get character-based alignment results. To avoid unnecessary processing (e.g. resulted from non-Chinese units in Chinese corpus), we in advance token the non-Chinese or non-Japanese letter and as one unit. For machine translation system, we use *Moses*[4]. To benchmark our method, we choose data segmented by *Kytea* as baseline. The reason we choose Kytea is that it always segments the corpus with a small degree (the most cases are morpholog-

---

[1] http://www.phontron.com/kytea/
[2] http://orchid.kuee.kyoto-u.ac.jp/ASPEC/
[3] https://github.com/moses-smt/mgiza
[4] http://www.statmt.org/moses/

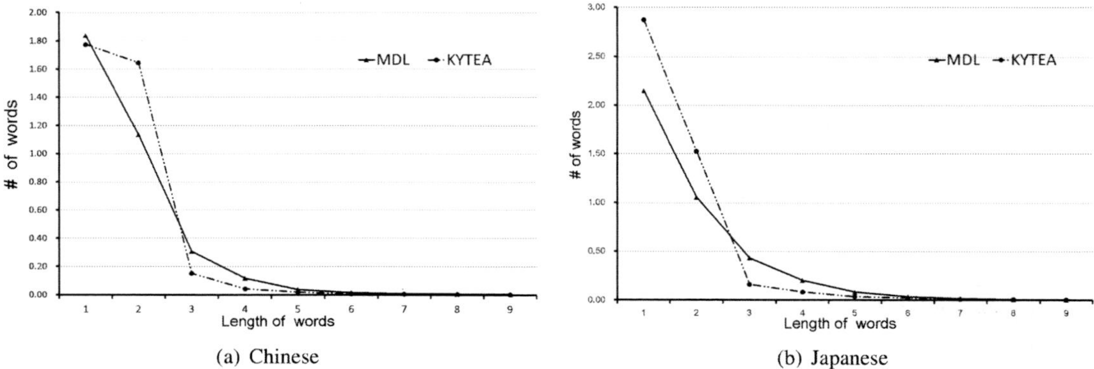

(a) Chinese

(b) Japanese

Figure 3: Frequency and length of words in corpus segmented by MDL and Kytea

1. Kytea (monolingual segmentation method) have different granularity of the segmentation in Chinese and Japanese. However, bilingual MDL-based method **share similar granularity** across both languages.

2. Words segmented by Kytea have small granularity. However, our method (MDL-based segmentation) have **smoother distribution and larger segmentation granularity.**

ical level). We suppose it could show the unbalance problem in Chinese and Japanese more clearly. Table 1 illustrates the data setting of SMT experiment.

4.2   Result and analysis

The total number of iterations of our algorithm are 8 times. Figure 4 illustrates changes of each iteration in data cost, model cost and total cost. We found that MDL principle provides any candidates an evidence through introducing a change in two parts cost. MDL principle would find a best balanced cost of model and data. Figure 3 illustrates the frequency distribution of different length of words. The granularity of segmentation given by Kytea and our method is different, and our method assign a smoother frequency distribution than kytea. We also can found such phenomenon shown in data setting of SMT system (Table 1). In Table 1, we found average of length of words segmented by our method is longer than Kytea.

Due to different segmentation standards, we need to unify them in the evaluation step. Here, we evaluate translation accuracy in characters. Likewise, non-Chinese and non-Japanese are tokenized as one unit. Table 4.2 shows that the BLEU (Papineni et al., 2002) scores have improved **2.01%** in Chinese

to Japanese. For NIST (Doddington, 2002) scores, we found that there are improvements in both translating directions.

5   Conclusion and Future Work

5.1   Conclusion

We propose a bilingual segmentation method using MDL, which aims at improving translation quality. Our method could simultaneously segment bilingual corpus and generates corresponding bilingual lexicon. Thus, our work also can be treated as a bilingual lexicon induction. Since our segmentation method achieves a slightly better translation result shown in Table 4.2, we conclude that our bilingual MDL-based segmentation method is more effective than previous monolingual segmentation method. Besides, we also found that MDL-based method could give more balanced trade-off between segmentation granularity and frequency. Differ with previous works using MDL-based method on monolingual segmentation, we extended the MDL-based method into bilingual segmentation and improved translation quality.

Our contributions in this work can be summa-

Data	Seg.	Sent.	Chinese		Japanese	
			Tokens	Length	Tokens	Length
Train	Kytea	135.0 k	3.66 M	10.82	4.74 M	11.33
	MDL		3.46 M	11.82	3.98 M	12.27
Tune	Kytea	3.0 k	84.1k	7.71	108.1 k	8.28
	MDL		79.4 k	8.36	90.4 k	9.03
Test	Kytea	11.0 k	308.4 k	8.94	396.6 k	9.47
	MDL		290.9 k	9.44	331.1 k	10.06

Table 1: Data setting
Length: average length of types in corpus;
Tokens.: number of word tokens in corpus;
Sent.: number of sentences in corpus;

	Seg.	BLEU	p-value	NIST	p-value
ja-zh	Kytea	36.68±0.28	<0.01	9.84±0.03	<0.01
	MDL	**38.69±0.28**		**10.24±0.04**	
zh-ja	Kytea	40.46±0.28	0.1	9.81±0.03	<0.01
	MDL	**40.35±0.28**		**10.08±0.03**	

Table 2: Experiment result

1. BLEU and NIST: translation accuracy metrics (based on characters)

2. p-value < 0.05 means the improvements are statistically significant different.

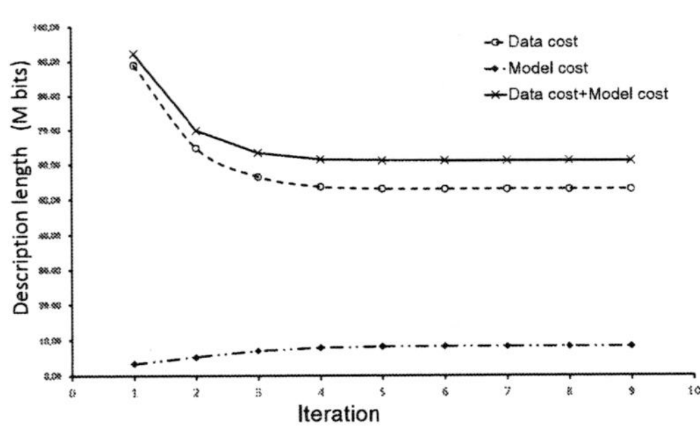

Figure 4: The data and model cost with iteration

5.2 Future Work

For languages written with the Latin alphabet, the basic unit is very limited. The current alignment tools will filter a large amount of characters alignment results. Thus, the bottom-to-top method cannot be applied. As mentioned in Section 3, there is also another strategies (top-down) which can be used to solve the problem. It will be in our future work. In addition, the initial model in our method depends on character-based alignment results. The quality of character-based word alignments is an influential factor in our final segmentation. A better method could be generate the initial model without any alignment tool. This could lead to better segmentation. For calculation of description length, we will be working on designing more accurate formula. Due to our method is initial step of NLP task, in this experiment we use translation accuracy of building SMT system as evaluation of our method. However, we also suggest that our segmentation method could be evaluated with other machine translation system.

rized as in three folds. Firstly, we propose a bilingual segmentation method instead of the monolingual method as an initial step of machine translation. Secondly, we choose MDL as main technology in our segmentation. This technology could be prone to produce more balanced word pairs in segmentation and gives a better inference on bilingual lexicon. Thirdly, our method is an unsupervised method based on characters which is also can be applied to any other languages writing in CJK characters.

References

Shlomo Argamon, Navot Akiva, Amihood Amir, and Oren Kapah. 2004. Efficient unsupervised recursive word segmentation using minimum description length. In *Proceedings of the 20th international conference on Computational Linguistics (COLING 2004)*, volume 2, pages 1058–1064, Genève, August.

Ruey-Cheng Chen. 2013. An improved MDL-based compression algorithm for unsupervised word segmentation. In *Proceedings of the 51st Annual Meeting of the Association for Computational Linguistics (ACL 2013)*, volume 2, pages 166–170, Sofia, Bulgaria, August. Association for Computational Linguistics.

Carl De Marcken. 1996. *Unsupervised Language Acquisition*. Ph.D. thesis, Massachusetts Institute of Technology.

George Doddington. 2002. Automatic evaluation of machine translation quality using n-gram co-occurrence statistics. In *Proceedings of the second international conference on Human Language Technology Research*, pages 138–145. Morgan Kaufmann Publishers Inc.

Jesús González-Rubio and Francisco Casacuberta. 2015. Improving the minimum description length inference of phrase-based translation models. In *Proceedings of the Iberian Conference on Pattern Recognition and Image Analysis*, pages 219–227. Springer.

Peter Grünwald. 2005. A tutorial introduction to the minimum description length principle. In *Advances in Minimum Description Length: Theory and Applications*. MIT Press.

Daniel Hewlett and Paul Cohen. 2011. Fully unsupervised word segmentation with bve and mdl. In *Proceedings of the 49th Annual Meeting of the Association for Computational Linguistics: Human Language Technologies (ACL-HLT 2011)*, pages 540–545. Association for Computational Linguistics.

Philipp Koehn, Hieu Hoang, Alexandra Birch, Chris Callison-Burch, Marcello Federico, Nicola Bertoldi, Brooke Cowan, Wade Shen, Christine Moran, Richard Zens, et al. 2007. Moses: Open source toolkit for statistical machine translation. In *Proceedings of the 45th annual meeting of the ACL-2007 on interactive poster and demonstration sessions*, pages 177–180. Association for Computational Linguistics.

Philipp Koehn. 2005. Europarl: A parallel corpus for statistical machine translation. In *Proceedings of Machine Translation Summit X (MT summit X)*, volume 5, pages 79–86.

Adrien Lardilleux, François Yvon, and Yves Lepage. 2012. Hierarchical sub-sentential alignment with anymalign. In *Proceedings of the 16th annual conference of the European Association for Machine Translation (EAMT 2012)*, pages 279–286.

Kishore Papineni, Salim Roukos, Todd Ward, and Wei-Jing Zhu. 2002. Bleu: a method for automatic evaluation of machine translation. In *Proceedings of the 40th annual meeting on association for computational linguistics*, pages 311–318. Association for Computational Linguistics.

Jorma Rissanen. 1978. Modeling by shortest data description. *Automatica*, 14(5):465–471.

Markus Saers, Karteek Addanki, and Dekai Wu. 2013. Unsupervised transduction grammar induction via minimum description length. In *Proceedings of the Second Workshop on Hybrid Approaches to Translation (HyTra)*, pages 67–73.

Sami Virpioja, Jaakko J Väyrynen, Mathias Creutz, and Markus Sadeniemi. 2007. Morphology-aware statistical machine translation based on morphs induced in an unsupervised manner. In *Proceedings of Machine Translation Summit XI (MT Summit XI)*, pages 491–498.

Hua Yu. 2000. Unsupervised word induction using mdl criterion. In *Proceedings of the International Symposium of Chinese Spoken Language Processing (ISCSL 2000)*, Beijing.

Valentin Zhikov, Hiroya Takamura, and Manabu Okumura. 2010. An efficient algorithm for unsupervised word segmentation with branching entropy and mdl. In *Proceedings of the 2010 Conference on Empirical Methods in Natural Language Processing (EMNLP 2010)*, pages 832—842. Association for Computational Linguistics, Oct.

The Importance of Automatic Syntactic Features in Vietnamese Named Entity Recognition

Thai-Hoang Pham
R&D Department
Alt Inc
Hanoi, Vietnam
phamthaihoang.hn@gmail.com

Phuong Le-Hong
College of Science
Vietname National University in Hanoi
Hanoi, Vietnam
phuonglh@vnu.edu.vn

Abstract

This paper presents a state-of-the-art system for Vietnamese Named Entity Recognition (NER). By incorporating automatic syntactic features with word embeddings as input for bidirectional Long Short-Term Memory (Bi-LSTM), our system, although simpler than some deep learning architectures, achieves a much better result for Vietnamese NER. The proposed method achieves an overall F_1 score of 92.05% on the test set of an evaluation campaign, organized in late 2016 by the Vietnamese Language and Speech Processing (VLSP) community. Our named entity recognition system outperforms the best previous systems for Vietnamese NER by a large margin.

1 Introduction

Named entity recognition (NER) is an essential task in natural language processing that falls under the domain of information extraction. The function of this task is to identify noun phrases and categorize them into a predefined class. NER is a crucial preprocessing step used in some NLP applications such as question answering, automatic translation, speech processing, and biomedical science. In two shared tasks, CoNLL 2002[1] and CoNLL 2003[2], language independent NER systems were evaluated for English, German, Spanish, and Dutch. These systems focus on four named entity types namely person, organization, location, and remaining miscellaneous entities.

Lately, an evaluation campaign that systematically compared NER systems for the Vietnamese language has been launched by the Vietnamese Language and Speech Processing (VLSP)[3] community. They collect data from electronic newspapers on the web and annotate named entities in this corpus. Similar to the CoNLL 2003 share task, there are four named entity types in VLSP dataset: person (PER), organization (ORG), location (LOC), and miscellaneous entity (MISC).

In this paper, we present a state-of-the-art NER system for Vietnamese language that uses automatic syntactic features with word embedding in Bi-LSTM. Our system outperforms the leading system of the VLSP campaign utilizing a number of syntactic and hand-crafted features, and an end-to-end system described in (Pham and Le-Hong, 2017) that is a combination of Bi-LSTM, Convolutional Neural Network (CNN), and Conditional Random Field (CRF) about 3%. To sum up, the overall F_1 score of our system is 92.05% as assessed by the standard test set of VLSP. The contributions of this work consist of:

- We demonstrate a deep learning model reaching the state-of-the-art performance for Vietnamese NER task. By incorporating automatic syntactic features, our system (Bi-LSTM), although simpler than (Bi-LSTM-CNN-CRF) model described in (Pham and Le-Hong, 2017), achieves a much better result on Vietnamese NER dataset. The simple architecture also contributes to the feasibility of our system in

---

[1]http://www.cnts.ua.ac.be/conll2002/ner/
[2]http://www.cnts.ua.ac.be/conll2003/ner/

[3]http://vlsp.org.vn/

31st Pacific Asia Conference on Language, Information and Computation (PACLIC 31), pages 97–103
Cebu City, Philippines, November 16-18, 2017

practice because it requires less time for inference stage. Our best system utilizes part-of-speech, chunk, and regular expression type features with word embeddings as an input for two-layer Bi-LSTM model, which achieves an F_1 score of 92.05%.

- We demonstrate the greater importance of syntactic features in Vietnamese NER compared to their impact in other languages. Those features help improve the F_1 score of about 18%.

- We also indicate some network parameters such as network size, dropout are likely to affect the performance of our system.

- We conduct a thorough empirical study on applying common deep learning architectures to Vietnamese NER, including Recurrent Neural Network (RNN), unidirectional and bidirectional LSTM. These models are also compared to conventional sequence labelling models such as Maximum Entropy Markov models (MEMM).

- We publicize our NER system for research purpose, which is believed to positively contributing to the long-term advancement of Vietnamese NER as well as Vietnamese language processing.

The remainder of this paper is structured as follows. Section 2 summarizes related work on NER. Section 3 describes features and model used in our system. Section 4 gives experimental results and discussions. Finally, Section 5 concludes the paper.

2   Related Works

We categorize two main approaches for NER in a large number of research published in the last two decades. The first approach is characterized by the use of traditional sequence labelling models such as CRF, hidden markov model, support vector machine, maximum entropy that are heavily dependent on hand-crafted features (Florian et al., 2003; Lin and Wu, 2009; Durrett and Klein, 2014; Luo and Xiaojiang Huang, 2015). These systems made an endeavor to exploit external information instead of the available training data such as gazetteers and unannotated data.

In the last few years, deep neural network approaches have gained in popularity dealing with NER task. With the advance of computational power, there has been more and more research that applied deep learning methods to improve performances of their NLP systems. LSTM and CNN are prevalent models used in these architectures. Firstly, (Collobert et al., 2011) used a CNN over a sequence of word embeddings with a CRF layer on the top. They nearly achieved state-of-the-art results on some sequence labelling tasks such as POS tagging, chunking, albeit did not work for NER. To improve the accuracy for recognizing named entities, (Huang et al., 2015) used Bi-LSTM with CRF layer for joint decoding. This model also used hand-crafted features to ameliorate its performance. Recently, (Chiu and Nichols, 2016) proposed a hybrid model that combined Bi-LSTM with CNN to learn both character-level and word-level representations. Instead of using CNN to learn character-level features like (Chiu and Nichols, 2016), (Lample et al., 2016) used BI-LSTM to capture both character and word-level features.

For Vietnamese, VLSP community has organized an evaluation campaign that follows the rules of CoNLL 2003 shared task to systematically compare NER systems. Participating systems have approached this task by both traditional and deep learning architectures. In particular, the first-rank system of the VLSP campaign which achieved an F_1 score of 88.78% used MEMM with many hand-crafted features (Le-Hong, 2016). Meanwhile, (Nguyen et al., 2016) adopted deep neural networks for this task. They used the system provided by (Lample et al., 2016), which consists of two types of LSTM models: Bi-LSTM-CRF and Stack-LSTM. Their best system achieved an F_1 score of 83.80%. More recently, (Pham and Le-Hong, 2017) used an end-to-end system that is a combination of Bi-LSTM-CNN-CRF for Vietnamese NER. The F_1 score of this system is 88.59% that is competitive with the accuracy of (Le-Hong, 2016).

3 Methodology

3.1 Feature Engineering

Word Embeddings We use a word embedding set trained from 7.3GB of 2 million articles collected through a Vietnamese news portal[4] by word2vec[5] toolkit. Details of this word embedding set are described in (Pham and Le-Hong, 2017).

Automatic Syntactic Features To ameliorate a performance of our system, we incorporate some syntactic features with word embeddings as input for Bi-LSTM model. These syntactic features are generated automatically by some public tools so the actual input of our system is only raw texts. These additional features consist of part-of-speech (POS) and chunk tags that are available in the dataset, and regular expression types that capture common organization and location names. These regular expressions over tokens described particularly in (Le-Hong, 2016) are shown to provide helpful features for classifying candidate named entities, as shown in the experiments.

3.2 Long Short-Term Memory

Long short-term memory (LSTM) (Hochreiter and Schmidhuber, 1997) is a special kind of Recurrent Neural Network (RNN) which is capable of dealing with possible gradient exploding and vanishing problems (Bengio et al., 1994; Pascanu et al., 2013) when handling long-range sequences. It is because LSTM uses memory cells instead of hidden layers in a standard RNN. In particular, there are three multiplicative gates in a memory cell unit that decides on the amount of information to pass on to the next step. Therefore, LSTM is likely to exploit long-range dependency data. Each multiplicative gate is computed as follows:

$$\mathbf{i}_t = \sigma(\mathbf{W}_i\mathbf{h}_{t-1} + \mathbf{U}_i\mathbf{x}_t + \mathbf{b}_i)$$
$$\mathbf{f}_t = \sigma(\mathbf{W}_f\mathbf{h}_{t-1} + \mathbf{U}_f\mathbf{x}_t + \mathbf{b}_f)$$
$$\mathbf{c}_t = \mathbf{f}_t \odot c_{t-1} + \mathbf{i}_t \odot \tanh(\mathbf{W}_c\mathbf{h}_{t-1} + \mathbf{U}_c\mathbf{x}_t + \mathbf{b}_c)$$
$$\mathbf{o}_t = \sigma(\mathbf{W}_o\mathbf{h}_{t-1} + \mathbf{U}_o\mathbf{x}_t + \mathbf{b}_o)$$
$$\mathbf{h}_t = \mathbf{o}_t \odot \tanh(\mathbf{c}_t)$$

---

[4]http://www.baomoi.com
[5]https://code.google.com/archive/p/word2vec/

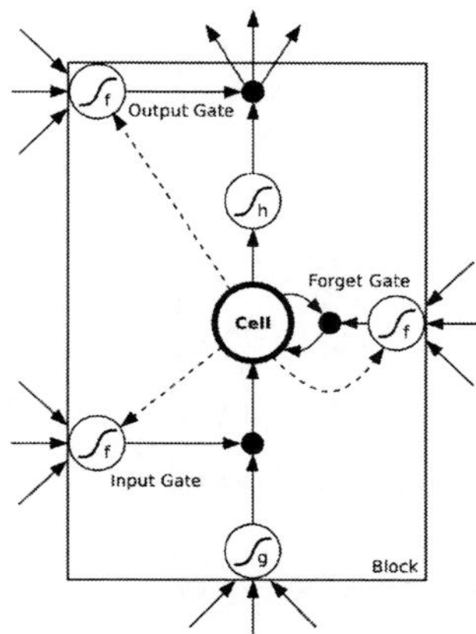

Figure 1: LSTM memory cell

where σ and $\odot$ are element-wise sigmoid function and element-wise product, $\mathbf{i}$, $\mathbf{f}$, $\mathbf{o}$ and $\mathbf{c}$ are the input gate, forget gate, output gate and cell vector respectively. $\mathbf{U}_i, \mathbf{U}_f, \mathbf{U}_c, \mathbf{U}_o$ are weight matrices that connect input $\mathbf{x}$ and gates, and $\mathbf{U}_i, \mathbf{U}_f, \mathbf{U}_c, \mathbf{U}_o$ are weight matrices that connect gates and hidden state $\mathbf{h}$, and finally, $\mathbf{b}_i, \mathbf{b}_f, \mathbf{b}_c, \mathbf{b}_o$ are the bias vectors. Figure 1 illustrates a single LSTM memory cell.

3.3 Bidirectional Long Short-Term Memory

The original LSTM uses only past features. For many sequence labelling tasks, it is beneficial when accessing both past and future contexts. For this reason, we utilize the bidirectional LSTM (Bi-LSTM) (Graves and Schmidhuber, 2005; Graves et al., 2013) for NER task. The basic idea is running both forward and backward passes to capture past and future information, respectively, and concatenate two hidden states to form a final representation. Figure 2 illustrates the backward and forward passes of Bi-LSTM.

3.4 Our Deep Learning Model

For Vietnamese named entity recognition, we use a 2-layer Bi-LSTM with softmax layer on the top to detect named entities in sequence of sentences. The inputs are the combination of word and syntactic features, and the outputs are the probability distributions over named entity tags. Figure 3 describes the details of our deep learning model. In the next sections, we present our experimental results.

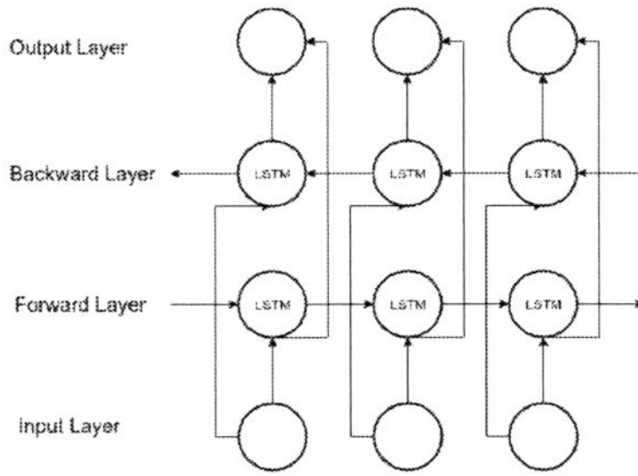

Figure 2: Bidirectional LSTM

4 Results And Discussions

4.1 VLSP Corpus

We conduct experiments on the VSLP NER shared task 2016 corpus. Four named entity types are evaluated in this corpus including person, location, organization, and other named entities. Definitions of these entity types match with their descriptions in the CoNLL shared task 2003.

There are five columns in this dataset including surface word, automatic POS and chunking tags, named entity and nested named entity labels, of which the first four columns conform to the format of the CoNLL 2003 shared task. We do not use the fifth column because our system focuses on only named entity without nesting. Named entities are labelled by the IOB notation as in the CoNLL 2003 shared tasks. In particular, there are 9 named entity labels in this corpus including B-PER and I-PER for persons, B-ORG and I-ORG for organizations, B-LOC and I-LOC for locations, B-MISC and I-MISC for other named entities, and O for other elements. Table 1 presents the number of annotated named entities in the training and testing set.

Entity Types	Training Set	Testing Set
Location	6,247	1,379
Organization	1,213	274
Person	7,480	1,294
Miscellaneous names	282	49
All	15,222	2,996

Table 1: Statistics of named entities in VLSP corpus

Because we use early stopping method described in (Graves et al., 2013) to avoid overfitting when training our neural network models, we hold one part of training data for validation. The number of sentences of each part of VLSP corpus is described in Table 2.

Data sets	Number of sentences
Train	14,861
Dev	2,000
Test	2,831

Table 2: Size of each data set in VLSP corpus

4.2 Evaluation Method

We evaluate the performance of our system with F_1 score:

$$F_1 = \frac{2 * \texttt{precision} * \texttt{recall}}{\texttt{precision} + \texttt{recall}}$$

Precision and recall are the percentage of correct named entities identified by the system and the percentage of identified named entities present in the corpus respectively. To compare fairly with previous systems, we use an available evaluation script provided by the CoNLL 2003 shared task[6] to calculate F_1 score of our NER system.

4.3 Results

In this section, we analyze the efficiency of word embeddings, bidirectional learning, model configuration, and especially automatic syntactic features.

Embeddings To evaluate the effectiveness of word embeddings, we compare the systems on three types of input: skip-gram, random vector, and one-hot vector.

The number of dimensions we choose for word embedding is 300. We create random vectors for words that do not appear in word embeddings set by uniformly sampling from the range $[-\sqrt{\frac{3}{dim}}, +\sqrt{\frac{3}{dim}}]$ where dim is the dimension of embeddings. For random vector setting, we also sample vectors for all words from this distribution. The performances of the system with each input type are represented in Table 3.

We can conclude that word embedding is an important factor of our model. Skip-gram vector significantly improves our performance. The improve-

---

[6]http://www.cnts.ua.ac.be/conll2003/ner/

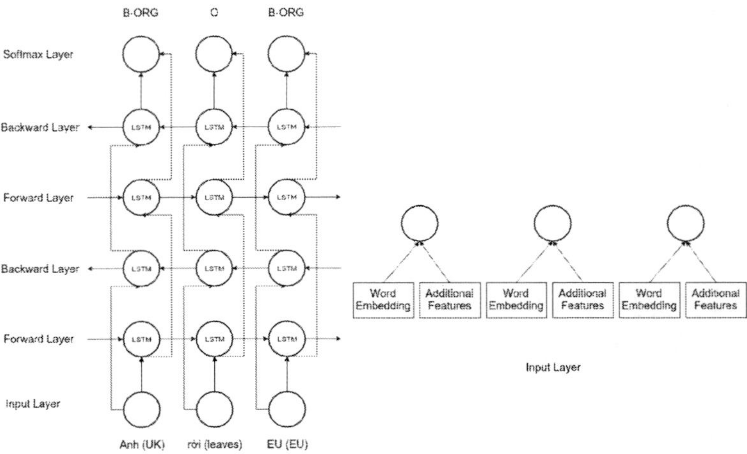

Figure 3: Our deep learning model

Entity	Skip-Gram			Random			One-hot		
	Pre.	Rec.	F_1	Pre.	Rec.	F_1	Pre.	Rec.	F_1
LOC	83.63	82.48	83.05	79.39	66.37	72.26	79.21	72.37	75.63
MISC	84.14	78.37	81.07	65.23	69.80	76.70	82.14	46.94	59.74
ORG	49.85	50.51	50.07	35.19	19.56	25.11	30.56	12.04	17.28
PER	72.77	65.73	69.06	70.76	50.35	58.83	69.13	52.09	59.41
ALL	75.88	72.26	**74.02**	72.99	55.23	62.87	57.68	72.88	64.39

Table 3: Performance of our model on three input types

ment is about 11% when using skip-gram vectors instead of random vectors. Thus, we use skip-gram vectors as inputs for our system.

Effect of Bidirectional Learning In the second experiment, we examine the benefit of accessing both past and future contexts by comparing the performances of RNN, LSTM and Bi-LSTM models. In this task, RNN model fails because it faces the gradient vanishing/exploding problem when training with long-range dependencies (132 time steps), leading to the unstable value of the cost functions. For this reason, only performances of LSTM and Bi-LSTM models are shown in Table 4.

Entity	Bi-LSTM			LSTM		
	Pre.	Rec.	F_1	Pre.	Rec.	F_1
LOC	83.63	82.48	83.05	74.60	77.38	75.96
MISC	84.14	78.37	81.07	2.15	2.04	2.09
ORG	49.85	50.51	50.07	32.22	34.60	33.60
PER	72.77	65.73	69.06	67.95	60.73	64.12
ALL	75.88	72.26	**74.02**	66.61	65.04	65.80

Table 4: Performance of our model when using one and two layers

We see that learning both past and future contexts is very useful for NER. Performances of all of the entity types are increased, especially for ORG and MISC. The total accuracy is improved greatly, from 65.80% to 74.02%.

Number of Bi-LSTM Layers In the third experiment, we investigate the improvement when adding more Bi-LSTM layers. Table 5 shows the accuracy when using one or two Bi-LSTM layers. We observe a significant improvement when using two layers of Bi-LSTM. The performance is increased from 71.74% to 74.02%

Entity	Two layers			One layer		
	Pre.	Rec.	F_1	Pre.	Rec.	F_1
LOC	83.63	82.48	83.05	82.22	80.64	81.41
MISC	84.14	78.37	81.07	85.15	74.29	79.32
ORG	49.85	50.51	50.07	44.10	40.88	42.39
PER	72.77	65.73	69.06	72.70	62.15	66.91
ALL	75.88	72.26	**74.02**	74.83	68.91	71.74

Table 5: Performance of our model when using one and two layers

Effect of Dropout In the fourth experiment, we compare the results of our model with and without dropout layers. The optimal dropout ratio for our experiments is 0.5. The accuracy with dropout is 74.02%, compared to 68.27% without dropout. It proves the effectiveness of dropout for preventing overfitting.

Entity	Dropout = 0.5			Dropout = 0.0		
	Pre.	Rec.	F_1	Pre.	Rec.	F_1
LOC	83.63	82.48	83.05	80.98	76.79	78.79
MISC	84.14	78.37	81.07	84.09	64.49	72.73
ORG	49.85	50.51	50.07	41.09	32.92	36.43
PER	72.77	65.73	69.06	67.35	59.23	62.97
ALL	75.88	72.26	**74.02**	71.97	64.99	68.27

Table 6: Performance of our model with and without dropout

Syntactic Features Integration As shown in the previous experiments, using only word features in deep learning models is not enough to achieve the state-of-the-art result. In particular, the accuracy of this model is only 74.02%. This result is far lower in comparison to that of state-of-the-art systems for Vietnamese NER. In the following experiments, we add more useful features to enhance the performance of our deep learning model. Table 7 shows the improvement when adding part-of-speech, chunk, case-sensitive, and regular expression features.

Features	Pre.	Rec.	F_1
Word	75.88	72.26	74.02
Word+POS	84.23	87.64	85.90
Word+Chunk	90.73	83.18	86.79
Word+Case	83.68	84.45	84.06
Word+Regex	76.58	71.86	74.13
Word+POS+Chunk+Case+Regex	90.25	92.55	91.39
Word+POS+Chunk+Regex	91.09	93.03	**92.05**

Table 7: Performance of our model when adding more features

As seen in this table, adding each of these syntactic features helps improve the performance significantly. The best result we get is adding part-of-speech, chunk and regular expression features. The accuracy of this final system is 92.05% that is much higher than 74.02 of the system without using syntactic features. An explanation for this problem is possibly a characteristic of Vietnamese. In particular, Vietnamese named entities are often a noun phrase chunk.

Comparision with Other Languages In the sixth experiment, we want to compare the role of syntactic features for NER task in other languages. For this reason, we run our system on CoNLL 2003 data set for English. The word embedding set we use for English is pre-trained by Glove model and is provided by the authors[7]. Table 8 shows the performances of our system when adding part-of-speech and chunk features.

Features	Vietnamese			English		
	Pre.	Rec.	F_1	Pre.	Rec.	F_1
Word	75.88	72.26	74.02	87.39	89.66	88.51
Word + POS + Chunk	90.39	92.59	91.48	87.08	89.59	88.31

Table 8: The importance of syntactic features for Vietnamese compared to it for English

For English NER task, adding the syntactic features does not help to improve the performance of our system. Thus, we can conclude that syntactic features have the greater importance in Vietnamese NER compared to their impact in English.

Comparison with Previous Systems In VLSP 2016 workshop, there are several different systems proposed for Vietnamese NER. These systems focus on only three entities types *LOC*, *ORG*, and *PER*. For the purpose of fairness, we evaluate our performances based on these named entity types on the same corpus. The accuracy of our best model over three entity types is 92.02%, which is higher than the best participating system (Le-Hong, 2016) in that shared task about 3.2%.

Moreover, (Pham and Le-Hong, 2017) used a combination of Bi-LSTM, CNN, and CRF that achieved the same performance with (Le-Hong, 2016). This system is end-to-end architecture that required only word embeddings while (Le-Hong, 2016) used many syntactic and hand-crafted features with MEMM. Our system surpasses both of these systems by using Bi-LSTM with automatically syntactic features, which takes less time for training and inference than Bi-LSTM-CNN-CRF model and does not depend on many hand-crafted features as MEMM. Table 9 presents the accuracy of each system.

Models	Types	F_1
(Le-Hong, 2016)	ME	88.78
(Pham and Le-Hong, 2017)	Bi-LSTM-CNN-CRF	88.59
Our model	Bi-LSTM	92.02

Table 9: Performance of our model and previous systems

[7]https://nlp.stanford.edu/projects/glove/

5 Conclusion

In this work, we have presented a state-of-the-art named entity recognition system for the Vietnamese language, which achieves an F_1 score of 92.05% on the standard dataset published by the VLSP community. Our system outperforms the first-rank system of the related NER shared task with a large margin, 3.2% in particular. We have also shown the effectiveness of using automatic syntactic features for Bi-LSTM model that surpass the combination of Bi-LSTM-CNN-CRF models albeit requiring less time for computation.

Acknowledgement

The second author is partly funded by the Vietnam National University, Hanoi (VNU) under project number QG.15.04. Any opinions, findings and conclusion expressed in this paper are those of the authors and do not necessarily reflect the view of VNU.

References

Yoshua Bengio, Patrice Simard, and Paolo Frasconi. 1994. Learning long-term dependencies with gradient descent is difficult. *IEEE transactions on neural networks*, 5(2):157–166.

Jason P.C. Chiu and Eric Nichols. 2016. Named entity recognition with bidirectional lstm-cnns. *Transactions of the Association for Computational Linguistics*, 4:357–370.

Ronan Collobert, Jason Weston, Léon Bottou, Michael Karlen, Koray Kavukcuoglu, and Pavel Kuksa. 2011. Natural language processing (almost) from scratch. *Journal of Machine Learning Research*, 12:2493–2537.

Greg Durrett and Dan Klein. 2014. A joint model for entity analysis: Coreference, typing, and linking. *Transactions of the Association for Computational Linguistics*, 2:477–490.

Radu Florian, Abe Ittycheriah, Hongyan Jing, and Tong Zhang. 2003. Named entity recognition through classifier combination. In Walter Daelemans and Miles Osborne, editors, *Proceedings of CoNLL-2003*, pages 168–171. Edmonton, Canada.

Alex Graves and Jürgen Schmidhuber. 2005. Framewise phoneme classification with bidirectional lstm networks. In *Proceedings of 2005 IEEE International Joint Conference on Neural Networks*, volume 4, pages 2047–2052, Montreal, QC, Canada. IEEE.

Alex Graves, Abdel rahmand Mohamed, and Geoffrey Hinton. 2013. Speech recognition with deep recurrent neural networks. In *Proceedings of 2013 IEEE international conference on acoustics, speech and signal processing*, pages 6645–6649, Vancouver, BC, Canada. IEEE.

Sepp Hochreiter and Jürgen Schmidhuber. 1997. Long short-term memory. *Neural computation*, 9(8):1735–1780.

Zhiheng Huang, Wei Xu, and Kai Yu. 2015. Bidirectional lstm-crf models for sequence tagging. *arXiv preprint arXiv:1508.01991*.

Guillaume Lample, Miguel Ballesteros, Sandeep Subramanian, Kazuya Kawakami, and Chris Dyer. 2016. Neural architectures for named entity recognition. *arXiv preprint arXiv:1603.01360*.

Phuong Le-Hong. 2016. Vietnamese named entity recognition using token regular expressions and bidirectional inference. In *Proceedings of The Fourth International Workshop on Vietnamese Language and Speech Processing*, Hanoi, Vietnam.

Dekang Lin and Xiaoyun Wu. 2009. Phrase clustering for discriminative learning. In *Proceedings of the Joint Conference of the 47th Annual Meeting of the ACL and the 4th International Joint Conference on Natural Language Processing of the AFNLP*, volume 2, pages 1030–1038. Association for Computational Linguistics.

Gang Luo and Zaiqing Nie Xiaojiang Huang, Chin-Yew Lin. 2015. Joint entity recognition and disambiguation. In *Proceedings of the 2015 Conference on Empirical Methods on Natural Language Processing*, pages 879–888. Association for Computational Linguistics.

Truong Son Nguyen, Le Minh Nguyen, and Xuan Chien Tran. 2016. Vietnamese named entity recognition at vlsp 2016 evaluation campaign. In *Proceedings of The Fourth International Workshop on Vietnamese Language and Speech Processing*, Hanoi, Vietnam.

Razvan Pascanu, Tomas Mikolov, and Yoshua Bengio. 2013. On the difficulty of training recurrent neural networks. In *The 30th International Conference on Machine Learning*, volume 28, pages 1310–1318, Atlanta, USA.

Thai-Hoang Pham and Phuong Le-Hong. 2017. End-to-end recurrent neural network models for vietnamese named entity recognition: Word-level vs. character-level. In *Proceedings of The 15th International Conference of the Pacific Association for Computational Linguistics*, pages 251–264.

Multiple Nominative Constructions in Japanese:
An Incremental Grammar Perspective

Tohru Seraku
Hankuk University of Foreign Studies
seraku@hufs.ac.kr

Abstract

This article defends an "incremental grammar" view, where syntactic puzzles are accounted for in terms of how a sentence is parsed online. To this end, we focus on the Multiple Nominative Construction (MNC) in Japanese, offering new data involving "rightward displacements." The displacement patterns of nominative NPs are shown to follow from the way an MNC string is parsed left-to-right. Our incremental account is formalised in Dynamic Syntax, with the upshot that only the licit ordering of nominative NPs in MNC leads to a legitimate structure update.

1 Introduction

Japanese allows Multiple Nominative Construction (MNC), where more than one NP is nominative-marked within a (seemingly) single clause (Kuno, 1973; see also references in §2.3).

(1) *Ken-ga kami-ga nagai*
K-NOM hair-NOM long
'Ken's hair is long.'

In (1), both *Ken* and *kami* 'hair' are marked by the nominative case particle *ga*. The initial *ga*-marked element *Ken* in (1) is often called "major subject" (Kuroda, 1978; 1986; 1988).[1]

In this article, we provide new data on MNC in connection with rightward displacements (§2), and argue that these data are adequately handled from

the perspective of "incremental grammar," a view where syntactic puzzles are solved as a reflection of the way a sentence is parsed time-linearly (§3). Our analysis is formalised within Dynamic Syntax (Cann et al, 2005), with the bonus of predicting the "left-right asymmetries" (§4).

2 Empirical Findings

2.1 Domain of Enquiry

We begin by clarifying our target. In Japanese, an object NP is typically accusative-marked, but some stative predicates may select a nominative-marked object NP (Koizumi, 2008; Kuno, 1973; 1983).

(2) *Ken-ga eigo-ga hanas-eru*
K-NOM English-NOM speak-POT
'Ken can speak English.'

This article does **not** analyse MNC data such as (2) which involve a nominative-marked object.

In generative syntax, some scholars have argued that MNC (1) is derived from (3).

(3) *Ken-no kami-ga nagai*
K-GEN hair-NOM long
'Ken's hair is long.'

In Kuno (1973), "subjectivization" applies to the genitive-marked NP *Ken-no*, which turns it to the nominative-marked subject NP *Ken-ga*. Analyses along with these lines include "nominativization" (Shibatani, 1977), "possessor raising" (Ura, 1996), and "genitive raising" (Tateishi, 1991).

The type of MNC sentences such as (1), which is related to "genitive"-involving sentences like (3), has been studied most extensively. Since the other kinds of MNC have distinct syntactic and semantic properties (Kikuchi, 1996; Kobayashi, 2010), we focus on the type of MNC illustrated in (1).

---

[1] A major subject is generally in focus, giving rise to an "exhaustive listing" reading (Kuno, 1973). Thus, a more appropriate translation of (1) would be 'It is Ken whose hair is long.' See Heycock and Doron (2003: §4) for an explanation of why a major subject generally (but not always) endangers an exhaustive interpretation.

31st Pacific Asia Conference on Language, Information and Computation (PACLIC 31), pages 104–113
Cebu City, Philippines, November 16-18, 2017

It is further noted that more than two *ga*-marked NPs are licensed in the (1)-type of MNC, as shown in (4). Examples with more than two *ga*-marked NPs are also addressed in our study.

(4) *Ken-ga   imouto-ga   kami-ga   nagai*
    K-NOM   sister-NOM hair-NOM long
    'Ken's younger sister's hair is long.'

2.2 MNC and Rightward Displacements

Having clarified our research target, we now offer new data on MNC in connection with "rightward displacement" where the term *displacement* is used for the purposes of description. Compared with the simple sentence (5), Japanese has three rightward-displacement constructions: relatives (6), clefts (7), and postposing (8). In (6)-(8), *sushi* appears to the right of the clause in question. (*e* in (6)-(8) is used to notate "gap" in a theory-neutral manner.)

(5) *Ken-ga   sushi-o   tabeta*
    K-NOM   sushi-ACC   ate
    'Ken ate sushi.'

(6) [[*Ken-ga e tabeta*] *sushi*]-*wa   yasui*
    [[K-NOM   ate]   sushi]-TOP   cheap
    'The sushi Ken ate is cheap.' <relatives>

(7) [[*Ken-ga e tabeta*] *no*]-*wa   sushi-da*
    [[K-NOM   ate]   NMNS]-TOP sushi-COP
    'It is sushi that Ken ate.' <clefts>

(8) *Ken-ga   e tabeta-yo, sushi*(-*o*)
    K-NOM   ate-FP   sushi(-ACC)
    'Ken ate sushi.' <postposing>

In (7), *no* is a nominalising complementiser (Kizu, 2005). In (8), *yo* is a final particle, indicating that (8) is uttered colloquially; though Japanese is verb-final, a non-verbal item may appear to the right of the sentence in casual speech (Kuno, 1978).

For an MNC string which contains the *n*-number of *ga*-marked NPs in a single clause (setting aside *ga*-marked object NPs; see §2.1), let us notate the sequence of such NPs as $<NP_1, NP_2, ..., NP_n>$. We then put forward the following generalisation:

(9) <u>Generalisation</u>
    For MNC with $<NP_1, NP_2, ..., NP_n>$, only the leftmost NP_1 may be "right-displaced."

Below, we shall illustrate (9) with MNC examples.

Relatives. Consider the MNC sentence (10). While NP_1 *sono-otoko* 'that man' may be a head noun (i.e.

appear to the right of the relative clause) as in (11), this is not the case with NP_2 *imouto* 'younger sister' and NP_3 *kami* 'hair' as shown in (12)-(13).

(10) *sono-otoko-ga imouto-ga kami-ga nagai*
     that-man-NOM sister-NOM hair-NOM long
     'That man's younger sister's hair is long.'

(11) [*e imouto-ga kami-ga   nagai*] *sono-otoko*
     [sister-NOM hair-NOM long]   that-man
     'That man whose younger sister's hair is long'

(12) *[sono-otoko-ga e kami-ga   nagai*] *imouto*
     [that-man-NOM   hair-NOM long]   sister

(13) *[sono-otoko-ga imouto-ga e nagai*] *kami*
     [that-man-NOM sister-NOM   long]   hair

Clefts. In MNC (10), only NP_1 *sono-otoko* 'that man' may be in focus (i.e. appear to the right of the presupposition clause of the cleft). That is, neither NP_2 *imouto* 'younger sister' nor NP_3 *kami* 'hair' can be at a focus position of the cleft.

(14) [[*e imouto-ga   kami-ga   nagai*]
     [[sister-NOM hair-NOM long]
     no]-*wa   sono-otoko-da*
     NMNS]-TOP that-man-COP
     Lit. 'It is that man$_i$ that his$_i$ younger sister's hair is long.'

(15) *[[sono-otoko-ga e kami-ga   nagai*]
     [[that-man-NOM   hair-NOM   long]
     no]-*wa   imouto-da*
     NMNS]-TOP sister-COP

(16) *[[sono-otoko-ga imouto-ga e nagai*]
     [[that-man-NOM sister-NOM   long]
     no]-*wa   kami-da*
     NMNS]-TOP hair-COP

Postposing. In MNC sentence (10), what may be postposed (i.e. appear to the right of the sentence) is NP_1 *sono-otoko* 'that man' alone.

(17) *e imouto-ga kami-ga   nagai-yo,*
        sister-NOM hair-NOM long-FP
     sono-otoko(-*ga*)
     that-man(-NOM)
     'That man's younger sister's hair is long.'

(18) *sono-otoko-ga e kami-ga   nagai-yo,*
     that-man-NOM   hair-NOM long-FP
     imouto(-*ga*)
     sister(-NOM)

(19) *sono-otoko-ga   imouto-ga   e   nagai-yo,
     that-man-NOM   sister-NOM   long-FP
     kami(-*ga*)
     hair(-NOM)

We have exemplified the generalisation (9), but the following examples may pose a problem.

(20) *nihon-ga   GDP-ga   takai*
     Japan-NOM GDP-NOM high
     'Japan's GDP is high.'

(21) [*e   GDP-ga   takai*]   *nihon*
     [GDP-NOM high]   Japan
     Lit. 'Japanᵢ such that GDP is high in itᵢ.'

(22) [*nihon-ga   e   takai*]   *GDP*
     [Japan-NOM   high]   GDP
     Lit. 'GDPᵢ such that itᵢ is high in Japan.'

In particular, it is (at first glance) unexpected that (22), where NP$_2$ *GDP* in (20) occurs to the right of the clause, seems fine. (22) may not be completely acceptable, but our contention is that for those who accept (22), (23) would also be acceptable.[2]

(23) *GDP-ga   nihon-ga   takai*
     GDP-NOM   Japan-NOM   high
     'It is GDP that is high in Japan.'

Provided that (23) is a basis for (22), acceptability of (22) is not problematic for the generalisation (9) since NP$_1$ in (23) is *GDP*.

In a similar vein, the cleft sentence (24) and the postposing sentence (25), where NP$_2$ *GDP* occurs to the right of the clause, do not pose a problem for the generalisation (9), given that they are related to the MNC sentence (23).

(24) [*nihon-ga   e   takai*] *no*]-*wa*   *GDP-da*
     [Japan-NOM   high] NMNS]-TOP   GDP-COP
     'It is GDP that is high in Japan.'

(25) *nihon-ga   e   takai-yo,   GDP-ga*
     Japan-NOM   high-FP   GDP-NOM
     'GDP is high in Japan.'

We illustrated (9) with MNC (10) that involves three *ga*-NPs. The generalisation, we believe, also holds of MNC with more than three *ga*-NPs. Such

---

[2] (23) is reasonably acceptable (or much better than the *-marked ones above) if it serves as an answer to (i).

(i) [*nihon-ga   takai no*]-*wa   dono-shihyou desu-ka*
    [Japan-NOM high NMNS]-TOP   which-index COP-Q
    'Which national index is high in Japan?'

examples, however, are hard to construct due to performance factors; see Heycock (1993: 204) and Kuroda (1986: §8) for related discussion.

2.3   Previous Studies

The data in §2.2 have not been noted in past works (e.g. Akiyama, 2005; Fukui, 1988; Heycock, 1993; Heycock and Doron, 2003; Hiraiwa, 2001; Kiss, 1981; Kuno, 1973; Kuroda, 1986; Mihara, 1994; Mihara and Hiraiwa, 2006; Muromatsu, 1997; Nagai, 1999; Ohtani and Valverde, 2012; Shibatani, 1977; Takami and Kamio, 1996; Takezawa, 1987; Tateishi, 1991; Ura, 1996; Vermeulen, 2005; Whitman, 2001); see also Kobayashi (2010; 2011) for a meticulous review of previous studies.

The exception is Nakamura et al. (2009) (cf. Nakamura (2002)), but their findings are limited. They consider MNC with exactly two *ga*-NPs and do not survey postposing. Thus, our generalisation (9), which concerns *leftmost* and *postposing*, is not obtainable from their data. Moreover, they do not examine the left-right asymmetries (see §4). Lastly, their account is formally illicit (Seraku, 2016).

Past analyses are divided into two types in terms of how multiple *ga*-NPs are licensed:

- *Ga*-NPs are licensed at multiple Specs of a single projection (Hiraiwa, 2001; Ura, 1996; Vermeulen, 2005; among others).

- *Ga*-NPs are licensed at multiple adjunction sites for a Spec (Heycock, 1993; Kuno, 1973; Mihara, 1994; among others).

In both approaches, it is not obvious how the data in §2.2 are treated. In Japanese, it has been widely assumed that relativisation, (caseless) clefting, and (caseless) postposing are island-insensitive (Hoji, 1990; Kuno, 1973; Tanaka and Kizu, 2007). Thus, it must be worked out how displacement of non-leftmost *ga*-NPs in <NP$_1$, NP$_2$, …, NP$_n$> (in the sense of (9)) is precluded.[3]

It may be possible to reconcile the past analyses with the issues raised here by postulating further constraints on syntactic derivations/representations. In this article, however, we pursue another line of analysis, arguing that the generalisation (9) follows from the modelling of incremental parsing.

---

[3] Sakai (1994) opens up the view that Japanese relatives are island-sensitive, but the problem still remains of how to prevent non-leftmost NPs from being extracted in relatives (as well as clefts and postposing).

3 Incremental Analysis

"Incrementality" in time-linear parsing has been a basis for some recent linguistic theorising (Cann et al., 2011). Our claim is that if we adopt (26) and give formal substance to them, we can capture the generalisation (9) (and further properties of MNC).

(26) <u>Assumptions adopted in this study</u>
  a. A string of words is parsed progressively as it is produced.
  b. Each parse state is associated with a structure, gradually updated as the parse proceeds.
  c. This structure is semantic in that it represents an interpretation of the string parsed.

These assumptions are made precise with the tools of Dynamic Syntax (Cann et al., 2005; Kempson et al., 2001). For reasons of brevity, we omit as many dispensable technical details as possible.

3.1 Dynamic Syntax

Dynamic Syntax (DS) specifies, for each language, a set of (i) procedures to build a semantic structure and (ii) constraints on its gradual update.

To take (27) as an example, a semantic structure is built up as it is incrementally parsed, as shown in each step of (28)-(30). Within DS, a structure is expressed in binary-branching tree format.

(27) *Ken-ga   ne-ta*
    K-NOM   sleep-PAST
    'Ken slept.'

(28) Parsing *Ken-ga*

$$?t$$

$$Ken' : e$$

(29) Parsing *Ken-ga ne-ta* (ignoring tense)

$$?t$$

$$Ken' : e \quad sleep' : e{\to}t$$

(30) Final state (representing the content of (27))

$$sleep'(Ken') : t$$

$$Ken' : e \quad sleep' : e{\to}t$$

Note that the structure is **semantic**; thus, *Ken'* and *sleep'* are not natural-language expressions but are semantic contents. Each content is specified for a semantic type. For instance, *Ken'* is of type e (i.e. entity), *sleep'(Ken')* is of type-t (i.e. proposition),

and *sleep'* is of type e→t (i.e. function from a type-e content to a type-t content).

In (28)-(29), the symbol ?t is used. Generally, ?α requires that the node be decorated with α before the parse process finishes. The constraint ?t is met in (30), where the type-t content (i.e. proposition that Ken sleeps) appears at the node in question.

There are two types of procedures for structure update: (i) general action and (ii) lexical action. An example of (i) is Functional Application. As shown in (29)-(30), the function *sleep'* applies to *Ken'*, with the output *sleep'(Ken')*. An example of (ii) is a set of actions encoded in *Ken*, which is to decorate a ?e-node with the content *Ken'* and its type e.

(31) Illustration: lexical action encoded in *Ken*

Not only *Ken* but also all the other lexical items in a language encode a set of actions for tree update.

Before closing, another formal apparatus, LINK, needs to be mentioned. LINK pairs structures.

(32) Illustration: LINK

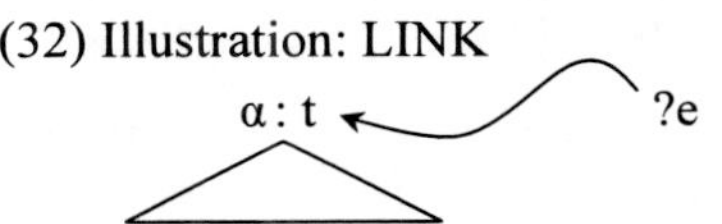

LINK (32) models relatives. α is the content of a relative clause. This structure is LINKed to another node where the head noun of the relative clause is parsed. LINK pairs two structures irrespective of sematic types of connected nodes. In (32), a type-t node is LINKed to a type-e node. In §3.2, we shall see a LINK relation between two type-e nodes.

3.2 Analysis

The DS analysis of Japanese MNC is proposed in Seraku (2016). Consider MNC example (33).

(33) *Ken-ga   kami-ga   nagai*
    K-NOM   hair-NOM   long
    'Ken's hair is long.'

The parse of *Ken-ga* in (33) produces (34).

(34) Parsing *Ken-ga*

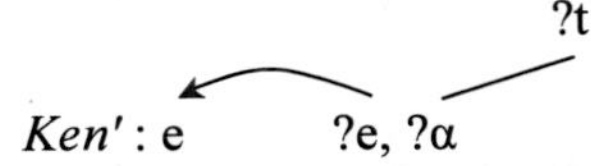

$$?t$$

$$Ken' : e \quad\quad ?e, ?α$$

where ?α is a requirement that this node be decorated with a content related to *Ken'*

For simplification, informal symbols such as ?α are used.[4] The requirement ?α is met by the parse of *kami* 'hair,' as reflected in the term α in (35).[5]

(35) Parsing *Ken-ga kami-ga*

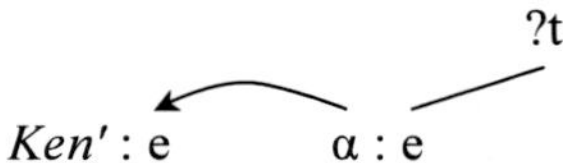

$$?t$$

$$Ken' : e \qquad \alpha : e$$

where α denotes the hair of Ken

The parse of *nagai* 'long' then creates a predicate node, and Functional Application yields the final state (36), where $long'(\alpha)$ expresses the proposition that Ken's hair is long.

(36) Parsing *Ken-ga kami-ga nagai*

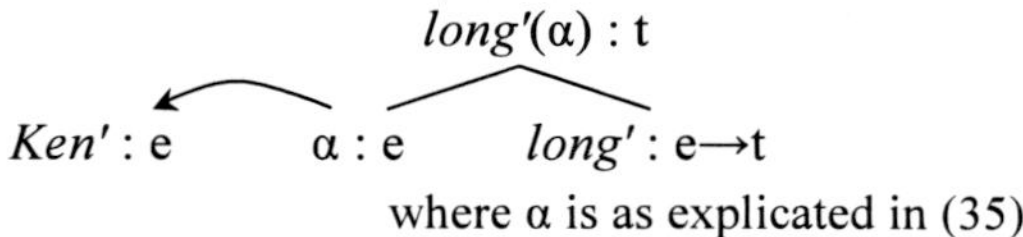

$$long'(\alpha) : t$$

$$Ken' : e \qquad \alpha : e \qquad long' : e{\rightarrow}t$$

where α is as explicated in (35)

A LINK relation can be reiterated, which deals with MNC strings with more than two *ga*-marked NPs. (For this, the "structural underspecification" device must be employed.) Based on this analysis, let us turn now to the examples presented in §2.2.

Relatives. A DS account of Japanese relatives is developed in Kempson and Kurosawa (2009).

(37) [*Ken-ga   e tabeta*] *sushi*
　　 [K-NOM   ate]   sushi
'The sushi which Ken ate' <relatives>

First, the parse of the relative clause *Ken-ga tabeta* builds (38). (x is a notation for the gap *e*.)

(38) Parsing *Ken-ga tabeta*

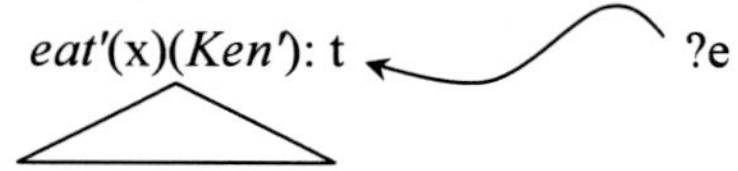

$$eat'(x)(Ken') : t \qquad ?e$$

Second, the parse of the head noun *sushi* decorates the ?e-node with α, as explicated in (39).

(39) Parsing *Ken-ga tabeta sushi*

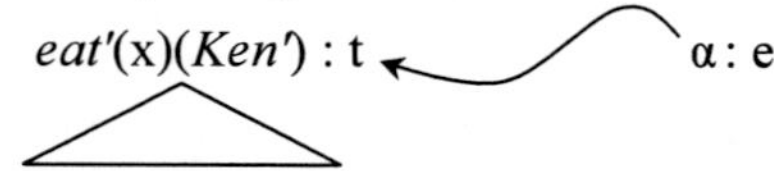

$$eat'(x)(Ken') : t \qquad \alpha : e$$

where α denotes an entity that is sushi and that Ken ate

Note that the term α reflects the content of the relative clause. In Cann et al. (2005) and Kempson and Kurosawa (2009), this process is formulated as the general action of LINK Evaluation.

Now consider (11)-(13), repeated as (40)-(42).

(40) [*e imouto-ga kami-ga   nagai*] *sono-otoko*
　　 [sister-NOM hair-NOM long]   that-man
'That man whose younger sister's hair is long'

(41) *[*sono-otoko-ga e kami-ga   nagai*] *imouto*
　　 [that-man-NOM   hair-NOM long]   sister

(42) *[*sono-otoko-ga imouto-ga e nagai*] *kami*
　　 [that-man-NOM sister-NOM   long]   hair

In (40), the parse of *imouto-ga kami-ga* builds up the structure (43).

(43) Parsing *imouto-ga kami-ga*

$$?t$$

$$\alpha : e \qquad \beta : e$$

where α denotes an individual that bears a "sister" relation to another individual x; β denotes the hair of α

The term α contains a variable x. This is because *imouto* 'younger sister' is a relational noun, which denotes a younger sister of another individual x. In virtue of LINK, this term is mapped onto β. Note that β also contains the variable x (as α is part of β) and that this variable has not yet been saturated.

The next stage is shown in (44), where the parse of *nagai* 'long' has created a predicate node.

(44) Parsing *imouto-ga kami-ga nagai*

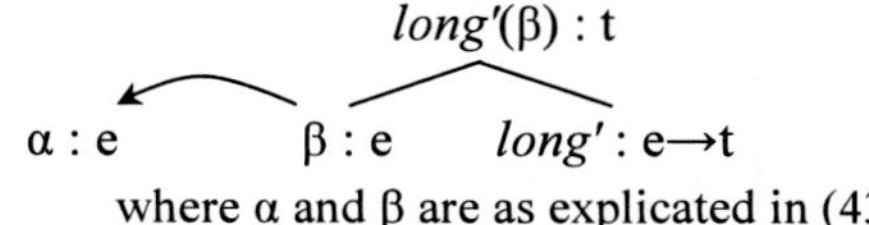

$$long'(\beta) : t$$

$$\alpha : e \qquad \beta : e \qquad long' : e{\rightarrow}t$$

where α and β are as explicated in (43)

The formula $long'(\beta)$ expresses that the hair of a younger sister of x is long.

Finally, the head noun *sono-otoko* 'that man' is parsed, with another LINK relation (cf. (39)). It is at this stage that the variable x is saturated in γ.

(45) Parsing *imouto-ga kami-ga nagai sono-otoko*

$$long'(\beta) : t \qquad \gamma : e$$

where β is as explicated in (43); γ denotes an individual such that he is a man and that the hair of his younger sister is long

---

[4] ?α is formally expressed as $?\exists x.Fo(x_{R(Ken')(x)})$.
[5] α is formally expressed as $(\iota, x, hair'(Ken')(x))$.

As reflected in γ, the variable x is saturated by the parse of *sono-otoko* 'that man.'

The tree update in (43)-(45) is licit, particularly because (i) what comes first in (40) is the relational noun *imouto* 'younger sister' that creates a variable and (ii) the sentence contains the head noun *sono-otoko* 'that man' which saturates this variable.[6]

On the other hand, the above points (i) and (ii) do not hold of (41)-(42), and this is why they are ungrammatical. For (41), the first element parsed is *sono-otoko* 'that man.' This does not introduce a variable, and there is no room in the derived tree into which the content of the head noun *imouto* 'younger sister' is incorporated.[7] Similarly, in (42), the first NP parsed *sono-otoko* 'that man' does not create a variable, and the same issue arises.

Recall that MNC allows an infinite number of *ga*-NPs in a single clause. Even in such cases, only NP_1 (in the sense of (9)) can be "right-displaced." If an NP other than NP_1 is displaced, the relative clause necessarily contains NP_1 but NP_1 does not introduce a variable in our targeted type of MNC. Thus, the aforementioned problem arises.

Clefts. A DS treatment of Japanese clefts has been offered in Seraku (2013).

(46) [[*Ken-ga e tabeta*] *no*]-*wa*   *sushi-da*
    [[K-NOM   ate]   NMNS]-TOP sushi-COP
    'It is sushi that Ken ate.' <clefts>

The parse of the presupposition part *Ken-ga tabeta* builds the structure containing a variable x (which corresponds to the gap *e*).

(47) Parsing *Ken-ga tabeta*

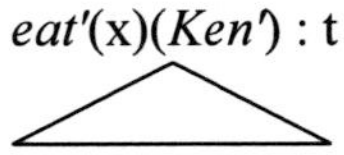

$$eat'(x)(Ken') : t$$

Seraku (2013) assumes that *no-wa* is a cleft marker that LINKs the structure of the presupposition part to a new structure where a focus is parsed. In (46),

the focus is provided by *sushi*. The copula *da* is treated as a propositional pro-form; *da* copies the structure of the presupposition part, into which the content of the focussed NP is incorporated.

(48) Parsing *Ken-ga tabeta no-wa sushi-da*

$$eat'(x)(Ken') : t \quad\longleftarrow\quad eat'(sushi')(Ken') : t$$

Setting aside the details of the tree update in (47)-(48), what is of note here is that the variable x is saturated by the parse of the focussed NP *sushi*.

Now consider (14)-(16), repeated as (49)-(51).

(49) [[*e imouto-ga   kami-ga   nagai*]
    [[sister-NOM hair-NOM   long]
    no]-*wa*   *sono-otoko-da*
    NMNS]-TOP that-man-COP
    Lit. 'It is that man$_i$ that his$_i$ younger sister's hair is long.'

(50) *[[*sono-otoko-ga e kami-ga   nagai*]
    [[that-man-NOM   hair-NOM   long]
    no]-*wa*   *imouto-da*
    NMNS]-TOP sister-COP

(51) *[[*sono-otoko-ga imouto-ga e nagai*]
    [[that-man-NOM   sister-NOM   long]
    no]-*wa*   *kami-da*
    NMNS]-TOP hair-COP

In (49), the parse of *imouto-ga kami-ga nagai* yields (52), exactly as in the case of relatives (44).

(52) Parsing *imouto-ga kami-ga nagai*

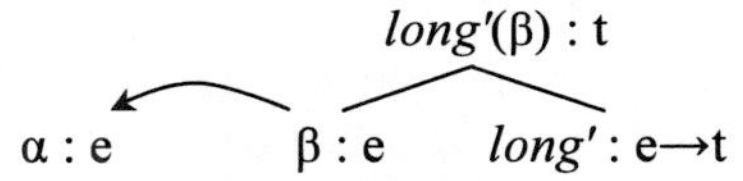

$$long'(\beta) : t$$
$$\alpha : e \qquad \beta : e \quad long' : e{\rightarrow}t$$
where α and β are as explicated in (43)

With the yet-unsaturated variable x (which lurks in α and β), *long'*(β) expresses the proposition that the hair of a younger sister of x is long.

The cleft marker *no-wa* subsequently LINKs the current structure to a new structure, to be fleshed out by the parse of *sono-otoko* 'that man' and the copula *da*. (Recall the tree update (47)-(48).)

(53) Parsing the whole string (49)

$$long'(\beta) : t \quad\longleftarrow\quad long'(\gamma)$$

where β is as explicated in (43); γ denotes the hair of a younger sister of that man

---

[6] As we address only the "genitive-type" MNC (§2.1), NP_2 in the sense of (9) (i.e. *imouto* in (40)) always introduces a variable. Other types of variable-introducing noun include part-whole nouns (e.g. *yane* 'roof of x'), inalienable nouns (e.g. *te* 'hand of x'), and so forth. See Shibatani (1978) for related discussion.

[7] The part *sono-otoko-ga kami-ga nagai* in (41) is grammatical, meaning 'That man's hair is long.' It is at the time of parsing *imouto* that the whole sentence of (41) becomes ungrammatical.

At this stage, the variable x, introduced by *imouto* 'younger sister,' is saturated by the parse of the focus *sono-otoko* 'that man.' (49) is thus mapped onto the valid structure (53).

In (50)-(51), however, such correct mapping is unachievable. For (50)-(51), the initial NP parsed is *sono-otoko* 'that man,' which does not introduce a variable. Therefore, the derived structure cannot accommodate the content of the focus (i.e. *imouto* 'younger sister' in (50), *kami* 'hair' in (51)).

The analysis in the last paragraph remains intact if MNC comprises more *ga*-NPs than (49)-(51). For <NP$_1$, NP$_2$, …, NP$_n$> (in the sense of (9)), the crux of our analysis lies in the distinction between NP$_1$ (which does not introduce a variable) and the other NPs in the NP cluster (all of which introduce a variable). This distinction remains the same in MNC with more *ga*-NPs than (49)-(51).

Postposing. A DS account of Japanese postposing is presented in Seraku and Ohtani (2016a; 2016b).

(54) *Ken-ga   e tabeta-yo,   sushi(-o)*
     K-NOM   ate-FP   sushi(-ACC)
     'Ken ate sushi.' <postposing>

The parse of *Ken-ga tabeta* outputs a propositional structure, with the variable (annotating the gap *e*). The final particle *yo* (which makes no contribution to the asserted content of (54)) is ignored.

(55) Parsing *Ken-ga tabeta-yo*

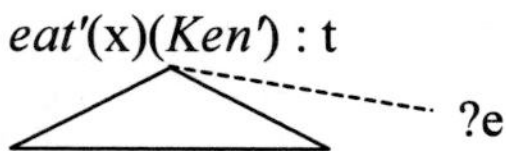
$eat'(x)(Ken') : t$

Seraku and Ohtani (2016a; 2016b) propose to make use of the general action of *Adjunction to parse the postposed element *sushi*.[8]

(56) Parsing *Ken-ga tabeta-yo* + *Adjunction

$eat'(x)(Ken') : t$
              ?e

*Adjunction creates a "structurally unfixed" node, a node whose position in a tree is not determined when it is introduced. (This structural uncertainty

---

[8] In the current DS setting (Cann et al., 2005; Kempson et al., 2001), the use of *Adjunction is prohibited in such environments as (55). Noting that postposing typically occurs colloquially, Seraku and Ohtani (2016a; 2016b) propose that such licensing constraints on *Adjunction are relaxed in colloquial register.

is visually shown by a dashed line in (56).) Note that *Adjunction creates a ?e-node, a place suitable for parsing the postposed NP *sushi*.

(57) Parsing *Ken-ga tabeta-yo sushi*

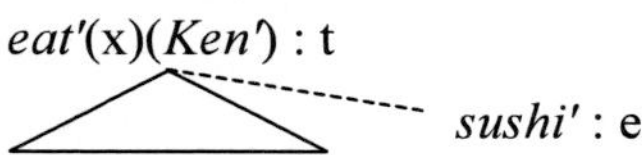
$eat'(x)(Ken') : t$
                 sushi' : e

Once the unfixed node is decorated with *sushi'*, it is incorporated into the propositional tree, with the result of saturating the variable x with *sushi'*.

(58) Final state (representing the content of (54))

$eat'(sushi')(Ken') : t$

There are two ways of incorporating an "unfixed node" into a structure, but this complication is not germane to our main points (see Cann et al. (2005: Ch. 2)). What is crucial here is that the parse of the postposed NP *sushi* leads to the saturation of the variable x.

Now consider (17)-(19), repeated as (59)-(61).

(59) *e imouto-ga   kami-ga   nagai-yo,*
     sister-NOM   hair-NOM   long-FP
    sono-otoko(-ga)
    that-man(-NOM)
    'That man's younger sister's hair is long.'

(60) **sono-otoko-ga e kami-ga   nagai-yo,*
    that-man-NOM   hair-NOM long-FP
    imouto(-ga)
    sister(-NOM)

(61) **sono-otoko-ga imouto-ga e nagai-yo,*
    that-man-NOM sister-NOM   long-FP
    kami(-ga)
    hair(-NOM)

In (59), as usual, the parse of *imouto-ga kami-ga nagai* constructs the structure (62) (= (52)).

(62) Parsing *imouto-ga kami-ga nagai*

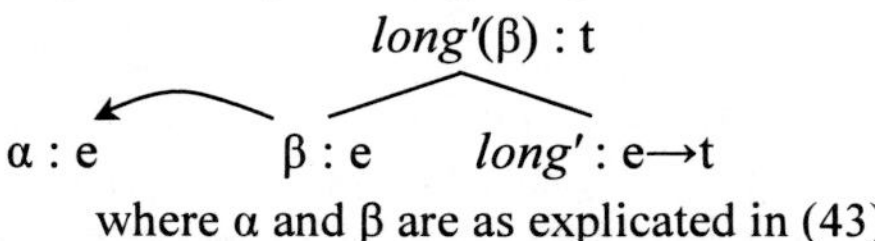
$long'(\beta) : t$
$\alpha : e$ $\beta : e$ $long' : e{\to}t$
where α and β are as explicated in (43)

The general action of *Adjunction is then applied, creating an "unfixed node" at which the postposed NP *sono-otoko* 'that man' is parsed.

(63) Parsing the whole string (59)

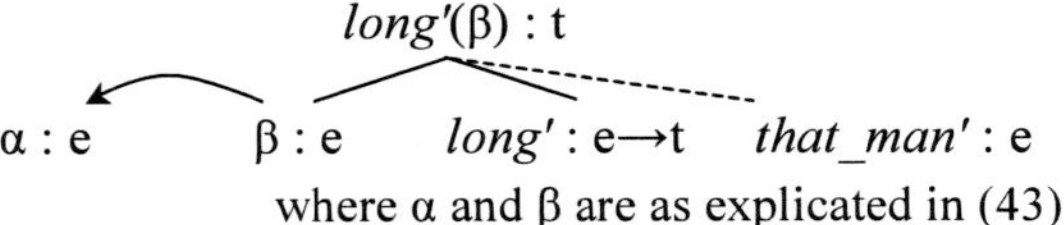

where α and β are as explicated in (43)

After the unfixed node is incorporated into the tree, the variable x (which lurks in β) is saturated by the content of *sono-otoko* 'that man.' Grammaticalness of (59) is thus captured.

The above analysis also accounts for why (60)-(61) are ungrammatical. For (60)-(61), the first NP parsed *sono-otoko* 'that man' does not introduce a variable, and no structural position is prepared for the incorporation of the content of the postposed NP (i.e. *imouto* in (60), *kami* in (61)).

Besides, the analysis carries over to MNC cases where more *ga*-marked NPs occur. No matter how many *ga*-NPs are present in $\langle NP_1, NP_2, ..., NP_n\rangle$ (see (9)), only NP_1 can be "right-displaced"; for, if another NP is postposed, the initial item parsed is NP_1, which prepares no structural position for the content of a postposed NP.

3.3 Summary

The key to our analysis is incrementality: only NP_1 in $\langle NP_1, NP_2, ..., NP_n\rangle$ may be right-displaced, so that the first item parsed must be an NP other than NP_1. We formalised this analysis in DS. It is worth stating that this formalisation itself contributes to the study of MNC since a strict translation from an MNC sentence to its interpretation has rarely been attempted (see Nakamura (2002) and Ohtani and Valverde (2012) for accounts within Combinatory Categorial Grammar (Steedman, 2000).)

4 Extension: Left-Right Asymmetries

We have considered **right** displacements. One may wonder how MNC is related to **left** displacements, and this is where we find left-right asymmetries.

Japanese displays scrambling and topicalisation as instances of left displacements. We restrict our attention to topicalisation as (i) scrambling of *ga*-NPs in MNC is subject to cross-speaker variations (Kobayashi, 2010: 120) and (ii) scrambling of a subject NP is contentious (Tateishi, 1991: 186).

MNC and topicalisation have been extensively investigated, but no due attention has been paid to data such as (64)-(66) (see Kuno (1973), Masuoka (1979), and Nishiyama (2003) for discussion):

(64) *sono-otoko-ga kami-ga   nagai*
    that-man-NOM hair-NOM long
    'That man's hair is long.'

(65) *sono-otoko-**wa** kami-ga   nagai*
    that-man-TOP hair-NOM long

(66) *kami-**wa**   sono-otoko-ga nagai*
    hair-TOP that-man-NOM long

Compared with the non-topicalised sentence (64), NP_1 *sono-otoko* is topicalised in (65) and NP_2 *kami* is topicalised in (66). Notably, (66), where NP_2 is topicalised, is acceptable (in a context where the hearer is looking for a long-haired person). (66) is not based on (67), which itself is not acceptable.

(67) **kami-ga   sono-otoko-ga nagai*
    hair-NOM that-man-NOM long

It then seems that extraction constraints like (9) are not imposed on topicalisation.[9]

Within DS (Cann et al., 2005: §6.4), the topic particle *wa* LINKs the node for a topicalised NP to the propositional structure for the rest of the string, with the requirement that the content of the NP be located at some node below the LINKed node.

(68) Parsing *sono-otoko-wa* in (65)

    that_man' : e ⟶ ?t, ?α

        where ?α is a requirement that a node somewhere below the current node be decorated with *that_man'*

In (65)-(66), when the node for the gap (containing a variable) is created, it is **immediately** decorated with the content of the topicalised NP, due to ?α. So, the interpretations of (65)-(66) with respect to the topicalised NPs are incrementally ensured.

5 Conclusion

We have made a case for an incremental grammar perspective by exploring Japanese MNC. In future research, we hope to extend our account to other types of MNC (§2.1) and MNC in other languages (Heycock and Doron, 2003; Kim et al., 2007).

---

[9] Topicalisation of a non-leftmost *ga*-NP in MNC is not always possible, however, presumably due to semantic and/or pragmatic factors such as "presupposition" (Nishiyama, 2003: 225-31). Our claim is that, setting aside such factors, topicalisation of a non-leftmost *ga*-NP in MNC is grammatically allowed. This contrasts with the data in §2.2, which are grammatically illicit.

Acknowledgements

I am grateful to the two PACLIC referees, Koji Kamada, and Mika Kizu for their beneficial comments on earlier versions of the present article. This work was supported by the Hankuk University of Foreign Studies Research Fund of 2017.

References

Akiyama, M. 2005. On the general tendency to minimize moved elements. *The Linguistic Review* 22 (1), 1-68.

Cann, R., Kempson, R., and Marten, L. 2005. *The Dynamics of Language*. Oxford: Elsevier.

Fukui, N. 1988. Deriving the differences between English and Japanese. *English Linguistics* 5, 249-70.

Heycock, C. 1993. Syntactic predication in Japanese. *Journal of East Asian Linguistics* 2, 167-211.

Heycock, C. and Doron, E. 2003. Categorical subjects. *Gengo Kenkyu* 123, 95-135.

Hiraiwa, K. 2001. Multiple agree and the defective intervention constraint in Japanese. In Matushansky, O. et al. (eds.) *MIT Working Papers in Linguistics* 40, Cambridge, MA: MITWPL, 67-80.

Hoji, H. 1990. *Theories of Anaphora and Aspects of Japanese Syntax*. Ms., University of Southern California.

Kempson, R., Gregoromichelaki, E., and Howes, C. (eds.) 2011. *The Dynamics of Lexical Interfaces*. Stanford, CA: CSLI Publications.

Kempson, R. and Kurosawa, A. 2009. At the syntax-pragmatics interface. In Hoshi, H. (ed.) *The Dynamics and Mechanism of Language*. Tokyo: Kuroshio Publishers.

Kempson, R., Meyer-Viol, W., and Gabbay, D. 2001. *Dynamic Syntax*. Oxford: Wiley-Blackwell.

Kikuchi, Y. 1996. "X-*ga* Y-*ga* Z"-bun-no seiri. (Classification of "X-*ga* Y-*ga* Z"-sentences) *Bulletin of International Center, the University of Tokyo* 6, 1-46.

Kim, J., Sells, P., and Yang, J. 2007. Parsing two types of multiple-nominative constructions. *Language and Information* 11 (1), 1-17.

Kiss, K. 1981. On the Japanese "double subject" constructions. *The Linguistic Review* 1, 155-70.

Kizu, M. 2005. *Cleft Constructions in Japanese Syntax*. New York: Palgrave.

Kobayashi, A. 2010. Multiple subject constructions (1). *Shimane Daigaku Houbun Gakubu Kiyou* 29, 77-122.

Kobayashi, A. 2011. Multiple subject constructions (2). *Shimane Daigaku Houbun Gakubu Kiyou* 31, 53-109.

Koizumi, M. 2008. Nominative object. In Miyagawa, S. and Saito, M. (eds.) *The Oxford Handbook of Japanese Linguistics*. Oxford: Oxford University Press, pp. 141-64.

Kuno, S. 1973. *The Structure of the Japanese Language*. Cambridge, MA: MIT Press.

Kuno, S. 1978. *Danwa-no Bunpou*. (Grammar of discourse) Tokyo: Taishukan.

Kuno, S. 1983. *Shin Nihon Bunpou Kenkyu* (New studies on Japanese grammar) Tokyo: Taishukan.

Kuroda, S.-Y. 1978. Case-marking, canonical sentence patterns, and counter equi in Japanese. In Hinds, J. and Howard, I. (eds.) *Problems in Japanese Syntax and Semantics*. Tokyo: Kaitakusha, 30-51.

Kuroda, S.-Y. 1986. Movement of noun phrases in Japanese. In Imai, T. and Saito, M. (eds.) *Issues in Japanese Linguistics*, Dordrecht: Foris, 229-71.

Kuroda, S.-Y. 1988. Whether we agree or not. *Linguisticae Investigationes* 12, 1-47.

Masuoka, T. 1979. Double subject constructions in Japanese. *Papers in Japanese Linguistics* 6, 219-36.

Mihara, K. 1994. *Nihongo-no Tougo Kouzou*. (Syntactic structure of Japanese) Tokyo: Shohakusha.

Mihara, K. and Hiraiwa, K. 2006. *Shin Nihongo-no Tougo Kouzou*. (Syntactic structure of Japanese, new edition) Tokyo: Shohakusha.

Muromatsu, K. 1997. Two types of existentials. *Lingua* 101, 245-69.

Nagai, N. 1999. Complex passives and major subjects in Japanese. *Linguistics* 29 (6), 1053-92.

Nakamura, H. 2002. Double subject, double nominative object and double accusative object constructions in Japanese and Korean. In Lee, I.-H. et al. (eds.) *Proceedings of the 16th Pacific Asia Conference*, Seoul: KSLI, 358-69.

Nakamura, H., Yoshimoto, K., Mori, Y., and Kobayashi, M. 2009. Multiple subject construction in Japanese. In Hattori, H. et al. (eds.) *New Frontiers in Artificial Intelligence (LNAI 5447)*. Dordrecht: Springer, 103-18.

Nishiyama, Y. 2003. *Nihongo Meishiku-no Imiron-to Goyouron*. (The Semantics and pragmatics of noun phrases in Japanese) Tokyo: Hituzi Syobo Publishing.

Noda, H. 1996. "Wa"-*to* "Ga." (*Wa* and *ga*) Tokyo: Kuroshio Publishers.

Ohtani, A. and Valverde, M. 2012. Nominative-marked phrases in Japanese tough constructions. In Manurung, R. and Bond, F. (eds.) *Proceedings of the 26th Pacific Asia Conference on Language, Information, and Computation.* Jawa Barat: Faculty of Computer Science, Universitas Indonesia, 272-79.

Sakai, H. 1994. Complex NP constraint and case-conversions in Japanese. In Nakamura, M. (ed.) *Current Topics in English and Japanese.* Tokyo: Hituzi Shobo Publishing.

Seraku, T. 2013. *Clefts, Relatives, and Language Dynamics.* DPhil thesis, University of Oxford.

Seraku, T. 2016. A "maximal exclusion" approach to structural uncertainty in Dynamic Syntax. In Park, J. C. and Chung, J. W. (eds.) *Proceedings of the 30th Pacific Asia Conference on Language, Information, and Computation.* Seoul: Institute for the Study of Language and Information, Kyung Hee University, 39-47.

Seraku, T. and Ohtani, A. 2016a. *Wh*-licensing in Japanese right dislocations. In Piñón, C. (ed.) *Empirical Issues in Syntax and Semantics* 11. Paris: CSSP, 199-224.

Seraku, T. and Ohtani, A. 2016b. The word-order flexibility in Japanese novels. In Ogata, T. and Akimoto, T. (eds.) *Computational and Cognitive Approaches to Narratology.* Hershey, PA: IGI Global, 213-44.

Shibatani, M. 1977. Grammatical relations and surface cases. *Language* 53, 789-809.

Shibatani, M. 1978. *Nihongo-no Bunseki.* (The analysis of Japanese) Tokyo: Taishukan.

Steedman, M. 2000. *The Syntactic Process.* Cambridge, MA: MIT Press.

Sugimoto, T. 1990. Nihongo-no daishugo-to shudai. (Major-subject and topic in Japanese) *Kitakyushu Kougyou Daigaku Jouhou Kougakubu Kiyou*, 3, 165-82.

Takami, K. and Kamio, A. 1996. Topicalization and subjectivization in Japanese. *Lingua* 99, 207-35.

Takezawa, K. 1987. *A Configurational Approach to Case-Marking in Japanese.* PhD thesis, University of Washington.

Tanaka, H. and Kizu, M. 2007. Island insensitive constructions in Japanese. *York Papers in Linguistics* 2, 219-34.

Tateishi, K. 1991. *The Syntax of Subjects.* Stanford, CA: CSLI Publications.

Ura, H. 1996. *Multiple Feature-Checking.* PhD thesis, MIT.

Vermeulen, R. 2005. Possessive and adjunct multiple nominative constructions in Japanese. *Lingua* 115, 1329-63.

Whitman, J. 2001. Kayne 1994: p. 143, fn. 3. In Alexandrova, G. M. and Arnaudova, O. (eds.) *The Minimalist Parameter*, Amsterdam, Philadelphia: John Benjamins, 77-100

BTG-based Machine Translation with Simple Reordering Model using Structured Perceptron

Hao Wang
Graduate School of Information,
Production and Systems,
Waseda University
oko_ips@ruri.waseda.jp

Yves Lepage
Graduate School of Information,
Production and Systems,
Waseda University
yves.lepage@waseda.jp

Abstract

In this paper, we present a novel statistical machine translation method which employs a BTG-based reordering model during decoding. BTG-based reordering models for *preordering* have been widely explored, aiming to improve the standard phrase-based statistical machine translation system. Less attention has been paid to incorporating such a reordering model into decoding directly. Our reordering model differs from previous models built using a syntactic parser or directly from annotated treebanks. Here, we train without using any syntactic information. The experiment results on an English–Japanese translation task show that our BTG-based decoder achieves comparable or better performance than the more complex state-of-the-art SMT decoders.

1 Introduction

The phrase-based method (Koehn et al., 2003) and the syntax-based method (Yamada and Knight, 2001) are two of the representative methods in statistical machine translation (SMT). On the one hand, in the phrase-based model, the lexical reordering model is a crucial component, but it is often be criticized, especially when translating a language pair with widely divergent syntax like English-Japanese, as the naïve distance-based lexical reordering model does not work so well when applied to longer reorderings. On the other hand, in syntax-based SMT method, word reordering is implicitly addressed by translation rules. The performance is thus directly subject to the parsing errors of the syntactic parser.

Syntax-based translation models are usually built from annotated treebanks to extract grammar rules for reordering (Genzel, 2010). Such reordering models are thus more difficult to train. Between these two models, some loose hierarchical structure models have been proposed: the hierarchical phrase-based model (Chiang, 2007) and or the Bracketing Transduction Grammar (BTG) based model (Wu, 1997). Compared with the hierarchical phrase-based model, the BTG model has many advantages like its simplicity. Also, its well-formed rules avoid extracting a large number of rare or useless translation rules, as is the case of the hierarchical phrase-based model.

In recent proposals, phrase-based statistical machine translation has been shown to improve when BTG-based preordering is applied as a preprocessing (DeNero and Uszkoreit, 2011; Neubig et al., 2012; Nakagawa, 2015). The idea behind preordering is to reduce the structural complexity. It is preferable to apply the reordering operations in advance rather than during decoding as this benefits the word alignment step.

In this paper, following (Xiong et al., 2008), we propose to incorporate the BTG-based reordering model directly into the decoding step of a BTG-based SMT system using a simple Structured Perceptron (Rosenblatt, 1958; Collins and Roark, 2004). The rest of the paper is organized as follows. Section 2 briefly introduces previous BTG-based reordering methods both for preordering or determining the reorderings during decoding. Section 3 describes the principal model used in BTG-based machine translation. Section 4 gives the details of the

31st Pacific Asia Conference on Language, Information and Computation (PACLIC 31), pages 114–123
Cebu City, Philippines, November 16-18, 2017

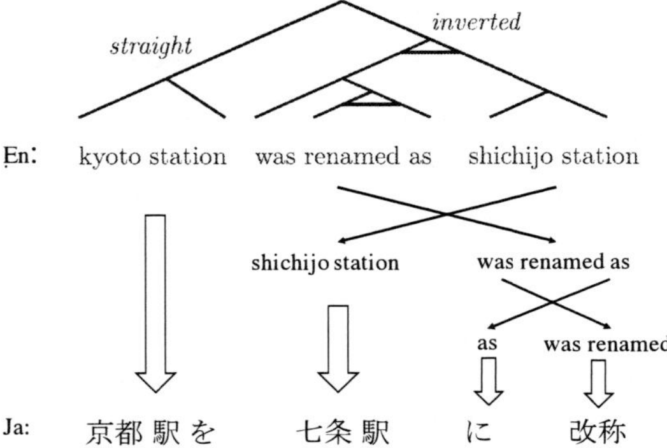

Figure 1: Example of translating a source sentence (English) into Japanese while reordering at the same time using a BTG tree.

proposed method and the model combination in the system construction. Section 5 reports the results of the experiment on an English-to-Japanese translation task. We conclude in Section 7.

2 Using Linguistic Contexts for BTG-based Reordering

A common problem in the distortion reordering models (Tillmann, 2004; Koehn et al., 2005; Galley and Manning, 2008) used in phrase-based SMT (PB-SMT) method is that they do not take contexts into account. Hence, we draw our attention on using linguistic-context information for reordering.

Bracketing Transduction Grammar (BTG) (Wu, 1997) is a binary and simplified synchronous context-free grammar with only one non-terminal symbol. It has three types for the right hand side of the rules γ: S–*straight* keeps the order of child nodes, I–*inverted* reverses the order, and T–*terminal* generates a terminal symbol.

$$X \to \gamma = \begin{cases} [X_1 X_2] & straight \\ < X_1 X_2 > & inverted \\ f/e & terminal \end{cases} \quad (1)$$

where X, X_1, X_2 are non-terminal symbols and f/e is a source/target phrase pair. BTG provides an easy and simple mechanism for modeling word permutation across languages. Figure 1 illustrates this mechanism.

There exists some solutions for BTG grammar induction, which typically focus on unsupervised approaches, like inside-outside algorithm (Pereira and Schabes, 1992) for probabilistic context-free grammar (PCFG), monolingual bracketing representation (Klein and Manning, 2002) or bilingual bracketing grammar induction (Wu, 1995). The common problem is that these models suffer from a higher computational complexity.

Some supervised versions focus on supervised approach, ranging from simple flat reordering model (Wu, 1997), maximum-entropy based model (Zens and Ney, 2006; Xiong et al., 2008) and Tree Kernel-based SVM (Zhang and Li, 2009). Other approaches, use pre-annotated treebanks to train a monolingual/synchronous parser (Collins and Roark, 2004; Genzel, 2010). In this case, the rules are learned directly from the treebank. The majority of works (Zhang and Gildea, 2005; Xiong et al., 2008) rely on syntactic parsers available in one of a source or target language.

However, bilingual parallel treebanks are not always available. As to building a bilingual synchronous parser using the BTG formalism, there exist rare works without the use of such a constituency/dependency parser, and sometimes bilingual parallel treebanks are not always available. Zens and Ney (2006) and DeNero and Uszkoreit (2011) proposed semi-supervised approaches for synchronous grammar induction based on source-side information only when bilingual word alignments are given in advance, instead of training the parser in a supervised way on pre-annotated treebanks. This strategy does not require syntactic annotations in the training data, making training easier.

Rather than developing a novel BTG-decoder incorporated with a BTG-based reordering model, using reordering models for *preordering* have been widely explored to improve the standard phrase-based statistical machine translation system. Neubig et al. (2012) present a bottom-up method for inducing a preorder for SMT by training a discriminative model to minimize the loss function on the hand-aligned corpus. Their method makes use of the general framework of large margin online structured prediction (Crammer et al., 2006). Lerner and Petrov (2013) present a simple classifier-based preordering approach using the source-side dependency tree. Nakagawa (2015) further develop a more efficient top-down incremental parser for preordering

via online training using simple structured Perceptron algorithm. Differing from the mentioned methods to pre-reorder the sentence before the phase of
decoding, in this paper; we propose to build a reordering model directly for building a BTG-based
decoder.

3 BTG-based Machine Translation

Given the three types of rules in Equation 1, we
define a BTG derivation $\mathcal{D}$ as a sequence of independent operations $d_1, \ldots, d_K$ that apply bracketing rules $X \to \gamma$ as each stage when parsing a
source-target sentence pair $< \mathbf{f}, \mathbf{e} >$. We write
$\mathcal{D} = [d_1, \ldots, d_k, \ldots, d_K]$. We can produce one
single BTG tree accordingly for one given $\mathcal{D}$. The
probability of a synchronous derivation (parse tree)
under the framework of Probabilistic Synchronous
Context Free Grammar (PSCFG) is computed as:

$$P(\mathcal{D}) = \prod_{d \in \mathcal{D}} P(d : X \to \gamma) \qquad (2)$$

where $d : X \to \gamma$ stands for the derivation with the
grammar rule $X \to \gamma$. Given an input sentence pair
$< \mathbf{f}, \mathbf{e} >$ and the word alignment $\mathbf{a}$, the problem of
finding the best derivation $\tilde{\mathcal{D}}$ can be defined as:

$$\tilde{\mathcal{D}} = \arg\max_{\mathcal{D}} P(\mathcal{D}|\mathbf{e}, \mathbf{f}, \mathbf{a}) \qquad (3)$$

In the real case of machine translation, we do not
know the word alignment $\mathbf{a}$ when training set is the
parallel corpus. In order to find the best translation
$\tilde{\mathbf{e}}$ from all translation candidates, we assume two latent variables $\mathbf{a}, \mathcal{D}$ were required as following:

$$\tilde{\mathbf{e}} = \qquad \arg\max_{\mathbf{e}} P(\mathbf{e}|\mathbf{f}) \qquad (4)$$

$$\propto \qquad \arg\max_{\mathbf{e}} P(\mathbf{e}, \mathcal{D}, \mathbf{a}|\mathbf{f}) \qquad (5)$$

$$\propto \quad \arg\max_{\mathbf{e}} P(\mathcal{D}|\mathbf{a}, \mathbf{f}, \mathbf{e}) \times P(\mathbf{a}|\mathbf{f}, \mathbf{e}) \times P(\mathbf{e}) \quad (6)$$

In Equation 6, $P(\mathbf{e})$ is the language model and $\mathbf{a}, \mathcal{D}$
are latent variables that should be learnt from the
training data. The generative story of Equation 6
is understood as follows: Once we found the hidden word alignment $\mathbf{a}$ with an alignment model
$P(\mathbf{a}|\mathbf{f}, \mathbf{e})$ and the hidden derivation $\mathcal{D}$ using BTG-
based reordering model $P(\mathcal{D}|\mathbf{a}, \mathbf{f}, \mathbf{e})$, we can trans-
late the input source sentence $\mathbf{f}$ with the target trans-
lation $\tilde{\mathbf{e}}$.

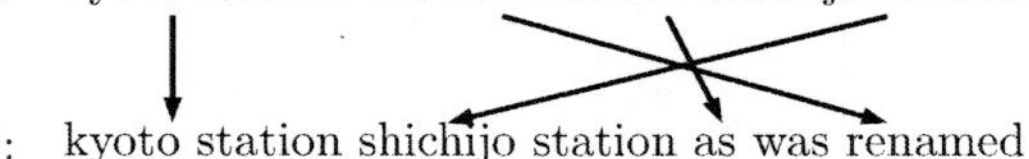

Figure 2: Example of preordering a source sentence given
the target word order.

3.1 Training Alignment Model

There are two sub-models in Equation 6, one is the
alignment model $P(\mathbf{a}|\mathbf{f}, \mathbf{e})$ and the other one is the
reordering model $P(\mathcal{D}|\mathbf{a}, \mathbf{f}, \mathbf{e})$. Since state-of-the-
art alignment methods yield high-quality word-to-
word alignments, it is not necessary to design a new
alignment model to obtain the intermediate variable
$\mathbf{a}$. We use the standard method to get word-to-word
alignments.

3.2 Training Reordering Model

Recently, some research also showed that treating
the parse tree as latent variables (Loehlin, 1998)
can benefit the BTG tree inference but for preordering (see Figure 2). The reordering model is trained
to maximize the conditional likelihood of trees that
license the reorderings implied by observed word
alignments in a given parallel corpus. For example, Neubig et al. (2012) proposed a BTG-based reordering model trained from word-aligned parallel
text directly. With assuming that there is an under-
lying derivation $\mathcal{D}$ that produced $\mathbf{f}'$, where $\mathbf{f}'$ is the
reordered source sentence given the corresponding
target word orders under the constraints of BTGs.

$$\mathbf{f} \xrightarrow[\mathbf{a}]{\text{preordering with } \mathcal{D}} \mathbf{f}' \qquad (7)$$

To learn such a reordering model, they handled
the derivations $\mathcal{D}$ as a latent variable directly from
the source side linguistic contexts. The objective
function in their work can be represented as:

$$\tilde{\mathbf{f}}' = \arg\max_{\mathbf{f}'} Score(\mathbf{f}', \mathcal{D}|\mathbf{f}) \qquad (8)$$

Since their model is based on reorderings $\mathbf{f}'$ licensed
by BTG derivations $\mathcal{D}$, notes $\mathcal{D} \to \mathbf{f}'$, the objective
function also can be written as:

$$\tilde{\mathcal{D}} = \arg\max_{\mathcal{D} \to \mathbf{f}'} Score(\mathcal{D}|\mathbf{f}) \qquad (9)$$

The learning problem defined here is fairly simple. With treating the derivation $\mathcal{D}$ as the latent variable, they want to find the derivation with maximal score of $Score(\mathcal{D}|\mathbf{f})$. Furthermore, following (Collins, 2002; Collins and Roark, 2004), they assume that $Score(\mathcal{D}|\mathbf{f})$ is the linear combination of feature functions defined over $\mathcal{D}$ and $\mathbf{f}$.

Because it is also possible to apply the score function $Score(\mathcal{D}|\mathbf{f})$ as a reordering model during the BTG-based decoding, following (Neubig et al., 2012; Nakagawa, 2015), we propose to build such a reordering model with latent derivation for decoding instead of preordering. The natural difference between their works and our work is as follows: In (Neubig et al., 2012; Nakagawa, 2015), they train an incremental parser for preordering, following the order in the target language before decoding, but we do reordering while decoding. In other words, we adopt their model but make use of it as an online reordering heuristic during decoding.

4 Proposed Methods

In our method, we propose to train and use a BTG-based reordering model in three steps. Firstly, we train the BTG parser on the source side with shallow annotations (only POS-tags and word classes (Brown et al., 1992)) on word-aligned bilingual data. Then we select a large mount of features of unigrams, bigrams, and trigrams to represent the current parser state and we estimate feature weights using a Structured Perceptron (Nakagawa, 2015). Finally, the log-linear combination score for the current state is computed again during decoding. This works as an additional heuristic score and helps the decoder to select the best candidates in sub-hypothesis combination.

4.1 Reordering

We define a reordering model Φ_{RM} as a model composed of a *straight* reordering model Φ_{RMs} and an inverted reordering model Φ_{RMi}. $\mathcal{R}$ stands for the composition of Φ_{RMs} and Φ_{RMi}.

$$\mathcal{R} = \{\Phi_{RMs}, \Phi_{RMi}\} \qquad (10)$$

Given a source sentence $\mathbf{f}$, we define the score for $\mathcal{R}$ the weighted sum of the score $\mathcal{P}(d)$ of the sub-derivation d at each parse state defined over D given

$\mathbf{f}$: kyoto station was renamed as shichijo station
  1   2   3   4   5   6   7

Derivations:

1. $f_1^7 \rightarrow [f_1^2\ f_3^7]$ 2. $f_1^2 \rightarrow [f_1\ f_2]$

3. $f_3^7 \rightarrow \langle f_3^5\ f_6^7 \rangle$ 4. $f_3^5 \rightarrow [f_3^4\ f_5]$

5. $f_3^4 \rightarrow \langle f_3\ f_4 \rangle$ 6. $f_6^7 \rightarrow [f_6\ f_7]$

Figure 3: Example of step-by-step atomic derivations.

a source sentence $\mathbf{f}$.

$$\mathcal{R}(\mathcal{D}|\mathbf{f}) = \sum_{d \in \mathcal{D}} \mathcal{P}(d : X \rightarrow \gamma) \qquad (11)$$

Each atomic derivation d which belongs to $\mathcal{D}$ is weighted with various features in a log-linear form as (Xiong et al., 2008; Duan et al., 2009):

$$\mathcal{P}(d : X \rightarrow \gamma) = \sum_{\phi_i \in d} \pi_i \phi_i \qquad (12)$$

where ϕ_i is the ith feature function and π_i is the ith weight can be trained on the training data.

Suppose that we know the word alignment $\mathbf{a}$. We want to train a parser which maximizes the number of times the source sentences in the training data are successfully parsed under the constraints of BTGs. Nakagawa (2015) propose an efficient top-down parser via online training for this problem. He uses a simple structured perceptron algorithm.

We assume that the parser has an independent state in each step. We define the parse state as a triple $\langle X, r, d \rangle$, where X is an unparsed span. For example, following the deductive proof system representations (Shieber et al., 1995; Goodman, 1999), $[X, p, q]$ covers $f_p, \ldots, f_q$. $d = \langle r, X \rightarrow \gamma \rangle$ is the derivation at the current state with r is the splitting position between f_{r-1} and f_r and $X \rightarrow \gamma$ is the applied BTG rule. To extract the features used to score the model, we assume that each word in a sentence has three types of features: lexical form, part-of-speech (POS) tag and word class (Brown et al., 1992) as (Nakagawa, 2015). We extract the unigrams, bigrams, and trigrams at each parse state and compute the model score defined in Equation 12[1].

---

[1] We use the same set of features described in (Nakagawa, 2015)

Algorithm 1: Training the Reordering Model

Input : Training data $\{\langle \mathbf{e}, \mathbf{f}, \mathbf{a}\rangle\}_0^L$
Output: Feature weights π for $\mathcal{R}$

1 **foreach** *iteration* t **do**
2   **foreach** *example* $\langle \mathbf{e}, \mathbf{f}, \mathbf{a}\rangle$ **do**
3      $\hat{\mathcal{D}} = \arg\max_{\mathcal{D}} \mathcal{R}(\mathcal{D}|\mathbf{f})$;
4      $\mathcal{D}^* = \arg\max_{\mathcal{D}\wedge Constraint(\mathcal{D},\mathbf{a},\mathbf{e},\mathbf{f})} \mathcal{R}(\mathcal{D}|\mathbf{f})$;
5   **if** $\hat{\mathcal{D}} \neq \mathcal{D}^*$ **then**
6        $\pi \leftarrow \pi + \mathcal{R}(\mathcal{D}^*, \mathbf{f}) - \mathcal{R}(\hat{\mathcal{D}}, \mathbf{f})$;
7   **end**
8   **end**
9   **return** π;
10 **end**

The training algorithm (see Algorithm 1) can be described briefly as following: The parser first produces a *system derivation* $\hat{\mathcal{D}}$ with the maximum model score given $\mathbf{f}$. If $\hat{\mathcal{D}}$ is not licensed by BTG constraints also given $(\mathbf{e}, \mathbf{a})$, we consider the parser entered a failure state and stop it. Another *oracle derivation* $\mathcal{D}^*$ was also selected, which satisfied the constraint of BTGs (notes $Constraint(\mathcal{D}, \mathbf{a}, \mathbf{e}, \mathbf{f}) = true$). If the *system derivation* $\hat{\mathcal{D}}$ and the *oracle derivation* $\mathcal{D}^*$ are not equivalent, we update the model weights π towards $\mathcal{D}^*$.

Like all structured prediction learning frameworks, the online Structured Perceptron is costly to train as training complexity is proportional to inference, which is frequently non-linear in the length of example. To train the reordering model, we employ an in-house parser[2] which uses Batch Perceptron. It is a modified and boosted version of the original top-down parser (Nakagawa, 2015), which allows us to train on the whole training set[3].

4.2 Decoding

In decoding, we follow (Och and Ney, 2002; Chiang, 2007). That is, we remove the target side and use a more general linear model composition over derivations:

$$\tilde{\mathbf{e}} = \arg\max_{\mathbf{e}} P(\mathbf{e}, \mathcal{D}|\mathbf{f}) \tag{13}$$

$$\propto \arg\max_{\mathcal{D}\to\mathbf{e}} \prod_i \Phi_i(\mathcal{D})^{\lambda_i} \tag{14}$$

where each Φ_i is a sub-model score function and λ is the corresponding weight. For each arbitrary score function Φ_i with a derivation D, we decompose it as a chain of independent derivations d with BTG rules $X \to \gamma$:

$$\Phi_i(\mathcal{D}) = \prod_{d\in\mathcal{D}} \Phi_i(d : X \to \gamma) \tag{15}$$

Therefore, given an input sentence $\mathbf{f} = f_1, \ldots, f_n$, notes f_1^n, the task to translate an input source sentence can be solved by finding the derivation with maximal score in Equation 14, which uniquely determines a target translation $\hat{\mathbf{e}}$ (e_1^m) with this latent derivation $\mathcal{D}$.

The decoder needs to generate all derivations for each segment spanning from f_i to f_j ($0 \leq i < j \leq n$). Since our goal is to find the best derivation $\hat{\mathcal{D}}$ that covers the whole input sentence $[f_1, \ldots, f_n]$, we employ a CKY-style decoder to generate the best derivation $\hat{\mathcal{D}}$ for each source sentence. This yields the best translation $\hat{\mathbf{e}}$ (e_1^m) at the same time.

4.2.1 The *-LM -RM* Decoder

The integration of a standard n-gram-based language model into a CKY-style decoder is not easy as in the standard phrase-based method (Koehn et al., 2003). Following (Chiang, 2007), we first introduce the *-LM -RM* model in which the reordering and language model are removed from the decoding model:

$$w(\mathcal{D}) = \prod_{i\notin\{RM,LM\}} \Phi_i(\mathcal{D})^{\lambda_i} \tag{16}$$

Using the deductive proof system (Shieber et al., 1995; Goodman, 1999) to describe our *-LM -RM* decoder, the inference rules are the following:

$$\frac{X \to f/e}{[X, p, q] : w} \tag{17}$$

$$\frac{X \to \langle X_1, X_2\rangle : \quad [X_1, p, r] : w_1 \ [X_2, r+1, q] : w_2}{[X, p, q] : w_1 w_2} \tag{18}$$

$$\frac{X \to [X_1, X_2] : \quad [X_1, p, r] : w_1 \ [X_2, r+1, q] : w_2}{[X, p, q] : w_1 w_2} \tag{19}$$

---

[2]https://github.com/wang-h/HieraParser

[3]We skip the sentences which cannot be parsed under the constraints of BTGs.

where $X \to \gamma$ is the derivation rule, $[X, p, q]$ is the subtree rooted in a non-terminal X (see Section 2), w is the model score defined in Equation 16. When all terms on the top line are true, the item on the bottom line is derived. The final goal for the decoder is $[\mathbf{f}, 1, n]$, where $\mathbf{f}$ is the whole source sentence.

During decoding, the *-LM -RM* decoder flexibly explores the derivation without taking reordering into account. This strategy is a simple way to build a CYK-style decoder, but the decoder requires very large beam size to find the true best translation. Incorporating the *LM* and *RM* model directly into the translation construction will improve efficiency.

4.2.2 The +*LM* +*RM* Decoder

The computational complexity of online strategy is reduced by using dynamic programming and incorporating the language model and the reordering model into decoding. The similar method has been described in (Chiang, 2007). The decoder integrated with the n-gram language model is called: "+*LM* decoder". In our case, we also need to integrate the reordering model, so we call it "+*LM* +*RM* decoder". Given the inference rules described in Equations 17–19, we describe the +*LM* +*RM* decoding algorithm using Equations 20–23.

In our case, the reordering model affects computing the language model score if the derivation requires to swap the target sub-charts. We can calculate $\Phi_{RM}(X)$ by just taking the model score as the product of two sub-charts $\Phi_{RM}(X_1)$ and $\Phi_{RM}(X_2)$ with current reordering score $\Phi_{RM}(X \to \gamma)$. Since $\mathcal{R}$ is a log-linear expression, we compute the reordering score $\mathcal{R}(X)$ for a given span $X : [X, p, q]$ that consists of $X_1 : [X_1, p, r]$ and $X_2 : [X_2, r+1, q]$ with a grammar rule $X \to \gamma$ as:

$$\mathcal{R}(X) = \mathcal{R}(X_1) + \mathcal{R}(X_2) + \mathcal{P}(X \to \gamma) \quad (24)$$

When we merge the chart $X_1 : [X_1, p, r]$ with $X_2 : [X_2, r+1, q]$ using the rule $X \to \gamma$, we update the total score for the composition model after applying each rule dynamically, we call this the +*RM* strategy. The BTG *terminal* rule ($T : X \to f/e$) is used to translate the source phrase f into the target phrase e while the *straight* and *inverted* rules ($S : X \to [X_1X_2]$ and $I : X \to\ < X_1X_2 >$) are used to concatenate two neighbouring phrases with

a *straight* or *inverted* order as following:

$$e_x^y = \begin{cases} e_1 \cdot e_2, & X \to [X_1X_2] \\ e_2 \cdot e_1, & X \to \langle X_1X_2 \rangle \end{cases} \quad (25)$$

where $\cdot$ stands for concatenation between strings. After having decided the word order on the target side, we compute the score in the language model, noted $\mathcal{L}(\cdot)^4$. The language model score $P_{LM}(e_x^y)$ depends on the preceding $N - 1$ words for any $e_x^y(|e_x^y| \geq N, 1 \leq x < y \leq m)$. It is computed as:

$$P_{LM}(e_x^y) = \prod_{x \leq z \leq y} p(\hat{e}_{z+N-1}|\hat{e}_z \ldots \hat{e}_{z+N-2}) \quad (26)$$

The language model score function $\mathcal{L}(e_x^y)$ depends on the rule type γ as follows:

$$\mathcal{L}(e_x^y) = \begin{cases} P_{LM}(e_x^{y+1}), & |e_x^y| = |e_1^m| \\ 0, & |e_x^y| < N \\ P_{LM}(e_{x+N}^y), & \text{otherwise} \end{cases} \quad (27)$$

To determine whether we have the case $|e_x^y| = |e_1^m|$, we assume that, if the span of $X : [X, p, q]$ covers the entire source sentence f_1^n as $X : [X, 1, n]$, then the target translation e_x^y should also cover the entire target sentence. On the basis of +*RM* decoder, we add the +*LM* component into the decoder and build a +*LM*+*RM* decoder for CYK-style bottom-up decoding. cube pruning (Chiang, 2007) was also applied to speedup the decoder.

4.2.3 Model Combination

HieraTrans is our newly-developed in-house BTG-based SMT translation platform. It adopts the constraints of BTG in both phrase translation and reordering. We combine the models in a log-liner manner as shown in Equation 14. The feature functions employed by HieraTrans are:

- Phrase-based translation models (TM): direct and inverse phrase translation probabilities, direct and inverse lexical translation probabilities.

- Language model (LM)

---

⁴For the case of start-of-the sentence and end of the sentence, we wrap the target sentence $\mathbf{e}$ (e_1^m) as $\hat{\mathbf{e}} = \hat{e}_1^{m+h} = \langle s \rangle^{N-1} e_1^m \langle \backslash s \rangle$.

$$\frac{X \to f/e}{[X, p, q] : w[\mathcal{L}(e)]^{\lambda_\mathcal{L}}} \tag{20}$$

$$\frac{X \to \langle X_1, X_2 \rangle : \quad [\exp \mathcal{P}(X \to \langle X_1, X_2 \rangle)]^{\lambda_\mathcal{R}} \quad [X_1, p, r] : w_1 \; [X_2, r+1, q] : w_2}{[X, p, q] : w_1 w_2 [\exp \mathcal{R}(X)]^{\lambda_\mathcal{R}} [\mathcal{L}(e_2 + e_1)]^{\lambda_\mathcal{L}}} \tag{21}$$

$$\frac{X \to [X_1, X_2] : \quad [\exp \mathcal{P}(X \to [X_1, X_2])]^{\lambda_\mathcal{R}} \quad [X_1, p, r] : w_1 \; [X_2, r+1, q] : w_2}{[X, p, q] : w_1 w_2 [\exp \mathcal{R}(X)]^{\lambda_\mathcal{R}} [\mathcal{L}(e_1 + e_2)]^{\lambda_\mathcal{L}}} \tag{22}$$

$$X_1 \to f_1/e_1, X_2 \to f_2/e_2 \tag{23}$$

- Reordering models (RM): *straight* and *inverted* scores combined within the log-linear framework.

- Penalties (PM): word penalty, phrase penalty, unknown word penalty.

The weights for each feature are tuned and estimated using the minimum error rate training (MERT) algorithm (Och, 2003).

5 Experiment

5.1 Experimental Setup

To evaluate our system, we conducted translation experiments on the KFTT Corpus (English–Japanese) and compared our system with baseline phrase-based (PB) and hierarchical phrase-based (HPB) SMT implementations in Moses[5] (Koehn et al., 2007). For each language, the training corpus is around 330,000 sentences. The development set contains nearly 1,235 sentences and nearly 1,160 sentences used for testing. We use the default training set for training translation model, and traditional lexical (Koehn et al., 2005) reordering model or our proposed BTG-based reordering model, and also target language model. We use the default tuning set for tuning the parameters and the default test set for evaluation.

For word alignment, we train word alignments in both directions with the default settings, i.e., the standard bootstrap for IBM model 4 alignment in GIZA++ ($1^5 H^5 3^3 4^3$). We then symmetrize the word alignments using *grow-diag-final-and* (*+gdfa*) and the standard phrase extraction heuristic (Koehn et al., 2003) for all systems. In our experiment, the maximum length of phrases entered into phrase table

is limited to 7, and we input only the top 20 translation candidates. The language model storage of target language uses the implementation in KenLM (Heafield, 2011) which is trained and queried as a 5-gram model. For distortion model in phrase-based SMT baseline, we set the distortion limit to 6.

Word alignments used for training the reordering model are the intersection of both asymmetrical alignments in each mono-direction output by GIZA++[6] (Och and Ney, 2003). For pos-tagging, we make use of the Stanford Log-linear POS Tagger[7] (Toutanova and Manning, 2000). To produce word class tags for each source word, we use the implementation of (Liang, 2005) [8] of Brown's clustering algorithm (Brown et al., 1992). The size of the class tags is fixed to 256.

For tuning, the optimal weights for each feature are estimated using the minimum error rate training (MERT) algorithm (Och, 2003) and parameter optimization with ZMERT[9] (Zaidan, 2009).

5.2 Experiment Results

For evaluation of machine translation quality, standard automatic evaluation metrics are used, like BLEU (Papineni et al., 2002) and RIBES (Isozaki et al., 2010) in all experiments. BLEU is used as the default standard metric, RIBES takes more word order into consideration. Table 1 shows the performance of MT systems on the KFTT test data, which are (1) Moses, trained using the phrase-based model (PB-SMT). (2) Moses, trained using the hierarchical phrase-based model (HPB-SMT) and last one (3) HieraTrans, trained using the BTG-based model

---

[5] http://www.statmt.org/moses/

[6] http://www.statmt.org/moses/giza/GIZA++.html
[7] https://nlp.stanford.edu/software/tagger.shtml
[8] https://github.com/percyliang/brown-cluster
[9] http://www.cs.jhu.edu/ ozaidan/zmert/

	BLEU	RIBES
Moses (PB-SMT)	20.81	67.50
Moses (HPB-SMT)	**21.67**	66.58
HieraTrans (BTG-SMT)		
(beam=40)	**21.15**	65.80
(beam=100)	**21.24**	66.33

Table 1: Results on phrase-based baseline system, hierarchical phrase-based system and our BTG-based system. Bold scores indicate no statistically significant difference at $p < 0.05$ from the best system (Koehn, 2004).

(BTG-SMT).

5.3 Analysis

Compared with the PB-SMT, BTG-based SMT uses weak linguistic annotations on the source side which provides additional information for reordering. We found that this strategy does help tree structure construction and finding final translations. However, our BTG-based method underperformed the HPB-SMT method. Increasing the beam size will gain improvement slightly.

There are two explanations for the result: First, final machine translation performance is also related to the used tools, which is sensitive to parse errors, alignment errors or annotation errors. Inaccurate labeling hurts the performance. Second, strict constraints of BTGs makes the decoder difficult to find some discontinuous phrases (translations).

6 Conclusion

In this paper, we proposed a novel BTG-based translation approach using a BTG-based reordering model directly trained from the training data. Training such a reordering model does not require any syntactic annotations, hence no use of treebanks or parsers. This approach provides an alternative to building a BTG-based machine translation system using syntactic information. We also made several improvements over (Xiong et al., 2008): First, we developed a novel BTG-based parser using Batch Perceptron. It allows training the reordering model on the whole training set. Second, we made the reordering model serve as a model which can be queried during decoding. We compared and validated our method can achieve the comparable performance with state-of-the-art SMT approaches. For further improvements, we will work on towards higher-speed decoder and make the decoder open available.

Acknowledgments

This work is supported in part by China Scholarship Council (CSC) under the CSC Grant No.201406890026. We also thank the anonymous reviewers for their insightful comments.

References

Peter F Brown, Peter V Desouza, Robert L Mercer, Vincent J Della Pietra, and Jenifer C Lai. 1992. Class-based n-gram models of natural language. *Computational linguistics*, 18(4):467–479.

David Chiang. 2007. Hierarchical phrase-based translation. *Computational Linguistics*, 33(2):201–228.

Michael Collins and Brian Roark. 2004. Incremental parsing with the perceptron algorithm. In *Proceedings of the 42nd Annual Meeting on Association for Computational Linguistics*, page 111. Association for Computational Linguistics.

Michael Collins. 2002. Discriminative training methods for hidden markov models: Theory and experiments with perceptron algorithms. In *Proceedings of the ACL-02 conference on Empirical methods in natural language processing-Volume 10*, pages 1–8. Association for Computational Linguistics.

Koby Crammer, Ofer Dekel, Joseph Keshet, Shai Shalev-Shwartz, and Yoram Singer. 2006. Online passive-aggressive algorithms. *Journal of Machine Learning Research*, 7(Mar):551–585.

John DeNero and Jakob Uszkoreit. 2011. Inducing sentence structure from parallel corpora for reordering. In *Proceedings of the Conference on Empirical Methods in Natural Language Processing*, pages 193–203. Association for Computational Linguistics.

Xiangyu Duan, Deyi Xiong, Hui Zhang, Min Zhang, and Haizhou Li. 2009. I2r's machine translation system for iwslt 2009. In *IWSLT*, pages 50–54.

Michel Galley and Christopher D Manning. 2008. A simple and effective hierarchical phrase reordering model. In *Proceedings of the Conference on Empirical Methods in Natural Language Processing*, pages 848–856. Association for Computational Linguistics.

Dmitriy Genzel. 2010. Automatically learning source-side reordering rules for large scale machine translation. In *Proceedings of the 23rd international conference on computational linguistics*, pages 376–384. Association for Computational Linguistics.

Joshua Goodman. 1999. Semiring parsing. *Computational Linguistics*, 25(4):573–605.

Kenneth Heafield. 2011. Kenlm: Faster and smaller language model queries. In *Proceedings of the Sixth Workshop on Statistical Machine Translation*, pages 187–197. Association for Computational Linguistics.

Hideki Isozaki, Tsutomu Hirao, Kevin Duh, Katsuhito Sudoh, and Hajime Tsukada. 2010. Automatic evaluation of translation quality for distant language pairs. In *Proceedings of the 2010 Conference on Empirical Methods in Natural Language Processing*, pages 944–952. Association for Computational Linguistics.

Dan Klein and Christopher D Manning. 2002. A generative constituent-context model for improved grammar induction. In *Proceedings of the 40th Annual Meeting on Association for Computational Linguistics*, pages 128–135. Association for Computational Linguistics.

Philipp Koehn, Franz Josef Och, and Daniel Marcu. 2003. Statistical phrase-based translation. In *Proceedings of the 2003 Conference of the North American Chapter of the Association for Computational Linguistics on Human Language Technology*, volume 1, pages 48–54. Association for Computational Linguistics.

Philipp Koehn, Amittai Axelrod, Alexandra Birch, Chris Callison-Burch, Miles Osborne, David Talbot, and Michael White. 2005. Edinburgh system description for the 2005 iwslt speech translation evaluation. In *IWSLT*, pages 68–75.

Philipp Koehn, Hieu Hoang, Alexandra Birch, Chris Callison-Burch, Marcello Federico, Nicola Bertoldi, Brooke Cowan, Wade Shen, Christine Moran, Richard Zens, et al. 2007. Moses: Open source toolkit for statistical machine translation. In *Proceedings of the 45th Annual Meeting of the ACL on Interactive Poster and Demonstration Sessions*, pages 177–180. Association for Computational Linguistics.

Philipp Koehn. 2004. Statistical significance tests for machine translation evaluation. In *EMNLP*, pages 388–395. Citeseer.

Uri Lerner and Slav Petrov. 2013. Source-side classifier preordering for machine translation. In *EMNLP*, pages 513–523.

Percy Liang. 2005. *Semi-supervised learning for natural language*. Ph.D. thesis, Massachusetts Institute of Technology.

John C Loehlin. 1998. *Latent variable models: An introduction to factor, path, and structural analysis*. Lawrence Erlbaum Associates Publishers.

Tetsuji Nakagawa. 2015. Efficient top-down btg parsing for machine translation preordering. In *ACL (1)*, pages 208–218.

Graham Neubig, Taro Watanabe, and Shinsuke Mori. 2012. Inducing a discriminative parser to optimize machine translation reordering. In *Proceedings of the 2012 Joint Conference on Empirical Methods in Natural Language Processing and Computational Natural Language Learning*, pages 843–853. Association for Computational Linguistics.

Franz Josef Och and Hermann Ney. 2002. Discriminative training and maximum entropy models for statistical machine translation. In *Proceedings of the 40th Annual Meeting on Association for Computational Linguistics*, pages 295–302. Association for Computational Linguistics.

Franz Josef Och and Hermann Ney. 2003. A systematic comparison of various statistical alignment models. *Computational Linguistics*, 29(1):19–51.

Franz Josef Och. 2003. Minimum error rate training in statistical machine translation. In *Proceedings of the 41st Annual Meeting on Association for Computational Linguistics*, volume 1, pages 160–167. Association for Computational Linguistics.

Kishore Papineni, Salim Roukos, Todd Ward, and Wei-Jing Zhu. 2002. Bleu: a method for automatic evaluation of machine translation. In *Proceedings of the 40th Annual Meeting of the Association for Computational Linguistics*, pages 311–318. Association for Computational Linguistics.

Fernando Pereira and Yves Schabes. 1992. Inside-outside reestimation from partially bracketed corpora. In *Proceedings of the 30th annual meeting on Association for Computational Linguistics*, pages 128–135. Association for Computational Linguistics.

Frank Rosenblatt. 1958. The perceptron: A probabilistic model for information storage and organization in the brain. *Psychological review*, 65(6):386.

Stuart M Shieber, Yves Schabes, and Fernando CN Pereira. 1995. Principles and implementation of deductive parsing. *The Journal of logic programming*, 24(1):3–36.

Christoph Tillmann. 2004. A unigram orientation model for statistical machine translation. In *Proceedings of HLT-NAACL 2004: Short Papers*, pages 101–104. Association for Computational Linguistics.

Kristina Toutanova and Christopher D Manning. 2000. Enriching the knowledge sources used in a maximum entropy part-of-speech tagger. In *Proceedings of the 2000 Joint SIGDAT conference on Empirical methods in natural language processing and very large corpora: held in conjunction with the 38th Annual Meeting of the Association for Computational Linguistics-Volume 13*, pages 63–70. Association for Computational Linguistics.

Dekai Wu. 1995. Stochastic inversion transduction grammars, with application to segmentation, bracketing, and alignment of parallel corpora. In *Proceedings of the 14th International Joint Conference on Artificial Intelligence*, volume 95, pages 1328–1335.

Dekai Wu. 1997. Stochastic inversion transduction grammars and bilingual parsing of parallel corpora. *Computational Linguistics*, 23(3):377–403.

Deyi Xiong, Min Zhang, Aiti Aw, and Haizhou Li. 2008. Linguistically annotated btg for statistical machine translation. In *Proceedings of the 22nd International Conference on Computational Linguistics-Volume 1*, pages 1009–1016. Association for Computational Linguistics.

Kenji Yamada and Kevin Knight. 2001. A syntax-based statistical translation model. In *Proceedings of the 39th Annual Meeting on Association for Computational Linguistics*, pages 523–530. Association for Computational Linguistics.

Omar Zaidan. 2009. Z-mert: A fully configurable open source tool for minimum error rate training of machine translation systems. *The Prague Bulletin of Mathematical Linguistics*, 91:79–88.

Richard Zens and Hermann Ney. 2006. Discriminative reordering models for statistical machine translation. In *Proceedings of the Workshop on Statistical Machine Translation*, pages 55–63. Association for Computational Linguistics.

Hao Zhang and Daniel Gildea. 2005. Stochastic lexicalized inversion transduction grammar for alignment. In *Proceedings of the 43rd Annual Meeting on Association for Computational Linguistics*, pages 475–482. Association for Computational Linguistics.

Min Zhang and Haizhou Li. 2009. Tree kernel-based svm with structured syntactic knowledge for btg-based phrase reordering. In *Proceedings of the 2009 Conference on Empirical Methods in Natural Language Processing: Volume 2-Volume 2*, pages 698–707. Association for Computational Linguistics.

Arabic-English Text Translation Leveraging Hybrid NER

Emna Hkiri
Latice Laboratory
Faculty of sciences Monastir
Emna.hkiri@gmail.com

Souheyl Mallat
Latice Laboratory
ISIM of Monastir
Souheyl.mallat@gmail.com

Mounir Zrigui
Latice Laboratory
Faculty of sciences Monastir
Mounir.zrigui@fsm.rnu.tn

Abstract

Named Entities (NEs) are a very important part of a sentence and their treatment is a potentially useful preprocessing step for Statistical Machine Translation (SMT). Improper translation of NE lapse the quality of the SMT output and it can hurt sentence's human readability considerably. Dropping NE often causes translation failures beyond the context, affecting both the morphosyntactic formedness of sentences and the word sense disambiguation in the source text. Due to peculiarities of the written Arabic language, the translation task is however rather challenging. In this work, we address the challenging issues of NEs treatment in the context of SMT of Arabic into English texts. We have experimented on three types of named entities which are: Proper names, Organization names and Location names. In this paper, we present integration between machine learning and rule based techniques to tackle Arabic NER problem in attempt to improve the final quality of the SMT system output. We show empirically that each aspect of our approach is important, and that their combination leads to the best results already after integration of NER into SMT. We show improvements in terms of BLEU scores (+4 points) and reduction of out of vocabulary words over a baseline for the News Commentary corpus.

1 Introduction

Named entities recognition is essential for many tasks of natural language processing, whether monolingual or multilingual, as information retrieval or machine translation. In this work, we are interested in the processing of NE in the context of statistical machine translation from Arabic into English, in which the processing of NE poses particular problems. A statistical machine translation (SMT) system learns to translate based on examples of translations already made, extracted from parallel corpus.

In so far as these training corpus are relatively small in size, this raises the question of translation of words that are not seen during training(Hkiri et al., 2015a). This is particularly critical in case of Arabic texts. Arabic is indeed a morphologically complex language (Habash, 2011), many possible forms are rarely observed in the corpus (Heintz, 2008). This requires, at least, implementing morphological analysis to define the source inventory units of the translation system.

A study carried out by Habash (2008) on unknown words in a journalistic corpus for Arabic-English language reports that about 40% of unknown words correspond to proper names. The SMT systems use a default strategy to treat these unknown words; it copies their forms in the output target language. This strategy is sometimes operative especially for person names when the source and target languages use the same alphabet. Unfortunately, this strategy is unsuitable in the case of Arabic into English translation.

To overcome this problem, a common strategy consists to transliterate unknown words in the Latin alphabet (Al-Onaizan and Knight, 2002b), in case of person names and Places (Hermjakob et al., 2008), or even to consult bilingual dictionaries (Hal and Jagarlamudi, 2011).

Treatment of unknown words in Arabic texts in SMT context requires distinguishing between different types of unknown forms, in order to apply differential treatment. In this context, identifying NE appears as a requirement for the text translation. This identification is however difficult in Arabic, in particular because of the lack of distinction between upper and lower case letters which is a valuable indicator to identify proper names in languages using the Latin alphabet. A word form in Arabic texts may refer to different meanings or words according to their context and their diacritics for example the no vowelized word "حافظ" could be a verb (save) for

124

31st Pacific Asia Conference on Language, Information and Computation (PACLIC 31), pages 124–131
Cebu City, Philippines, November 16-18, 2017

the vowel (FAT'HA) and a personal name for the vowel (Kassra).

Other factors combine to make the identification of NE more challenging. In particular, the use common names as parts of name or surnames or the use of prefixes like (Abd) (servant) associated with a name that describes God. Or, the word Ben (son of) is a part of many names of people from North Africa. The instability of spelling of proper names in various Arabic regions and their diversified transliteration in languages using the Latin alphabet is another source of difficulty. For example "Philippines" is spelled differently: الفليبين or الفليبيين.

In this work, we propose an approach for integrating Named Entities recognition and translation within SMT, which tries to address all these issues at the same time. The objective of applying the treatment of NEs in our statistical machine translation system is to reinforce and improve the quality of Arabic to English text translation. We used DBpedia Linked Data for NER, and the parallel corpus for translation of the recognized NE. For the NER component, we adopted a hybrid approach. We have reproduced the annotator ANNIE incorporated into the GATE tool to serve as baseline rule based component. For machine learning component we exploited the discriminant models using conditional random fields. The rest of the paper is structured as follows. In section2, we will give a literature review of Arabic NER in the SMT. Section 3describes data collection, the architecture of the proposed system and details the main components. Section 4 reports the results of our experiments. In the last section we draw conclusions and discuss some future works.

2 State of the art

For the machine translation (MT) of a text from one natural language to another, named entities require special attention. The MT system should decide whether to translate or transliterate the named entity (Al-Onaizan and Knight, 2002b; Hassan and Sorensen, 2005). In practice, this depends on the type of NE (Chen et al, 2003). For example, personal names tend to be transliterated. The organization names are different, most of them are translated. In contrast, many proper names vary from one language to another. Automatic translation of NEs is one of the most delicate problems; a significant part of mistakes made by the search engines and the most powerful MT tools is

caused by NE translation; its bad translation often produce absurd results (Agrawal and Singla. 2012).

Some studies resolve this problem by developing techniques and algorithms for NE transliteration (Santanu, 2010; Hermjakob et al, 2008; Zhang et al, 2011) or by creating domain dictionaries for translation. These last are dictionaries of frequent named entities in a specific area. The quality of the NER system affects the quality of translations (Hkiri et al.,2015). Therefore, the translation of NEs is a fundamental task for most multilingual applications systems (Babych and Hartley, 2003).

There have been few successful attempts on the translation of Arabic named entities. Benajiba (2010) translated directly NE using the automatic alignment of words. Hassan (2007) used the similarity metrics to extract the named entities from bilingual comparable and parallel corpora. Moore (2003) also used the parallel corpus to translate the named entities. The source language in its process is English, so it was based on the initial capitalization to detect proper names. Fehri (2011) translated Arabic entities named using the NooJ platform. Abdul Rauf (2012) improved the translation of entities based on comparable corpus and dictionaries that contain unfamiliar words. Ling (2011) used web links to the translation of NE.

Other published work that uses named entities recognition for machine translation has been directed towards transliterating NEs. The work proposed by Ulf Hermjakob and Kevin Knight et. al. (2008) for Arabic-English translation demonstrates that improvement in translation can be achieved by transliterating NEs instead of trying to translate them. Their work is based on the hypothesis that MT system mistranslates or drops named entities when they do not exist in the training data.

Al-Onaizan (2002a) (2002b) combined translation and transliteration of NE using bilingual and monolingual resources to obtain the best translation of NE. Kashani (2007) transliterates unknown words to improve the performance of the translation system. Jiang (2007) combined the transliteration with data from the web to achieve the best translation of NEs. Azab (2012) reduced the out of vocabulary words of the translation system by automating the translation or transliteration decision from English into Arabic. Abdul Jaleel and Larkey (2003) described their statistical technique of transliteration of the English-Arabic names.

Recently Nasredine and Saadane (2013) developed a system for automatic transliteration of the Arabic proper names in the Latin alphabet.

3   Proposed system
3.1   Data collection

Various linguistic resources are important and necessary in order to develop our Arabic NER system with scope of three different categories of NEs(Hkiri et al.,2016). In the literature, the corpora are commonly used for training, evaluation and comparing with existing systems. The corpora have been cleaned prepared and annotated using our XML format (three named entity tags; one for each NE type person, organization and location).

United nations[1] corpus: is one of the biggest available corpora involving the Arabic language. To obtain our training corpus, we used about 15000 sentences from 2005 Dataset folder. Before using these data files we applied linguistic preprocessing to obtain data in the appropriate automatic processing format.

-ANERcorp[2] dataset is developed by Yassine Benajiba. It is exploited for the training phase of the ML for NER component.

News Commentary 2012[3] Corpus: This corpus consists of political and economic comments from the Project Syndicate website. It has no NE annotations and originally designed to support statistical machine translation in Arabic NLP. Therefore in this research, these datasets have been manually annotated in order to support the NER task. In our study the corpus is used as a reference corpus for NER and SMT evaluation, therefore we extracted and annotated 500 sentences in which we have 350 person names, 410 locations and 151 organizations.

Another type of linguistic resources used is our bilingual NE lexicon[4]: This lexicon is built based on linked datasets of DBpedia and it includes person, place and organization named entities for the couple of Arabic-English languages (Hkiri et al.,2017) (see Table 1).

Named Entities extracted from DBpedia Linked Data	Arabic-English
Person	27480
Organization	17237
Location	4036
Overall	48753

Table1. Bilingual Named Entities lexicon

The described data collection is used for the system development. Our system is based on two relevant components. The NER component is used to detect NE in the source text. This component is based on rule based and machine learning techniques. The second component is dedicated for the Named entities translation (NET component).

3.2   NER component

Both rule based approach and Ml approach have their weakness and strength. By combining them in one hybrid system they may achieve a better performance than operating each of them separately. Our hybrid NER system is a combination of rule-based and ML approaches. The rule-based component is a reproduction of ANIIE system, which is integrated in GATE framework. The ML component uses the CRF model. The system consists of two pipelined components detailed in the following sub-sections:

The rule based component: The rule-based component in our system is a reproduction of the ANNIE system (A Nearly New Information Extraction system) integrated in GATE framework. It is dedicated mainly to the extraction of NE for English. Later the developers have integrated a module for the Arabic language. Nevertheless, the number of Gazetteers for Arabic is much lower compared to that of the English. Time consuming and tedious construction of Arabic Gazetteers lead us to question the way of acquiring an acceptable number of them to ensure better performance of NER system. To overcome this problem we used our bilingual lexicon of NE. In this step, we have exploited the Arabic part of our lexicon; we have mapped our Arabic named entities to predefined gazetteers of GATE as detailed in the following table.

ANNIE/Gate	Predefined entities	Enriched entities from our lexicon
Person	1700	27480
Organization	96	17237

---

[1] http://www.euromatrixplus.net/multi-un/

[2] http://users.dsic.upv.es/~ybenajiba/downloads.html

[3] http://www.casmacat.eu/corpus/news-commentary.html

[4] https://github.com/Hkiri-emna/Named_Entities_Lexicon_Project

Location	485	4036

Table 2 : Enrichment of predefined Gazetteers of GATE using our lexicon

Moreover, ANNIE is based on the combination of gazetteers and JAPE rules. The idea was to put aside the gazetteers of ANNIE of named entities that we do not need to annotate (such as "URL", "id", "Phone", etc.). We have halved the number of gazetteers. Thus, we simplified the extraction process and we noted a considerable gain in the response time. Similarly, we observed that the JAPE transducer includes a significant n umber of phases (under the .jape file format). Each phase includes a lot of rules, some of which could be inactivated in response to our needs of annotation (annotation rules of the "URL", "id", "Phone", etc.). We believe that these points help to simplify and speed up the base system.

Machine learning based component: The union of rule-based component with the ML component generates the NER hybrid system, which aims to improve the performance of the translation system. The hybridization process is to automatically annotate the test corpus by the rule-based component. The test corpus is annotated again by CRF ++, considering that NE annotated by our rule-based component are correct and CRF ++ is used only to predict areas that have not been annotated. The ML module requires a large amount of annotated data; to do this we used about15000 sentences of United Nations Organization corpus (UN). This corpus is annotated automatically by the rule based module. In addition we used the ANER corpus Benajiba and Rosso.

The latter consists of 4871 sentences. Our supervised ML module uses the Conditional Random Fields model, which is a generalization of Bayesian networks. In our application we used the CRF ++ [5] to annotate sequences of named entities (person, place and organization).

Integrating CRF into Arabic NER : We have used CRF ++ as a development environment for the ML component. This last is based on the set of features, the classification algorithm and the output of the rule-based component. The output of the classification component is used in the prediction phase to generate the final annotation of the NEs. In our study, the output of the hybrid system is analyzed and used to improve the rule-based component.

The selection of features involves selecting a combination of classification functions from the global characteristics space. The features studied in our application are divided into various types: rule-based features, morphological features, POS (morphosyntactic) features and gazetteers features. Each existence x of an element of one of these categories results in testing boolean functions x with each label and each n-gram of the possible labels.

The set of features that are used for NE extraction includes:

Rule-based Characteristics: These contextual elements are the main contribution of the rule-based component to the hybrid system. They come from decisions based on rules defined in terms of a sliding window of size 5 for the immediate right and left neighbors of the candidate word.

Morphological features are derived from the morphological analysis. These characteristics help distinguish the entity named from regular text based on its morphological state. These characteristics are respectively: the aspect, mode and status of the verb, the number of gender, person, voice, whether or not proclitics (such as conjunctions proclitic (Fa), subordinating conjunction (Wa), particles, prepositions (Fi, Bi), the jussive (Li), a marker of future (Sa) negative particles, relative pronouns, etc.

POS feature: is the morphosyntactic category of the target word estimated by SAPA tool[6]. This feature allows the classifier to learn the morphosyntactic labels whose named entities occurring with. These labels are: name, number, proper noun, adjective, adverb, pronoun, verb, particle, preposition, conjunctions and punctuation.

Gazetteer features: check the class of the named entity (person, place and organization): a binary function to check if the word (left neighbor / right neighbor of the current word) belongs to predefined Gazetteers categories (person, location, organization). This feature helps to reveal the context of named entities.

Punctuation: This feature indicates whether the word has a point adjacent, for example, at the beginning or the end of the sentence or it is part of an abbreviation. This function allows using the position of text within the classification model

---

[5] http://crfpp.sourceforge.net/

[6] https://github.com/SouhirG/SAPA

3.3 Named Entities Translation component

The difference of this phase compared to the standard SMT is that we offer hypothesis/proposals of NEs translations to the decoder. During preprocessing step, the Arabic text is segmented and NEs are extracted. Depending on the type of named entities detected, the bilingual lexicon is consulted (Person, location and organizations) in order to avoid ambiguities: a person's name (PERS) can be identical to the name of a street (LOC) as if "الحبيب بورقيبة" this name can be a person's name, airport name or street name. Translations proposals of this named entity, extracted from the bilingual lexicon, are injected in the source text as tags. For example, to name the person "والحبيب بورقيبة" ("Habib Bourguiba"), translations of this NE are proposed to the decoder in the format:
<n translation="Habib Bourguiba || Habib Ben Ali Bourguiba|| Al Habib Bourguiba "> AlHbybbwwrqybp < =n>

4 Experiments and evaluation

4.1 Baseline system

For machine translation, we used our baseline translation system. It integrates GIZA ++ aligner for the training phase. The translation table is formed by aligned segments whose length is up to seven words. The Baseline system was built following the steps in the tutorial of EACL 2009 workshop on statistical machine translation. The difference is that we exploited the UN corpus. The system has been trained and tested on a corpus of about 3.4 million parallels sentences. For Arabic texts, the pipeline of experiences for preprocessing is accomplished on several stages. The first stage is dedicated to the transliteration of texts. The second is devoted to morphological analysis. The next step is normalization. In the last stage, a segmentation of the text is performed to separate the proclitics from the basic word form.

For English text corpus, the main task is tokenization in order to separate punctuation from words. Then, we convert, except for proper names, upper letters by lowercase letters. The final step in this process is data cleaning, it is essential to obtain a high quality translation. In practice, it is difficult to get a perfect set of data or close to perfection. By cleaning our training corpus, we removed:

The source- target repetitive segments, misaligned or identical,
- Too short or too long segments or those who violate the Giza ++ limit ratio,
- Internet links (email, FTP / FTPS, HTTP / HTTPS addresses).

The table below shows the results of preprocessing and cleaning of the UN corpus

	Training Corpus		test Corpus	
Language	Arabic	English	English	Arabic
N° of tokens	38291993	32645500	8161375	9572998
N° of sentences	1370508	1370508	342627	342627
Avg of tokens /sentence	27,94	23,82	23,82	27,94

Table 3: Statistics: the total number of tokens in Arabic and English corpus

To show the impact of hybridization and the injection of the lexicon as a strengthening NER resource, we conduct an evaluation on News Commentary corpus

4.2 Detection of NE in the News Commentary corpus

This corpus is parallel and it offers us the opportunity to evaluate the translation and recognition of NEs. The News Commentary corpus is extracted from political and economic sites whose topics are close to those of our basic learning corpus, which is extracted from the united nations organization works (UN) .The table below shows performance of baseline NER system, optimized NER system and the hybrid NER system on the News Commentary corpu using standard measures (precison, recall and f-measure)

Named entities		Rule Based NER	Rule Based + NE lexicon	Hybrid NER
Person	P	48.3	80.6	84.3
	R	45.7	79.8	83.34
	F	46.96	80.19	83.81
Organizati on	P	52.12	71.54	86.24
	R	33.4	59.12	62.5
	F	40.71	64.73	72.47
Location	P	59.5	86.7	89.86
	R	44.6	80.35	89.5
	F	50.98	83.40	89.67
F-measure		46.21	76.10	81.9

Table 4 : Comparison of Baseline, optimized and hybrid NER system on the News Commentary corpus.

-The Baseline system is the rule-based annotator integrated in GATE tool: This mode presents modest scores precision, recall and F-measure for all NE classes. This is explained by the lack of Arabic Gazetteers in this annotator. We remind that it is mainly developed for English and later was upgraded for Arabic language processing.

The Baseline system + lexicon is the optimized version: We have enriched the baseline system by our bilingual lexicon. We mapped the Arabic part of the bilingual lexicon to GATE Gazetteers. As a result, we note an improvement in precision for all classes. The strength is the recognition of the place entities, which is attributed to the high coverage of the NE lexicon containing DBpedia datasets.

It is important to note that our system has a good recall for person names, which were more abundant in the UN corpus and in our lexicon (27480 Person NE). Besides, the corpus was a heterogeneous mixture of proper names of persons not only in Arabic countries but also in the continents of Africa, Asia and America ("أنان كوفي" / Kofi Annan, "مون كي بان" / Ban Ki-moon "أوباما باراك" / Barack Obama). A good percentage of recall for the person NE is encouraging because the named entities of South Asia and America have no phonetic similarity with the names of person in Arabic countries. A detailed review of the results shows that our NER system works poorly for organizations in the corpus, in fact, our system does not effectively manages acronyms or abbreviations.

The Hybrid system is the final version. The results show an improvement in overall F-measure of NE classes (+5 points) compared to previous results. Note that the hybrid model improves recognition of all NEs and especially the recognition of places since the lexicon-based system has better performance on the recognition of places.

4.3 Evaluation of the impact of NER on the SMT system

For SMT, we used the Moses decoder that integrates GIZA ++ aligner used in the training phase. The translation table generated consists of segments up to seven words. The SAPA tool is used for pretreatment of Arabic texts.

We remind that the basic principle of our translation method is to propose translations of NE to the decoder. During the preprocessing phase, the Arabic text is pretreated and the named entities are annotated. Depending on the class or category of NE detected, the bilingual lexicon is consulted (people, places and organizations) to avoid ambiguities in polysemic entities. Proposals of translations extracted from the NE lexicon are injected in the text to be translated in two modes of translation (inclusive and exclusive). The annotation of NE in source and target News Commentary corpus allows us to automatically evaluate the quality of the translation of NEs. We evaluated three modes of translation summarized below.

The Default mode: As the name indicates, in this mode no treatment of named entities is accomplished. It presents the translation generated by our baseline system.

The Exclusive mode: In this mode, only proposals of translations offered by the lexicon are considered in the calculation of the best translation score.

The Inclusive mode: In this mode the translations provided by the lexicon and the translations from the translation table are considered in calculating the score.

We remind that we have achieved learning on the UN corpus and for evaluation experiments we used the News Commentary corpus. The results of the evaluation are in terms of BLEU score. Table below shows the translation results in the three modes of translation. The total of out of vocabulary words (OOV) is also presented.

	BLEU	Mots OOV
Default	32.35	145
Inclusive	36.2	115
Exclusive	32.14	115

Table 5: BLUE and OOV scores for the Arabic-English translation of 500 sentences of the News Commentary2012 corpus.

Comparing the exclusive mode by default mode, we notice a slight decrease in BLEU score. This is because some translations proposed by our lexicon differ from those of the reference. A more detailed analysis shows that our lexicon does not provide incorrect translations, but they are different from those of the reference. An example is the translation "منظمة حلف شمال الأطلسي" in our lexicon the word is translated by North Atlantic Treaty Organization, while for the reference is abbreviated to "NATO". In some cases, our translations correct those of the reference as an example of the place "سيريلانكا" it is translated in the reference by Srilanka, while our system, it says Sri Lanka. Also, using this mode some named entities translations are improved. They are translated correctly by our system but they are incorrect for the Baseline system (default). Cite the example of NE " الرئيس جورج بوش الأب " it is translated by the Baseline system "President Bush" whereas the reference is "president George Herbert Walker Bush"

The exclusive mode does not improve translation quality, but it affects the rate of OOV words. The percentage declined, he passed by 145 in the default mode to reach 115 for the exclusive mode.

According to the BLEU score, inclusive mode is the best, with a decrease of OOV words. Therefore, we can say that the idea of integrating translations extracted from the bilingual lexicon, improves translation quality while ensuring, as shown above, better coverage of the named entities.

For evaluating the translation of named entities, we will limit to the inclusive mode. The rate of correctly translated NEs was calculated for each class on the test corpus. The calculation is made by comparing NE translated to those in the reference.

	Person	Location	Organization
Default	53.36%	73.50%	46.42%
Inclusive	80.05%	86.31%	62.80%

Table 6: evaluation of effect of NE Translation on the News Commentary corpus.

Using the inclusive method improves the rate of NE translated correctly compared to the default system. These quantitative results show that the use of the lexicon does affect the translation of named entities, although this is not always reflected by a significant increase in BLEU score.

5   Conclusion

In this work, we addressed the main problems of NE integration into an SMT system. Our approach integrates a hybrid NER system, and allows choosing adapted NE translations for each NE. In conclusion, it can be said that using NEs does help in providing better SMT. we did improve the BLEU score over baseline system, a number of translated sentences show improvement with the use of these techniques. There was a considerable reduction in mistranslation and dropping of NEs. This helped enhancing human readability as well. Analysis of our models also revealed a number of insights and scopes for further improvement. There is also a space for using different ML techniques other than CRF, and how this will impact on the performance of the NER system

References

AbdulJaleel Nasreen, and Leah S. Larkey. 2003. Statistical transliteration for English-Arabic cross language information retrieval. Proceedings of the twelfth international conference on Information and knowledge management. ACM,

Abdul Rauf Sadaf. 2012. Efficient corpus selection for Statistical Machine Translation. PhDthesis. Le Mans, France.

Al-Onaizan Yaser, Knight Kevin. 2002a. Machine transliteration of names in Arabic text. Proc. of the ACL-02 workshop on Computational approaches to semitic languages: 1-13.

Al-Onaizan Yeser, Knight Keven 2002b. Translating named entities using monolingual and bilingual resources. Proc. of the 40th Annual Meeting on ACL, ACL '02, Philadelphia, PA, USA: 400-408.

Agrawal Neeraj and Singla Ankush. 2012. Using named entity recognition to improve machine translation. Technical report, Standford University, NaturalLanguage Processing..

Babych, Bogdan, and Anthony Hartley.2003. Improving machine translation quality with automatic named entity recognition. In: Proceedings of the 7th International EAMT workshop on MT and other Language Technology Tools, Improving MT through other Language Technology Tools: Resources and Tools for Building MT. EAMT '03. Budapest, Hungary: Association for Computational Linguistics: 1-8.

Benajiba Yassine, Zitouni Imed. 2010. Enhancing mention detection using projection via aligned corpora. In: Proceedings of the 2010 conference on empirical methods in natural language processing, Cambridge. Association for Computational Linguistics:993-1001.

Chen, Hsin-Hsi, Changhua Yang, and Ying Lin. 2003.Learning formulation and transformation rules for multilingual named entities. Proceedings of the ACL 2003 workshop on Multilingual and mixed-language named entity recognition- 15(1). Association for Computational Linguistics.

Fehri Hela., Haddar Kais., Ben Hamadou Abdelmajid. 2011. Recognition and Translation of Arabic Named Entities with NooJ Using a New Representation Model.2011. In M. Constant, A. Maletti, A. Savary (eds), FSMNLP, 9th International Workshop:134-142,.

Habash Nizar.2008. Four techniques for online handling of out-of-vocabulary words in Arabic-English statistical machine translation. Proc. of the 46th Annual Meeting of the Association for Computational Linguistics on Human Language Technologies:57-60.

Habash Nizar, 2011.Arabic Natural Language Processing, Synthesis Lectures on Human Language Technologies, organ & Claypool Publishers.

Daumé III, Hal, and Jagadeesh Jagarlamudi. 2011 . Domain adaptation for machine translation by mining unseen words, Proceedings of the 49th Annual Meeting of the ACL :HLT : short papers - Volume 2, HLT '11, ACL, Stroudsburg, PA, USA, p. 407-412.

Hammersley John M. and Peter Cliford. 1971. Markov fields on finite graphs and lattices.

Hassan, Ahmed, Haytham Fahmy, and Hany Hassan. 2007. Improving Named Entity Translation by Exploiting Comparable and Parallel Corpora. In: Proceedings of the Conference on Recent Advances in Natural Language Processing (RANLP '07).

Hassan, Hany, and Jeffrey Sorensen. 2005. An integrated approach for Arabic-English named entity translation. In Proceedings of the ACL Workshop on Computational Approaches to Semitic Languages, Semitic '05, ACL:87-93,

Heintz Ilana..2008. Arabic Language Modeling with Finite State Transducers. In Proc. of the ACL-08 :

HLT Student Research Workshop, ACL, Columbus, Ohio, p. 37-42.

Hermjakob, Ulf, Kevin Knight, and Hal Daumé III. 2008. Name Translation in Statistical Machine Translation - Learning When to Transliterate. Proc. of ACL-08 : 389-397

Hkiri Emna, Mallat Souheyl, and Zrigui Mounir.2017.Constructing a Lexicon of Arabic-English Named Entity using SMT and Semantic Linked Data. IAJIT, vol.6, to appear November 2017.

Hkiri Emna, Mallat Souheyl, and Zrigui Mounir, 2016. Events Automatic Extraction from Arabic Texts. IJIRR, vol. 6(1), pp. 36-51.

Hkiri Emna, Mallat Souheyl, and Zrigui Mounir.2015.Improving coverage of rule based NER systems," ICTA, pp.1-6.

Hkiri Emna, Mallat Souheyl, and Zrigui Mounir.2015a.Automating Event Recognition for SMT Systems. ICCCI, pp.494-502.

Jiang, Long, Zhou, Ming, Chien, Lee-Feng. 2007. Named Entity Translation with Web Mining and Transliteration. In: Proceedings of the 20th International Joint Conferenceon Artificial Intelligence:1629-1634

Mehdi M. Kashani, Simon Fraser, Eric joanis, George Foster, Fred Popowich 2007. Integration of an Arabic transliteration module into a statistical machine translation system.

Lafferty, John, Andrew McCallum, and Fernando CN Pereira. 2001. Conditional random fields: Probabilistic models for segmenting and labeling sequence data.

Ling, Wang, Calado, Pável, Martins, Bruno 2011. Named Entity Translation using Anchor Texts. In: Proceedings of the International Workshop on Spoken Language Translation (IWSLT).

Moore Robert C. 2003. Learning Translations of Named-Entity Phrases from Parallel Corpora. In: In Proc. Of Eacl: 259-266.

Nasredine Semmar, Saadane Houda.2013. Using Transliteration of Proper Names from Arabic to Latin Script to Improve English-Arabic Word Alignment. IJCNLP :1022-1026, 2013.

PAL, Santanu, Kumar Naskar, Sudip, Pecina, Pavel, 2010. Handling Named Entities and Compound Verbs in Phrase-Based Statistical Machine Translation. In: Proceedings of the COLING 2010 Workshop on Multiword Expressions: from Theory to Applications (MWE 2010):46-54,

Zhang, Min, Haizhou Li, Kumaran Ming L. 2011. Report of NEWS2011 Machine Transliteration Shared Task. In: Proceedings of 2011 Named Entities Workshop. Chang Mai, Thailand.

#ActuallyDepressed: Characterization of Depressed Tumblr Users' Online Behavior from Rules Generation Machine Learning Technique

Czarina Rae C. Cahutay

University of the Philippines Cebu

Gorordo Avenue, Lahug, Cebu City

czarinacahutay@gmail.com

Aileen Joan O. Vicente

University of the Philippines Cebu

Gorordo Avenue, Lahug, Cebu City

aovicente@up.edu.ph

Abstract

The ubiquitous data provided by social networking sites paved the way for researchers to understand netizens behavior with psychological ailments such as depression. However, most of these researches are aimed at classifying users with depression using blackbox algorithms such as SVM. This does not allow data exploration or further understanding the characteristics of depressed individuals. This research aims to characterize depressed Tumblr users online behavior from rules generation . Characterization is done by collecting affective, social, cognitive and linguistic style markers collected from the respondents posts. Rules are then generated from these features using CN2 algorithm — a rules generating machine learning technique. The rules are analyzed and are compared with observations in prior literature on depressive behavior. We observed that depressed respondents in Tumblr have more photo content in posts rather than just pure textual posts, posts are more negative, and there is an evident use of self-referencing words. These characteristics are also evident in offline behavior of depressed individuals based on prior literature

Keywords: Depression, Characterization, Rules Generation, CN2 Algorithm

1. Introduction

According to the World Health Organization (WHO) (2001), depression is a serious mental issue and may be the second leading cause of disease by 2020. Amy Courtney (2014) argues that blogging reduces the symptoms brought about depression. Blogging allows the public to access and comment on such work, allowing additional psychological benefits.

Microblogging is an easier way of blogging that allows users to create short contents shared with an audience in real-time. This creates an easier and more convenient way of sharing content and information through the web (Nations, 2015). Contents vary from text, to visual, audio, audiovisual and even the use of links to redirect to other websites. This study aims to characterize the online behavior of depressed individuals using machine learning technique. Further, this research is guided by the following questions:

RQ1. What are the characteristics of depressed individuals on Tumblr in terms of their affective, behavioral, cognitive, and linguistic style attributes?

RQ2. How do these characteristics compare to offline behavior of depressed individuals in literature? Are they any different?

This study focuses on Tumblr because there have not been a lot of studies focusing on adolescents social media postings. Other studies on depression online are focused on an adult age group. Moreover, we find that because Tumblr allows anonymity of users there might be a more genuine response with regards to their posting and the results that we gather since they are not bound to their true identity in person similar to the study of Warner et al (2016).

The research covers 17 features of depressed individuals that are explored in other studies as classification problems. With these 17 features, 13 are coming from the posts, while the other 4 are basic information about the user (age, civil status, highest education attained and gender).

Despite a number of studies correlating with depression, we extracted features from 4 different processes or style attributes. These are: (1) affective, (2) social, (3) cognitive, and (4) linguistic. In other studies (Reece, 2016; De Choudhury, 2014; Moreno, 2011), only cognitive and linguistic patterns have been extracted. By extending the depression studies to include its social and affective process and allowing a more varied set of attributes, this research aims to create a wholistic characterization of such users.

2. Background and Related Work

2.1. Depression Studies on Social Media

A prominent work by De Choudhury et al (2013) reveals how depression can be predicted in twitter based on linguistic patterns. The researchers crowdsourced labels as ground truth data for Major Depressive Disorder (MDD). Using Amazon's Mechanical Turk interface, they successfully design human intelligence task for crowdworkers to take standardized clinical depression survey.

The researchers used a CESD questionnaire as a primary tool for determining depression levels which is a self-report scale to measure depressive symptoms. The range of the score of this scale varies from 0 - 60.

Another study by Hu et al (2015) explored on Predicting Depression of Social Media User on Different Observation Windows. The study is done to predict a user's depression based on Weibo data, thus building a regression model to predict the CES-D score of any user. The study featured around 900 features but deemed only 200 to be used. The goal of the study by Hu et al (2015) only considered the accuracy and performance of the regression models that the researchers have developed without taking focus on the specific behaviors of such depressed individuals.

2.2. Characterization Methods in Social Media Studies

There are a number of researches that aim to understand or characterize various types of behavior and phenomena on social media. Most of these characterization methods involve deriving patterns from statistical data such as means and p-values.

To describe their posting patterns, they create Cumulative Distribution Functions (CDF) of different variables. They focus on the variables such as popularity, reciprocity, retweet_ratio, url_ratio, mention_ratio, hashtag_ratio. Moreso, they create a heatmap that shows the tweet frequencies for different days and hours on a four-month period. They answer research questions they have identified in their study from their characterization.

A notable characterization study was made by De Choudhury et al (2015) on characterizing anorexia on Tumblr. By using the Tumblr API, they collect 55,334 public language posts from 18,923 unique blogs. They manually examined these posts and obtained a list of 28 tags relating to eating disorder and anorexia.

They characterize Tumblr through affective, social, cognitive and linguistic style processes to determine the features used. By using statistical methods such as p-scores and z-scores, they were able to translate qualitative data into quantitative data.

The features of the depression studies of De Choudhury et al (2013) and Hu et al (2015) focus on blackbox algorithms such as SVM where the understanding of these features are not explored in detail. These aforementioned studies have focused on predicting and not understanding the behavior of such users.

3.   Methodology

This research is developed through understanding the behavior of such users through a rule generation machine learning technique using a Sequential Covering Algorithm. The rules generated are analyzed further to get characteristics of the online behavior of depressed individuals.

3.1.   Data Collection

Tags such as #depressed, #actuallydepressed, #depressing, #depression, and #actuallyborderline are used to initially gather information about depressive posts. The tags are used to retrieve other tags associated with depression. Tags that do not necessarily characterize or which may not automatically correlate with depression such as #sad, #family, #words are removed from the set of tags so that the tags only pertaining to depression or its types are used. We only include the tags that are associated with depression or its symptoms such as feeling suicidal.

The initial set of usernames are collected through crawling the tags and posts during the initial data collection. An invitation is sent to these pre-processed users to answer the survey which contains the Center for Epidemiologic Studies Depression (CESD) Scale (http://cesd-r.com/) and Primary Health Questionnaire - 2 (PHQ-2) questionnaires. Only processed users who post

English content that has posts with tags correlated to depression are used in this study.

The information collected from the users are the posts coming from the first 20 pages of their accounts. The number of posts ranges from 100 to 228 posts per user depending on the individual layouts done by the user on their webpages. Tumblr allows users to customize their profiles according to their liking thus there is no specific number of posts per page.

A set of 20 tags collected from tag-crawling are used to gather information about depressive posts. 447 users are contacted through the instant messaging feature on Tumblr. These users have been initially screened to meet the corpus requirements that they: (1) only post English-content posts, and (2) have posted media in their microblogs with a tag correlating with depression. Of the 447 messaged users, only 130 users responded. It is expected that a larger number of responses will be categorized as depressed as the data collection is aimed at collecting posts from depressed individuals.

The survey responses gathered from 130 respondents are analyzed to be able to ascertain that the respondents are really depressed. From the 130 respondents, 70 are actually depressed, 19 are not depressed , and 41 are invalid.

3.2.   Feature Extraction

Affective, cognitive, social and linguistic features are retrieved from the collected data of these users.

Affective processes are feelings, responses (usually quantified as positive or negative), emotion-laden behavior and beliefs (StateUniversity.com, 2016). For affective processes, the positive, negative and neutral reaction from data collected from these users is measured through subjectivity and positivity. Using the NTLK library from python, we attach subjectivity and positivity scores to the dataset. Positivity is a range from -1 to 1 determining the emotion generated from the text. A lower positivity score would mean that the post shows more negative emotion a post has based on the NTLK. Subjectivity is based on the emotive expression being detected from the posts. It is a range from 0 to 1, where 0 determines that the post is more objective.

For cognitive processes, we measure the user posting and behavior. There are six types of measures that are used: (1) self-referencing (I, me, my, etc.) which is also one of the many signs and symptoms of depression (Segrin, 2000), (2) average number of articles (a, an, the) a feature also used in the study of Hu et al (2015), (3) big words defined as greater than 6 letters, also used in the study of Hu et al (2015). We also consider the words that are (4) Social and personal concerns pertaining to, family, friends, work and home.

Social Processes are collected through the following measures: (1) gender of the individual, (2) level of education, (3) civil status, as these three components are linked to determining if the person is more prone to depression based on prior research (Ross & Mirowsky, 1989), (4) Number of photo posts (Segrin, 2000) is also collected as this determines whether these individuals prefer posting content with photos, (5) the average difference between each post which determines how much the user interacts with the set of followers that he has, and determines how often he shares content.

Linguistic Features are extracted through (1) verbal fluency as the number of words in a post, (2) number of sentences in a post, (3) number of unique tags in a post which would determine how specific the user is using the tags to determine a specific post.

3.3. Characterization Using Rule Extraction

This study will explore rule extraction through a Sequential Covering Algorithm (CN2) for rule generation. A free open-source software, Orange (https://orange.biolab.si/) developed by the University of Ljubljana, is used to implement the algorithm. The algorithm is provided with nominal and numeric features and a target variable of 0 or 1 that indicates whether or not the user is depressed.

The CN2 Algorithm was developed by Clark and Niblett in 1989 as an improved version of the ID3 and AQ algorithm that are used for rules generation and tree generating algorithms. CN2 algorithm uses entropy to determine the best complex found. A complex is a condition that when satisfied, will minimize the number of examples that the algorithm needs to explore to determine the label of the class. Rules are determined by an if-then condition where the complex and labels complete the condition, if <complex> then predict <label> where <complex>. The algorithm determines the new complex by finding the set of examples that the complex covers. The entropy function prefers a large number of examples of a single class with a few examples of another class, resulting that these complexes perform well on the training data.

CN2 rule induction results in an ordered or unordered list of if-then rules, removing the items in the training data that are captured by the consecutive set of rules, finishing off with a sequence of if-then statements that determine the label of the data. The heuristics used by the CN2 algorithm uses entropy to determine the *best complex* found. A complex is a condition that when satisfied, will minimize the number of examples that the algorithm needs to explore to determine the label of the class. Rules are determined by an if-then condition where the complex and labels complete the condition, if *<complex>* then predict *<label>* where *<complex>*. The algorithm determines the new complex by finding the set of examples that the complex covers.

3.4. Rule Validation and Rule Interpretation

Orange (http://orange.biolab.si/) has a built-in Test and Score function that offers a "leave one out" testing method. Although the study is not aiming for classification, the validation is needed to verify if the rules generated by the CN2 Algorithm are quality rules with good performance based from the data. The entire dataset is used in both training and testing due to the limited number of respondents.

The testing validation used by the Orange (http://orange.biolab.si/) software returns recall, precision and F1-score. The three being the most commonly used testing validations for classification problems. This would also help in determining our confidence with the rules that were derived by the CN2 Algorithm to correctly understand the data.

3.5. External Validation

The general patterns on the findings of the data are discussed in detail and and understood in the context of depression. An attempt to compare such retrieved behavior with offline behavior of the patients is also be explored to answer the research question presented prior to the specific objectives.

4. Results and Discussion

4.1. Dataset Description

Based on the collected data from Tumblr users, most of the depressed Tumblr users are at the ages of 16-19. The distribution of these respondents can be found in Figure 4.1.

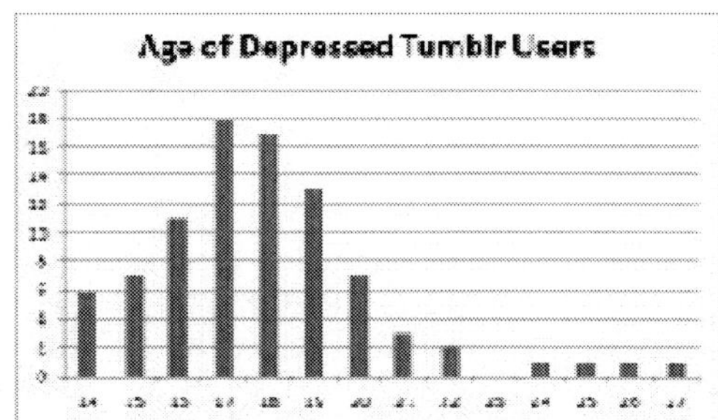

Figure 4.1. Age distribution of Depressed Tumblr Users

The age distribution would suggest that most of these users lie at the high school age group. Most of the depressed user respondents high school level as their highest educational degree attained.

It would also hold that these depressed Tumblr users would have similar civil status. Thus, it shows that only 2 out of the 70 depressed users are married while the rest are single.

The gender distribution of the depressed respondents is found in Figure 4.2. Depressed respondents are predominantly female. It is followed by other genders composed of the following genders: bisexual, agender, genderfluid, agendertransexual, genderflux, non-binary males and females, and cisgender.

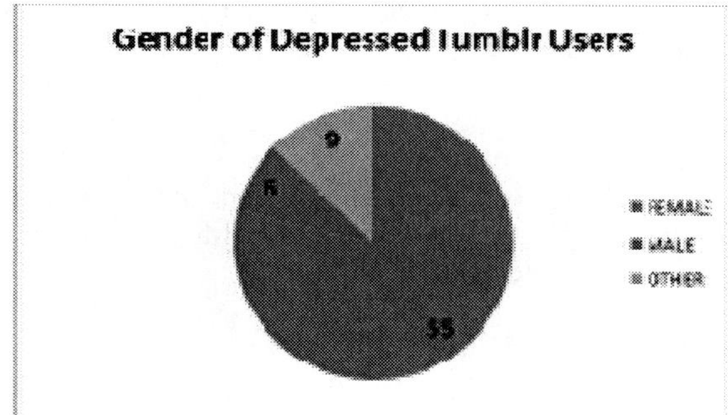

Figure 4.2 Different Genders of Depressed Tumblr Users

General descriptions of the features used in this study are described in the succeeding tables.

Table 4.1 Affective Processes: Polarity and Subjectivity of User Posts

	Polarity	Subjectivity	Polarity Range	Subjectivity Range
Non-Depressed	0.108752	0.300021	-0.00672 to 0.327344	0.06008 to 0.502567
Depressed	0.065096	0.22518	-0.04871 to 0.180963	0.02293 to 0.465965

Table 4.2 Social Processes: Posting Frequency and Photo Use

	Average Time Difference	Average percentage of posts with photo	Average number of photos per photo post
Non-Depressed	1393.913	0.408430	1.011022
Depressed	1165.601	0.625631	1.015832

Table 4.3 Cognitive Processes: Self-referencing, Articles and Themes Used

	Average self-referencing words	Average articles used	Average number the theme was mentioned
Non-Depressed	1.190897	1.947048	0.072669
Depressed	0.782567	1.54454	0.049233

Table 4.4 Linguistic Processes: Form and Context of User Posts

	Average tags per post	Average number of words more than 6 letters	Average number of sentences per post	Average number of words per post	Total number of tags
Non-Depressed	3.41023	11.90891	2.260369	41.22556	137.8421
Depressed	1.95896	7.700895	1.502773	36.33325	86.1

4.2. Respondents

Of the 447 messaged users, only 130 users responded. It is expected that a larger number of responses would be categorized as depressed as the data collection is aimed at collecting posts from depressed individuals.

Based on the analysis of the survey responses of the 130 respondents, 70 are actually depressed, 19 are not depressed and 41 were invalid. Quality responses are achieved by two measures:

a. The results for both PHQ-2 and CESD-R should be the same. That is, if a user scores depressed on the PHQ-2 scales, the user must also score similarly on the CESD-R scale.

b. The control question in between the CESD-R questionnaire should be correctly answered to eliminate the responses from respondents who did not read the questions carefully giving dishonest answers.

Other responses have also been considered invalid even if they passed both quality measures because their Tumblr blogs are private and they requested to keep its privacy.

4.3. Tags Used

Although the tags that have been used to retrieve the pool of respondents were related to depression, a number of non-depressed users (19 out of 130 respondents) have also responded.

Figure 4.4a is a tag cloud containing the top 25 tags that are used by depressed users while Figure 4.4b contains that top 25 tags used by non-depressed users. Each tag is associated with a weight that corresponds to the number of times the tag has been used. The larger the tag appears on the tag cloud, the more frequent it has been used.

Depressed users often incorporate tags in their posts that were used in retrieving the usernames of potential respondents. Most of their tags present depressive content and often employs the word depression.

On the other hand, non-depressed users do not have any of the 20 tags that the study used in order to retrieve the potential respondents. The tags are rarely used and are overpowered by the tags found in Figure 4.4b that they are frequently using. Non-depressed users often use depression-associated tags within their posts encouraging depressed users to seek help or when only a limited number of posts are aimed at depression. Some of these non-depressed users may be only mildly depressed depending on the scores of both PHQ-2 and CESD-R questionnaires.

(a)   (b)

Figure 4.4 Tag Clouds Generated from the Top 25 Tags Used by (a) Depressed and (b) Non-Depressed Users

4.4. Rules Generated

Six (6) unordered rules are generated from CN2 Rule Induction given maximum coverage of 4% (3 out of 89) and a statistical significance of 1 (default alpha). As this study focuses on the behavior of depressed Tumblr users, only the rules with a class label of 1 are analyzed. The rules can be found in Table 4.6 which contains two columns that describe the rules: (1) if <complex>, (2) then <class>. The complex contains the condition that is to be satisfied in order for one to receive a label of a class.

Table 4.5 Unordered Rules

	IF <complex>	THEN <class>
1	polarity >= 0.163177578	label = 0
2	time elapsed >= 163.8604768	label = 0
3	total tags >= 13	label = 0
4	has image >= 0.8739	label = 1
5	polarity <= 0.090295132	label = 1
6	self referring words <= 3.225	label = 1

Several different types of features were included in the study in the hope of gathering as much information about depressed online users. Apparently, only three (3) features significantly characterizes depressed online users covering affective, social and cognitive behaviors.

The most prominent characteristic based on the rules generated would be that depressed Tumblr users most likely posts with photo content. Reece and Danforth (2016) support this characteristic in their study where users can be found depressed based on their photo posts. Moreso, this study would support this such that depressed individuals also post more images frequently as compared to non-depressed individuals.

Polarity is found as a feature in both depressed and non-depressed individuals. However, a polarity closer to 1 would entail a more positive post while a polarity score closer to 0 would mean a more negative post. From the rules, depressed individuals tend to post more negative posts as compared to non-depressed individuals. The idea of depressive realism explored by Burton (2012) would reflect a depressive characteristic that depressed individuals often have a negative perspective in life allowing them to be more objective. A study by Gotlib and Joormann (2010) find that depression is characterized by an increase in the elaboration of negative information, difficulties in disengaging from negative which may be reflective in their posts.

Lastly, the use of self referring words can also characterize depressed individuals. Despite the depressed Tumblr users average use of self-referring words being 0.7, the threshold retrieved from the rules is at 3. Because of this, it is enough to say that depressed users highly use self-referencing words. There have been linguistic markers of depression as studied by Hargitay, et. al(2007). These linguistic markers are found the self-narratives of depressed individuals that feature the pronouns 'I' and 'myself'. The linguistic markers can be seen as "reflecting pervasive and enduring psychological processes" (Hargitay et al, 2007). Another study by Rude et al (2004), depressed individuals used the word "I" more than never depressed participants.

4.5.   Rule Validation Results

While this study is not intended to classify, we find it imperative to assure the quality of the rules. After a leave-one-out cross validation, the classification performance metrics are generated. The summary is found in Table 4.7

Table 4.6. Evaluation Metrics

F1 Score	Precision	Recall
0.885	0.802	0.986

The F1-Score of 88.5% is a relatively good performance metric that can signify a relatively strong confidence in the rules generated and consequently, its interpretation. The skewness of the data where there are 70 depressed users and only 19 non-depressed users may be accounted for the low precision and recall scores. This is because the data gathering is targeted towards users who have posted depressed content based on the gathered tags.

5.   Conclusion

Depression is a pressing issue, and will continue to haunt individuals making it one of the possible leading causes of deaths in adolescents by 2020. The study observed the posting patterns of 89 Tumblr users, 70 of which are depressed according to the PHQ-2 and CESD-R scales. The mean age of the individuals who participated in the study was between 16-19 years old.

Therefore, a depressed Tumblr user is characterized by photo content in posts rather than just pure textual posts, posts are more negative, and the evident use of self-referencing words.

The study concludes that it is possible to use a rule generation machine learning technique in characterizing online behavior.

6.   Recommendations

This study only covers the characterization of 70 depressed Tumblr users. Moreover, we have not covered linguistic features that are evident in depressed Tumblr users. Increasing the number of respondents and the number of depressed user posts in the study will allow us to cover other processes and features that are not year clear in this study.

Classification problems that have been using black box algorithm methods such as the work of Hu et al (2015) use 200-900 different features. This study only focuses on 17 features so increasing the number of features would allow more characterization rules to be evident.

References

All about depression: Diagnosis. (2013). Retrieved December 7, 2016, from All About Depression, http://www.allaboutdepression.com/dia_03.html

American Psychological Association. (2016). Center for epidemiological studies depression (CESD). Retrieved December 7, 2016, from American Psychological Association, http://www.apa.org/pi/about/publications/caregivers/practice-settings/assessment/tools/depression-scale.aspx

American Psychological Association. (2016). Patient health questionnaire (PHQ-9 & PHQ-2). Retrieved December 09, 2016, from http://www.apa.org/pi/about/publications/caregivers/practice-settings/assessment/tools/patient-health.aspx

Beattie, G.S. (2005, November). Social Causes of Depression. Retrieved May 31, 2017, from http://www.personalityresearch.org/papers/beattie.html

Burton, N. (2012, June 5). Depressive Realism. Retrieved May 31, 2017, from https://www.psychologytoday.com/blog/hide-and-seek/201206/depressive-realism

Clark, P., Niblett, T. (1988, October 25). The CN2 induction Algorithm. Retireved May 10, 2017, from https://pdfs.semanticscholar.org/766f/e3586bda3f36cbcce809f5666d2c2b96c98c.pdf

De Choudhury, M., Counts, S., Horvits, E., & Hoff, A. (2014). Characterizing and Predicting Postpartum Depression from Shared Facebook Data.

De Choudhury, M., Gamon, M., Couns, S., & Horvitz, E. (2013). Predicting Depression via Social Media.

Gotlib IH, Kasch KL, Traill S, Joormann J, Arnow BA, Johnson SL. (2010) Coherence and specificity of information-processing biases in depression and social phobia. J Abnorm Psychol. 2004;113(3): 386-98.

Gotlib, I. H., & Hammen, C. L. (1992). Psychological aspects of depression: Toward a cognitive-interpersonal integration. New York: Wiley.

Gotlib IH, Joormann J. Cognition and depression: current status and future directions. Annu Rev Clin Psychol. 2010;6:285-312.

Hu, Quan, Ang Li, Fei Heng, Jianpeng Li, and Tingshao Zhu. "Predicting Depression of Social Media User on Different Observation Windows." 2015 IEEE/WIC/ACM International Conference on Web Intelligence and Intelligent Agent Technology (WI-IAT) (2015): n. pag. Web.

Koopman, C., Ismailji, T., Holmes, D., Classen, C., Palesh, O., & Wales, T. (2005, March). The Effects of Expressive Writing on Pain, Depression and Posttraumatic Stress Disorder Symptoms in Survivors of Intimate Partner Violence.

Lowe, N. (n.d.).Social Support Networks and Their Role in Depression. Retrieved May 31, 2017, from http://www.personalityresearch.org/papers/beattie.html

Ramirez-Esparza, N., Chung, C.K., Kacewicz, E., & Pennebaker, J.W. (2008). The psychology of word use in depression forums in English and in Spanish: Testing two text analytic approaches. Association for the Advancement of Artificial Intelligence, 102-108.

Reece, A., Reagan, A., LM Lix, K., Dodds, P. S., Danforth, C., & Langer, E. (2016, August). Forecasting the onset and course of mental illness with Twitter data.

Smith, M., Segal, R., & Segal, J. (2016, November). How to recognize the symptoms and get effective help. Retrieved November 15, 2016, from http://www.helpguide.org/articles/depression/depression-signs-and-symptoms.htm

StateUniversity.com. (2016). Individual differences - Affective and Conative processes. Retrieved December 7, 2016, from http://education.stateuniversity.com/pages/2081/Individual-Differences-AFFECTIVE-CONATIVE-PROCESSES.html

Thapar, A. K., Collishaw, S., & Pine, D. S. (2012). Depression in adolescence. , 379(9820), . Retrieved from https://www.ncbi.nlm.nih.gov/pmc/articles/PMC3488279/

World Health Organization. (2001). The World Health Report 2001: Mental Health: New Understanding, New Hope. Retrieved from http://www.who.int/whr/2001/en/whr01_en.pdf

A Parallel Recurrent Neural Network for Language Modeling with POS Tags

Chao Su[1,3]**, Heyan Huang**[1,2]**, Shumin Shi**[1,2,*]**, Yuhang Guo**[1]**, Hao Wu**[1]

[1]School of Computer Science and Technology, Beijing Institute of Technology,
Beijing 100081, China
[2]Beijing Engineering Research Center of High Volume Language Information Processing and
Cloud Computing Applications, Beijing 100081, China
[3]Beijing Advanced Innovation Center for Imaging Technology, Capital Normal University,
Beijing 100048, China
`{suchao,hhy63,bjssm,guoyuhang,wuhao123}@bit.edu.cn`

Abstract

Language models have been used in many natural language processing applications. In recent years, the recurrent neural network based language models have defeated the conventional n-gram based techniques. However, it is difficult for neural network architectures to use linguistic annotations. We try to incorporate part-of-speech features in recurrent neural network language model, and use them to predict the next word. Specifically, we proposed a parallel structure which contains two recurrent neural networks, one for word sequence modeling and another for part-of-speech sequence modeling. The state of part-of-speech network helped improve the word sequence's prediction. Experiments show that the proposed method performs better than the traditional recurrent network on perplexity and is better at reranking machine translation outputs.[1]

1 Introduction

Language models (LMs) are crucial parts of many natural language processing applications, such as automatic speech recognition, statistical machine translation, and natural language generation. Language modeling aims to predict the next word given context or to give the probability of a word sequence in textual data. In the past decades, n-gram based modeling techniques were most commonly used in such NLP applications. However, the recurrent neural network based language model (RNNLM) and

its extensions (Mikolov et al., 2010; Mikolov et al., 2011) have received a lot of attention and achieved the new state of the art results since 2010. The most important advantage of RNNLM is that it has the potential to model unlimited size of context, due to its recurrent property. That is to say, the hidden layer has a recurrent connection to itself at previous timestep.

Part-of-speech (POS) tags capture the syntactic role of each word, and has been proved to be useful for language modeling (Kneser and Ney, 1993; A. Heeman, 1998; Galescu and Ringger, 1999; Wang and Harper, 2002). Jelinek (1985) pointed out that we can replace the classes with POS tags in language model. Kneser and Ney (1993) incorporated POS tags into n-gram LM and got 37 percents improvement. But they got only 10 percents improvement with classes through clustering. A. Heeman (1998) redefined the objective of automatic speech recognition: to get both the word sequence and the POS sequence. His experiments showed 4.2 percent reduction on perplexity over classes.

It is common to build probabilistic graphical models using many different linguistic annotations (Finkel et al., 2006). However, the problem to combine neural architectures with conventional linguistic annotations seems hard. This is because neural architectures lack flexibility to incorporate achievements from other NLP tasks (Ji et al., 2016). To address the problem, (Ji et al., 2016) used a latent variable recurrent neural network (LVRNN) to construct language models with discourse relations. LVRNN was proposed by Chung et al. (2015) to model variables observed in sequential data.

---

*Corresponding author

[1]Our code is available at `https://github.com/chao-su/prnnlm`

31st Pacific Asia Conference on Language, Information and Computation (PACLIC 31), pages 140–147
Cebu City, Philippines, November 16-18, 2017

Inspired by the POS language models and the LVRNN models above, we use POS features to improve the performance of RNNLM. We assume that if we know the next POS tag, the search range to predict the next word will be shrinked; and the next POS is closely related with the POS sequence that has been seen before. Not the same as Ji et al. (2016), who used a latent variable to model the language annotation, we designed a parallel RNN structure, which consists two RNNs to model the word sequence and POS sequence respectively. And further the state of POS network has an impact on the word network.

In summary our main contributions are:

- We propose to model words and POS tags simultaneously by using a parallel RNN structure that consists of two recurrent neural networks, word RNN and POS RNN.

- We propose that the current state of the word network is conditioned on the current word, the previous hidden state, and also the state of POS network.

- We demonstrate the performance of our model by computing lower perplexity. We conducted our experiments on three different corpora, including Penn TreeBank, Switchboard, and BBC corpora.

The rest parts of this paper are organized as follows. Section 2 introduces the background techniques, including RNNLM and evaluation for language models. Section 3 elaborates our POS tag language model. Section 4 reports the experimental results. Section 5 reviews related work and Section 6 concludes the paper.

2　Background

In this section, we introduce the background techniques on which our work is based on. Recurrent neural network language models (RNNLMs) are important bases of our work. And the introduced evaluation method (perplexity) is used in this paper.

2.1　RNN Language Model

Mikolov et al. (2010) proposed to use recurrent neural network (RNN) to construct language model. By

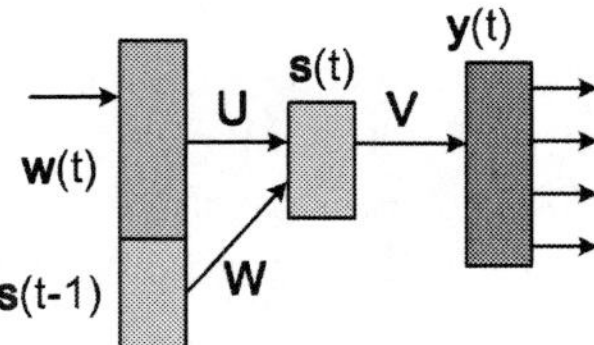

Figure 1: A simple Recurrent Neural Network.

using RNN, context information can cycle inside the network for arbitrarily long time. Though it is also claimed that learning long-term dependencies by stochastic gradient descent can be quite difficult. We simply introduce Mikolov et al. (2010)'s recurrent neural network language model and its extensions (Mikolov et al., 2011) here.

We assume that a sentence consists of words, and each word is represented as $y(t)$, where t is current time step and $y(t) \in Vocab$. The architecture of RNNLM is shown in Fig. 1. Input to the network at time t is $w(t)$ and $s(t-1)$, where $w(t)$ is a one hot vector representing the current word $y(t)$, and $s(t-1)$ is the hidden layer s at previous time $t-1$. The hidden layer $s(t)$ is the current state of the network. Output layer $y(t)$ represents probability distribution of next word. Hidden and output layers are computed as:

$$s_i(t) = f\left(\sum_j w_j(t)u_{ij} + \sum_k s_k(t-1)w_{ik}\right) \tag{1}$$

$$y_k(t) = g\left(\sum_i s_i(t)v_{ki}\right) \tag{2}$$

where $f(z)$ is sigmoid activation function:

$$f(z) = \frac{1}{1+e^{-z}} \tag{3}$$

and $g(z)$ is softmax function:

$$g(z_m) = \frac{e^{z_m}}{\sum_k e^{z_k}} \tag{4}$$

In 2011, Mikolov et al. (2011) proposed some extensions of RNNLM. Those include a training algorithm for recurrent network called backpropagation through time (BPTT), and two speedup techniques. One is factorizing the output layer by class layer, and the other is adding a compression layer between the hidden and output layers to reduce the size of the weight matrix V. In this paper, we use two extensions, BPTT and class layer. But we still use the simple RNNLM architecture in figures for simplicity.

2.2 Evaluation

The quality of language models is evaluated both intrinsically by perplexity and extrinsically by quality of reranking machine translation outputs. The perplexity (PPL) of a word sequence w is defined as

$$PPL = \sqrt[K]{\prod_{i=1}^{K} \frac{1}{P(w_i|w_{1...i-1})}} \quad (5)$$
$$= 2^{-\frac{1}{K}\sum_{i=1}^{K} \log_2 P(w_i|w_{1...i-1})}$$

Perplexity can be easily evaluated and the model which yields the lowest perplexity is in some sense the closest to the true model which generated the data.

Language model is an essential part of statistical machine translation systems, for measuring how likely it is that a translation hypothesis would be uttered by a native speaker (Koehn, 2010). Under the same conditions, a better language model brings a better translation system. Thus, we also evaluate our language model by evaluating the translation system who uses it. We use the most popular automatic evaluation metric for translation system, BLEU (Bilingual Evaluation Understudy) (Papineni et al., 2002); higher is better.

3 Parallel RNN LM with POS Feature

The traditional RNNLM models word sequences but ignores other linguistic knowledge. POS is such a kind of linguistic knowledge. It is easy to acquire with high annotation accuracy. We now present a parallel RNN structure over sequences of words and POS tag information. In this structure, we train two RNNs simultaneously, one for word sequence and another for POS sequence. We integrate the state of POS RNN with the word RNN.

3.1 Parallel RNN

The structure of the parallel RNN is shown in Fig. 2. The parallel RNN consists of two RNNs, word

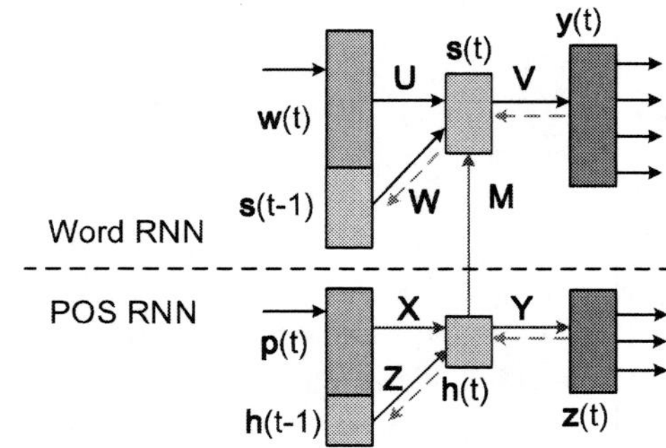

Figure 2: Structure of the Parallel RNN

RNN and POS RNN. The word RNN is almost the same as the traditional RNN, except that its hidden state $s(t)$ is also affected by an output from the state of POS RNN. The input layer of POS RNN consists two parts. One is the current POS tag $p(t)$ and the other is the previous state of POS RNN. The hidden layer of POS RNN represents the current state of the network. The output layer represents the probability distribution of the next POS tag.

We can see that the structure of the word RNN is similar with traditional RNN. The hidden layer of RNNLM theoretically contains all the information of the words those have been seen before. Similarly, the hidden layer of POS RNN contains the POS information in history. In order to use these information to predict the next word, we add a connection matrix between the hidden layers of word RNN and POS RNN.

In Fig. 2, the blue solid lines represent the forward computation, while the red dashed lines represent the back propagation of errors. Note that there is no error propagation from the hidden layer of word RNN to that of POS RNN. It is more likely that the latter affects the former like a latent variable in (Ji et al., 2016).

The hidden layer $h(t)$ and output layer $z(t)$ of POS RNN are computed as

$$h_i(t) = f\left(\sum_j p_j(t)x_{ij} + \sum_k h_k(t-1)z_{ik}\right) \quad (6)$$

142

$$z_k(t) = g\left(\sum_i h_i(t) y_{ki}\right) \qquad (7)$$

The hidden layer of word RNN should be affected by that of POS RNN. So it is computed as

$$s_i(t) = f\left(\sum_j w_j(t) u_{ij} + \sum_k s_k(t) w_{ik} + \sum_l h_l(t) m_{il}\right) \qquad (8)$$

3.2 Learning

In language model scenery, our purpose is to get the best word sequence. The training of the word RNN is the same as the traditional RNN. Though using the hidden layer of POS RNN to compute the state of the word RNN, we do not propagate the latter's error vector to the former. This is why we tend to treat the former also as a latent variable affecting the word sequence.

We train the POS RNN to maximize the log-likelihood function of the training data:

$$O = \sum_{i=1}^{T} \log d_{l_t}(t) \qquad (9)$$

where T is the total number of POS tags in training examples, and l_t is the index of the correct POS tag for the t'th sample. The error vector in the output layer $e_o(t)$ is computed as

$$e_o(t) = d(t) - z(t) \qquad (10)$$

where $d(t)$ is the one-hot target vector that represents the POS tag at time t.

We update the parameters of POS RNN using stochastic gradient descent method. For example, the matrix Y is updated as

$$y_{jk}(t+1) = y_{jk}(t) + h_j(t) e_{ok}(t)\alpha - y_{jk}(t)\beta \qquad (11)$$

where β is L2 regularization parameter. And the error vector propagated from the output layer to the hidden layer is

$$e_{hj}(t) = h_j(t)(1 - h_j(t)) \sum_i e_{oj}(t) y_{ij} \qquad (12)$$

The update of the matrices X and Z is similar to equation (11). The error vector propagated from the hidden layer to its previous is similar to equation (12).

4 Experiments

We evaluated the proposed model in two ways: using perplexity (PPL) and reranking machine translation outputs.

4.1 Perplexity Setup

We evaluated our model on three corpora, including Switchboard-1 Telephone Speech Corpus (SWB), Penn TreeBank (PTB)[2], and BBC[3]. The former two corpora was used by Ji et al. (2016), while the last one was used by Wang and Cho (2016). We took all their work as comparisons. We splitted all the corpora into train, valid, and test sets, just like Ji et al. (2016) and Wang and Cho (2016) did. Statistics of the corpora are listed in Table 1. We tokenized all the corpora with tokenizer written by Pidong Wang, Josh Schroeder, and Philipp Koehn [4], and POS tagged with the Stanford POS Tagger [5].

We implemented our model based on Mikolov's RNNLM Tookit[6]. We considered the value 100 for the hidden dimension, and 10K for the vocabulary size.

The POS tagger's tagset consists of 48 tags. We counted the times of each tag appeared in the BBC corpus and sorted them in descending order (see Table 2). To verify the effect of POS tags, we gradually expanded our tagset's size (5, 10, 15, 20, 25, 30, 35, 40, 45) in the experiments. The size of POS RNN's hidden layer was set to one-fifth of the tagset's size. For example, $varsize = 40$ represents that we use the first 39 tags in Table 2 and reduce other tags to the $OTHER$ tag and the hidden size of POS RNN is set to be $40/5 = 8$.

---

[2] LDC97S62 for SWB, and LDC99T42 for PTB

[3] http://mlg.ucd.ie/datasets/bbc.html

[4] https://github.com/moses-smt/mosesdecoder/blob/master/scripts/tokenizer/tokenizer.perl

[5] http://nlp.stanford.edu/software/tagger.shtml

[6] http://www.fit.vutbr.cz/~imikolov/rnnlm/

	SWB		PTB		BBC	
	#Sents	#Words	#Sents	#Words	#Sents	#Words
Train	211K	1.8M	37K	1M	37K	879K
Valid	3.5K	32K	3.6K	97K	2K	47K
Test	4.4K	38K	3.3K	91K	2.2K	51K

Table 1: Statistics of the Corpora SWB, PTB, and BBC

Order	POS	Times	Order	POS	Times
1	NN	121,359	21	"	11,010
2	IN	92,042	22	PRP$	8,939
3	NNP	88,331	23	"	7,961
4	DT	75,397	24	POS	7,711
5	JJ	52,851	25	:	5,219
6	NNS	47,003	26	FW	4,041
7	.	37,146	27	WDT	3,916
8	,	31,840	28	RP	3,583
9	VBD	31,575	29	JJR	2,990
10	VB	29,429	30	WP	2,865
11	RB	27,261	31	WRB	2,424
12	PRP	26,519	32	JJS	2,215
13	CC	22,554	33	NNPS	1,904
14	TO	22,440	34	EX	1,440
15	VBN	22,096	35	RBR	1,295
16	VBZ	20,795	36	$	1,127
17	CD	17,696	37	RBS	438
18	VBG	15,773	38	PDT	402
19	VBP	15,409	39	WP$	114
20	MD	11,015	OTHER		199

Table 2: Times of Each Tag Appeared in BBC Corpora

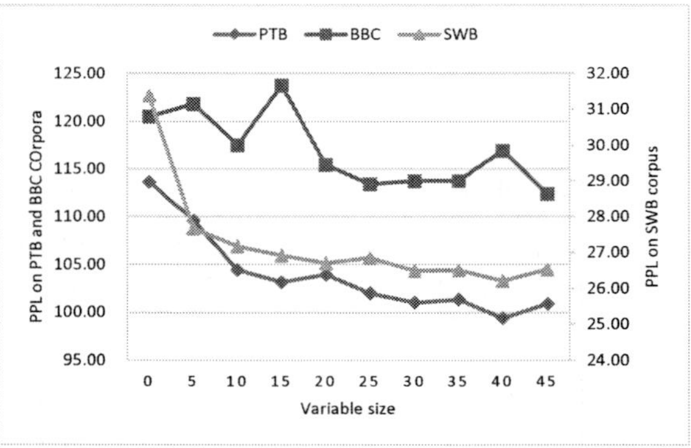

Figure 3: Perplexity Reduction with the Growth of Variable size

Model	SWB	PTB	BBC
5-gram	32.10	120.18	127.32
RNNLM	31.38	113.63	120.49
(Ji et al., 2016)	39.60	108.30	-
(Wang and Cho, 2016)	-	126.20	**105.60**
p-RNNLM	**26.20**	**99.36**	112.35
PPL reduction	16.5%	12.6%	6.8%

Table 3: Perplexity Comparison with Other Works

4.2 Perplexity Results

The perplexities of language modeling on the three corpora are summarized in Figure 3 and Table 3.

In Figure 3, we demonstrate the results using different number of most frequent POS tags, where the variable size is actually the size of POS RNN's hidden layer. Note that $varsize = 0$ represents a traditional RNNLM. We can see that the perplexity tends to reduce as the tagset size grows.

In Table 3, we compared our model with classic 5-gram model, Mikolov et al. (2010)'s RNNLM, Ji et al. (2016)'s, and Wang and Cho (2016)'s work. We can see that our parallel RNN (p-RNN) performs better than most of them except Wang and Cho (2016)'s work on BBC corpus. And our model gets 6.8%-16.5% PPL reduction over Mikolov et al. (2010)'s RNNLM.

4.3 MT Reranking Setup

We also performed reranking experiments on Chinese-English machine translation (MT) task. We evaluated the proposed parallel RNN language model by rescoring the 1000-best candidate translations produced by a phrase-based MT system. The decoder used was Moses(Koehn et al., 2007). The MT system was trained on FBIS (Foreign Broadcasting Information Service) corpus[7] containing about 250K sentence pairs and tuned with MERT (Minimum Error Rate Training) (Josef Och, 2003) on NIST MT02 test set. Our test sets included NIST

---

[7]LDC2003E14

MT 03, 04, and 05.

In reranking phase, we first performed MERT on two features, the MT score (got from MT system) and a LR score (the length ratio of the target language sentence to the source one), as a baseline. Both the RNNLM and p-RNNLM were trained on some news corpora[8] which contains about 2M sentences. We considered the values {100, 300, 500} for the hidden dimension of the word RNN, and 80K for the vocabulary size. We also performed POS tagging using the Stanford POS Tagger. We used the two trained models to rescore the 1000-best outputs from MT system and got RNNLM score and p-RNNLM score. Then we combine the two scores with MT score and LR score respectively to perform MERT to get their own weights. We tuned the weights for MT, LR, and RNNLM/p-RNNLM scores by using Z-MERT (Zaidan, 2009), which is a easy-to-use tool for MERT.

4.4 MT Reranking Results

The results for MT reranking is shown in Table 4. Both the RNN and p-RNN models outperform the baselines, Moses or MT+LR. The p-RNN model with 500 dimension size gets 0.59-1.04 BLEU improvement than MT+LR and at most 0.31 BLEU improvement than RNN model. Most of the improvements are statistically significant. The p-RNN model outperforms the RNN model on every test set with each dimension size.

5 Related Work

This paper draws on previous work language modeling including structured count-based and neural LMs.

5.1 Structured LMs

Efforts to incorporate linguistic annotations into language model include the structured LMs. Chelba et al. (1997) proposed a dependency language model using maximum entropy model. Chelba and Jelinek (1998) developed a language model that used syntactic structure to model long-distance dependen-

cies. Charniak (2001) assigned the probability to a word conditioned on the lexical head of its parent constituent. Peng and Roth (2016) developed two models that captured semantic frames and discourse information.

POS-based LM originated from class-based LM (Jelinek, 1985; F. Brown et al., 1992), since POS tags captured the syntactic role of each word and could be seen as the equivalence classes. Kneser and Ney (1993) reported a perplexity reduction when combined their model with POS tags. A. Heeman (1998) redefined the speech recognition problem to find the best both word and POS sequences and incorporated POS-based LM.

5.2 Neural LMs

Bengio et al. (2003) proposed to use artificial neural network to learn the probability of word sequences. The feedforward network they used has to use fixed length context to predict the next word. Mikolov et al. (2010) used recurrent neural network to encode temporal information for contexts with arbitrary lengths.

In recent years, there was an increasing number of research integrating knowledge into RNN. Mikolov and Zweig (2012) incorporated topic information as a feature layer into RNNLM. Ji et al. (2015) employed the hidden states of the previous sentence as contextual information for predicting words in the current sentence. Ji et al. (2016) modeled discourse relation with Latent Variable Recurrent Neural Network (LVRNN) for language models. Ahn et al. (2016) proposed a language model which combined knowledge graphs with RNN. Dieng et al. (2016) proposed a TopicRNN to capture the global topic information for language modeling.

6 Conclusions

We proposed a parallel RNN structure to model both word and POS tag sequences. The structure consists of two RNNs, one for words and another for POS tags. The connection between the two network's hidden layers enabled the POS information to help to improve the word prediction. The role of POS RNN's hidden layer is similar to that of the latent variable in Ji et al. (2016)'s work. The perplexity of LM trained based on that structure got a reduction of

---

[8]LDC2003E14, LDC2000T46, LDC2007T09, LDC2005T10, LDC2008T06, LDC2009T15, LDC2010T03, LDC2009T02, LDC2009T06, LDC2013T11, LDC2013T16, LDC2007T23, LDC2008T08, LDC2008T18, LDC2014T04, LDC2014T11, LDC2005T06, LDC2007E101, LDC2002E18

System	MT02	MT03	MT04	MT05
Moses	28.09	24.38	28.03	24.19
MT+LR	28.07	24.40	28.11	24.26
MT+LR+RNN-100	28.25	25.16**	28.48**	24.39*
MT+LR+p-RNN-100	28.46***+	25.23**	28.70***++	24.53***+
MT+LR+RNN-300	28.57*	25.16**	28.72**	24.50**
MT+LR+p-RNN-300	28.62***+	25.26**	28.85**+	24.79***++
MT+LR+RNN-500	28.48**	25.38**	28.72**	24.59**
MT+LR+p-RNN-500	**28.66*****+	**25.44****	**28.84*****+	**24.90*****++

Table 4: MT Reranking Results. */**: significantly better than Moses ($p < 0.05/0.01$); +/++: significantly better than MT+LR+RNN ($p < 0.1/0.05$)

6.8%-16.5%. We used the LM to rerank MT outputs and got improvement on BLEU score.

Next, we will explore the expandability of the parallel RNN structure. We need to incorporate more linguistic knowledge to improve the performance of neural networks.

Acknowledgments

This work was supported by the National Basic Research Program (973) of China (No. 2013CB329303), the National Natural Science Foundation of China (Nos. 61132009, 61671064, 61502035), and Beijing Advanced Innovation Center for Imaging Technology (BAICIT-2016007).

References

Peter A. Heeman, 1998. *Sixth Workshop on Very Large Corpora*, chapter POS Tagging versus Classes in Language Modeling.

Sungjin Ahn, Heeyoul Choi, Tanel Pärnamaa, and Yoshua Bengio. 2016. A neural knowledge language model. *CoRR*, abs/1608.00318.

Yoshua Bengio, Réjean Ducharme, Pascal Vincent, and Christian Janvin. 2003. A neural probabilistic language model. *Journal of Machine Learning Research*, 3:1137–1155.

Eugene Charniak. 2001. Immediate-head parsing for language models. In *Association for Computational Linguistic, 39th Annual Meeting and 10th Conference of the European Chapter, Proceedings of the Conference, July 9-11, 2001, Toulouse, France.*, pages 116–123. Morgan Kaufmann Publishers.

Ciprian Chelba and Frederick Jelinek. 1998. Exploiting syntactic structure for language modeling. In *Proceedings of the 36th Annual Meeting of the Association for Computational Linguistics and 17th International Conference on Computational Linguistics, COLING-ACL '98, August 10-14, 1998, Université de Montréal, Montréal, Quebec, Canada.*, pages 225–231. Morgan Kaufmann Publishers / ACL.

Ciprian Chelba, David Engle, Frederick Jelinek, Victor Jimenez, Sanjeev Khudanpur, Lidia Mangu, Harry Printz, Eric Ristad, Ronald Rosenfeld, Andreas Stolcke, and Dekai Wu. 1997. Structure and performance of a dependency language model. In *Fifth European Conference on Speech Communication and Technology, EUROSPEECH 1997, Rhodes, Greece, September 22-25.* ISCA.

Junyoung Chung, Kyle Kastner, Laurent Dinh, Kratarth Goel, Aaron C. Courville, and Yoshua Bengio. 2015. A recurrent latent variable model for sequential data. In *Advances in Neural Information Processing Systems 28: Annual Conference on Neural Information Processing Systems 2015, December 7-12, 2015, Montreal, Quebec, Canada*, pages 2980–2988.

Adji B. Dieng, Chong Wang, Jianfeng Gao, and John William Paisley. 2016. Topicrnn: A recurrent neural network with long-range semantic dependency. *CoRR*, abs/1611.01702.

Peter F. Brown, Peter V. deSouza, Robert L. Mercer, T. J. Watson, Vincent J. Della Pietra, and Jenifer C. Lai. 1992. Class-based n-gram models of natural language. *Computational Linguistics, Volume 18, Number 4, December 1992.*

Rose Jenny Finkel, D. Christopher Manning, and Y. Andrew Ng, 2006. *Proceedings of the 2006 Conference on Empirical Methods in Natural Language Processing*, chapter Solving the Problem of Cascading Errors: Approximate Bayesian Inference for Linguistic Annotation Pipelines, pages 618–626. Association for Computational Linguistics.

Lucian Galescu and Eric K. Ringger. 1999. Augmenting words with linguistic information for n-gram language models. In *Sixth European Conference on Speech Communication and Technology, EUROSPEECH 1999, Budapest, Hungary, September 5-9, 1999*. ISCA.

F. Jelinek. 1985. Self-organized language modeling for speech recognition. *Technical Report*.

Yangfeng Ji, Trevor Cohn, Lingpeng Kong, Chris Dyer, and Jacob Eisenstein. 2015. Document context language models. *CoRR*, abs/1511.03962.

Yangfeng Ji, Gholamreza Haffari, and Jacob Eisenstein. 2016. A latent variable recurrent neural network for discourse-driven language models. In *Proceedings of the 2016 Conference of the North American Chapter of the Association for Computational Linguistics: Human Language Technologies*, pages 332–342, San Diego, California, June. Association for Computational Linguistics.

Franz Josef Och. 2003. Minimum error rate training in statistical machine translation. In *Proceedings of the 41st Annual Meeting of the Association for Computational Linguistics*.

Reinhard Kneser and Hermann Ney. 1993. Improved clustering techniques for class-based statistical language modelling. In *Third European Conference on Speech Communication and Technology, EUROSPEECH 1993, Berlin, Germany, September 22-25, 1993*. ISCA.

Philipp Koehn, Hieu Hoang, Alexandra Birch, Chris Callison-Burch, Marcello Federico, Nicola Bertoldi, Brooke Cowan, Wade Shen, Christine Moran, Richard Zens, Chris Dyer, Ondrej Bojar, Alexandra Constantin, and Evan Herbst. 2007. Moses: Open source toolkit for statistical machine translation. In *Proceedings of the 45th Annual Meeting of the Association for Computational Linguistics Companion Volume Proceedings of the Demo and Poster Sessions*, pages 177–180. Association for Computational Linguistics.

Philip Koehn. 2010. *Statistical Machine Translation*. Cambridge University Press.

Tomas Mikolov and Geoffrey Zweig. 2012. Context dependent recurrent neural network language model. In *2012 IEEE Spoken Language Technology Workshop (SLT), Miami, FL, USA, December 2-5*, pages 234–239. IEEE.

Tomas Mikolov, Martin Karafiát, Lukás Burget, Jan Cernocký, and Sanjeev Khudanpur. 2010. Recurrent neural network based language model. In *INTERSPEECH 2010, 11th Annual Conference of the International Speech Communication Association*, pages 1045–1048.

Tomas Mikolov, Stefan Kombrink, Lukás Burget, Jan Cernocký, and Sanjeev Khudanpur. 2011. Extensions of recurrent neural network language model. In *Proceedings of the IEEE International Conference on Acoustics, Speech, and Signal Processing, ICASSP 2011, May 22-27, 2011, Prague Congress Center, Prague, Czech Republic*, pages 5528–5531. IEEE.

Kishore Papineni, Salim Roukos, Todd Ward, and Wei-Jing Zhu. 2002. Bleu: a method for automatic evaluation of machine translation. In *Proceedings of the 40th Annual Meeting of the Association for Computational Linguistics, July 6-12, 2002, Philadelphia, PA, USA.*, pages 311–318. ACL.

Haoruo Peng and Dan Roth. 2016. Two discourse driven language models for semantics. In *Proceedings of the 54th Annual Meeting of the Association for Computational Linguistics (Volume 1: Long Papers)*, pages 290–300, Berlin, Germany, August. Association for Computational Linguistics.

Tian Wang and Kyunghyun Cho. 2016. Larger-context language modelling with recurrent neural network. In *Proceedings of the 54th Annual Meeting of the Association for Computational Linguistics (Volume 1: Long Papers)*, pages 1319–1329. Association for Computational Linguistics.

Wen Wang and Mary P. Harper. 2002. The superarv language model: Investigating the effectiveness of tightly integrating multiple knowledge sources. In *Proceedings of the ACL-02 Conference on Empirical Methods in Natural Language Processing - Volume 10*, EMNLP '02, pages 238–247, Stroudsburg, PA, USA. Association for Computational Linguistics.

Omar F. Zaidan. 2009. Z-MERT: A fully configurable open source tool for minimum error rate training of machine translation systems. *The Prague Bulletin of Mathematical Linguistics*, 91:79–88.

Identifying Deception in Indonesian Transcribed Interviews through Lexical-based Approach

Tifani Warnita
School of Electrical Engineering and
Informatics
Institut Teknologi Bandung
tifaniwarnita@gmail.com

Dessi Puji Lestari
School of Electrical Engineering and
Informatics
Institut Teknologi Bandung
dessipuji@gmail.com

Abstract

This paper aims to present a lexical-based approach in order to identify deception in Indonesian transcribed interviews. Using word calculation from the psychological point of view, we classify each subject utterance into two classes, namely lie and truth. We find that the intentions of the people in both telling the truth and hiding the fact can affect the words used in their utterances. We also find that there is an interesting pattern for Indonesian people when they are answering questions with lies. Despite the promising result of lexical-based approach for detecting deception in the Indonesian language, there are also some cases which cannot be handled by only using the lexical features. Hence, we also present an additional experiment of combining the lexical features with acoustic/prosodic features using the recorded sound data. From the experiment, we find that the combination of lexical features with other features such as acoustic/prosodic can be used as the initial step in order to get better results in identifying deception in Indonesian.

1 Introduction

Human social behavior has successfully led to the ubiquitous human communication. In this regard, it is also very possible for people to commit lies when communicating with others. Deceit or commonly referred to as lie is any actions of making others believe what we perceived as false, without the receivers know that they are being fooled (Ekman, 1992; Vrij, 2008). A lie can be divided into a variety of classes when viewed from various aspects involved in such actions. For example, when viewed from how bad a lie is, a lie can be classified into a white lie, gray lie, and real lie (Bryant, 2008).

Various motivations may underlie a lie. Based on interviews with children and questionnaire survey results from adults by Ekman (1989), according to most of the children and the adults, someone might lie in order to avoid punishment. Referring to this phenomenon, especially if we focus on the realm of interrogation for solving crimes, it is a compelling matter when people are challenged to be able to tell which utterances contain lies. However, for many people, it seems difficult to recognize any deception, considering that the cues to deception can be reflected from diverse aspects (DePaulo et al., 2003) as well as the need for specific experience in related scientific fields.

As in other computational linguistic studies, in order to obtain the best result, sometimes the geographic location of the speakers have to be taken into account when finding the salient features. The location of the speakers can affect their way of thinking, and also their way of speaking. A feature might be very dominant in a particular language yet only considered as an additional feature in other languages. That being said, currently, there is only a small number of deception detection studies using Indonesian language.

A lot of studies have been conducted in order to find the best method for distinguishing deception within human communication. Not only in the field of psychology (Ekman et al., 1991) which is the root of this engaging topic, but also in other areas such as text processing (Mihalcea & Strapparava, 2009; Newman et al., 2003) and speech processing (Benus et al., 2006; Hirschberg et al., 2005; Levitan et al., 2016). In this paper, we present our approach of identifying deception, especially in Indonesian, based on lexical approach. Moreover, we also perform an additional experiment of combining lexical features and acoustic/prosodic features.

2   Related Studies

Deception in people can be seen from various aspects such as the choices of words when committing lies. There are at least three cues of deception in the lexical domain, which are fewer uses of self-referencing words (*I*, *we*, *us*, etc.), more uses of negative emotion words, and fewer uses of cognitive-complex words (Newman et al., 2003). The fewer uses of self-referencing words might be caused by a lot of reasons. For instance, this is due to the unwillingness of the people to be involved or being responsible for their lies. It can also be the result of people telling something that they have never done before hence they subconsciously not mentioning themselves in their lies (Knapp et al., 1974).

The second cue, the uses of negative emotion words, can arise as the result of guilty feelings after telling lies (Ekman, 1992). The examples of negative emotion words are *hate, worry, jealous, anxious*, and *envy*. In addition to the uses of negative emotion words, according to Newman et al. (2003), there is also a tendency of the fewer uses of exclusive words such as *but, except*, and *without*. This cue is closely related to the third cue mentioned above because it will be difficult for people who are lying to think more information contrary to what they had said before. In this case, people who are lying rarely using that kind of words because at the time they are lying, they have to think carefully in order to make their lies to be

as perfectly possible. Therefore, they tend to refuse using words which require the brain to think more.

Recently, there are a lot of studies related to the exploration of automatic identification of detecting lies in people through lexical approach. One of the experiment was conducted using English dataset containing statements of some people when they are being asked about their opinions towards the death penalties, abortion, and best friend (Mihalcea & Strapparava, 2009). From the study, using the classes of words as defined in the Linguistic Inquiry and Word Count (LIWC), it can be inferred that the first cue, the fewer uses of self-referencing words, also takes an important part for detecting deception. It is said that the subjects tend to use human-related word classes, avoid mentioning about themselves as trying to not involve themselves in their lies. The words expressing certainty are also often used in deceptive opinions in order to emphasize the fake and hide the lies. Besides, based on another study, words in pleasantness dimension extracted from Whissell's Dictionary of Affect in Language (DAL) (Whissell, 2009) become promising features in predicting lying utterances (Hirschberg et al., 2005).

3   Indonesian Deception Corpus

In order to know the difference between deceptive utterance and truth utterance, we use Indonesian Deception Corpus (IDC) as the dataset. The corpus contains 30 interviews with different subjects (16 males, 14 females) along with the transcription of the interview sessions. The construction of the corpus is similar to the recording paradigm of Columbia/SRI/Colorado (CSC) Corpus of deceptive speech (Hirschberg et al., 2005).

At first, the participants were told that they were being involved in an experiment for selecting any participant who matches with the target profile of the top entrepreneurs in Indonesia. The interview process began with giving a pre-test for the participants to answer some questions in six areas (politics, music, foods, geography, social, economy). At a later stage, the participants were informed about their result in the previous task with some adjustment for the corpus creation purpose. For every participant, they were told that they got matching scores in two areas, lower score in two areas, and higher score in two areas.

Indonesian	English*
TRUTH	
Karena mungkin dalam bergaul saya cukup cukup lumayan.	Because maybe in mine I'm pretty pretty good.
Di FTTM sering jadi PJ PJ, terus di Menwa juga cukup aktif.	In FTTM often become PJ PJ, continue in Menwa also quite active.
Jadi maupun di fakultas maupun di unit cukup bagus, untuk sekarang.	So as well as in the faculty and in the unit is pretty good, for now.
LIE	
Seperti apa, perubahan kurs mata uang, mata uang rupiah.	Like what, the exchange rate changes, the rupiah currency.
Dan apa, kayak harga minyak juga, suka mengikuti.	And what, like oil prices too, likes to follow.

* Translated using automated machine translation

Table 1: Sample of truth and lie statements in IDC transcription

Based on their result from the previous task, the subjects have to lie to the interviewer for the second task, telling them that they successfully got match scores with the generalization of the Indonesian top entrepreneurs. All of the participants were being motivated to commit such lies with financial reward. After the interview session, we label each speech segment as lie or truth. From the corpus, we collected the total of 5,542 sentence-like segments, specifically 1,127 lying utterances and 4,415 truthful utterances. From each utterance, we also have the transcription which transcribed manually by humans as can be seen in Table 1.

4 Lexical-based Approach

4.1 Experimental Setup

As the attempt of automatically detecting deception in people, we try to explore deception cues within the choices of words when lying to others. In this experiment, we use Linguistic Inquiry and Word Count (LIWC) (Pennebaker et al., 2007) and Whissell's Dictionary of Affect in Language (DAL) (Whissell, 2009) in order to determine the psychological scores for each

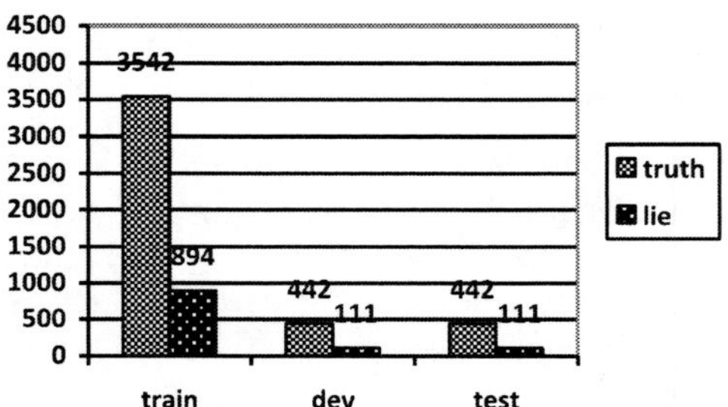

Figure 1: Proportion of data used for experiment

sentence. Using LIWC, we extract 72 features which comprise of word class scores and also scores for non-word elements of the sentence such as punctuations and parenthesis.

From IDC, we use 9:1 of all data as learning data and the rest of them as testing data. For the learning experiment, we use 8:1 of all learning data as training data and developing data as can be seen in Figure 1. We use three classifiers, Random Forest, linear Support Vector Machine (SVM), and Neural Networks.

Due to the unavailability of Indonesian dictionary in both of LIWC and DAL, we have to automatically translate the transcription into English using machine translation. However, because the psychological scores are calculated based on the word occurrences, incorrect word ordering in the translated text will not affect much. Hence we have to focus on how to make all the words from the transcriptions can be translated. Therefore, for the preprocessing steps, we use Indonesian sentence formalization of inaNLP (Purwarianti et al., 2016) to formalize any slangs or incorrectly transcribed text, followed by the second step of formalization using our own Indonesian formal dictionary that contains pairs of slang, non-standard word, or abbreviation along with its formal phrase. After that, we translate the transcription using automatic machine translation for Indonesian-English.

4.2 Result of Experiment

Using the three classifiers, we obtained the best result using Random Forest with 80.29% accuracy and 74.12% for F-measure as can be seen in Table 2. The imbalanced dataset made most of the data to be classified into the majority class, which is the

	Accuracy (%)	F-*measure* (%)
RF	80.29	**74.12**
SVM	79.93	71.01
NN	55.15	59.61

Table 2: Experiment result of Random Forest (RF), Support Vector Machine (SVM), and Neural Network (NN)

Model	Resampling Techniques	Acc (%)	Fm (%)	Truth Acc (%)	Lie Acc (%)
RF	-	80.29	**74.12**	98.19	9.01
	SMOTE	79.93	71.01	100.00	0.00
	RUS	55.15	59.61	54.98	55.86
SVM	-	79.93	71.01	100.00	0.00
	SMOTE	56.42	60.70	58.14	49.55
	RUS	52.08	56.79	51.13	55.86
NN	-	78.65	73.28	95.79	14.29
	SMOTE	36.89	39.09	27.15	32.50
	RUS	58.41	62.15	63.12	27.67

Table 3: Experiment result of Random Forest (RF), Support Vector Machine (SVM), and Neural Network (NN) models using several resampling techniques

truth class. We obtained 98.19% accuracy for classifying the truth data and only 9.01% for classifying the lie data.

In order to handle the imbalance data problem, we also try to apply two resampling techniques, Synthetic Minority Over-sampling Technique (SMOTE) for increasing the minority classes and Random Under-sampling (RUS) for decreasing the majority classes in training data. By applying the two resampling techniques, we manage to increase the ability of the classifiers in detecting deception. However, it also decreases the ability in detecting truth as well. This causes the F-measure score for each classifier to decrease as can be seen in Table 3.

We also try to identify the most dominant LIWC word classes of the data by calculating the coverage of each word class for both lie and truth data. After that, we calculate the ratio between the two coverage scores to get dominance of each word class (Mihalcea & Strapparava, 2009). The calculation is performed on every data in the IDC corpus. As can be seen in Table 4, the result shows

Score	Class
	Lie
1.45	See: view, see
1.38	Insight: think, know, consider
1.26	Cause: because, effect, therefore, hence
1.23	Body: cheek, hands, spit
1.19	We: we, us, our
	Truth
0.00	Death: kill, die, death
0.37	They: they, their
0.50	Female: she, her, female
0.63	Anger: hate, kill, annoying
0.67	Work: job, majors

Table 4: Dominant word classes from each label

the most dominant word classes of every data category along with the examples of the words for each class (Pennebaker et al., 2007). Word classes with scores higher than 1 mean the classes are dominant in lie data and less than 1 mean the otherwise.

The dominant words result shows a different perspective from previous studies. *Self-referencing* words, specifically 'we', appear mostly in deceptive statement instead of truth statement. This is due to the tendency of subjects to relate their lies with other people. This can be the result of the subjects not wanting to take the responsibility for themselves and also wanting to defend their lies. Therefore, the subjects tend to use the word 'we' with the intention to build a perception as if many people support what they say. Besides, according to the data, most of the 'we' that subjects use in their lies are not referred to 'we' as a small group of people but related to 'we' as almost all people in particular location or even around the globe. There is also an interesting finding in the second most dominant word class of the lie data, which is *insight*. When the subjects are lying, they tend to use 'I think' as if there is a slight doubt when they are speaking. It can also be caused by not having any evidence from the outside world to support their ideas. Thus they choose to say it with 'I think' instead of answering the interviewer's questions directly.

Moreover, some of the dominant classes are caused by the tendency of the subjects to answer certain topics of the corpus in a similar way. This

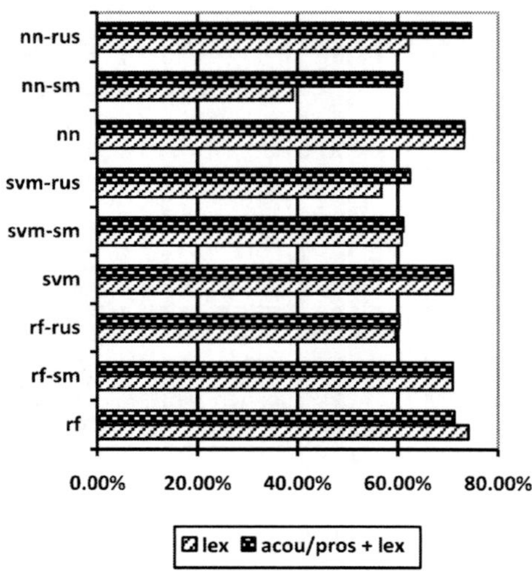

Figure 2: F-measure comparison of the use of lexical only features and the combination of acoustic/prosodic with lexical

Model	Resampling Techniques	Acc (%)	Fm (%)	Truth Acc (%)	Lie Acc (%)
RF	-	79.93	71.35	99.77	0.90
	SMOTE	79.93	71.01	100.00	0.00
	RUS	55.88	60.26	55.20	58.56
SVM	-	79.93	71.01	100.00	0.00
	SMOTE	56.78	61.03	58.37	50.45
	RUS	58.41	62.45	60.18	51.35
NN	-	80.36	73.32	99.09	6.31
	SMOTE	56.60	60.85	58.60	48.65
	RUS	75.23	**74.64**	85.97	32.43

Table 4: Additional experiment result of Random Forest (RF), Support Vector Machine (SVM), and Neural Network (NN) models using several resampling techniques

is due to there are only 6 topic areas that are being discussed in the interview session. For example, the female word class appears to be very dominant in truth class because there are a lot of subjects who answer the question with something related to cooking with their mothers. Besides, the word class anger which comes from negative emotion words is also very dominant in the truth class because the subjects mostly answer questions about cheating without lying.

In addition to the analysis of LIWC based word classes, for DAL, there are three classes, which are pleasantness (how pleasant the word when it is used), activation (how active the word is), and imagery (how easy the word is to evoke an image). From the three categories, the imagery class seems to be the most promising category amongst all. When the imagery score is high enough, there is a bigger probability that the instance is closely related to lying utterances.

Regarding the incorrect classification of some instances, it might be caused by several reasons. First, we only explore one sentence-segment for each instance. There might be some correlations between the segments we are exploring with the previous and/or next segment. For example, when people are lying at the first sentence, they are likely to lie again in the next sentence they say as

they want to defend their previous statement. There are also some possibilities that when the subjects answer the question with lying, the whole answer may show the deception cues. However, taking consideration only some part of the whole answer can make us lose the pattern.

Furthermore, some of the instances contain only 'yes' or 'no' answer which caused the deception to be unidentifiable by only using the lexical approach. Using only word analysis will only cause the instance to be classified into the majority class. In this case, the experiment result shows that for some model, all instances are classified into truth label as it is the majority class. Regarding the same sentence with a different class, speech analysis can be performed for increasing the deception detection performance. This is due to when we explore the recorded sound data, especially for instance with 'yes' or 'no' answer, there are a slightly different pitch pattern and silence duration from lying utterances and truthful utterances. It has also been confirmed that there has been a significant increase in pitch of the deceptive speech over truthful speech (Ekman, Sullivan, Friesen, & Scherer, 1991).

5 Additional Experiments

5.1 Experimental Setup

As the result of the low accuracy in detecting deception, we perform an additional experiment. In this case, we also try to use features from the

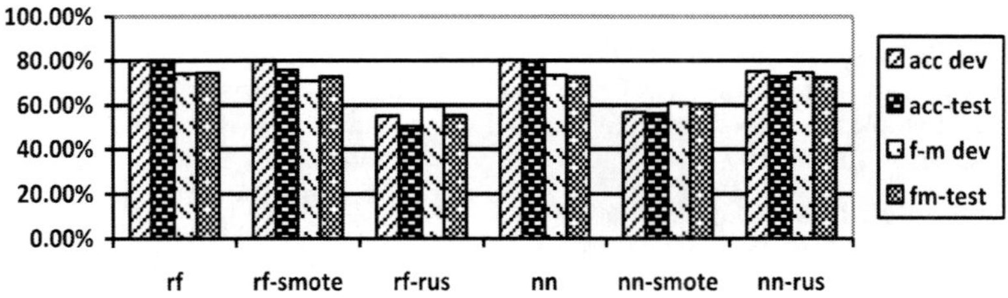

Figure 3: Comparison accuracy and F-measure between using development data and test data

acoustic/prosody that can be extracted from the recorded sound data of IDC. In accordance with previous research related to detecting deception using speech analysis (Enos, 2009; Graciarena et al., 2006; Hirschberg et al., 2005), we use features from silence, energy, and pitch category then apply some normalization techniques to the extracted features.

From the silence category, we calculate the time taken by the subjects to answer the questions, duration between sentences, the number of silence, and the duration of all silence in each instance. For the energy and pitch category, we calculate the number of changing energy and pitch (falling, rising, doubling, halving), the maximum, minimum, and mean values of energy and pitch, also other energy and pitch related features. For the normalization techniques, we calculate the difference from the mean, the ratio with the mean, and z-score for each score.

5.2 Result of Experiment

From the combination of lexical and acoustic/prosody features, we can see a better result compared with using only lexical features as can be seen in Figure 2. The best classifier in this experiment obtained the best result with F-measure of 74.64% and accuracy of 75.23% using Neural Network and RUS as can be seen in Table 4. However, for the other classifiers, the combination of lexical and acoustic/prosodic approach does not affect much. We can see that the combination of the two feature categories gives a better result for both SMOTE Neural Network and RUS Neural Network compared with the previous experiments.

We also test our model using the testing data that we have introduced before. For each experiment, we select the best classifier to be tested. We select Random Forest for the lexical-based only approach and Neural Network for the other approach and get the result as shown in Figure 3. We can see that there are not any significant differences between the result using development data and testing data. From this, we can also say that the corpus that we use in this experiment can be considered as consistent.

6 Conclusion and Future Works

In this paper, we have described the explorations on analyzing deception in Indonesian transcribed interviews using the data collected from IDC. Seeing that the experiments give promising results, we can use the lexical approach as an initial step for detecting deception in people. Besides, we can also combine the lexical approach with using acoustic/prosodic features. In future works, we plan to combine the lexical features along with other speech related features for identifying deception as it can give broader information about the data. We will also take into consideration the correlation between the previous sentence and also the following sentence that the subjects say.

References

Aldert Vrij. 2008. Detecting Lies and Deceit: Pitfalls and Opportunities. Wiley Series in the Psychology of Crime, Policing and Law. John Wiley & Sons.

Ayu Purwarianti, Alvin Andhika, Alfan Farizki Wicaksono, Irfan Afif, Filman Ferdian. 2016. InaNLP: Indonesia natural language processing toolkit, case study: Complaint tweet classification. 2016 International Conference on Advanced Informatics: Concepts, Theory And Application (ICAICTA).

Bella M. DePaulo, James J. Lindsay, Brian E. Malone, Laura Muhlenbruck, Kelly Charlton, and Harris

Cooper. 2003. Cues to deception. Psychological Bulletin, 129(1), 74–118.

Cynthia Whissell. 2009. Using the Revised Dictionary of Affect in Language to Quantify the Emotional Undertones of Samples of Natural Language. Psychological Reports, 105(2), 509–521.

Erin M. Bryant. 2008. Real Lies, White Lies and Gray Lies: Towards a Typology of Deception. Kaleidoscope: A Graduate Journal of Qualitative Communication Research, 7, 23–48.

Frank Enos. 2009. Detecting Deception in Speech. Ph.D. Dissertation. Columbia Univ., New York, NY, USA. Advisor(s) Julia B. Hirschberg.

James W. Pennebaker, Roger J Booth, and Martha E. Francis. 2007. Operator's Manual: Linguistic Inquiry and Word Count - LIWC2007, 1–11.

Julia Hirschberg, Stefan Benus, Jason M. Brenier, Frank Enos, Sarah Friedman, Sarah Gilman, Cynthia Girand, Martin Graciarena, Andreas Kathol, LauraMichaelis, Bryan Pellom, Elizabeth Shriberg, and Andreas Stolcke. 2005. Distinguishing Deceptive from Non-Deceptive Speech. Interspeech 2005, 1833–1836.

Mark L. Knapp, Roderick P. Hart, Harry S. Dennis. 1974. An Exploration of Deception as a Communication Construct. Human Communication Research, 1(1), 15–29.

Martin Graciarena, Elizabeth Shriberg, Andreas Stolcke, Frank Enos, Julia Hirschberg, and Sachin Kajarekar. 2006. Combining Prosodic, Lexical and Cepstral Systems for Deceptive Speech Detection. Proceedings of IEEE ICASSP, 1033–1036.

Matthew L. Newman, James W. Pennebaker, Diane S. Berry, and Jane M. Richards. 2003. Lying Words: Predicting Deception From Linguistic Styles. Personality and Social Psychology Bulletin, 29(5), 665–675.

Paul Ekman, Mary Ann Mason Ekman, and Tom Ekman. 1989. Why Kids Lie: How Parents Can Encourage Truthfulness. Penguin Books.

Paul Ekman, Maureen O'Sullivan, Wallace V. Friesen, and Klaus R. Scherer. 1991. Face, voice, and body in detecting deceit. Journal of Nonverbal Behavior, 15(2), 125–135.

Paul Ekman. 1992. Telling Lies: Clues to Deceit in the Marketplace, Politics, and Marriage. New York: W W Norton & Co Inc.

Rada Mihalcea and Carlo Strapparava. 2009. The Lie Detector: Explorations in the Automatic Recognition of Deceptive Language. Proceedings of the ACL-IJCNLP 2009 Conference Short Papers, (August), 309–312.

Sarah Ita Levitan, Guozhen An, Min Ma, Rivka Levitan, Andrew Rosenberg, Julia Hirschberg. 2016. Combining Acoustic-Prosodic, Lexical, and Phonotactic Features for Automatic Deception Detection. Proceedings of the Annual Conference of the International Speech Communication Association, INTERSPEECH, 08–12–Sept, 2006–2010.

Stefan Benus, Frank Enos, Julia Hirschberg, and Elizabeth Shriberg. 2006. Pauses in Deceptive Speech. Speech Prosody 2006, 18, 2–5.

Foreign Influence and Sound Change: A Case Study of Cantonese Alveolar Affricates

Yizhou Lan

Nagoya University of Commerce and Business

4-4 Komenoki, Nisshin, Aichi Prefecture, Japan

anthonylan@nucba.ac.jp

Abstract

Language contact is one major factor for language change. In some cases such changes are brought from a language of higher status. The present study examines a systematic phonological change among current young Hong Kong Cantonese speakers. L1 Cantonese Speakers of both genders in three age groups were tested for production of Cantonese alveolar affricates /ts/ and /tsʰ/ phonemes in a carrier sentence. English and Cantonese control sounds were also added to the reading list. Results show that speakers of the younger generation have a larger tendency in substituting /tsʰ/ and /ts/ with the English sound /ʧ/ in the back-vowel context. Two probable reasons to such change, language contact and gestural proximity, were identified. The findings clearly acknowledge a sociolinguistic change of /tsʰ/ > [ʧ] for the younger generation in contrast to the elder, and suggest that foreign influence that could be possibly traced back to the influence of the English language.

1   Introduction

Language change through languages contact has been recorded in ways including lexical or structural borrowing [1]. However, structural borrowing, especially that of sound change, is less commonly documented. This study explores a sound change occurring in Cantonese by a probable language contact from English. The sound change under investigation is usually found among Cantonese speakers of younger generation. Recent studies have exemplified that many segmental (e.g., the merge between /n/ and /l/ [2]) and supra-segmental (e.g., tone merging between Cantonese tone 2 and tone 4 [3] [4]) sound changes had taken place in Cantonese. However, apart from the sound change within Cantonese itself, as has illustrated above, could it be probable that this dialect can accommodate foreign influences as well? The present study intends to test whether young speakers in their 20s will produce the Cantonese alveolar affricates /ts/ /tsʰ/ with an "English touch" as the post-alveolar laminal affricate [tʃ]. It attempts to tackle language change not from an evolutionary point view but from one of foreign contact: i.e., the language under investigation borrowing some new features from another language. To investigate this question, a production experiment sampling speakers from different age groups producing Cantonese and English sounds was performed.

2   Literature Review

Hong Kong Cantonese, a variant from the canonical Cantonese language or the *Yue* dialect, has a rich consonantal inventory including alveolar affricates (/ts/ and /tsʰ/) but without post-alveolar laminal affricates (/ʧ/ and /dʒ/). On the other hand, standard British and American English have a three-way distinction of /ts/, /ʧ/ and /dʒ/.

Descriptive and pedagogical literature has shown the phonetic similarity of these alveolar and post-alveolar affricates [5] [6] [7]. For example, investigations from AHSA [6] show that the English /tʃ/ & /dʒ/ are acoustically similar to the Cantonese sounds [tsʰ] & [ts] respectively. On one hand, the English /tʃ/ & /dʒ/ are palato-alveolar, the former being voiceless and the latter being voiced. But on the other hand, the Cantonese [tsʰ] & [ts] are alveolar, and both are voiceless. Despite the phonetic similarity, these post-alveolar affricates are still regarded as difficult sounds for Cantonese learners to acquire [5] [7]. Other studies, however, identify the Cantonese [ts] sound as an equivalent to English /tʃ/ among others in the Cantonese inventory [8], but such studies are extremely scarce.

Even though the pedagogical literature [7] [8] suggested pronunciation techniques to avoid the influence of Cantonese [tsʰ] & [ts] on /tʃ/ & /dʒ/ (which is an underlining support to the clear-cut differences of these sounds), the real Cantonese speech by young generation suggests something different. Anecdotal records have shown that the productions of fricatives are undergoing changes among young speakers of Cantonese.

Similar processes have been identified in some other languages in literature. From a diachronic point of view, language change influenced by foreign languages, or creolization, may take place within or across typological boundaries [9]. For example, a Mayan dialect has palatalized the nasal sounds /m, n/ under the influence of a neighboring communities (ibid.). Sri Lanka Creole has stress pattern rules transferred from Portuguese. A colonial inheritance was also identified from the latter, whose speakers are perceived to have more power and as higher-class individuals. Similarly, Lai & Gooden [10] identified the socio-phonetic change of [ɻ]>[l] in Yami, a language in Taiwan, due to language contact with a more powerful language.

The reason for proposing foreign influence to resolve the current problem also lies in the observed instability of the alveolar affricates in Cantonese. Labov [11] denotes that the instability, usually age or class differences within a phoneme is a signpost for socio-phonetic change. Thus, the present study brings about a new possible explanation of foreign influence to the sound change of Cantonese in the current multilingual landscape of Hong Kong. Such an explanation differs from mainstream theory suggesting these changes being mostly intrinsic within the evolution of a single language.

Thus, as backed up by previous literature, the study intends to investigate the following research questions:

1. How do Cantonese speakers of different age groups produce Cantonese words with /tsʰ, ts/ and English words with /tʃ/?

2. Can the sound change /tsʰ/ /ts/ > /tʃ/ be identified from any of these age groups?

3. If yes, what may be the underlying reason(s) for such sound change?

3   Methods

The study intends to test whether young speakers in their 20s produce the Cantonese alveolar affricate /tsʰ/ and /ts/ in an English accent as the post-alveolar laminal affricate [tʃ]. A production experiment is designed. In the experiment, 12 native Cantonese-speaking participants from three age groups read out both English and Cantonese stimuli in a recording booth. All recorded sounds are identified by three trained phoneticians.

3.1   Participants

Participants are twelve speakers in three age groups, namely 20s, 30s and 60s (mean age=25.5, 37.4 and 61.6, std<3.506). The gender ratio is 1:1. They are all native Cantonese speakers, children of monolingual Cantonese parents, and are all educated with English. The 20s group are all college students and learned English from elementary school. No speech or hearing disorder has been reported. They are asked to read aloud the stimuli in front of a MD recorder in a sound booth.

3.2   Stimuli

Stimuli words in the experiment consist of both target stimuli and control words. The target stimuli are 15 Cantonese character with their pronunciation having /tsʰ/ and /ts/ as the initial consonant. A series of control sound are also chosen to test the hypothesis of English foreign influence. Firstly, 15 Chinese characters whose pronunciation begins with /tʰ/ sounds are recorded for controlling age groups. Secondly, 10 monosyllabic English words with /tʃ/ as the initial consonant are also recorded for controlling language. All stimuli are grouped with vowel four contexts: high front (/i, y/), high back (/u/), low front (/a, ɛ/), and low back (/ɔ/). The number of stimuli of each vowel context is not balanced because of the lack of words for some conditions. The complete list of stimuli Chinese characters and English words are listed in Table 1.

Chinese	English
/tʰ/	/tʃ/
他 濤 塔 投 肚 聽 天 提 太 臺 腿 湯 童 禿 屯	charge chirp chap chore check chuck choose choke cheek chick
/tsʰ/, /ts/	
擦 炒 遮 柴 癡 超 徹 拆 猜 徐 昌 沖 速 邨 黜	

Table 1: Chinese and English Stimuli

3.3 Procedure

The production experiment took place in a sound-proof booth in Hong Kong. First, the participants were asked to read aloud the Cantonese stimuli in a carrier sentence "佢嘅名系唔系叫＿＿＿吖 (Is his name called＿＿＿?)". For English words, a similar sentence "Now I say＿＿＿ again" was used. Both Cantonese and English carrier sentences were controlled for V__V phonetic environment for the acoustic clarity of segmenting the target affricate for analysis. Participants were asked to read these carrier sentences for 10 times each in randomized order. The total number of tokens for Cantonese is 15 words × 2 word groups × 10 repetitions = 600 and for English, the total number is 10 words × 10 repetitions = 100. All carrier sentences were recorded by a Shure SM 57 Microphone with the sampling rate of 44100Hz in mono channel.

Then, the target sound in both Cantonese and English tokens were segmented from the sentence and stored as isolated sound tokens. The data of which was transferred to a laptop PC with a headphone for sound classification and judgement. To measure and classify the production in terms of phonemic transcription, three phonetically-trained Cantonese speakers listened to both Cantonese and English productions, and then judged their phonetic categorization.

4 Results

The results of the production experiment are presented in this section. For both Cantonese and English speech, we present statistical comparisons of the dependent variable of correct percentages of productions judged by the phonetically trained listeners, and the comparisons were grouped by the independent variables of age groups (participants in their 20, 30 and 60s) and vowel contexts.

4.1 Cantonese Speech

Overall, for Cantonese speech, the main factor of age group and the intermediate factor of vowel were examined for two groups of Cantonese words, the /tʰ/ control group and the experiment group. The inter-rater reliability for the Cantonese speech was 86%. Rater confidence was also high.

For the control group, 100% sound were pronounced as /tʰ/ as predicted, and we did not see any of the tokens with a palatalized sound change. Therefore, no further statistical comparison was done for the control group.

For the experiment group, overall findings of statistical comparisons showed that the 20s and 40s speakers are producing significantly different patterns for the sounds /tsʰ/ and /tʃ/. In detail, for age groups, it was found that only the 20s showed significantly more /tʃ/ sound tokens.

As for the effect of vowel context, the substitution of /tʃ/ only occured after vowels of /ɔ/ and /u/ (p<.001), which are all back vowels (see Table 2). However, the /tsʰ/sound remained less changed or even unchanged in vowels of /i/, /y/, /ɛ/, and /a/. One-way ANOVA comparisons showed that the differences between the three age groups were significant [F(2, 543)=3.245, p<.01]. Within the 20s and 30s group, the effect of the independent variable of vowel condition was significant, with the 20s' age group having a larger significance. However, there was no significance of vowel quality for the 60s group [20s: F(5, 215)=3.245, p<.001; 30s: F (5, 149)=2.468, p<.05; 60s: F(5, 227)=2.045, p=.267].

Vowels	Stimuli	20s	30s	60s
/a/	擦 柴 炒 拆	85%	85%	90%
/ɛ/	遮 昌	100%	100%	100%
/i/	超 徹 癡	90%	100%	100%
/ɔ/	猜 徐 沖	42%	71%	89%

| /u/ | 速 黜 | 24% | 56% | 89% |
| /y/ | 村 | 89% | 85% | 100% |

Table 2: Percentage of Cantonese /ts//tsʰ/ tokens pronounced correctly by three age groups, perceived by three phonetically-trained persons.

4.2 English Speech

The English speech of speakers from each age group was also investigated for qualitative analysis by phonetic judgement. The inter-rater reliability for the Cantonese speech is 92%. Rater confidence was very high. The results were shown below.

The correct English pronunciation of /tʃ/ is much higher for 20s young age group as expected. However, in terms of vowel context variability, the correct tokens of /tʃ/ productions mostly occurred after vowels of /ɔ/ and /u/ (see Table 3). One-way ANOVA comparisons showed that the differences between the three age groups were significant [$F_{(2, 97)}$=2.253, $p<.01$]. The effect of the independent variable of vowel condition was significant as in the Chinese speech for all three age groups, with the 20s' age group having a larger significance.

Vowels	Stimuli	20s	30s	60s
/a/	charge chap chuck	43%	25%	22%
/ɛ/	chirp check	47%	30%	32%
/i/	chick cheek	48%	37%	32%
/ɔ/	chore choke	80%	71%	67%
/u/	choose	85%	65%	58%

Table 3: Percentage of English tokens pronounced correctly as /tʃ/ by three age groups, perceived by three phonetically-trained persons.

4.3 Summary

If we combine the vowel groups /i/ and /y/ for Cantonese, data in both languages can be divided into 5 vowel groups (/a, ɛ, i ɔ, u/). The Cantonese and English data could show some common tendencies when they were superimposed together for each age group (See Figure 1). The English and Cantonese percentages seem inversely proportional for all groups but the 20s group shows the highest tendency in all three groups.

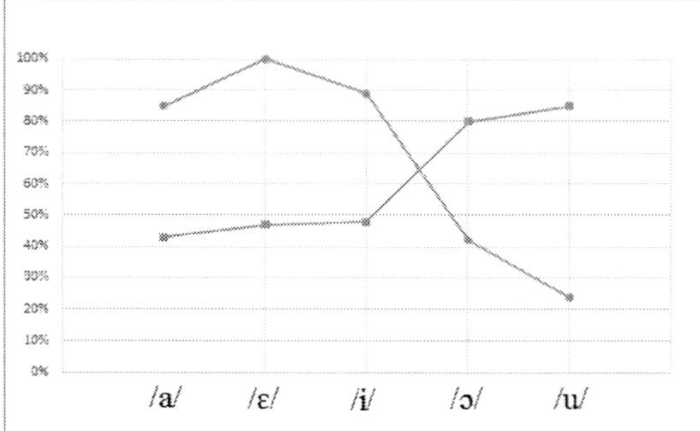

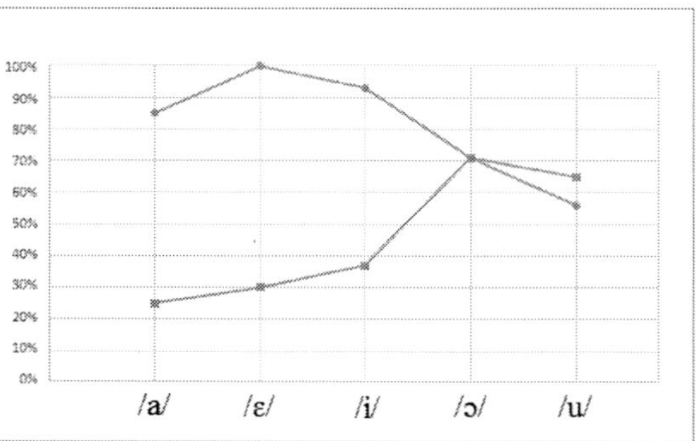

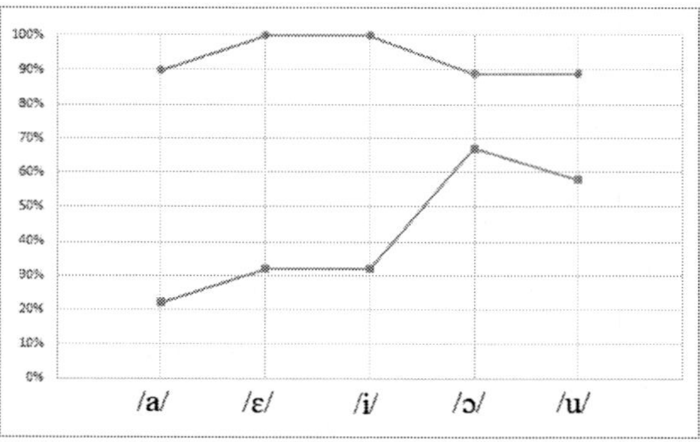

Figure 1: Average percentage of correct instances for the 20s (upper) 30s (center) and 60s (lower) age groups. The blue line represents Cantonese/ts//tsʰ/ and the red line represents English /tʃ/.

5 Discussions

In answering the research questions 1 and 2, we may conclude that the language change under discussion did exist. Speakers of all ages exhibited, at least to some extent, both [tsʰ] and [tʃ] in their productions of Cantonese /tsʰ/. We may also regard the "newly" discovered [tʃ] as an allophone of /tsʰ/ in the Cantonese inventory, especially for the 20s generation. In other words, the substitution of /tsʰ/

158

could be regarded as a sound change /ts^h/ /ts/ > /tʃ/ in the group of young speakers. However, for 30s and 60s generations, the overall percentage of /tʃ/ tokens appeared significantly fewer compared with the 20s generation. Another important finding is that the difference in rates of correct production lies primarily in back vowel conditions (/ɔ, u/), as has been confirmed by post-hoc tests of the statistical analyses. The reasons for the language change and especially the effect of back vowel conditions will be addressed in the following.

As an attempt to answer research question 3, the rest of this section explains the reasons to this language change by proposing effects of (1) the universal gestural economy conditions in vowel contexts and (2) sociolinguistic contact of foreign sounds.

Firstly, the vowel condition can be attributed to anticipatory gestural economy. Results has shown that labialization is especially evident for words with back vowels. It is argued that this may be driven by speakers' gestural economic strategy to approximate these two sounds [12] seen in socio-phonetic changes. The backward movement of the tongue body involved in the alveolar → post-alveolar change is in accordance with the backward movement of the tongue body in back vowels [13], hence the greater inclination of this change.

Moreover, the English speech results show that the speakers had not pronounced the sound fully as English /tʃ/ but having a similar pattern of vowel variation, as shown in the inverse proportion of /ts, ts^h/ and /tʃ/ in Figure 1. This further agrees with the gestural hypothesis of the language change stated above. The gestural economy of moving the tongue body up to form an affricate in anticipation of back vowels as pulling the tongue backward has made the sound change easier in gestural terms.

Secondly, the sound change of /ts/ > /tʃ/ as a whole can be regarded as from language contact. The Cantonese phonological inventory contains no post-alveolar sounds in general, and that the Chinese dialectal system is rare with laminal post-alveolar affricates. It is more plausible to consider this case as from foreign influence, despite the scarcity of such cases [14].

But what might have motivated the change from language contact? The /tʃ/ sound has affected the Cantonese language systematically in phonology instead of just through loan words. One reason of such systematic change might be the social drive for the younger generation to acculturate or even assimilate to the western way of speaking. The "language identity" factor may had hoisted this sound as a more socially accepted norm in the peer group than the conventional /ts^h/.

Tracing back the foreign influence leads to the sociolinguistic impact of such trend of changing. The senior and young participants of this study, without any linguistic knowledge, showed divided opinions towards it as the researcher seek their attitudes towards the change. When the researcher randomly sampled the senior group (60s)'s attitude towards such linguistic use, the response was that such usage "comes from younger generations", which is valid. They commented that such usage is *"talking when biting the tongue"*, *"pretentious"* and *"almost a kind of polluted language"*. However, when the researcher asks younger participants (20s), irrespective of whether they do use /tʃ/ or not, they responded that *"everybody does that"*, *"it's cute and lovely"* and *"I think it is going to be a norm in the future"*. Such polarized perceptions towards the same phenomenon in language change clearly portraits the ideological construct of a linguistic form; and in that new linguistic forms may or may not be welcomed by social ideals. A similar viewpoint was proposed by Labov [15] where the Canadian French /r/ sound pronunciation witnessed the coexistence of some clear-cut different productions, namely apical /r/ and uvular /r/, by speakers from two generations. He thus concluded that parental influence on the next generation often accelerates the polarization of sounds undergoing language change.

6   Conclusion

The study provides empirical evidence to an ongoing sound change in Hong Kong Cantonese. Young college students in around their 20s has been using a different variety of alveolar affricates /ts^h/ and /ts/, producing it as the post-alveolar laminal affricate [tʃ]. Since this sound, with its place of articulation, does not appear in Cantonese phonology and is spoken only by younger generations, we speculate that language contact may be responsible for this undergoing sound change. Also, the cross-linguistic tendency of /tʃ/-substitution exists mainly in back vowel conditions was found in both Cantonese and English, as a probable result from anticipatory gestural configurations. From the above two findings, we have identified an interwoven influence of articulatory phonetics and foreign influence. For future studies, there could be more foreign influences on other phonemes could be identified as young Cantonese speakers continue to be exposed to and identify themselves with the English language. In the long run, such features in the phonemic inventory may be preserved.

References

McMahon, A. M. (1994). Understanding language change. Cambridge University Press.

Yang, C. (2013). Predicting language change, paper presented at the CUHK linguistic seminar.

Zhang, C., Peng, G., & Wang, W. S. (2011). Inter-talker Variation as a Source of Confusion in Cantonese Tone Perception. Proceedings of ICPhS XVII, 2276-2279.

Mok, P. P., Zuo, D., & Wong, P. W. (2013). Production and perception of a sound change in progress: Tone merging in Hong Kong Cantonese. Language Variation and Change, 25(03), 341-370.

EDUHK. (2017). English Pronunciation Tips. Retrieved from URL= http://webcache.googleusercontent.com/search?q=cache:eWPsLlzCZAwJ:ec-concord.ied.edu.hk/phonetics_and_phonology/wordpress/learning_website/comparison_of_english_and_canton.htm.

AHSA, (2017). Cantonese Inventory. Retrieved from URL= http://www.asha.org/uploadedFiles/practice/multicultural/CantonesePhonemicInventory.pdf.

Hung, T. T. (2002). Towards a phonology of Hong Kong English. Hong Kong English: autonomy and creativity, 1, 119.

Rogerson-Revell (2011). English Phonology and Pronunciation Teaching, Bloomsbury Publishing.

Thomason, S. G., & Kaufman, T. (1992). Language contact, creolization, and genetic linguistics. Univ of California Press.

Lai, L., & Gooden, S. (2014). Sociophonetic Variation in the voiced alveolar lateral fricative in Yami. Poster presented at NWAV, 43, 23-26.

Labov, W. (1994). Principles of linguistic change. Vol. 1: Internal factors. Oxford: Blackwell

Lawson, E., Scobbie, J. M., & Stuart-Smith, J. (2013). Bunched/r/promotes vowel merger to schwar: An ultrasound tongue imaging study of Scottish sociophonetic variation. Journal of Phonetics, 41(3), 198-210.

Gick, B. (2003). Articulatory correlates of ambisyllabicity in English glides and liquids. Phonetic Interpretation: Papers in Laboratory Phonology VI, 222-236.

Pavlenko, A. (2000). L2 Influence on L1 in Late Bilingualism. Issues in Applied Linguistics, 11(2), 175-205.

Labov, W. (2014). The sociophonetic orientation of the language learner. Advances in sociophonetics, 15, 17-29.

Unsupervised Method for Improving Arabic Speech Recognition Systems

Mohamed Labidi
LaTICE laboratory
Unit of Monastir
5000 Monastir, Tunisia
labidi8mohamed@gmail.c
om

Mohsen Maraoui
Computational
Mathematics Laboratory,
Tunisia
5000 Monastir, Tunisia
maraoui.mohsen@gmail.c
om

Mounir Zrigui
LaTICE laboratory
Unit of Monastir
5000 Monastir, Tunisia
mounir.zrigui@fsm.rnu.tn

Abstract

One of the big challenges connected to large vocabulary Arabic speech recognition is the limit of vocabulary, which causes high out-of-vocabulary words. Also, the Arabic language characteristics are another challenge. These challenges negatively affect the performance of the created systems. In this work we try to handle these challenges by proposing a new unsupervised graph-base method. Finally, we have obtained a 4.6% relative reduction in the word error rate. Comparing our suggested method with other methods in the literature, it has given better results. Moreover, it has presented a major step towards solving this problem. In addition, it can be easily adaptable to other languages.

1 Introduction and state of the art

One of the big challenges in speech recognition is how to cover all possible words by a speech recognition system. The vocabulary of a conventional large-vocabulary continuous speech recognition system is finite, and this vocabulary limits the terms that appear in speech transcriptions. The words that do not occur in the vocabulary of the recognizer are called "out-of-vocabulary" words. This problem is a perennial challenge for speech recognition, where the out-of-vocabulary words are badly recognized. A larger vocabulary for the automatic speech recognition system is not the solution, since language is in constant growth and new words are steadily enriching the vocabulary. In (Ng and Zue, 2000), an analysis of news text demonstrated that the vocabulary size would continue to grow as the dataset got larger. In other words, it was not possible to create single large vocabulary that would eliminate the out-of-vocabulary problem. Consequently, it was not possible to create a language model that would cover all the words of any language. Furthermore, under certain conditions, adding more words could compromise the recognition performance of words already in the vocabulary. According to (Logan et al., 2005), up to 10% of all query words in a typical application that used a word-based recognizer with large vocabulary could be out-of-vocabulary words. Of course it was possible to update the vocabulary of the Automatic Speech Recognition (ASR) systems by adding new words to the language model. However, as noted by (Logan et al., 2005), it could be difficult to obtain enough training data to train the language model for new words. Additionally, for most application scenarios, it would not be feasible to re-recognize spoken content once the initial transcription was generated, due to the high computation cost of the ASR process and the huge sizes of daily spoken content collections. For these reasons, the out-of-vocabulary problem was a formidable one.

For the Arabic language, this problem limits the performances of speech recognition systems. As noted in the previous paragraph, it is not practical to recreate a new language model each time we want to enrich our systems by new vocabulary. To deal with these problems, some superficial work has been done. In (Novotney et al., 2011), a morpho-base language model was used in speech recognition systems for four morphologically rich languages which were Turkish, Finnish, colloquial Egyptian Arabic and Estonian. The authors said that the experiments showed that the morph models performed fairly well on out-of-vocabulary words without compromising the recognition accuracy on in-vocabulary ones. Nevertheless, they reported that the Arabic language was the exception where their proposed method failed. They noted that

31st Pacific Asia Conference on Language, Information and Computation (PACLIC 31), pages 161–168
Cebu City, Philippines, November 16-18, 2017

this might be due to the Arabic language characteristics. The second work belongs to (El-Desoky et al., 2009), where the authors addressed the out-of-vocabulary problem and the non-appearance of diacritical-marks at the Arabic written transcriptions. The authors introduced a morphological decomposition, as well as a diacritization in Arabic language modeling. Their experiments showed a reduction in the Word Error Rate (WER) by 3.7%. However, they still suffer from the new words in languages and diacritical marks in the Arabic words, which present a big problem for Arabic speech recognition. Other work related to this topic has been done in other domains, as in (Al-Shareef and Hain, 2012), (Razmara et al., 2013), (Creutz et al., 2007), (Diehl et al., 2009) and (Habash, 2009).

In our work, we investigate a graph-based method to deal with the present challenge. We use our web crawler to collect text data from the Internet on a regular, continuous and up-to-date basis. We use the collected text for the construction of an oriented weighted graph, where each node presents a word and each arc presents the relationship of succession between two words in the Arabic language. After that, we use a graph search method to detect the false words in the transcription. Finally, we discover the best words that can be replacements.

The paper is organized as follows. In section 2, we present our methodology of performing false-word correction and we deal with out-of-vocabulary words. Our experiments are discussed in section 3, while section 4 gives the conclusions.

2   Methodology

In this section we describe how the corrections of false words are performed. Figure 1 describes the steps of the work.

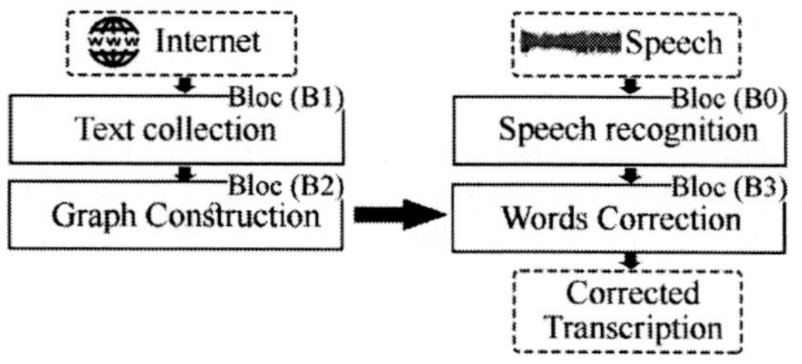

Figure 1: Architecture of the proposed system.

2.1   Linguistic tools

Our acoustic model is built with the help of the CMU Sphinx (Lamere et al., 2003). We train it using 51h of audio material for the modern standard Arabic, recorded by 41 native speakers. Each audio file is accompanied by its transcription. The audio files are converted to 16 kHz, 16 bits, mono speakers, and in an MS WAV format, as required by the Sphinx trainer. The phonetic dictionary is similarly used by almost all researchers in the construction of Arabic speech recognition systems (Ali et al., 2009).

Our language model training corpora consist of around 200 million running full words including data from Ajdir Corpora, Tashkeela corpora (Zerrouki and Balla, 2017), Abbas corpora (Abbas et al., 2011), OSAC corpora (Saad and Ashour, 2010) and collected corpora. Our statistical language model is constructed using the SRILM toolkit (Stolcke and others, 2002).

To evaluate the recognition performance, our small audio corpus of 8h for all our experiments is divided into 12 audio files. Each one contains almost 40 minutes of speech. They contain almost 48,000 Arabic words where 2,000 of them are out of vocabulary (they do not exist in the vocabulary of the system).

For the construction of the oriented weighted graph we use our web crawler to collect text from the Internet and our Java implementation to construct the graph, where each sentence in the collected corpus is transformed to a set of connected words in the graph (i.e., each node of the graph contains one word).

2.2 Speech recognition (B0)

To make the speech correction, it is much easier to work on the text more than spoken documents. For this reason, we have to use a speech recognition system to get the transcriptions of the spoken documents.

We use the CMU Sphinx tools to construct our speech recognition systems. The utilized data are described in the linguistic tools section (section 2.1) and the obtained results are described in section 3. The system gives us the transcriptions for the recognized speech files.

2.3 Text collection (B1)

The text collection is a process to collect Arabic texts from the Internet to establish a corpus of

Arabic text. We use our web crawler in this task. It proceeds as follows:

- Search for the addresses of Arabic web sites in the Internet using API search engines.

- Only Keep addresses of authentic sites: (using the WOT tool, which is a tool powered by 140 million users, machine learning, which is a free browser extensions, and mobile app and API, which let us check whether a website is safe and contains correct information before reaching it).

- Save the authentic addresses in a database.

- Parse the authentic web pages and collect the Arabic texts.

- Save the collected Arabic texts in files (text corpus).

The first successful execution of our web crawler allows collecting more than 2,981 Arabic text files. The advantage of our web crawler is that it systematically updates the corpus. That way we guarantee that our corpus is updated and increased each time. We guarantee also that each new word in the language will be added as soon as possible. The collected corpus is used to create our oriented weighted graph in the next section.

The graph is systematically auto-updated by new texts from the Internet, which make it bigger day after day. The update of the corpus follows the next steps:

- Search for the addresses of Arabic web sites in the Internet using API search engines.

- Only Keep addresses of authentic site: (using the WOT tool).

- For each found authentic address check whether it does not exist in our database, then save it; else do not save it.

- Parse the authentic web pages and collect the Arabic texts.

- Save the collected Arabic texts in files (text corpus).

2.4 Graph construction (B2)

Using the collected corpus in the previous section, where our web crawler is issued, we create an oriented weighted graph that depicts the Arabic language words succession (Figure 2). Each word in the corpus is transformed to a node in the graph. And each two words that succeed in the corpus they will linked by an arc in the graph as described in the following table.

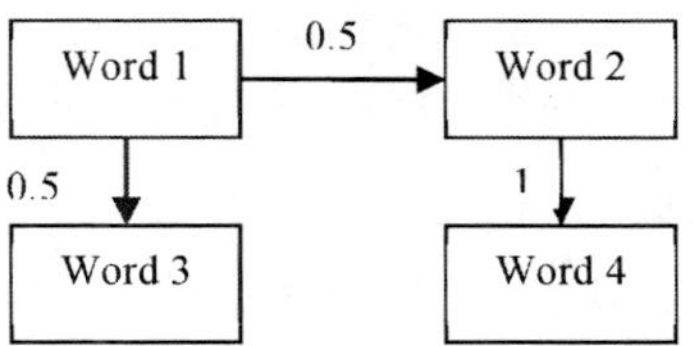

(a) Graph illustration

Node
Word
Number of occurrences
Date of first use
Next nodes
Weight of next relations

(b) Node structure

Figure 2: Illustration of the constructed oriented weighted graph and the structure of its nodes.

The graph of Figure 2 presents the relationship of succession between the four words and the probabilities of these successions. Where the value (0.5) that exist on the arc between "word 1" and "word 2" presents the probability P("word 2"| "word 1"). It is systematically auto-updated by new texts from the Internet, which make it bigger day after day. This graph is used to correct false words in the transcription.

Each node in the graph is a word from the corpus. Also, it contains only one Arabic word and the information related to it. (a) describes the node structure and its fields. Hence, each sentence in the corpus is transformed to a set of connected nodes in the graph. The following points describe the following node fields.

- Word: Field containing the word

- Number of occurrences: Field containing the number of occurrences of the word in the corpus

- Date of first use: Field containing the first appearance of the word in the Internet or in documents

- Next nodes: Links to the next nodes

- Weight of the next relations: Field containing the weight of the relations between the current word and the next words.

To create our graph we pass by the following steps:

- Create for each word in the corpus a node in the graph. Each word has only one node in the graph, even if it exists several times.

- If a word "X" comes after another word "Y" in the textual corpus, then the node of the word "X" will be linked by an arc to the node of the word "Y" in the graph. The following example explains how two words can be transformed to the graph and how we make the link between them.

In the text	In the graph
« Hello word »	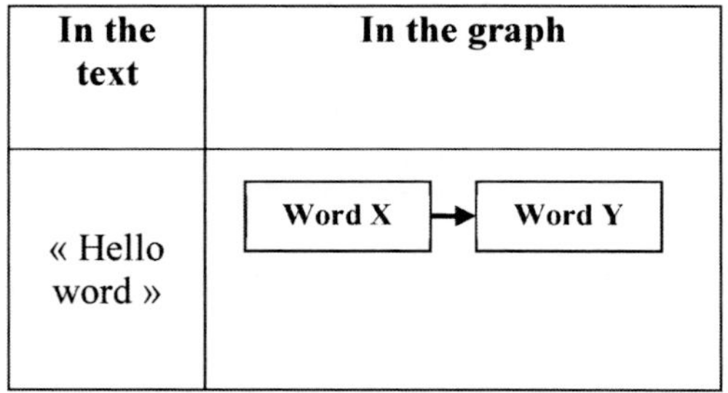

Table 1: Illustration of the arc construction between words.

The arc between any two words "W" and "Y" is weighted by P(W|Y), which is the probability of the appearance of "W" and "Y" together such as that "Y" arrives after "W".

2.5 Word correction (B3)

Our goal in this section is to correct the false words in the transcriptions using the graph created in section 2.4. The correction passes by the steps explained in the next sections:

Suppose we have the following sentence, which contains a false word (Word 3).

Word1 Word2 Word3 Word4 Word5 Word6

To correct the false word (Word 3) we follow the following steps:

2.5.1 False-word detection

First of all, we should detect the false words in the transcriptions, for that we use the oriented weighted graph created in section 2.4. The graph contains the Arabic words collected from the Internet, books, journals, etc. Added to that, the graph is automatically updated by the new words that appear in the language. Logically, any correct word in the transcription should be presented in the graph. To know whether a word is false or not, we search for it in our created graph. If it exists, then it will be correct. Else, it will be considered as a false word and it will pass to the correction step.

2.5.2 Context-window construction

The context window is a set of words that appears with the false word in the same sentence or in the same phrase. It contains N words from both the left and the right of the false word. The context window is used to search correct words that appear in the same context as our false word. Table 2 gives an example of the context-window construction.

Therefore, each false word has more than one context window. Each context window has a different size. The size of the context windows for a false word starts from N=1 (one word from the left and one word from the right of the false words) and reaches N=N, which is the maximum number of words that appear with the false word in the transcription.

We vary the size of the context window for each false word in order to search for the most appropriate context window size that filters out the best possible replacements for the false word. We consider the best context window size as the size that gives us the minimum of possible replacements. We make this choice because we consider that the context window which gives the minimum number of replacements is a better semantic filter than the windows which give more replacements.

The false word (Word 3) in the following example :

Word1 Word2 Word3 Word4 Word5 Word6

has 2 words on the left and 3 words on the right. Two or more of these words can describe the context of the false word that we want to replace. The number of words of the context window (N words) cannot exceed 3 in the example provided in section 2.5, because this is the maximum number of words that can be found with the false word (Word 3) in one of its two sides (left and right).

Context window size	N=1	N=2	N=3
Left side	Word 2	(Word2-Word1)	(Word2-Word1)
Right side	Word 4	(Word4-Word5)	(Word4-Word5-Word6)

Table 2: Example of context-window construction.

2.5.3 Search for possible replacements

After the construction of the context windows, we search for possible replacements of false words, using the context windows created in the previous section. We search in the graph for the word that has the same context window as our false word. We take the words order of the context windows into consideration. For example, if the false word "word3" appears between the two words "word4" and "word2" in the transcription, then we search in the graph for replacements that appear between "word4" and "word2".

The result of this search step is a set of words. Each set contains a set of possible replacements for the false word. Also, each set presents the search results using one of the context windows of the false word; i.e., for each context window for the false word, this step will give us a set of possible replacements. Table 3 describes the created context windows for the false word (Word 3) given in as example in the following sentence : "Word1 Word2 Word3 Word4 Word5 Word6".

Context window size	N=1	N=2	N=3
Possible founded replacement	Word X Word Y Word Z Word W	Word X Word Z	Word Y Word Z Word W

Table 3: Example of searching possible replacements.

The next section describes the selection of the best set of replacements for the false word.

2.5.4 Selection of best set of replacements

The best context window is the one that gives us the replacements that are semantically the closest to the false word in its context. Then, the best context window will give us the minimum possible of replacements because it filters the words well and it proposes only the semantically closest words to the false one. Thus, the best set of replacements is the one that contains the minimum number of replacements. This step is explained in Table 3 and Table 4.

Context window size	N= 2
Possible replacement	Word X Word Z

Table 4: Example of selecting the best replacement set.

2.5.5 Replacement of false word

In the previous step, we chose the set of replacements that were semantically closest to the false word because they have the same context and it works as a semantic filter. Researchers usually choose one word as a substitute to the wrong one. For us, we opt for replacing the false word by all possible replacements selected from the previous step. On the other hand, each replacement is put with its probability of succession that appears in the graph. This probability defines its relationship of succession of the replacement with its successor and predecessor. This process is explained in the following example.

We suppose that the replacements appear in the graph as represented in Figure 3 where

"Word X" and "Word Z" are the possible correct replacements of the false word.

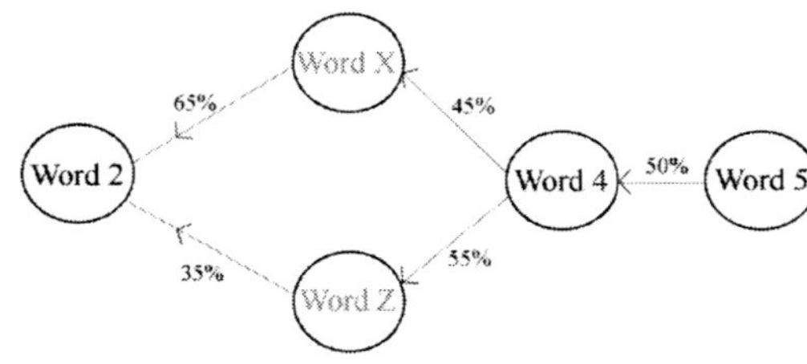

Figure 3: Replacement relations in the graph.

These two possible replacements will replace the false word in the transcription as described in Table 5. Where, the false word is replaced by its possible replacements. And each replacement is accompanied by its probabilities of successions between it and the words of the contextual window.

Replacing false word by the selected ones
Word1 Word2 (65%)WordX (45%) Word4 Word5 Word6
Word1 Word2(35%)WordZ (55%) Word4 Word5 Word6

Table 5: Replacing the false word.

3   Experiments

Our experiments are decomposed in two parts. The first one is the post-correction experiments where we evaluate our speech recognition system performance before the use of our proposed method. The second one is the correction experiments where we evaluate our suggested method. We evaluate our correction method twice: the first one before updating the graph and the second one after updating it. The material used in the experiments is described in the experimental setup section just after the introduction. We use the WER metric, because it is mostly used by researchers to evaluate automatic speech recognition systems (Ali et al., 2009), (Diehl et al., 2009).

3.1 Experiments results

WER% before correction	12.5%
WER% after first correction	8.11%
WER% after second correction (after updating the graph)	7.9%

Table 6: Tests results.

Table 6 shows the obtained results. The first line describes the WER obtained with our speech recognition system before the correction step. The obtained WER is 12.5% ,which means that the transcription contains 6,000 wrongly recognized words, including the 2,000 out-of-vocabulary words. After that, to decrease the WER we execute our proposed method. The second line of Table 6 contains the WER% obtained after the execution of our correction approach, which is 8.11%. This execution was released with the graph constructed in section 3.3. We notice that the WER is decreased. We have recorded a gain of 4.39% in terms of WER, which means a reduction in the number of the false words. We pass from 6,000 to 3,896 false words in the transcriptions. Then, 2,104 words are corrected and 956 of them are out-of-vocabulary words.

After the correction step, we update our graph automatically. Then, we relaunch the correction again, but this time with a richer graph. Line 3 of Table 6 indicates the obtained results. The WER becomes 7.9%, with a reduction of 0.21% from the previous correction; i.e., we pass from 6,000 false words in the transcription to 3,792 ones. However, the number of the corrected out-of-vocabulary words is bigger this time. We pass from 956 corrected out-of-vocabulary words in the first correction to 1,148 ones in the second correction, which proves that the update of the graph has added new words and has positively influenced the correction process.

Work	Gain in WER%
(El-Desoky et al., 2009)	3.7%
Our method	4.6%
(Messaoudi et al., 2006)	1.2%
(Afify et al., 2005)	1.4%

Table 7: Comparison between methods.

The obtained results show the efficiency of our proposed method in the detection and correction of false words. In addition, the results show the ease, speed and performance of our method in the enrichment of the corpus and in correction, unlike the classical language models and the difficulties of their enrichment. As cited in the methodology section, our method does not replace the false word by another word from the possible replacements, but it replaces it by all possible replacements accompanied by their probabilities, which gives a huge advantage to the transcription so that it can be used in various fields. Moreover, any researcher can utilize any selection method to give preference to the suitable word. Furthermore, Table 8 shows that our proposed method gives better results and deals better with false words and out-of-vocabulary ones in the Arabic speech recognition systems than that of the most recent work in the field.

3.2 Discussion

We have proposed a method to correct badly recognized words by any Arabic speech recognition system. Our method shows a good performance in the correction task. Furthermore, it shows an admirable performance in dealing with out-of-vocabulary words. This is thanks to our proposed graph which is systemically auto-updated by new vocabulary and texts from the Internet. Also, it gives a probabilistic description for the words succession in the language. Our method shows a better correction rate than other methods in the literature (El-Desoky et al., 2009), (Creutz et al., 2007) especially for out-of-vocabulary words. In addition, our proposed method provides better results because it takes into consideration the Arabic language characteristics. All this gives our method a great advantage over other ones. Besides, our proposed method can be adapted to other languages easily.

We believe that the correction of false recognized words in any transcription given by any Arabic automatic speech recognition system should take into account two major points. The first is the language characteristics and the second is the new vocabulary that is appearing in the language day after day. Our proposed method is a good step in this field and it can be improved by other methods like the rule-based ones. This is going to be our goal during the next work.

4 Conclusion

In this paper we have tried to deal with the challenges of the limit of vocabulary and the Arabic language characteristics in large vocabulary Arabic speech recognition systems. We have tested a graph-based method. It has given a good reduction by 4.6% in terms of WER. Furthermore, it has fairly dealt with the Arabic language characteristics. The proposed method presents a good step in this field and in dealing with the challenges. Another important thing is that our method can be easily adapted to work with other languages.

References

Mourad Abbas, Kamel Smaïli, and Daoud Berkani. 2011. Evaluation of Topic Identification Methods on Arabic Corpora. *JDIM*, 9(5):185–192.

Mohamed Afify, Long Nguyen, Bing Xiang, Sherif Abdou, and John Makhoul. 2005. Recent progress in Arabic broadcast news transcription at BBN. In *Interspeech*, volume 5, pages 1637–1640.

Mohamed Ali, Moustafa Elshafei, Mansour Al-Ghamdi, and Husni Al-Muhtaseb. 2009. Arabic phonetic dictionaries for speech recognition. *Journal of Information Technology Research (JITR)*, 2(4):67–80.

Sarah Al-Shareef and Thomas Hain. 2012. CRF-based Diacritisation of Colloquial Arabic for Automatic Speech Recognition. In INTERSPEECH, pages 1824–1827.

Mathias Creutz, Teemu Hirsimäki, Mikko Kurimo, Antti Puurula, Janne Pylkkönen, Vesa Siivola, Matti Varjokallio, Ebru Arisoy, Murat Saraçlar, and Andreas Stolcke. 2007. Morph-based speech recognition and modeling of out-of-vocabulary words across languages. ACM Transactions on Speech and Language Processing (TSLP), 5(1):3.

Frank Diehl, Mark JF Gales, Marcus Tomalin, and Philip C Woodland. 2009. Morphological analysis and decomposition for Arabic speech-to-text systems. In INTERSPEECH, pages 2675–2678.

Amr El-Desoky, Christian Gollan, David Rybach, Ralf Schlüter, and Hermann Ney. 2009. Investigating the use of morphological decomposition and diacritization for improving Arabic LVCSR. In Interspeech, pages 2679–2682.

Nizar Habash. 2009. REMOOV: A tool for online handling of out-of-vocabulary words in machine translation. In Proceedings of the 2nd International Conference on Arabic Language Resources and Tools (MEDAR), Cairo, Egypt.

Paul Lamere, Philip Kwok, William Walker, Evandro B Gouvêa, Rita Singh, Bhiksha Raj, and Peter Wolf. 2003. Design of the CMU sphinx-4 decoder. In INTERSPEECH. Citeseer.

Beth Logan, J-M Van Thong, and Pedro J Moreno. 2005. Approaches to reduce the effects of OOV queries on indexed spoken audio. IEEE transactions on multimedia, 7(5):899–906.

Abdelkhalek Messaoudi, J Gauvain, and Lori Lamel. 2006. Arabic broadcast news transcription using a one million word vocalized vocabulary. In Acoustics, Speech and Signal Processing, 2006.

ICASSP 2006 Proceedings. 2006 IEEE International Conference on, volume 1, pages I–I. IEEE.

Kenney Ng and Victor W Zue. 2000. Subword-based approaches for spoken document retrieval. Speech Communication, 32(3):157–186.

Scott Novotney, Richard M Schwartz, and Sanjeev Khudanpur. 2011. Unsupervised Arabic Dialect Adaptation with Self-Training. In INTERSPEECH, pages 541–544.

Majid Razmara, Maryam Siahbani, Reza Haffari, and Anoop Sarkar. 2013. Graph Propagation for Paraphrasing Out-of-Vocabulary Words in Statistical Machine Translation. In ACL (1), pages 1105–1115. Citeseer.

Motaz K Saad and Wesam Ashour. 2010. Arabic morphological tools for text mining. Corpora, 18:19.

Andreas Stolcke and others. 2002. SRILM-an extensible language modeling toolkit. In Interspeech, volume 2002, page 2002.

Taha Zerrouki and Amar Balla. 2017. Tashkeela: Novel corpus of Arabic vocalized texts, data for auto-diacritization systems. Data in Brief, 11:147–151.

Remarks on Epistemically Biased Questions

David Y. Oshima
Graduate School of Humanities, Nagoya University
Furo-cho, Chikusa-ku, Nagoya, Japan 466-8601
`davidyo@nagoya-u.jp`

Abstract

Some varieties of polar interrogatives (polar questions) convey an epistemic bias toward a positive or negative answer. This work takes up three paradigmatic kinds of biased polar interrogatives: (i) positively-biased negative polar interrogatives, (ii) negatively-biased negative polar interrogatives, and (iii) rising tag-interrogatives, and aims to supplement existing descriptions of what they convey besides asking a question. The novel claims are: (i) a positively-biased negative polar interrogative conveys that the speaker assumes that the core proposition is likely to be something that is or should be activated in the hearer's mind, (ii) the bias induced by a negatively-biased negative polar interrogative makes reference to the speaker's assumptions about the hearer's beliefs, and (iii) the biases associated with the three constructions differ in strength, the one of the rising tag-interrogative being the strongest.

1 Introduction

Some varieties of polar interrogatives (polar questions) convey an epistemic bias toward a positive or negative answer. While previous research has revealed much on how different varieties of biased interrogatives contrast with each other in their syntactic and semantic properties, there is a great deal of complexity and subtlety concerning the usage of each type that calls for further investigations.

This work takes up three paradigmatic kinds of biased interrogatives, (i) positively-biased negative polar interrogatives (*Isn't she home already?*), (ii) negatively-biased negative polar interrogatives (*Isn't she home yet?*), and (iii) rising tag-interrogatives (*She is home, isn't she?*), and aims to supplement existing descriptions of what they convey besides asking a question.

2 Negative Polar Interrogatives and Tag-Interrogatives

This section provides a brief overview of the basic facts about the three kinds of marked polar interrogatives.

2.1 Positively-Biased Negative Polar Interrogatives

Positively-biased negative polar interrogatives, or "outside-negation (outside-NEG)" interrogatives (the term due to Ladd, 1981), convey a positive bias toward the core proposition (p_c), i.e., the proposition denoted by *the radical minus the negation*.[1]

(1) H:　John is such a philanthropist.
　　 S:　Yeah, doesn't he even run some sort of charity group?
　　 (S thinks that p_c: "John (even) runs some sort of charity group" is likely to be true.)

(2) H:　OK, now that Stephen has come, we are all here. Let's go!
　　 S:　Isn't Jane coming too?
　　 (S thinks that p_c: "Jane is coming (too)" is likely to be true.)
　　 (adapted from Romero and Han, 2004: 611)

---

[1] In examples and main text, "S" and "H" are used as abbreviations of "the speaker" and "the hearer" respectively.

31st Pacific Asia Conference on Language, Information and Computation (PACLIC 31), pages 169–177
Cebu City, Philippines, November 16-18, 2017

Outside-NEG interrogatives (i) are compatible with a positive polarity item (e.g., *too* as in (2)) and (ii) do not license a negative polarity item. On this ground, McCawley (1988: 499, 571) characterizes the negations in outside-NEG interrogatives (and some instances of "postnuclear" rising tag-interrogatives; see below) as "fake" negations, which do "not count as negative for the purposes of syntactic rules that are sensitive to negation".[2]

2.2 Negatively-Biased Negative Polar Interrogatives

Negatively-biased negative polar interrogatives, or "inside-negation (inside-NEG)" interrogatives, convey a negative bias toward p_c (= a positive bias toward $\neg p_c$).

(3) H: There is nothing John can help with here.
    S: Doesn't he even know how to keep accounts?
        (S thinks that p_c: "John does not (even) know how to keep accounts" is likely to be true.)

(4) H: So we don't have any phonologists in the program.
    S: Isn't Jane coming either?
        (S thinks that p_c: "Jane is not coming (either)" is likely to be true.)
        (adapted from Romero and Han, 2004: 611)

Inside-NEG interrogatives (i) are not compatible with a positive polarity item, and (ii) license a negative polarity item (e.g, *either* as in (4)). This suggests that the negation involved is "genuine", rather than "fake".

2.3 Rising Tag-Interrogatives

Rising (or "non-falling") tag-interrogatives ("nuclear" rising tag-interrogatives, to be precise; see below) convey a positive bias toward the proposition denoted by the host clause (p_h). They contrast with falling tag-interrogatives, to be briefly taken up below, in prosody as well as in function. The prosodic contours that characterize rising and

falling tag-interrogatives can be equated with those that characterize canonical polar interrogatives and canonical declaratives, the exact phonological characterstics of which are not of concern for the purpose of the current work.

The term "tag-interrogatives" has been used in two different ways in the literature, either referring to the complex structure consisting of the host clause and the short polar interrogative ("tag") following it, or referring only to the latter. In this work, I adopt the former terminology, according to which α rather than γ in (5) is a tag-interrogative.

(5) $[_\alpha[_\beta$ Jane is coming], $[_\gamma$ isn't she]]?
    α = tag-interrogative, β = host (clause), γ = tag

The distributions of polarity items within tag-interrogatives are determined by the polarity of the host clause.

(6) a. Jane is coming (too/*either), isn't she?
         (The speaker thinks that p_h: "Jane is coming" is likely to be true.)
    b. Jane isn't coming (*too/either), is she?
         (The speaker thinks that p_h: "Jane is not coming" is likely to be true.)

2.4 Other Varieties of Negative Polar Interrogatives and Tag-Interrogatives

There are some varieties of negative polar interrogatives and tag-interrogatives which exhibit considerable similarities with the types mentioned above but nevertheless are distinct. I will provide brief descriptions of three such varieties, in purpose to clarify what exactly falls under the scope of the current work.

2.4.1 Unbiased Negative Polar Interrogatives

In English (and some other languages; Romero and Han, 2004), the unbiased interpretation of a negative polar interrogative is possible, but only when the negation is realized in non-preposed (post-verbal) position.

(7) (**Situation**: S is organizing a party and she is in charge of supplying all the non-alcoholic beverages for teetotalers. S is going through a list of people that are invited. She has no previous be-

---

[2] Ito and Oshima (2015) make a similar remark on positively-biased negative interrogative in Japanese, which exhibit the same pattern as outside-NEG interrogatives as to the compatibility with polarity items, and furthermore are prosodically differentiated from their negatively-biased counterparts.

lief or expectation about their drinking habits.)

H: Jane and Mary do not drink.
S: OK. What about John? Does he not drink (either)?
S': #OK. What about John? Doesn't he drink (either)?

(Romero and Han, 2004: 610)

Patterning the same as the negatively-biased variety, unbiased negative polar interrogatives may contain a negative polarity item but is not compatible with a positive polarity item.

It should be noted that negative polar interrogatives with non-preposed negation, like ones with preposed negation, can be used as a positively-biased or negatively-biased question. There appears to be a tendency such that negative polar interrogatives with preposed negation are more easily interpreted as positively rather than negatively biased, and ones with non-preposed negation are more easily interpreted as negatively rather than positively biased; for some speakers, for example, (8S), the version with non-preposed negation, seems to be significantly preferred to (8S') in the described context.

(8) (**Situation**: S is going to the movies.)

H: Have fun!
S: Oh, aren't you coming?
S': Oh, are you not coming?

How speakers' intuitions may vary on the preferred interpretations of negative polar interrogatives with preposed and non-preposed negation is an interesting question, which I must leave to future research.

2.4.2 Falling Tag-Interrogatives

Falling tag-interrogatives have the same structure as rising ones except that the tag is associated with a falling intonation.

(9) a. Jane is coming (too/*either), isn't she.
   b. Jane isn't coming (*too/either), is she.

While there is room for debate as to what the discourse function of the falling tag-interrogative is,[3] it

seems to be largely agreed that their function is better characterized as making a statement rather than asking a question.

2.4.3 Postnuclear Tag-Interrogatives

"Postnuclear" tag-interrogatives are similar to regular (or "nuclear") rising tag-interrogatives in terms of the final intonation within the tag, but involve a weaker prosodic boundary (indicated by the equal sign in (10)) between the host and the tag.

(10) Jane isn't coming=is she?

Reese (2007) points out that postnuclear tag-interrogatives come in two varieties. Ones of the first variety are semantically equivalent to the corresponding regular rising tag-interrogatives, and exhibit the same pattern as to the compatibility with polarity items, as in *Jane isn't coming either=is she?/Jane is coming too=isn't she?*.

Postnuclear tag-interrogatives of the second type always have a host with a ("fake") negation, which may contain a positive polarity item, as in *Jane isn't coming too=is she?*. Reese characterizes their meaning as a "neutral question". Huddleston (2002: 894) remarks that they convey that the speaker is "afraid that the positive answer is the true one", also suggesting that it may involve a mild degree of positive bias.

2.5 Section Summary: The Semantic Contrast

The three marked kinds of polar interrogatives – the positively-biased negative polar interrogative (outside-NEG interrogative), the negatively-biased negative polar interrogative (inside-NEG interrogative), and the rising tag-interrogative – semantically contrast with the unmarked polar interrogative, and with one another, in terms of the presence and direction of the bias:

(11) a. *unmarked positive polar interrogative*
       Is Jane coming?
       [neutral (no bias)]
    b. *inside-NEG polar interrogative*
       Isn't Jane coming (too)?
       [positive bias]

---

[3]Some ideas suggested in the literature are: (i) to signal "something like a hedge" (Ladd, 1981: 167), (ii) to "seek acknowledgment that the anchor [= host clause] is true" (Huddleston, 2002: 894), and (iii) to indicate that the speaker is aware that the hearer already knows the content of the host clause (Oshima, 2014: 442).

c. *outside-NEG polar interrogative*
   Isn't Jane coming (either)?
   [negative bias]

d. *rising tag-interrogative (with a positive/negative host clause)*
   Jane is coming, isn't she? / Jane isn't coming, is she?

The summary above, however, leaves out some important semantic features of the three constructions. In the following, I will argue that outside-NEG and inside-NEG interrogatives convey additional, subtle meanings that cannot be reduced to the presence and direction of a bias, and that rising tag-interrogatives convey a stronger bias than negative polar interrogatives do.

3 A Brief Note on Existing Research

In this work, I adopt the view that the three kinds of biased interrogatives conventionally implicate epistemic biases and other subtle meanings (to be discussed below) as part of their constructional meanings (in the Construction-Grammatical sense).

Alternative ideas have been put forth, according to which such meaning components are derivative of (i) other independently motivated features of the three constructions, and/or (ii) more general processes including conversational implicature (e.g., van Rooy and Šafářová, 2003; Romero and Han, 2004; Romero, 2005; Reese, 2007; Farkas and Roelofsen, 2017; Krifka, 2017). This work does not aim to make any claim against such "reductionist" theories. My goal here is to provide thorough descriptions of the meanings of the three constructions, which hopefully will contribute to the discussion of how and to what extent different kinds of reductionist approaches are useful in accounting for the relevant semantic/pragmatic phenomena.

4 Inside-NEG Interrogatives and the "Inference on the Spot" Condition

Ladd (1981) points out that an inside-NEG interrogative indicates that the speaker previously expected $\neg p_c$ to be true, but "has just inferred" $\neg p_c$ in the discourse situation. Romero and Han (2004), in a similar vein, state that the speaker "starts with the positive belief or expectation" when asking an inside-NEG interrogative. (12) exemplifies a felicitous utterance that satisfies this "inference on the spot" condition. (13), on the other hand, is infelicitous due to violation of this constraint.

(12) (**Situation**: Pat and Jane are two phonologists who are supposed to be speaking in the workshop tomorrow.)
   H: Pat is not coming. So we don't have any phonologists in the program.
   S: Isn't Jane coming either?
   (adapted from Romero and Han, 2004: 611)

(13) (**Situation**: S is preparing lunch for Jane. S thinks that Jane is probably not a vegetarian, but wants to make sure. He sees Nancy, Jane's sister, and asks her:)
   S: #Hey, isn't Jane a vegetarian?
   S': Hey, Jane is not a vegetarian, is she?

In this sense, the inside-NEG interrogative can be said to have a flavor of *mirativity*, which DeLancey (1997, 2001) defines as "linguistic marking of an utterance as conveying information which is new or unexpected to the speaker".

The "inference on the spot" condition as put forth by these authors leads to the prediction that (14) conveys that S had estimated the chance of Jane's coming to be significantly higher than 50%, rather than been neutral on the matter. Speakers' judgments on this point could be subtle, but the experimental results presented by Filippo et al. (2017) seem to support their intuition.

(14) (**Situation:** S and Nancy are going to the movies. S is waiting for Nancy, who went to check if Jane would want to join them. Nancy comes back by herself. S asks:)
   Isn't she coming?

5 Outside-NEG Interrogatives and the "Matter of Interest" Condition

Unlike the inside-NEG interrogative, the outside-NEG interrogative does not implicate that the (positive) epistemic bias has been formed in the discourse situation. The following example illustrates this point:

(15) (**Situation**: S's roommate comes back from a
trip to a conference. S has previously heard
from Jane, S and H's mutual friend, that she
was planning to attend the same conference.)

S_1: How was the conference?

H: It was pretty good. My talk went okay, and
I got to talk to quite a few people.

S_2: Wasn't Jane there too?

Outside-NEG interrogatives, however, appear to
be subject to be a subtle pragmatic constraint that
has not been explicitly discussed in the literature.
Observe that outside-NEG interrogatives (16S') and
(18S') are less natural than the corresponding (i)
positive polar interrogatives and (ii) rising tag-
interrogatives with a positive host, and that the same
sentences are fully acceptable in the alternative contexts specified in (17) and (19).

(16) (**Situation**: S needs assistance from somebody
who speaks Chinese. He has heard that Amy
speaks Chinese, but wants to make sure. He
asks his roommate.)

S: Does Amy speak Chinese? (positive polar
interrogative)

S': ?Doesn't Amy speak Chinese? (outside-
NEG)

S": Amy speaks Chinese, doesn't she? (rising
tag)

(17) (**Situation**: S has heard that Amy speaks Chinese.)

H: Prof. Li is looking for a TA for his Chinese linguistics course. Can you think of
anybody? He would prefer somebody who
speaks Chinese.

S: Does Amy speak Chinese? (positive polar
interrogative)

S': Doesn't Amy speak Chinese? (outside-
NEG)

S": Amy speaks Chinese, doesn't she? (rising
tag)

(18) (**Situation**: S needs some postage stamps. He
thinks that the nearby convenience store should
have them, but he is not completely sure. He
goes to the living room and asks his wife:)

S: Can you buy postage stamps at convenience stores? (positive polar interroga-

tive)

S': ?Can't you buy postage stamps at convenience stores? (outside-NEG)

S": You can buy postage stamps at convenience stores, can't you? (rising tag)

(19) (**Situation**: S's wife asks him if he can quickly
drive to the post office to buy some postage
stamps. He thinks that it will be easier to go to
the nearby convenience store, but is not completely sure if they have postal stamps. So he
asks her:)

S: Can you buy postage stamps at convenience stores? (unmarked polar interrogative)

S': Can't you buy postage stamps at convenience stores? (outside-NEG)

S": You can buy postage stamps at convenience stores, can't you? (rising tag)

Utterances (16S') and (18S'), though fully interpretable, sound deviated from the natural dynamics
of conversation. They give the hearer the impression
that the speaker has failed to provide some relevant
preliminary information, much like in cases of presupposition failure. I suggest that an outside-NEG
interrogative conveys that the speaker assumes that
the core proposition is likely (i) to hold true, and,
furthermore, (ii) to be something that is activated
in the hearer's mind (as in (15)) or that the hearer
should pay attention to (as in (17)/(19)).

It can be easily confirmed, with a discourse like
(20), that the inside-NEG interrogative is not subject to this constraint, which I tentatively name the
"matter of interest" constraint.

(20) (**Situation**: S has always thought Jane is a vegetarian. One day, he sees a picture of her holding a chicken wing on her website. Surprised,
he says to Nancy, her sister, who happened to
be sitting next to him:)

Oh, isn't Jane a vegetarian? (inside-NEG)

6   Truth vs. Accepted Truth

Another difference between the inside-NEG interrogative on the one hand and the outside-NEG interrogative and the rising tag-interrogative on the
other is that only the former makes reference to

the speaker's assumptions (expectations) about the hearer's beliefs.

Outside-NEG interrogatives and rising tag-interrogatives can be felicitously used when it is contextually clear that p_c is *not* part of the hearer's beliefs, with the intention to suggest the hearer to revise his beliefs. (21S, S') illustrate this point.

(21) (**Situation**: H is Jane's brother.)

    H: Jane really should stop lazing around and get a job.

    S: Aren't you too harsh on your sister? You know what the current job market is like.

    S': You are too harsh on your sister, aren't you? You know what the current job market is like.

I suggest that an inside-NEG interrogative conveys that the speaker believes not only that $\neg p_c$ is likely to be true, but also that $\neg p_c$ is likely to be part of the hearer's beliefs. This supposition is motivated by the contrast illustrated in the following set of examples. (Notice that p_c/p_h for (22S)/(22S') and $\neg p_c$ for (22S") are truth-conditionally equivalent.)

(22) (**Situation**: S and H are organizing an academic colloquium. On the day before the colloquium, H shows S the room that he has arranged. S expected H to choose a larger room, and thinks that the arranged room will be too small to accommodate the audience. S says:)

    S: Isn't this room {too small/not large enough}? (outside-NEG)

    S': This room is too small, isn't it? / This room is not large enough, is it? (rising tag)

    S": #Isn't this room large enough? (inside-NEG)

The infelicity of (22S") cannot be attributed of the violation of the "on the spot" condition, as in the provided scenario it is clear that S's assumption that the room is likely not to be large enough (likely to be too small) did not exist prior to the discourse, and was formed right before his utterance. The infelicity of (22S") should rather be attributed to the fact that S cannot sensibly expect H to share the belief that the room is likely not to be large enough before his utterance.

7 Degrees of Likelihood

To summarize the discussions so far, the three marked polar interrogative constructions contrast with the unmarked positive polar interrogative and with each other in the following way (CI stands for "conventional implicature"):

(23) a. *unmarked positive polar interrogative*
    Is Jane coming?
    CI: none

    b. *outside-NEG interrogative*
    Isn't Jane coming (too)?
    CI: S believes that p_c is likely to (i) hold true and (ii) be a matter of interest for H.

    c. *inside-NEG interrogative*
    Isn't Jane coming (either)?
    CI: S previously believed that p_c was likely to be true, and has just come to believe that $\neg p_c$ is likely to (i) hold true and (ii) be part of H's beliefs.

    d. *rising tag-interrogative*
    Jane is coming, isn't she?
    CI: S believes that p_h is likely to hold true.

A further question that needs to be addressed is: Are the three marked interrogatives associated with the same *degree* of epistemic bias? Lassiter (2017) argues that markers of epistemic modality, including the auxiliaries *must* and *might*, indicate that the likelihood (probability) of the semantically embedded proposition's holding true is above or below some threshold value. More specifically, he proposes that the threshold values associated with *might*, *must*, *possible*, *likely*, and *certain* are ordered as in (24), and that each marker indicates that the likelihood of the embedded proposition exceeds its threshold value.

(24) $\theta_{possible} < \theta_{might} < \theta_{likely} < \theta_{must} < \theta_{certain}$
    (Lassiter, 2017: 140)

The relative order between *might* and *likely*, for example, can be confirmed by observing the contrast between (25) and (26).

(25) (**Situation**: The estimated chances of John's being in his office/the library/the cafeteria are 60%/20%/20% respectively.)

    a. John might be in his office.

b. John is likely to be in his office.

(26) (**Situation**: The estimated chances of John's being in his office/the library/the cafeteria are 34%/33%/33% respectively.)

   a. John might be in his office.
   b. #John is likely to be in his office.

It can be shown that the epistemic biases conveyed by the three marked interrogatives are, in a similar vein, associated with different degrees of likelihood.

7.1 The Outside-NEG Interrogative vs. the Rising Tag-Interrogative

The bias conveyed by a rising tag-interrogative is stronger than that conveyed by an outside-NEG interrogative. This can be illustrated with discourse sets like the following.

(27) (**Situation**: A guard sees a group of youth drinking beer on a river bank. They look like about **16 years old**. (The drinking age here is 21.) The guard asks:)

   S: Aren't you guys under age?
   S': You guys are under age, aren't you?

(28) (**Situation**: A guard sees a group of youth drinking beer on a river bank. They look like about **19 years old**. (The drinking age here is 21.) The guard asks:)

   S: Aren't you guys under age?
   S': ?You guys are under age, aren't you?

(29) (**Situation**: H goes to the library to see if John is there. S estimates the chance of John's being there is about **95%**. H comes back, and S asks her:)

   S: Wasn't John there?
   S': John was there, wasn't he?

(30) (**Situation**: H goes to the library to see if John is there. S estimates the chance of John's being there is about **75%**. H comes back, and S asks her:)

   S: Wasn't John there?
   S': ?John was there, wasn't he?

The outside-NEG interrogative and the rising tag-interrogative semantically differ in that only the lat-

ter is subject to the aforementioned "matter of interest" condition. Thus, the choice between them cannot be fully reduced to the matter of the degree of certainty. Utterance pairs (27S/S') and (28S/S'), and utterance pairs (29S/S') and (30S/S'), however, differ only with respect to the degree of likelihood that the speaker assigns to $p_{c/h}$. To account for the observation that only the acceptability of the rising tag-interrogatives is sharply affected by the decrease of the estimated likelihood, it must be concluded that the rising tag-interrogative is associated with a higher threshold value on the scale of likelihood than the outside-NEG interrogative, i.e., $\theta_{Out\text{-}NEG\text{-}Int} < \theta_{Rising\text{-}Tag\text{-}Int}$.

7.2 The Inside-NEG Interrogative vs. the Rising Tag-Interrogative

To compare the strength of the biases conveyed by a rising tag-interrogative and by an inside-NEG interrogative, we need to construct discourse situations where (i) the "on the spot" condition is met and (ii) "$\neg p_c$ is true and known to H" and "p_h is true" practically entail each other. Discourse sets (31)–(34) satisfy these criteria.

(31) (**Situation**: S and H know that Jane eats meat very infrequently – **at most a couple of times a year**. S notices that there is a sandwich on the table, and asks H whose it is.)

   H: I bought this for Jane, but she cannot come. You can have it if you like.
   S: So, doesn't it have any meat?
   S': So, it doesn't have any meat, does it?

(32) (**Situation**: S and H know that Jane eats meat sparingly – **about 2–3 times in a week**. S notices that there is a sandwich on the table, and asks H whose it is.)

   H: I bought this for Jane, but she cannot come. You can have it if you like.
   S: So, doesn't it have any meat?
   S': ?So, it doesn't have any meat, does it?

(33) (**Situation**: S and H are roommates. H told S in the morning that he would go to the city library. When H goes to the city library, he **always** checks out three or more books and put them in the bookcase in the living room. S comes home in the evening, and notices that

there is no library book in the bookcase. S asks:)

S: Didn't you go to the library?
S': You didn't go to the library, did you?

(34) (**Situation**: S and H are roommates. H told S in the morning that he would go to the city library. When H goes to the city library, he **usually** checks out some books and put them in the bookcase in the living room, but sometimes he does not check out any books. S comes home in the evening, and notices that there is no library book in the bookcase. S asks:)

S: Didn't you go to the library?
S': ?You didn't go to the library, did you?

The illustrated contrasts between (31) and (32) and between (33) and (34) indicate that the threshold value of likelihood for the rising tag-interrogative is higher than the one for the inside-NEG interrogative, i.e., $\theta_{In\text{-}NEG\text{-}Int} < \theta_{Rising\text{-}Tag\text{-}Int}$.

7.3 The Outside-NEG Interrogative vs. the Inside-NEG Interrogative

The remaining question is: How do the outside-NEG and inside-NEG interrogatives compare in terms of the strength of bias? The procedure of constructing minimal pairs and placing them in different contexts, which was used above to compare the rising tag-interrogative and the two kinds of negative polar interrogatives, cannot be easily applied here, because it is hard to construct discourse situations where (i) either an outside-NEG interrogative or the inside-NEG interrogative corresponding to it can be felicitously uttered (without violating the "matter of interest" or "inference on the spot" condition), where the correspondence relation is defined as: outside-NEG Q_1 corresponds to inside-NEG Q_2 (and vice versa) if and only if p_c of Q_1 is equivalent (in the context) to $\neg p_c$ of Q_2, and furthermore (ii) the "$\neg p_c$" for the inside-NEG is practically equivalent to "$\neg p_c$ is known to H".

I do not attempt to provide a definitive answer to this question. It can be pointed out, however, that the two constructions seem to exhibit a subtle difference as to their compatibility with hedge phrases such as *maybe* and *possibly*; that is, the outside-NEG interrogative seems to be more tolerant to the occurrence of a hedge phrase following it, after a intonation-phrase boundary.

(35) a. Is Jane coming too, {maybe/possibly}?
     b. Isn't Jane coming too, {maybe/possibly}?
     c. Isn't Jane coming either, {?maybe/?possibly}?

This contrast, if proven to be real, may be taken as evidence that the inside-NEG interrogative conveys a stronger bias than the outside-NEG interrogative. Arguably, such hedge phrases are used to convey that the speaker's estimate of the likelihood of the relevant proposition does *not* exceed a certain threshold value, which is designated here as α for convenience. In (35a,b), the hedge phrases indicate that the speaker's estimate of $prob(\textbf{Jane-is-coming})$ does not exceed α. In (35c), the hedge phrases would indicate that the speaker's estimate of $prob(\neg\textbf{Jane-is-coming})$ does not exceed α.[4] The contrast between (35b) and (35c) can be accounted for if we hypothesize that α is, at least typically, set higher than $\theta_{Out\text{-}NEG\text{-}Int}$ but lower than $\theta_{In\text{-}NEG\text{-}Int}$ (i.e., $\theta_{Out\text{-}NEG\text{-}Int} < \alpha < \theta_{In\text{-}Tag\text{-}Int}$), leading to inconsistency between a "high" expectation conveyed by an inside-NEG interrogative and a "not-so-high" expectation signaled by a hedge phrase.

8 Summary

This work examined the semantic contrasts between the three kinds of marked polar interrogatives: (i) the positively-biased negative polar interrogative (the outside-NEG interrogative), (ii) the negatively-biased negative polar interrogative (the inside-NEG interrogative), and (iii) the rising tag-interrogative. It was argued that (i) a positively-biased negative polar interrogative conveys that the speaker assumes that the core proposition is likely to be something that is or should be activated in the hearer's mind, (ii) the bias associated with a negatively-biased negative polar interrogative makes reference to the speaker's assumptions about the hearer's beliefs, and (iii) the biases associated with the three constructions differ in strength, the one of the rising tag-interrogative being the strongest.

---

[4]Given that the negation involved in an inside-NEG interrogative is a regular kind of negation (§2.2), it is natural to expect that it falls under the scope of a hedge phrase.

Acknowledgments

Many thanks to David Beaver, John Beavers, Michael Everdell, Daniel Lassiter, Maribel Romero, Yasutada Sudo, and Stephen Wechsler for helpful comments and discussions. This work was supported by JSPS KAKENHI Grant Number 15K02476.

References

Scott DeLancey. 1997. Mirativity: The grammatical marking of unexpected information. *Linguistic Typology*, 1(1):33–52.

Scott DeLancey. 2001. The mirative and evidentiality. *Journal of Pragmatics*, 33(3):369–382.

Donka F. Farkas and Floris Roelofsen. 2017. Division of labor in the interpretation of declaratives and interrogatives. *Journal of Semantics*, 34(2):237–289.

Domaneschi Filippo, Maribel Romero, and Bettina Braun. 2017. Bias in polar questions: Evidence from English and German production experiments. *Glossa: A Journal of General Linguistics*, 2(26):1–28.

Rodney Huddleston. 2002. Clauset type and illocutionary force. In Rodney Huddleston and Geoffrey K. Pullum, editors, *The Cambridge Grammar of the English Language*, pages 851–946. Cambridge University Press, Cambridge.

Satoshi Ito and David Y. Oshima. 2016. On two varieties of negative polar interrogatives in Japanese. In Michael Kenstowicz, Ted Levin, and Ryo Masuda, editors, *Japanese/Korean Linguistics*, volume 23, pages 229–243. CSLI Publications, Stanford.

Manfred Krifka. 2017. Negated polarity questions as denegations of assertions. In Chungmin Lee, Ferenc Kiefer, and Manfred Krifka, editors, *Contrastiveness in Information Structure, Alternatives and Scalar Implicatures*, pages 359–398. Springer, Heidelberg.

D. Robert Ladd. 1981. A first look at the semantics and pragmatics of negative questions and tag questions. In *Proceedings of the 17th Annual Meeting of Chicago Linguistic Society*, pages 164–171.

Daniel Lassiter. 2017. *Graded Modality: Qualitative and Quantitative Perspectives*. Oxford University Press, Oxford.

James D. McCawley. 1988. *The Syntactic Phenomena of English*, volume 2. The University of Chicago Press, Chicago.

David Y. Oshima. 2014. On the functional differences between the discourse particles *ne* and *yone* in Japanese. In *Proceedings of the 28th Pacific Asia Conference on Language, Information and Computation*, pages 442–451.

Brian Reese. 2007. *Bias in Questions*. Ph.D. thesis, University of Texas Austin.

Maribel Romero and Chung-Hye Han. 2004. On negative "yes/no" questions. *Linguistics and Philosophy*, 27(5):659–658.

Maribel Romero. 2005. Two approaches to biased *yes/no* questions. In John Alderete, Chung-hye Han, and Alexei Kochetov, editors, *Proceedings of the 24th West Coast Conference on Formal Linguistics*, pages 352–360. Cascadilla Press, Somerville.

Robert van Rooy and Marie Šafářová. 2003. On polar questions. In Robert B. Young and Yuping Zhou, editors, *Proceedings of Semantics and Linguistic Theory XIII*, pages 292–309. CLC Publications, Ithaka.

The blocking effect and Korean *caki*

Hyunjun Park
Department of Chinese Language and Literature
Chungbuk National University
Chengju, South Korea 28644
tudorgepark@gmail.com

Haihua Pan
Department of Linguistics and Modern Languages
The Chinese University of Hong Kong
Shatin, New Territories, Hong Kong
panhaihua@cuhk.edu.hk

Abstract

When the Chinese reflexive *ziji* is located far from its antecedents, it is not uncommon to see the blocking effect, since the long-distance binding of *ziji* is normally blocked by the presence of a first (or second) person pronoun intervening in the reported speech. Conversely, it has generally been accepted that Korean *caki* does not manifest any blocking effects. However, in this paper, we propose that the blocking effect exists in the long-distance binding of Korean *caki*.

1 Introduction

When the Chinese reflexive *ziji* is located far from its antecedents, it is not uncommon to see the blocking effect, since the long-distance binding of *ziji* is normally blocked by the presence of a first (or second) person pronoun intervening in the reported speech (Y.-H. Huang 1984, Cole et al. 1990, Huang and Tang 1991, Huang and Liu 2001, Pan 2001, Cole et al. 2006, among others), as shown in (1) and (2).

(1) Zhangsan$_i$ renwei Lisi$_j$ zhidao Wangwu$_k$
Zhangsan think Lisi know Wangwu
xihuan ziji$_{i/j/k}$.
like self
'Zhangsan$_i$ thinks Lisi$_j$ knows Wangwu$_k$ likes self$_{i/j/k}$.'

(Cole et al. 1990:1)

(2) Zhangsan$_i$ renwei wo$_j$ zhidao Wangwu$_k$
Zhangsan think I know Wangwu
xihuan ziji$_{*i/*j/k}$.
like self

'Zhangsan$_i$ thinks that I$_j$ know that Wangwu$_k$ likes him$_{*i}$/me$_{*j}$/himself$_k$.'

(Cole et al. 1990:15)

The antecedent of Chinese *ziji* in (1) can be the matrix subject *Zhangsan*, the intermediate subject *Lisi*, or the most embedded subject *Wangwu*. In contrast, *ziji* in (2) can only be coreferential with the local antecedent *Wangwu* rather than the matrix subject *Zhangsan* or the intermediate subject *wo* of a first person pronoun. This phenomenon of Chinese *ziji* has long been accounted for in terms of the blocking effect, which occurs when an immediately higher noun phrase differs in the person feature from a lower noun phrase. Therefore, in (2), the intermediate subject *wo* 'I' serves as a blocker because the person feature of *wo* 'I' differs from the third person *Wangwu*.

Conversely, it has generally been accepted that Korean *caki* does not manifest any blocking effects (Yoon 1989, Cole et al. 1990, Sohng 2004, Cole et al. 2006, Han and Storoshenko 2012, Kim 2013, among others), as exemplified in (3).[1]

(3) Chelswu$_i$-nun nay$_j$-ka caki$_{i/*j}$-lul
Chelswu-Top I-Nom self-Acc
cohaha-n-ta-ko sayngkakha-n-ta.
like-Prs-Decl-Comp think-Prs-Decl
'Chelswu$_i$ thinks I$_j$ like him$_i$/myself$_{*j}$.'

---

[1] Cole et al. (1990), contrary to *caki*, assume that long-distance *casin* is subject to the blocking effect, as shown in (i).
(i) *Chelswu$_i$-nun nay$_j$-ka casin$_i$-ul saranha-n-ta-ko
Chelswu-Top I-Nom self-Acc love-Prs-Decl-Comp
sayngkakha-n-ta.
think-Prs-Decl
'*Chelswu thinks I like himself.'

(Cole et al. 1990:18)

However, we will not discuss the long-distance binding of *casin* here.

178

31st Pacific Asia Conference on Language, Information and Computation (PACLIC 31), pages 178–186
Cebu City, Philippines, November 16-18, 2017

(Cole et al. 1990:19)

In (3), *caki* can only refer to the matrix subject *Chelswu* while it does not refer to the first person pronoun *nay*. However, even if the matrix subject *Chelswu* and the first person pronoun *nay* in the embedded clause are switched, the coreferential relationship remains unchanged. Here is the relevant example.

(4) Na$_i$-nun Chelswu$_j$-ka caki$_{*i/j}$-lul
    I-Top   Chelswu-Nom self-Acc
    cohaha-n-ta-ko   sayngkakha-n-ta.
    like-Prs-Decl-Comp think-Prs-Decl
    'I$_i$ think Chelswu$_j$ likes me$_{*i}$/himself$_j$.'

Nonetheless, the question then arises as to how we can explain what blocks Korean *caki*, in a certain context, from referring to the long-distance potential antecedent, as illustrated in (5).

(5) Hyengsa$_i$-nun nay$_j$-ka caki$_{*i/j}$ pwumo-lul
    detective-Top I-Nom self   parents-Acc
    salhayha-n phaylyunpem-i-lako
    kill-Adn   reprobate-being-Comp
    sayngkakha-n-ta.
    think-Prs-Decl
    'The detective thinks that I am a reprobate who
    killed his (*the detective's/speaker's) parents.'
                    (Park 2016:102)

We assume that the first person pronoun *nay* in (5) functions as a blocker since it is unnatural for *caki* to refer to the matrix subject *Hyengsa* in this discourse.[2] Thus, based on the observed fact, this paper would like to show that a blocking effect does hold in Korean as well and to suggest the analysis of the blocking effect in Korean *caki* in terms of a unified account in line with that of Chinese *ziji*.

The organization of the paper is as follows. In the section 2, we discuss what has been said about Korean *caki*, especially with respect to the properties of *caki*. Then, in section 3, we review Huang and Liu's (2001) analysis on blocking effects. And in section 4, the blocking effect of Korean *caki* is considered. Section 5 summarizes our findings and conclusions, with a discussion of some predictions that follow from the current analysis.

2   Korean *caki*'s puzzle

Since Lee's (1973) observation, it has generally been held in the literature (Kim 1976, Cho 1985, O'Grady 1987, Yoon 1989, Cole et al. 1990, Sohng 2004, Han and Storoshenko 2012, among others) that *caki* can only have a third person human noun as its antecedent. Thus, Sohng (2004) argues that *caki* has inherent Φ-features with a third person. Such a distinction could be demonstrated by the following sentences.

    pemin-i-lako   sayngkakha-n-ta.
    criminal-being-Comp think-Prs-Decl
    'The people think that I am a criminal who killed his
    (*their/the speaker's) parents.'
The matrix subject *Salamtul* 'people' cannot be the antecedent of *caki* in this sentence while *nay* 'I' can. On the other hand, in the following example, as pointed out by an anonymous reviewer, the internal speaker *Chelswu* is much more likely to be the antecedent of *caki* here rather than the external speaker *nay* unlike (ii).
(iii) Chelswu$_i$-un nay$_j$-ka caki$_{i/*j}$ pwumo-lul salhayha-n
    Chelswu-Top I-Nom self   parents-Acc kill-Adn
    pemin-i-lako   sayngkakha-n-ta.
    criminal-being-Comp think-Prs-Decl
    'Chelswu thinks that I am a criminal who killed his
    (Chelswu/??the speaker's) parents.'
In this case, we can only conjecture that this is attributed mainly to the typical property of *caki* to refer to an attitude holder. In other words, Korean *caki* functions as a logophor in the majority of cases unless particular clues are provided in the discourse. In the same vein, *caki* in (i) can have two readings in that it is coreferential with *hyungsa* when used as a logophor while it is also coindexed to *nay* when the actual speaker objectively describes the situation from the detective's perspective, as in Kuno's (1987) empathy. Ultimately, likelihood of the story depends on the context.

Based on the observed facts, we assume here that a blocking effect does hold in Korean as well. Further discussion is included in section 4.

---

[2] Some may claim that (5) is a kind of a special occasion in this context and thus the blocking of *caki*'s referring to *hyengsa* is attributed just to the lexical property of *phaylyunpem* 'reprobate', which means to harm one's own lineal ascendant and descendant. Thus, if *phaylyunpem* is replaced by neutral word *pemin* 'criminal', *caki* can also refer to either *hyengsa* or *nay*, as shown in (i).
(i) Hyengsa$_i$-nun nay$_j$-ka caki$_{i/j}$ pwumo-lul salhayha-n
    detective-Top I-Nom self parents-Acc kill-Adn
    pemin-i-lako   sayngkakha-n-ta.
    criminal-being-Comp think-Prs-Decl
    'The detective thinks that I am a criminal who killed his
    (the detective's/speaker's) parents.'
We agree with the view. If so, however, how should we account for the following sentence?
(ii) Salamtul$_i$-un nay$_j$-ka caki$_{*i/j}$ pwumo-lul salhayha-n
    people-Top I-Nom self   parents-Acc kill-And

(6) *Nay$_i$-ka caki$_j$-lul piphanhay-ess-ta.
   I-Nom self-Acc criticize-Pst-Decl
   'I criticized myself.'
(7) *Ney$_i$-ka caki$_j$-lul piphanhay-ess-ta.
   You-Nom self-Acc criticize-Pst-Decl
   'You criticized yourself.'
(8) Chelswu$_i$-ka caki$_j$-lul piphanhay-ess-ta.
   Chelswu-Nom self-Acc criticize-Pst-Decl
   'Chelswu criticized himself.'

In comparison with *caki*, *ziji* seems to be much more versatile in that it can be used to refer to all persons, as shown in (9) and (10).

(9) Zhangsan$_i$ juede {wo/ni}$_j$ dui ziji$_{*i/j}$
   Zhangsan think I/you   to self
   mei xinxin.
   not confidence
   'Zhangsan thinks I/you have no confidence in myself/yourself/*him.'
(10) Zhangsan$_i$ zhidao Lisi$_j$ dui ziji$_{i/j}$ mei xinxin.
   Zhangsan think Lisi to self not confidence
   'Zhangsan thinks Lisi has no confidence in him/himself.'

(Pan 2001:280)

On the other hand, Yoon (1989:486) points out that the incompatibility of *caki* with first or second person antecedents can be readily accounted for in terms of the notion of a logophor since it could be very awkward for an external speaker or an addressee participating in the current discourse to report their own thoughts or feelings in an indirect way.[3] For this reason, she further argues that the behaviors of *caki* binding fit nicely into the notion of logophoricity. In fact, Pearson (2013) reports that logophoric pronouns in Ewe are necessarily construed as referring to the reported speaker and the attitude holder is preferentially occupied by a third person.[4] The relevant data are from Pearson (2013).

(11) a. *M xɔse   be yè nyi sukuvi nyoe de.
       Pro believe that Log Cop student good Art
       'I believe that I am a good student.'
    b. M xɔse   be m nyi sukuvi nyoe de.
       Pro believe that Pro Cop student good Art
       'I believe that I am a good student.'
(12) a. *O xɔse   be yè nyi sukuvi nyoe de.
       Pro believe that Log Cop student good Art
       'You believe that you are a good student.'
    b. O xɔse   be o nyi sukuvi nyoe de.
       Pro believe that Pro Cop student good Art
       'You believe that you are a good student.'

(Pearson 2013:449-50)

The only difference between (11a) and (11b) is that a logophor *yè* in (11a) is used in the complement clause and it is replaced by the first person pronoun *m* in (11b). However, it is incorrect when *yè* refers to the first person pronoun in the matrix subject while the first person pronoun *m* can refer. It is not correct in (12a), either when *yè* refers to the second person pronoun *o* in the matrix subject.

It seems that there is a clear relationship between the role of a logophor and the absence of blocking effects in Korean *caki*. A blocking effect does not usually occur in a logophoric environment since a logophor preferentially occurs with a third person antecedent. The following examples illustrate this point.

(13) Kofi$_i$ xɔ   agbalẽ tso gbɔ-nye$_j$ be
    Kofi receive letter from side-Pro that
    yè$_{i/*j}$-a-va   me kpe na m.
    Log-T-come cast block for Pro
    'Kofi$_i$ got a letter from me saying that he$_i$ should come cast blocks for me.'
(14) Me$_i$-xɔ   agbalẽ tso Kofi$_j$ gbɔ be
    Pro-receive letter from Kofi side that
    ma$_i$-va   me kpe na yè$_j$.
    Pro/T-come cast block for Pro
    'I$_i$ got a letter from Kofi$_j$ saying that I$_i$ should come cast blocks for him$_i$.'

---

[3] As pointed out by many authors working on Korean *caki*, there are two different uses. One is a syntactic anaphor and the other is a logophor. We do not discuss here the syntactic anaphor, which is related to locally bound *caki*.

[4] As is seen in (9) and (10), *ziji* can refer to the antecedents regardless of person features. Thus, Pan (2001) contends that the long-distance binding of *ziji* should not be treated as a logophor. In addition, *ziji* in the complement clause can be coindexed to the first (or second) person pronoun in the matrix subject, as shown in (i) and (ii).
(i) Wo$_i$ zhidao Lisi$_j$ de baogao hai-le   ziji$_{i/j}$.

I   know Lisi DE report hurt-Perf self
'I knew that Lisi's report hurt me/him.'
(ii) Ni$_i$ xiang mei xiang guo Lisi$_j$ conglai jiu
   You think not think Guo Lisi never Conj
   mei xihuan guo ziji$_{i/j}$?
   not like   Guo self
   'Have you ever thought about the idea that Lisi never liked you/himself?'

(Pan 2001:283-4)

The first person pronouns intervening between the logophor *yè* and the higher potential antecedent *Kofi* both in (13) and (14) really do not affect the long-distance binding of logophors. The behaviors of long-distance binding of *caki* exactly correspond to those of a logophor. Consider the related examples in Korean *caki*, repeated here in (15) and (16) from (3) and (4).

(15) Chelswu$_i$-nun nay$_j$-ka caki$_{i/*j}$-lul
    Chelswu-Top I-Nom self-Acc
    cohaha-n-ta-ko   sayngkakha-n-ta.
    like-Prs-Decl-Comp think-Prs-Decl
    'Chelswu$_i$ thinks I$_j$ like him$_i$/myself$_{*j}$.'
(16) Na$_i$-nun Chelswu$_j$-ka   caki$_{*i/j}$-lul
    I-Top   Chelswu-Nom self-Acc
    cohaha-n-ta-ko   sayngkakha-n-ta.
    like-Prs-Decl-Comp think-Prs-Decl
    'I$_i$ think Chelswu$_j$ likes me$_{*i}$/himself$_j$.'

Then now let's go back to the blocking effect of *caki*, repeated here in (17) from (5).

(17) Hyengsa$_i$-nun nay$_j$-ka caki$_{*i/j}$ pwumo-lul
    detective-Top I-Nom self   parents-Acc
    salhayha-n phaylyunpem-i-lako
    kill-Adn   reprobate-being-Comp
    sayngkakha-n-ta.
    think-Prs-Decl
    'The detective thinks that I am a reprobate who killed his (*the detective's/speaker's) parents.'

Caki in (17) may be coreferential with the first person pronoun *na(y)* here, even though the long-distance binding of *caki* is blocked by the person mismatch. If the sentence is grammatical, it should be noted that the notion of logophoricity is not functioning properly here. Thus, we would like to propose an alternative analysis for blocking effects in the next section.

3   Reanalysis of Huang and Liu (2001)

Huang and Liu (2001) give a plausible account of the so-called blocking effect of long-distance binding in Chinese by relying on the notion of logophoricity. The crucial thing is that a blocking effect arises as a consequence of a conflict of perspective in the process of switching from direct to indirect speech.

(18) [1 [1 ... ziji ...]]
        ↑______________|

(19) [2 [2 ... ziji ...]]
        ↑______________|

(20) [3 [3 ... ziji ...]]
        ↑______________|

According to their view, (18) to (20) do not induce the blocking effect since the referents are homogeneous in a single context. On the other hand, the blocking effects occur in the following situation instead.

(21) *[3 [1 ... ziji ...]]
        ↑______________|

(22) *[3 [2 ... ziji ...]]
        ↑______________|

Thus the following examples are the typical cases of blocking effects in Chinese.

(23) Zhangsan$_i$ juede {wo/ni}$_j$ zai piping ziji$_{*i/j}$.
    Zhangsan think   I/you   at   criticize self
    'Zhangsan$_i$ thinks that {I/you}$_j$ are criticizing him$_{*i}$/myself$_j$/yourself$_j$.'
                   (Huang and Liu 2001:161-2)

However, blocking effects are much more complicated than they predicted. Here is the evidence in favor of this view.

(24) Mama$_i$ shuo jia   chuqu-de nüer$_j$
    mother say marry go.out-DE daughter
    yijing hui   lai   ziji$_{i/*j}$-de jia   le.
    already return come self-DE home Asp
    'Mother$_i$ said that the married daughter$_j$ had already come back to her$_{i/*j}$ home.'
(25) Mama$_i$ shuo jia   chuqu-de nüer$_j$
    mother say marry go.out-DE daughter
    yijing hui   qu ziji$_{*i/j}$-de jia   le.
    already return go   self-DE   home Asp

'Mother$_i$ said that the married daughter$_j$ had already gone back to her$_{*i/j}$ home.'

(Liu 1999:39)

Only third person referents, such as *mama* 'mother' and *nüer* 'daughter', exist in (24) and (25). Nonetheless, *ziji* cannot be bound by the long-distance antecedent *mama* 'mother' in (25) whereas it can be bound in (24). In that case, a third person intervener can serve as a blocker, as in (26).

(26) *[3 [3 ... ziji ...]]

This is totally opposed to what Huang and Liu expected, as shown in (20).[5] Here are more examples to support this point.

(27) Lisi$_i$ shuo tamen$_j$ chang piping ziji$_{i/j}$.
Lisi say they often criticize self
'Lisi$_i$ said that they often criticized him$_i$/themselves$_j$.

(28) Tamen$_i$ shuo Lisi$_j$ chang piping ziji$_{*i/j}$.
they say Lisi often criticize self
'They$_i$ said that Lisi$_j$ often criticized them$_{*i}$/himself$_j$.

(29) Tamen$_i$ shuo tamen$_j$ chang piping ziji$_{*i/j}$.
they say they often criticize self
'They$_i$ said that they$_j$ often criticized them$_{*i}$/themselves$_j$.

(Huang and Liu 2001:164-5)

An instance such as (27) shows that there is no blocking effect. However, number features, a singular noun phrase in (28) and plural noun phrase in (29), may cause blocking effects for long-distance binding even with the same person feature.

The first person plural noun phrase in (30) and the second person plural noun phrase in (31) may trigger the blocking effect of long-distance binding in Chinese.

(30) Wo$_i$ zhidao women$_j$ dui ziji$_{*i/j}$
I know we to self
mei you xinxin.
not have confidence

'I know that we have no confidence in ourselves.'

(31) Ni$_i$ zhidao nimen$_j$ dui ziji$_{*i/j}$
you(sg) know you(pl) to self
mei you xinxin.
not have confidence
'You know that you have no confidence in yourselves.'

(Xu 1993:133-4)

If this is a correct judgment, it could be opposed to what was expected as in (18) and (19).

Pan (2001), followed by Huang and Liu (2001), claim for the first time that the blocking effect in Chinese is asymmetrical: an intervening first and second person pronoun can block a third person long-distance antecedent from being coindexed with *ziji* whereas an intervening third person referent does not necessarily block a first and second person antecedent from being coindexed with *ziji*, as exemplified in (32).

(32) Wo$_i$ bu xihuan Lisi$_j$ guan ziji$_{i/j}$
I not like Lisi interfere self
de shi.
DE matter
'I$_i$ don't like Lisi$_j$ interfering in my$_i$ (own) business.'

(33) Lisi$_i$ bu xihuan wo$_j$ guan ziji$_{*i/j}$
Lisi not like I interfere self
de shi.
DE matter
'Lisi$_i$ does not like me$_j$ interfering in my$_j$ (own) business.'

(Pan 2001:283)

The person asymmetry of the blocking effect basically does not admit a third person blocker. However, as mentioned before, a third person intervener can also trigger the blocking effect.

(34) Ni$_i$ shuo Zhangsan$_j$ chang piping ziji$_{*i/j}$.
you say Zhangsan often criticize self
'You$_i$ said that Zhangsan$_j$ often criticized you$_{*i}$/himself$_j$.'

(Huang and Tang 1991:277)

The intervening third person referent *Zhangsan* in (34) does block *ziji* from referring to the second person long-distance antecedent, as shown in (35).

---

[5] Korean *caki* and Japanese *zibun* as well as Chinese *ziji* also exhibit the blocking effect by means of a third person intervener. We will discuss this matter again in section 4.

(35) *[2 [3 ... ziji ...]]

Furthermore, a closer look reveals a much more complicated situation with respect to the blocking effect. Consider the following examples.

(36) Lisi$_i$ shengpa wo$_j$ chaoguo ziji$_{i/*j}$.
    Lisi worry   I   surpass self
    'Lisi$_i$ was afraid that I$_j$ would surpass him$_i$/ myself$_{*j}$.'
             (Pollard and Xue 2001:321)

(37) Zongtong$_i$ qing wo$_j$ zuo zai ziji$_{i/*j}$ de shenbian.
    president ask I sit at self DE side
    'The president$_i$ asked me$_j$ to sit beside him$_i$/ himself$_{*j}$.'
             (Pollard and Xue 2001: 321)

(38) Wo$_i$ juede AlphaGo$_j$ yudao ziji$_{*i/j}$
    I think AlphaGo face self
    meixiangdao de yishouqi shi
    unexpected   DE situation when
    duiying nengli xiajiang.
    react   ability fall
    'I think it revealed some kind of bug when AlphaGo faced unexpected positions.'
        (Lee Se-dol' interview, 13 March, 2016)

In (36) and (37), as is well known, the intervening first person does not function as a blocker. Besides, (38) presents a very interesting fact: the inanimate feature as well as person and number can trigger the blocking effect in Chinese.[6]

In short, the blocking effect of the long-distance bound *ziji* has long been explained in terms of the notion of logophoricity. However, it cannot elucidate the nature of the blocking effect properly. For the evidence, we propose the data from Korean *caki* in the next section.

4   The blocking effect revisited and *caki*

As previously mentioned, a common thread in the literature on the blocking effect of the long-distance anaphor has mainly been concerned with the mismatch of person features between potential candidates. In addition, blocking effects have long been treated exclusively in connection with Chinese *ziji*. However, we propose here that the blocking effect in the long-distance binding of Korean *caki* also exists.[7]

It is well known that Korean *caki* is not compatible with first or second person antecedents locally as well as at a distance. Contrary to this, we propose that Korean *caki*, in some contexts, can refer to a first or second person as its referent. The following example is compatible with this idea.[8]

(39) Na$_i$-nun caki$_j$ casik-ul   cwuki-n api-lo
    I-Top   self child-Acc kill-Adn father-as
    kiloktoylkesita.
    be recorded
    'I$_i$ will be remembered as a father who killed my own child.'
    (Slightly modified from the movie 'The Throne' (2015))

Based on this fact, we further argue that the blocking effect of long-distance binding is observed in Korean as well. We repeat the relevant example here.

(40) Hyengsa$_i$-nun nay$_j$-ka caki$_{*i/j}$ pwumo-lul
    detective-Top I-Nom self   parents-Acc
    salhayha-n phaylyunpem-i-lako
    kill-Adn   reprobate-being-Comp
    sayngkakha-n-ta.
    think-Prs-Decl
    'The detective thinks that I am a reprobate who killed his (*the detective's/speaker's) parents.'

---

[6] Tang (1989) argues that the antecedent of *ziji* is inherently animate. However, we think that inanimate noun phrase can be the antecedent of *ziji*. It will be discussed for Korean *caki* in section 4.

[7] Nishigauchi (2014) also reports the existence of the blocking effect in Japanese *zibun* while no one has yet reported its presence for Korean *caki*. Here are the examples.
(i) *Taroo$_i$-wa boku$_j$-ga zibun$_i$-ni kasi-te kure-ta
    Taroo-Top I-Nom self-Dat lend   benef-Pst
    okane-o   nakusi-ta rasii.
    Money-Acc lose-Pst   seem
    '*Taroo$_i$ seems to have lost the money that I$_j$ had loaned him$_i$ (as a favor).'
    (Nishigauchi 2014:198)
[8] Im (1987) also claims that *caki* can be coreferential with a first (or second person), as shown in (i).
(i) Hyeng$_i$-un   nay$_j$-ka caki$_{i/j}$-lul piphanha-n-untey
    elder brother-Top I-Nom self-Acc criticize-Prs-about
    insaykha-ta-ko   sayngkakha-n-ta.
    stingy-Prs-Comp think-Prs-Decl
    'The older brother thinks that I am stingy with criticizing myself.' (Im 1987:150)

In this case, the long-distance binding of *caki* is blocked by the presence of an argument differing in person, as in (41).

(41) *[3 [1 ... caki ...]]

There is reason to believe that it does. Below we display the relevant examples.

(42) Emeni$_i$-nun sicip-ka-n   nay$_j$-ka
     mother-Top marry-go.out-Adn I-Nom
     caki$_{*i/j}$ cip-ulo tola-ka-ass-tako
     self   home-to return-go-Pst-Comp
     malha-yss-ta.
     say-Pst-Decl
     'Mother$_i$ said that I$_j$, who is married, had already gone back to her$_{*i/j}$ home.'
(43) Emeni$_i$-nun sicip-ka-n   ne$_j$-ka
     mother-Top marry-go.out-Adn you-Nom
     caki$_{*i/j}$ cip-ulo tola-ka-ass-tako
     self   home-to return-go-Pst-Comp
     malha-yss-ta.
     say-Pst-Decl
     'Mother$_i$ said that you$_j$, who is married, had already gone back to her$_{*i/j}$ home.'

The blocking effect is induced by the intervening first person pronoun *nay* in (42) and (43) shows that the intervening second person pronoun can act as a blocker of long-distance binding in Korean. It can be represented as in (44).

(44) *[3 [2 ... caki ...]]

A third person intervener may also trigger the blocking effect in Korean, as in (45) and (46).

(45) John$_i$-i   Mary$_j$-eykey Tom$_k$-i   caki$_i$-lul
     John-Nom Mary-Dat   Tom-Nom self-Acc
     pole-o-ass-tako   malha-yess-ta.
     see-come-Pst-Comp say-Pst-Decl
     'John$_i$ told Mary that Tom came to see/visit him$_i$.'
(46) *John$_i$-i   Mary$_j$-eykey Tom$_k$-i   caki$_i$-lul
     John-Nom Mary-Dat   Tom-Nom self-Acc
     pole-ka-ass-tako   malha-yess-ta.
     see-go-Pst-Comp say-Pst-Decl

'John$_i$ told Mary that Tom went to see/visit him$_i$.'

(Yoon 1989:486)

The blocking effect occurs only in (46), but not in (45). This is because the embedded subject *Tom* should be reported by the external speaker as the empathy locus to which *ka*- 'go' refers. However, the actual speaker empathizes with the internal speaker if *caki* refers to the matrix subject *John*. Thus the third person, *Tom*, blocks long-distance binding of *caki*, as in (47).

(47) *[3 [3 ... caki ...]]

In addition, multiple occurrences of *caki* in the same clause must refer to the same antecedent, as in (48).[9]

(48) John$_i$-i   Bill$_j$-i   caki-uy   emma-ka
     John-Nom Bill-Nom caki-Gen mother-Nom
     caki-lul silhehanta-ko sayngkakhanta-ko
     self-Acc hate-Comp   think-Comp
     malhayssta.
     said
     'John$_i$ said that Bill$_j$ thought that his$_i$ mother hates him$_i$.'
     'John$_i$ said that Bill$_j$ thought that his$_j$ mother hates him$_j$.'
     *'John$_i$ said that Bill$_j$ thought that his$_i$ mother hates him$_j$.'
     *'John$_i$ said that Bill$_j$ thought that his$_j$ mother hates him$_i$.'

(Park 2014)

We can observe that it is grammatical when the two occurrences of *caki* refer to the same antecedents whereas it is not grammatical when they refer to different antecedents. Thus a third person referent functions as a blocker if multiple instances of *caki* are not coreferential. Consider the following examples.

(49) Chelswu$_i$-nun salam-tul$_j$-i   caki$_{i/*j}$-lul
     Chelswu-Top people-Pl-Nom   self-Acc

---

[9] Huang and Liu (2001) also point out that multiple occurrences of *ziji* must be coreferential, which was originally coined by Pan (1997).

piphanha-yess-tako   sayngkakha-n-ta.
criticize-Pst-Comp   think-Prs-Decl
'Chelswu$_i$ thinks that people$_j$ criticized him$_i$/themselves$_j$.'

(50) Salam-tul$_i$-un Chelsw$_j$-ka   caki$_{*i/j}$-lul
people-Top   Chelswu-Nom   self-Acc
piphanha-yess-tako   sayngkakha-n-ta.
criticize-Pst-Comp   think-Prs-Decl
'People$_i$ think that Chelswu$_j$ criticized them$_{*i}$/himself$_j$.'

(51) Salam-tul$_i$-un   cemata Chelsw$_j$-ka
people-Pl-Top each   Chelswu-Nom
caki$_{i/j}$-lul piphanha-yess-tako
self-Acc   criticize-Pst-Comp
sayngkakha-n-ta.
think-Prs-Decl
'People$_i$ each think that Chelswu$_j$ criticized them$_i$/himself$_j$.'

The third person *Chelswu* in (50) can induce the blocking effect as well.

Although it has been noted in the literature that the property of the antecedent of *caki* is limited to animate noun phrase, we propose that *caki* can refer to an inanimate noun phrase. At this time, an inanimate referent can induce the blocking effect as well.

(52) Na$_i$-nun AlphaGo$_j$-ka   caki$_{*i/j}$-ka
I-Top   AlphaGo-Nom self-Nom
sayngkakhaci moshan swu-ka
think   not   move-Nom
nawassul ttay   tayche-nunglyek-i
come.out when react-ability-Nom
ttelecintako sayngkakha-n-ta.
fall   think-Prs-Decl
'I think it revealed some kind of bug when AlphaGo faced unexpected positions.'

Therefore, in order to accommodate these new types of blocking effect in Korean *caki* as well as in Chinese *ziji*, the alternative approach should be proposed in terms of a unified account.[10]

---

[10] We think that empathy theory, firstly proposed by Kuno and Kaburaki (1979) and developed by Oshima (2007), Nishiguchi (2014), and Wang and Pan (2014, 2015), could be an appropriate solution. We leave it to future research to elaborate on the detail.

5 Conclusion

The blocking effect of long-distance binding in Chinese *ziji* has commonly been explained in terms of the notion of logophoricity and a person asymmetry. In addition, the blocking effect has long been treated exclusively in connection with Chinese *ziji*. However, this paper proposes that the blocking effect exists in Korean *caki* as well. Moreover another type of blocker is presented for both Chinese *ziji* and Korean *caki*. In order to accommodate various blocking effects across languages, we need an alternative approach.

Acknowledgements

This research is a part of the project Long-distance Reflexives—an Asian Perspective, which is supported by a GRF grant from the Research Grants Council of Hong Kong (No. CUHK 11407214). We also appreciate the suggestions and comments made by two anonymous reviewers of PACLIC 31. All the remaining errors are, of course, ours.

References

Cole, Peter, Gabriella Hermon, and Li-May Sung. 1990. Principles and parameters of long-distance reflexives. *Linguistic Inquiry* 21: 1-22.

Cole, Peter, Gabriella Hermon, and C.-T. James Huang. 2006. Long-distance anaphors: an Asian perspective. In *SYNCOM*. Blackwell Publishers.

Han, Chung-hye and Dennis Ryan Storoshenko. 2012. Semantic binding of long-distance anaphor *caki* in Korean. *Language* 88: 764-790.

Huang, C.-T. James and C.-C. Jane Tang. 1991. The local nature of the long-distance reflexives in Chinese. In J. Koster and E. Reuland, eds., *Long-distance anaphora*, 263-282. Cambridge: Cambridge University Press.

Huang, C.-T. James and C.-S. Luther Liu. 2001. Logophoricity, attitudes, and *ziji* at the interface, In *Long-distance reflexives: Syntax and semantics 33*, ed. by Peter Cole, Gabriella Hermon, and C.-T. James Huang, 141-195. New York: Academic Press.

Im, Hong-Pin. 1987. *Kwuke-uy caykwysayenkwu* (A study on the reflexive *caki* in Korean). Seoul: Sinkwumwunhwasa.

Kim, Wha-Chun Mary. 1976. The theory of anaphora in Korean syntax. Ph.D. thesis, MIT.

Kim, Ilkyu. 2013. On blocking effects in Chinese: Syntactic, pragmatic, or both? *Korean Journal of Linguistics* 38: 305-325.

Lee, Chungmin. 1973. Abstract syntax and Korean with reference to English. Bloomington. Ph.D. thesis, University of Indiana.

Liu, Chensheng. 1999. Anaphora in Mandarin Chinese and binding at the interface. Ph.D. thesis, UC Irvine.

O'Grady, William. 1987. The interpretation of Korean anaphora: The role and representation of grammatical relations. *Language* 63: 251-277.

Pan, Haihua. 1997. *Constraints on reflexivization in Mandarin Chinese*. New York: Garland Publishing, Inc.

Pan, Haihua. 2001. Why the blocking effect? In *Long-distance reflexives: Syntax and semantics 33*, ed. by Peter Cole, Gabriella Hermon, and C.-T. James Huang, 279-316. New York: Academic Press.

Park, Hyunjun. 2016. Long-distance anaphors and the blocking effect revisited: An East Asian perspective. In *Proceedings of the 30th Pacific Asia Conference on Language, Information and Computation* (PACLIC 30), pages 95-103.

Park, Yangsook. 2014. Indexicals and the long-distance reflexive *caki* in Korean. In *Proceedings from SALT XIV*. CLS Publications.

Pearson, Hazel. 2013. The sense of self: Topics in the semantics of *de se* expressions. Ph.D. dissertation, Harvard University.

Pollard, Carl and Ping Xue. 2001. Syntactic and non-syntactic constraints on long-distance binding. In P. Cole, C.-T. J. Huang, and G. Hermon, eds., Long-distance reflexives, vol.33 of Syntax and semantics, pages 317-342. New York: Academic Press.

Sohng, Hong-Ki. 2004. A minimalist analysis of X0 reflexivization in Chinese and Korean. *Studies in Generative Grammar* 14: 375-96.

Tang, C.-C. Jane. 1989. Chinese reflexives. *Natural Language and Linguistic Theory* 7: 93-121.

Xu, Liejiong. 1993. The long-distance binding of *ziji*. *Journal of Chinese Linguistics* 21: 123-142.

Yoon, Jeong-Me. 1989. Long-distance anaphors in Korean and their cross-linguistic implications. In *Papers from the 25th Annual Meeting of the Chicago Linguistic Society*, ed. by Caroline Wiltshire, Randolph Graczyk, & Music Bradley, pages 479-495. Chicago: Chicago Linguistic Society.

Expressing prediction and epistemicity with Korean *-(u)l kes-i* and Mandarin Chinese *hui*

Eunson Yoo

Department of Chinese Language and Literature, Sun Yat-sen University
135 West Xingang RD., Guangzhou 510275, P.R. China
eunsun77@hotmail.com

Abstract

Due to the non-factual nature of futurity, there is an ongoing ambiguity between modality and futurity. The same ambiguity persists in Korean *-(u)l kes-i* and Mandarin Chinese *hui* that both express an estimation of the likelihood that the state of affairs will be realized in the world, involving the speaker's conjecture. A conjecture can be a statement expressing a prediction about what might happen or an epistemic assumption that draws a conclusion about the past and current course of events. This paper aims to show that *-(u)l kes-i* can express both prediction and epistemicity whereas the use of *hui* is limited to prediction. The present paper argues that *-(u)l kes-i* encodes the reasoning process which can be reversible from cause to consequence and consequence to cause, whereas *hui* encodes linkage between events in a forward direction whereby cause precedes consequence.

Keywords: *-(u)l kes-i, hui,* conjecture, prediction, epistemicity, cause, consequence

1 Introduction

Commonly, *-(u)l kes-i* and *hui* both encode prediction based on the speaker's observation. In Korean, *-(u)l kes-i*, which is based on a periphrastic construction, [1] is explained by Kim (1987) as expressing the speaker's volition or supposition and is used for both a definite future and a probable present or past. In addition, the adnominal ending *-(u)l* adds uncertainty as it indicates that an event has not yet occurred. [2]

(1) kkamakwi-ka wul-ko   iss-ta
    crow-Nom   cry-Con   exist-Dec
    mwen-ka   pwulkilha-n   il-i
    something-Nom be:ominous-Adn thing-Nom
    ilena-l   kes-i-ta
    happen-Adn thing-Cop-Dec
    'A crow is crying. Something bad will happen'.
    [3] (Kim 2012:39)

---

[1] *-(u)l kes-i* is a combination of an adnominal form *-(u)l* and the pronominal kes 'thing' and the copula i 'be'.

[2] A reviewer made a comment that instead of *-(u)l kes-i* as a modal auxiliary, the meanings of prediction and epistemicity can better be attributed to the adnominal ending *-(u)l* as opposed to *-(nu)n*. There has been an approach to dividing *-(u)l* and *-(nu)n* as irrealis and realis markers, which involves the concept of modality and defines them as modal markers. However, there is an ongoing debate over the usage of *-(u)l*. Pak (2009) argues that *-(u)l* still requires a periphrastic construction such as *-(u)l kes kath* to fully express the speaker's

conjecture. Lim (2008) defines *-(u)l kes-i* as an epistemic modal that draws a conclusion based on common knowledge. Given this, this paper defines *-(u)l kes-i* as a modal marker instead of a modal auxiliary.

[3] Abbreviations used in this paper: Acc (accusative), Adn (adnominal), Cl (classifier), Cop (copula), Comp (complementizer), Con (Connective), Dec (declarative), Ind (indicative morpheme), Nom (nominative), Nmlz (nominalization), Prs (present), Pst (past), Part (particle), Sfp (sentence-final particle), Top (topic)

In Mandarin Chinese, with no morphological tenses, it is commonly believed that other factors such as tense and aspect particles contribute to expressing futurity. The modal auxiliary verb *hui* 'may, will' presents the speaker's judgment of the possibility of a situation.[4] Fei Ren (2008) argues that when using *hui*, the speaker makes a predication based on what is observed and evaluates the possibility of a situation at the moment of speaking, based on information not explicitly stated in the sentence.

(2) Kan yangzi,   hui xiayu
    Look-appearance, Mod-rain
    'It looks like it will rain.'   (Zhu 1982: 63)

As seen above, *-(u)l kes-i* and *hui* express a prediction which is derived from the construction that q is contingent upon p. Lim (2008: 222, 237-238) claims that *-(u)l kes-i* is an epistemic modal marker that draws a conclusion based on common knowledge and denotes a conjecture based on internally-processed information. As a result, *-(u)l kes-i* expresses the speaker's conjecture based on the knowledge or beliefs of the speaker or others, as opposed to *-keyss* that expresses the speaker's conjecture based on the speaker's perception on the spot or his/her perceptivity, as illustrated below by Lim:

(3) a. ya, masiss-keyss-ta
     oh, be:delicious-Mod-Dec
     'Oh, it must be delicious.'
  b. ne-to masiss-ul ke-ya
     you-too be:delicious-Adn-Sfp
     'you will like it too.'

Lim explains that (3a) denotes the speaker's conjecture about the food that is just ordered on the spot, whereas (3b) implies a conjecture based on past knowledge about the food that the speaker is already acquainted with.

In his analysis of Mandarin Chinese modal verbs, *neng* and *hui*, Min (2007: 77) argues that *neng* and *hui* are often found in complex sentences, in which *hui* establishes the presence of a logical and causal relation between the main and subordinate clauses, in contrast to *neng* that does not imply causation. According to Jiun-Shiung Wu (2010), *hui* involves a statement based on knowledge, whereas *jiang* expresses a pure future in which the speaker simply presents a situation that will occur in the future without providing any information.

Puente, et al. (2009) explain that causation is a useful way of generating knowledge and providing explanations and is a type of relationship between two entities, cause and effect, and at the same time, causality not only concerns causal statements but also conditional sentences. In conditional statements, causality emerges from the relationship between antecedent and consequent.

In addition to this common feature of *-(u)l kes-i* and *hui*, the process of predicting an effect from a cause can also be reversed, and reasoning backward requires the process of inferring a cause from an effect. In terms of two reasoning processes, this paper aims to examine how *-(u)l kes-i* and *hui* are realized: 1) in predictive statements, constructed in the cause to consequence order, including generics and habituals in which general information is used to predict future consequences; 2) in epistemic statements[5] which provide an account of the state of the conjecture from the known effect; and 3) in the causal and conditional constructions through a corpus investigation. It will be argued that in the cause to consequence (p→q) order, *-(u)l kes-i* and *hui* are both used to denote prediction, while in the consequence to cause (q→p) order, only *-(u)l kes-i* can be applied to express an epistemic assumption.

2   Predictions and Generics/Habituals

Prediction entails a causal relationship in which the cause under a certain condition gives rise to the effect. According to Dancygier (1998), in the construction of predictive conditionals, a causal

---

[4] Mandarin Chinese *hui* is a polysemous modal auxiliary. Chang (2000), Hsieh (2002), Liu (1996: 40-51), etc. claim that *hui* expresses a future/prediction meaning, a generic meaning, a habitual meaning and an epistemic meaning. *-(u)l kes-i* is also known to express different meanings. Seo (1978) claims that *-(u)l kes* has five meanings: undefined object, prediction, intention, command, and explanation.

[5] Sweetser (1984, 1990) has argued for a distinction between content conditionals and epistemic conditionals, which follow the speaker's reasoning process and set up an epistemic space. Reasoning processes operate either from known cause to likely effect, or from known effect to possible cause. Effect-to-cause reasoning is frequently manifested in epistemic conditionals.

relation between the two events exist and then creates an environment that entails a sequential relation, as illustrated by Dancygier (1998:86) in the following example:

(4) a. If Mary goes to the dentist, she'll be late.

Like the English *will*, in Korean and Mandarin Chinese, *-(u)l kes-i* and *hui* are used to express prediction.

(4) b. Mali-nun chikwa-ey ka-myen nuc-ul
     Mary-Top dentist-at go-if   be:late-Adn
     kes-i-ta
     thing-Cop-Dec
  c. Mali ruguo qu yake   jiu hui chidao
     Mary-if -go-dentist-then-Mod-be:late

Not only in a typical conditional which predicts a likely result in the future if the condition is fulfilled, but also in past hypothetical and counterfactual situations whereby a prediction about the occurrence of a hypothetical or counterfactual [6]event is still contingent on the given circumstance, *-(u)l kes-i* and *hui* are equally used to denote a hypothetical predictive meaning as illustrated in (5):

(5) a. ku-ka   sala-iss-ta-myen   nay phyen
     he-Nom be:alive-exist-Dec-if my side
     tul-ess-ul   kes-i-ta
     take-Pst-Adn thing-Cop-Dec   (from Internet)
     'If he were alive, he would have taken my
     side.'
  b. youqi ruguo xianzai hai huo zhe yiding
     youqi-if - now-still-alive-Part-certainly
     hui   hen gaoxing ba
     Mod- very-happy-Part
     'If Youqi were alive, he would be very
     happy' .   (Mi(迷): 175)

The cause-consequence order is also argued to be found in generic truths and habitual actions which are often expressed by *will* in English. Ziegeler (2006) claims that *will* can indicate generics due to the operation of inductive inferences by generalizing from the truth of p (at all times, including the future) to p as a future event. In the

similar manner, in Mandarin Chinese, *hui* can indicate genericity. With regard to *hui*, Iljic (1985) argues that the predictive meaning of *hui* comes from the generalization of a potential property as in "When the fruit on the tree is ripe, it will naturally fall down" (shushang de guozi shu le ziran hui diao xia).

As seen in the following examples, *will* and *hui* are both used to indicate generic truths.

(6) a. Oil will float on water.   (Huddleston 1995)
  b. you yudao shui hui piao zai shui mianshang
     oil-meet-water-Mod-float-in-water-above
  c. kilum-un mwul-ey ttu-ki
     oil-Top water-at   float-Comp
     malyen-i-ta
     provision-Cop-Dec

Unlike (6a) and (6b), *-(u)l kes-i* cannot be used to express generality as seen in (6c). In Korean, law-like events are expressed by other modals such as -*ki maryeonida* or *nun pep ita*, or a generic truth is realized using an if-statement constructed with a regular declarative sentence in the main clause. Park (2013) claims that in Korean, generic truths are constructed by an if-clause with the Korean conditional marker that encodes a strong belief of the speaker towards the proposition of the apodosis, as illustrated by Park (2013:295):

(7) pi-ka   manhi o-myen kang-mwul-i
    Rain-Nom a lot   come-if river-water-Nom
    pwut-nun-ta.
    flood-Ind-Dec
    'If it rains a lot, the river will flood'.

Generality that describes generic characteristics exists as repeatable events, and this repetitive propensity of *will* and *hui* can also express habituality as in (8a) and (8b), in contrast to (8c) in Korean which describes a habitual behavior as a fact in the unmarked indicative form.

(8) a. They'll go on for hours without speaking to
     each other using a specific subject.
     (Huddleston 1995)

---

[6] According to Ziegeler (2006:140), the difference between hypothetical and counterfactual concepts is the absence and presence of contextual knowledge.

b. ta meitian   dou hui   wushui
   he-everyday-also-Mod-take:a:nap
   'He takes a nap everyday'
c. ku-nun mayil   naccam-ul ca-n-ta
   he-Nom everyday nap-Acc sleep-Ind-Dec

In Korean, not only generality but also habituality is expressed by a specific modal that describes a habitual event or an if-statement accompanied by the indicative form in the main clause as in (9a) and (9b).

(9) a. kutul-un   yennyensayng i-la
      they-Top siblings:born:within:a:year   be-as
      kotcal tathwu-kon ha-n-ta
      often argue-Comp do-Ind-Dec
      'Since they are born within a year of each other, they tend to argue often.'   (Internet)
    b. kutul-un manna-ki-man   ha-myen
      they-Top meet-Nmlz-only do-if
      tathwu-n-ta
      argue-Ind-Dec
      'Whenever they meet, they argue.'   (Internet)

In the cause-to-effect reasoning which is a typical process of predicting an event from a piece of knowledge, *-(u)l kes-i* and *hui* can both be used to express a conjecture in hypothetical and counterfactual situations as well. In the same vein, generics and habituals are constructed on the cause-consequence structure to predict an event which is not yet actualized. Ziegeler (2013) claims that in generics, the English modal *will* allows for a possible future prediction to be made. In Mandarin Chinese, like the English *will*, *hui* is often used to indicate generic and habitual events, whereas Korean denotes generality and habituality through specific modals or an if-statement constructed with the unmarked declarative main clause to indicate a factual statement. [7]

As will be presented later in epistemicity, not only in a causal conjunction but also in a conditional conjunction, when there is a strong causal relation with an apparent sequentiality, Korean uses the indicative form to describe factual knowledge or

belief, in contrast to Mandarin Chinese that employs *hui*. Let us consider (10):

(10) a. ku-key   ppalli meku-myen cheyha-n-ta
      That-thing fast eat-if   indigest-Ind-Dec
      'If you eat fast, you will have stomachache.'
                                        Park (2013: 291)
    b. ruguo ni chi de tai kuai, jiu hui shanghai
      if-you-eat-Part-too-fast, then-Mod-damage
      ni de wei
      you-Gen-stomach   (吃对了，病就少)

3   Epistemicity and assumptions

A process of prediction can be reversed. With backward reasoning, an inference can be derived in the consequence to cause order. Dancygier (1998:86) claims that causal and predictive sentences can be seen as reversed, expressing inferences, not predictions, and the relation is based on assumptions as in:

(11) "If Mary is late, she went to the dentist".

According to Dancygier, since epistemic conditionals are non-predictive, they are infelicitous with hypothetical forms, and the epistemic modal 'must' can be used, which is then understood as 'it means that'.

In Mandarin Chinese, *hui* cannot be used to express an epistemic relation. Instead, it is rephrased with epistemic modals such as *yinggai*. However, the Korean modal *-(u)l kes-i* can still be applied to denote this reasoning process in the reverse direction, as illustrated in (12) :

(12) a.manyak kil-i   cec-ess-ta-myen, ecey
      in:case road-Nom wet-Pst-Dec-if, yesterday
      pam-ey pi-ka   w-ass-ul   kes-i-ta
      night-at rain-Nom com-Pst-Adn-thing-Cop-
      Dec   (Yeom 2005:11)
    b. ruguo di shi le，   zuotian yinggai/*hui
      If-ground-wet-Part, yesterday-Mod
      xia guo yu
      come-Part-rain

---

[7] Chung (2012:221) argues that in Korean, an inference mechanism is utilized to indicate indirect evidence but when evidence is direct, things that are generally known, such as universal truth and generic situations, are expressed by regular declarative non-evidential sentences.

190

'If the road is wet, last night, it must have
rained'

In fact, in Korean, *-(u)l kes-i* can also be used with the causal connective *-nikka*. Park (2013:155) shows that the reading of the causal connective *-nikka* is determined by the presence of a modal in the main clause. In his analysis about the Korean causal connective *-nikka*, Park presents that if the proposition of the main clause includes an epistemic modal such as *thullimepsta* 'must' or *-(u)l kesita* 'will', *-nikka* encodes a reason to justify the outcome of the main clause. On the other hand, if a modal is not realized in the proposition of the main clause, the *nikka* clause just expresses causality.[8]

As observed above in generics and habituals, in Korean, generic and habitual statements with a tight causal relation can also be realized by an if-construction with the unmarked indicative form in the main clause, while a predictive statement that indicates a specific outcome contingent upon a specific piece of information is expressed by *-(u)l kes-i*.

In contrast, in Mandarin Chinese, when expressing a causal conjunction with a causal connective *yinwei*, *hui* cannot have an epistemic meaning that expresses the speaker's epistemic assumption but still encodes a linkage between propositions in which q is contingent on p as in (13):

(13) yinwei you ai, cai   hui qidai
     because-exist-love, only:then-Mod-expect
     'We expect because there is love.' (a novel title)

Then, the question remains why in epistemic relations, *-(u)l kes-i* remains applicable. The reason can be found in the fact that *-kes-i*, which can also be realized in combination with *-(nu)n* to indicate present and past situations, actually offers a reason for an inference made from the known facts. Jung (2016) argues that the most essential function of *-*

(nu)n kes-i is to explain a cause or reason derived from the background knowledge as in (14):

(14) ku-nun "Eureka"-lako oychi-mye mwul
     he-Nom 'Eureka -as   shout-while water
     pakk-ulo ttwichyenaw-ass-ta.
     outside-to come:out-Pst-Dec
←   haykyel-pangan-ul palkyenha-n kes-i-ta
     solution-Acc discover-Adn thing-Cop-Dec
     'He jumped out of the bathtub, shouting,
     Eureka! He found a solution.'
     (Jung 2016:250)

Lycan (2002) argues that explanation and epistemology are closely related, since the notion of explanation is itself exactly an epistemic notion. The function of *kes-i* to provide an account of reason is also supported by Foong *et al.* (2011:485) who claim that *kes-i* entails an epistemic meaning of strong probability, since *kes-ita* as in *-(nu)n kes-i* itself encodes the presence of evidence, which is presupposed by the speaker. In addition to the justification of a reason embedded in *kes-i*, due to the meaning of *-(u)l* that indicates non-actuality [9], *-(u)l kes-i* can provide predictive and epistemic readings at the same time depending on the reasoning process.

Unlike *-(u)l kes-i*, *hui* is based on the cause-and-effect reasoning that normally entails sequentiality, which then naturally encodes prediction, but it cannot derive an inference to justify the accepting of a conclusion as seen in (12b).

The fact that *hui* in positive statements especially with a stative verb that describes a state of being cannot have an epistemic reading can be supportive of this claim. It has been observed that the epistemic meaning of *hui* is more natural in negatives and interrogatives (Tsang 1981).[10] The meaning of *hui* in positive statements is not epistemic, as illustrated by Tsang (1981:155):

(15) a. Ta hui bu hui shi ge jingcha?

---

[8] Examples proposed by Park (2013:155) are as follows:
a. onul mina-ka   hakkyo-ey an o-ass-unikka
   today Mina-Nom school-to not come-Pst-because
   aphun key thullimeps-ta.
   sick Comp sure-Dec
   'Mina must be sick, because she didn't come to school today.'
b. hay-ka ci-nikka   pakk-i kkamkkamhata.
   sun-Nom go:down-because outside-Nom dark

'Because the sun has set, it is dark outside.'
[9] Lim and Chang (1995) explain that the relativizer *-l* denotes an event status that the event has not yet occurred, whereas the relativizer *-n* expresses a past situation and the relativizer *-nun*, progressiveness.
[10] Palmer (1986) explains that this is possibly because negatives and interrogatives are non-assertive, which reinforces uncertainty.

he-may-not-may-be-Cl-policeman
'May he be a policeman?'
b. Ta bu hui shi yi ge jingcha.
    he-not-may-be-one-Cl-policeman
    'He may not be a policeman'.
c. Ta hui shi yi ge jingcha.
    he-may-be-one-Cl-policeman
    'He will become a policeman.' [11]

Especially in realis contexts, *hui* appears to express an epistemic claim instead of a prediction, as the utterance expresses a realis state at some point in the past. However, it is actually impossible to make an epistemic conjecture about definite things. In fact, in realis contexts, *hui* does not encode an epistemic assumption by reasoning backwards but still a prediction by reasoning forward just from the event time set in the past. Let us consider the examples illustrated by Lu (1999:278) as in (16):

(16) a. mei xiang dao hui zhenme shunli
        Not-think-Part-Mod-this-smoothly
        'It was not expected that things would go so
        smoothly.'
     b. ta zenme hui zhidao?
        he-how-Mod-know
        'How would he know?'

Lu explains that when expressing probability, *hui* can be used in realis situations. As a matter of fact, (16a) and (16b) indicate surprise at an unexpected realization. In other words, they reflect the speaker's surprise as something goes against what was predicted at some point in the past. The hypothetical sense becomes stronger when the subject in (16b) is replaced by the first person as in the following example (17) which yields a counterfactual conditional reading, 'If X did not happen, I would not know Y'.

(17) wo zenme hui zhidao ne?
     I-how-Mod-know-Sfp?

How would I know this?

In fact, in an epistemic statement, the first person subject cannot be allowed, since it does not make sense that the speaker questions his own state of knowledge.[12] As such, in the interrogative form, -*(u)l kes-i* is not allowed. According to Yeom (2005), in Korean, when the speaker states something in a strong and definite way, -*(u)l kes-i* is infelicitous in interrogatives. Instead, -*(u)l kka*, combined with -*kka*, an interrogative sentence-type suffix, can be used, however its usage is allowed only with the second and third person subjects as in (18).[13]

(18) *nay-ka/ney-ka/chelswu-ka   sayngkak ha-ki
     *I-Nom/you-Nom/Chelswu-Nom think-Nmlz
     ey ku mwuncey-ka   elyewu-l-kka?
     Top that question-Nom difficult-Adn-Int?
     '*As for me/as for you/as for Chelswu,
     this question would be difficult?'
                                   (Yeom 2005:16)

In addition to the infelicitous use of *hui* in positive statements accompanied by stative verbs, when referred to past events, the use of *hui* in positive statements is not allowed either for epistemicity. Nuyts (2001:196) claims that the chances for an epistemic reading increase when there exists a discrepancy between the time of the state of affairs and that of the qualification. Let us consider the example as illustrated by Iljic (1985):

(19) zuotian wanshang ta yinggai (*hui) zai jia li
     yesterday-night- she-Mod -at-home-inside
     'Last night, she must have been at home.'

Yang (2006) claims that when predicting past events, sometimes with a past time adverbial, *hui* denotes a law-like event that occurred in the past, however, when the verb itself indicates pastness in combination with particles such as *le* and *guo*, *hui*

---

[11] In the original text, 'Ta hui shi yi ge jingcha.'was translated as 'he will be a policeman.'. However, in this paper, it is translated as 'he will become a policeman' to make it clear that it has a predictive reading, as opposed to the epistemic *will* which was proposed by Huddleston as in "That will be the postman" which receives an epistemic reading due to the stativity of the complement verb 'be'.

[12] Papafragou (2006) and Dorr & Hawthorne (2010) claim that epistemics are often taken to express possibilities given what the speaker knows.

[13] In Kim (2014)'s analysis on the relativizer -*l*, like -*kes*, -*kka* is also considered as a head noun. Kim claims that the fusion of -*l* and -*kka* expresses suggestion, as illustrated in:
nayil yenghwa   po-le ka-lkka?
tomorrow movie watch-to go-lkka
'Let's go to watch a movie tomorrow.'

cannot be used. Instead, *keneng* indicates probability as illustrated by Yang (2006) in (20):

(20) yao fuguan keneng jie guo hun
    yao-general-may - marry-Part
    'General Yao may have been married.'

The examples in (19) and (20) do not predict what might happen in the future but derive a conclusion from what is already known. As seen in (19) and (20), *hui* is not allowed in the backward process as in q → p. However, in Korean, the epistemic readings in (15c), (19), (20) can be expressed by -*(u)l kes-i* with no such restriction.

4. Corpus investigation

In order to further investigate how the features of *hui* and -*(ul) kes-i* are realized in cause-effect relationships in each language, a corpus-based investigation of causative and conditional constructions has been conducted. 118 phrases of *hui* in the conditional construction *ruguo..., hui...* and 127 phrases of *hui* in the causal construction *yinwei..., hui...* have been collected from the CCL (Center for Chinese Linguistics) corpus. As for -*(ul) kes-i*, 217 phrases in the conditional construction -*myen..., -(ul) kes-i* and 57 phrases in the causal construction [14] have been collected from the Sejong Corpus.

One of the findings to emerge from this investigation is that *yinwei..., hui...* entail general conjectures based on general knowledge, generality, and habituality. Out of the 127 phrases, 24 *hui* refer to conjectures based on general knowledge and 20 phrases denote generality and habituality, marked by adverbs expressing frequency such as *wangwang, jingchang, youshihou, suishidou, and xuduo.* In these cases, in Korean, the main phrases will not be marked by -*(ul) kes-i* but will be realized in the

unmarked indicative mood. Let us see some examples from the CCL corpus:

(21) laonianren   yinwei huodongliang buzu,
    elderly:people-because-activities-not:enough,
    sheru de nengliang duoyu, ye hui fapang
    aborb-Gen-ability-excessuve,also-Mod-get:fat
    'Because elderly people lack activities, increased intake of foods will make them fat.'

(22) yinwei jinchang chi tianpin，guoliang de
    because-often-eat-sweets, excessive-Part-
    tang hui zhengjia yidaosu de fenmi
    sugar-Mod-increase-insulin-Part-secretion
    'Because (if you) often eat sweets, excessive sugar will increase insulin secretion.'

(23) yinwei yidan huan ganbing, baiyanqiu
    Because-once-have-liver:disease, whites
    de bufen jiu hui chuxian huangdan
    Part-area-then-Mod-appear-jaundice
    'Because once (you) get liver disease, the whites of the eyes will become yellow.'

(24) yinwei wo jingchang jibuzhu ci, youdeshihou
    Because-I-often-forget-lyrics, sometimes
    zai tai shang chang zhe jiu hui wang ci
    on-stage-up-sing-Part-then-Mod-forget-lyrics
    'Because I often don't remember lyrics, sometimes on stage, while singing, I will forget lyrics.'

As for -*(ul) kes-i* in the causal construction, out of 57 phrases[15], 36 phrases are based on the structure of deriving a prediction from a given circumstance as seen in (25):

(25) kulemulo milay-uy inkansang-un Atlas
    therefore future-of human:image-Top Atlas
    sin-ul   talmaka-l kes-i-ta

---

[14] As for the causal construction in Korean, phrases semantically interpreted as causative including causal markers such as ttalase, kulayse, kulemulo, kunikka, ttaymwun, inhay, -(u)ni, and etc. have been included due to a relatively small sample pool, compared to the Mandarin Chinese causal connective *yinwei*. In fact, not only for Korean but also for Mandarin Chinese phrases, the frequency of occurrence of *hui* and -*(ul) kes-i* is significantly higher in the conditional construction than in the causal construction. Although all the phrases of the CCL corpus have not been sorted manually to verify eligibility, the total number of data matches for

ruguo...,hui... is 20,247, as opposed to 6,160 matches for *yinwei..., hui...* .

[15] 15 phrases are found to have the construction of giving an account first and then a reason. In order to indicate an epistemic reason to support the account, -*(ul) kes-i* is realized, for which *hui* is infelicitous. However, for simplicity and clarity, the scope of the investigation of this paper is limited to conditional and causal complex phrases, since -*(ul) kes-i* is often realized in single phrases as a continuity of causal or conditional statements, as in "Drinking two grams of cyanide causes death", which is approximately the same as saying "If somebody drinks two grams of cyanide, they will die" (Puente, et al. 2009)

God-Acc resemble-Adn thing-Cop-Dec
'Therefore, the image of the future men will resemble God Atlas.'

However, unlike *yinwei..., hui...*, 6 phrases marked by *-(ul) kes-i* entail an epistemic justification of an inference derived from what is known. In this case, *hui* is infelicitous as in the example (26):

(26) ku-to nwunchi-ka ppalun salam-i-ni nauy
he-too sense-Nom quick person-be-as my
komin-ul alachaly-ess-ul kes-i-ta
worries-Acc sense-Pst-Adn thing-Cop-Dec
'Since he is also a sensitive person, he must have sensed my concern.'

As to *hui* which is realized in the conditional construction, *ruguo...,hui...*, the process of reasoning is forward, indicating that an effect becomes possible when its premises hold, among which 3 phrases of generality and 5 phrases of habituality marked by *hui* are found as in (27):

(27) ruguo shi wo xiugai, nuer wangwang hui
if -be- I-correct, daughter-often-Mod
bufuqi, jinchang hui yu wo zhengbian
reject, often-Mod-with-me-argue
'If I corrected her, my daughter would reject it and often argue with me.'

With regards to *-(ul) kes-i* which is realized in the conditional construction, the forward reasoning process is still applied to most of the phrases, however, without a strong cause-and-effect relationship between the hypothesis and conclusion of a conditional statement, an epistemic judgement about the current or past state of affairs is identified in 7 phrases as in (28).

(28) nay-key khomphulleyksu-ka hana issta-ko
I-to complex-Nom one exist-Comp
ha-myen palo khi-i-l kes-i-ta
do-if then height-Cop-Adn thing-Cop-Dec
'If I have one complex about myself, that must be my height.'

From the corpus-based investigation, it is noticed that *hui* tends to entail a causal relationship, often indicating generality and habituality abundantly in the causal construction but also in the conditional construction, albeit fewer in number. Causality is derived from the accumulated or realized knowledge so that it is easy to derive a more concrete consequence whereby *hui* appears more in the causal construction than in the conditional construction to mark law-like events. Anscombe (1971) claims that causal relations are instances of exceptionless generalizations and presuppose some kind of law.

As for *-(ul) kes-i*, in addition to predicting an effect from a cause, the feature of expressing an epistemic assumption and judgement is identified in the corpus, which is more frequently realized in the causal construction whereby an inference about the state of affairs is made based on a circumstance that has been known, as opposed to a conditional statement in which a condition is a cause which has not yet been realized at the time of speaking.

5. Conclusion

This paper has examined the Korean and Mandarin Chinese modals, *-(ul) kes-i* and *hui* which are often used to express the speaker's conjecture and thus are sometimes considered to have future reference. Inspired by two thinking processes, one in which the events are linked in a cause-consequence order and the other in which events are realized in a consequence-cause order, this paper has shown how *-(ul) kes-i* and *hui* are used in the two reasoning processes. As for the process of prediction whereby cause leads to consequence, *-(ul) kes-i* and *hui* are both used. However, in generics and habituals which are also based on the cause-consequence framework, unlike *hui*, *-(ul) kes-i* cannot be applied. In generics and habituals that describe general property, *-(ul) kes-i* cannot be used, but it is applicable when specific episodes are expressed based on the construction of a specific condition resulting in a specific consequence. It can be explained by the essential function of *kes-i* that tends to derive a certain explanation from the known facts. In the same vein, in a consequence-cause order, *-(ul) kes-i* is used as giving an epistemic reason. Through a corpus-based investigation of causative and conditional constructions marked by *hui* and *-(ul) kes-i*, it is noted that the feature of *hui* is strongly relevant to generality, while that of *-(ul) kes-i* does not indicate law-like generalizations but can indicate epistemic assumptions about specific episodes based on specific accounts.

References

Bak, Jae Yeon. 2009. The Meanings of Korean Adnominal Endings and Their Grammatical Category. Korean Linguistics 43, 151-177

Chung, Kyung-Sook. 2012. Space in Tense: The interaction of tense, aspect, evidentiality and speech. John Benjamins Publishing Company.

Dancygier, Barbara. 1998. Conditionals and Prediction: Time, Knowledge and Causation in Conditional Constructions. Cambridge University Press.

Dancygier, Barbara & Sweetser, Eve. 2009. Mental Spaces in Grammar: Conditional Constructions. Cambridge University Press; Reissue edition.

Fei, Ren. 2008. Futurity in Mandarin Chinese. Doctoral dissertation: The University of Texas at Austin.

Foong Ha Yap, Karen Grunow-Hårsta and Janick Wrona. 2011. Nominalization in Asian Languages: Diachronic and Typological Perspectives. Amsterdam & Philadelphia: John Benjamins.

Hacquar, Valentine, Wellwood, Alexis. 2012. Embedding epistemic modals in English: A corpus-based study. Semant. Pragmatics 5(4), 1-29.

Iljic, Robert. 1985. HUI: propriété virtuelle et modalité du déductible. Cahiers de linguistique Asie Orientale, Vol. XIV n. 2, 217-230.

Jung, Sangcheol. 2016. On the discourse functions of written Korean "-n kes-ita". Textlinguistics 41, 245-267.

Kim, Dongmin. 2014. The Korean relativizer -l from the viewpoint of linguistic evolution. Korean Linguistics 62, 123-147.

Kim, Joung Min. 2012. Evidentiality and Mirativity on Sentence-Final Predicates in Japanese and Korean: A particular attention to 'Kes-ita' and 'Noda'. The Journal of the Humanities Vol.- No.66.

Kim, Nam-Kil. 1987. Korean. In B. Comrie (Ed.) The world's major languages. New York: Oxford University Press, 881-898.

Li, Ren Xhi. 2003. Modality in English and Chinese: A typological perspective. Doctoral dissertation: University of Antwerp.

Lim, Dong-hoon. 2008. The Mood and Modal Systems in Korean. Korean Semantics 26, 211-249

Lu, Shuxiang (Ed.). (1999). Xiandai Hanyu Babai Ci ['Eight Hundred Words of Modern Chinese'] (Expanded edition). Beijing: Commercial Press.

Min, Xing Ya 2007 Cognitive research on Modal Auxiliaries "neng" and "hui". PhD. Dissertation, Shanghai Normal University.

Nuyts, Jan. 2001. Epistemic modality, language, and conceptualization: A cognitive-pragmatic perspective. Amsterdam: Benjamins.

Park, Na Ree. 2013. The discourse-pragmatic functions of factual conditional '-myen'-focusing on relations between its morphological-syntactic meaning. Journal of Korean Linguistics, Vol.6.

Park, Yugyeong. 2013. A Unified Approach to Korean Causal Connective -nikka. Volume 19 Issue 1 Proceedings of the 36th Annual Penn Linguistics Colloquium.

Puente, Cristina, et al. 2009. Extraction of Conditional and Causal Sentences from Queries to Provide a Flexible Answer. 8th International Conference on Flexible Query Answering Systems, Roskilde (Denmark), Springer Berlin Heidelberg NewYork, 477-487.

Seo, Jeongsoo. 1978. About '-(u)l kes'- in comparison with '-keyss'. Journal of Korean Linguistics, Vol 6, 85-110.

Tsang, Chui Lim (1981) A Semantic Study of Modal Auxiliary Verbs in Chinese. Doctoral dissertation: Stanford University.

William G. Lycan. 2002. 'Explanation and Epistemology.' In Paul K. Moser (ed.), The Oxford Handbook of Epistemology, Oxford: Oxford University Press, 408–433.

Yang, Hui. 2006. The function of 'hui' from the interpersonal theme aspect. Journal of Soochow University, Engineering Science Edition.

Yeom, Jae-Il. 2005. The comparative study of the modalities of -keyss and -(u)l kes in Korean. Language and Information, Vol.9 No.2, 55-65.

Ziegeler, Debra. 2006. Interfaces with English Aspect: Diachronic and empirical studies. John Benjamins Publishing Company.

Ziegeler, Debra. 2013. 'On the generic argument for the modality of will' In: J.I. Marín-Arrese, M. Carretero, J.A. Hita and J. van der Auwera (eds.), 221-250.

Remarks on Denominal *-Ed* Adjectives

Tomokazu Takehisa
Niigata University of Pharmacy and Applied Life Sciences
265-1 Higashijima, Akiha-ku, Niigata 956-8603, Japan

takehisa@nupals.ac.jp

Abstract

This paper discusses denominal adjectives derived by affixation of *-ed* in English in light of recent advances in linguistic theory and makes the following three claims. First, unlike recent proposals arguing against their denominal status, the paper defends the widely held view that these adjectives are derived from nominals and goes on to argue that the nominal bases involved are structurally reduced: *n*P. Second, the paper argues that the suffix *-ed* in denominal adjectives shows no contextual allomorphy, which is a natural consequence that follows from the workings of the mechanism of exponent insertion in Distributed Morphology (Halle and Marantz, 1993). Third, the meaning associated with denominal *-ed* adjectives stems from the suffix's denotation requiring a relation, which effectively restricts base nominals to relational nouns, derived or underived. It is also argued that the suffix is crucially different from possessive determiners in English (e.g., *'s*) in that, while the former imposes type shifting on non-relational nouns, the latter undergo type shifting to accommodate them.

1. Introduction

Denominal adjectives derived by the adjectivizing suffix *-ed*, as in (1) below, are quite common in English and seem to have received the attention they deserve from grammarians and linguists. [1,2]

(1) a. blue-eyed
     b. bearded
     c. red-roofed
     d. black-jacketed

The syntactic and semantic properties of these adjectives are intuitively clear; they are adjectives derived from suffixation of *-ed* to the nominal base N, either a nominal compound or a noun phrase, and they have the meaning related to possession such as 'possessing N' or 'provided with N', etc.

The aim of this paper is to discuss denominal -*ed* adjectives in light of recent advances in linguistic theory and make the following claims about their structure, morphology and semantics. Specifically, on the fundamental assumption in the framework of Distributed Morphology (Halle and Marantz, 1993; Marantz, 1997, 2001) that there is no component dedicated to word formation, this paper defends the view that the *-ed* adjectives in question are denominal and argues that bases for -*ed* are reduced nominal structures, *n*P. It is shown that facts pertaining to number marking and interpretation support the *n*P-based analysis of denominal *-ed* adjectives. Incidentally, an analysis of the singular and plural forms of foreign nouns in English is offered along the way.

---

[1] Since so many cases of denominal *-ed* adjectives can be analyzed as verb-based as well (e.g., *armed, knobbed*, etc.), much care is taken to present unambiguously denominal ones, i.e., ones which have no verbal counterparts or with prenominal modifiers.

[2] See, among many others, Jespersen (1942), Hirtle (1970), Hudson (1975), Ljung (1976), Gram-Andersen (1992), Bauer and Huddleston (2002) and the references cited therein. See also Miller (2006:175ff.) for discussion of the Latinate counterpart *-(a)te/-ated*.

Second, we argue that the adjectivizing suffix -*ed* has no contextually determined allomorphs in denominal adjectives. Putative counterexamples are claimed to be stative participles in the sense of Embick (2003, 2004), which are deradical, not denominal.

Third, we discuss the source of the possession meaning associated with denominal adjectives and argue that it stems from the adjectivizing suffix's denotation which takes a relation as input. This effectively restricts the types of nominals which appear as bases for the suffix: intrinsically relational nouns and relational nouns derived by type shifting. We also argue that the suffix is in sharp contrast with possessive determiners in English: the former imposes type shifting on its non-relational bases, while the latter undergo type shifting to accommodate non-relational possessees.

The paper is organized as follows: in section 2, after seeing that the *-ed* adjectives in question are undeniably denominal, we will argue that their nominal bases are structurally reduced: *n*Ps. In section 3, building on the conclusion reached at in section 2, we will argue that no contextual allomorphy is possible in denominal adjectives and show that putative counterexamples can receive a different analysis. In section 4, we will consider the source of the possession meaning and propose an analysis in which the adjectivizing suffix is required to take a relation as input, which serves to restrict the types of nominal bases appearing in the adjectives. Section 5 will conclude the paper.

2.   An *n*P-Based Analysis

2.1   Denominal *-Ed* Adjectives Are Denominal

The fact that *-ed* adjectives, as in (1) above, are based on nominals can be demonstratively shown by the following examples where *-ed* attaches to bases with nominalizing suffixes such as *-age*, *-ance/-ence*, *-ing*, *-ion*, *-ment*, *-th/-t*, and the like. The relevant suffixes are underlined in the examples in (2) below:

(2) a.   sour-vis<u>age</u>d
     b.   good-appear<u>ance</u>d, average-intellig<u>ence</u>d
     c.   low-ceil<u>ing</u>ed
     d.   fair-complex<u>ion</u>ed
     e.   battle<u>ment</u>ed
     f.   average-leng<u>th</u>ed, gif<u>t</u>ed

The suffixes in (2) are indeed nominalizers, as can be confirmed by the following.[3]

(3) a. *-age*
        cover<u>age</u>, leak<u>age</u>, volt<u>age</u>, yard<u>age</u>, etc.
     b. *-ance/-ence*
        arrog<u>ance</u>, ridd<u>ance</u>, abs<u>ence</u>, depend<u>ence</u>, etc.
     c. *-ing*
        build<u>ing</u>, danc<u>ing</u>, meet<u>ing</u>, paint<u>ing</u>, etc.
     d. *-ion*
        fash<u>ion</u>, miss<u>ion</u>, reg<u>ion</u>, un<u>ion</u>, etc.
     e. *-ment*
        apart<u>ment</u>, base<u>ment</u>, move<u>ment</u>, pay<u>ment</u>, etc.
     f. *-th/-t*
        grow<u>th</u>, tru<u>th</u>, heig<u>ht</u>, sig<u>ht</u>, etc.

Recently, Nevins and Myler (2014) have proposed an analysis of *-ed* adjectives of the type discussed here, where *-ed* adjectivizes category-neutral √P, citing examples like **beautiful-singinged* as an argument against the involvement of nominalizers. However, their analysis has no way to account for the examples in (2) unless it is modified in such a way that *-ed* can also adjectivize *n*P, or alternatively, it is shown that the nominal bases in (2) are in fact √P, which is highly unlikely in face of the examples in (3). Note, however, that there are *-ed* adjectives based on √P, as Nevins and Myler (2014) conjecture. I will argue in section 3 that they are stative participles in the sense of Embick (2003, 2004).

Moreover, Bruening (2016), while admitting that *-ed* adjectives as in (1) and (2) are formed from nouns, suggests an analysis whereby their derivation involves an intermediate, non-existent verb form derived from an N and meaning 'possessing N', with the verbalizer being a null affix corresponding to the English prefix *be-*, as in *bejeweled, beringed, beribboned*, etc. Thus, this analysis treats the *-ed* adjectives in question as deverbal rather than denominal.

This view receives initial support from the fact that some *-ed* adjectives (used to) have forms with and without *be-*: *booted/bebooted, ringed/beringed, gartered/begartered*, etc. However, this null *be-*prefixation analysis seems to be limited in its empirical coverage and work only for cases involving bare nouns, i.e., when the nominal base

---

[3] See, for instance, Plag (2003:86ff.) for an overview of nominal suffixes in English.

is simple in form, and it is not at all clear how this analysis could handle *fair complexion* and other modified nominal bases, as given in (2). In fact, a cursory search of the Oxford English Dictionary found no examples of *be*-prefixed *-ed* adjectives based on modified nominal bases, suggesting that *be-* could not form verbs with modified nominals even when it was most productive in its history. Thus, I conclude that, even though the phonologically null version of the verbalizing prefix *be-* might attach to a bare nominal base and feed the formation of *-ed* adjectives as adjectival passives, this analysis cannot be extended into covering cases involving modified nominal bases. In section 4, I will propose an alternative approach to derive the possession meaning, whereby there is no need to invoke null *be*-prefixation in the formation of denominal *-ed* adjectives.

2.2　Number Marking

It is clear now that denominal *-ed* adjectives are undeniably denominal. Next, considerations of number marking and interpretation in the adjectives further reveal that they are based on reduced nominal structures, *n*Ps.

No regular plural morpheme appears inside denominal *-ed* adjectives, as in the case of most compounds and suffixed words in English.[4] The absence of plural marking leaves the nominal base of an *-ed* adjective unspecified for number. As a result, the nominal base is compatible with both singular and plural interpretations, as shown in (4).

(4)　a.　one-eyed, one-armed
　　　b.　two-faced, two-bedroomed
　　　c.　three-toed, three-cornered

When the nominal base has no numeral in it, the unspecified cardinality of the nominal referent is inferred on the basis of the encyclopedic knowledge, as exemplified in (5)a and (5)b. (5)c shows that the same holds for non-count nouns, which suggests that the nominal base is unspecified for mass/count as well as number.[5]

(5)　a. Singular interpretation
　　　　　a *big-bellied* man has a big belly
　　　　　a *strong-minded* woman has a strong mind
　　　　　a *rubber-tipped* stick has a rubber tip
　　　b. Plural interpretation
　　　　　a *hard-featured* actor has hard features
　　　　　a *fine-boned* head has fine bones
　　　　　a *low-spirited* Alice is in low spirits
　　　c. Non-count interpretation
　　　　　a *grey-haired* poet has grey hair
　　　　　a *middle-aged* person is of middle age
　　　　　a *cold-blooded* animal has cold blood
　　　　　　　　　　　　(Gram-Andersen, 1992:22)

Moreover, pluralia tantum nouns can form *-ed* adjectives, as in (6) below, without losing their interpretations.[6] This shows that what is necessary for their interpretation is not lost when they appear in *-ed* adjectives and that overt plural marking per se is not essential in obtaining the interpretation of a pluralia tantum noun.[7]

(6)　a. good-mannered
　　　b. long-trousered
　　　c. sharp-scissored
　　　d. spectacled
　　　e. sunglassed

(7)

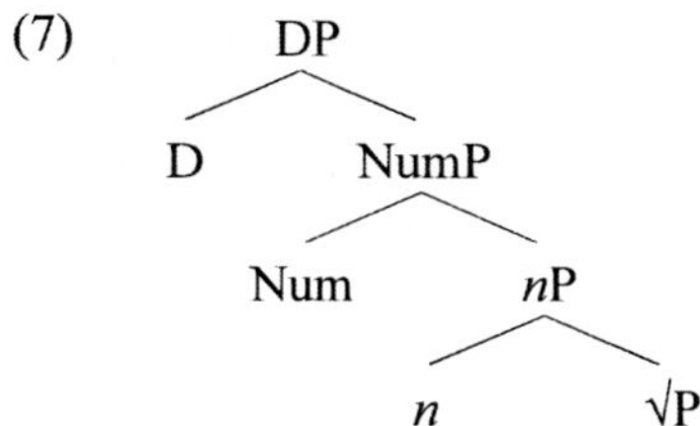

Given the full-fledged DP structure in English in (7), the absence of determiners suggests that nominal bases for *-ed* are not DPs, which is

---

[4] As is well known, there are cases where irregular plural forms or pluralia tantum nouns appear inside compounds. See Sproat (1985) for discussion.

[5] See Borer (2005) for an approach which derives these distinctions structurally.

[6] When it serves as a modifier, a plural tantum noun like *scissors* can appear in singular form and receives the singular interpretation, e.g., *a scissor blade*.

[7] Gram-Andersen (1992) reports *queer-looksed* and *baggypantsed* as the only cases he found where the regular plural morpheme *-s* appears. Notice that both are plural tantum nouns. The former and its like example *more pleasanter-looksed*, which is unacceptable in PDE, can be found in Jespersen (1942), whose source was the 19th-century writer George Elliot's novel, *Silas Marner*. For the latter, *pants* can appear as it is in other compounds as well (e.g., *pants dress*, *pants pocket, pant(s) skirt*, etc.). One possible interpretation is that, for those who allow these compounds, *pants* is registered as a group noun. See also footnote 11 below.

supported by the fact that they are not referential and do not introduce a discourse referent. See (8).

(8) When a four-wheeled vehicle goes through a turn, each of {the (four) wheels/*them} turns at a different speed.

        (Google search, with minor changes)

The absence of plural marking further suggests that the Num head and its projection are entirely missing from the structure as well, with nP being the base for *-ed*, as we have tacitly assumed.[8]

The same analysis holds in the case of nouns with irregular plural inflection as in (9), with ancillary assumptions concerning irregular plural marking. In this case as well, the absence of Num is crucial in deriving *-ed* adjectives based on them.

(9) a. sheep-Ø, men-Ø, mice-Ø, feet-Ø
    b. ox-en, child-(r)en
    c. curricul-a, foc-i, larv-ae, ax-es, criteri-a, temp-i, ind-ices

In the framework of Distributed Morphology, where all words are created in syntax, both regular and irregular plural forms have the same structure: [nP Num]. After the syntactic computation, the morphosyntactic features in the terminal nodes in the structure are realized as exponents by the Vocabulary Insertion rules, as in (10):

(10) VI rules for English plural inflection
    a. [−singular] ↔ -s
    b. [−singular] ↔ Ø / X__
       X = {√SHEEP, √MAN, √MOUSE, √FOOT, …}
    c. [−singular] ↔ en / {√OX, √CHILD…}__

In some cases, readjustment rules apply after VI, which bring about stem changes, as in *man~men-Ø, mouse~mice-Ø, foot~feet-Ø*, and *ox~ox-en*.[9]

Moreover, consider nouns with distinct suffixes for singular and plural forms like *curricul-um~curricul-a, foc-us~foc-i, larv-a~larv-ae, criteri-on~criteri-a, ax-is~ax-es, temp-o~temp-i, ind-ex~ind-ices*, and *matr-ix~matr-ices*.[10] In these nouns, the suffix in the singular form is an exponent of n, and the suffix in the plural form is more specified and is an exponent of n and the plural feature fused together.

Thus, in the case of singular *curricul-um*, whose structure is represented in (11)a, *-um* is the exponent of n, and Ø is the exponent of [+singular], as in (12)a and (12)c. respectively. In the case of plural *curricul-a* in (11)b, n and [−singular] undergoes the rule of fusion in (12)d under linear adjacency before VI, and the feature complex [n, −singular] is realized as *-a*, according to (12)b.

(11) a. *curriculum* b. *curricula*

```
(11) a. curriculum                     b. curricula
            Num                                Num
           /   \                              /   \
          n    Num                           n   ( Num  )
         / \   [+sing]                      / \  ( [-sing] )
   √CURRICUL  n                       √CURRICUL  ( n  FUSED )
        ↓     ↓    ↓                        ↓          ↓
     curricul -um  Ø                     curricul     -a
```

(12) a. n ↔ -um / {√CURRICUL, …}__
    b. [n, −singular] ↔ -a / {√CURRICUL, …}__
    c. [+singular] ↔ Ø
    d. n⌢[−singular] → [n, −singular]

In this analysis, what appears to be the singular and plural suffixes in the above foreign nouns are the exponents of n and the feature complex of n and [−singular], respectively. This treatment is justified by the fact that some of these nouns can have the regular plural suffix *-s*, and, when they do so, they always have the surface form, *Root + n + -s*, and the irregular plural endings never show up with the regular plural suffix, as shown in (13) below:

---

[8] Alternatively, the absence of plural marking might suggest that Num is present in syntax but its morphosyntactic feature undergoes deletion before phonological realization, thereby never appearing on the surface. In DM terms, the feature undergoes an impoverishment rule before Vocabulary Insertion. It is technically possible to implement such an analysis, but the trigger of the impoverishment rule is unclear. Thus, I do not pursue this possibility, though it is hard to distinguish between the nP analysis in the text and the NumP-cum-impoverishment analysis empirically.

[9] The necessity of readjustment rules in DM has been called into question. See Haugen (2016) for a recent discussion. In this paper, I follow Halle and Marantz (1993) and assume readjustment rules changing nominal stems for expository purposes. Their effects can be restated without making recourse to readjustment rules.

[10] Note that many of these nouns involve bound roots, which can be categorized by a differemt category-determining head: e.g., *curricul-ar, foc-al, larv-al, criteri-al, ax-ial*, etc.

(13) a. curricul-um-s   *curricul-a-s
      b. foc-us-es   *foc-i-s
      c. criteri-on-s   *criteri-a-s
      d. temp-o-s   *temp-i-s
      e. ind-ex-es   *ind-ices-es

This fact can be straightforwardly explained if we assume the VI rules for the *n* head such as (12)a and for the regular plural morpheme in (10)a apply, as a result of the rule of fusion in (12)c not having applied in the structure (11)b.

Turning back to denominal *-ed* adjectives, they can be formed from nouns with irregular plural marking. Crucially, the nominal bases involved are singular (or non-plural) forms, as in (14). Given the discussion so far, this strongly suggests that *n*P, not NumP, is the base for the suffix *-ed*.[11]

(14) a. beautiful-kimonoed
      b. three-footed
      c. raidused
      d. antennaed
      e. two-axised
      f. slow-tempoed

Furthermore, the *n*P-based analysis works well with pluraria tantum nouns, with ancillary assumptions. Specifically, I follow Arregi and Nevins's (2014) analysis of pluralia tantum nouns, where these nouns are assumed to have their *n* head specified for [−group], and, if Num is present in structure, they must appear with the Num head specified as [−singular].[12] The latter requirement is satisfied vacuously in the absence of Num, e.g., in denominal *-ed* adjectives. The relevant structure is represented in (15) below:

(15)

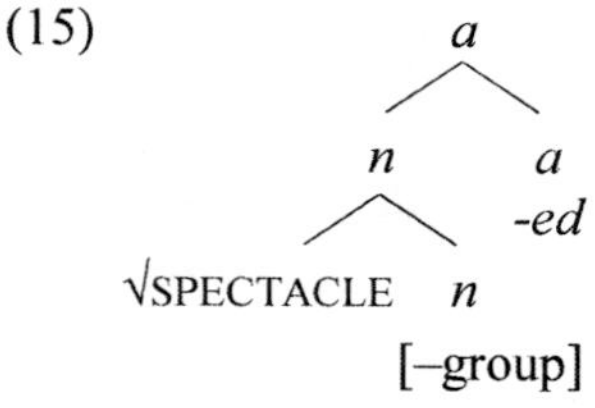

This way, the plural tantum interpretation, as in (6), can be guaranteed without having overt plural marking, which requires the presence of Num.

All in all, we can safely conclude that denominal *-ed* adjectives involve reduced nominal structures, and they are *n*Ps.

3. No Contextual Allomorphy

Another claim that I would like to put forth is that denominal adjectives show no contextual allomorphy, which will be explicated step-by-step.

First, the *-ed* suffix of denominal adjectives behaves in the same way as that of adjectival and verbal passives in displaying phonologically conditioned allomorphy, as shown in (16).

(16) Phonologically Conditioned Allomorphy
     [əd, ɪd]: red-headed, talented
     [d]: thick-skinned, winged[13]
     [t]: smooth-faced, forked
                    (Gram-Andersen, 1992:18)

Moreover, as has long been noted in the literature (e.g., Quirk *et al.* (1985) and Bauer and Huddleston (2002), among many others), a handful of *-ed* adjectives which do not end with [t] or [d] deviate from the above pattern, having syllabic *-èd* ([əd, ɪd]), either instead of or as well as non-syllabic *-ed* ([d, t]).

(17) a. with *-èd* only
        crooked, dogged, ragged
     b. with *-èd* or *-ed*[14]
        aged, forked, hooked, jagged, legged

Consider the adjectives with syllabic *-èd* in (17). Bauer and Huddleston (2002) treat them as "lexicalized" cases, along with other adjectives like *naked*, *wicked*, and *wretched*. This treatment is compatible with the fact that the regular form of the suffix in question was syllabic *-èd* in Middle English (Harley, 2006). Building on Bauer and Huddleston's insight, I argue that the lexicalized adjectives above are amenable to a different analysis. Specifically, I argue that they are stative participles in the sense of Embick (2003, 2004)

---

[11] Some speakers accept *-ed* adjectives based on irregular plural forms like *many-peopled*, *buck-teethed*, and the like. I treat their nominal bases as having [+group] specified in the *n* head, together with assumptions of the VI rules deriving their surface forms.

[12] Arregi and Nevins's analysis is based on Harbour's (2011) analysis of Kiowa collective nouns and pluralia tantum nouns.

[13] Note that *winged* has an alternative pronunciation with syllabic *-èd* (Embick, 2000:220 fn.).

[14] Some *-ed* adjectives like *forked* and *hooked* may be derived from their verbal forms.

200

and that syllabic *-èd* in these adjectives is a case of contextual allomorphy determined by the Root involved.[15,16,17] The structure of stative participles is given in the following:

(18) a. 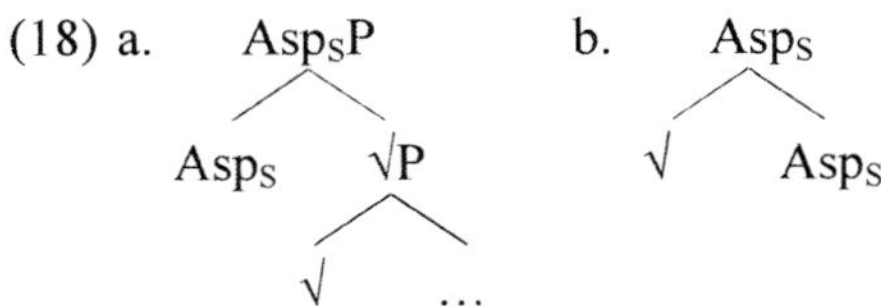

Asp$_S$ is a head which defines a simple state, and, in (18)a, it serves as a category-defining head and adjectivizes a category-neutral Root in its complement.[18] The complex head in (18)b is created in the structure in (18)a, and it undergoes VI from the Root out.

Specifically, for the lexicalized cases above, I argue that they are derived by the VI rule in (19)a below, which Embick (2003) proposes for stative participles like *allegèd*, *blessèd*, and *learnèd*. This amounts to saying that adjectives like *crooked*, *ragged*, and other adjectives with syllabic *-èd* are not denominal and on a par with *allegèd* and the like. On the other hand, those with non-syllabic *-ed* undergoes the VI rule in (19)b.

(19) a. Asp ↔ -èd/{√bless, √allege, √age, ...} __
    b. Asp ↔ -ed

(Embick, 2003:158)

This analysis is corroborated by the fact that some adjectives with syllabic *-èd* have meanings unpredictable from their putative nominal bases. Specifically, as we saw at the outset, the meanings of denominal *-ed* adjectives are predictable from their nominal bases fairly easily, construed as 'having N' or 'provided with N', etc. However, the adjectives with syllabic *-èd* in (20) have meanings unpredictable from their components.[19]

(20) a. crooked: 'bent or twisted'
                  not 'having a crook/crooks'
    b. dogged: 'having tenacity'
                  not 'having a dog/dogs'
    c. ragged: 'torn and in a bad condition'
                  not 'having rags'

This is what is expected under the theory of word formation developed by Marantz (2001).[20] According to his theory, the interpretation of a category-neutral Root is negotiated against the encyclopedic knowledge in the context of the functional head that categorizes it, as a result of which special meanings can arise. Given this, it is strongly suggested that the adjectives in (20) are Root-derived rather than denominal.[21]

The present analysis provides a simple and consistent answer to the cases we have seen so far. However, *leggèd* and related forms appear to resist an explanation along the line suggested here.[22] Specifically, on the assumption that syllabic *-èd* appears as a result of Root-determined contextual allomorphy, *leggèd* is predicted not to appear in denominal adjectives owing to the VI rule in (19)b. However, as (21) shows, *leggèd* can appear with a modifier unlike Root-derived adjectives.[23]

(21) a. three-leggèd
    b. long-leggèd
    c. cross-leggèd

---

[15] See Dubinsky and Simango (1996) for the relation between the syllabic and non-syllabic participial suffixes and adjectival and verbal passives.

[16] As an alternative to the widely held two-way distinction between adjectival and verbal passives, Embick (2003, 2004) proposes for a three-way distinction of so-called past participles: stative, resultative and eventive participles. The first two correspond to (stative) adjectival passives, and the last one to (eventive) verbal passives.

[17] Morita (2015) argues, adopting Nevins and Myler's (2014) √P-based analysis, that denominal *-ed* adjectives are stative participles. I have no objection to equating *-ed* adjectives based on √P with stative participles. However, as we saw in section 2, what we call denominal adjectives are based on *n*Ps and thus should be kept distinct from stative participles.

[18] I assume that several types of Asp in Embick (2003, 2004) and the *a* head forming denominal *-ed* adjectives belong to the same family, while differing in their "flavors," which are reflected in their semantic function. See Embick (2004) for Asp$_S$ which defines a simple state, and Asp$_R$ which takes a *v*P and defines a state out of an event subcomponent.

[19] See Kiparsky (1982) and Arad (2005) for related observations.

[20] See Marantz (2013) and Anagnostopoulou and Samioti (2013) for more recent developments.

[21] Nevins and Myler (2014) argue for the same point, citing adjectives like *blue-blooded* 'noble'. However, their examples are all based on A-N compounds, which can be idiomatic on their own (e.g., *blue blood* 'membership in a noble family').

[22] The alternative with non-syllabic *-ed* poses no problems.

[23] There is considerable variation in the pronunciation of *legged* among speakers, reflecting differences, at least, in region and age. The source of variation is reducible to whether √*leg* is in the list of the VI rule (19)a and whether the adjective is based on √P or *n*P, to which we will turn shortly.

Thus, we have the situation that the modification relation suggests the structure of the complex head in (22)a, while the contextually determined allomorph suggests that in (22)b. As is clear by now, the adjectives in (21) are cases of bracketing paradox.

(22) a. [$_{\text{Asp}}$ [$_n$ [$_\sqrt{}$ [$_a$ √three a] √leg] n] -ed]
    b. [$_{\text{Asp}}$ [$_a$ √three a] [$_{\text{Asp}}$ √leg -ed]]

To resolve the situation, I tentatively propose that complex forms like *three-legged* with syllabic -*èd* are adjectives derived from complex Roots.[24] The relevant structure is represented in (23):

(23) [$_{\text{Asp}}$ [$_\sqrt{}$ [$_a$ √three a] √leg] -ed]

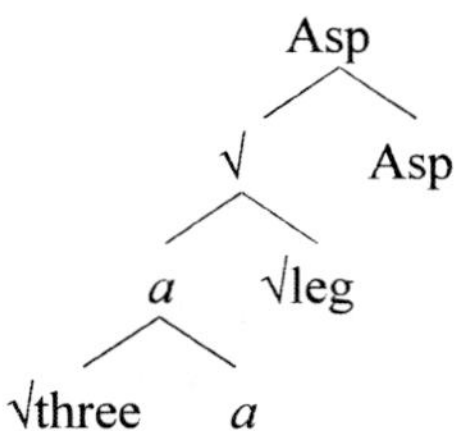

Recall that we have rejected the structure as in (23) as an analysis of denominal -*ed* adjectives in favor of an *n*P-based analysis. What I argue here then is that, although it is not tenable as an analysis of denominal -*ed* adjectives, the √P-based analysis is particularly suitable for complex adjectives involving *leggèd* and thus should be adopted as an ad hoc measure to account for the peculiar aspect of √*leg*. This treatment seems justified considering the variation in the distribution of *leggèd* among native speakers.[25]

____

[24] This is the structure proposed by Nevins and Myler (2014) for denominal -*ed* adjectives in general. See Harley (2009) for a DM analysis of compounds, where complex Roots as in (23) are formed.

[25] One might wonder at this point why denominal adjectives show no contextual allomorphy unlike English past participles. For reasons of space, I cannot discuss this issue in detail, but a brief answer is that, given that contextual allomorphy is restricted to cases where a node can see another node when it is concatenated with it, the Asp head deriving participles can see the Root involved despite the intervening heads, i.e., *v* and Voice, while the adjectivizing head -*ed* cannot due to the *n* head, as we saw in the text. See Embick (2010) for a proposal that can derive the distinction between these heads.

    Alternatively, the distinction can be captured by the notion of span and the Span Adjacency Hypothesis (Merchant, 2015),

To sum up this section, it can be concluded that denominal -*ed* adjectives show no contextual allomorphy and that the putative allomorph, syllabic -*èd*, is in fact the exponent of Asp$_S$ which can be realized only in the context of a limited number of Roots.

4. The Source of Possession Meaning

As we saw at the outset, the meaning of a denominal -*ed* adjective is fairly predictable and construed as 'possessing N' or 'provided with N'. Pretheoretically, it might appear that the meaning of possession arises as a result of affixation of -*ed*.

To account for this semantic property of denominal -*ed* adjectives, I follow Nevins and Myler (2014) and propose that the adjectivizing suffix -*ed* has the following denotation:

(24) $[\![\,a(\text{-}ed)\,]\!] = \lambda R \lambda x \exists y [R(x,y)]$

Here R is a variable for a 2-place relation, and this ensures that *n*P is restricted to relational nouns like nouns of inalienable possession.

The denotation in (24) is quite reminiscent of that of possessive determiners in English (e.g., the Saxon genitive, *'s*), and one might suspect that -*ed* is the adjectival version of the possessive determiner. However, the two cannot be equated even if the categorial difference is taken into consideration. Specifically, the adjectivizing suffix and the possessive D are crucially different in that the latter, which is semantically transparent as in (25)a below, can undergo type-shifting so that it can accommodate non-relational possessees, while the former cannot. Thus, when a possessee is a non-relational noun, the type-shifting operator in (25)b kicks in, thereby allowing the possessee to be in a free, pragmatically controlled relation with the possessor (Barker, 1995; 2011).[26]

(25) a. $[\![\,D_{\text{POSS}}\,]\!] = \lambda R[R]$
    b. $\pi = \lambda P \lambda x \lambda y [P(y) \wedge R(x,y)]$

As a result, both relational and non-relational nouns can appear as a possessee in possessive DPs, as shown in (26) and (27), respectively.

____

which makes reference to the notion of extended projection (Grimshaw, 2005).

[26] See also Partee and Borshev (2003).

(26) $[\![John\text{'s } leg]\!] = [\![\mathrm{D_{POSS}}\, leg]\!]([\![John]\!])$
$= ([\![\mathrm{D_{POSS}}]\!]([\![leg]\!]))(\mathbf{j})$
$= (\lambda R[R](\lambda x \lambda y[\mathbf{leg}(x,y)])(\mathbf{j})$
$= \lambda x \lambda y[\mathbf{leg}(x,y)](\mathbf{j})$
$= \lambda y[\mathbf{leg}(\mathbf{j},y)]$

(27) $[\![John\text{'s } log]\!] = (\pi\,([\![\mathrm{D_{POSS}}\, log]\!]))([\![John]\!])$
$= (\pi\,([\![\mathrm{D_{POSS}}]\!]([\![log]\!])))(\mathbf{j})$
$= (\pi\,(\lambda R[R](\lambda y[\mathbf{log}(y)])))(\mathbf{j})$
$= (\pi\,(\lambda y[\mathbf{log}(y)]))(\mathbf{j})$
$= (\lambda x \lambda y[\mathbf{log}(y) \wedge R(x,y)])(\mathbf{j})$
$= \lambda y[\mathbf{log}(y) \wedge R(\mathbf{j},y)]$

In the case of the adjectivizing suffix, since the suffix does not undergo type-shifting, the nominal bases are restricted, as (28) shows:

(28) a. relational
white-haired, hot-blooded, strong-willed, thick-voiced, simple-minded, good-natured, beaked, hoofed, horned, tailed, petalled, barked, branched, fringed, etc.
b. non-relational: clothes and accessories
white-capped (nurse), gloved (hand), silver-sandaled (feet), gold-ringed (finger), white-aproned (landlord), etc.

What is to note is that a class of non-relational nouns denoting clothes and accessories can be nominal bases for the adjectivizing suffix, whose denotation is fixed as in (24). I argue that this is possible because this class of nouns are coerced into relational nouns. Specifically, by building on the insight of Vikner and Jensen (2002), I argue that they can undergo type-shifting on the basis of their telic function (i.e., clothes are to wear), as a result of which the concomitant meaning-shift operation derives the relational denotation in (29) from the original, non-relational one: $\lambda x[\mathbf{CLOTHES}(x)]$ (where $\mathbf{CLOTHES}$ stands for any noun denoting clothes or accessories).[27]

(29) $\lambda y[\lambda x[\mathbf{CLOTHES}(x) \wedge \mathbf{wear}(y,x)]]$

I further argue that the meaning shift is possible as a result of negotiation with the encyclopedic knowledge, in particular, what we know about clothes: In a nutshell, cloths are for wearing, and wearing necessitates physical contact with body-parts, which allows them to be treated as relational. This meaning shift basically explains why denominal -ed adjectives based on this class of nouns are used for situations where they are worn, not possessed.

Therefore, it seems plausible to say that, for type-shifting of non-relational nouns to relational ones to be successful, concomitant meaning-shift must be such that it supports the relational interpretation. This presumably explains why the following adjectives are unacceptable.

(30) a. *two-carred (man)
b. *big-officed (president)
c. *good-jobbed (student)

To sum up this section, the adjectivizing suffix has the denotation in (24), which serves to restrict only relational nouns, underived and derived, to appear in denominal -ed adjectives. This is in sharp contrast with the possessive determiners in English, which can accommodate both relational and non-relational nouns, undergoing type-shifting if necessary.

5. Conclusion and Further Issues

We have discussed denominal -ed adjectives in light of recent advances in linguistic theory and have shown that, once you specify the adjectivizing suffix as taking a relational nP as input, all the properties discussed in this paper follow as consequences of independently motivated principles of grammar and the external system. However, I have left out many interesting issues concerning denominal -ed adjectives such as the derivation of their nominal bases, their stress patterns, their non-literal meanings, which are derived from their primary meanings, and so on. Needless to say, more research is needed for further understanding.

Acknowledgments

I am grateful to an anonymous reviewer for providing invaluable comments on an earlier version of this paper. The usual disclaimers apply.

---

[27] Vikner and Jensen's (2002) analysis, originally proposed to account for genitive possesssives, is couched within the framework of Generative Lexicon Theory (Pusktejovsky, 1995). I remain agnostic about whether the information in the qualia structure is part of lexical knowledge or not.

References

Anagnostopoulou, Elena and Yota Samioti. 2013. Allosemy, Idioms, and the Domains: Evidence from Adjectival Participles. In R. Folli, C. Sevdali, and R. Truswell, eds. *Syntax and its Limits*, pp.218–250. Oxford University Press, Oxford.

Arad, Maya. 2005. *Roots and Patterns: Hebrew Morpho-syntax*. Springer, Dordrecht.

Arregi, Karlos and Andrew Nevins. 2014. A Monoradical Approach to Some Cases of Disuppletion. *Theoretical Linguistics* 40(3/4):311–330.222

Barker, Chris. 1995. *Possessive Descriptions*, CSLI Publications, Stanford, CA.

Barker, Chris. 2011. Possessives and Relational Nouns. In C. Maienborn, K. von Heusinger, and P. Portner, eds., *Semantics: An International Handbook of Natural Language Meaning*, pp.1108–1129. Mouton de Gruyter, Berlin.

Bauer, Laurie and Rodney Huddleston. 2002. Lexical Word-Formation. In R. Huddleston and G. K. Pullum, eds., *The Cambridge Grammar of the English Language*, pp.1621–1721. Cambridge University Press, Cambridge, UK.

Borer, Hagit. 2005. *Structuring Sense Volume I: In Name Only*. Oxford University Press, Oxford.

Bruening, Benjamin. 2014. Word Formation Is Syntactic: Adjectival Passives in English. *Natural Language and Linguistic Theory* 32(2):363–422.

Dubinsky, Stanley and Silverster Ron Simango. 1996. Passive and Stative in Chichewa: Evidence for Modular Distinction in Grammar. *Language* 72(4):749–781.

Embick, David. 2000. Feature, Syntax, and Categories in the Latin Perfect. *Linguistic Inquiry* 31(2):185–230.

Embick, David. 2003. Linearization and Local Dislocation: Derivational Mechanics and Interactions. *Linguistic Analysis* 33(3/4):303–336.

Embick, David. 2004. On the Structure of Resultative Participles in English. *Linguistic Inquiry* 35(3):355–392.

Embick, David. 2010. *Localism versus Globalism in Morphology and Phonology*. MIT Press, Cambridge, MA.

Gram-Andersen, Knud. 1992. *The Purple-Eyed Monster and its Relations*. The Book Guild, Sussex.

Grimshaw, Jane. 2005. *Words and Structure*. CSLI Publications, Stanford, CA

Halle, Morris and Alec Marantz. 1993. Distributed Morphology and the Pieces of Inflection. In K. Hale and S.J. Keyser, eds., *The View from Building 20*, pp.111–176. MIT Press, Cambridge, MA.

Harbour, Daniel. 2011. Valence and Atomic Number. *Linguistic Inquiry* 42(4):561–594

Harley, Heidi. 2006. *English Words: A Linguistic Introduction*. Blackwell, Oxford.

Harley, Heidi. 2009. Compounding in Distributed Morphology. In R. Lieber and G. Scalise, eds., *The Oxford Handbook of Compounding*, pp.129–144. Oxford University Press, Oxford.

Haugen, Jason D. 2016. Readjustment: Rejected? In D. Siddiqi and H. Harley, eds., *Morphological Metatheory*, pp.303–342. John Benjamin, Amsterdam.

Hirtle, W.H. 1970. *-Ed* Adjectives like 'Verandahed' and 'Blue-Eyed'. *Journal of Linguistics* 6(1):19–36.

Huddleston, Rodney and Geoffrey K. Pullum, eds. 2002. *The Cambridge Grammar of the English Language*. Cambridge University Press, Cambridge, UK.

Hudson, R. A. 1975. Problems in the Analysis of Ed-Adjectives. *Journal of Linguistics* 11(1):69–72.

Jespersen, Otto. 1942. *A Modern English Grammar on Historical Principles, Volume VI: Morphology*. Munksgaard, Copenhagen. [Republished edition by Routledge, London]

Kiparsky, Paul. 1982. Word Formation and the Lexicon. In F. Ingeman, ed., *Proceedings of the Mid-America Linguistics Conference*, 3–29. University of Kansas, Lawrence, KS.

Ljung, Magnus. 1976. *-Ed* Adjectives Revisited. *Journal of Linguistics* 12(1):159–168.

Marantz, Alec. 1997. No Escape from Syntax: Don't Try Morphological Analysis in the Privacy of Your Own Lexicon. *University of Pennsylvania Working Papers in Linguistics* 4(2):201–225.

Marantz, Alec. 2001. Words. Paper presented at the 20th West Coast Conference on Formal Linguistics, University of Southern California, 23-25 February.

Marantz, Alec. 2013. Locality Domains for Contextual Allomorphy across the Interfaces. In O. Matushansky and A. Marantz, eds., *Distributed Morphology Today: Morphemes for Morris Halle*, pp.95–115. MIT Press, Cambridge.

Merchant, Jason. 2015. How Much Context Is Enough? Two Cases of Span-Conditioned Stem Allomorphy. *Linguistic Inquiry* 46(29):273–303.

Miller, D. Gary. 2006. *Latin Suffixal Derivatives in English and their Indo-European Ancestry*. Oxford University Press, Oxford.

Morita, Chigusa. 2015. A Note on Physical Attribute Expressions in Japanese and English. *Linguistic Research: Working Papers in English Linguistics* 30:81–90. University of Tokyo, Tokyo.

Nevins, Andrew and Neil Myler. 2014. A Brown-Eyed Girl. In Carson T. Schütze and Linnaea Stockall, eds., *UCLA Working Papers in Linguistics* 18:243–257.

Partee, H. Barbara and Vladimir Borshev. 2003. Genitives, Relational Nouns, and Argument-Modifier Ambiguity. In E. Lang, C. Maienborn, and C. Fabricius-Hansen, eds., *Modifying Adjuncts*, pp.67–112. Mouton de Gruyter, Berlin.

Plag, Ingo. 2003. Word-Formation in English. Cambridge University Press, Cambridge, UK.

Pustejovsky, James. 1995. *The Generative Lexicon*. MIT Press, Cambridge, MA.

Quirk, Radolph, Sidney Greenbaum, Geoffrey Leech, and Jan Svartvik. 1985. *A Comprehensive Grammar of the English Language*. Longman, London.

Sproat, Richard. 1985. On Deriving the Lexicon. Ph.D. Thesis. MIT.

Vikner, Carl and Per Anker Jensen. 2002. A Semantic Analysis of English Genitive. Interaction of Lexical and Formal Semantics. *Studia Linguistica* 56(2):191–226.

Subjecthood and Grammatical Relations in Korean: An Experimental Study with Honorific Agreement and Plural Copying

Ji-Hye Kim
Department of English Education
Korea National University of Education
Cheongju, Korea
jkim@knue.ac.kr

Yong-hun Lee
Department of English Literature & Language
Chungnam National University
Daejeon, Korea
yleeuiuc@gmail.com

James Hye-Suk Yoon
Department of Linguistics

University of Illinois, Urbana-Champaign
U. S. A.
jyoon@illinois.edu

Abstract

The present study investigated the following: i) how NPs bearing differing GRs behave with respect to two proposed subject diagnostics – Honorific Agreement (HA) and Plural Copying on adverbs (PC) and ii) whether scrambling allows non-Subject GRs to control these properties. An experimental investigation using Magnitude Estimation (ME) was conducted. The result revealed that the sentences with Subject NP controller got higher acceptability scores compared to non-Subject NP controllers for both diagnostics and that scrambling did not have an effect on acceptability. While both HA and PC showed a similar pattern of preference for Subject controllers, the contrast between Subject and non-Subject controllers was more pronounced with HA.

1 Introduction: Subjecthood diagnostics in Korean

The question of whether Grammatical Relations (GRs) such as Subject or Object are universal has been a matter of debate. While there are theories that posit GRs are theoretically central notions (Relational Grammar, Lexical Functional Grammar), there are others that do not countenance them at all but instead try to derive properties traditionally attributed to GRs from other aspects of the organization of a sentence, such as c-command among arguments (Government and Binding theory, Minimalist Program). Another debate has centered on whether GRs, as primitives or as derived notions, play a role in the grammar of all languages. Li and Thompson (1976) famously argued that there are languages where the syntactic articulation of a clause does not reference GRs but discourse relations like Topic instead. Topic-prominent languages like Chinese are argued not to utilize GRs at all, whereas Subject-prominent languages like English employ GRs centrally in the syntactic articulation of a clause. They argued that Korean may be both Topic and Subject prominent, given that it possesses signature properties of both types of languages. Against this backdrop, Sohn (1980) has argued that Korean is only Topic-prominent, with the notion of Subject playing no role. Sohn's (1980) position has been an outlier, however. The vast majority of generative works on Korean assumes that GRs, whether as primitive or as derived notions, are central in the grammar of Korean, and many properties of Korean have been analyzed using the vocabulary of GRs and related ideas. The most extensive defense of the role of GRs/Subjects in the grammar of Korean comes from works in the RG tradition, where a representative list of properties identifying Subjecthood (Subjecthood diagnostics) was proposed (Youn 1990, Gerdts 1991, Gerdts & Youn 2001, etc.).

(2) Subject Diagnostics in Korean

    a. Controller of optional plural-marking
       (i.e., Plural Copying)
    b. Controller of subject honorification
       (i.e., Honorific Agreement)

c. Controller of PRO in complement
(obligatory) control
d. Antecedent of (subject-oriented) anaphors
e. Controller of PRO in adjunct control
f. Controller of null coordinate subjects

Aside from the issue of the etiology of these diagnostics (which prompts us to deconstruct Subjecthood, either in structural or functional terms), a recurring challenge to diagnostic-based attempts to identify Subjects is that not all of the proposed diagnostics converge on a unique nominal in a clause. The responses to this challenge have proceeded in two directions; one line of research (RG) sought to answer the question of split Subjecthood by looking at Subjecthood in derivational terms, while a different line of research (inspired by Keenan 1976) has sought to group subject diagnostics into different classes (e.g., coding vs. behavioral properties, Keenan 1976), in order to understand the split.

While it is necessary to address the etiology question and to explore the implications of split Subject behavior for theories of Subjecthood and GRs in general, a more fundamental challenge for Subjecthood research in the context of Korean comes from recent experimental syntactic studies that show that judgments of non-linguist native speakers may differ from those of linguists regarding the proposed diagnostics (Kim, Lee & Kim 2015, Lee, Kim & Kim 2015, Kim, Kim & Yoon 2016, etc.). These works call for a fundamental re-examination of the empirical basis of Subjecthood diagnostics previously established through the intuitions of native speaker linguists. Despite their important contribution, a drawback of these particular studies is that they did not investigate the behavior of Subjects by comparing it with the full range of non-Subject GRs. The most common non-Subject GR with which a Subject was contrasted was the Possessor-of-Subject, since the focus of these papers was to investigate whether the Subject-like nominal (Major Subject) in a Multiple Subject Construction (MSC) can control certain Subject diagnostics. Since the Major Subject (MS) regularly alternates with the Possessor of a sentence with a single Subject, it was natural to restrict the range of non-Subject GRs in that way.

However, the Possessor-of-Subject GR is not representative of how non-Subject NPs behave, since it has sometimes been argued to have prominence over the Subject. Specifically, the Possessor-of-Subject can scope or bind out of the Subject in certain circumstances, as noted by Kayne (1994). In the case of Korean, it has been argued that the Possessor-of-Subject can control certain Subject properties such as Subject Honorification, especially when the head noun can be construed as a metonym of the Possessor (cf. C. Park 2010; K-S Hong 1994).

These considerations call for a systematic comparison of Subjects with a wide variety of non-Subject GRs, over the full range of proposed Subject diagnostics. It is only in this way that we can guarantee that subsequent investigations of Subjecthood and related issues (such as split Subjecthood) rest on a solid empirical foundation.

In the present study, we focused on two hypothesized Subject properties – Honorific Agreement (HA) and Plural Copying on adverbs (PC). With the Possessor-of-Subjects, we took particular care to control for any effects of metonymy, for reasons noted in the following section.

Overall results reveal that sentences with Subject controller – in both HA and PC – were significantly more acceptable than those with non-Subject GRs, validating their status as diagnostics for Subjecthood, and giving tentative support to the position that GRs like Subject play an important explanatory role in the grammar of Korean.

1.1 Honorific Agreement

It is commonly assumed that Subjects serve as the controller/trigger of honorific *-si* marking on the predicate (Yoon 1986, Youn 1990, Hong 1991, 1994, Yoon 2008, 2009). (1a), where the [+hon] Subject *halapeci* 'grandfather' co-occurs with *–si*, is well-formed, whereas (1b), where *–si* occurs with a [-hon] Subject *Cheli*, is ill-formed. And (1c) with a [-hon] Subject *Minswu* is ungrammatical, even in the presence of a [+hon] Object (*sensayngnim*), which shows that HA is Subject-controlled. Finally, (1d) shows that even when the [+hon] Object is fronted/scrambled, it does not license *–si* marking on the predicate, unlike certain proposed Subject diagnostics (i.e., reflexive binding) where a scrambled Object can behave similarly to a Subject in the scrambled position (Saito 1985, Miyagawa 2001).

(1)

a. **Halapeci**-ka cikum o-**si**-nta.
   Grandfather-NOM now come-HON-DECL
   'Grandfather is coming now.'

b. *****Cheli**-ka cikum o-**si**-nta.
   Cheli-NOM now come-HON-DECL
   'Cheli is coming now.'

c. *Minswu-ka **sensayngnim**-ul manna-**si**-ess-ta.
   M-NOM teacher-ACC meet-HON-PST-DECL
   'Minswu met the teacher.'

d. *****Sensayngnim**-ul Minswu-ka manna-**si**-ess-ta.
   Teacher-ACC M-NOM meet-HON-PST-DECL
   'The teacher, Minswu met.'

While the results so far are consistent with HA being controlled by a Subject, (2a) indicates that sometimes the honorific Possessor of a non-honorific Subject nominal can seemingly function as the controller of HA, though the fact that not all such sentences are acceptable (cf. 2b,c) requires further explanation.

(2)

a. **Sensayngnim**-uy nwun-i khu-**si**-ta.
   Teacher-GEN eye-NOM be.big-HON-DECL
   'The teacher's eyes are big.'

b. ?**Sensayngnim**-uy atul-i eli-**si**-ta.
   Teacher-GEN son-NOM be.young-HON-DECL
   'The teacher's son is young.'

c. *?**Sensayngnim**-uy cha-ka pissa-**si**-ta.
   Teacher-GEN car-NOM expensive-HON-DECL
   'The teacher's car is expensive.'

Based on sentences like (2), some scholars have questioned whether HA is always controlled by Subjects (Hong 1991, 1994), or whether it is subject to pragmatic constraints (Choe 2004 vs. Choi 2010). This debate calls for a more systematic investigation of HA as a Subjecthood diagnostic.

1.2 Plural Copying

Plural copying on constituents within the predicate (such as adverbs) is another diagnostic that is assumed to be controlled by Subjects, as shown in the contrast between (3a) and (3b). When –*tul* occurs with a plural Subject as in (3a), the sentence is grammatical, whereas the sentence becomes unacceptable when the Subject is singular, even when there is another nominal within the VP that is plural, as shown in (3b).

(3)

a. Ku tayhak-uy **kyoswu-tul**-i
   That university-GEN professor-PL-NOM
   chongcang-lul manhi-**tul** coahan-ta
   president-ACC much-PL like-DECL
   'The professors in the university like the president very much.'

b.*?Ku tayhak-uy chongcang-i
   That university-GEN president-NOM
   kyoswu-**tul**-lul manhi-**tul** coahan-ta
   professor-PL-ACC much-PL like-DECL
   'The president of the university likes the professors very much.'

c. Cheli-ka pang-eyse kuliko Yenghi-ka
   Cheli-NOM room-LOC and Yenghi-NOM
   kesil-eyse swukcey-lul yelsimhi-**tul**
   livingroom-LOC homework-ACC hard-PL
   ha-ko-iss-ta
   do-and-be-PRGES-DECL
   'Cheli in the room and Yenghi in the living room are doing their homework hard.'

While most instances of plural copying are licensed by plural Subjects, it has been noted that singular Subjects may license them in certain instances, as in (3c) (Chung, D. 2004). In (3c), the copied plural seems to function as a marker of distributivity (Song, S. 1975, Song, J. 1997).

Based on facts like these, some (Hong 1991) have questioned whether PC is a valid Subjecthood diagnostic.

1.3 Scrambling and Subject Position

In the literature on A-scrambling, it has been observed that a non-Subject that undergoes A-scrambling can take on certain properties typical of Subjects, such as the ability to act as binder of reflexives, and to take wide scope (Miyagawa 2001). Therefore, in the current experimental investigation, we wanted to see if scrambling can lead a non-Subject to function as controller of HA and PC when the Subject lacks the features to function as controller.

2 Research Method

2.1 Research Question and Hypotheses

The research questions of the current study are the following:

Research Questions:
1) Are Honorific Agreement (HA) and Plural Copying on adverbs (PC) controlled by Subjects?
2) Can a scrambled non-Subject control these properties when the Subject lacks the relevant features?

Our specific hypotheses and predictions are the following:

1) Korean speakers will judge sentences where HA and PC are controlled by the Subject to be significantly better than those where they are controlled by non-Subjects, because these properties are controlled only by Subjects.

2) A scrambled non-Subject will not be able to function as controller of HA and PC, unlike reflexive binding and wide scope. This is because HA and PC are properties controlled by the lower Subject position (SpvP, according to Yoon 2008, 2009), while (A)-scrambling places the non-Subject in a high Subject position (SpTP).

2.2 Participants

Sixty Korean native speakers (age m=23.05, sd=3.314) residing in and near Seoul, South Korea, who are either current university students or graduates, participated in the experiment.

2.3 Task, Materials, and Procedure

The main task was an acceptability judgment using online Magnitude Estimation (ME), where the participants were asked to judge the degree of naturalness of the target sentences relative to their judgment of a modulus sentence, of intermediate acceptability. The test items were composed of 170 Korean sentences (80 targets and 90 fillers). The target items were constructed so that either a Subject NP or one of the 4 non-Subject GRs (Possessor-of-Subject, Direct Object, Indirect Object, Adjunct) had the feature relevant for HA or PC (that is, [+hon] or [pl]). There were 4 tokens for each sentence type. Since there were 5 conditions and the same sentences were also varied in terms of word order, we had 40 sentences for each diagnostic, making a total of 80 test items.

The target items for HA with intended controllers ([+hon] NPs) in bold are shown in (4) below, in canonical order sentences.

(4) Canonical sentences with different GRs
a. **Halapeci-ka**   kkoma   Mincay-lul
   Grandfather-NOM   little-boy   M-ACC
cohaha-**si**-ess-ta.
like-HON- PST-DECL
'Grandfather likes the little Mincay.'
                    [Subject]

b. Kkoma   Mincay-ka   **halapeci-lul**
   Little-boy   M-NOM   grandfather-ACC
cohaha-**si**-ess-ta.
like-HON- PST-DECL
'Little Mincay likes his grandfather.'
                    [Direct Object]

c. Haksayng   tayphyo-ka   **chongcangnim-eykey**
   Student   chairman -NOM   chancellor -DAT
phyenci-lul   ponay-**si**-ess-ta.
letter-ACC   send-HON- PST-DECL
'The student chairman sent a letter to the chancellor.'   [Indirect Object]

d. **Ku   sacangnim –uy** alpasayng -i
   That president-GEN   part-time-worker-NOM
kkoma   sonnimtul-ul   cohaha-**si**-ess-ta.
little-kid   customers-ACC   like-HON-PST-DECL
'The part-time worker of the president liked the little kid customers.' [Possessor of Subject]

e. Pwulhyocasik-i   **pwumonim-ttaymwuney**
   Bad son-NOM   parents -because
wu-**si**-ess-ta.
weep-HON-PST-DECL
'The bad son wept because of the parents.'
                    [Adjunct]

In addition to varying the type of controller of HA between Subjects and non-Subjects, we also manipulated word order, as illustrated below in (5), which gives us additional contrast (i.e., scrambled order vs. canonical order) to our original experimental design.

(5) Scrambled sentences
a. Kkoma   Mincay-ka **halapeci-lul**
   Little-kid   M-NOM   grandfather-ACC
cohaha-**si**-ess-ta.

like-HON- PST-DECL
'Little Mincay likes grandfather.'

b. **Halapeci-lul**   kkoma   Mincay-ka
   Grandfather-ACC   little-kid   M-NOM
cohaha-**si**-ess-ta.
like-HON- PST-DECL
'Little Mincay likes grandfather.'

The word order variation was introduced in order to evaluate research question 2.

2.4   Statistical Analysis

Scores were extracted for the target sentences and were encoded with four linguistic factors as shown in Table 1 below: DIAGTYPE represents the Subject properties, HA and PC. The value of AGREETYPE is NP1 (Subject) and NP2 (non-Subject), with NP2 divided further into 4 GRs. WORDORDER ranges over canonical vs. scrambled order. SCORE represents acceptability scores of the sentences containing relevant factors. The scores were converted into the z-scores using mean and standard deviation, following Gries (2013) and Lee (2016).[1]

Factor	Value
DIAGTYPE	HA, PC
AGREETYPE	Direct Object, Indirect Object, Possess of Subject, Adjunct
AGREEMENT	NP1(Subject), NP2(non-Subject)
WORDORDER	Canonical, Scrambled
SCORE	Acceptability scores

Table 1: Encoded Factors

3   Results

3.1   HA + Canonical

The results with HA in sentences occurring in canonical order are shown below. In the results, sentences where Subjects control HA are divided into 4 types, depending on the GR borne by the competitor NP, where the competitor is the other NP in the sentence that bears the feature appropriate for HA when the Subject NP does not. We separated the results for the Subject controller condition in this way because the ratings for the Subject controller are different depending on the GR of the competitor.[2]

As we see in Figure 1, the sentences where the [+hon] Subject controls HA (black bars) got high acceptability scores regardless of the GR of the competitor NP. By contrast, sentences where a [+hon] competitor NP is intended as the controller of HA (white bars) were judged as unacceptable (i.e., worse than the modulus).

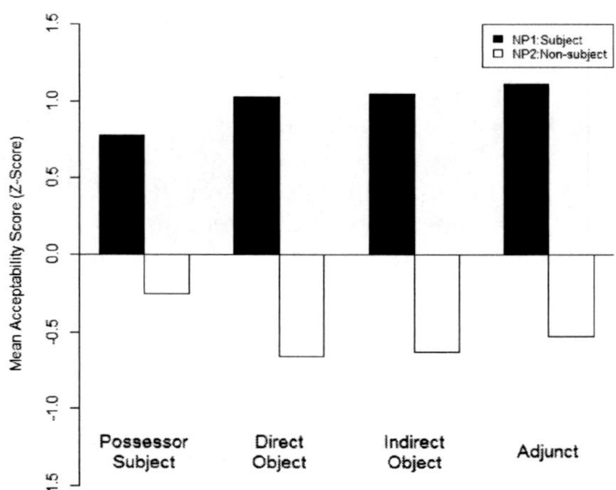

Figure 1: HA + Canonical

3.2   HA + Scrambled

The results with the sentences containing HA with scrambled order (NP2 preceding NP1) are shown in Figure 2. As you can see, the manipulation of NP1-NP2 order had no effect. The difference among various GRs in canonical vs. scrambled order was not significant (p=0.3080222).

---

[1] The acceptability score ranged from -2.938 to 3.585 in z-scores, where the acceptability scores of modulus sentences used in Magnitude Estimation are represented to be 0. Thus, 3.585 represents the highest acceptability with respect to the modulus sentence (i.e., meaning that the sentence is considered more acceptable than the modulus sentence to that degree) while -2.938 represents the lowest acceptability compared to the modulus sentence.

[2] In target items with more than one non-Subject NP, we took care to ensure that only one NP had the potential to be a competitor. For example, since HA is possible only with animate/human NPs, we took care to ensure that besides the Subject, there was only one other NP that is animate/human.

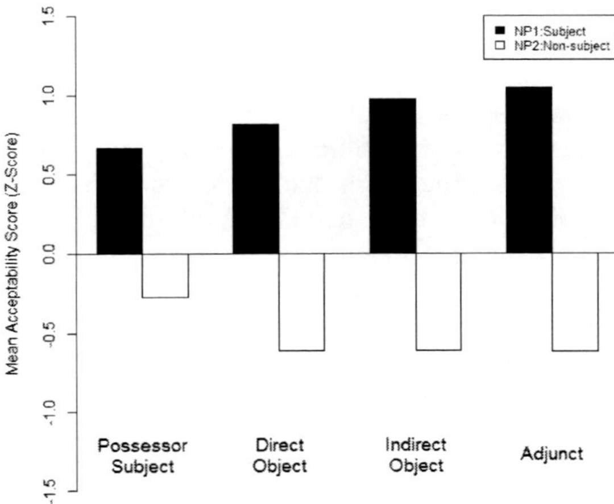

Figure 2: HA + Scrambled

3.3 PC + Canonical

As for PC, we found a similar pattern of results between the sentences where plural *-tul* was controlled by Subject (i.e., black bars) or by non-Subject GRs (i.e., white bars). Korean native speakers showed significantly higher acceptability with sentences like (3a) with Subject controller, compared to the sentences like (3b) with non-Subject controllers.

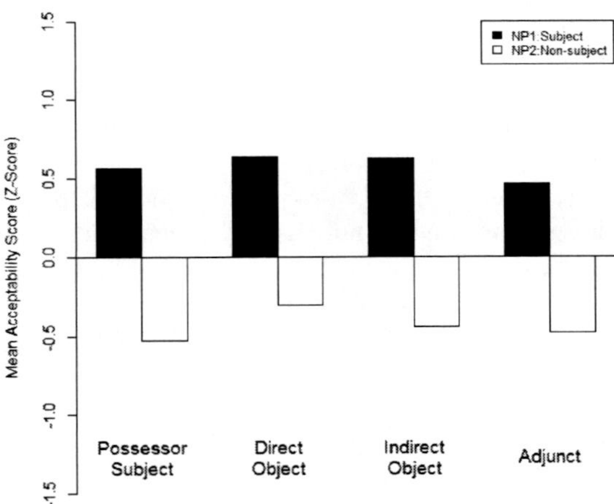

Figure 3: PC + Canonical

What is noticeable is the comparison between HA and PC in their contrast between Subject vs. non-Subject controllers. If we compare Figure 1 and Figure 3, we can see that i) overall acceptability scores for sentences with Subject controllers are lower in PC compared to HA, and ii) the magnitude of difference between sentences

with Subject controllers (black bars) and those with non-Subject controllers (white bars) is greater across the full range of competitor NPs in Figure 1 than Figure 3.

3.4 PC + Scrambled

Finally, the sentences containing PC in scrambled order showed the similar pattern as well, with respect to their contrast between Subject controller and non-Subject GRs. The difference among various non-Subject GRs in canonical vs. scrambled orders was not significant (p=0.2614641).

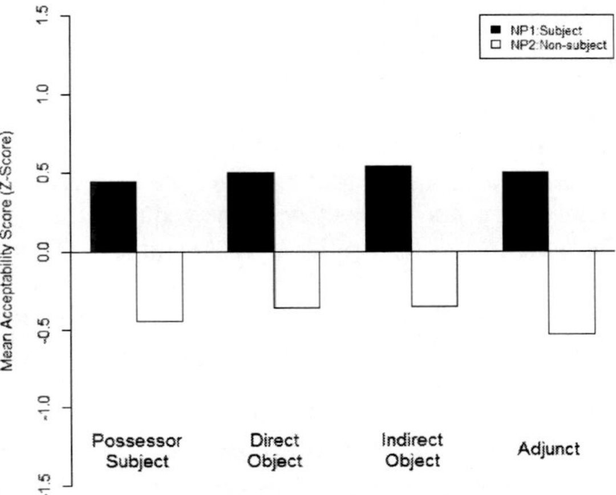

Figure 4: PC + Scrambled

4 Discussion

The specific hypotheses and predictions for the study were the following:

1) Korean speakers will judge sentences where HA and PC are controlled by the Subject to be significantly better than those where they are controlled by non-Subjects, because these properties are controlled only by Subjects.

2) A scrambled non-Subject will not be able to function as controller of HA and PC, even though scrambled non-Subjects can sometimes behave in a manner similar to Subjects. This is because HA and PC are properties controlled by the lower Subject (Yoon 2008, 2009), while (A)-scrambling places the non-Subject in a high Subject position (SpTP).

The results of our experiment are consistent with the predictions of our hypotheses. First of all, the sentences where Subject controls the diagnostic property showed significantly higher acceptability than those where non-Subject NPs do. The pattern of the results were similar for both HA and PC. This result seems to imply that HA and PC can be used reliably as diagnostics of Subjecthood in Korean, despite the existence of data that seem to challenge it. This in turn suggests a strategy for looking at such data. One strategy is to control for potential noise, or confounds, that may mask the underlying generalization. In the case of most common pretender to the throne, Possessor-of – Subjects, the culprit is metonymy. When metonymic interpretation is carefully controlled, Possessor-of-Subject does not approximate the Subject in terms of being able to function as controller of Subjecthood diagnostics.[3]

Secondly, word order variation had no effect in enabling a non-Subject with the requisite features to function as controller of HA and PC. This is interesting in light of the literature on local scrambling that found that a scrambled non-Subject can take on some properties typical of Subjects in the derived position. Our results did not show such behavior.

This could be due to a couple of reasons. The explanation we proffered is based on the division of Subject properties in Korean into low vs. high Subject properties. HA and PC have been claimed to be controlled by the nominal in the low Subject position (Yoon 2008, 2009), while the landing site of (A)-scrambling has been taken to be SpTP, the high Subject position. Under this view, scrambling of a non-Subject to SpTP will not imbue it with the ability to control Subject properties that are within the purview of the nominal in the lower Subject position.

However, it should be noted that we did not force an A-scrambling parse on the relevant sentences. Therefore, the possibility exists that speakers took the scrambling in question to be A'-scrambling, in which case we do not expect the A'-scrambled nominal to behave in a way similar to Subjects. Future work must control for this confound.

In addition, though HA and PC behaved similarly in being controlled by Subjects, there was a difference in magnitude of discrimination between Subject and non-Subject controllers between HA and PC, with speakers reporting a much more pronounced degree of discrimination with HA.

5 Conclusion

The current study investigated how nominals bearing different GRs behave with respect to the two diagnostics claimed to pick out Subjects (HA and PC). Through an experimental investigation, this study confirmed that these properties are indeed controlled by Subjects. A broad spectrum of non-Subject GRs cannot approximate the Subject in terms of being able to function as controller of HA and PC.

We can take the results to be consistent with the utility of Subject as a theoretically important notion in the grammar of Korean.

However, the non-Subject nominals we investigated have not usually been claimed to participate in split Subject behavior. What remains to be done is to examine a wider range of nominals in order to determine whether Subjecthood (as theoretically understood in various traditions of generative grammar) is still relevant in the grammar of Korean. Yoon (2008, 2009) argued that the utility of Subjecthood can be maintained in the case of Multiple Subject/Nominative Constructions, which show split Subject behavior between the Major Subject and the Grammatical Subject, once a decompositional approach to Subjecthood diagnostics is adopted (McCloskey 1997, Falk 2006). And Kim et al (2015, 2016) provided experimental support for this proposal. Additional research needs to be done to defend the utility of Subjecthood for other potential split Subject

---

[3] Counter-examples to the Subject control generalization of PC, such as (3c), are harder to account for if PC is controlled by a local plural Subject.

A possible analysis of (3c) that makes it consistent with the plural Subject controller generalization might be to view as a version of the following, where the RNR-ed string has a phonologically null plural Subject, which is overtly realized in (i) below.

(i) Cheli-ka   pang-eyse   kuliko   Yenghi-ka(nun)
    Cheli-$_{NOM}$ room-$_{LOC}$ and   Yenghi-$_{NOM(TOP)}$
    kesil-eyse   **twul-i**   swukcey-lul   yelsimhi
    livingroom-$_{LOC}$ two-$_{NOM}$ homework-$_{ACC}$ hard
    ha-ko-iss-ta
    do-and-be-$_{PRGES-DECL}$
    'Cheli in the room and Yenghi in the living room are doing
     their homework hard.'

constructions (Non-nominative Subject Constructions, A-Scrambling Constructions, etc.).

References

Sungeun Cho. 2000. Three Forms of Case Agreement in Korean. *Doctoral dissertation*, State University of New York at Stony Brook

Jae-Woong Choe. 2004. Obligatory Honorification and the Honorific Feature. *Studies in Generative Grammar* 14(4): 545-559.

Kiyong Choi. 2010. Subject Honorification in Korean: In Defense of Agr and Head-Spec Agreement. *Language Research* 46: 59-82.

Donna B. Gerdts. 1991. Outline of a relational theory of case. *In Simon Fraser University Working Papers in Linguistics* 1, Paul McFetridge (ed.), 25–51.

Donna B. Gerdts and Cheong Youn. 2001. Korean dative experiencers: The evidence for their status as surface subjects. *Harvard Studies in Korean Linguistics* 9, 317-327.

Yehuda Falk. 2006. Subjects and Universal Grammar. Cambridge, MA: Cambridge University Press.

Stefan de Gries. 2013. *Statistics for Linguistics with R: A Practical Introduction*. Berlin: Mouton.

Ki-Sun Hong. 1991. Argument Selection and Case-Marking in Korean. *Doctoral dissertation*, Stanford University

Ki-Sun Hong. 1994. Subjecthood Tests in Korean. *Language Research* 30:99-136.

Beom-Mo Kang. 2002. *Pemcwu Mwunpep: Hankwuke-uy Hyengthaylon, Thongsalon, Thaipnonlicek Uymilon* (Categorial Grammar: The Morphology, Syntax, and Type-Logical Semantics of Korean). Seoul: Korea University Press.

Richard Kayne. 1994. *The Antisymmetry of Syntax*. Cambridge: MIT Press.

Edward L Keenan. 1976. Towards a universal definition of subject. *In Li, C. N. (ed.) Subject and Topic*, New York: Academic Press, pp. 303–333

Ji-Hye Kim, Yong-hun Lee, and Eunah Kim. 2015. Obligatory Control and Coordinated Deletion as Korean Subject Diagnostics: An Experimental Approach. *Language and Information* 19(1):75-101.

Ji-Hye Kim, Eunah Kim and James H-S Yoon. 2016. An Experimental Study of Subject Properties in Korean Multiple Subject Constructions (MSCs).

Proceedings of 2016 Pacific Asia Conference on Languages, Information and Computation 30.

Yong-hun Lee. 2016. *Corpus Linguistics and Statistics Using R*. Seoul: Hankook Publishing Company.

Yong-hun Lee, Eunah Kim, and Ji-Hye Kim. 2015. Reflexive Binding and Adjunct Control as Subject Diagnostics in Korean: An Experimental Approach. *Studies in Language Research* 31.2:427-449.

Charles Li and Thompson, Sandra. 1976. Subject and Topic: A New Typology of Language. *In Charles N. Li. Subject and Topic*. New York: Academic Press. pp. 457–489.

James McCloskey. 1997. Subjecthood and Subject Positions. In Elements of Grammar, Liliane Haegeman, ed., Dordrecht, Boston & London: Kluwer Academic Publishers: 197–235.

Shigeru Miyagawa. 2001. The EPP, scrambling, and wh-in-situ. *In Kenstowicz (ed.), Ken Hale: A life in language*, pp. 293-338.

Chongwon Park. 2010. The Role of Metonymy in the Interpretation of Korean Multiple Subject Constructions. *Language Sciences*, 33(1): 206-228

Ho-min Sohn. 1980. The State of the Art in the Historical-Comparative Studies of Japanese and Korean. *Korean Studies* 4, 29-50.

Jae Jung Song. 1997. The So-called Plural Copy in Korean as a Marker of Distribution and Focus. *Journal of Pragmatics* 27: 203-224.

Seok Choong Song. 1975. Bare Plural Marking and Ubiquitous Plural Marker in Korean. *In Papers from the 11th Regional Meeting of Chicago Linguistic Society*, 536-46.

James Hye-Suk Yoon. 1986. Some Queries Concerning the Syntax of Multiple Subject Constructions in Korean. *Studies in the Linguistic Sciences* 16: 215-236, Department of Linguistics, University of Illinois, Urbana-Champaign.

James Hye-Suk Yoon. 2008. Subjecthood and Subject Properties in Multiple Subject Constructions. *Talk presented at the East Asian Linguistics Seminar*, Oxford University.

James Hye-Suk Yoon. 2009. The Distribution of Subject Properties in Multiple Subject Constructions. *Japanese/Korean Linguistics* 19:64-83. Stanford, CA: CSLI.

Youn, Cheong. 1990. A Relational Analysis of Korean Multiple Nominative Constructions. *Doctoral dissertation*, State University of New York at Buffalo.

A Stylistic Analysis of a Philippine Essay, "The Will of the River"

Pilar S. Caparas
Western Mindanao State University
Zamboanga City, Philippines
pilarcaparas@gmail.com

Abstract

The continuous study of stylistics has been regarded as significant in identifying the border between language and literature. Hence the study presented a stylistic analysis of Alfredo Q. Gonzales's essay "The Will of the River." The lexis-grammar complementary analysis on the personal narrative of the author focused on the vocabulary of the essay and the grammatical structure of the sentence primarily the use of sentence-initial adjuncts that leads to the unraveling of the essay's general theme of man and nature.

1 Introduction

Understanding the depth and craftsmanship of any literary pieces poses challenges. It requires the analysis of the language to provide an objective interpretation and meaning of the literary text. It demands awareness on how the language works, its functions and components. From this point, understanding stylistics is quintessential.

The essay, "The Will of the River," by Alfredo Q. Gonzales is the literary text under study. It is a narrative essay about the river, *Bacong*, whose resolute journey towards the sea is likened to the life of a man. The author's style in writing exemplifies a pattern of structure foregrounded by an unconventional means of opening sentences which are the sentence-initial adjuncts, also called clause-initial adjuncts (Ernst, 2002). Its dominant pattern led to the consideration of the lexicon since adjuncts involve lexical selections as well, its grammatical and semantic functions and other major grammatical components of the text that provided a fertile and challenging ground for stylistic analysis. Significantly, this study hoped to contrib-

ute to the academic enrichment of Philippine Literature as a starting point in appreciating local literary writers and literary style of writing.

The essay seemed to involve a journey, a personal association with the narrator and a strong allusion to the duties and values of man. These initial observations led to the consideration of the chief gesture of stylistics that is to closely examine the 'linguistic particularities of a text' that leads to the 'understanding of the anatomy and functions of the language' (Toolan, 1998, p. ix). In other words, it is significant to pay attention to the language in the text to gain understanding and meaning of the literary piece because 'literature is made of language' (Watson & Zyngier, 2007, p. xii), and stylisticians uphold this principle for several years. This view is emphasized by Wellek and Warren (1977 in Yeibo, 2011) who posit that "language is the material of literature as stone or bronze is of sculpture, paints of picture, or sounds of music" (p. 137).

The paper took an eclectic approach as regards to the theoretical framework. The most important sources are the semantic categories in Biber et al. (1999), the analysis provided in Halliday and Hasan (1976) and Blake (1990). Blake's conventions of clause elements are: a) subject, it refers to the one that performs the verb; b) predicator, the verb performed by the subject; c) object, the receiver of the action of the verb which could be a person or a thing in the sentence besides the subject; d) complement, refers to the subject; and e) adjunct, refers to anything that does not belong to the first four categories.

Furthermore, Halliday's (1994) definition of adjuncts corroborates Blake's when he says that "an adjunct is an element that has not got the potential of being subject. It is typically realized by an adverbial group or a prepositional phrase" (p.

31st Pacific Asia Conference on Language, Information and Computation (PACLIC 31), pages 214–221
Cebu City, Philippines, November 16-18, 2017

80). Essentially, an adjunct is a grammatical function of adverbial and that adjunct is a realization of adverbial (Quirk et al., 1985).

Biber et al., (1999) classified adverbials by their functions: circumstance adverbials, to add circumstantial information about the proposition in the clause; stance adverbials, to express speaker/writer's stance towards the clause; and linking adverbials, to link the clause to some other unit of discourse.

Circumstance adverbials are the most varied class, as well as the most integrated into the clause structure. They add information about the action or state describe in the clause, answering questions such as 'how, when, where, how much, to 'what extent' and 'why.' (Biber, et al., 1999).

The seven major semantic categories of circumstance adverbials in Biber et al. (1999) are place, time, process, contingency, extent/degree, additive/restriction and recipient. Place circumstance adverbials convey distance, direction, or position. Distance adverbials typically answer the question 'How far', and include both general description of distance and specific measurements. Direction adverbials describe the pathway of an action. Position adverbials occur most often with stative verbs. They also occur with communication and activity verbs.

Time circumstance adverbials used to convey four-time related meanings: position in time, duration, frequency, and temporal relationship between two events or states. Process circumstance adverbials cover a wide range of semantic roles and are a less unified group than place or time adverbials. The most common subcategory of process adverbials is manner which describes the way in which something is done.

Process circumstance adverbials also include the category of means while instrument and agentive adverbials specify the agent of an action and are used with passive construction.

Furthermore, like the category of the process, contingency is a more diverse category than time and place. This category covers circumstance adverbials that show how one event or state is contingent upon another, including cause, reason, purpose, concession, condition, and result. While extent/degree circumstance adverbials function as intensifiers or diminishers, additive adverbials show that a current proposition is being added to a previous one. Finally, recipient adverbials typically expressed by *for*-phrases express the target of an action.

The second classification of adverbials is stance Adverbials whose primary function in the clause is to provide comment on the content or style of a clause. Their semantic categories include epistemic stance adverbial, attitude adverbial, and style adverbial. The third classification of adverbials is the linking adverbials whose primary function is to state the speaker/ writer's perception of the relationship between two units of discourse. Because they explicitly signal the connections between passages of text, linking adverbials are important devices for creating textual cohesion, alongside coordinators and subordinators. Their semantic categories include enumeration and addition, summation, apposition, result/inference apposition, contrast/ concession, and transition.

Essentially, the syntactic realizations of adverbials are varied ranging from single adverbs and adverb phrases, noun phrases (including single nouns), prepositional phrases, finite clauses, nonfinite clause and its subclasses: *ing*-clauses, *ed*-clauses, *to*-infinitive clauses, and verbless clauses (Biber et al., 1999).

Among the realizations of adverbials in the essay, predominant is the prepositional phrase and coordinating conjunctions. According to Quirk et al. (1985), prepositional phrases can perform some syntactic functions such as post modifiers in a noun phrase, adverbials of different kinds, verbs and adjective complements, clause subjects, and semi adjectives. Factually, Zihan's (2014) study highlighted two important arguments in comprehending the differences between linking adverbials and conjunctions. First, linking adverbials mark a meaning relationship at discourse level while conjunctions provide a structural link at clause complex level. Second, when a word form which can be used as a conjunction (e.g. and, so) is used as a discourse marker, it no longer belongs to the grammatical class of conjunction. Instead, it is a clause component which functions as a linking adverbial grammatically.

Applying these categories and concepts to explore the lexical behavior and grammatical components of the language used in the essay, the analysis would like to answer the following questions:

1. What are the occurrences of the initial position adjuncts found in the essay?

2. How do these initial position adjuncts unravel the meaning of the essay?

3. What other grammatical features found in the text that help shed the central theme of the essay?

2 Analysis

2.1 The Physical Structure

The essay consists of 15 paragraphs with 53 sentences and 1,356 words. The highest number of words in a paragraph is 229 which occurred in the last paragraph. It also has the greatest number of sentences, and the lowest number of words is 22 which occurred in the 9th paragraph, the only paragraph which contains only one sentence. The physical structure of the essay is shown in Table 1.

Table 1. The Physical Structure of the Essay

Paragraph	Number of Words	Number of Sentences	Number of Initial Position Adjuncts	Number of Initial Position Adjuncts in Series
1	124	5	4	2
2	124	6	7	3
3	66	2	3	1
4	52	4	5	1
5	92	3	5	1
6	33	2	2	1
7	141	3	1	0
8	117	4	0	0
9	22	1	1	0
10	44	2	0	0
11	59	4	1	0
12	122	4	5	2
13	55	3	1	1
14	47	2	3	1
15	227	8	11	4
Total 15	1,325	50	49	17

The essay showed a high proportional use of initial adjunct adverbials including the adjuncts that appear in series in a clause. Thirteen out of fifteen paragraphs have initial position adjuncts which include coordinating conjunctions functioning semantically as adjuncts. The highest number of adjuncts is in the last paragraph in which the number of occurrences is almost one-fourth of the total initial adjuncts while the second higher in number occur in paragraph 2 with half of the total

number of the highest occurrences. Paragraphs 4, 5 and 12 have the third highest number of occurrences with the same distribution. The least occurrences are in paragraph 1, 3, 6 and 14 while single occurrences are recognized in paragraphs 7, 9, 11 and 13.

The syntactic realization of these initial sentence adjuncts ranged from single adverbs to adverb phrases, clauses and coordinating conjunctions. Most of these series are a combination of single word and phrase or word and clause or clause and another clause in a clause. These series may affect the comprehension of the readers on the essay. However, Gonzales seemed to follow the principle of end weight in his distribution of series of adjuncts occurring in the same clause. It is said that this principle showed a "preferred distribution of elements in the clause by their weight […] the tendency for long and complex elements to be placed towards the end of the clause" (Biber et al., 1999, p. 899). In the essay, the [ ] is used to show the series of initial adjuncts.

(1) [And] [yet], [continuing our way into the hills], we found the river grow deeper and stronger than it was as it passed by our cottage.
(2) [Verily], [if a man derives his strength and inspiration from a low and feeble source,] he will fail to "arrive."
(3) [Unless a man draws his power from some source of heavenly altitude], [unless the stream of his life issues from a never-failing source], [unless], [in other words], his soul is fed from heights of infinite power, he may well fear that he will not reach the sea.

In (1) a combination of conjunctions semantically functioning as linking adverbials and a circumstantial contingency adverbial come in series while in (2) a circumstantial manner and circumstance contingency adverbial come in series. In (3), a series of circumstance conditionals occur. According to Biber et al., (1999), this kind of distribution eases comprehension by the reader who does not then have the burden of retaining complex information from earlier in a clause in short-memory while processing the remainder. The said distribution also provides the reason that even the compound and complex sentences in the essay do not leave a burden on the reader.

2.2 The Semantic Categories of the Initial Position Adjuncts

The classified adjuncts in the initial positions facilitated in the analysis of the meaning of the essay. Table 2 includes only the categories identified in the essay.

Table 2. Distribution of Initial Position Circumstance Adjuncts

Classification of Adjuncts	Occurrences of Initial Positions	Percentage
1.Circumstance Adjuncts	26	53.06
1.1 Place		
1.1.1. Position	2	4.08
1.1.2 Direction	1	2.04
1.2 Time		
1.2.1 Position in time	3	6.12
1.2.2 Temporal	2	4.08
1.2.3 Duration	1	2.04
1.3 Restriction	1	2.04
1.4 Process		
1.4.1 Comparison	2	4.08
1.4.2 Accompaniment	1	2.04
1.5 Contingency	2	4.08
1.5.1 Condition	8	16.32
1.5.2 Result	2	4.08
1.6 Agent	1	2.04
2. Stance Adjuncts	4	8.16
2.1 Epistemic		
2.1.1 Doublt/Certainty	1	2.04
2.1.2 Viewpoint or perspective	3	6.12
3. Linking Adjuncts	19	38.77
3.1 Contrast/Concession	3	6.12
3.2 Result/Inference	2	4.08
3.3 Conjunctions	14	28.57

Table 2 shows the distribution of the occurrences of initial position adjuncts within the three classifications: circumstance adjuncts, stance adjuncts, and linking adjuncts. The initial adjuncts were classified further into their categories and subcategories. The occurrences of circumstance adjuncts are one-half of the total initial position adjuncts dominated by contingency adjuncts that express condition while linking adverbials occur more than three-fourth of the total adjuncts which are predominantly conjunctions functioning semantically as linking adverbials. Stance adverbials have less and single distributions.

2.3 The Initial Position Adjuncts and Grammatical Functions Expressing Semantic and Pragmatic Meanings

The essay opened with a locative prepositional phrase function as a subject of the sentence. As a subject, it does not function as an adverbial. It fulfills a syntactically nominal function. But since it answers the question where it denotes a semantically adverbial function. It expresses circumstance.

(4) [BY MY WIFE'S ancestral home] flows a river.

The subject of the clause itself identifies the location of the river in the essay. According to Busse (2012), a *by my* construction is lexically primed because "the persons, concepts or things referred to are usually held high in high esteem by the speaker. Also, they are thought to be appreciated by the hearer" (Hoey, 2005 in Busse, 2012 p.302). This said construction seems to tell us that the river is very significant to the narrator.

Essentially, the succeeding clauses of the essay show initial position adjuncts of circumstance time providing more information of time duration and temporal position that make the narration of the author vivid.

(5) [For a dozen summers] I have visited it, and almost every year I make an effort to trace its course back to its source in the neighboring hills; I do not consider my vacation there complete without doing this.

(6) [But] [this past summer] I saw something I had never seen before, though I know that if I had been sufficiently observant in other abnormally dry years, I am sure I could not have failed to notice the same thing earlier.

(7) [One morning] [last April], [in company with a student friend and my elder son], I started out for the hill to spend the day by the rapids and cascades at a place called Intongasan.

Circumstance time duration in the initial position in (5) informed the reader of the number of times the speaker has visited the river. The lexicon *summer* in the Philippines usually refers to either in the month of April or May where most Filipinos have their vacation by spending it to some beautiful destinations or visit their relatives in the provinces just like what the narrator did in the essay. The duration of time suggests not only the fondness and value of the river to the narrator but also its deep familiarity with him. Evidently, the narrator has known the river for so long. Initial adjuncts in (6) contribute to cohesion by being anaphoric through the repeated word such as summer that exemplifies cohesion of the text.

In (7), a series of two circumstance position in time adjuncts plus a circumstance accompaniment process adjunct that express accompaniment appears in the initial position. Each type of adjunct does not modify each other but amplify the information provided. According to Murar, Trantescu and Pisoschi (2011), "time adverbials can be a hierarchical relationship: the order of the adverbials depends in part on information focus, but the tendency is for the adverbial denoting the most extended period to come last" (p. 55). Thus, one morning precedes last April showing this hierarchy. This series of temporal adverbials corroborate to the claim made by the authors that temporal adjuncts can be placed initially. However, the position of the process adverbial in the series shifted the emphasis from the temporal adjuncts to process adjuncts.

Significantly, the river and its journey were described by the speaker through the initial adjuncts as illustrated in the following.

(8) [In common with other streams of its kind], our river suffers much from the summer drought.
(9) [After we had walked a kilometer or more], I saw that the river had disappeared and its bed was dry.
(10) [But] [where we stood] [at the moment] there was no water to be seen. All about us, the wide river bed was hot and dry.
(11) [And] [yet], [continuing our way into the hills], we found the river grow deeper and stronger than it was as it passed by our cottage.
(12) [Flowing down from its cradle] [in the mountains] [just] [as it left the last foothills], the river had been checked by the long, forbidding stretch of scorching sand.
(13) [But] Bacong- because that is the name of our river - determined to reach the sea, tunneled its way, so to speak, under its sandy bed, of course choosing the harder and lower stratum beneath, until at last it appeared again, limpid and steady in its march to sea.

Process circumstance in which expresses comparison describes the kind of journey the river had as observed by the narrator. This kind of comparison has the intention of amplifying the subject since the speaker seemed to characterize the river as ennobling in character (Lowth, 1825).

Substantially, initial place adjuncts in (9) *where we stood* and in (12) *flowing down from its cradle, in the mountains* allow information to connect more specifically with the clause content, and can have scope over the entire clause and can be used to set the scene for the direction (Biber et al., 1999). Result contingency circumstance in (11) *continuing our way into the hills* and (12) *as it left the last foothills* express information of the destination of the river.

Moreover, circumstance adverbials are dominated with conditional adjuncts which foregrounded the message of the essay. Conditional adjuncts can present a rhetorical condition. When clauses take the form of a conditional but combined with the main clause, they make a strong assertion (Biber et al., 1999). Thus, the essay brought forth a strong assertion as exemplified in the following lines:

(14) [If our river had not remained faithful to its duty,] [instead of a landscape with the varied green of foliage of shrubs and trees and gay with the voices of the birds singing and calling to one another in the branches] [that April morning], there would have been spread before us a wide expanse of desolate and lifeless land, fit only for the wandering of Cain.

This sentence asserts the fulfillment of the river's duty to play its part in the processes of nature, to live, in other words, for the rest of the creation; that the river had lived not for itself but of others. In comparison with the duty of man, the line further asserts that because of the faithfulness of the river to its duty, we will not experience a desolate and lifeless land.

(15) [For] [if in the face of obstacles it lacks the strength of will to continue keeping itself fit to serve and seeking new opportunities for service], it will ultimately become useless to others.
(16) [Unless a stream draws its power from a source of sufficient height and magnitude], it cannot do as our river did this summer.

In (15) and (16), the conditional adjuncts emphasize that the result of the assertion on the determination of the river will have an unfavorable result if the river is weak. The same conditions were presented to man if he wishes to reach his goal in life as exemplified in the sentences below. On the other hand, the stance adjunct verily did not only contribute to cohesion but also emphasized the importance of the assertion.

(17) [Verily], [if a man derives his strength and inspiration from a low and feeble source], he will fail to 'arrive'.
(18) [Unless a man draws his power from some source of heavenly altitude], [unless the stream of his life issues from a never-failing source], [unless, in other words, his soul is fed from heights of infinite power], he may well fear that he will not reach the sea.
(19) [But] [if his spirit is impelled and nourished by an inexhaustible power] he will in spite of all obstruction, finish the course...

Gonzales must have strongly brought forth the message of the essay using conditional adjuncts in sentences (17), (18) and (19). These arguments were presented in the last part of the sentence, but they emerged as the focal point of the essay which made the great impact on the reader. It provided strong arguments.

Looking at other circumstance adjuncts, the place, and manner adjuncts were also dominant in the essay. Gonzales was also concerned with mental images that he used other circumstance adverbials to create a mental picture that brought out the landscape of the mountainous areas where the river flowed and narrated its 'journey' towards the sea using initial position adjuncts.

Furthermore, the essay also showed a minimal use of stance adverbials, but their semantic roles expressed the assertion of the author on his comparison of the river and the life of man from his experience and evaluative assessment as exemplified in the passages:

(20) [To most people], I suppose, there is nothing significant in this.
(21) [To me], [however], it was a new experience, and it impressed me like all new experiences.
(22) [To me], it was not merely strange, it suggested a spiritual truth.

Initial viewpoints adjuncts here, *to most people*, and *to me* assert more truth in the author's perspective and indicate that other people who experienced the same presence of the river in the community may hold another view about the river.

Significantly, the author has effectively woven the events using linking adverbials which are important devices for creating textual cohesion (Biber et al., 1999). The author employed them to organize and connect long stretches of clauses and to help readers follow the preceding discourse. In the essay, most occurrences of this classification are conjunctions which introduce another context

with their pragmatic meaning while others retained their semantic meanings. They function as linking adjuncts as shown in the following lines in the essay:

(23) [But] [this past summer] I saw something I had never seen before...
(24) [But] [where we stood at the moment] there was no water to be seen.
(25) [And] [yet], [continuing our way into the hills], we found the river grow deeper...
(26) [But] Bacong - because that is the name of our river determined to reach the sea...
(27) [And] [then] I thought of human life.
(28) [But] I thought most of all of those who, like our river...
(29) [On the other hand], think of other lives that, ...
(30) [And] what is the duty of a river?
(31) [For] part of the ministering duty of a river is to flow on and on...
(32 [And] does this not suggest that the river of man's life should be likewise?
(33) [For] [if in the face of obstacles] it lacks the strength...
(34) [For] Bacong was able to carry on...
(35) [But] [if his spirit is impelled and nourished] [by an inexhaustible power] he will...

The coordinating conjunctions *and, then, but,* and *for* in sentences 27 to 35 can be "deleted without causing any grammatical concern" (Zihan, 2014). Thus, they function as adverbials and not conjunctions. They mark meaning between sentences. In (23), *but* marks a meaning difference in what the speaker notices about the flow of the river in his time of writing. In (24), *but* introduces additional information about the flow of the river. In (25) linking adverbials *and* and *yet* occurring with circumstance manner expressing concession relationship initiated another important piece of information about the river whose flow has grown stronger. The concession circumstance is important because it is a means of presenting new arguments.

Essentially, the initial linking adverbials connect previous events that made the narrative connected. They help refer to the past events. Linking adverbials carried what Halliday & Hasan (1976) called retrospective effect or 'retrojective' as a better word according to them. They further explained that this retrospective effect is significant because it made the action/events in the text whole. Seemingly, the retrospective quality of *and* provided a useful insight into the meaning of *but* in the essay. The word *but* "expresses a relation which is not additive but adversative [...], but contains within itself also the logical meaning of and; it is a sort of portmanteau, or shorthand form, of *and however*. The evidence for this is the fact that *but* is also retrospective – but the meaning which it projects in his way is not *but* but *and*' (Halliday & Hasan, 1976, p. 237). This concept is exemplified in (23), (24), (26), (28) and (35). Then in (27) it is also anaphoric. As these linking adverbials express retrospective and anaphoric element, they are thereby cohesive. Linking adverbial in (29) is important to show the contrasting relationship of meaning.

2.4 Focalization

Since the literary piece is a narrative essay, it encompasses authorial omniscience, his personal version of events. The writer serves as the first-person-actional participant since the main character tells his story. This focalization has a clear authorial viewpoint which projects the coherence or purpose and human perception.

The essay has 23 occurrences of personal pronoun *I* which justifiably indicate the subject. However, there is also greater occurrences of the pronoun *it* with 18 occurrences, referring to the river, which justifies the significance of the river throughout the essay. The term *river* occurs 19 times and *Bacong* five times. For the first time, *Bacong* was in introduce in sentence (20) But '*Bacong-because that is the name of our river-determined to reach the sea, tunneled its way, so to speak, under its sandy bed, of course choosing the harder and lower stratum beneath, until at last it appeared again, limpid and steady in its march to sea.*' It was introduced like a very close entity to the narrator as realized in the use of pronoun *our* in the passage. It was mentioned the second time in the sentence (26) '*Another lesson I learned from Bacong is found in the fact that the river was not merely determined to flow just anywhere; it was determined to reach the sea, to reach the great end.*' Here the narrator described its determination to reach the sea. Then third in the sentence (43) '*Bacong, by continuing its march to the sea, kept itself fit for the service of nature and man; and not only it expanded its field of usefulness.*' In this sentence, *Bacong* is in the vocative case as it is addressed directly by the narrator. In sentence (46) '*As I marveled at the power of Bacong to push its way through such a seemingly impassable barrier, I discerned the secret-a secret that has a message for all of us.*' The narrator saw the power of *Bacong* to push its way to the sea; and finally, in the sentence (47) '*For Bacong was able to carry on, to continue its watery pilgrimage and reach the immensity and sublimity of the sea, only because its source is the vast and lofty mountains.*' The narrator acknowledges the great source of power that helped *Bacong* reached its destination.

3   Conclusion

The essay is foregrounded with the use of initial position adjuncts dominated by the circumstance adjuncts followed by linking adjuncts and very few stance adjuncts. The initial circumstance adjuncts particularly the initial conditional adjuncts have the greatest number of occurrences in the essay. They showed the strong argument of the essay on the comparison of the river to the life of man. The essay also exemplified greater occurrences of personal pronoun *I* which refer to the narrator and pronoun *it* that refers to the river. These language components have facilitated the understanding of the meaning of the essay.

Further analysis showed that the analyses are in the domains of physical, psychological, social and philosophical aspects although the comparisons were not provided explicitly. The river was presented and described in the first part of the essay from sentence 1 to 27 where the essayist paused with the statement *How like so many lives* which explicitly brought the comparison further in the essay. Firstly, the physical aspects of the river were described in sentences (13) and (43). Secondly, the psychological aspects centered on the determination of the river to reach the destination, the sea, as it surmounted from the various obstacles along its way, and how it had overcome and under come obstacles as it tunneled its way through. Thirdly, the social aspects centers on the duty of the river as it flows not only for itself but at the service of man and nature. Finally, in the philosophical aspects, the river is faithful to its duty, and its source of power had come from the sufficient height and magnitude as compared to the source of power of man from heavenly altitude. These descriptions of the river in four aspects were reflected in the life of man on earth in a comparison showed implicitly and explicitly in the essay.

Implicitly, the narrator would question how men keep himself fit for service, what is his duty, how faithful he is in his duty and where does he draw his inspiration and source of power to live for him and others. These arguments were clearly presented using initial condition adjuncts.

Significantly, it was also noted that these arguments are from the personal viewpoints and perspectives of the narrator which were pointed out using the initial viewpoint or perspective adjuncts. The initial viewpoint or perspective adjuncts showed that to the narrator; this is how he perceived his personal experience, relationship and lessons and realizations in life with the river in the community where his wife lives. These perspectives also mean that his insights will surely be different from the insights and experiences of other people about the river in the community where the river is located.

Further, the initial contrastive/concessive adjuncts which are subcategories of linking adjuncts presented the comparison between the flow of the river and the life of man on earth which is the central theme of the essay. More than revealing the central theme of the essay, they also serve as cohesive devices. Halliday & Hasan (1976) define cohesion as "the relation between sentences in a text, and the sentences of a text can only follow one after the other" (p.227). The conjunctive adjuncts together with the other types of adjuncts forming continuum or cluster or series of adjuncts faithfully perform their cohesive functions making a general impression that the initial position adjuncts serve explicitly as the text strategy of the text. They further indicate the movements in the text and navigate through the text as the various information were presented in adjacent with the other elements in the clause in mostly long and complex stretches of sentences shaping the meaning of the essay.

Indeed, the lexical and grammatical analyses provide the description and understanding of the ecological psychology of nature and the relationship to man and vice versa. This essay, which is river-personified, reminds us of the inexhaustible power – the omnipotent God; we are destined to reflect his glory.

References

Beatrix Busse. 2012. Historical Text Analysis: Underlying Parameters and Methodological Procedures. In W. Bisang (ed.), Methods in Contemporary Linguistics.KG, Berlin/Boston:Walter de Gruyter Gmbh &Co.

Douglas Biber, Stig Johansson, Geoffrey Leech, Susan Conrad & Edward Finegan. 1999. Longman Grammar of Spoken and Written English. Harlow, England: Longman.

Ebi Yeibo. 2011. Patterns of Lexical Choices and Stylistic Function in J. P. Clark-Bekederemo's poetry. International Journal of English Linguistics 1(1) 137-149.

Greg Watson and Sonia Zyngier. (Eds.). 2007. Literature and Stylistics for Language Learner's Theory and Practice. New York: Palgrave Macmillan.

Ioana Murar, Ana-Maria Trantescu. & Claudia Pisoschi. 2011. English Syntax the Simple Sentence. Retrieved From http://cis01.central.ucv.ro/litere/idd/cursuri/an_2/lb_straina/engleza/lec_an2_sem1_trantescu.pdf

Michael Alexander Kirkwood Halliday.1994. An Introduction to Functional Grammar (2nd ed.). People's Republic of China: Edward Arnold, Ltd.

Michael Alexander Kirkwood Halliday & Ruqaiya Hasan. 1976. Cohesion in English. Harlow : England.

Michael Hoey.(2005). Lexical Priming: A New Theory of Words and Language. New York: Routledge.

Michael Toolan. 1998. Language in Literature an Introduction to Stylistics. London, New York: Routledge Taylor & Francis Group.

Norman Francis Blake. 1990. An Introduction to the Language of Literature. London: Macmillan.

Robert Lowth. 1825. Lectures on the Sacred Poetry of the Hebrews. London: JF Dove, St. John's Square.

Randolph Quirk, Sidney Greenbaum, Geoffrey Leech, G. & Jan Svartvik. 1985. A Comprehensive Grammar of the English language. London:Longman.

René Wellek, and Austin Warren. 1977. Theory of Literature (3rd ed.). New York, London: Harcourt, Brace Jovanovich, - A Harvest/HBJ book.

Thomas Ernst. 2002. The Syntax of Adjuncts. Cambridge: Cambridge University Press.

Zihan Yin. 2004. Linking Adverbials in English. Ph. D. Dissertation, Victoria University of Wellington.

A Corpus-based Analysis of Near-Synonymous Sentence-final Particles in Mandarin Chinese: "*bale*" and "*eryi*"

Xuefeng Gao
Department of Chinese and Bilingual Studies
The Hong Kong Polytechnic University
Hong Kong
gaoxuefeng0812@163.com

Sophia Yat-mei Lee
Department of Chinese and Bilingual Studies
The Hong Kong Polytechnic University
Hong Kong
ym.lee@polyu.edu.hk

Abstract

This paper explores the differences between two near-synonymous disyllabic sentence-final particles in Mandarin Chinese *bale* and *eryi* based on a corpus-based approach. We argue that there is a close interaction between adverbs and sentence-final particles. Firstly, the usage of adverbs in the local proposition of two different SFPs has a strong tendency. 仅 jin 'only' is only used in the local proposition of *eryi*, and 仅仅 jin-jin 'only' tends to use in the local propositions of *eryi*. 最多 zui-duo/顶多 ding-duo/至多 zhi-duo 'at most' are only used in the local propositions of *bale*, while 决不是 jue-bu-shi/绝非 jue-fei/决非 jue-fei/绝不 jue-bu 'definitely not' are only used in the local propositions of *eryi*. *Eryi* expresses minimal value and *bale* expresses maximal value. Moreover, the position of the adverbs also presents a tendency: the adverbs in the local proposition of *bale* are always in the initial position, while *eryi* in the middle position. In addition, the polarity of the local propositions of two SFPs are also different: the local proposition of *bale* tends to express negativity, while the local proposition of *eryi* obtains a tone of neutrality. We believe that this study will significantly enhance the research on sentence-final particles and second language teaching.

1 Introduction

罢了 *bale* and 而已 *eryi* are two Chinese disyllabic sentence-final particles (SFPs) which are believed to be almost equivalent in terms of meaning and usage (Lü 1980, Wang 1984, Hou 1998, Zhang 2001), and can be used interchangeably in most cases (Fang 2006). For instance:

（1）有些人认为，所谓野人，不过是一些猿猴<u>罢了/而已</u>。
you3xie1 ren2 ren4wei2, suo3wei4
some people think so-called
ye3ren2, bu2guo4 shi4 yi4xie1 yuan2hou2
savages merely is some monkey
ba4le/er2yi3.
BALE/ERYI
'Some people think that the so-called savages are merely some monkeys.'

（2）从另一个角度说，生活又是极其简单的，它只不过是过去的简单重复<u>而已/罢了</u>。
cong2 ling4yi2ge4 jiao3du4 shuo1,
from another point of view say
sheng1huo2 you4 shi4 ji2qi2 jian3dan1
life also is extremely simple
de, ta1 zhi3bu2guo4 shi4 guo4qu4
DE it just is past
de jian3dan1 chong2fu4 er2yi3/ba4le.
DE simple repetition ERYI/BALE
'On another point of view, life is extremely simple, and it is just a simple repetition of the past.'

There is no difference when the two SFPs interchange in (1) and (2). Yet, there remain some cases where the two SFPs *bale* and *eryi* cannot be used interchangeably. For example:

（3）卢梭一生清贫，但他的清贫和我们当时的清贫之间有着一个本质的区别：我们是物质匮乏，迫不得已；而卢梭则是自

222

愿贫困。无衣可穿时打补丁称不上朴素，不过是不折不扣地穷<u>罢了</u>。

Lu2suo1 yi4 sheng1 qing1pin2, dan4 ta1
Rousseau one life poor but he
de qing1pin2 he wo3men de qing1pin2
DE poor with we DE poor
zhi1jian1 you3zhe yi2 ge4 ben3zhi4 de
between have one CL essential DE
qu1bie2, wo3men shi4 wu4zhi4 kui4fa2,
difference we is material short
po4bu4de2yi3; er2 Lu2suo1 ze2shi4
be forced while Rousseau is
zi4yuan4 pin2kun4. wu2 yi1
of one's own accord poor no clothes
ke3 chuan1 shi2 da3bu3ding1 cheng1
have wear when put a patch called
bu2shang4 pu3su4, bu2guo4 shi4
not simplicity merely is
bu4zhe2bu2kou4 de qiong2 ba4le.
completely DE poor BALE
'Rousseau's life is poor, but there is an essential difference between his poverty and our poverty at that time: we lack material things and it is forced, while Rousseau is poor of his own accord. It cannot be called simplicity when there are not clothes to be worn and put a patch, but just completely poor.'

（4） 詹姆斯对此事的参与也仅止于此。老布什更只是写了封推荐信<u>而已</u>。

Zhan1mu3si1 dui4 ci3 shi4 de
James for this matter DE
can1yu4 ye3 jin3 zhi3 yu2 ci3.
participation also only stop PERP here
lao3bu4shi2 geng4 zhi3shi4 xie3
Bush the Elder even more just write
le feng1 tui1jian4xin4 er2yi3.
LE CL recommendation letter ERYI
'James's participation in this matter just only ended here. Bush the Elder even just wrote a letter of recommendation.

In (3) and (4), the alternation of two SFPs will have influence on the meaning and the acceptability of the sentences.

The current study aims to examine the semantic and pragmatic differences between the two near-synonymous SFPs *bale* and *eryi* based on a corpus-based approach.

This paper is organized as follows: Section 2 discusses the related work on two SFPs: *bale* and *eryi*. Section 3 describes the data collection and agreement test. Section 4 presents the data analysis and results. Section 5 concludes the paper and highlights the contributions of this work.

2 Related Work

The study of the sentence final particles (SFP) is one of the most popular studies in recent years. One of the reasons is that the SFPs is a special element in Chinese compared with other European languages. We find that the study of SFPs focused more on the typical monosyllabic ones, such as 吧 ba, 吗 ma, 呢 ne, 啊 a etc., but not the disyllabic SFPs, such as 罢了 ba-le, 而已 er-yi, 得了 de-le, 着呢 zhe-ne, etc.

It is believed that *bale* always uses in the sentence final position of the declarative sentences which indicating 'that is it' and there is the tone of unimportance. It always collocates with 不过 bu-guo 'merely', 无非 wu-fei 'nothing but', 只是 zhi-shi 'just', etc. (Lü 1980, Zhang 2001, Qi 2011). Tang and Zhou (1989), Hou (1998) argue that *bale* can dilute the sentence meaning and often use with 不过 bu-guo 'merely', 只 zhi 'just', 无非 wu-fei 'nothing but', 只有 zhi-you 'only', 只好 zhi-hao 'have no choice but', etc. It is the same as *eryi*, but *bale* is often used in the spoken language. Liu and Shao (2012) argue that *bale* has three grammatical meanings. Liu (2013) states that there are three functional meanings of *bale*: (1) *bale* emphasizes a part of information (2) *bale* expresses dissatisfied, negative, despised and sarcastic emotion (3) *bale* obtains the attitudes of tolerance, euphemism and modesty.

There are also some discussions on *eryi*. Some scholars argue that *eryi* is often used in the final position of declarative sentences which contains a kind of tone of smallness. It always collocates with 不过 bu-guo 'merely', 无非 wu-fei 'nothing but', 只 zhi 'just', 仅仅 jin-jin 'only'. *Eryi* often used in the written language (Lü 1980, Zhang 2001), which dilutes the mood of sentence meaning at the end of the sentence (Wang 1984, Hou 1998, Qi 2001). Chu (1986) and Liu (2000) believe that *eryi* expresses the mood of limitation.

Compared with these two SFPs, some scholars believe that *bale* and *eryi* are almost equivalent in terms of meaning and usage, and the only difference is that *bale* often use in spoken language while *eryi* in written language. Fang (2006) also made a comparative study of two SFPs. He claims that the usage of the two SFPs have a kind of tendency. The numeral phrases often correlate with *eryi*, but not in *bale*. There are also differences on the mood of the two SFPs.

3   Corpus Data

The data was retrieved from Center for Chinese Linguistics PKU (CLC), from which 4652 sentences containing *bale* and 8579 sentences containing *eryi* are extracted. Firstly, all the data are retrieved from the corpus. Secondly, a manually analysis is processed to find the sentences that the two SFPs *bale* and *eryi* cannot be used interchangeably. We find that 6.5% (304 sentences) of the sentences which contain *bale* and 5.2% (452 sentences) of the sentences which contain *eryi* cannot be used interchangeably. Therefore, our dataset has 756 sentences which the two SFPs cannot be used interchangeably.

In order to verify the manually analysis results, a questionnaire is designed. Eight sentences which contain *bale* and eight sentences which contain *eryi* are extracted from the dataset randomly (see Appendix A). 15 participants with linguistic academic background and 15 participants without linguistic academic background fill out our questionnaire. The 30 participants are all native speakers of Mandarin Chinese.

We collected the questionnaire via Wechat and then do the statistical work. We calculate the accuracy which means the answer what the participants choose is same as the original text in the corpus. The SFPs which the original text is used are in gray shade on frequency and percentage in Table 1. The majority of the answers of each question are in accordance with the original text. As Table 1 shows, the agreement is 88.25%. It proves that our preliminary observation is efficient and can be used to do the following analysis and comparison.

The meaning and usage of the two sentence-final particles are too close to be distinguished, but the native speakers have the intuition to judge the accurate situations to use two SFPs respectively. A

No.	Bale		Eryi		Bale / Eryi	
	Frequency	Percentage	Frequency	Percentage	Frequency	Percentage
1	27	90%	0	0	3	10%
2	0	0	29	97%	1	3%
3	25	83%	3	10%	2	7%
4	30	100%	0	0	0	0
5	3	10%	24	80%	3	10%
6	1	3%	28	93%	1	3%
7	2	7%	23	77%	5	17%
8	28	93%	1	3%	1	3%
9	2	7%	25	83%	3	10%
10	28	93%	0	0	2	7%
11	30	100%	0	0	0	0
12	2	7%	26	87%	2	7%
13	2	7%	22	73%	6	20%
14	0	0	27	90%	3	10%
15	25	83%	1	3%	4	13%
16	27	90%	0	0	3	10%
Agreement			88.25%			

Table 1. The result of the questionnaire

word always has different word senses based on the context of the word's usage in a sentence. As for near-synonymous words, they have some common word senses, but differ in others. So the two SFPs that can be used interchangeably in these sentences share the same word sense, while those cannot be used interchangeably contain different word senses. In this study, we analyze 13231 sentences and find that 756 sentences (5.7%) cannot be used interchangeably. It is an exhaustive data analysis of CLC on two SFPs. In other words, native speakers can demonstrate the usage of two SFPs in different situations precisely, which proves that the two SFPs have obvious differences on word sense. Otherwise, the two SFPs can be used interchangeably in all situations. Therefore, even though the dataset is relatively small, it is efficient to compare the two SFPs and analyze their different word senses more precisely. Based on the analysis of the context to narrow down the possible senses to the probable ones, we can find the accurate meaning of each word and the differences between the two SFPs.

4 Data Analysis

Of the 756 sentences analyzed, we find some different features between *bale* and *eryi*. Most of the sentences of *bale* and *eryi* collocate adverbs in their local propositions, e.g. 只 zhi 'only', 不过 bu-guo 'merely', 最多 zui-duo 'at most', 仅仅 jin-jin 'only'. The local proposition means that the clause contains the SFPs. But there is a tendency for using different adverbs in the local propositions between *bale* and *eryi*. There is a list for the top 10 collocating adverbs (see Table 2).

Adverb in *bale*	Token	Percentage	Adverb in *eryi*	Token	Percentage
不过 *bu-guo*	60	28.57%	仅 *jin*	102	29.57%
只是 *zhi-shi*	37	17.62%	只是 *zhi-shi*	94	27.25%
只不过 *zhi-bu-guo*	20	9.52%	仅仅 *jin-jin*	32	9.28%
也 *ye*	16	7.62%	不过 *bu-guo*	22	6.38%
无非 *wu-fei*	15	7.14%	只 *zhi*	20	5.80%
只好 *zhi-hao*	8	3.81%	只不过 *zhi-bu-guo*	20	5.80%
最多/顶多/至多 *zui-duo/ding-duo/zhi-duo*	7	3.33%	只有 *zhi-you*	17	4.93%
只 *zhi*	6	2.86%	无非 *wu-fei*	12	3.48%
只能 *zhi-neng*	6	2.86%	决不是/绝非/决非/绝不 *jue-bu-shi/jue-fei/jue-fei/jue-bu*	7	2.03%
只有 *zhi-you*	4	1.90%	只能 *zhi-neng*	6	1.74%

Table 2. Distribution of co-occurrence between adverbs and SFPs (Top 10 adverbs)

Of the 756 sentences analyzed, there are 188 sentences that use adverbs in their local propositions of *bale* and 298 sentences in *eryi*. Moreover, some sentences use more than one adverb in one sentence. For example:

（5）　至于苏伦和弗兰克·肯尼迪的失利，她根本就不放在心上，**最多只**暗中冷冷地笑笑罢了。

zhi4yu2　su1lun2　he2　Fu2lan2ke4
as for　　Sullen　and　Frank

Ken3ni2di2　de shi1li4, ta1 gen1ben3 jiu4
Kennedy　DE　loss she totally thus

bu2　fang4　zai4　xin1 shang4, zui4duo1
NEG　put　PREP heart　on　　at most

zhi3　an4zhong1　leng3leng3　de
just　secretly　coldly　DE

xiao4xiao　ba4le.
sneer　　BALE

'As for the loss of Sullen and Frank Kennedy, she totally put it behind her. She at most sneered secretly.'

（6） 而且她父亲常来北京，她母亲也有可能
再到北京学习、进修。我们这一次分别，
仅仅不过是为下一次会面创造条件<u>而已</u>。
er2qie3 ta1 fu4qin chang2 lai2
and she father often come
Bei3jing1, ta1 mu3qin ye3 you3
Beijing she mother also have
ke3neng2 zai4 dao4 Bei3jing1 xue2xi2,
possibility again come Beijing study
jin4xiu1. wo3men zhe4 yi2 ci4
advanced study we this one CL
fen1bie2, jin3jin3 bu2guo4 shi4 wei4
separate only merely is for
xia4yi2ci4 hui4mian4 chuang4zao4
next meet make
tiao2jian4 er2yi3.
condition ERYI
'And her father often comes to Beijing.
Her mother may also come to Beijing to
study. This parting is just for making a
condition to union.'

In (5) and (6), two adverbs are used in one
sentences: 最多 zui-duo 'at most' and 只 zhi 'just'
in (5); 仅仅 jin-jin 'only' and 不过 bu-guo 'merely'
in (6)

4.1 Adverbs and SFPs

Based on the analysis above, adverb is a very
important part in the local proposition of SFPs *bale*
and *eryi*. Of the 756 sentences analyzed, 486
sentences (64%) collocate one or more adverbs in
their local propositions. Different adverbs are used
collocating with different sentence-final particles.

As shown in Table 2, there are some features
can be identified:

- 仅 jin 'only' is only used in the local
  proposition of *eryi*, and 仅仅 jin-jin 'only'
  tends to use in the local proposition of *eryi*
  (9.28% in *eryi*, while 1.43% in *bale*). 最多
  zui-duo/ 顶多 ding-duo/ 至多 zhi-duo 'at
  most' are only used in the local proposition
  of *bale*.

仅 jin 'only' is an adverb in Mandarin Chinese,
which means only, solely, merely and just. 仅 jin
'only' expresses limitation in (7). And the SFP *eryi*
is used in the final position indicating a minimal

value---only one. So we argue that *eryi* indicates
minimal value.

（7） 十字路口没有路灯，亦很少有警察，有
的重要路口亦**仅**有一块"停"的牌子<u>而已</u>。
shi2zi4lu4kou3 mei2you3 lu4deng1, yi4
crossroad NEG streetlight also
hen3 shao3 you3 jing3cha2, you3de
very less have police officer some
zhong4yao4 lu4kou3 yi4 jin3 you3 yi2
important junction also only have one
kuai4 ting2 de pai2zi er2yi3.
CL STOP DE sign ERYI
'There are no streetlights at the crossroads,
and there are very few police officers.
Some important junctions have only one
"stop" sign.'

最多 zui-duo/ 顶多 ding-duo/ 至多 zhi-duo
means at most. So *bale*, collocating with 最多 zui-
duo/ 顶多 ding-duo/ 至多 zhi-duo 'at most',
expresses maximal value. It can be seen that
maximum value performs a kind of expectation of
the speaker. As in (8) and (9), *treating it as a
guided principle* and *watching the sunrise* express
maximal value of the speaker. As in (8), the
intention of the speaker is the neglect of his
response and he also told the listener treating it as a
guided principle only. So *treating it as a guided
principle* is the maximal value / maximal
expectation.

（8） 我所草拟的答复，你不必交去，**最多**把
它看作是一个指导原则<u>罢了</u>。
wo3 suo3 cao3ni3 de da2fu4, ni3 bu2
I PREP draft DE response you NEG
bi4 jiao1 qu4, zui4duo1 ba3 ta1
need hand in PREP at most BA it
kan4zuo4 shi4 yi2 ge4 zhi3dao3
treat is one CL guided
yuan2ze2 ba4le.
principle BALE
'You don't have to hand in the response
that I draft. You can treat it as a guided
principle at most.'

（9） 卡拉蒙漫不经心的乱瞄，心想着没啥大
不了的，**顶多**就是看个日出<u>罢了</u>。
Ka3la1man4 man4bujing1xin1 de
Karaman insouiance DE

luan4   miao1, xin1 xiang3 zhe mei2
carelessly aim   heart think ZHE NEG
sha2   da4bu4liao3 de,   ding3duo1
what   a big deal   DE   at most
jiu4 shi4 kan4 ge   ri4chu1 ba4le.
thus is   see CL   sunrise BALE
'Karaman aimed carelessly. He thought it
is not a big deal. At most, it is to see the
sunrise.'

Based on the analysis above, we argue that *bale*
expresses maximal value while *eryi* expresses the
minimal value collocating with adverbs.

- 决不是 jue-bu-shi/绝非 jue-fei/决非 jue-
  fei/绝不 jue-bu 'definitely not' are only used
  in the local proposition of *eryi*.

决不是 jue-bu-shi/绝非 jue-fei/决非 jue-fei/绝
不 jue-bu means definitely not. Eryi, collocating
with 决不是 jue-bu-shi/绝非 jue-fei/决非 jue-fei/
绝不 jue-bu 'definitely not', contains a strong tone
of subjectivity. The sentence-final particles are
always used to express mood or tone. As shown in
(10) and (11), *alive and still breath* and *a simple
repetition of previous works* contain a strong tone
of speaker's subjectivity collocating with the
adverb 绝非 jue-fei 'definitely not'. The speakers
want to express their own mood and tone, which
may different from other people.

（10） 这块闲章，**绝非只是** "活着还有一口气"
      而已。
      zhe4   kuai4 xian2 zhang1, jue2fei1
      this   CL   free   seal definitely not
      zhi3shi4 huo2 zhe   hai2   you3
      only   alive ZHE still have
      yi4   kou3   qi4   er2yi3.
      one   CL   breath ERYI
      'This piece of free seal is not only "alive
      and still breath".'

（11） 江枫的译文，有他个人的特色，**绝非**是
      前人劳动成果的简单重复**而已**。
      Jiang1feng1 de   yi4wen2,   you3 ta1
      Jiang Feng   DE translation work have he
      ge4ren2 de   te4se4,   jue2fei1   shi4
      personal DE   style   definitely not is
      qian2   ren2   lao2dong4 cheng2guo3
      previous people   work   achievement

de   jian3dan1   chong2fu4   er2yi3.
DE simple   repetition   ERYI
'Jiang Feng's translation work has his own
personal style. It is not a simple repetition
of previous works.'

- 不过 bu-guo 'merely' may inclined to use in
  the local proposition of *bale* (28.57%).

As shown in Table 2, the most commonly used
adverbs in our dataset is 不过 bu-guo 'merely'
(28.57%) in the local proposition of *bale* and 仅 jin
'only' (29.57) in the local proposition of *eryi*. 只是
zhi-shi 'just' is the second most commonly adverbs
used in both *bale* and *eryi*. 也 ye 'also' may also
inclined to use in the local proposition of *bale* in
our dataset (7.62%).

It can be seen that the usage of the adverbs has
strong tendency. It can also be concluded that
adverb is a very important part of the sentences
which collocate with SFPs in the final position.
And there is a close interaction between adverbs
and sentence-final particles.

4.2   Position of adverbs

The position of adverbs in the local proposition of
bale and *eryi* is also different from each other. As
shown in Table 3, the adverbs in the proposition of
bale incline to use in the initial position (see 12),
while *eryi*'s tend to use in the middle of the
sentence (see 13).

（12） 照王守仁的说法，"致知"就是"致良知"。
      自我的修养，**不过**是遵从自己的良知而
      行罢了。
      zhao4   Wang2shou3ren2 de shuo1fa3,
      according to Wang Shouren DE argument
      "zhi4zhi1"   jiu4 shi4 " zhi4liang2zhi1".
      know   thus   is   conscience
      zi4wo3 de   xiu1yang3, bu2guo4 shi4
      self   DE   cultivation   merely   is
      zun1cong2   zi4ji3   de   liang2zhi1
      comply with   own   DE   conscience
      er2   xing2   ba4le.
      with   do   BALE
      'According to Wang Shouren's argument,
      "to know" is "to conscience." Self-
      cultivation merely complies with their own
      conscience to do things.'

（13） 我还没打算退休，也许这本书出版后我
会被迫退休。我又在讲笑话了，我希望
仅仅是笑话<u>而已</u>。

wo3 hai2 mei2 da3suan4 tui4xiu1, ye3xu3
I   still NEG   intend   retire   maybe
zhe4 ben3 shu1 chu1ban3 hou4 wo3
this   CL book publish   after I
hui4 bei4po4 tui4xiu1, wo3 you4
will be forced retire   I   also
zai4 jiang3 xiao4hua4 le, wo3
PREP talk   joke   LE I
xi1wang4 jin3jin3 shi4 xiao4hua4 er2yi3.
hope   only   is   joke   ERYI
'I have not intended to retire, and maybe I
will be forced to retire after this book
published. I'm talking about jokes again,
and I hope it's only a joke.'

		Initial Position	Middle Position
bale	Token	141	69
	Percentage	67.14	32.86
eryi	Token	100	245
	Percentage	28.99	71.01

Table 3. The position of adverb

We find that the adverbs in the local proposition
of *bale* are often used in the initial position, while
there are subjects, pronouns or other kinds of
constituents in the initial position of the local
proposition of *eryi*.

We can conclude that the structures of the local
proposition of two SFPs are:

- Adverb + clause + *bale*
- Subject / other constituent + adverb + clause + *eryi*

4.3 Polarity and SFPs

Sentence-final particles are always used to express
speaker's mood and tone. Benveniste (1971)
argues that language is the instrument of
communication and taken over by the man who is
speaking and within the condition of
intersubjectivity. Therefore, people can use a lot of
methods to express their mood and tone. Sentence-
final particle is a very important element in
Chinese to express different mood and tone.
Polarity is often used to classify and detect

sentiment and it can be classified to positive,
negative, both and neutral (Wilson et al. 2005). In
order to compare the polarity of the local
proposition between *bale* and *eryi*, a polarity
analysis is conducted. Firstly, we extract all the
local propositions in the corpus. Then, analyze
them based on the sentiment of the local
proposition and context to classify them into
positivity, negativity and neutrality. The analysis
result shows in Table 4.

		Positive	Neutral	Negative
bale	Token	14	119	171
	Percentage	4.61	39.14	56.25
eryi	Token	2	420	30
	Percentage	0.44	92.92	6.64

Table 4. Polarity of the local proposition

It can be seen that *bale* always expresses a tone
of negativity, while *eryi* always obtains a tone of
neutrality. It can be seen that when people express
their mood or tone, they have a strong tendency to
choose different sentence-final particles. It is also a
way to describe the SFPs more precisely in
pragmatics. For example:

（14） 倘若硬要认定何处是"家"，不过是回
到牢笼<u>罢了</u>。

tang3ruo4 ying4yao4 ren4ding4 he2chu4
if   insist   affirm   where
shi4 "jia1" bu2guo4 shi4 hui2dao4
is   home   merely   is   back to
lao2long2 ba4le
cage   BALE
'If you insist that it is "home", we will just
go back to the cage.'

（15） 说到这个组委会，它不是什么体育组织，
仅仅是赤柱居民联谊会<u>而已</u>。

shuo1dao4 zhe4 ge4 zu3wei3hui4,
speaking of this CL   committee
ta1 bu2 shi4 shen2me ti3yu4
it NEG is   what   sports
zu3zhi1, jin3jin3 shi4 Chi4zhu4
organization only   is   Stanley
ju1min2 lian2yi2hui4 er2yi3.
resident association ERYI
'Speaking of this committee, it is not a
sports organization, but only the Stanley
Resident Association.'

In (14), the local proposition has a strong tone of negativity. *We will just back to the cage* express the speaker's sentiment is negative. The key word is 牢笼 lao-long 'cage'. While (15) just expresses that it is a kind of tone of neutrality. *But just the Stanley Resident Association* doesn't contain any sentiment in the context. Based on the analysis above, we argue that polarity can also become a feature to define the usage of *bale* and *eryi*.

5 Conclusion

This paper explores the differences between two disyllabic sentence-final particles in Mandarin Chinese *bale* and *eryi* based on a corpus-based approach. We argue that there is a close interaction between adverbs and sentence-final particles. Firstly, the usage of adverbs in the local proposition of two different SFPs has a strong tendency. 不过 buguo 'merely' may incline to use in the local proposition of *bale* (28.57%). 只是 zhi-shi 'just' is the second most commonly adverbs in the local proposition of both *bale* and *eryi*. 仅 jin 'only' is only used in the local proposition of *eryi*, and 仅仅 jin-jin 'only' tends to use in the local propositions of *eryi*. 最多 zui-duo/顶多 ding-duo/至多 zhi-duo 'at most' are only used in the local propositions of *bale*, while 决不是 jue-bu-shi/绝非 jue-fei/决非 jue-fei/绝不 jue-bu are only used in the local propositions of *eryi*. *Bale* expresses maximal value while *eryi* expresses the minimal value collocating with different adverbs. Moreover, the position of the adverbs also presents a tendency: the adverbs in the local proposition of *bale* are always used in the initial position, while *eryi* in the middle position. In addition, the polarity of the local propositions of two SFPs are also different: the local proposition of *bale* tends to express negativity, while the local proposition of *eryi* obtains a tone of neutrality. We believe that this study will significantly enhance the research on sentence-final particles and second language teaching.

Acknowledgement

This research work is supported by a General Research Fund project sponsored by the Research Grants Council, Hong Kong (Project No. B-Q50Z) and a Faculty Research Grant sponsored by the Hong Kong Polytechnic University (Project No. 1-ZEVK).

References

Benveniste, Emile. 1971. Subjectivity in Language. *Problems in general linguistics*, 1: 521-524.

Chu, Yongan. 1986. (ed). *Functional Words of Ancient Chinese*. Beijing: China Renmin University Press.

Fang, Xujun. 2006. The Sentence-final Particles: bale and eryi. *Journal of Language Science*, 5(3): 49-54.

Hou, Xuechao. 1998. (ed). *A Dictionary of Contemporary Chinese Functional Words*. Beijing: Peking University Press.

Liu, Dehui. 2000. A Study on eryi. *Journal of Zhuzhou Normal Junior College*, 5(1): 1-2.

Liu, Feilu. 2013. The Functional Meaning of Particle bale and the Topic Marker bale. *Journal of Huaihua College*, 32(6): 82-84.

Liu, Xiaoqing, and Jingmin Shao. 2012. The Grammaticalization of bale and the Change of Meaning. *Journal of Study on Ancient Chinese*, 2: 66-73.

Lü, shuxiang. 1980. (ed). 800 Words of Contemporary Chinese. Beijing: The Commercial Press.

Qi, Huyang. 2011. (ed). *A Dictionary of Usage for Contemporary Chinese Mood Constituents*. Beijing: The Commercial Press.

Tang, qiyun, and Rijian Zhou. 1989. (eds). *A Dictionary of Chinese Functional Words*. Guangdong: Guangdong Renmin Press.

Wang, Ziqiang. 1984. (ed) *A Dictionary for Usage of Contemporary Chinese Functional Words*. Shanghai: Shanghai Lexicographical Publishing House

Wilson, Theresa, Janyce Wiebe, and Paul Hoffmann. 2005. Recognizing Contextual Polarity in Phrase-level Sentiment Analysis. In *Proceedings of the conference on Human Language Technology and Empirical Methods in Natural Language Processing*, 347–354.

Zhang, bin. 2011. (ed). *A Dictionary of Contemporary Chinese Functional Words*. Beijing: The Commercial Press.

Appendix A. The questionnaire of the agreement test

序号	句子	罢了	而已	罢了/而已
1	卢梭一生清贫，但他的清贫和我们当时的清贫之间有着一个本质的区别：我们是物质匮乏，迫不得已；而卢梭则是自愿贫困。无衣可穿时打补丁称不上朴素，不过是不折不扣地穷_____。			
2	世上的毒大致可分两种,一种是草木之毒,一种是蛇虫之毒,能自草木中提炼毒药的人较多,能提取蛇虫之毒的人较少,能以蛇虫杀人于无形的，普天之下,也只不过仅有一两人_____。			
3	这(活动宫殿)在当时可算是一种发明，可惜只是供隋炀帝一个人享乐_____。			
4	现在我不能不实说，我确实没听魏元忠说过反对陛下的话，只是张昌宗逼我做伪证_____。			
5	(女足门票)说是卖出去了 10 万张票，但除了瑞典队比赛外，其余各场观众寥寥，仅数百人_____。			
6	真是出乎人意料，小王可是大型企业的 CEO，原来年薪也只不过 10 万_____。			
7	的确有人把范文搬到考场上得了高分，但那毕竟是少数幸运儿_____。			
8	七巧就在兰仙的椅子上坐下了，一手托着腮，抬高了眉毛，斜瞅着季泽道："她跟我生了气么？"季泽笑道："她干嘛生你的气？"七巧道："我正要问呀！我难道说错了话不成？留你在家倒不好？她倒愿意你上外头逛去？"季泽笑道："这一家子从大哥大嫂起，齐了心管教我，无非是怕我花了公帐上的钱_____。"			
9	说话间，200 余名旅客已通过了海关，时间不过 30 分钟。被开箱检查的仅一两人_____。			
10	"不。不能算是家。不如说来做客_____。老人家照顾不了我。"			
11	但几千年婚姻专制的中国，两性的结合，几乎完全由于"父母之命"、"媒妁 之言"，买卖包办或强迫_____。			
12	在上万种新药中，经临床筛选能脱颖而出的仅一两种_____。			
13	在不少科研单位，工学博士的研究课题一般在本人毕业后 3--4 年也未能变成产品，有的甚至永远只是一篇文章_____。			
14	《大公报》的一篇专栏文章指出,为了提高选民登记率，港英当局花费了大量纳税人的金钱，而登记率仅在10%至30%_____。			
15	光绪进了宫，什么也不懂，一切全听凭慈禧和慈安的摆布。慈安又作不了多大的主，她只是听从慈禧的旨意_____。			
16	遗憾的是，日本人的说话能力几乎为零。话题空洞、毫无事前准备、缺乏服务精神以及广泛的社交性，顶多只能和自己的亲朋好友谈谈家务_____。			

Poster Papers

Extracting a Lexicon of Discourse Connectives in Czech from an Annotated Corpus

Pavlína Synková, Magdaléna Rysová, Lucie Poláková, Jiří Mírovský
Charles University
Faculty of Mathematics and Physics
Institute of Formal and Applied Linguistics
Malostranské nám. 25, Prague, Czech Republic
`{synkova|magdalena.rysova|polakova|mirovsky}@ufal.mff.cuni.cz`

Abstract

We discuss a process of exploiting a large corpus manually annotated with discourse relations – the Prague Discourse Treebank 2.0 – to create a lexicon of Czech discourse connectives (CzeDLex). The data format and the data structure of the lexicon are based on a study of similar existing resources and are adapted for a uniform representation of both primary (such as in English *because, therefore*) and secondary connectives (e.g. *for this reason, this is the reason why*). The main principle adopted for nesting entries in the lexicon is a discourse-semantic type expressed by the given connective word, which enables us to deal with a broad formal variability of connectives. We present a technical solution based on the (XML-based) Prague Markup Language that allows for an efficient incorporation of the lexicon into the family of Prague treebanks – it can be directly opened and edited in the tree editor TrEd, processed from the command line in btred, interlinked with its source corpus and queried in the PML-Tree Query engine – and also for interconnecting CzeDLex with existing lexicons in other languages.

1 Introduction

Recent years witnessed a vivid development of corpora annotated with discourse relations. In connection with this development, electronic lexicons of discourse connectives began to be built, although they are so far much less common. These lexicons present an important source not only for theoretical research of text coherence but they may be also helpful in NLP tasks such as discourse parsing (disambiguation of connective and non-connective usages, determining the semantic type of discourse relations), machine translation, text generation and information extraction. This paper presents the process of developing an electronic lexicon of Czech discourse connectives. The chosen approach is inspired by existing electronic lexicons – most of all by DiMLex (Stede, 2002; Scheffler and Stede, 2016), and also by LexConn (Roze et al., 2012), XML-based inventories of discourse connectives for German and French, respectively, and it follows the theoretical framework for designing a lexicon of discourse connectives outlined in Mírovský et al. (2016b).

The text of this paper is organized as follows: Section 2 presents the discourse-annotated treebank used as the source data for the lexicon, in Section 3, the structure of the lexicon and properties of its entries are described, and CzeDLex is also compared to (mostly) DiMLex. Section 4 describes technical aspects of the lexicon development, including the data format and the automatic extraction of connective properties from the treebank data, and also mentions necessary automatic and manual post-processing steps.

2 Prague Discourse Treebank 2.0

The Prague Discourse Treebank 2.0 is built upon the data of the Prague Dependency Treebank (Hajič et al., 2006; Bejček et al., 2013), which is a richly annotated corpus with a multilayer annotation of approx. 50 thousand sentences of Czech journalistic texts. The Prague Dependency Treebank con-

232

31st Pacific Asia Conference on Language, Information and Computation (PACLIC 31), pages 232–240
Cebu City, Philippines, November 16-18, 2017

	PDiT 1.0 (2012)	PDT 3.0 (2013)	PDiT 2.0 (2016)
Primary connectives	yes	updated	updated
Second relations		yes	updated
Secondary connectives			yes

Table 1: Major changes in the annotation of discourse relations in various published versions of the data.

tains morphological information on each token and two layers of syntactic annotation for each sentence (shallow and deep structure), both layers are represented by dependency trees. Besides, there is an annotation of information structure, coreference, bridging anaphora and multiword expressions. Annotation of discourse relations was carried out on top of deep-syntactic trees (on the so called tectogrammatical layer, see Example 1 and Figure 1) and covers relations expressed by a surface-present connective. A connective is defined as a predicate of a binary relation opening two positions for two text spans as its arguments and signalling a semantic or pragmatic relation between them (compare Prasad et al., 2008). The set of discourse types is inspired by the Penn Discourse Treebank 2.0 sense hierarchy (Prasad et al., 2008) and syntactico-semantic labels used for representation of compound sentences on the tectogrammatical layer (the complete set can be found in Zikánová et al., 2015). The annotation reflects a division of connectives into primary and secondary ones (the terms established by Rysová and Rysová, 2014) and it had two phases – in the first one, primary connectives (i.e. grammaticalized expressions such as *because* or *therefore*) were captured, taking into account only those that anchored relations between arguments containing finite verb forms (Poláková et al., 2013). The second phase covered secondary connectives (i.e. not yet fully grammaticalized phrases with connecting function such as *the reason was* or *for this reason*), involving also relations with a noun phrase as its argument (Rysová and Rysová, 2015).

The first version of the annotation of discourse relations in the data of the Prague Dependency Treebank was published in 2012 as the Prague Discourse Treebank 1.0 (Poláková et al., 2012) and described

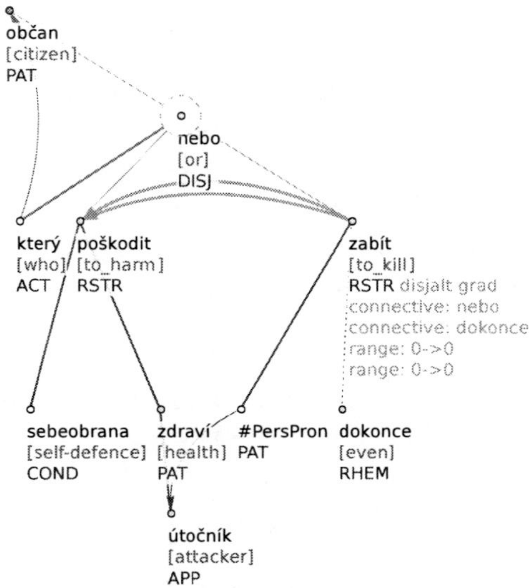

Figure 1: Annotation of discourse relations in PDiT 2.0. The relations are represented by two orange arrows connecting roots of the arguments. Information about the discourse types and connectives is given at the starting node of the relations.

in detail in Poláková et al. (2013). An updated version of the annotation of discourse relations of the same data was published in the Prague Dependency Treebank 3.0 (Bejček et al., 2013), with newly annotated second relations (see Example 1) and newly added rhematizers as parts of connectives (the updates were reported in Mírovský et al., 2014). A detailed study dedicated to different aspects of discourse relations and coherence in Czech, elaborating on various types of annotations of discourse-related phenomena in the data of the Prague Dependency Treebank, can be found in Zikánová et al. (2015). The most recent version of the annotated data, published as the Prague Discourse Treebank 2.0 (Rysová et al., 2016), newly brings annotation of discourse relations marked by secondary connectives. This last version of the annotations was used as the source data in the development of CzeDLex, as reported in the present paper. Table 1 summarizes the most significant changes of the annotation of discourse relations in various versions of the published data.

Example 1 offers an illustration of discourse relations annotated in PDiT 2.0. It contains two intra-sentential discourse relations – a disjunctive alternative expressed by the connective *nebo* [*or*], and a gradation expressed by the connective *dokonce* [*even*]; the tectogrammatical tree of the relevant part of the sentence, along with the discourse annotation, is depicted in Figure 1.

(1)   *Občané, kteří v sebeobraně poškodili zdraví útočníka* **nebo** *ho* **dokonce** *zabili, bývají za své jednání často nespravedlivé stíháni.*
(PDiT 2.0)

[*Lit.: Citizens who in self-defence harmed health of the attacker* **or even** *killed him, are often unfairly prosecuted for their actions.*]

3   Theoretical Issues

In this section, we first briefly compare our approach to the principles of development of related lexicons and then we provide a list of connective properties in CzeDLex, accompanied by description of necessary modifications made due to practical issues.

3.1   Inspiration from Other Lexicons

In the initial phase of the lexicon development, we kept in mind to be theoretically and technically as close to existing electronic lexicons of connectives as possible for the purposes of future lexicon linking and usability for translation. As stated earlier, the main source of inspiration was the German machine-readable Lexicon of Discourse Markers, DiMLex, developed since 1998 (Stede and Umbach, 1998) and continuously enhanced (DimLex 2, Scheffler and Stede, 2016). Like DiMLex, CzeDLex is encoded in XML (see Section 4.1 below), covers the part-of-speech, syntactic and semantic properties of the items described. Semantic properties are described via similar frameworks – a variant of the PDTB sense taxonomy (the PDTB version 3 for DiMLex versus Prague adjustments of the PDTB version 2.0 for CzeDLex). The core of the category of discourse connectives/markers is determined quite in agreement, although independently: DiMLex adopts the definition from Pasch et al. (2003), CzeDLex is inspired by the definition in the PDTB (see Section 2). Items covered in DiMLex include also several prepositions, or, more precisely, adpositions (*-halber, um ... Willen*), which is so far not the case for CzeDLex. In contrast, CzeDLex cov-ers also some frequent secondary discourse connectives (similar to the "AltLex" category in the PDTB approach). Inclusion of both these groups of expressions in electronic inventories is quite a novel approach and can support further research on connectives in different languages and lexicographic projects. Nesting of lexicon entries in DiMLex follows the syntactic category of discourse markers. CzeDLex is structured differently, according to the discourse types (senses) of each lemma, see Section 3.2. The latter approach is also taken in the lexicon of French connectives, LexConn (Roze et al., 2012).

3.2   List of Connective Properties in CzeDLex

As PDiT 2.0 covers annotation both of primary and secondary connectives, CzeDLex contains both these groups. These two types of connectives differ lexico-syntactically as well as semantically and thus the linguistic information in the entries varies in several aspects. We first describe an entry of a primary connective and then for a secondary connective.

The theoretical basis of the structure of the lexicon entries and their properties has been adopted from the theoretical framework developed in Mírovský et al. (2016b). The entries in CzeDLex are structured according to a two-level nesting principle. On the first level, entries are nested according to the lemma of a connective. Apart from the lemma and its approximate English translation, the level-one entry contains the following linguistic information:

- type of the connective (primary vs. secondary),
- structure of the connective (whether the connective is single like *a* [*and*], *ale* [*but*] or complex like *i když* [*even though*]),
- variants of the connective (variants may be of a different kind, cf. stylistic variants like *tedy* [*so.neutral*] vs. *teda* [*so.informal*] or orthographic variants like *protože* vs. *proto, že*, both meaning [*because*] or inflection variants, e.g. the form *čehož* is the second case form of the connective with the first case form *což* [*which*]),
- connective usages – a list of level-two entries representing semantico-pragmatic relations the connective expresses and their properties,

- non-connective usages – another list of level-two entries, representing contexts where the lemma does not function as a discourse connective (e.g. "mum and dad").

Level-two nesting for primary connectives reflects the discourse-semantic types (condition, opposition etc.).[1] It is the lemma in combination with the discourse type, not the lemma alone, which allows for searching for the connective's counterparts in translation and lexicon linkage. Entries for the individual semantic types of a connective (called "usages" in the data structure) then contain the following pieces of information:

- semantic type of the discourse relation (condition, opposition etc.),
- gloss (an explanatory Czech synonym),
- English translation,
- part of speech of the connective,
- argument semantics (for asymmetric relations like reason–result, it is necessary to determine whether the argument syntactically associated with the connective expresses reason (e.g. *protože* [*because*]) or result (e.g. *proto* [*therefore*])),
- ordering , i.e. position of the argument syntactically associated with the connective in relation to the other (external) argument (e.g. Czech coordinating conjunctions, adverbs and particles are placed in the linearly second argument),
- integration, i.e. placement of a connective in an argument (e.g. Czech subordinating conjunctions are placed at the beginning of a clause),[2]
- list of the connective modifications (a modified connective contains an expression further specifying the relation, e.g. *hlavně protože* [*mainly because*]),
- list of complex connectives containing the given connective (a complex connective contains two or more connective words like *a proto* [*and therefore*]),
- examples from PDiT (i.e. a context for the given discourse relation) and their English translations,

- is_rare (set to '1' for rare usages),
- register (formal, neutral, informal).

An entry for a secondary connective contains several modifications. On level one of the lexicon structure, entries are nested according to the lemma of the core word for a secondary connective (core words are words such as *důvod* [*reason*] in *z tohoto důvodu* [*for this reason*], *to je důvod, proč* [*that is the reason why*] etc., or *podmínka* [*condition*] in *podmínkou bylo* [*the condition was*], *za těchto podmínek* [*under these conditions*]). A level-two entry then contains the following properties (we list here the additional properties assigned only to the secondary connectives).

- syntactic characteristics of the structure (e.g. *z tohoto důvodu* [*for this reason*] is a prepositional phrase),
- dependency scheme (general pattern) for each structure (e.g. *z tohoto důvodu* [*for this reason*] = "z ((anaph. Atr) důvod.2)", i.e. a preposition *z* [*for*] plus an anaphoric attribute and the word *důvod* [*reason*] in genitive),
- realizations of the dependency scheme (e.g. *z tohoto důvodu* [*for this reason*], *z daných důvodů* [*for the given reasons*], *z uvedených důvodů* [*for the stated reasons*]).

3.3 Unifying Changes

The theoretically pure data schema of the lexicon (described shortly above) was slightly modified in the implementation of the lexicon in several aspects, making it more suitable for practical use. The most important changes involved:

(i) On the second level of the lexicon structure, the secondary connectives are nested not only according to the discourse type they express, but also according to the syntactic structure of similar surface realizations of the connective. A purer solution would result in a three-level hierarchy for the secondary connectives. This more practical solution keeps the data structure almost identical for the primary and secondary connectives.

(ii) The part of speech of the secondary connectives (their core words) should be on the first level, as it cannot differ in various connective or non-connective usages. On the other hand, the part of speech of a primary connective word can be differ-

---

[1] Level-two nesting of non-connective usages is based on the part of speech of the lemma.

[2] The names of the elements ordering and integration are taken from DiMLex.

ent (at least for connective vs. non-connective usages), and therefore it has to be placed at the second level. For unification reasons, the part of speech was placed at the second level also for the secondary connectives.

The positive impact of these modifications becomes probably most evident in querying the lexicon, significantly simplifying queries concerning both the primary and secondary connectives (we mention a querying tool later in Section 4.1).

4 Practical Implementation

This section describes the practical implementation of the lexicon in the Prague Markup Language framework (PML, see below) and advantages this choice brings. Two short examples show in detail how the data format looks like, to demonstrate a relative ease of using the PML formalism and possibly encourage others to use it in their practical research. We also shortly describe technical steps in the process of extracting the lexicon from the Prague Discourse Treebank and mention a few post-processing steps needed to improve the quality of the final data, and connective properties that need to be inserted into the lexicon manually.

4.1 Prague Markup Language

The primary format used for the Prague Dependency Treebank since version 2.0 is called the Prague Markup Language (PML, Hana and Štěpánek, 2012).[3] It is an abstract XML-based format designed for annotation of linguistic corpora, especially treebanks. It is completely independent of a particular annotation schema and can capture simple linear annotations as well as annotations with one or more richly structured interconnected annotation layers, dependency or constituency trees. The PML format has since been used for many other treebanks, most importantly the Prague Discourse Treebank but also the Prague Czech-English Dependency Treebank (Hajič et al., 2012), all treebanks in the HamleDT project (Zeman et al., 2015), and many others.

Representing data in the PML format immediately brings the following advantages:[4]

- The data can be browsed and edited in TrEd, a fully customizable tree editor (Pajas and Štěpánek, 2008). TrEd is written in Perl and can be easily customized to a desired purpose by extensions that are included in the system as modules.[5]
- The data can be processed using scripts written in btred – a command line version of TrEd.
- The data can be searched in the PML-TQ (Prague Markup Language–Tree Query, Pajas and Štěpánek, 2009), a powerful, yet user friendly, graphically oriented system for querying linguistically annotated treebanks.

The listing in Figure 2 is a short example from the PML-schema for CzeDLex, i.e. from the definition of the format of the lexicon data in the PML, namely a definition of the format for level-one entries (the lemmas). Notice the declarations of roles (role="#NODE", role="#CHILDNODES", lines 2 and 9), defining which data structures should be understood (i.e. represented) as tree nodes, and also the declaration of the identifier role (role="#ID", line 3), defining which element should be understood as the key for the records.

The following example shows the respective part of the resulting lexicon entry for the connective *tedy* [*therefore*]:

```
<lemma id="l-tedy" pdt_count="576">
    (a level-one entry)
  <text>tedy</text> (the lemma itself)
  <type>primary</type> (vs. secondary)
  <struct>single</struct>
        (vs. complex)
  <variants>
    <variant register="informal"
            pdt_count="1">
    teda (an informal variant)
    </variant>
  </variants>
  <usages>
    (lists of connective and
    non-connective usages)
  </usages>
</lemma>
```

---

[3] http://ufal.mff.cuni.cz/jazz/PML/

[4] And, of course, as the PML format is technically an XML, any general XML tool can be used for the data as well.

[5] Such a module was used also for the annotation of discourse relations in the PDT, see Mírovský et al. (2010).

```
01 <type name="c-lemma.type">
02   <structure role="#NODE">
03     <member as_attribute="1" name="id" role="#ID" required="1">
          <cdata format="ID"/></member>
04     <member as_attribute="1" name="pdt_count">
          <cdata format="nonNegativeInteger"/></member>
05     <member name="text" required="1"><cdata format="any"/></member>
06     <member name="type" type="c-type.type"/>
07     <member name="struct" type="c-struct.type"/>
08     <member name="variants" type="c-variants.type"/>
09     <member name="usages" type="c-usages-all.type" role="#CHILDNODES"/>
10   </structure>
11 </type>
```

Figure 2: A small piece from the PML-schema for CzeDLex, defining the data structure for the level-one entry – a lemma.

Similar type definitions need to be provided for all other parts of the lexicon data structure, i.e. for the types referred to in Figure 2 (such as `type="c-variants.type"`, line 6) and all other data types needed in the lexicon.

Figure 3 shows the lexicon loaded in the tree editor TrEd, allowing an annotator to make manual changes in the data. It displays an entry for the lemma *tedy* [*so*], with an opened dialog window for editing the connective usage representing the discourse type reason–result, and a roll-down list of available options for the value of the element `arg_semantics`. Individual lemmas (level-one entries), lists of connective usages, lists of non-connective usages, and individual usages (level-two entries) are represented by tree nodes.

Using the PML for the lexicon CzeDLex brings, apart from the three advantages named above, another possibility – the lexicon can be easily inter-linked with the source data, i.e. the Prague Discourse Treebank, by adding identifiers of the lexicon entries to the respective places in the treebank, using so called PML references. The query system PML-TQ then allows for incorporating information both from the treebank and the lexicon into a single query, allowing – for example – to search for all discourse relations in the treebank with connectives that have the ability to express (in different contexts) more than 2 different discourse types (senses).[6]

<hr>

[6] See Mírovský et al. (2014) and Mírovský et al. (2016a) for examples of using the PML-TQ for searching in discourse-annotated treebanks (PDT 3.0 and PDTB 2.0, respectively).

4.2 Data Extraction

The automatic extraction of the lexicon entries from the data of the Prague Discourse Treebank 2.0 (PDiT) was implemented in btred, a command line version of the tree editor TrEd. As an input, it used lists of lemmas accompanied by lists of variants, complex forms and modifications, which were created manually from the list of all connectives annotated in PDiT. In this all-connective list, each different string of words (e.g. *ale* [*but*] vs. *ale zároveň* [*but at the same time*] vs. *ale také* [*but also*]) formed a separate item. Primary and secondary connectives were distinguished automatically (in over 20 thousand annotated discourse relations in the treebank, there were approx. 700 different items for primary connectives and 350 for the secondary ones). Then, starting from the most frequent single connectives as lemmas, their variants, complex forms and modifications possibly belonging together under this lemma were selected manually from this all-connective list.

Based on this material, the script processed the whole data of PDiT, found all occurrences of the lemmas (and their variants etc.) and sorted them into the lexicon according to their type of usage (connective vs. non-connective) and the discourse type of the relations (or the part of speech for non-connective usages). For each usage, the part of speeach was automatically set and a number of the shortest examples were collected (the annotators later chose the most suitable ones and added their English translations). For each connective usage,

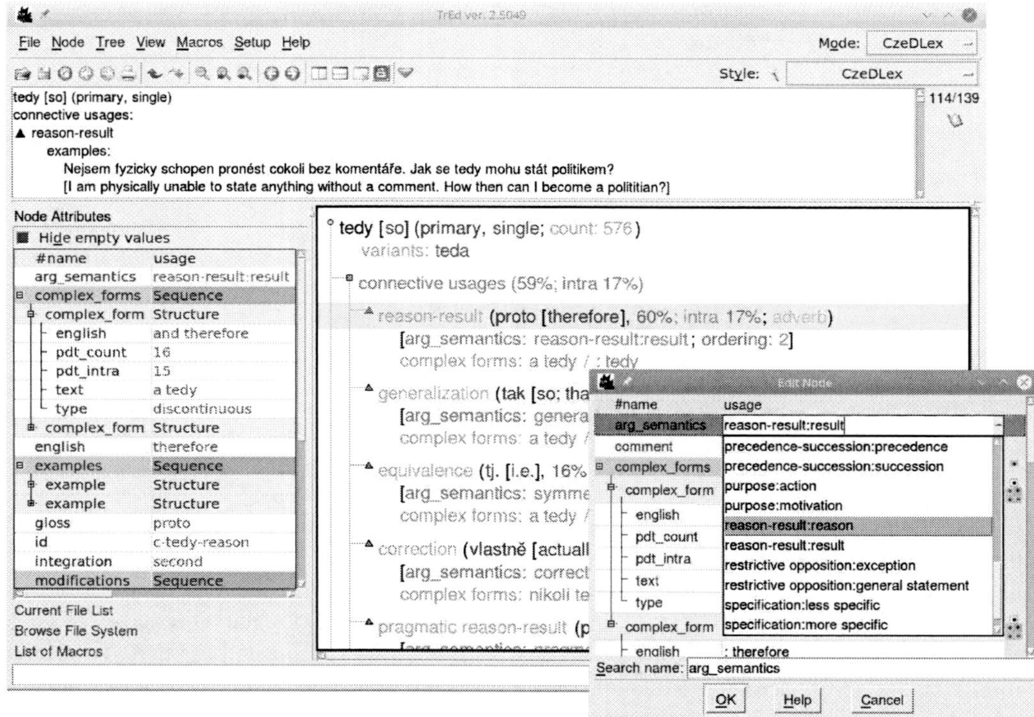

Figure 3: CzeDLex opened in the tree editor TrEd.

in moste cases, the argument semantics and ordering were assigned according to the orientation of the discourse arrow and position of the connective in an argument. Numbers of occurrences in PDiT were added to all individual variants, complex forms and modifications, as well as to connective and nonconnective usages (level-two entries) and the whole lemmas (level-one entries).

After the lexicon was extracted from the annotated treebank, a few automatic or semi-automatic post-processing and data validity checking steps were performed. All counts of appearances of various lexicon data structures in the source treebank data have been checked (e.g. if counts of individual connectives sum up to counts of the usages and the lemmas). Another important verifying step checked for each complex form (e.g. *ale také* [*but also*]) that its basic lemma (the respective level-one entry, say *ale* [*but*]) appeared in the treebank with the same discourse type. If not, the complex form was removed from that lemma (being for the moment left

as a complex form of the other lemma forming the complex form, in our case *také* [*also*]). If the complex form was by this process removed from all its basic lemmas, a new level-one entry for this complex form was created, with the value complex in the element struct.

Several properties required manual work, as the treebank data either did not contain this information at all (English translations, Czech synonyms, register, rareness, constituency-based syntactic characteristics of secondary connectives, structure) or the data were not big enough to cover all existing possibilities (integration, dependency scheme, sometimes ordering).

5 Conclusion

We presented the development process and implementation of an electronic lexicon of discourse connectives in Czech (CzeDLex). First, theoretical lexicographic aspects of building a lexicon for both primary and secondary connectives were addressed.

Second, the practical approach was discussed, starting with the description of the data format used – the Prague Markup Language – and advantages this choice brings. We followed by an elaboration on the actual process of exploiting the Prague Discourse Treebank 2.0 – a large corpus manually annotated with discourse relations – to build the raw basis of the lexicon, with subsequent automatic and manual checks, corrections and additions. To make the lexicon readable for non-Czech speakers, all names of elements, attributes and their values (with the obvious exception of Czech word entries and Czech corpus examples) are in English. In addition, each entry in Czech was supplemented by its English translation, including all corpus examples.

The first version of CzeDLex will be published this year in the Lindat/Clarin repository[7] under the Creative Commons license. It will cover an essential part of the connectives used in the Prague Discourse Treebank 2.0.[8] The second version of CzeDLex, planned to be published next year, will cover all connectives annotated in the treebank.

Acknowledgment

The authors gratefully acknowledge support from the Ministry of Education, Youth and Sports of the Czech Republic (project COST-cz LD15052), and the Grant Agency of the Czech Republic (project GA17-06123S). The research reported in the present contribution has been using language resources developed, stored and distributed by the LINDAT/CLARIN project of the Ministry of Education, Youth and Sports of the Czech Republic (project LM2015071). The authors are also grateful for inspiration coming from meetings and work realized within the European project TextLink (COST Action IS1312).

References

Eduard Bejček, Eva Hajičová, Jan Hajič, Pavlína Jínová, Václava Kettnerová, Veronika Kolářová, Marie Mikulová, Jiří Mírovský, Anna Nedoluzhko, Jarmila Panevová, Lucie Poláková, Magda Ševčíková, Jan Štěpánek, and Šárka Zikánová. 2013. Prague Dependency Treebank 3.0. Data/software.

Jan Hajič, Eva Hajičová, Jarmila Panevová, Petr Sgall, Ondřej Bojar, Silvie Cinková, Eva Fučíková, Marie Mikulová, Petr Pajas, Jan Popelka, Jiří Semecký, Jana Šindlerová, Jan Štěpánek, Josef Toman, Zdeňka Urešová, and Zdeněk Žabokrtský. 2012. Announcing Prague Czech-English Dependency Treebank 2.0. In *Proceedings of LREC 2012*. ELRA, European Language Resources Association, İstanbul, Turkey, pages 3153–3160.

Jan Hajič, Jarmila Panevová, Eva Hajičová, Petr Sgall, Petr Pajas, Jan Štěpánek, Jiří Havelka, Marie Mikulová, Zdeněk Žabokrtský, Magda Ševčíková-Razímová, and Zdeňka Urešová. 2006. Prague Dependency Treebank 2.0. Data/software.

Jirka Hana and Jan Štěpánek. 2012. Prague Markup Language Framework. In *Proceedings of LAW 2012*. Association for Computational Linguistics, Association for Computational Linguistics, Stroudsburg, pages 12–21.

Jiří Mírovský, Pavlína Jínová, and Lucie Poláková. 2014. Discourse Relations in the Prague Dependency Treebank 3.0. In Lamia Tounsi and Rafal Rak, editors, *Proceedings of Coling 2014 System Demonstrations*. Dublin City University (DCU).

Jiří Mírovský, Lucie Mladová, and Zdeněk Žabokrtský. 2010. Annotation Tool for Discourse in PDT. In Chu-Ren Huang and Dan Jurafsky, editors, *Proceedings of Coling 2010*. Chinese Information Processing Society of China, Tsinghua University Press, Beijing, China, volume 1, pages 9–12.

Jiří Mírovský, Lucie Poláková, and Jan Štěpánek. 2016a. Searching in the penn discourse treebank using the PML-tree query. In Nicoletta Calzolari et al., editor, *Proceedings of LREC 2016*. European Language Resources Association, Paris, France, pages 1762–1769.

Jiří Mírovský, Pavlína Synková, Magdaléna Rysová, and Lucie Poláková. 2016b. Designing CzeDLex – A Lexicon of Czech Discourse Connectives. In *Proceedings of PACLIC 2016*. Kyung Hee University.

---

[7] http://lindat.cz

[8] All those that will have undergone all checks and manual additions by that time.

Petr Pajas and Jan Štěpánek. 2008. Recent Advances in a Feature-Rich Framework for Treebank Annotation. In Donia Scott and Hans Uszkoreit, editors, *Proceedings of Coling 2008*. The Coling 2008 Organizing Committee, Manchester, pages 673–680.

Petr Pajas and Jan Štěpánek. 2009. System for Querying Syntactically Annotated Corpora. In Gary Lee and Sabine Schulte im Walde, editors, *Proceedings of the ACL–IJCNLP 2009 Software Demonstrations*. Association for Computational Linguistics, Suntec, pages 33–36.

Renate Pasch, Ursula Brauße, Eva Breindl, and Ulrich Hermann Waßner. 2003. *Handbuch der deutschen Konnektoren. Linguistische Grundlagen der Beschreibung und syntaktische Merkmale der deutschen Satzverknüpfer (Konjunktionen, Satzadverbien und Partikeln).* Walter de Gruyter.

Lucie Poláková, Pavlína Jínová, Šárka Zikánová, Eva Hajičová, Jiří Mírovský, Anna Nedoluzhko, Magdaléna Rysová, Veronika Pavlíková, Jana Zdeňková, Jiří Pergler, and Radek Ocelák. 2012. Prague Discourse Treebank 1.0. Data/software.

Lucie Poláková, Jiří Mírovský, Anna Nedoluzhko, Pavlína Jínová, Šárka Zikánová, and Eva Hajičová. 2013. Introducing the Prague Discourse Treebank 1.0. In *Proceedings of IJCNLP 2013*. Asian Federation of Natural Language Processing, Nagoya, pages 91–99.

Rashmi Prasad, Nikhil Dinesh, Alan Lee, Eleni Miltsakaki, Livio Robaldo, Aravind Joshi, and Bonnie Webber. 2008. The Penn Discourse Treebank 2.0. In Nicoletta Calzolari et al., editor, *Proceedings of LREC 2008*. European Language Resources Association, Marrakech, pages 2961–2968.

Charlotte Roze, Laurence Danlos, and Philippe Muller. 2012. LEXCONN: a French lexicon of discourse connectives. *Discours. Revue de linguistique, psycholinguistique et informatique* (10).

Magdaléna Rysová and Kateřina Rysová. 2014. The Centre and Periphery of Discourse Connectives. In Wirote Aroonmanakun, Prachya Boonkwan,

and Thepchai Supnithi, editors, *Proceedings of PACLIC 2014*. Chulalongkorn University.

Magdaléna Rysová and Kateřina Rysová. 2015. Secondary connectives in the Prague Dependency Treebank. In Eva Hajičová and Joakim Nivre, editors, *Proceedings of Depling 2015*. Uppsala University.

Magdaléna Rysová, Pavlína Synková, Jiří Mírovský, Eva Hajičová, Anna Nedoluzhko, Radek Ocelák, Jiří Pergler, Lucie Poláková, Veronika Pavlíková, Jana Zdeňková, and Šárka Zikánová. 2016. Prague Discourse Treebank 2.0. Data/software.

Tatjana Scheffler and Manfred Stede. 2016. Adding Semantic Relations to a Large-Coverage Connective Lexicon of German. In *Proceedings of LREC 2016*. European Language Resources Association, Paris, France.

Manfred Stede. 2002. DiMLex: A lexical approach to discourse markers. In V. Di Tomaso A. Lenci, editor, *Exploring the Lexicon - Theory and Computation*. Alessandria (Italy): Edizioni dell'Orso.

Manfred Stede and Carla Umbach. 1998. DiMLex: A Lexicon of Discourse Markers for Text Generation and Understanding. In *Proceedings of Coling 1998*. Association for Computational Linguistics, pages 1238–1242.

Daniel Zeman, David Mareček, Jan Mašek, Martin Popel, Loganathan Ramasamy, Rudolf Rosa, Jan Štěpánek, and Zdeněk Žabokrtský. 2015. HamleDT 3.0.

Šárka Zikánová, Eva Hajičová, Barbora Hladká, Pavlína Jínová, Jiří Mírovský, Anna Nedoluzhko, Lucie Poláková, Kateřina Rysová, Magdaléna Rysová, and Jan Václ. 2015. *Discourse and Coherence. From the Sentence Structure to Relations in Text*. Studies in Computational and Theoretical Linguistics. ÚFAL, Praha, Czechia.

Word Learning by Young Bilinguals: Understanding the Denotation and Connotation Differences of "Cut" Verbs in English and Chinese

Keng Hwee Neo
School of Humanities
Nanyang Technological University
NEO016@e.ntu.edu.sg

Helena Hong Gao
School of Humanities
Nanyang Technological University
helenagao@ntu.edu.sg

Abstract

This paper discusses the semantic differences of four "cut" verbs in Chinese *jiǎn, qiē, xiū, gē* and their English counterparts *cut* (with scissors), *slice/cut, trim/prune* (away/off) and *cut* (off/out) and challenges that young bilingual children may encounter in word learning. The fine differences of the verbs were first identified with references to usage notes in dictionaries and thesaurus and then represented with an approach for lexical differentiation adopted from DiMarco et al., (1992).The nuances and subtleties of the denotation and connotation of the "cut" verbs were illustrated accordingly for the understanding of bilingual word learning by young children.

1   Introduction

"Cut" verbs belong to a sub-class of physical action verbs (PA verbs) named "hand action verbs with instrument" (Gao, 2001, 2015). The basic conceptual knowledge that forms the semantics of the verbs include the information of body part, the hand(s) in this case, the cut action in a specific manner, a particular instrument used, degree of force applied, motion direction of the hand(s), and/or a causative result. *Cut* in English and *qiē* in Chinese are the basic verbs of "cut" verb class. English speaking children were found to be able to use the verb *cut* in a causative syntactic frame

around 3 years old (Sethuraman and Goodman, 2004). Chinese speaking children started to produce the first "cut" verbs *qiē* 'cut' at 17 months old. This shows that children before 3 years old have had observations or even physically conducted cutting actions (e.g., cutting a cake or an apple, etc.). Other studies have shown that action words naming movable and manipulative objects that can be used when playing with hands or feet are among the first acquired vocabulary of young children (Tomasello 1992; Gao 2015; Ma et al. 2009; Tardif et al. 2009). Such action words are either PA verbs or verbs that indirectly denote certain physical actions. For example, in Gao's (2001; 2015) studies, a total of 143 PA verbs in Mandarin were found to have been used by children between 1.9 and 2.3 years old. These verbs can be classified into 12 categories and close to half of them depict hand actions with or without an instrument. Mu's (2009) study also found that PA verbs were the first and core vocabulary of Mandarin-speaking children between 1 to 2 years of age. Zhang's (2010) corpus-based analysis of the Chinese language use by children between 3 to 6 years of age discovered that the frequencies of their noun and verb usage were comparable and highly dominant in their production. Out of the 100 mostly frequently produced words by the children, 31 were identified as verbs.

The above and other studies pertaining to lexical acquisition of Mandarin by 1-to-6-year olds have highlighted the fact that verb acquisition is the most dominant among other word classes and that PA verbs represent the core of domain-specific lexical development that occurs in parallel with

31st Pacific Asia Conference on Language, Information and Computation (PACLIC 31), pages 241–248
Cebu City, Philippines, November 16-18, 2017

cognitive development in children during this age period.

Due to the fact that the PA verbs acquired by young children are mostly those that depict physical actions involving everyday activities, monolingual children may not find it difficult to acquire them. However, for children who are acquiring two languages at the same time in places like Singapore, bilingual lexical development may not occur easily, since it does not solely depends on natural input, familiarity or physical experience of the actions. In bilingual lexical development, when L1 words are in close proximity to the semantics of L2 words, "functional equivalence" (cf. Nida, 1964) mapping may easily occur. Thus, the proximity of equivalence in the process of mapping between two words from two languages being acquired plays a crucial role. In the case of lexical near-equivalents, particularly for a set of near-synonyms with subtle differences in the semantic meanings, understanding the non-equivalent semantic features of seemingly paired words between two languages becomes more important in the study of bilingual lexical development. We assume that employing usage notes from dictionaries and thesaurus would be the first step, or the basis for identifying the fine differences between paired words from two languages before asking or accounting for why bilingual children acquired or used this word in L1 at this age but its paired word in L2 at a different age and why their word choices of certain pairs are correct and appropriate but certain others are not. We believe that an analysis of such bilingual word pairs would enable us to understand the differences in the process of bilingual word learning.

This paper first analyses the semantic differences of the highly frequently used Chinese physical action verbs, *jiǎn, qiē, xiū, gē* and their English counterparts *cut(with scissors), slice/cut, trim/prune(away/off)* and *cut (off/out)* that may influence Chinese-English bilingual children's acquisition of the lexical semantic meanings of the words from the two languages, and then discusses the acquisition challenges for bilingual children in associating words from L1 or L2 with words from L2 or L1 with the above four paired words as examples. Employing the usage notes of dictionaries and thesaurus as reliable resources for illustrating the fine differences of the verbs, we

adopted the approach of a two-part representation for lexical differentiation proposed by DiMarco et al. (1992) to demonstrate the nuances and subtleties of the denotation and connotation of the verbs that may explain why they can be challenges in bilingual word learning by bilingual children.

2   Chinese PA Verbs Acquired by Young Chinese-English Bilingual Children

Physical action verbs (PA verbs) in Chinese that express single actions or events are monosyllabic words (e.g., *ná* 'take', *hē* 'drink, etc.). According to Gao (2001), there are 494 monosyllabic PA verbs in Chinese that can be classified into seven categories based on the action features expressed by the lexical words, such as body part, contact, motion, motion direction, force, instrument, intention, patient object, and so on (Gao, 2001).

In this study, the 494 Chinese PA verbs in Gao's list were selected to compile a PA verb database. They were first collated with three parameters to illustrate the possibility of a full or near conceptual equivalence mapping of one Chinese verb with one counterpart in English that expresses an identical action concept. When one counterpart failed to do so, partial translation equivalence mapping was applied to match one Chinese verb with two or more synonymous English verbs expressing a similar physical action concept. The collating procedure was as follows:

(a) Each monosyllabic hand action verb in Chinese and its collocations in the form of bi-syllabic words or phrases were identified based on the meaning definitions found in the Dictionary of Contemporary Mandarin (DOCM) and the Modern Chinese Database designed by the Centre for Chinese Linguistics, Peking University (CCL-PKU).

(b) Corresponding equivalents in English of the monosyllabic physical action verbs in Chinese and their collocations in the form of bi-syllabic words or phrases were identified based on the meaning definitions found in the translation dictionaries, such as the Dictionary of Mandarin-English (DOME) and Oxford English Dictionary (OED).

(c) Use frequency of each monosyllabic physical action verbs in Chinese and their corresponding collocations found in CCL-PKU were identified accordingly.

(d) Remarks were added to those verbs in the database that have one of the following three types of translation equivalence:

(i) Type 1: Full or near translation equivalence mapping of one Chinese verb to one English verb expressing a similar action concept.

(ii) Type 2: Near or partial translation mapping of one Chinese verb to several other synonymous English verbs expressing a similar action concept and vice versa.

(iii) Type 3: Near or partial translation mapping of several English verbs to several other synonymous Chinese verbs expressing a similar physical action concept and vice versa.

For the purpose of illustrating Type 3, another word-use frequency list of the meaning equivalence correspondence of the PA verbs from English to Mandarin were established on the basis of the above list to illustrate the degree of translation equivalence mapping of one English verb to several other synonymous Chinese ones expressing a similar action concept.

In order to identify a specific group of highly frequently used PA verbs in Chinese and their counterparts in English, the verbs produced by bilingual children aged from 1 to 6 years were selected for the lexical semantic analysis. The Chinese data were first drawn from Mu (2009)'s study on the early acquisition of verbs in young children aged from 1 to 2 years old and Zhang's (2010) corpus-based analysis of the language use by children aged from 3 to 6 years old. The children's productions of the various word classes in both studies were then examined and those PA verbs were selected for comparing with the Mandarin-speaking children's word production for action in Tardif's (2006) study. Twenty most frequently used action words were selected based on the above studies and the Mac-Arthur-Bates Communicative Development Inventory (CDI) for both English and Mandarin children aged 16 months old and Naigles's (2009) study on infants' learning of first verbs within the first two years of life. Subsequently, a specific group of highly frequently used verbs by children within the age range of 1 to 6 years old were found. Among them "cut" verbs *jiǎn* 'cut (with scissors)', *qiē* 'slice/cut', *xīu* 'trim/prune(away/off)' *and ge* 'cut (off/out)' were found. After the frequently used verbs were

identified, the usage notes of dictionaries and thesaurus demonstrating the fine differences of the verbs were employed in a two-part representation for lexical differentiation (DiMarco et al., 1992). The results are expected to reveal the nuances and subtleties of the denotation and connotation of words that belong to a same class and that are near-synonymous in Chinese and English.

3   Lexicons for Lexical Choice: Synonymy and Plesionymy within and between Languages

According to Dimarco and Hirst (1995), "the problem of lexical choice in text generation is to determine the word that conveys most precisely the denotation and connotation that are to be expressed." (Dimarco and Hirst, 1995: 1). The key issue is thus to distinguish between lexical near-equivalents which may occur in the form of near-synonyms or plesionyms (Cruse, 1986). As opposed to absolute synonyms, near-synonyms or plesionyms differ in their nuances of denotation or connotation which result in their non-interchangeability depending on the situated context owing to their varying shades of meanings and of style or interpersonal emphasis.

We consider the two dimensions along which synonyms can differ in terms of semantically (denotative) and stylistically (connotative) both across and within English and Mandarin respectively. More specifically, while denotation represents the semantic meaning of the word, connotation often refers to the style and interpersonal emphasis of its usage in a specific context. However, the boundary between denotation and connotation may not be at times all that distinct owing to some overlap of meaning within the set of near-synonyms (See further explanations of this in Section 5). Our main purpose is then to locate and highlight the differences between near-synonyms or plesionyms both between and within English and Mandarin respectively for the highly frequent used "hand action verbs with instrument", *jiǎn* 'cut (with scissors)', *qiē* 'slice/cut', *xīu* 'trim/prune (away/off)' and *gē* 'cut (off/out)' respectively.

4   Usage Notes: Structure, Content and an Illustrations of 13 "Cut" Verbs in English

We adopt the claim by DiMarco et al. (1992) that "it is usually the explicit purpose of the usage notes from the dictionary or thesaurus to explain to the ordinary dictionary user the differences between groups of near synonyms." Table 1 shows a typical example of the list of 13 near-synonyms for the concept of CUT from the Online Thesaurus of LDOCE.

No/Word	Meaning	Usage
1. cut	to divide something into two or more pieces, especially using a knife or scissors	---to cut the cake ---cut off the lower branches
2. snip	to quickly cut something, especially using scissors	---snipped the label off. ---snipped away at her hair
3. slit	to make a long narrow cut through something, especially using a knife	---slit the envelope open with a penknife. ---slit through the plastic covering.
4. slash	to cut something quickly and violently with a knife, making a long thin cut	---slashed the tyres on his car. ---slash his wrists
5. saw	to cut wood, using a saw (=a tool with a row of sharp points)	---Saw the wood to the correct length.
6. chop	to cut wood, vegetables, or meat into pieces	---chopping up firewood with an axe. ---chopped down the old tree. ---finely chopped onion
7. slice	to cut bread, meat, or vegetables into thin pieces	---slice the cucumber. ---Slice the bread thinly.
8. dice	to cut vegetables or meat into small square pieces	---dice the apple into cubes.
9. grate	to cut cheese or a hard vegetable by rubbing it against a special tool	---Grate the cheese and sprinkle it over the vegetables.
10. peel	to cut the outside part off something such as a potato or apple	---peeled the potatoes
11. carve	to cut thin pieces from a large piece of meat	---carved the turkey.
12. mow	to cut the grass in a garden, park etc.	---mowing the lawn.
13. trim	(also clip) to cut a small amount off something, especially to make it look neater	---trimming his beard. ---Trim the excess fat off the meat.

Table 1. Usage notes for the 13 near--synonyms for the concept of CUT from the Online Thesaurus of LDOCE

The structure and content of the usage notes of dictionaries and thesaurus contain invaluable reference on lexical discrimination for computational use in machine translation. According to DiMarco and Hirst (1995: 6), "while the style and length of usage note entries varies somewhat, the following structure is characteristic:

a statement of the meaning that is central or common to the set of words being discriminated and a description of the factors that distinguish each word in the set such as implications (denotational differences between the meanings of words), connotations (nuances that 'colour' a word's meaning) and applications (restrictions on a word's use), coupled with examples of the use of each word in the set." The content of usage notes then refer to the denotative and connotative dimensions and features of the language descriptions of distinguishing factors particular to the notes.

The above table explicitly distinguishes the differences in usage of the 13 "cut' verbs. Through examining the regularities within these explanations, the key factors in lexical differentiation could be determined. Referencing on the 26 dimensions for denotation and 12 for connotation described more fully by DiMarco et al. (1993), the following lexical features for differentiation of the 13 verbs are illustrated in the Figure1.

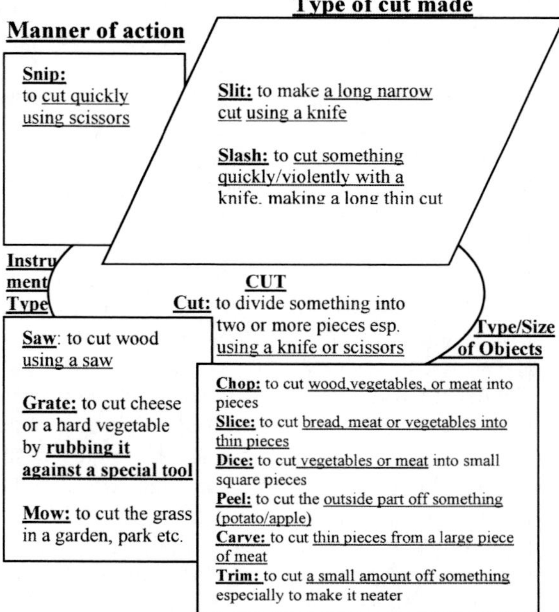

Figure. 1. Dimensions for the concept of CUT in English

The above figure clearly highlighted the lexical features for the differentiation of the 13 CUT verbs. The prototypical meaning of these verbs pertaining to the concept of the CUTTING ACT is essentially to divide something into two or more pieces esp. using a cutting instrument (a knife or scissors). In terms of the denotation dimensions, there are 5 aspects ranging from the manner of action, i.e. speed and strength of cutting, the type of instrument for the cutting act, type of cut made from the action of cutting and the type and or size of the object being cut which would differentiate the semantic meaning of each of these verbs. For example, SNIP can only be used to denote the quick manner of cutting an object using scissors, which distinguish it from CUT which could include the use of knife in the cutting of an object without any specification of its manner of cutting. Consequently, the above-mentioned 5 lexical features in the denotational dimension distinguish the subtle nuances of the semantic meaning of each of the synonymous verbs respectively, though with some occasional overlap among these features. For instance, while both SLICE and DICE both refers to the cutting of specific objects such as meat or vegetables, the former requires the cutting into thin pieces as opposed to the latter which necessitates the cutting into small square pieces.

Within the denotative differentiae, the connotative differentiae could also co-exist in the form of emphasis of one of the components of the semantic meaning of a word such as the pair of synonyms SLIT and SLASH, while both denotes the use of a knife to render something into a thin, long, narrow cut, SLASH highlights the rapid and violent action which connotes an intended brutal act.

5   Lexical Differentiation: Denotation and Connotation

In this study, several highly frequently used PA verbs in Chinese that have near or partial conceptual equivalence in English are selected to account for the possible asymmetries in the children's acquisition of bilingual lexicon. By examining Gao's (2014) 494 Chinese PA verbs against various lists of action verbs found in Mu (2009), Zhang (2010), Tardif (2006), and Naigles' (2009) studies, we identified *jiǎn* 'cut (with scissors', *qiē* 'slice/cut', *xīu* 'trim/prune(away/off' and *gē* 'cut (off/out' that have near or partial conceptual equivalence between the two languages and are also most frequently used by bilingual children aged from 1 to 6 years old. Based on the operating principles of the usage notes methodology advocated by DiMarco et al. (1993), we then perform a lexical differentiation of these synonymous PA verbs in both Chinese and English in terms of their denotation and connotation distinctions to demonstrate the subtle differences in their word senses.

5.1   Lexical Differentiation of *Jiǎn, Qiē, Xīu* and *Gē* in Chinese: Denotation and Connotation

Table 2 shows a consolidated usage notes of the 4 near-synonyms *jiǎn, qiē, xīu* and *gē* for the concept of CUT from both the Dictionary of Contemporary Mandarin (DOCM) and Dictionary of Mandarin-English (DOME), with the translations of the Mandarin verbs meaning and collocation in English and the Mandarin to English verbs translation equivalents.

Mandarin Character	Piny in	English Meaning	Mandarin Verbs Meaning and Collocation	Translations of The Mandarin Verbs Meaning And Collocation in English	Mandarin to English Verbs Translation Equivalent
剪	jiǎn	**cut with scissors**, clip, trim, snip, shear	**1.用剪刀等使东西断开**（剪裁/剪纸/剪指甲/剪几尺布做衣服） **2.剪裁**: 缝制衣服时把衣料按照一定尺寸断裁开	**1. cut (with scissors)/** clip/trim/snip/ shear (cut open/ shear a sheep/ trim one's nails/the letter was cut open) **2. cut out** (a garment)/tailor: (the coat was well cut and well made)	剪---cut with scissors, clip, trim, snip, shear 剪(裁)--- cut out
切	qiē	**cut, slice**	**1.用刀把物品分成若干部分**（切西瓜/把肉切成丝儿） **2.切割**: 用刀等把物品截断	**1.cut /slice** (cut up vegetables/ cut into halves/ slice meat/sliced into his fingers by accident when cutting vegetables) **2. slicing/cutting** (cutting part)	切(割)---- cut, slice
修	xiū	**trim, prune (away/off)**	**1.剪或削, 使整齐**（修树枝/指甲） **2.修剪**: 用剪子一类的工具修（枝叶、指甲、毛发等）: （修剪松墙/八字胡修剪得十分整齐）	**1. trim/prune** (prune away/off branches /trim /manicure one's fingernails)	修(剪)--- trim, prune (away/off)
割	gē	**cut (off/out),** slice, mow, excise, chop up	**1.用到截断**（割腕/麦子） **2.割除**: 割掉; 出去（割除肿瘤） **3.割断**: 截断; 切断（割断绳索）	**1. cut/mow** (cut paddy/cut apart/ break up) **2. cut off/cut out/excise** (cut off/remove the tonsil) **3. cut off/chop up** (cut off connections with)	割---cut (off/out), mow 割(除)--- cut (off/ out), excise, remove 割(断)--- cut off/ chop up

245

Table2. Usage notes for jiǎn, qiē, xīu and gē from DOCM and DOME

The above table explicitly distinguishes the differences in usage of the 4 "cut" verbs. Through examining the regularities within these explanations, the key factors in lexical differentiation could be determined. Referencing on the 26 dimensions for denotation and 12 for connotation described more fully by DiMarco et al., (1993), the lexical features for differentiation of *jiǎn, qiē, xīu* and *gē* are illustrated in the following Figure 2.

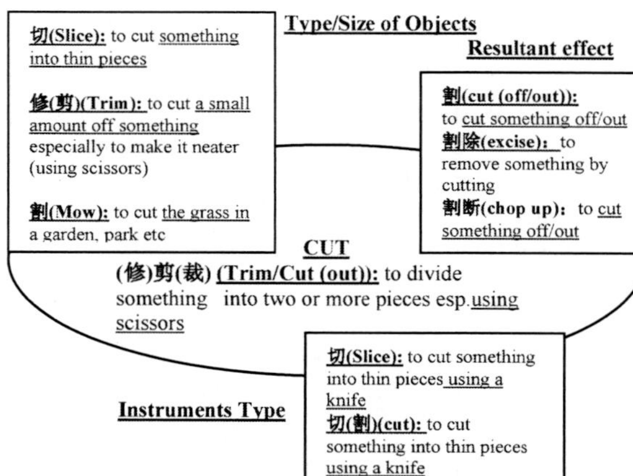

Figure. 2. Dimensions for the concept of CUT in English

The above figure clearly highlighted the lexical features for differentiation of *jiǎn, qiē, xīu* and *gē*. The prototypical meaning of these synonymous verbs pertaining to the concept of the CUTTING ACT realized by the lexicon *jiǎn* is essentially to divide something into two or more pieces esp. using scissors. In terms of the denotation dimensions, there are 3 aspects: the resultant effect of cutting, the type of instrument for the cutting act and the type and or size of the object being cut which would differentiate the semantic meaning of each of these verbs. For example, *qiē* can only be used to denote the cutting of an object into thin pieces using a knife, which distinguish it from *jiǎn* which refers to the use of scissors in the cutting of an object into mere pieces without any specification on its thickness. Additionally, though *jiǎn* and *xīu* both share the same denotational dimension of using scissors in the act of cutting, *xīu* specifically denotes the cutting of a small part off something especially to make it neat, which distinguishes it from *jiǎn* denoting the cutting of an

object into mere pieces without any specification on its sizes. Interestingly, owing to the bi-syllabic structure lexicon formation of Modern Chinese, both the monosyllabic lexicon *xīu* and *jiǎn* could combine into a bi-syllabic lexicon *xīu jiǎn* to denote specifically the cutting of a small part off something especially to make it neat using scissors.

Consequently, the above-mentioned 3 lexical features in the denotational dimension distinguish the subtle nuances of the semantic meaning of each of the synonymous verbs respectively, though with some occasional overlap among these features. For instance, the monosyllabic word *gē* in Chinese has the following denotational meanings:

1. **Type/Sizes of Objects:**

gē 'mow': to cut the grass in a garden, park etc.

2. **Instrument Type:**

qiē (*gē*) *cut*: to cut something into thin pieces using a knife

3. **Resultant Effects:**

gē 'cut (off/out)': to cut something off/out

gē chú 'excise' : to remove something by cutting

gē duàn 'chop up': to cut something off/out

Firstly, in the lexical feature of the type or sizes of objects, *gē* 'mow' specifically denotes the cutting of the grass in a garden or a park, etc. Secondly, in the lexical feature of the type of instrument, when combined with the word *qiē* 'slice' to form the bi-syllabic Chinese lexicon *qiē gē* 'cut', it then denotes specifically the cutting of something into thin pieces using a knife, which emphasizes the original denotational meaning of *qiē* instead of *gē*. Thirdly, in the lexical feature of the resultant effects of the cutting act, *gē* 'cut (off/out)' denotes the act of cutting to render something off/out as the resultant effect which could also be denoted with a greater emphasis on the removal of something through the act of cutting by either combining the monosyllabic verb *chú* 'remove' and *duàn* 'break' to form *gē chú* 'excise' denoting the removal of something by cutting and *gē duàn* 'chop up' denoting the cutting off or out of something respectively.

Within the denotative differentiae, the connotative differentiae could also co-exist in the form of emphasis of one of the components of the semantic meaning of a word such as the pair of synonyms *gē chú* 'excise' and *gē duàn* 'chop up': while both denote the removal of something through the act of cutting possibly with a cutting instrument like a knife, *gē chú* 'excise' highlights the excising action which connotes the complete removal of something undesirable while *gē duàn* 'chop up' emphasizes the forceful act of chopping up or hacking of something for the purpose of breaking it.

5.2 Challenges for Bilingual Children in "Cut" Verb Learning

In sections 4 and 5, the semantics of thirteen "cut" verbs in English and four "cut" verbs in Chinese that are frequently used in daily life were illustrated with usage notes. The illustrations show that the semantic differences between the words within and between the two languages are big enough to cause challenges for young bilingual children to acquire the verbs easily. For example, the manner distinctions and causative results of the different cut actions may not be easily acquired by young bilingual children through daily life experience. To understand how the process of learning happens at an early age and whether there is an order of learning of the verbs within a PA verb class, an analysis of the semantics of the verbs from learners' perspective becomes necessary. The semantic differences between the paired verbs in the two languages can also become evident through a comparative illustration of the verb semantics.

From the illustration of the denotation and connotation differences between the "cut" verbs in English and Chinese, we can see that it would require more linguistic and real-world knowledge for bilingual children to be able to acquire fully "cut" verbs, which explains why empirical studies of Chinese-English bilingual word learning have not shown any data of bilingual children's full acquisition of all the "cut" verbs in their preschool years.

6 Conclusion

It This paper discusses the semantic and stylistic differences of the highly frequently used Chinese physical action verbs, such as *jiǎn, qiē, xīu, gē* and their English counterparts *cut* (with scissors), *slice/cut, trim/prune*(away/off) and *cut* (off/out) that may influence Chinese-English bilingual children's acquisition of these differences between the two languages. Employing the usage notes of dictionaries and thesaurus as a methodology, the fine differences of the verbs were demonstrated in a two-part representation for lexical differentiation (DiMarco et al., 1992). The nuances and subtleties of the denotation and connotation of the "cut" verbs were illustrated accordingly.

Acknowledgments

We acknowledge the support by the Academic Research Fund (AcRF) of Ministry of Education and Nanyang Technological University, Singapore. . We hope that this approach will be able to serve as a reference point in explaining why bilingual children tend to have preferences or make incorrect choices in their use of certain PA verbs that are commonly used and heard from a young age. The result of such a study could be applied to the study of other word classes

References

Aneta Pavlenko. 2009. The Bilingual Mental Lexicon: Interdisciplinary Approaches. Bristol, United Kingdom: Multilingual Matters.

Chang L. L. et al. 2000. A Lexical Semantic Analysis of Mandarin Chinese Verbs: Representation and Methodology. In Computa-tional Linguistics and Chinese Language Processing. 5(1): 1-18. Taiwan: The Association for Computational Linguistics and Chi-nese Language Processing.

Christina Gitsaki. 1999. Second Language Lexical Acquisition: A Study of the Development of Collocational Knowledge. San Fran-cisco: International Scholars Publications

Costa, A. 2005. Lexical Access in Bilingual Production. In J. Kroll and A.M.B. De Groot (eds.) Handbook of Bilingualism: Psycho-linguistics Approaches: 308-325. Oxford: Oxford University Press.

David Singleton. 1999. Exploring the Second Language Mental Lexi-con. Cambridge, United Kingdom: Cambridge University Press.

Dictionary of Mandarin-English (吴光华编著《汉英大词典（第 3 版）》（上海：上海译文出版社，2010）。)

Dictionary of Contemporary Mandarin (中国社会科学院语言研究所词典编辑室《现代汉语词典（第 6 版）》（北京：商务印书馆出版社，2005。)

DiMarco, C. & Hirst, G. 1995. Usage Notes as the Basis for a Repre-sentation of Near-Synonyms for Lexical Choice.

DiMarco, C., Hirst, G. & Stede, M. 1992. The Semantic and Stylistic Differentiation of Synonyms and Near-Synonyms.

Eve V. Clark. 1993. The Lexicon in Acquisition. Cambridge, London: Cambridge University Press.

Gao H. 2015. Chinese Children's Production of Physical Action Verbs. In C. F. Sun, W. S-Y Wang & Y. Tsai (ed.), Oxford Handbook of Chinese Linguistics. 641-653.Oxford, UK: Oxford University Press.

Gao H. 2001. The Physical Foundation of the Patterning of Physical Action Verbs: A Study of Chinese Verbs. Lund: Lund University Press.

Gao H. 2001. A Specification System for Measuring Relationship among Near-Synonyms of Physical Action Verbs. In Proceedings of the 2nd Chinese Lexical Semantics Workshop (第二届汉语词汇语义学研讨会论文集). 45-51. Beijing, China.

Kong Lingda, Youyang Junlin, Chen Changhui, ding Lingyun, Wang Xiangrong, Zhu Wanxi, fu Manyi, Yao Wenbing. (孔令达， 胡德明， 欧阳俊林， 陈长辉， 丁凌云， 王祥荣， 朱万喜， 傅满义， 姚文兵). 2004. A Study of Concrete Word Acquisition By Chinese Children (汉族儿童实词习得研究). Anhui University Press (安徽大学出版社).

Kroll, J. 1993. Accessing Conceptual Representations for Words in a Second Language. In R. Schreuder and B. Weltens (eds.). The Bi-lingual Lexicon: 53-81. Amsterdam: John Benjamins.

Kroll, J., and De Groot, A.M.B. 1997. Lexical and Conceptual Memory in the Bilingual: Mapping Form to Meaning in Two Lan-guages. In A.M.B. De Groot and J. Kroll (eds.). Tutorials in Bilin-gualism: Psycholinguistic Perspectives: 169-199. Mawhah, N.J.: Lawrence Erlbaum.

Kroll, J. and Sunderman, G. 2003. Cognitive Processes in Second Language Learners and Bilinguals: The Development of Lexical and Conceptual Representations. In C. Doughty and M. Long (eds.). The Handbook of Second Language Acquisition: 104-129. Malden, MA: Blackwell.

Letitia R. Naigles. 2009. A General Description of Early Verb Growth and Use. In Flexibility in Early Verb Use: Evidence from a Multi-ple-n Diary Study. Letitia R. Naigles, Erika Hoff, Donna Vea, Mi-chael Tomasello. Wiley-Blackwell.2009.

Longman Dictionary of Contemporary English (LDOCE), 2017. http://www.ldoceonline.com/dictionary/cut/ 12 May2017.

Modern Chinese Database, Centre for Chinese Linguistics, Peking University (北京大学中国语言学研究中心现代汉语语料库), in http://ccl.pku.edu.cn:8080/ccl_corpus/. 16 Jan 2017.

Natasha Tokowicz. 2015. Lexical Processing and Second Language Acquisition. New York: Taylor and Francis.

Oxford Advanced Learners Dictionary (OALD), 2017. http://www.oxfordlearnersdictionaries.com/definition/english/cut_1?q=cut/ 12 May 2017.

Oxford English Dictionary. Second Edition. CD-ROM (v. 4.0). Ox-ford University Press, 2009.

Sethuraman, N. and J.C. Goodman. 2004. Learning to Generalized Verbs to New Syntactic Environments. In E.V. Clark (Ed.), Proceedings of the 2004 Stanford Child Language Research Forum: Constructions and Acquisition. CSLI Publications, 78-87.

Twila Tardif. 2006. But Are They Really Verbs? Chinese Words for Action. In Action Meets Word: How Children learn verbs. Kathryn A. Hirsh-Pasek and Robert M. Golinkoff. Oxford Schol-arship Online.2010.

Twila Tardif et al. 2008. Baby's First 10 Words. In Developmental Psychology. 44(4): 929-938. The American Psychological Associa-tion. 2008.

A corpus-based study on synesthesia in Korean ordinary language

Charmhun Jo
Faculty of Humanities,
The Hong Kong Polytechnic
University, Hong Kong
jch337@hotmail.com

Abstract

Synesthesia means an involuntary neurological phenomenon where "sensory events in one modality take on qualities usually considered appropriate to another" (Marks, 1982, p. 15). More generally, it indicates an experiential mapping of one sense domain with another, such as "sweet sound". The study reported in this paper is to test Ullmann's (1963) theoretical framework of "hierarchical distribution" through the synesthetic data coming out of Korean National Corpus (KNC), focusing on modern daily Korean. The research questions here are (a) what are the routes for Korean synesthetic transfers like?, (b) what are the predominant source and target domain for the transfers?, and (c) what are the universal and/or culture-specific aspects in the association? Based on Strik Lievers et al.'s (2013) methodology, the study extracts synesthetic data from KNC. As a result, the data analysis shows that (a) Korean synesthesia conforms to Ullmann's (1963) general scheme in the metaphoric mappings, (b) the predominant source domain is touch while the predominant target is hearing, which matches with Ullmann's (1963) study as well, and (c) there could be a delicate cultural dependency, which means "taste" occupies a significant position together with "touch" in Korean synesthetic metaphors.

comes from the Ancient Greek σύν syn, "together", and αἴσθησις aisthēsis, "sensation". Basically, synesthesia refers to an involuntary neurological phenomenon where "sensory events in one modality take on qualities usually considered appropriate to another" (Marks, 1982, p. 15). To be more general, it means an experiential association of one sense domain with another, such as "sweet sound" and "cold color". In linguistics, synesthesia is understood in terms of metaphor (Williams, 1976; Geeraerts, 2010), which means that a perceptual experience of one sense is described by lexical expressions associated with another. For example, "sweet sound" is linguistically synesthetic because the speaker expresses a perception of sound ("sound") using a word related to taste ("sweet"), where "sound" becomes the target domain of the transfer and "sweet" is the source. The synesthetic metaphors were introduced by S. Ullmann (1963), where he proposed his theoretical framework of "hierarchical distribution" as a probable universal principle in the process of synesthetic mapping. In this light, the objective of the study is to test Ullmann's (1963) theoretical framework using the synesthetic data from Korean National Corpus (KNC). Therefore, the research questions here are (a) what are the routes for Korean synesthetic transfers like?, (b) what are the predominant source and target domain for the transfers?, and (c) what are the universal and/or culture-specific aspects in the association?

1 Introduction

Synesthesia (also spelled synæsthesia or synaesthesia) has been an interesting research topic in diverse academic fields. The term synesthesia

2 Brief literature review

As the seminal work of synesthetic metaphors, Ullmann (1963), analyzing poetic writings of the nineteenth century in English, French, and Hungar-

31st Pacific Asia Conference on Language, Information and Computation (PACLIC 31), pages 249–254
Cebu City, Philippines, November 16-18, 2017

ian, proposed his theoretical framework of "hierarchical distribution", where he concluded three overall tendencies in synesthetic mappings. First of all, the majority of synesthetic transfers show the following direction: touch → heat → taste → smell → sound → sight. This transfers tend to move from the "lower" to the "higher" sensory domains, which is called "hierarchical distribution". Second, based on the first tendency, the most frequent source domain of transfers is touch, the lowest level of sensation. Third, the most frequent target domain for synesthetic transfers is sound rather than sight.

Based on Ullmann's (1963) study on data from poetry, Williams (1976) investigated the synesthetic transfer in daily language, namely, the historical change of meaning of synesthetic adjectives in daily English (together with some evidence from other Indo-European languages and Japanese as well). In sum, his results support Ullmann's (1963) framework of "hierarchical distribution", generalized as follows:

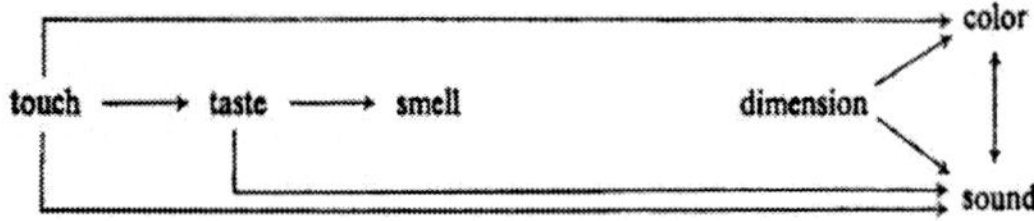

Figure 1. Synesthetic transfer route of Williams (1976)

Following Ullmann (1963) and Williams (1976), Yu (1992) applied their approaches to the data collected from Chinese literary and daily language. The conclusion of the research shows that Chinese synesthetic metaphors basically conform to their general schemes in metaphoric mappings. Yu (2003) also found almost the same results from the analysis of synesthetic data extracted from literary works written by current eminent Chinese novelist Mo Yan, examining synesthesia based on a cognitive perspective.

From the perspective of cognitive poetics, following Ullmann's (1963) approach, Shen (1997) explored the directionality of transfer for synesthetic metaphors in Hebrew on the basis of the literary analysis of modern poetry and two experimental data. His findings reinforce Ullmann's (1963) observation about the mapping in linguistic synesthesia. That is to say, the synesthetic expressions in the Hebrew language tend to map lower senses on to higher ones in their hierarchy. By way of the notion of "accessibility", Shen (1997) claims that the "low to high" transfer comes from the general cognitive constraints, where "a mapping from more 'accessible' or 'basic' concepts onto 'less accessible' or 'less basic' ones seems more natural and is preferred over the opposite mapping" (p. 51). Also, he points out that sight and sound are less accessible because they do not involve any direct contact with the perceived entity.

Recently, Strik Lievers (2015) reported a noticeable study about linguistic synesthesia by making use of corpora to investigate synesthetic transfers of English and Italian. Via a semi-automatic method for extracting synesthesiae from corpora, developed in Strik Lievers et al. (2013), she found large-scale data results and more clearly presented that the so-called principle of directionality just reflects the "frequency" of synesthetic connection types, adding a few interesting interpretations about the motivation of English and Italian synesthetic mappings.

3 Methodology

Sensory domains

Prior to the examination into synesthetic mappings in the linguistic text, sensory domains, or sensory modalities, are first to be designated. As a matter of fact, there is no agreement among scholars over how many sensory modalities there exist, and they can vary depending on researchers' viewpoints and classificatory criteria (Strik Lievers et al., 2013; Strik Lievers, 2015). Most of synesthetic studies now follow the Aristotelian five-sense system of touch, taste, smell, hearing, and sight (cf. Cytowic, 1989; Shen, 1997; Strik Lievers 2015). Some of the studies, on the other hand, makes an adjustment to the above system. For instance, Ullmann (1963) separated "heat" from "touch" [1], and Williams (1976) divided sight into two categories of "dimension" and "color". Day (1996) is based on Ullmann's (1963) taxonomy, while Yu (1992, 2003) follows Williams's (1976). Lin and Hsien (2011) add "emotion" on the six senses of touch, temperature, taste, smell, hearing, and vision, and Zhao and Huang (2015) also take "emotion" into consideration along with the traditional five senses.

[1] However, Ullmann (1963) mentioned: "There is of course no harm in combining the two sets of data; actually this would only throw an even more glaring light on the general pattern". (p. 278)

This study chooses the general Aristotelian sensory modes for broader reviews and comparisons.

Data and corpus

In this study, the synesthetic data will be collected from Korean National Corpus (KNC) well known as "21st century Sejong Project". The 21st century Sejong Project is a comprehensive project aiming to build various kinds of language resources including Korean corpora, comparable to British National Corpus (BNC) (Aston & Burnard, 1998), and Korean electronic dictionaries. The KNC data basically have the raw corpora of modern Korean (written and spoken), North Korean, Korean used overseas, old Korean, and oral folklore literature. They include parallel corpora consisting of Korean and other languages such as English and Japanese, morph-tagged corpora, part-of-speech (POS)-tagged corpora, sense-tagged corpora, and a parsed corpus as well. Among them, the parsed corpus of modern written Korean will be selected for this study, because it is the only syntactically analyzed corpus and the contents are all composed of daily linguistic data. The Korean parsed corpus had been set up for 4 years from 2002 to 2006, and the size is 43,828 sentences (around 433,839 words) (NIKL, 2011).

How to extract synesthetic metaphors from the corpus

The study refers to Strik Lievers et al.'s (2013) methods to extract synesthetic data from KNC. The author firstly sets up the lexical items subdivided by five sensory modes respectively in terms of POS categorization of noun (N), adjective (A) and verb (V)[2], and secondly, as for the synesthesia extraction from the corpus, a simplest method is applied that just lists all the sentences containing at least two perception-related words, given the fact that this simplest way can possibly collect the largest number of candidate sentences and the candidates will be affordable for the final manual checking because the corpus is not big. Finally, to sort out "true" synesthesiae, it is necessary to do a

handwork inspection of the extracted candidate output.

4   Results and discussion

Sense-related word lists

The total number of perception-related lexemes collected for this survey is 417 words. The summary is as follows:

	Touch	Taste	Smell	Sight	Hearing
N	31	15	28	68	54
A	52	31	8	47	6
V	12	8	12	25	20
Sub-total	95	54	48	140	80
Total	417				

Table 1. The distribution of sense-related words collected for the study

Results

The first finding is the whole result of synesthesia extraction from KNC, as summarized in Table 2. This data can show an overall outlook of corpus work on Korean synesthetic phenomena.

Total Corpus Sentences (TCS)	Extracted Positive Sentences (EPS)	True Positives (true synesthesiae) (TP)	TP / EPS (%)	TP / TCS (%)
43,828	1,250	100	8	0.23

Table 2. The total result of synesthesia extraction

The second is the overall synesthetic transfer route in Korean. It is directly concerning what the routes for Korean synesthetic transfers found in the corpus data are like. The result is displayed in the following figure:

Touch → Taste → Smell → Sight → Hearing

Figure 2. Overall synesthetic transfer route in Korean

The third one is the distribution of synesthetic mappings among sensory modes. This is practical informational data, which represent how frequent each mapping is and how many forward or backward transfers exist. The above result 2 is generalized from this data.

---

[2] Regarding the POS matter of linguistic synesthesia, three parts of speech of noun, adjective and verb have to be taken into account because they are all able to engage in synesthetic connections (Strik Lievers et al., 2013). For example, "She has a golden [Adj/Source] voice [N/Target]", "The flowers smell [V/Target] sweet [Adj/Source]" (Strik Lievers et al., 2013, p. 4).

Source \ Target	Touch	Taste	Smell	Sight	Hearing	Total
Touch	0	3	3	11	20	37
Taste	1	0	8	9	15	33
Smell	0	0	0	1	2	3
Sight	2	1	4	0	13	20
Hearing	0	1	1	5	0	7
Total	3	5	16	26	50	100

Table 3. The distribution of Korean synesthetic mappings among sensory domains (TOKEN)[3]

General discussion

The first issue to be discussed here is regarding the directionality of Korean synesthetic mappings. In a word, the result reported in this research at large conforms to the theory of "hierarchical distribution" by Ullmann (1963), as showed in Figure 2. The predominant source is touch, while the predominant target is hearing, as seen in Table 3, which also matches with the conclusion of Ullmann (1963). The above reports are confirmed again by Strik Lievers (2015) as well.

However, the universal tendency, as Strik Lievers (2015) noted, is not unidirectional but frequency-based. That is because some opposite transfers, or backward transfer types, are found, although the number of cases is remarkably low. More importantly, there could be found a delicate cultural dependency, or a subtle culture-based difference. In a closer observation on the finding data, a very noticeable point is detected in Korean synesthetic metaphor phenomena. It is with regard to the gustatory domain, taste, which works as a sec-

Source \ Target	Touch	Taste	Smell	Sight	Hearing	Total
Touch	0	2	3	9	14	28
Taste	1	0	7	8	12	28
Smell	0	0	0	1	2	3
Sight	2	1	4	0	10	17
Hearing	0	1	1	5	0	7
Total	3	4	15	23	38	83

[3] Table 4. The distribution of Korean synesthetic mappings among sensory domains (TYPE)

ond largest source modality of Korean synesthetic mappings investigated. The key point here is in that the difference of the proportion between the most and second frequent source sensory domains is very slight, as indicated in Table 5.

Touch	Taste	Sight	Hearing	Smell
37	33	20	7	3

Table 5. Korean source sensory domains in frequency-decreasing ordering (%)

This observation is comparable to Strik Lievers's (2015) data in Table 6.

	Touch	Taste	Sight	Hearing	Smell
English	49.3	25.7	21.8	3.0	0.2
Italian	55.6	20.2	19.1	4.6	0.2

Table 6. English and Italian source sensory domains in frequency-decreasing ordering (%), adapted from Strik Lievers (2015)

On the other hand, the frequency of target modes in Korean synesthetic transfers is similar to the finding of Strik Lievers (2015). The comparison is displayed as follows:

	Hearing	Sight	Smell	Taste	Touch
Korean	50	26	16	5	3
English	52.3	28.0	12.4	5.3	2.1
Italian	50.2	42.5	3.8	3.0	0.2

Table 7. Target sensory domains in frequency-decreasing ordering in Korean, English, and Italian (%), merged with the data presented in Strik Lievers (2015)

Accordingly, this situation can imply that together with the tactile domain, touch, the sense of taste takes up a significant position in Korean or Asian cultural context, and so people in the cultural circle more often tend to describe something in terms of gustation or tactility, compared with western people. Such point of view can be strongly supported by Zhao and Huang (2015), who came to the following conclusion from their study on synesthetic metaphors in modern Chinese:

Figure 3. The hierarchy of synesthetic transfers among taste, touch, and smell in Chinese, excerpted from Zhao and Huang (2015)

References

Aristotle. Poetics. Translated by S. H. Butcher. (http://www.gutenberg.org/files/1974/1974.txt)

Aston, G., & Burnard, L. (1998). The BNC handbook: exploring the British National Corpus with SARA. Capstone.

Baron-Cohen, S. (n.d.). Historical Perspective. UK Synesthesia Association Site: http://www.uksynaesthesia.com/histiorical.htm.

Chung, I. (1997). Synaesthetic Transfer of Korean Adjectives. Studies in Modern

Grammatical Theories, 11, 163-180. [in Korean]

Cytowic, R. E. (1989). Synesthesia: A Union of the Senses. New York: Springer-Verlag.

Cytowic, R. E. (1993). The man who tasted shapes: A bizarre medical mystery offers revolutionary insights into reasoning, emotion, and consciousness. New York: Putman.

Day, S. (1996). Synaesthesia and synaesthetic metaphors. Psyche, 2(32), 1-16.

Geeraerts, D. (2010). Theories of lexical semantics.

Harris, R., & Taylor, T. J. (1997). Landmarks in linguistic thought 1: The western tradition from Socrates to Saussure (Vol. 1). Psychology Press.

Huang, C. R. (2015). Towards a Lexical Semantic Theory of Synaesthesia in Chinese. In Keynote Speech in the 16th Chinese Lexical Semantics Workshop (CLSW-16). Beijing.

Kang, B. & Kim H. (2004). Sejong Korean Corpora in the Making. Paper presented at the International Conference on Language Resources and Evaluation. Retrieved April 2, 2015, from http://www.lrec-conf.org/proceedings/lrec2004/pdf/66.pdf.

Karwoski, T. F., Odbert, H. S., & Osgood, C. E. (1942). Studies in synesthetic thinking: II. The role of form in visual responses to music. The Journal of general psychology, 26(2), 199-222.

Lakoff, G., & Johnson, M. (1980). Metaphors we live by. University of Chicago press.

Lakoff, G., & Turner, M. (1989). More than cool reasoning: A field guide to poetic metaphor. University of Chicago press.

Lee, S. (2015). A study on synesthetic metaphor shown in Korean and Chinese advertisement from the viewpoint of cognitive linguistics. [in Korean]

Liddell, H. G., Scott, R., & Jones, H. S. (1940). A Greek-English lexicon.

Lievers, F. S. et al. (2015). Methods for the extraction of synaesthetic associations from corpora (unpublished).

Liu, H. & Huang, C. R. (2015). The automatic extraction and mapping directionality of synaesthetic sentences of modern Chinese. [in Chinese]

Marks, L. E. (1982). Synesthetic perception and poetic metaphor. Journal of Experimental Psychology: Human Perception and Performance, 8(1), 15.

National Institute of Korean Language (NIKL). (2011). 21C Sejong Project final result (revised). https://ithub.korean.go.kr

Park, G., (1978). Synesthetic mapping of poetic diction. Korean Language and Literature, No.78. [in Korean]

Ramachandran, V. S., & Hubbard, E. M. (2001). Psychophysical investigations into the neural basis of synaesthesia. Proceedings of the Royal Society of London B: Biological Sciences, 268(1470), 979-983.

Sacks, Oliver (2007). Musicophilia. New York: Alfred A. Knopf.

Shen, Y. (1997). Cognitive constraints on poetic figures. Cognitive Linguistics, 8(1), 33-72.

Shin, S. (2005). Automatic Pattern Extraction for Korean Sentence Parsing. Proceedings from the Corpus Linguistics Conference Series (Vol. 1, no. 1). University of Birmingham. Available on-line from http://www.corpus.bham.ac.uk/PCLC.

Simner, J., & Hubbard, E. M. (Eds.). (2013). Oxford handbook of synesthesia. Oxford University Press.

Stanford, W. B. (1936). Greek metaphor: studies in theory and practice. B. Blackwell.

Stefanowitsch, A., & Gries, S. T. (Eds.). (2007). Corpus-based approaches to metaphor and metonymy (Vol. 171). Walter de Gruyter.

Strik Lievers, F. (2015). Synaesthesia: A corpus-based study of cross-modal directionality. Functions of Language, 22(1), 69-95.

Strik Lievers, F., et al. (2013). A methodology for the extraction of lexicalized synaesthesia from corpora. Paper presented at ICL 19 (International Congress of Linguists). Geneva, Switzerland.

Takada, M. (2008). Synesthetic metaphor: perception, cognition, and language. VDM Publishing.

Ullmann, S. (1938). Synästhesien in der dichterischen Werken von Oscar Wilde. Englische Studien, 72, 245–256.

Ullmann, S. (1963). The Principles of Semantics (2nd ed., 3rd Impression). Oxford: Basil Blackwell.

Williams, J. M. (1976). Synesthetic Adjectives: A possible law of semantic change. Language, 52, 461-478.

Yoon, H. (1970). Structurality of synesthetic metaphors. Korean Language and Literature, No.49-50. [in Korean]

Yu, N. (1992). A possible semantic law in synesthetic transfer. SECOL Review, 16(1), 20-40.

Yu, N. (2002). Body and emotion: Body parts in Chinese expression of emotion. Pragmatics & cognition, 10(1), 341-367.

Yu, N. (2003). Synesthetic metaphor: A cognitive perspective. Journal of Literary Semantics, 32(1), 19-34.

Zhao, Q. & Huang, C. R. (2015). A corpus-based study on synaesthetic adjectives in modern Chinese.

Zhao, Q., Huang, C. R., & Xu, H. (2015). Auditory Synaesthesia and Near Synonyms: A Corpus-Based Analysis of sheng1 and yin1 in Mandarin Chinese.

Intrusions of Masbate Lexicon in Local Bilingual Tabloid

Cecilia F. Genuino
De La Salle University
2401 Taft Ave., Manila, Philippines
cecilia.genuino@dlsu.edu.ph

Romualdo A. Mabuan
Lyceum of the Philippines University
Intramuros, Manila, Philippines 1002
romualdo.mabuan@lpu.edu.ph

Abstract

Philippinization of English has come full circle: It has penetrated not only the center but also the periphery. This paper demonstrates a trend of nativization of English in a rural area as seen in a local daily. Thirty newspaper articles from *The Stalwart Journal*, a province-wide weekly circulating bilingual journal in the island province of Masbate, Bicol Region in the Philippines, were examined to identify the local lexical intrusions in the English text. The borrowing and assimilation of local lexical terms were analyzed and categorized. These lexical items were found in various categories: people, cultural events, cultural groups, public and private organizations, government programs, program units, government agencies, places, broadcast and social media, transportation, food, animals, human descriptions, public services, and other items. English nativization is shown in the borrowing and switching to local or native lexis in the news articles of the local daily.

1 Introduction

'English is the global language' (Crystal, 2003). English has developed a special role that is recognized in every country in the world. It has covered important domains in the global society such as telecommunications, business, commerce, air control, and social media, to name a few. The use of English has privileged some and marginalized others resulting in some sort of 'linguistic deprivation'. In praise of the English language, Simon Jenkins (1995 in J. Jenkins, 2009) stated: 'English has triumphed. Those who do not speak it are at a universal disadvantage against those who do. Those who deny this supremacy merely seek to keep the disadvantaged deprived.' The dominance of the English language in the rapidly globalizing world resulted in linguistic inequality and induced some feeling of anxiety to who cannot speak it (Tsuda, 2005 in David & Dumanig, 2008). Today, with over 6,800 languages in the world, English has proven its power and dominance, which has spread in almost two-thirds of the world's population (Crystal, 2003).

Considered as the language of prestige and power, English has continuously expanded throughout the world, which gives birth to the emergence of different varieties now commonly called as *World Englishes*. These Englishes have embraced the world's English and appropriated it to suit their local cultures and contexts based on the needs of their communities. Sik and Anping (2004 in David & Dumanig, 2008) suggests that with its imperialist and globalizing force, English has penetrated many non-English speaking communities results in a linguistic phenomenon called 'code-switching', which also leads to the nativization or indigenization of English throughout the world. This Englishization of non-English contexts, according to B. Kachru (2011), gives birth to 'transplantation' of English to different areas creating various varieties. Saghal (1991 in David & Dumanig, 2008) defines nativization as 'a process of transferring a local language to a new cultural environment.' This process of transference is situated and contextualized; it is socially conditioned and determined and takes into the account the various needs and nuances of the cultures. The sociolinguistic realities of the speech communities are considered in order to articulate the people's local, social, cultural and religious identities (Kachru, 1997).

Honna (in David & Dumanig, 2008) stresses that 'when English migrates to foreign countries, it diffuses and internationalizes, acculturates and indigenizes, and adapts and diversifies,' which leads to localized or lexical items. These local

31st Pacific Asia Conference on Language, Information and Computation (PACLIC 31), pages 255–264
Cebu City, Philippines, November 16-18, 2017

terminology may or may not have equivalents in the English language. This nativization process of English in local contexts creates localized varieties of English that exist to serve the needs of their local speakers.

Much research has already been done exploring the nativization of English in Asia or what linguists refer to as Asianization of English, as cited by David and Dumanig (2008): Malaysia, the Philippines and Thailand (Powell, David & Dumanig, 2008), Brunei (David & McLellan, 2007), Singapore and Pakistan (David, Kuang & Qaisera, 2008), Malaysia (Pillai, 2006), and the Philippines (Bautista, 1997). These studies have found that, although coming from one original Anglophone source, these English varieties have distinct characteristics and vary from each other graphologically, phonologically, and lexically.

These new varieties of English engage in language contact with English and their speakers, in their attempt to express themselves fully in a foreign language, engage in direct lexical borrowings, which initial appear as code-switches. Haugen (1956, p. 26 in David & Dumanig, 2008) describes code-switching as the "alternative use of two languages". Code-switching, according to David (2001) and Kow (2003) functions to build solidarity, to exclude others, to practice power, and to maintain the authenticity of the original source.

In the Philippines, the linguistic phenomenon of code-switching is commonly called as Taglish" or Tagalog-English, which appears in both spoken and written discourses. Written discourses include computer-mediate communication (CMC) such as e-mail and chat as well as newspaper prints. Several studies on Taglish have already been conducted (Bautista, 1997), but it is very rare (at least to the author's knowledge at the moment of writing) to come across studies of nativization of English within a local Philippine English variety. This paper aims to fill in such research gap as it explores the linguistic intrusions of local lexical items in English news articles in a local town within the Philippines. The lexical items in focus are the occurrences of code-switches in the English texts.

1.1 General Information on Masbate

Masbate is an island province located in the Bicol Region in the Philippines. The province lies roughly at the center of the Philippine archipelago between latitudes 11 degrees 43 minutes north and 21 degress 36 minutes north, 123 degrees 9 minutes east and 124 degrees 15 minutes east. It is composed of a wedge-shaped mainland (Masbate), two major islands (Ticao and Burias) and 14 small islands. It is bounded on the north by Burias and Ticao Pass, east by San Bernardino Strait, south by the Visayan Sea, and west by the Sibuyan Sea. Relative to Mainland Bicol, the province faces the southwestern coasts of Camarines Sur, Albay, and Sorsogon areas. Masbate is at the crossroads of two island groups: Luzon and Visayas. Being administratively assigned to the Bicol Region, it is politically part of the Luzon island group. However, from a biogeographic and sociolinguistic perspective, Masbate has a stronger affiliation with Visayas.

Masbate had a population of 892,393 in the 2015 Census of Population, with a density of 210 inhabitants per square kilometer or 540 inhabitants per square mile. The province covers a total land area of 4,151.78 square kilometers (1,603.01 sq mi). It is politically subdivided into three congressional districts, 20 municipalities, one city and 550 barangays.

Masbate is a melting pot of dialects and cultures due to its geographic location. Masbatenyos speak different languages based on their areas of residence. Residents in the capital town of Masbate speak the native Masbatenyo (sometimes Masbateño or Minasbate) with a mixture of the Bicol dialect; natives of Cataingan, Palanas, and Dimasalang along its east coast use Samar-Visayan; residents from Pio V. Corpus, Cataingan and Placer in the south speak Bohol and Cebu Visayan; along the western coast of Mandaon and Balud, people speak in Hiligaynon and Capiznon; natives of Ticao and Burias Islands converse in variants of the Bicol dialect and Visayan due primarily to the droves of migrants to the island during the sixties (Rosero, 2011). Masbatenyos speak English as a second language (ESL), but most students formally learn the English language when they start their elementary education.

With the aim of examining the nativization of English in a local variety Philippine English, this study examines the local lexical items in newspaper articles in a local daily in the province of Masbate.

1.3 Research Questions

1. How is nativization of Philippine English reflected in the lexical items in the news articles of a Masbatenyo English daily?
2. What are the uses of these local lexical items?

2 Methodology

2.1 Data

Thirty English news articles were purposively gathered from *The Stalwart Journal*, the only bilingual newspaper in the island province of Masbate in Bicol Region (Region V), the Philippines, from January to October 2015. *The Stalwart Journal* releases issues on a weekly basis with province-wide circulation. It is tabloid size (432 x 279 mm or 17 x 11 inches) and consists of eight pages.

2.2 Data Treatment

After the selection process of the 30 English news articles, the researcher perused each of them in paragraph and full-text levels in order to identify the local lexical intrusions in the English texts. For the purposes of this study, local lexical intrusions refer to local terms or vocabulary that are native or indigenous in Masbate or the Philippines and that are not part of Standard English lexicon. These local lexical terms were highlighted in the texts; then, they were encoded in the MS-Excel format together with the sentences that carry them to provide the context. Headlines or titles and dates of issue were also noted.

The identified local lexical terms were categorized into related semantic groups and were cited in the results section.

3 Results

The findings reveal that nativization of English in the Masbateño local daily occurs through code-switching from English to local language. The local lexical items that have been enmeshed and entrenched in the English language fall under the following categories:

A. people (titles, honoraries, and labels)
B. cultural events,
C. cultural groups,
D. public and private offices or organizations,
E. government programs,
F. program units,
G. government agencies,
H. places,
I. broadcast and social media,
J. transportation,
K. food,
L. animals,
M. human descriptions,
N. public services, and
O. other items.

3.1 People (Titles, honoraries, and labels). Language binds people and their social and cultural experiences. Culture-specific events and objects are usually labelled with local or native languages to reflect indigeneity. These labels or references can be in the form of titles and honorific terms, and are commonly used to show respect and to name people, events, and objects. In the Philippines, people from different regions use different titles to indicate respect to older people or even to strangers. Some of these terms include *kuya, ate, noy (nonoy), ne (nene), dong (dodong),* and *day (inday)*. The extracts below show how some of the local titles like *Barangay Captain, Barangay Kagawad* and *Sultan* are entrenched in the writing of English news articles.

(1) The report said the motorized ***banca*** named FB/CA "Marjun 2" – with length of 10.0 meters, breadth of 1.2 meters, 2.98 gross tonnage, engine make 4DR5 and serial number # 392801 – was owned by Constantino G. Sampayan, 65 and former ***Barangay Captain*** of Barangay Canomay. ("Unidentified men burn boat in Masbate," *The Stalwart Journal*, March 16-22, 2015, p. 2)

(2) During the forum, Jacel confirmed the meeting between her uncle ***Sultan*** Bantilan Esmail Kiram II and Interior Secretary Manuel Roxas II. ("Ninoy Aquino betrayed the Philippines – Sold Sabah to Malaysia for power ambition," *The Stalwart Journal*, April 13-19, 2015, p.8)

(3) He has been tagged as the "***berdugo***" (buster) of illegal activities like illegal gambling, illegal drugs, and illegal fishing. ("Bicol top cop set to head CIDG," *The Stalwart Journal*, August 17-23, 2015, p.7)

(4) He said the choice of Deona was not based on his being a *mistah*, nor his mere impression of the Bicol police chief, but on the latter's accomplishments and impressive record as a police officer. ("Bicol top cop set to head CIDG," *The Stalwart Journal*, August 17-23, 2015, p.7)

(5) The initiative is a directive from the Higher Headquarters to guarantee a crime-free summer within the Area of Responsibility (AOR) and facilitates a hassle-free travel of tourists and *Balikbayans*. ("Security plan for Rodeo Masbateño Festival set," *The Stalwart Journal*, April 6-12, 2015, p.6)

Six titles of people were noted, which include *Barangay Captain, Sultan, Barangay Kagawad, berdugo, mistah,* and *balikbayans. Barangay Captain* is the title given to the head of the barangay, *Sultan* is the title given to the head of a Muslim group, *Brgy. Kagawad* is the title given to the elected councilor who assists the Barangay Captain. Other titles found in the local newspaper are *berdugo* which refers to a man who puts criminals to death, *mistah* which refers to a military slang for 'batchmates', and *Balikbayans* which refers to Filipinos returning to the Philippines especially after having lived overseas for an extended period of time.

The six terms are considered intrusion in the local newspaper as some of these lexical terms are not flagged by italics, quotation marks or even translations, which means that they have already been entrenched into the local English language variety, while some, such as in (4) are still flagged, which could mean that they are not frequently occurring and hence their meaning is not as common as the others.

a.   Cultural Events. In 1940, Ralph Linton defined culture as the sum total of knowledge, attitudes and habitual behaviour patterns shared and transmitted by the members of a particular society. Language mediates culture and events. People in a speech community name significant events in the society, which in turn become established and celebrated regularly. The data below shows cultural events referring to religious rites that are observed and participated in by the local communities:

(6) The lead dancer of Tribu Himag-ulaw of Placer, Masbate bested 15 others to win the 2015 *Sinulog Festival* Queen title. ("Masbateña hailed as Sinulog Festival Queen 2015," *The Stalwart Journal*, January 26 – February 1, 2015, p.2)

(7) The joined meeting was purposely called to discuss in detail the Re-routing Scheme duly enacted by the Sangguniang Panglungsod, which enumerates the traffic scheme during the *Rodeo Masbateño Festival* effective April 5 – 20, 2015. ("Security plan for Rodeo Masbateño Festival set," *The Stalwart Journal*, April 6-12, 2015, p.6)

Two cultural events, *Sinulog Festival* and *Rodeo Masbateño*, were noted from the local newspaper. Though the term *festival* is an English lexicon, the terms *Sinulog* and *Rodeo Masbateño* are considered local intrusions incorporated in the text. *Sinulog* in Masbate means 'river current', while *Rodeo Masbateño* means an annual competition of bull riding in the province of Masbate. The use of these two lexical items may be attributed to the lack of English counterpart, hence, the intrusion in English sentences.

b.   Cultural Groups. Culture is shared by at least two or more people. For an idea, a thing, or a behaviour to be considered cultural, it must be shared by some type of social group or society (Ferraro 1998: 16). The present study identified cultural groups specifically referring to small groups of people who are natives of their indigenous communities and who act as representatives of these communities in national events. Extracts (9) and (10) illustrate these local lexical items.

(9) According to a Sun Star Cebu report, Delara told reporters that they were walking alongside the two Masbate contingents, *Kulturang Placereño* and *Tribu Himag-ulaw*, while they were headed from the grandstand. ("SWAT cop aims M-16 rifle at Gov. Dayan's son in Cebu," *The Stalwart Journal,* January 26 – February 1, 2015, p. 3)

Other occurrences of lexical intrusions are evident in cultural groups like *Kulturang Placereño* and *Tribu Himag-ulaw, Tribu Katbalugan. Kultura* is the Filipino term for 'culture', while *Placereño* is an adjective from of the town of Placer in Masbate. On the other hand, *tribu* is the Filipino term for 'tribe'. In the excerpts presented, *tribu* is used twice to introduce two proper names, *Himag-ulaw* and *Katbalugan. Himag-ulaw* is a tribe's name which means 'a ritual for a good harvest', while *Katbalugan* is derived from the name of the place Catbalogan.

c. Public and Private Offices/Organizations. Another common local lexical intrusion in English news articles is the use of native terminology to name public and private offices or organizations, which usually reflect their nature, advocacy, and functions. These local linguistic penetrations usually appear as sole local terms such as in (15) or co-occur with English words, as in (11), (12), (13), and (14):

(10) Likewise impleaded as co-accused are officers/representatives of the implementing agencies: technology Resource Center Director General Antonio Ortiz, Deputy Director General Dennis Cunanan and others;…and a number of officers/representatives of non-government organizations (NGOs), namely: the Countrywide Agri and Rural Economic and Development Foundation, ***Masaganang Ani para sa Magsasaka Foundation, Inc*….** ("Ombudsman junks Governor Lanete's appeal," *The Stalwart Journal*, January 19-25, 2015, p.2)

(11) Padua was head of the group which recently conducted the 3rd Joint WB-Asian Development Bank – Australian Department of Foreign Affairs and Trade (DFAT) Implementation Support Mission which looked into the enhancement of the ***Kapit-Bisig Laban sa Kahirapan-Comprehensive and Integrated Delivery of Social Services (Kalahi-CIDSS)*** in the region. ("Support mission assesses impacts of Kalahi Program in Bicol," *The Stalwart Journal*, April 20-26, 2015, p.7)

(12) Police records showed Ogad has a pending murder case at the Regional Trial Court Branch 53 in Sorsogon City for the killing of peasant leader Willy Jeruz of the ***Samahang Magsasaka ng Sorsogon***, an affiliate of ***Kilusang Magbubukid ng Pilipinas***, in April 2007. ("Soldier eyed in Masbate mining town massacre," *The Stalwart Journal*, May 4-10, 2015, p.2)

d. Government Programs. With purposes for social services and accommodation, government programs are commonly linguistically realized in local languages or are presented in conjunction with the English language.

(13) Said agency is now preparing to conduct its second round of household assessment under the ***Listahanan Program***, previously known as the National Household Targeting System for Poverty Reduction (NHTS-PR). ("DSWD Bicol to hire 3,450 field workers," *The Stalwart Journal*, February 2-8, 2015, p.2)

(14) Another livelihood project to be funded by BUB is ***"Nutri-bun ni Juan",*** a school-based bakery at Aroroy, West Elementary School. ("BUB funds livelihood project in Aroroy, Masbate," *The Stalwart Journal*, July 13-19, 2015, p.2)

The choice of localized lexical items for government programs is common. When included in English news articles, they are not translated or flagged with italics or quotation marks.

e. Government Units. This category is the most extensively used in the data. Local terms such as *purok, sitio,* and *barangay* have been observed to be present in many local news reports. These lexical items are not flagged and co-occur with English words in the texts. Some examples of their uses in the data are shown below.

(15) Rapsing, 39, was beheaded by still unknown men in an ambush at the National Road in ***Purok*** 2, ***Barangay*** Usab, Masbate City around 12:10 p.m. Saturday. ("Severed head found in Camarines Sur matches description of ambush victim," *The Stalwart Journal*, April 27-May 3, 2015, p.2)

(16) F/B Purification Martha – II skippered by: …3. Eduardo Yanong y Lape, 40 y/o, married, a resident of **Sitio** Maiton, Old Escalante, Negros Occidental;… ("24 fishermen arrested for illegal fishing in Placer, Masbate," *The Stalwart Journal*, June 8-14, 2015, p.2)

f. **Government Agencies.** Another common category reflective of local political culture or origin is the names of local government agencies, which include *Sangguniang Panglungsod* or City Council, *Sangguniang Panlalawigan* or Provincial Council, and *Sandiganbayan.* Some of these lexical items have English translations but it is now very common to see them in their local versions in both local and national English newspapers. The extracts below illustrate their uses in the data:

(17) The joined meeting was purposely called to discuss in detail the Re-routing Scheme duly enacted by the **Sangguniang Panglungsod**, which enumerates the traffic scheme during the Rodeo Masbateño Festival effective April 5 – 20, 2015. ("Security plan for Rodeo Masbateño Festival set," *The Stalwart Journal*, April 6-12, 2015, p.6)

g. **Places.** Names of places are referred to by the use of their native terminology such as shown in the extracts below.

(18) Lanete is currently detained at the Bureau of Jail Management and Penology (BJMP) Female Dormitory in **Camp Bagong Diwa** in Taguig City. ("Lanete asks court to allow her to post bail on 'pork'," *The Stalwart Journal*, March 16-22, 2015, p.2)

(19) He said his office has been coordinating with Bicol chief executives for the creation and reorganization of PMRB, including the establishment of **Minahang Bayan** in each province to end illegal small-scale mining operations. ("DENR intensifies information, education campaign on geohazard, responsible mining in Bicol," *The Stalwart Journal*, September 7-13, 2015, p.8)

In the local context, names of places are usually not placed within quotation marks and are not italicized, suggesting that they have already been adopted as part of Philippine English.

h. **Broadcast and Social Media.** The present data has also revealed local lexical instrusions in the broadcast and social media, which are rich environments for public discourse and information sharing. Below are some examples.

(20) **"Tarabil sa Masbate"** (Masbate Talks) facebook posted these reactions:…More reactions came in more than a week from Masbateños working abroad whose sardonic and statements of disgusts were downloaded but not printed on this paper. ("Masbate Board Members get flak from netizens," *The Stalwart Journal,*, March 23-29, 2015, p. 2)

Some lexical items such as in (28) are still flagged with quotation marks and presented with translations. However, this author believes that it is only a matter of time. As soon as the terminology has been fully exposed to the members of the virtual communities and they begin using it as part of their daily communication, these terms will soon be unflagged, which means that they have already been adopted as part of the local English variety.

3.6 **Transportation.** Reflecting local modes of movement and transport, local terms such as *habal-habal* and *banca/bangka* or *baruto* are used as flagged or unflagged in the English news articles. Examples are shown below.

(21) Earlier, Banua issued a press statement accusing the military of deliberately killing the alleged NPA members who she said were actually drivers of motorcycle-for-hire or **"habal-habal"** in Cawayan town, Masbate. ("Bloody encounter in Masbate: AFP debunks NDF massacre claim," *The Stalwart Journal*, August 17-23, 2015, p. 2)

(22) With eagle-eyes, our boat spotter observes a massive silhouette approaching our **banca.** ("The giants are back: Whale sharks again congregate in Donsol waters," *The Stalwart Journal*, June 29 – July 5, 2015, p. 3)

The term *habal-habal* in (30) is placed with quotation marks, in some news articles with English translation in parenthetical enclosures, and unflagged in others. This suggests that though belonging to the same newspaper company, some writers have different treatment with the local lexical items, with others seeing them as old terms mixed with a foreign language and others using them as if they were already of part of such language.

3.7   Food. Similar to transportation, food reflects ethnic or local tastes and flavours. Native terminologies are used to refer to names of local dishes, foods, fruits and vegetables, as shown in the extracts below.

(23) According to Nida Bagayusa, the livelihood worker of the Local Social Welfare and Development Office, the ₱860,000 has funded various livelihood project benefiting 105 Pantawid Pamilya beneficiaries of 35 recipients from the three barangays namely: ***Matalang talang with torones de mani*** and banana chips as their project, ***fish kropek***, for Barangay San Agustin and production of native bags and fan for barangays Malubi. ("BUB funds livelihood project in Aroroy, Masbate," *The Stalwart Journal*, July 13-19, 2015, p.2)

(24) The drive also netted 7 fishing vessels, 6 fishing boats, 1,339.5 kilos of assorted fish, 6 boxes of dynamited fish locally known as ***"tuloy"***, two bottles of explosive (dynamites), 5 bottles of ammonium nitrate with two blasting caps and other fishing paraphernalia were confiscated for the period covered. (Masbate police boasts success in anti-illegal fishing drive," *The Stalwart Journal*, August 10-16, 2015, p.2)

3.8   Animals. Animal names are also commonly expressed in local terminology to suggest that these are endemic in some areas. As has been observed also in the category of transportation, some of the terms referring to animals such as *butanding* are sometimes flagged with quotation marks and sometimes unflagged. Again, this author believes that it is an indication of transitory phase of the nativization process of the local lexis into the English language, where some writers have fully adopted them, while the others are gradually embracing them as part of their linguistic repertoire in writing English texts. This author also believes that it could be the journalist's communicative strategy to accommodate a wider audience particularly the foreign ones who cannot decipher the meanings of local terms.

(25) A town whose booming economy was fuelled by the ***butanding***, Donsol has risen from a fifth-class municipality since a community-based whale shark ecotourism program was established in 1998. ("The giants are back: Whale sharks again congregate in Donsol waters," *The Stalwart Journal*, June 29 – July 5, 2015, p. 3)

3.9   Human   Descriptions. Though less extensively used in the English news articles, physical descriptions referring to humans are also observed to have penetrated the English texts, as in the example below.

(26) "The head has the same ***"semi-kalbo"*** (semi-bald) haircut and an earring on the left ear, like Rapsing," Trilles said. ("Severed head found in Camarines Sur matches description of ambush victim," *The Stalwart Journal*, April 27-May 3, 2015, p.2)

Descriptions such as the one shown above are flagged with quotation marks and translations to indicate that they are in the process of nativization. Soon, when the members of the speech community begin to familiarize with their uses in the English texts, they will be unflagged and become part of the local English variety.

3.10   Public Services. Another category that has been observed to be penetrated by local lexical items are terms referring to services offered to the public. These local terms usually co-exist or co-occur with the English terms when they are presented in the text. They are not usually flagged, which suggests that they have already been entrenched into the local variety of English.

(27) Police reports said that the raid yielded three plastic sachets of suspected shabu, six unsealed plastic sachets with shabu residue, eleven strips of aluminium foils, improvised burner, pair of scissors, eight disposable lighters and sixteen receipts of **Palawan Express Pera Padala** – which maybe evidence of the illegal drug transactions. ("Masbate PNP scores anew on anti-illegal drugs campaign," *The Stalwart Journal*, June 22-28, 2015, p.2)

(28) The Department urges all those who will receive this text message not to respond, instead, immediately report to the nearest DSWD office or text to the **Pantawid Pamilya Grievance Text Hotline** 0918-912-2813. ("The DSWD Field Office V warns the public against text scam using Pantawid Pamilya," *The Stalwart Journal*, September 7-13, 2015, p.4)

3.11   Other Items. Finally, there are also observable occurrences of other local items in the data pertaining to drugs, promos, and other cultural items. The use of these lexis in the English news articles are usually unflagged, which means that the readers have become fully aware of them and have accepted them as part of the Philippine English variety.

(29) **Piccolo** is still the leading cause of injuries with 62 cases followed by **kwitis**, 5-star and other firecrackers including **bombshell, bawang** and **watusi**. ("DOH posts decrease in firecracker injuries in Bicol," *The Stalwart Journal*, January 12-18, 2015, p.2)

(30) The text message is sent by certain Hydee Gomez. It states "Congrats, from President Noy Noy Aquino Foundation. 4Ps Pantawid Pamilyang Pilipino Program. Your sim # won ₱950,000.00 2ⁿᵈ prize winner, **handog pangkabuhayan raffle promo**! DTI P#9513, S'15, pls. text complete NAME/ADDRESS/OCCUPATION." ("The DSWD Field Office V warns the public against text scam using Pantawid Pamilya," *The Stalwart Journal*, September 7-13, 2015, p.4)

4 CONCLUSION

The findings in this study reveal that nativization of English in the Philippines particularly in its provincial level is evident in the news articles of a local bilingual newspaper as it has already penetrated the domain of print media. Consistent with Edgar Schneider's (2003) notion of 'nativization', which he considers as the most vibrant phase of his five-stage *Dynamic Model of the Evolution of New Englishes*, the local lexical terms in the present study are seen to have been entrenched in the news articles in different categories such as people's titles and labels, government programs, government units, cultural events, cultural groups, transportation, food, broadcast and social media, inter alia. The presence of these lexical items in news articles are observed to have been flagged and unflagged with italicization, quotation marks, and parentheses. The former suggests that these local terms have already been entrenched in the English texts, while the latter points to a nativization process, which, following David and Dumanig's (2008) idea, has to take some time before they also become indigenized. This nativization or indigenization process through code-switching from English to a local language, Filipino or Tagalog, may be attributed to lack of English counterparts of the local terms, and may suggest that English has been Philippinized.

B. Kachru (2011) sees this dimension as a 'creation of a new culture', while Soyinka (1998: 88 in B. Kachru, 2010) refers to this as a 'new medium of communication'. Patel (2006 in David & Dumanig, 2008) calls this phenomenon one of the various 'reincarnations' of English, where people share the medium but use it to express native and local messages. The widespread linguistic assimilation, accommodation, and appropriation of the English language to suit local tastes and contexts have resulted in local lexical intrusions, which gives rise to the Asianization and Philippinization of the English language. Hence, it is evident that the colonization process has come full circle; however, in the process, the colonized have managed to talk back to the colonizer using the same medium but with local linguistic imprints according to the tastes of the local tongues.

Yoneoka (2002 in David & Dumanig, 2008) expresses it in a stronger view: "the colonized have subjugated the English language, beaten it on its head and made it theirs, and in adapting it to their use, in hammering it sometimes on its head and sometimes twisting its tail, they have given it a new shape, substance, and dimension" (p.98). It resonates what Chinua Achebe (1965) argues that 'the price a world language must be prepared to pay is submission to many different kinds of use…' Indeed, the global widespread of English is unstoppable, unavoidable, and unthinkable. English worldwide diaspora afforded it the undisputed crown of being the global language or world's lingua franca; it has also given birth to other varieties or World Englishes. The *English effect*, *English fever*, and *English invasion* may continue to linger and forever change the world's linguistic landscape, but in the eyes, hearts, and minds of the local speakers, they have already conquered English and made it their own.

References

Achebe, C. (1965). English and the African writer. *Transition* 4(18): 27-30.

Crystal, D. (2003a). *English as a Global Language*, 2nd edition, Cambridge: Cambridge University Press.

David, M.K. (2001). *The Sindhis of Malaysia: A sociolinguistic account*. London: Asean.

David, M.K. & Dumanig, F.P. (2008). Nativization of English in Malaysia and the Philippines as Seen in English Dailies. *Philippine Journal of Linguistics* *39*(1).

Jenkins, J. (2009). *World Englishes*. London: Routledge.

Kachru, B.B. (1997). 'World Englishes: resources for research and teaching' in L. Smith and M. Forman (eds) (1997).

Kachru, B.B. (2011). Asian Englishes beyond the Canon. Hong Kong: Hong Kong University Press.

Kow, Y. C. K. (2003). Code-switching for a purpose. Focus on pre-school Malaysian children. *Multilingua*, 22, 59-77.

Schneider, E. (2003). The dynamics of new Englishes: From identity construction to dialect birth. *Language*, 79(2), 233-81.

Appendices

Categories	Local Lexical Items
Public and Private Offices/ Organizations	• Butanding Interaction Office (BIO) • Kapit-Bisig Laban sa Kahirapan - Comprehensive and Integrated Delivery of Social Services (KALAHI-CIDSS) • Kilusang Magbubukid ng Pilipinas • Lingkod Banahaw MPC • Lukban Langgonisa Manufacturers (LUKLAMA) • Masaganang Ani Para sa Magsasaka Foundation, Inc. • Pag-ibig payments • Samahang Magsasaka ng Sorsogon • Sinulog Foundation Inc.
Government Programs	• Gawad KALASAG • "LIGTAS SUMVAC 2015" • Listahanan Program • OPLAN LIGTAS PASUKAN 2014 • Pantawid Pamilya • Pantawid Pamilyang Pilipino Program • Seal of Good Local Governance (SGLG) or Pagkilala sa Katapatan at • Kahusayan ng Pamahalaang Lokal
Titles and Lables	• Balikbayans • Barangay Captain • "berdugo" (buster) • Brgy Kagawad • mistah • Sultan
Government units	• barangay • purok • sitio
Government agencies	• Sangguniang Panglungsod • Sanggunian Panlalawigan • Sandiganbayan
Places	• Camp Bagong Diwa • Minahang Bayan
Cultural events	• Sinulog Festival • Rodeo Masbateno Festival
Transportation	• banca

	• "habal-habal"
Broadcast and Social Media	• Barkadahan Radio Program • "Tarabil sa Masbate" (Masbate Talks)
Cultural groups	• Kulturang Placereño • Tribu Himag-ulaw • Tribu Katbalaugan
Human description	• 'semi-kalbo' (semi-bald)
Food	• fisk kropek • 'Lukban Langgonisa' • malunggay noodle • matalang-talang with torones de mani • "tuloy" • "Nutri-bun ni Juan"
Animals	• butanding,
Public Services	• Palawan Express Pera Padala • Pantawid Pamilya Grievance Text Hotline
Other items	• bawang • kwitis • pla-pla • piccolo • shabu • "shabu" • watusi • handog pangkabuhayan raffle promo

Facebook Integration into University Classes:
Opportunities and Challenges

Romualdo A. Mabuan
Lyceum of the Philippines University
Intramuros, Manila, Philippines 1002
romualdo.mabuan@lpu.edu.ph

Gregorio P. Ebron, Jr.
Lyceum of the Philippines University
Intramuros, Manila, Philippines 1002
gregorio.ebronJr@lpu.edu.ph

Abstract

Following the principles of the TPACK Framework (Koehler & Mishra, 2009) and Blended Learning Framework (Horn & Staker, 2014), this study reports findings of integrating Facebook, a Social Networking Site (SNS), in facilitating English language classes at a private university in Manila, Philippines. It aimed to explore students' attitudes towards the use of a 'closed' class Facebook group in the English language classroom and to describe how they utilize it as part of their English language learning. Research participants were sophomore students enrolled at an English writing class in the first semester of the academic year 2016 – 2017. Research data come from surveys, students' wall posts, students' reflections, and individual and focus group interviews suggest that despite some technological limitations, students view and respond positively to the use of Facebook as an alternative platform for English language learning and as an innovative and strategic tool in enhancing lesson delivery, engaging students with the material, and creating a discourse space for self-expression. Pedagogical implications for ESL (English as a second language) and EFL (English as a foreign language) and researchers are offered in the light of these results.

1 Introduction

The influx of Information and Communications Technology (ICT) has revolutionized the teaching of English to ESL/EFL learners (Cequena, 2013). If students before were used to in-class traditional English language learning delivered within the walls of the classroom, today, the scenario has dramatically changed with the rise of modern technology. 21st century students now carry portable and handheld electronic and smart gadgets such as laptop, tablet, phablet, netbook, iPad, phone, and other devices and use them every day when doing their school and personal tasks. This '24/7/365 fingertip access' to information allows students to navigate the information superhighway, stay updated and connect interpersonally in virtual spaces with anyone, anytime, and anywhere. This trend extends to the academic world; in fact, in the last decade, research has shown how the World Wide Web or the Internet and other communication technologies have supported meaningful educational experiences (Belz & Kinginger, 2002, 2003; Garrison & Anderon, 2003; Sykes, 2005; Arnold & Ducate, 2006; O'Bryan & Hegelmeier, 2007; Lord, 2008; among others) to students deemed Digital Natives (Prensky, 2001, 2006).

These technological innovations are continually reshaping, redefining, and revolutionizing the phases and pathways of educational landscapes across the many parts of the globe. Hence, with this technological advancement dominating and permeating globally, it is imperative that the teaching of English, especially among English as second language (ESL) students, must be interactive, responsive, and relevant to make language learning more challenging and meaningful to the learners. The World Wide Web or the Internet's features of interactivity, connectivity and ubiquity make it a good platform for an alternative classroom engagement to trigger some 21st century skills namely critical thinking and problem solving, collaboration and communication, global awareness, and information literacy (Dohn, 2009). Today, educators can utilize social networking sites (SNS) such as Facebook, Twitter, YouTube, Instagram, Pinterest, Google Hangout, Blogger, and Tumblr as platforms for enhancing students' English language skills.

31st Pacific Asia Conference on Language, Information and Computation (PACLIC 31), pages 265–273
Cebu City, Philippines, November 16-18, 2017

Among these sites, Facebook is the most widely used domain by students for their virtual social activities.

Facebook is a SNS that boasts more than 1 billion monthly active users, and it is one of the fastest-growing and best-known sites on the Internet today ("Most famous social network sites," 2016). Established by Mark Zuckerberg in 2004, Facebook is a powerful learning tool that is not only built off of synchronous and asynchronous technologies that has transformed learning but also extended the reach of communicative tools (Blattner & Fiori, 2009). Facebook has a variety of interactive features that students can use. Students can create their own profiles, upload photos and videos, post on their wall posts, share information, join in groups as online communities, among others. Selwyn (2007) stated that Facebook has quickly become the social network site of choice by college students and an integral part of the "behind the scenes" college experience. Thompson (2007) added that the adoption rates of Facebook in universities and colleges are remarkable, i.e., 85% of college students that have a college network within Facebook have adopted it. Furthermore, Pempek (2009) reveals that Facebook enables teachers to provide constructive educational outcomes in a variety of fields. Hew (2011) furthered that Facebook allows teachers to practice a differential pedagogy, in the best interests of the students.

Several studies have already explored the pedagogical benefits of integrating Facebook in a language classroom (Selwyn, 2007; Stewart, 2008; Madge et al., 2009; Schroeder & Greenbowe, 2009; Yunus & Salehi, 2012; Shih, 2013; Yu, 2014; Ghani, 2015; Miron & Ravid, 2015; Low & Warawudhi, 2016). These studies have established the pedagogical potentials, benefits and implications of integrating a SNS, particularly Facebook, in the classroom. This study aims to contribute to these ongoing dialogs and explorations, to contextualize the use of Facebook in the Philippine ESL (English as a second language) classroom, and to respond to Prensky's (2006) challenge: "it's time for education leaders to raise their heads above the daily grind and observe the new language that's emerging." Following the tenets of the TPACK Framework (Koehler & Mishra, 2009), which urges the researchers to consider the complex interplay of the three primary forms of knowledge: Content (C), Pedagogy (P), and Technology (T) and their intersections in the language classroom context, the researchers drew implications from these intersections: PCK or Pedagogical Content Knowledge, which refers to the knowledge of pedagogy that is applicable to the teaching of specific content that a teacher intends to teach; TCK or Technological Content Knowledge, which refers to the knowledge of the relationship between technology and content; TPK or Technological Pedagogical Knowledge, which refers to the components and capabilities of various technologies as they used in teaching and learning; and finally the TPACK or Technological Pedagogical Content Knowledge, which is the intersection of the three components characteristic of true technology integration in the classroom. Furthermore, the study is anchored on Horn and Staker's (2014) Blended Learning Framework, employing one of the four models – the Flex Learning Model, which integrates technology into a regular face-to-face or in-class setup.

1.1 Research Questions

The main purpose of this study was to determine the pedagogical viability of integrating 'closed' Facebook groups in the ESL classroom. Specifically, the study attempted to answer the following questions: (1) How often do students access the class' Facebook groups, and what features of Facebook groups do they use during their access? (2) What are the students' attitudes towards Facebook as a learning tool in the English language classroom? And (3) What are the advantages and challenges in using Facebook groups in the English language classroom as perceived by the students?

2 Method
2.1 Participants

The study was conducted during the first semester of the academic year 2016 – 2017 which lasted approximately five months. The participants were 100 sophomore undergraduate students in a Writing in the Discipline class at the Lyceum of the Philippines University, Manila, Philippines. These students were majoring in Bachelor of Arts in Multimedia Arts. Their English levels range from Intermediate to Upper Intermediate based on their TOEIC scores in Listening and Reading

Tests. The researchers created Facebook groups for classes, and students were required to be members of those groups. The Facebook group name was given to the class, and they joined the group individually. The researchers acted as the group administrators and approved students' requests to join. As a classroom extension, the students were required to participate actively in the online activities such as responding to polls related to the lessons, posting responses to prompts, commenting on the teachers' and classmates' posts, replying to comments, tagging classmates to reply to posts, uploading and downloading files, among others. Group chat feature was also used to establish connection among members of the group. Occasionally, students sent PMs or private messages to ask questions or clarify something. All this was done to encourage students to practice what they have learned in the class and to solve the so-called 'three-hour problem' of learning English weekly.

2.2 Instruments and Data Analysis

The researchers utilized surveys, students' reflections, wall posts, individual interviews, and focus group discussions to gather data from the respondents. Before and after using the class Facebook groups, the students responded to two surveys via Survey Monkey (www.surveymonkey.org). The pre-FB-group survey aimed at exploring students' background and experience on using the features of Facebook and Facebook groups and their demographic profiles, while the post-FB-group survey explored the respondents' experiences and perceptions about using the group in the class. Individually, students were also asked to submit their reflections about how the class Facebook group affected their English language learning in the class. Students' wall posts were also analyzed to identify students' activities and participation in online discussions. Finally, the researchers posted an invitation for individual and group interviews on the FB groups' walls, and 15 students agreed to be interviewed at the college office during their free time.

2.3 Data Analysis

For the analysis of the demographic data, frequency and percentages were used. As for the open-ended survey questions and interviews, students' views were codified and categorized as emerging domain themes and analyzed accordingly. Students' reflections and Facebook wall posts were analyzed and used to give meaning and support to the other data.

3 Results
3.1 Frequency of Facebook group access

Table 1: Frequency of students' access to Facebook groups

	f	%
Whenever I get Facebook notifications	51	51
Every day, even if I don't get Facebook notifications	44	44
The day before the next English class	3	3
Every week	2	2
Not at all	0	0

One-hundred students participated in the study for a period of one semester or five weeks. Table 1 shows the frequency of students' access to the class' Facebook group. Majority of the students (51%) indicated that they accessed the group every time they were alerted by the notification feature of Facebook; others (44%) reported that they visited the group automatically even without notification alerts in order to check if there were class announcements. A small percentage stated they accessed the group a day before the English class schedule (3%) and every week (2%). Having mobile gadgets such as cellular phones and tablets, free campus Wi-Fi connection, and free data connection from telecommunication networks allowed students to stay online most of the time and get connected and updated with the online group. This happened despite some concerns on poor Internet connection in the campus or at home and lack of Internet-ready gadgets among some students. Others reported that they were willing to access the class' Facebook group regularly but could not to do so due to high volume of school tasks.

3.2 Facebook group activities of students

Facebook as the world's largest SNS has a wide array of features that allow its users to perform online activities using their electronic devices.

When students were asked to list the different activities that they performed whenever they accessed the group, they reported a total of 711 responses. Of these answers, 12.9% indicated that they visited the group primarily to see if there were announcements from the teacher such as a lecture file to be downloaded, a weblink to be accessed, a task to be completed, or a project to be submitted. Others stated that they accessed the group to like their teacher's and classmates' posts (12.2%), which is also a means to see for updates and to scan or skim some wall posts. These first two activities can be categorized as passive activities by the students because they do not necessarily have to perform something. This also includes seeing posts (10.7%), which also another way of checking information. In contrast, the other reported activities can be categorized as active activities because students have to do something to fulfil or accomplish certain tasks. These include the following: commenting on posts (9.3%), submitting tasks (9.3%), replying to posts or comments (7.6%), tagging teacher or classmates (5.8%), replying to teacher or classmates' comments (4.8%), posting ideas or photos (4.5%), sharing links, photos or videos (4.5%), chatting with classmates 4.4%), starting a discussion (2.7%), and chatting with the teacher (0.7%).

Table 2: Student activities while using class' Facebook group

	f	%
Check announcements from the teacher	92	12.9
Like posts	87	12.2
Comment on my classmates' posts	76	10.7
See posts	76	10.7
Comment on my teacher's posts	66	9.3
Submit assignments or tasks	66	9.3
Reply to my classmates' comments	54	7.6
Tag my teacher or classmates	41	5.8
Reply to my teacher or classmates' comments	34	4.8
Post random thoughts and/or photos	32	4.5
Share some links, photos, or posts	32	4.5
Chat with my classmates	31	4.4
Start a discussion	19	2.7
Chat with my teacher	5	0.7
Total	711	100

Facebook group's homepage contains the group's name, cover photo, share button, notifications section, and other features for adding people, sending message, managing group, editing group settings, removing the group from favorite list, and creating a new group.

Figure 1: A screenshot of a class' Facebook group

Figure 1 is a screenshot of one of the Facebook groups, which shows the interface of the group. On the left side are the links for newsfeed, events, favorites, groups, pages, apps, friends, interests, events, and payments. On the right side are the functions to add members to the group, description of the group, tags, group chats, recent group photos, and suggested groups. In the center is the main activity area for all of the group's members. Here, any member can access the discussion, members list, events, photos, and files. Below, the member can write a post, add a photo or video, and create a poll. The 'more' button allows the member to sell something, add a file, create a photo album, create a document, and create an event. Other features allow members to do the active and passive activities mentioned above. The area where members can write is called 'wall' and the written idea or uploaded photo or video is called a 'post'. Posting an idea can be more specific as the wall allows the member to add photos or a video to the post, tag people in the post, add what the member is doing or feeling, and indicate the member's location. Once the idea is successfully posted, other members can use any of the three buttons under the post: like, comment, or share. Facebook also indicates how many people have 'seen' the post. Other options with the post also allow any member to save the link, turn off notifications for a particular post, turn off commenting, pin or unpin post, refresh shared attachment, delete post, or start group chat. On top of that, any member can chat privately with any member or send a private message to others.

Table 3 illustrates Facebook features that the students commonly used whenever they accessed the group. Of the 474 responses, 329 or 69.41% can be categorized as active activities performed by the students. These include the following: commenting (18.8%), posting (12.9%), replying (11.8%), downloading (6.8%), uploading (4.6%), tagging (4.2%), sharing (3.8%), chatting 3.5%), and editing (3%). Meanwhile, 145 responses or 30.6% can be categorized as passive activities when they accessed the group (liking posts, 20.5%; seeing posts, 10.1%).

Table 3: Facebook group features used by the students

	f	%
Like	97	20.5
Comment	89	18.8
Post	61	12.9
Reply	56	11.8
See	48	10.1
Download	32	6.8
Upload	22	4.6
Tag	20	4.2
Share	18	3.8
Chat	17	3.5
Edit	14	3.0
Total	474	100

This data reveals how students utilize the available Facebook group features in performing online tasks and activities as part of their English language learning beyond the regular class hours outside the classroom. It further shows that students use these functions to accomplish both active and passive tasks – they complement one another for successfully carrying out activities virtually with or without teacher or peer assistance.

3.3 Learner-perceived benefits of class Facebook groups

Students' reflections as well as the results of the survey, individual, and group interviews revealed that all of them "liked" the idea of having a Facebook group for the class as a virtual classroom extension outside the campus. When asked about the benefits of using Facebook groups in the class, reasons why they liked it, and what challenges

they encountered in using it, students reported a variety of responses, as shown in Table 4 below.

Table 4: Students perceived benefits of using class' Facebook group

	f	%
Facilitates easy and fast information dissemination, class updates	61	36.3
Facilitates online communication and interaction with my teacher and my classmates	36	21.4
Promotes academic sharing and collaboration	16	9.5
Reinforces learning and enhances class participation	15	8.9
Helps develop English communication skills	14	8.3
Serves as classroom extension	13	7.7
Is easy to access	10	5.9
Facilitates file sharing	3	1.8
Total	168	100

Of the 168 responses, 36.3% (61 responses) indicated that Facebook groups facilitate easy, convenient and quick information dissemination among students. By accessing the group anywhere via Internet-ready electronic devices, students can get notifications and updates about the class seamlessly, without having to meet physically with the teacher. Thirty-six (21.4%) responses showed that Facebook groups act as an online platform to facilitate teacher-student and student-student interactions. Fifteen responses (9.5%) suggested that Facebook groups can promote sharing and collaboration among students. By using features like sharing, tagging, posting, commenting, replying, and chatting, teachers and students can easily establish online dialogs, forums, brainstorming sessions, and discussions about various topics and accomplish tasks by communicating with one another. Fifteen responses (8.9%) pointed out that Facebook groups can increase class participation and reinforce learning through continuous engagement among members. For instance, after class dismissal, the teacher may create a poll about the previously discussed concept in the class and invite students to respond to the question on their free time. This method engages the students to reflect on the lesson, provides opportunity to passive students in the class to participate, and extends the discussion for further understanding of ideas. Other feedback indicated that Facebook groups can develop the communication skills of the students (8.3%, 14 responses) particularly writing skills because students are given opportunities to post their ideas on the 'wall', respond to polls, engage in discussions via comment threads, and comment on posts. Depending on the guidelines agreed upon by the class, the teacher can ask the students to avoid posting or commenting using slang expressions or colloquialisms to help them develop formal writing skills. Some students also reported that Facebook groups serve as a good classroom extension beyond the physical classroom (7.7%, 13 responses), as an accessible platform for learning anytime anywhere (5.9%, 10 responses), and as a quick channel for file transfer and sharing (1.8%, 3 responses).

3.4 Challenges in using class' Facebook group

Table 5: Challenges encountered by the students in using class' Facebook group

	f	%
Weak internet connection	28	50
Difficulty in accessing Facebook, consumes extra time	15	26.8
No internet access at home	13	23.2
Total	56	100

As with any other educational undertaking, integrating class Facebook groups in the traditional English language classroom also comes with challenges and limitations. When students were asked what challenges they encountered while using the groups for the entire semester, they reported varied answers. Of the 56 responses, 50% complained about weak internet connection in the campus or at home. This was addressed by the university's continued efforts to increase the Wi-Fi connection inside the school premises and by encouraging students to use the university's e-library. Fifteen responses (26.7%) echoed a similar concern on difficulty accessing Facebook while logging in, downloading and uploading files, which could also be attributed to weak internet access. Thirteen responses (23.2%) reported that they did not have any internet connection at home; thus, they could not participate actively in the online discussions or comply promptly with the online tasks or assignments. Some students shared that they had to go out of their house and go to a computer shop just to do the online tasks, which required them to spend extra money and extra time.

4 Discussion

This study explored the educational value of integrating Facebook groups into the English language classroom by identifying how students used this media in performing classroom tasks online, how they viewed its relevance and usefulness to their English language learning, and what challenges they encountered in using it. Consistent with the findings of Low & Warawudhi (2016), this study revealed the pedagogical potential of using Facebook groups in managing large classes and in providing enhanced engagement among teachers and students beyond the physical classroom via virtual spaces. Because of its ubiquity and popularity among the learners, Facebook acts as an online rendezvous for the teachers and students; and since everybody is using Facebook, it is easy for the teacher to create an online community and ask the students to join and become members. Hence, the findings illustrate that Facebook groups can serve as a class management system that allows the teachers to create an exclusive virtual space, design it like an online meeting room, and use it as an extension of the physical classroom. Facebook groups act as a point of convergence where teachers and students connect with one another at any time and place with the power of the Internet.

The results of this study also corroborated with that of Shih's (2013) – integrating Facebook using a blended learning model such as the flex model based on Horn and Staker (2014), which combines face-to-face or in-class instruction with off-line or out-of-class interaction can help increase students' interest and motivation in the lesson and assist them in doing their classroom tasks. Because the teacher can upload learning materials as review tools, post useful websites for enhanced input, and communicate with students for consultation, the learners feel connected and engaged with the happenings of the class; thus, continuity of learning may occur. Various Facebook features such as 'post', 'upload', 'download', 'comment', 'reply', 'share', and 'chat' affords the teacher and the students to access and shares files quickly and easily.

Consistent with Miron and Ravid (2015), this study found that the use of Facebook groups for educational purposes is favored by the students because they appreciate the idea of using a social tool as a means for learning, where they can freely share their opinions and apply the lesson concepts learned in the classroom. This also resonates what Yu (2014) found in the context of university level learning in Taiwan where she also utilized Facebook groups to facilitate students' participation from in-class to online class discussion. Selwyn (2007) emphasized that this active participation and collaboration among students on Facebook reflects a good model of learning.

Although Madge et al. (2009) argued that the use of Facebook is solely for social purposes and sometimes for informal learning, we believe that careful teacher design can capitalize on the 'social power' of Facebook, and educators can tap its features to provide an educational dimension that can co-occur with its social function. Selwyn (2009) may view this as intruding students' social spheres in order to use Facebook for educationally 'appropriate' or 'valid' purposes, yet we cannot discredit its pedagogical potential as the participants in this study claimed to be helpful and useful in their learning process. Other concerns remain to be addressed pertaining to the availability of infrastructures, readiness and willingness of teachers to innovate their pedagogies, capability of the students to participate, flexibility of the curriculum, and appropriacy to the learning context.

While some educators and practitioners may be skeptical on the pedagogical viability of integrating SNSs such as Facebook into the language classroom, we believe that it can be one of the feasible and practical means to engage our modern learners – the 'digital natives' of the Generation Z – and address their changing needs and nature, and connect with their dynamic, fast-paced, and mobile lifestyle. As Mishra and Koehler (2009) recommended: teachers need to go beyond the "functional fixedness" of technology, and instead need to creatively repurpose it to make it pedagogically viable.

4.1 Pedagogical Implications

Ubiquity, mobility, and accessibility have become the buzz words of the 21st century. Social media such as networking sites (SNSs) are now part of the lifestyle of today's learners who are techno-savvy and adept at maneuvering networked systems. A decade ago, technology integration into the classroom was considered only as an option; now, it has become a significant part of the curriculum. Technology can now be utilized to "substitute, augment, modify, and redefine" (Puentedura, 2014) classroom practices to "enhance and transform" students' learning experience. The changing nature and needs of the 21st century learner implicates a reconfiguration in our pedagogical practices if we are to stay relevant, responsive and meaningful in this modern age.

5 Conclusion

The findings of this study must be set against its own limitations – the area of inquiry focused only on the class Facebook group, which is only one of the communication mechanisms available to the students to explore and utilize while they one online. The data showed the concurrent use of other Facebook features among the participants, with students referring to private messaging and chatting. Students' use of the class Facebook groups is part and parcel of the face-to-face mode interaction in the classroom, and it should be seen as only partial accounts of larger conversations taking place among students and their teachers about their studies. This may raise 'important questions about how universities will articulate their teaching with students' (Kitto and Higgins, 2003), how educational leaders acknowledge these innovative strategies (Prensky, 2006), and how we can harmoniously blend our time-tested pedagogies with the emerging models of teaching and learning.

Acknowledgements

This work is supported in part by the College of Arts and Sciences Faculty Development Fund. We would like to thank our college dean, Dr. Joyce M. Dy. We also thank the anonymous reviewers for their insightful comments.

References

Arnold, N., & Ducate, L. (2006). CALL: Where are we and where do we go from here? In L. Ducate & N. Arnold (Eds.), *Calling an CALL: From theory and research to new direction foreign language teaching* (pp. 1-20). San Marcos, TX: CALICO Monograph Series, 5.

Belz, J.A., & Kinginger, C. (2003). Discourse options and the development of pragmatic competence by classroom learners of German: The case of address forms. *Language learning, 53*(4), 591-647.

Blattner, G., & Fiori, M. (2009). Facebook in the Language Classroom: Promises and Possibilities. *International Journal of Instructional Technology and Distance Learning, 6*(1), 17-28.

Cequena, M. (2013). Does blogging facilitate the development of students' writing skills? *Philippine ESL Journal, 10*, 126-147.

Dohn, N.B. (2009). Web 2.0-mediated competence: Implicit educational demands on learners. *Electronic Journal of e-Learning, 7*(2), 111-118.

Garrison, D. R., & Anderson, T. (2003). E-Learning in tire 21st Century: A framework for research and practice. London: Routledge.

Ghani, M. B. (2015). Using Facebook in Teaching and Learning English. *The International Conference on Language, Literature, Culture and Education,* April 25-26.

Hew, K. F. (2011). Students' and teachers' use of Facebook. *Computers in Human Behaviour.* Article available at doi:10.1016/j.chb.2010. 11.020.

Horn, M., & Staker, H. (2014). Blended: Using Disruptive Innovation to Improve Schools. San Francisco, CA: Jossey-Bass.

Kitto, S., & Higgins, V. (2003). Online university education: Liberating the student? *Science as Culture, 12*(1), 23-58.

Koehler, M. J., & Mishra, P. (2009). What is technological pedagogical content knowledge? *Contemporary Issues in Technology and Teacher Education (CITE Journal), 9*(1), 60-70.

Lord, G. (2008). Podcasting communities and second language pronunciation. *Foreign Language Annals, 41*(2), 364-379.

Low, P., & Warawudhi, R. (2016). Undergraduates' Attitudes toward the Use of Facebook in Fundamental English Course. *International Journal of Information and Education Technology, 6*(12), 934-939.

Madge, C., Meek, J., Wellens, J., & Hooley, T. (2009). Facebook, Social Integration and Informal Learning at University: 'It is More For Socializing and Talking to Friends about Work Than Actually Doing Work'. *Learning, Media & Technology, 34*(2), 141-155.

Miron, E., & Ravid, G. (2015). Facebook Groups as an Academic Teaching Aid: Case Study and Recommendations for Educators. *Educational Technology & Society, 18*(4), 371–384.

Most famous social network sites worldwide. (2016). Retrieved from https://www.statista.com/statistics/ 272014/global-social-networks- ranked-by-number-of-users/

O'Bryan, A., & Hegelheimer, Y. (2007). Integrating CALL into the classroom: The role of podcasting in an ESL listening strategies course. *ReCALL, 19*(2), 162-180.

Pempek, T., et al. (2009). College Students' Social Networking Experiences on Facebook. *Journal of Applied Developmental Psychology, 30*(1), 227-238.

Prensky, M. (2001). Digital natives, digital immigrants. *On The Horizon , 9*(5), 1-6.

Prensky, M. (2006). Listen to the natives. *Educational Leadership, 63*(4).

Puentedura, R. (2014). *Learning, Technology, and the SAMR Model: Goals, Processes, and Practice.* Retrieved from http://www.hippasus. com/rrpweblog /archives/2014/06/29/ LearningTechnologySAMRModel.pdf

Schroeder, J., & Greenbowe, T. (2009). The chemistry of Facebook: using social networking to create an online community for the organic chemistry laboratory. *Journal of Online education, 5*(4).

Selwyn, N. (2007). Web 2.0 Applications as Alternative Environments for Informal Learning – A Critical Review. *OCEDKERIS International Expert Meeting on ICT and Educational*

Performance. Cheju Island, South Korea: Organization for Economic Co-Operation and Development.

Shih, R. (2013). Effect of using Facebook to assist English for Business Communication course instruction. *TOJET: The Turkish Online Journal of Educational Technology, 12*(1), 52-59.

Stewart, P. (2008). Facebook: A School Librarian's Tool for Building a Community of Readers. Retrieved from http://www.slideshare.net/verzosaf/social-networking-literacy-skills-recasting-the-readers-services-librarians-competencies-in-the-21st-century

Sykes, J. (2005). Synchronous CMC and pragmatic development: effects of oral and written chat. *CALICO, 22*, 399-431.

Thompson, J. (2007). *Is Education 1.0 Ready for Web 2.0 students? Innovate 3*(4). http://www.innovateonline.info/index.php?view=article&id=393&action=article. Retrieved on August 1, 2016 from http://webcitation.org/5aG19ykVH.

Yu, L. (2014). A case study of using Facebook in an EFL English writing class: The perspective of a writing teacher. *JALT CALL SIG, 10*(3), 189-202.

Yunus, M., & Salehi, H. (2012). The Effectiveness of Facebook Groups on Teaching and Improving Writing: Students' Perceptions. *International Journal of Education and Information Technologies, 1*(6), 88-96.

Semantic Similarity Analysis for Paraphrase Identification in Arabic Texts

Adnen Mahmoud
LATICE Laboratory Research Department of
Computer Science
University of Monastir, Tunisia
Mahmoud.adnen@gmail.com

Mounir Zrigui
LATICE Laboratory Research Department of
Computer Science
University of Monastir, Tunisia
Mounir.zrigui@fsm.rnu.tn

Abstract

Arabic plagiarism detection is a difficult task because of the great richness of Arabic language characteristics of which it is a productive, derivational and inflectional language, on the one hand, and a word can has more than one lexical category in different contexts allows us to have different meanings of the word what changes the meaning of the sentence, on the other hand. In this context, Arabic paraphrase identification allows quantifying how much a suspect Arabic text and source Arabic text are similar based on their contexts. In this paper, we proposed a semantic similarity approach for paraphrase identification in Arabic texts by combining different techniques of Natural Language Processing NLP, such as: Term Frequency-Inverse Document Frequency TF-IDF technique to improve the identification of words that are highly descriptive in each sentence; and distributed word vector representations using word2vec algorithm to reduce computational complexity and to optimize the probability of predicting words in the context given the current center word, which they would be subsequently used to generate a sentence vector representations and after applying a similarity measurement operation based on different metrics of comparison, such as: Cosine Similarity and Euclidean Distance. Finally, our proposed approach was evaluated on the Open Source Arabic Corpus OSAC and obtained a promising rate.

1 Introduction

Plagiarism is defined as the unauthorized use or closer imitation for the language and thought of another author and the representation of them that one's own original work based on a set of rules, such as for example: inadequate referencing, direct copy from one or more sources of the text by displacement of words in a sentence, paraphrase and rewrite texts by presenting other's ideas with different words, and translation by expressing an idea in one language into another one (Abderahman et al, 2016) (Gharavi et al, 2016).

However, the field of paraphrase detection in Arabic texts is a difficult task because of the great variability of morphological and typographical features of Arabic language where a plagiarized text can include more changes: in the vocabulary, or syntactic, and semantic representation of the text compared with other languages such as Latin or English and we also find that a word can have more than one lexical category in different contexts what changes the meaning of the sentence. Nowadays, Arabic paraphrase identification based on semantic similarity analysis between source text and suspicious text is a difficult task in Natural Language Processing NLP of which we examine the similarity degree of a given pair of texts, in varying in different levels such as word, sentence or paragraph (Vo et al., 2015). Thus, many distributional semantic approaches based on the resemblance determination of their signification and their semantic contain (Negre, 2013) have drawn a considerable amount of attention by research community. In this context, our work consists in detecting semantic relatedness between the suspect text and the source text by combining different Natural Language Processing NLP methods to detect paraphrase in Arabic texts by generating word vector representations using word2vec algorithm which they would be combined subsequently to generate sentence vector representations and thereafter applying a similarity measurement operation. In this paper, we start by present a state of the art in the field of Arabic plagiarism detection in section 2 describing the complexities of Arabic language, on the one hand, and the works that have been proposed in this field in the literature, on the other hand. Thereafter, we detail different phases that make up our proposed method in section 3. Finally, we present the evaluation in section 4 as well as the results obtained and we end by a conclusion and some future works to realize in the field of plagiarism detection especially in Arabic language in section 5.

2   State Of The Art

2.1   Complexities of Arabic Language

Arabic language is very rich of morphological and typographical features (Meddeb et al, 2016) (Zouaghi et al, 2008) which make Arabic semantic analysis a very difficult task for several reasons among which we can mention:

- Arabic language is very rich of morphological features. Thus, Arabic script is cursive whose most letters are tied and written from right to left whose letters change shape depending on whether they appear at the beginning, middle or end of the word, on the one hand, and it consists of: a stem composed by a consonant root and a pattern morpheme; more affixes include time markers, sex and/or number; and enclitics include some propositions, conjunctions, determinants and pronouns. (Meddeb et al, 2016) (Boudhief et al, 2014)

- A word can have more than one lexical category such as: noun, verb, adjective, subject, etc. and can have more than one meaning depending on the context in which it is used (Zrigui et al, 2016) where the identification of some words is very difficult because of the non-capitalization of proper noun, acronyms and abbreviations (Lihioui et al, 2014) as shown in table 1:

Example	Translation	Function
ذهب أحمد إلى الدكان	Ahmed <u>went</u> to the shop	Verb
ذهب هذا الرجل ممتاز	The <u>gold</u> of this man is excellent	Subject

Table 1: Influence of syntactic category on the disambiguation of the word "ذهب" (dhhb)

- Inflected language whose lexical units vary in number and in bending such as the number of names or verb tense according to the grammatical relationships which they have with other lexical units. (Boudhief et al, 2014)

- The absence of diacritic marks makes Arabic language more ambiguous (Meddeb et al, 2016) (Zrigui et al, 2016). Therefore, only the diacritics, the occurrence context, and in some cases the grammatical category of the ambiguous word can disambiguate its sense which complicates the automatic processing of Arabic language and especially in its semantic analysis of which there is not a consistent theoretical formalism capable of taking into account all the phenomena encountered in this language (Zouaghi et al, 2012) (Zouaghi et al, 2007) as indicated in table 1 and 2:

Word	Vocalization	Translation
عَمِلَ	amila	Worked
عُمِلَ	omila	was done
عَمَلٌ	amalon	Work
عَمِلَ	amila	Worked

Table 2: Influence of diacritics on the disambiguation of the word 'عمل' (aml)

- An Arabic word may have several possible divisions such as proclitic, flexive form and enclitic. Thus, clitics stick to nouns, verbs, and adjectives which they relate that makes Arabic language agglutinative, on the one hand, and increase the ambiguity of word segmentation, on the other hand. (Boudhief et al, 2014) (Zouaghi et al, 2012)

- Synonyms are widespread in which there are many words are considered synonyms which require the use of tools of morphological analysis to find synonyms of a word. (Zrigui et al, 2016)

- The presence of coordination conjunction with a space-free link makes it difficult to distinguish between 'و' as a letter of a word and the word 'و' having the role of conjunction of coordination, on the one hand, and plays an important role in the interpretation of a statement by identifying its proposals, on the other hand. (Lihioui, 2014) (Zouaghi et al, 2007) as illustrated in the following example:

لقد تم إكمال هذا الإنجاز بالحكمة والعمل الدؤوب من أبناء هذه المدينة

"This accomplishment has been completed with the wisdom and hard work of the people of this city."

To conclude, Arabic language is very difficult to treat automatically because of its properties and its morphological, syntactic and semantic specificities that we quoted above and which make also the field of Arabic paraphrase detection difficult because the change of the word order or its meaning in the suspect sentence causes an ambiguity during semantic analysis between the source text and suspect text whose a word can have more than one lexical category in different contexts which allows us to have different meanings of a word what changes the meaning of a sentence.

2.2 Related Work

This section provides an overview on related works that deal with Arabic plagiarism detection especially in paraphrase identification field based on semantic analysis to determine the relatedness between the suspect and source Arabic text documents. Thus, several similarity detection approaches between documents have been proposed in the literature of which there are three types of methods for computing relatedness according to the type of resources that have been used, we distinguish:

- Knowledge-based methods relies on some form of ontology using WordNet which is a well-known knowledge source to compute semantic similarity between words as in (Shenoy et al, 2012) that proposed a semantic plagiarism detection system using ontology mapping where ontologies are a computational model of some domain of the world by describing semantics of terms used in the domain.
- Web-based approach gathers co-occurrence statistics based on the search engine results and used that to compute word relatedness like Point-wise Mutual Information PMI (Niraula et al, 2015). Thus, (Shuka et al, 2016) showed that the use of a web based cross language semantic plagiarism detection approach helps authors and written to secure their files and to make their files sale.
- Corpus-based measurements compute word similarity and relatedness based on word vector representations obtained from a given corpus. Among the most popular methods for inferring word vector representations to select more discriminative features, we can cite:

(Hussein, 2015) showed that Arabic document similarity analysis using N-grams and Singular Value Decomposition SVD can generalize the eigen decomposition of a positive semi definite normal matrix[1]. Also, (Hafeez and Patil, 2017) showed that the author analyzed summary of Chinese expression habits using an adaptive weight of word position algorithm based on TF-IDF to dynamically determining the weight of a word position according to the word position. Thus, it introduced the Vector Space Model VSM and designed comparative experiment under the scene of Chinese document clustering of which TF-IDF-AP algorithm improved a promising results. Moreover, Latent Semantic Analysis LSA algorithm allows to measure similarity between texts which represents the meaning not only of individual words but also of whole passages such as sentences, paragraphs, and short essay (Bihi, 2017), as in (Kenter and Rijke, 2015) that proposed a method for inducing polarity to the document-term matrix before applying LSA which was novel and shown to effectively preserve and generalize the synonymous / antonymous information in the projected space. Also, Latent Dirichlet Allocation LDA which is a probabilistic model can capture polysemy where each word had multiple meanings and used to reduce dimensionality to themes that are useful building blocks for representing a gist of

---

[1] https://en.wikipedia.org/wiki/Singular_value_decomposition

what a collection contains, statically or over time as in (Yih et al, 2012) in order to support navigability between similar documents via dynamically hyperlinks using an LDA based on cosine similarity measurement.

But nowadays, distributed word vector representation is a branch of machine learning where each word is described by the surrounding context and thereafter a vector is generated automatically containing semantic and syntactic information about the word (Gharavi et al, 2016) of which the learned vectors explicitly encode many linguistic regularities and patterns (Towne et al, 2016). Indeed, distributed word representations in a vector refers as word embeddings where each vector can be located and visualized in multi dimensional space and helps learning algorithms to achieve better performance in Natural Language Processing NLP by grouping similar words and has dwarfed older methods for achieving distributed representations, like: Latent Semantic Analysis LSA (Towne et al, 2016) (Mikolov et al, 2013). In this context, several methods have been proposed, despite that there is little works have been proposed in the field of Arabic paraphrase detection, such as:

(Mikolov et al, 2013) showed that the inclusion of Twitter-based word embeddings using word2vec may yield better tagged sentences when it used to train systems designed for downstream NLP tasks. However, a generic and flexible method for semantic matching of short texts as in (Samuel, 2016) which leveraged word embeddings of different dimensionality obtained by different algorithms (GloVe and word2vec) and from different sources where the purpose was to go from word-level to short-text level semantics by combining insights from methods based on external sources of semantic knowledge with word embeddings. On the other hand, (Prazak et al, 2012) attempt to estimate the similarity score between chunks based upon estimating semantic similarity of individual words and compiling them into one number for a given chunk pair. After, it experimented with word2vec and GloVe to estimate similarity of words and compiled all word similarities in one number that reflected semantics of whole chunks via lexical semantic vectors. Moreover, (Niraula et al, 2015) showed that words relatedness and similarity can be measured by combining word representations, like: LSA, LDA, word2vec and GloVe to complement the coverage of semantic aspects of a word and thus better represent the word than individual representations.

3 Proposed Approach

Paraphrase detection between Arabic documents becomes a very important task in the recent years because of the great variability of Arabic language specificities, on the one hand, and the availability of enormous volume of information over the internet. In this context, we propose a method for Arabic paraphrase detection based on the identification of similarity between source document and suspect document using Natural Language Processing NLP techniques. Thus, our proposed approach allows extracting their semantic similarity to detect paraphrase which can be created by direct copy of sentences, replacement of words with similar ones, and changing the order of words or reconstructing the sentences (Sindhu and Idicula, 2015). Indeed, our proposed approach is composed by three phases, as follows:

1- We begin with a preprocessing phase to extract the relevant information from texts.
2- After, we apply a features extraction phase to extract more discriminant features.
3- Thereafter, a paraphrase detection phase is used to identify the rate of similarity between source document and plagiarized document.

Here is the general architecture of our approach for Arabic paraphrase identification as shown in the following figure 1:

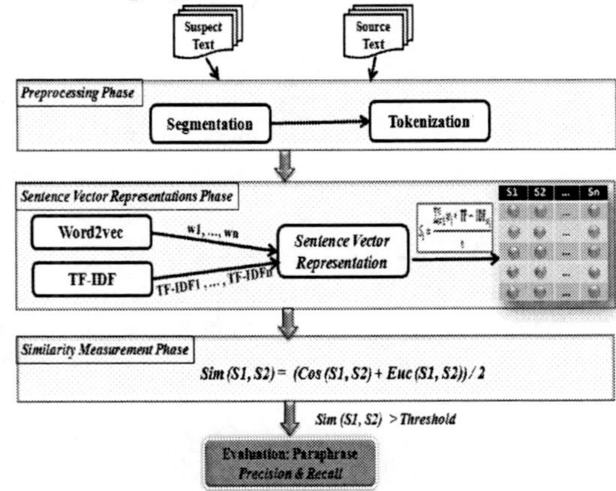

Figure 1.   General architecture of Arabic paraphrase detection

3.1 Preprocessing Phase

Our model begins with a preprocessing phase to facilitate further processing by cleaning the Arabic text from noisy information, on the one hand, and to reduce the complexity of Arabic paraphrase identification, on the other hand. So, we proceed by the following steps:

1. We begin by segmenting the source text and suspect text into sentences by identifying their boundaries in order to extract the meaningful information. Among the boundaries used in the literature, we can mention: "," ";" "." ".." "!" "?".

2. After, we try to extract tokens from running text where one Arabic word end and another Arabic word begin by detecting the space between them. (Aliwy, 2012)

3.2 Features Extraction Phase

Term Frequency-Inverse Document Frequency "TF- IDF": TF-IDF is used as a weighting factor in information retrieval and text mining of which it allows the construction of a vector space where each vector represent how a word is important to a document in a collection by the combination between Term Frequency TF (t,d) and Inverse Document Frequency IDF(w). (Shuka et al, 2016)

More formally, given the frequency of the occurrence of term in document d, in order to control the fact that some words are common than others by proceeding as follows (Abderahman, 2016):

- *Term Frequency TF:* is defined as the number of times a term occurs in a document as shown in equation (1). Moreover, a term can appear much more times in long documents than shorter ones since every document is different in length[2].

$$TF(t, d) = \frac{O}{T} \tag{1}$$

Where: O represent the number of times that a term t appears in a document, and T is the number of terms in the document.

- *Inverse Document Frequency IDF:* is a statistical weight used for measuring the importance of a term in a text document collection. Also, IDF feature is

incorporated which reduces the weight of terms that occur very frequently in the document set and increases the weight of terms that occur rarely as shown in the following equation 2:

$$IDF(t,d)\log = \frac{|D|}{N} \tag{2}$$

Where: |D| is the total number of documents and N is the number of documents with term t in it.

- *Term Frequency-Inverse Document Frequency TF-IDF:* is calculated for each term in the document by combining TF and IDF as shown in the following equation 3:

$$TF - IDF(t,d,f) = TF(t,d) * IDF(t,d) \tag{3}$$

Word Embeddings "word2vec": Word embeddings are based on a probabilistic feed forward neural network language model to learn a space of continuous word representations in which similar words are expected to be close to each other. Thus, word embeddings allows representing words with low dimensional and dense real-value vectors which capture useful semantic and syntactic features of words (Law and al, 2017), on the one hand, and reducing computational complexity, on the other hand. So, we use word2vec algorithm of which it consists two architectures for learning word embeddings that are less computationally expensive than previous models, such as: Continuous Bag Of Words CBOW and Skip-gram models. Indeed, we use the Skip-Gram model in our work because it showed better performance in Natural Language Processing NLP especially in semantic analysis.

Generally, each input word w is associated with a k-dimensional vector $v_w \in \Re^k$ called the input embedding and each context word wO is associated with a k-dimensional vector $v_{wO} \in \Re^k$ called the output embedding, the probability of observing wO in the context of w is modeled with a softmax function, as follows in equation 4:

$$P(wO|w) = \frac{\exp(v_{wO}^{T} v_w)}{\sum_{1}^{W} \exp(v_{wi}^{T} v_w)} \tag{4}$$

Also, given a sequence of training words $\{w1, \ldots, wn\}$ and a larger size of the training context

---

[2] http://www.tfidf.com/

c in more training examples to lead a higher accuracy at the expense of the training time, the objective of skip gram model is to maximize the average log probability for this sequence, as follows in equation 5 (Mikolov and al, 2013) :

$$\frac{1}{n}\sum_{t=1}^{n}\sum_{-c\leq j\leq c, j\neq 0}\log p\left(w_{t+j}\middle|w_t\right) \tag{5}$$

Distributed Word Vector Representations "word2vec and TF-IDF": In our work, we try to facilitate the identification of similarity between Arabic texts using word embedding representations and TF-IDF techniques, as follows: On the one hand, we capture semantic properties of words by exploiting vectors as word representation in a multi dimensional space using word2vec algorithm based on skip gram model to optimize the probability of predicting words in the context given the current center word and overcoming the problem of the data sparsity problem. On the other hand, we use TF- IDF technique in order to improve the identification of words that are highly descriptive in each sentence of which TF- IDF value is used as a weighting factor to increase proportionally the number of times a word appears in the document but it is counteracting by the frequency of the word in the corpus.

More formally, given a sentence S composed by n words, our distributed sentence representations of suspect text and source text is composed by the following steps:

1. We begin by determining the Term Frequency - Inverse Document Frequency $TF\text{-}IDF \in \Re$ of each word in the sentence. The output of this step is a set of values representing the importance of each word in the text, as follows in equation 6:

$$TF\text{-}IDF_{w1,...,n} = TF\text{-}IDF_{w1},\cdots,TF\text{-}IDF_{wn} \tag{6}$$

2. Then, we learn word embeddings using word2vec algorithm where the i-th word in the sentence S is mapped into a single vector $w_i \in \Re^k$ represented by a column w_i in a matrix M of size n*k. At the end of this operation, we have a sequence of n word vector representations of the sentence S, as follows in equation 7:

$$w_{1:n} = w_1, w_2,\cdots,w_n \tag{7}$$

3. The word-level skip-gram model predicts the context of words given the current word vector but our goal is the prediction of the context of

sentences given the vector representation of the current sentence vector. (Peng and Gildea, 2016)

So, we proceed as follows: we calculate an average of all word vector representations w_i extracted from W for each sentence S_i composed by n words, as follows in equation 8:

$$S_i = \frac{\sum_{i=1}^{n} w_i * TF\text{-}IDF_{w_i}}{n} \tag{8}$$

At the end of this step of sentence vector representations, each sentence Si will be mapped into a single vector represented by a column in a matrix V, which will be used in subsequent processing, as follows in equation 9:

$$V_{1:m} = S_1,\cdots,S_m \tag{9}$$

Where: m is the number of sentences in the text.

3.3 Arabic Texts Similarity Measurement

Our goal in this study is how identify the rate of similarity between Arabic texts to conclude that there is a paraphrase between them by combining different metrics of comparison to prove our proposed approach. So, given the sentence vector representations of suspect text S_1 and source text S_2 of dimension k, we compare each sentence of suspect document with all sentences of source document, as follows:

1. We identify the semantic relation between suspect and source sentence using Cosine Similarity based on the calculation of the number of similar words that exist in source sentence S_1 and suspect sentence S_2 to determine the score of similarity between them where the Cosine Similarity is measured using word vectors (Alaa et al, 2016), as follows in equation 10:

$$Cos(S_1,S_2) = \frac{S_1 \cdot S_2}{\|S_1\|\cdot\|S_2\|} \tag{10}$$

$$= \frac{\sum_{i=1}^{k} S_{1i}\, S_{2i}}{\sqrt{\sum_{i=1}^{k} S_{1i}^2}\sqrt{\sum_{i=1}^{k} S_{2i}^2}}$$

2. After, we use the Euclidean distance as another similarity measure which calculates the similarity between two documents as the distance between their vectors representations reduced to a single point (Negre, 2013) as follows in equation 11:

$$Euc(x, y) = \sqrt{\Sigma \left| x_i - y_j \right|^2} \qquad (11)$$

So, our proposed similarity method is based on the semantic similarity of sentences in Arabic texts to determine the degree of semantic relatedness between them by combining two methods, such as: Cosine Similarity *Cos* and Euclidean Distance *Euc*, as follows in equation 12:

$$Sim_{Comb}(S_1 \cdot S_2) = \frac{Cos(S_1 \cdot S_2) + Euc(S_1 \cdot S_2)}{2} \qquad (12)$$

If the result we found from (12) has also exceeded a threshold α, then, we find that there is actually plagiarism (paraphrase) between the source document and suspect document. Otherwise, it is considered to be not plagiarized (not paraphrase).

At the end of this step, we obtain a vector which contains different scores of similarity according to the suspect text document sizes until reaching the source document size.

4 Results and Discussion

Open Source Arabic Corpora OSAC[4] includes 22,429 text documents where each text document belongs to 1 of 10 categories such as: Economics, History, Entertainments, Education & Family, Religious and Fatwas, Sports, Heath, Astronomy, Low, Stories, Cooking Recipes). Indeed, the evaluation of our proposed approach is carried out on a collection of historical documents contains 3233 text documents of the Open Source Arabic Corpora (OSAC)[3].

The parameters we used and which made our approach efficient are:
- The word vector representations using word2vec based on Skip-gram model are checked in a matrix of size n*k. In our case, we used more than 350 millions words extracted from Wikipedia and we fixed k at 5 which represent the number of synonyms according to each word context where two words before the word in the middle target and two words after.
- The experiments of this study to identify paraphrase between Arabic texts included the implementation of two combined methods, which are: Cosine Similarity *Cos* and Euclidean Distance *Euc*.
- Two sentences are considered as plagiarism (paraphrase), if they pass the threshold (α) between the result of our proposed method for similarity detection $Sim_{Comb}(S_1 \cdot S_2)$ whose the threshold was fine-tuned by several trials on the training corpus and the results achieved when α = 0.3.

Each method was tested individually and the combination method gave us the final result of our proposed method as shown in the following table:

Proposed Approaches	Precision	Recall
TF- IDF + Sim_{Comb}	0.81	0.79
Word2vec + Sim_{Comb}	0.83	0.81
Final Combination: word2vec + TF- IDF + Sim_{Comb}	0.85	0.84

Table 3: Results of paraphrase identification approaches

To conclude, the combination between distributed word vector representations and TF-IDF method have shown good result when we applied each measure of comparison that we cited above (Cosine Similarity and Euclidean Distance), and especially when we have combined them with a set of different measures of similarity (Cosine Similarity and Euclidean Distance) of which a promised plagiarism detection rate was obtained in terms of precision and recall.

5 Conclusion and Future Works

We proposed a semantic textual similarity approach for paraphrase identification in Arabic texts based on the combination of different Natural Language Processing NLP such as: TF-IDF technique to improve the identification of words that are highly descriptive in each sentence, and distributed word vector representations using word2vec algorithm to reduce computational complexity and to optimize the probability of predicting words in the context which they would be subsequently used to generate a sentence vector representations and after applying a similarity measurement operation based on the combination of different metrics of comparison such as: Cosine Similarity and Euclidean Distance. Finally, our proposed approach was evaluated on the Open

---

[3] https://sites.google.com/site/motazsite/corpora/osac

Source Arabic Corpus OSAC and obtained a promising rate. Despite the promising results that we have obtained using our proposed approach, several improvements will be applied in our method later on, such as : the use of a Convolutional Neural Network CNN to improve the capability to capture statistical regularities in the context of sentences, on the one hand, and we will try to combine word vector representations to improve the similarity measure and to improve the weakness of each method, like: Latent Semantic Analysis LSA, Latent Dirichlet Allocation LDA and distributed representation of words word2vec.

References

Abderahman Y. A., Khalid A. and Osman I. M.. (2016). *A survey of plagiarism detection for Arabic documents, International Journal of Advanced Computer Technology IJACT*, volume 4, n. 6, pp. 34-38.

Alaa Z., Tiun S. and Abdulameer M. H. (2016). *Cross-language plagiarism of Arabic-English documents using linear logistic regressing, Journal of Theoretical and Applied Information Technology, 2005 - 2015 JATIT & LLS*, Volume 83. No.1, , pp. 20-33.

Aliwy A. H. (2012). *Tokenization as Preprocessing for Arabic Tagging System, International Journal of Information and Education Technology*, volume 2, No. 4, pp. 348-353.

Bihi A. (2017). *Analysis of similarity and differences between articles using semantics*, Université Malardalen, Sweden.

Boudhief A., Maraoui M. and Zrigui M. (2014). *Elaboration of a model for an indexed base for teaching Arabic language to disabled people, 6th International Conference on CIST*, pp110-116.

Gharavi E., Bijari K., Zahirnia K. and Veisi H.. (2015). A *deeplearning approach to Persian plagiarism detection*, India.

Hafeez S. and Patil B. (2017). *Using Explicit Semantic Similarity for an Improved Web Explorer with ontology and TF-IDF, International Journal of Advance Scientific Research and Engeneering Trends*, Volume 2, Issue 7, pp. 171-173.

Hussein A. S. 2017. *Arabic document similarity analysis using N-gram and Singular Value Decomposition, 9th International Conference on Research Challenges in Information Science RC IS*.

Kenter T. and Rijke M. D. (2015). *Short text similarity with word embeddings, International Conference on Information and Knowledge Management CIKM'15*, Australia.

Law J., Zhuo H. H., He J. and Rong E. (2017). *LTSG: Latent Topical Skip-Gram for Mutually Learning Topic Model and Vector Representations*, Cornell University Library, Coputer Science, Computation and language, United States.

Lihioui C., Zouaghi A. and Zrigui M. (2014). *Towards a hybrid approach to semantic analysis of spontaneous Arabic speech, International Journal of Computational Linguistics and Applications*, volume 5, n. 2, pp. 165-193.

Meddeb O., Maraoui M. and AlJawerneh S. (2016). *Hybrid modeling of an offline arabic handwriting recognition system AHRS, International Conference on Engineering & MIS ICEMIS*, Maroc

Mikolov T., Sustskever I., Chen K., Corrado G., and Dean J. (2013). *Distributed representations of words and phrases and their compositionality, Neural Information Processing Systems NIPS*, United States

Vo N. P. A., Magnolini S. and Popescu O. (2015). *Paraphrase identification and semantic similarity in Twitter with simple features, Proceedings of Social NLP* ,pp. 10-19, Colorado.

Negre E. (2013). *Comparaison de textes: quelques approche , Cahier du LAMSADE 338, Laboratoire d'Analyses et Modélisation de Systèmes pour l'Aide à la Décision UMR 7243*, Paris.

Niraula N. B., Gautam D., Banjadae R., N. Maharjan, and Rus V. (2015). *Combining word representations for measuring word relatedness and similarity, Twenty Eight International Florida Artificial Intelligence Research Society Conference*, Florida

Prazak O., Steinberger D., Konopik M., and Brychain T. (2012). *Interpretable semantic textual similarity with distributional semantics for chunks, Proceedings of the 2012 Joint Conference on Empirical Methods in Natural Language Processing and Computational Natural Language Learning*, pp1212-1222.

Peng X. and Gildea D. (2016). *Exploring phrase-compositionality in skip-gram models, Cornell University Library, Computer Science, Computation and language*, United States.

Samuel D. S. (2016). *On the use of vector representation for improved accuracy and currency of Twitter POS Tagging*, Dalhousie University, Halifax, Nova Scotia.

Shenoy M. K., Set D. C. and Achrya U. D. (2012). *Semantic plagiarism detection system using ontology mapping, Advanced Computing: An International Journal ACIJ*, volume 3, n. 3, pp. 59-62.

Shuka V., Khan F. and Mody K. (2016). *Plagiarism detection for document, International Journal on Recent and Innovation Trends in Computing and Communication*, volume 4, issue 2, pp. 175-178.

Sindhu L., and Idicula S. M. (November 2015). *SRL based plagiarism detection system for Malayalam documents, International Journal of Computer Science Issues IJCSI*, volume 12, issue 6, pp. 91-97.

Towne W. B., Rosé C. P. and Herbsleb J. D. (2016). *Measuring similarity: LDA and Human Perception, ACM Transaction on Intelligent Systems and Technology*, pp. 1-29, volume 7, n. 2.

Yih W. T., Zweig G. and Platt J. C. (2012). *Polarity inducing Latent Semantic Analysis, Proceedings of the 2012 Joint Conference on Empirical Methods in Natural Language Processing and Computational Natural Language Learning*, pp. 1212–1222, Korea.

Zouaghi A., Zrigui M., Ben Ahmed M. and Antoniadis G. (2007). *L'influence du contexte sur la compréhension de la parole spontanée, Proceedings de la Conference Traitement Automatique de La Langue Naturelle TALN'07*

Zouaghi A., Zrigui M. and Antoniadis G. (2008). *Compréhension automatique de la parole arabe spontanée , Traitement Automatique des Langues*, Beljique.

Zouaghi A., Marhbène L. and Zrigui M. (2012). *A hybrid approach for Arabic word sense disanbiguation, Internatonal Journal of Computer Processing of Languages*, volume 24, n.2, pp. 133-151.

Zrigui S., Zouaghi A., Ayadi R., Zrigui M. and Zrigui S. (2016). *ISAO: An intellgent system of opinion analysis, Research in Computing 110* , pp. 21-31.

An Empirical Study of Language Relatedness for Transfer Learning in Neural Machine Translation

Raj Dabre
Kyoto University,
Kyoto, Japan
prajdabre@gmail.com

Tetsuji Nakagawa
Google Japan,
Tokyo, Japan
tnaka@google.com

Hideto Kazawa
Google Japan,
Tokyo, Japan
kazawa@google.com

Abstract

Neural Machine Translation (NMT) is known to outperform Phrase Based Statistical Machine Translation (PBSMT) for resource rich language pairs but not for resource poor ones. Transfer Learning (Zoph et al., 2016) is a simple approach in which we can simply initialize an NMT model (child model) for a resource poor language pair using a previously trained model (parent model) for a resource rich language pair where the target languages are the same. This paper explores how different choices of parent models affect the performance of child models. We empirically show that using a parent model with the source language falling in the same or linguistically similar language family as the source language of the child model is the best.

1 Introduction

One of the most attractive features of Neural Machine Translation (NMT) (Bahdanau et al., 2015; Cho et al., 2014; Sutskever et al., 2014) is that it is possible to train an end to end system without the need to deal with word alignments, phrase tables and complicated decoding algorithms which are a characteristic of Phrase Based Statistical Machine Translation (PBSMT) systems (Koehn et al., 2003). It is reported that NMT works better than PBSMT only when there is an abundance of parallel corpora. In the case of low resource languages like Hausa, vanilla NMT is either worse than or comparable to PBSMT (Zoph et al., 2016). However, it is possible to use a previously trained X-Y model (parent model; X-Y being the resource rich language pair where X and Y represent the source and target languages respectively) to initialize the parameters of a Z-Y model (child model; Z-Y

being the resource poor language pair) leading to significant improvements (Zoph et al., 2016) for the latter. This paper is about an empirical study of transfer learning for NMT for low resource languages. Our main focus is on translation to English for the following low resource languages: Hausa, Uzbek, Marathi, Malayalam, Punjabi, Malayalam, Kazakh, Luxembourgish, Javanese and Sundanese. Our main contribution is that we empirically (and exhaustively; within reason) show that using a resource rich language pair in which the source language is linguistically closer to the source language of the resource poor pair is much better than other choices of language pairs.

2 Related Work

Transfer learning for NMT (Zoph et al., 2016) is an approach where previously trained NMT models for French and German to English (resource rich pairs) were used to initialize models for Hausa, Uzbek, Spanish to English (resource poor pairs). They showed that French-English as a parent model was better than German-English when trying to improve the Spanish-English translation quality (since Spanish is linguistically closer to French than German) but they did not conduct an exhaustive investigation for multiple language pairs. In this paper we extend this work to explore how language relatedness impacts transfer learning.

3 Overview of Transfer Learning

Refer to Figure 1 for an overview of the method. It is essentially the same as described in (Zoph et al., 2016) where we learn a model (parent model) for a resource rich language pair (Hindi-English) and use it to initialize the model (child model) for the resource poor pair (Marathi-English). Henceforth the source languages of the parent model and

31st Pacific Asia Conference on Language, Information and Computation (PACLIC 31), pages 282–286
Cebu City, Philippines, November 16-18, 2017

child models will be known as parent and child languages respectively and the corresponding language pairs will be known as the parent and child language pairs respectively. The target language vocabulary (English) should be the same for both the parent and the child models. Following the originally proposed method we focused on freezing[1] (by setting gradients to zero) the decoder embeddings and softmax layers when learning child models since they represent the majority of the decoder parameter space. This method can easily be applied in cases where we wish to use the X-Y pair to help the Z-Y pair where Y is usually English.

4 Experimental Settings

All of our experiments were performed using an encoder-decoder NMT system with attention for the various baselines and transfer learning experiments. We used an in house NMT system developed using the Tensorflow (Abadi et al., 2015) framework so as to exploit multiple GPUs to speed up training. To ensure replicability we use the same NMT model design as in the original work (Zoph et al., 2016). In order to enable infinite vocabulary we use the word piece model (WPM) (Schuster and Nakajima, 2012) as a segmentation model which is closely related to the Byte Pair Encoding (BPE) based segmentation approach (Sennrich et al., 2016). We evaluate our models using the standard BLEU (Papineni et al., 2002) metric[2] on the detokenized translations of the test set. However we report the only the difference between the BLEU scores of the transferred and the baseline models since our focus is not on the BLEU scores themselves but rather the improvement by using transfer learning and on observing the language relatedness phenomenon. Baseline models are simply ones trained from scratch by initializing the model parameters with random values.

4.1 Languages

The set of parent languages (and abbreviations) we considered is: Hindi (Hi), Indonesian (Id), Turkish (Tr), Russian (Ru), German (De) and French (Fr). The set of child languages (and abbreviations) consists of: Luxembourgish (Lb), Hausa (Ha), Somali (So), Malayalam (Ml), Punjabi (Pa),

Group	Languages
European	French, German, Luxembourgish
Slavic	Russian
Afro-Asiatic	Hausa, Somali
Turkic	Turkish, Uzbek, Kazakh
Austronesian	Indonesian, Javanese, Sundanese
Indian	Hindi, Marathi, Punjabi, Malayalam

Table 1: Language Groups in Experiments

Marathi (Mr), Uzbek (Uz), Javanese (Jw), Kazakah (Kk) and Sundanese (Su). Table 1 groups the languages into language families. For each child model we try around 3 to 4 parent models out of which one is mostly learned from a linguistically close parent language pair. The source languages vary but the target language is always English. Since there are no standard training sets for many of these language pairs, we use parallel data automatically mined from the web using an in-house crawler. For evaluation, we use a set of 9K English sentences collected from the web and translated by humans into each of the source languages mentioned above. Each sentence has one reference translation. We use 5K sentences for evaluation and the rest form the development set.

To give a rough idea of the corpora sizes consider the WMT14 dataset for German-English which contains around 5M lines of parallel corpora for training. The child language pair corpora sizes vary from being one decimal order of magnitude smaller to one decimal order of magnitude larger than the WMT14 German-English corpus. However the parent language pair corpora are two to three decimal orders of magnitude larger than the aforementioned dataset. From left to right, the languages above are ordered according to the size of their corpora with the leftmost being the one with the smallest dataset. Since these datasets are mined from the open web they represent a realistic scenario and hence it should be evident that the child language pairs are truly resource poor.

Our choice of languages was influenced by two factors:

- a. We wanted to replicate the basic transfer learning results (Zoph et al., 2016) and hence chose French, German for Hausa and Uzbek.

- b. We wanted to compare the effects of using parent languages belonging to the same lan-

---

[1]We also tried experiments where we froze the decoder LSTM layers as well but we omit the results for brevity.

[2]This is computed by the multi-bleu.pl script, which can be downloaded from the public implementation of Moses (Koehn et al., 2007).

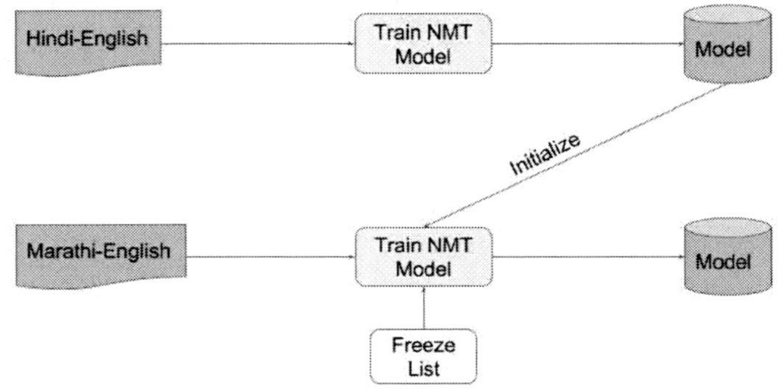

Figure 1: Transfer Learning for Low Resource Languages

guage family as the child languages (Hindi for Marathi) as opposed to unrelated parent languages (German for Marathi).

4.2 Settings

Following the aforementioned factors influencing our language choices we conducted our experiments in two stages as below:

- Exhaustive experimentation on 6 child languages (Hausa, Uzbek, Marathi, Malayalam, Punjabi and Somali) by using 4 parent languages (French, German, Russian and Hindi). This was done in order to verify whether there is any language relatedness phenomenon worth exploring or not. Based on these experiments we proposed a hypothesis that a parent language from the same or a closely related language family should be a lot more helpful than any other parent language.

- Opportunistic experimentation on 4 child languages (Kazakh, Javanese, Sundanese and Luxembourgish) by using 3 parent languages out of which one is from the same language family and the other two are from another language family. Turkish being the related language for Kazakh, German for Luxembourgish and Indonesian for Javanese and Sundanese.

The model and training details are the same as that in the original work (Zoph et al., 2016) but following are some specific settings:

- Model parts frozen (only when doing transfer learning): softmax and decoder embeddings layers (Decoder LSTMs were retrained)
- Embeddings: 512 nodes
- LSTM: 4 layers, 512 nodes output
- Attention: 512 nodes hidden layer

Child	Parent			
	Fr	De	Hi	Ru
Ha	+2.85	+2.17	+2.03	**+2.99**
Uz	+0.12	+0.22	**+0.46**	+0.34
Mr	-1.62	-0.38	**+0.57***	-0.55
Ml	+1.31	+1.89	**+2.80***	+1.45
Pa	+0.80	+0.67	**+2.41***	+0.69
So	**+3.17**	+2.69	+2.26	+2.89

Table 2: BLEU deltas for Exhaustive experimentation

- WPM vocabulary size: 16k (separate models for source and target)
- Batch size: 128
- Training steps: 5M
- Optimization algorithms: Adam for 60k iterations followed by SGD
- Annealing: Starts at 2M iterations followed by halving learning rate every 200k iterations
- Choosing the best model: Evaluate saved checkpoints on the development set and select checkpoint with best BLEU.

Note that the target language (English) vocabulary is same for all settings and the WPM is learned on the English side of the French-English corpus since it is the largest one amongst all our pairs. We deliberately chose this since we wished to maintain the same target side vocabulary for all our experiments (both baseline and transfer) for fair comparison. The parent source vocabulary (and hence embeddings) is randomly mapped to child source vocabulary since it was shown that NMT is less sensitive to it (Zoph et al., 2016).

284

Child	Parent			
	De	**Hi**	**Tr**	**Id**
Kk	+0.21	+0.40	**+0.48**	-
Jw	+1.10	+0.44	-	**+2.47***
Su	-0.13	+0.41	-	**+1.10***
Lb	**+8.58***	+6.44	+6.01	-

Table 3: BLEU deltas for Opportunistic experimentation

5 Results

Refer to Table 2 for the results of the exhaustive experimentation round and Table 3 for those of the opportunistic experimentation round. As mentioned before we only report the difference between the BLEU scores of the transferred and the baseline model. Entries in bold indicate the parent-child pair that performed the best amongst others. Furthermore, entries that have an "*" mark represent the parent-child pair with a BLEU difference that is statistically significant compared to the BLEU difference of other parent-child pairs.

5.1 Observations

One thing that stood out during the exhaustive experimentation phase (Table 2) is that Hindi as a parent language led to better gains (from +0.57 to +2.8) for all Indian languages as opposed to gains (-1.62 to +1.89) due to other parents. In the case of Marathi all other parent languages led to degradation in performance and Punjabi gained the most (+2.41) from Hindi as a parent where as the gains due to the others were at most +0.8. It makes sense that Punjabi being the closest language (linguistically speaking) to Hindi would gain the most followed by Marathi. It is also important to note that amongst all parent languages Hindi had the least amount of data and French had the most. This led us to believe that beyond a certain amount the size of the training data is not the real factor behind the gains observed due to transfer learning. Amongst the child languages Uzbek and Marathi were the most resource abundant ones and hence the gains to the transfer learning (less than 1 BLEU point) are notable only in cases where the baseline systems are not that strong.

Following this we decided to verify our hypothesis that: "A parent language from the same (or linguistically similar) language family as the child language will have a larger impact on transfer learning." From Table 3 it can be seen that this hypothesis is mostly true. The gain (+8.58) in the case of German as a parent for Luxembourgish is quite striking since the latter is known to be closely related to the former. Moreover using German gives an additional improvement of around 2 BLEU points over other parents. Indonesian, Javanese and Sundanese are close to each other in the same way that Punjabi is similar to Hindi. Thus Indonesian as a parent gives around 1 to 2 BLEU improvement for these language pairs over when other parents are chosen. Indonesian, Javanese and Sundanese use the same script but Hindi and Punjabi do not. In spite of this Hindi still acts as a better parent as compared to the others which means that the NMT system does learn certain grammatical features which provide the child models with a good prior when transferring the parameters. Finally, Kazakh received maximum benefit when using Turkish as a parent but the baseline model for Kazakh was too strong and thus it is difficult to draw any proper conclusion in this case since Hindi as a parent helped almost as much. We did try a scenario where Turkish was used as a parent for Uzbek (not in the tables) but failed to see any particular improvement over when other parents are used but it should be noted that, linguistically speaking, Turkish is a lot closer to Kazakh than it is to Uzbek.

Although we do not give details here due to lack of space transfer learning helps cut down the training time by more than half in most cases since more than half the model is already pre-trained.

6 Conclusions and Future Work

We presented our work on an empirical study of language relatedness for transfer learning in Neural Machine Translation. We showed that in general, transfer learning done on a X-Y language pair to Z-Y language pair has maximum impact when Z-Y is resource scarce and when X and Z fall in the same or linguistically similar language family. We did exhaustive experimentation to validate our hypothesis and it stands to be true in most cases. In the future we would like to experiment with transfer learning where we use Spanish as a parent for Italian with a slight modification where we force the Spanish vocabulary to resemble Italian by applying a segmentation mechanism (like BPE or WPM) trained on Italian to Spanish. This should help exploit cognates between closely related languages.

References

Martín Abadi, Ashish Agarwal, Paul Barham, Eugene Brevdo, Zhifeng Chen, Craig Citro, Greg S. Corrado, Andy Davis, Jeffrey Dean, Matthieu Devin, Sanjay Ghemawat, Ian Goodfellow, Andrew Harp, Geoffrey Irving, Michael Isard, Yangqing Jia, Rafal Jozefowicz, Lukasz Kaiser, Manjunath Kudlur, Josh Levenberg, Dan Mané, Rajat Monga, Sherry Moore, Derek Murray, Chris Olah, Mike Schuster, Jonathon Shlens, Benoit Steiner, Ilya Sutskever, Kunal Talwar, Paul Tucker, Vincent Vanhoucke, Vijay Vasudevan, Fernanda Viégas, Oriol Vinyals, Pete Warden, Martin Wattenberg, Martin Wicke, Yuan Yu, and Xiaoqiang Zheng. 2015. TensorFlow: Large-scale machine learning on heterogeneous systems. Software available from tensorflow.org.

Dzmitry Bahdanau, Kyunghyun Cho, and Yoshua Bengio. 2015. Neural machine translation by jointly learning to align and translate. In *In Proceedings of the 3rd International Conference on Learning Representations (ICLR 2015)*, San Diego, USA. International Conference on Learning Representations.

Kyunghyun Cho, Bart van Merriënboer, ÇaÄŞlar Gülçehre, Dzmitry Bahdanau, Fethi Bougares, Holger Schwenk, and Yoshua Bengio. 2014. Learning phrase representations using rnn encoder–decoder for statistical machine translation. In *Proceedings of the 2014 Conference on Empirical Methods in Natural Language Processing (EMNLP)*, pages 1724–1734, Doha, Qatar. Association for Computational Linguistics.

Philipp Koehn, Hieu Hoang, Alexandra Birch, Chris Callison-Burch, Marcello Federico, Nicola Bertoldi, Brooke Cowan, Wade Shen, Christine Moran, Richard Zens, Chris Dyer, Ondrej Bojar, Alexandra Constantin, and Evan Herbst. 2007. Moses: Open source toolkit for statistical machine translation. In *ACL*. The Association for Computer Linguistics.

Philipp Koehn, Franz Josef Och, and Daniel Marcu. 2003. Statistical phrase-based translation. In *Proceedings of the 2003 Conference of the North American Chapter of the Association for Computational Linguistics on Human Language Technology - Volume 1*, NAACL '03, pages 48–54, Stroudsburg, PA, USA. Association for Computational Linguistics.

Kishore Papineni, Salim Roukos, Todd Ward, and Wei-Jing Zhu. 2002. Bleu: A method for automatic evaluation of machine translation. In *Proceedings of the 40th Annual Meeting on Association for Computational Linguistics*, ACL '02, pages 311–318, Stroudsburg, PA, USA. Association for Computational Linguistics.

Mike Schuster and Kaisuke Nakajima. 2012. Japanese and korean voice search. In *2012 IEEE International Conference on Acoustics, Speech and Signal Processing, ICASSP 2012, Kyoto, Japan, March 25-30, 2012*, pages 5149–5152.

Rico Sennrich, Barry Haddow, and Alexandra Birch. 2016. Neural machine translation of rare words with subword units. In *Proceedings of the 54th Annual Meeting of the Association for Computational Linguistics (Volume 1: Long Papers)*, pages 1715–1725, Berlin, Germany. Association for Computational Linguistics.

Ilya Sutskever, Oriol Vinyals, and Quoc V. Le. 2014. Sequence to sequence learning with neural networks. In *Proceedings of the 27th International Conference on Neural Information Processing Systems*, NIPS'14, pages 3104–3112, Cambridge, MA, USA. MIT Press.

Barret Zoph, Deniz Yuret, Jonathan May, and Kevin Knight. 2016. Transfer learning for low-resource neural machine translation. In *Proceedings of the 2016 Conference on Empirical Methods in Natural Language Processing, EMNLP 2016, Austin, Texas, USA, November 1-4, 2016*, pages 1568–1575.

Rule-based Reordering and Post-Processing for Indonesian-Korean Statistical Machine Translation

Candy Olivia Mawalim, Dessi Puji Lestari, Ayu Purwarianti
School of Electrical Engineering and Informatics
Institut Teknologi Bandung
candyoliviamawalim@gmail.com, dessipuji@gmail.com, ayu@informatika.org

Abstract

This paper presents several experiments on constructing Indonesian–Korean Statistical Machine Translation (SMT) system. A parallel corpus containing around 40,000 segments on each side has been developed for training the baseline SMT system that is built based on n-gram language model and the phrase-based translation table model. This system still has several problems, including non-translated phrases, mistranslation, incorrect phrase orders, and remaining Korean particles in the target language. To overcome these problems, some techniques are employed i.e. POS (part-of-speech) tag model, POS-based reordering rules, multiple steps translation, additional post-process, and their combinations. We then test the SMT system by randomly extracting segments from the parallel corpus. In general, the additional techniques lead to better performance in terms of BLEU score compared to the baseline system

1　Introduction

Statistical Machine Translation (SMT) is a corpus-based MT for automatic translation. It has been growing rapidly since this approach gives some advantages, including language-independent and low-cost construction (Koehn, 2010). In the case of Indonesian–Korean translation, there has not been much research done in this field. It is probably because of the difficulty in constructing parallel

corpus since both Indonesian and Korean are low-resource languages.

As a valuable resource in developing SMT, we first construct a parallel corpus obtained from Korean learning books, drama and movie subtitles, and Bible text. By using this corpus, we construct the baseline SMT system. Phrase-based translation model is used since the previous studies have shown that phrase-based variant of SMT gives better performance than word-based variant of SMT (Koehn, 2010).

After the baseline system has been built, we analyze the problems found on the translation results. Based on these problems, we investigate several additional techniques which can be used to overcome them. These additional techniques are tested with random segments from the parallel corpus. The quality of each system is determined by using smoothed BLEU metric, known as BLEU+1 (Lin and Och, 2004). BLEU score is calculated by multiplying the geometric mean of the test corpus' modified precision scores with the exponential brevity penalty factor (Papineni, et al. 2002).

2　Related Work

Parallel corpus is a valuable component needed in SMT to train models, optimize the model parameters, and test the translation quality. However, a good parallel corpus of low-resource languages such as Indonesian and Korean is hard to obtain. Therefore, we do not only use books as the source for constructing, but also subtitles and Bible. Automatic parallel corpus extraction from movie subtitles has been introduced in (Caroline et al., 2007). From this study, it was reported that 37,625 aligned pairs with a precision of 92.3% was obtained from 40 movies. Using Bible as the parallel corpus source was also introduced in (Christodouloupoulos and Steedman, 2015). Even though there are missing words and the nature of Bible text problems, Bible corpus can be used as one of parallel corpus source.

The use of pivot language has been a common theme for constructing low resource languages SMT. This approach is also used by well-known available MT, Google Translate. It uses English and Japanese as pivot languages for Indonesian–Korean Translation (Balk et al., 2013). However, it has been reported that direct MT model gives better performance compared to pivot MT model (Costa-jussa et al., 2013). A former study about a speech-to-speech translation for 8 Asian languages in A-STAR project has found that this phenomenon also applies to Indonesian–Korean translation (Sakti et al., 2011).

In (Sakti et al., 2011), the SMT system is designed to translate commonly spoken utterances of travel conversations from a given source language into multiple target languages. Basic travel expression sentences (BTEC) with a comparison of training and testing data of 20:1 is used to construct the system. Each Asian language is treated in a different way. In the case of Korean language, they determine a sequence of morphemes as a word. The quality for this direct Indonesian–Korean SMT system in terms of BLEU score is 30.53 (ID–KR) and 23.62 (KR–ID).

The quality of SMT system for specific languages can be improved by adding models and/or techniques. For Indonesian–Japanese translation, experiments by adding lemma translation, particle elimination, and other processes have been reported to produce a better result (Simbolon and Purwarianti, 2013; Sulaeman and Purwarianti, 2015). Since Japanese and Korean has the most similar characteristics in grammar structures (Kim and Dalrymple, 2013), these additional techniques will also be explored as additional processes.

3 Characteristics of Indonesian and Korean Languages

There are some differences between Indonesian and Korean languages described in Table 1 (Kim et al., 2015).

Characteristics	Indonesian	Korean
Basic pattern	subject-predicate-object-adverb (S-P-O-A)	subject-adverb-object-predicate (S-A-O-P)
Adj. explaining noun	Post-modification	Pre-modification
Preposition	Pre-modification	Post-modification
Aux. verb	Pre-modification	Post-modification
Negation word	Pre-modification	Post-modification
Particle	No	Yes
Time marker	Inflection	Conjugation
Honorific form	No	Yes
Unit	Small to large	Large to small

Table 1: Differences between Indonesia and Korean languages

4 Baseline SMT System

The baseline model was built with the aim to find out the problems that exist in Indonesian–Korean SMT system. The development of this model was carried out using several combinations of the collected corpus. These combinations are conducted to observe which corpus is qualified to be used in constructing a SMT system. There are two main steps that need to be performed in constructing a baseline system.

4.1 Parallel Corpus

The parallel corpus is collected from books, subtitles, and Bible. The segment pairs from each source are taken differently. The book-sourced corpus consists of segments which are already available in two languages and the ones which are available only in one language. The segments which are available only in one language are translated manually.

Unlike (Caroline et al., 2007), corpus from subtitles is built by semi-automatically combining several monolingual drama and movie subtitles. Generally, subtitles for Indonesian are in SRT (Subtitle Resource Tracks) format while for Korean language format are in SAMI (Synchronized Accessible Media Interchange) format. SRT format consists of a number indicating the subtitle's sequence, the start and end time the subtitle is appeared and the caption text. However, SAMI file sets the time to milliseconds and the written style is similar to HTML and CSS. Due to these differences, the conversion of Korean subtitles from SAMI to SRT is needed. After the subtitles for both languages have the same format, both segments are paired based on the start time and ending time of each subtitle line. In automatic generation of these subtitle pairs, there are some errors that are then fixed manually. The errors are poorly paired subtitles, one subtitle line from one language consists of more/less than one segment from another language, incorrect translation, excessive punctuation, and undefined characters in this study (not alphanumeric or hangul characters).

Using the Bible as a corpus has several advantages. One of them is because it has been translated into numerous languages (Christodouloupoulos and Steedman, 2015). The version used for the Indonesian Bible is the Terjemahan Baru (TB) (published by Indonesian Bible Society) while the Korean Bible is the 현대인의성경 hyeondaein-uiseong-gyeong version (published by International Bible Society). Both of these Bible version are commonly used since they are translated by the official organizations. The unit used for Bible-sourced segments are the Bible verse. Having obtained the verses pairs for both languages, adjustment is needed for the Korean verse translation which has been merged in the previous verse.

After the corpus is collected, corpus cleaning is then performed. Corpus cleaning is employed by removing excessive whitespace characters, converting every word into a lowercase form and separating each punctuation and word with spaces. After that, tokenization is performed in accordance with the language. Tokenization for Indonesian corpus is based on spaces with the addition of tokenization to a word containing prefix ("ku-" and "kau-") and containing suffix ("-ku", "-mu" and "-nya"). This tokenization process is applied because the Korean has different syntax to Indonesian in case of writing proprietary phrases. In Indonesian the writing of proprietary phrases is united like "rumahku" while in Korean the writing is separated into "내 집".

On the other hand, tokenization for Korean corpus is based on Korean morphology by using Mecab class from KoNLPy (Park and Cho, 2014). Table 2 shows the number of paired segments obtained from each source which are used for building baseline system. The comparison between

training and testing data follows (Sakti et al. 2011). Besides using only one corpus source, this research also utilizes the combination of the corpus sources, i.e. books and subtitles (bs), books and Bible (bB), Bible and subtitles (Bs) and all.

Source	#paired segments		#vocabulary	
	train	test	ID	KR
books (b)	4,886	243	3,286	3,532
subtitles (s)	5,740	286	3,732	5,600
Bible (B)	28,922	1,446	13,775	13,629

Table 2: Number of paired-segments and vocabulary in corpus

4.2 SMT Model

Phrase-based model is used in constructing baseline system. Generally, it consists of language model, translation model, and decoder. We use the parallel corpus which has been cleaned and tokenized to build the language model and translation model. The n-gram based language model is developed by employing the IRSTLM toolkit (Federico et al. 2008). After that, we create the alignment model of each pair of segments using Giza++ (Och and Ney, 2003). Translation model is built based on the alignment model. We use phrase-based translation table as the translation model. This model was developed from the experiments performed by Dalmia (2014). In the translational model, all punctuation is removed except the hyphen (-) which states the reduplication in Indonesian language. The decoder is built based on stack decoding algorithm (Koehn, 2010).

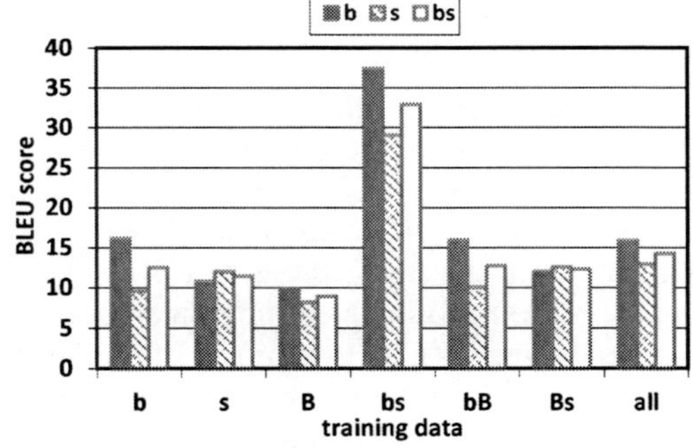

Figure 1: Average BLEU score from baseline system for ID-KR translation

Figure 1 and Figure 2 shows the average BLEU score from the baseline system by using several sources for training and testing data for Indonesian to Korean (ID–KR) and Korean to Indonesian (KR–ID) respectively. The training data used in this evaluation consists of corpus from each source (shown in Table 2) and their combinations (bs, bB, Bs, and all). The testing data consists of books, subtitles and their combination (bs). Table 3 shows the examples of the translation result from the baseline system.

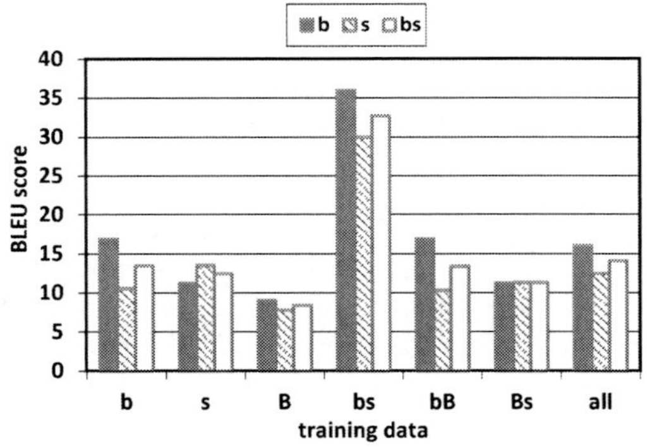

Figure 2: Average BLEU score from baseline system for KR-ID translation

ID–KR	
Source	aku tak sabar bertemu orang-orang
Reference	사람 들 을 정말 만나 보 고 싶 어
Hypothesis	나 tak sabar 만나 서 사람 들
KR–ID	
Source	사람 들 을 정말 만나 보 고 싶 어
Reference	aku tak sabar bertemu orang-orang
Hypothesis	orang-orang di 을 정말 만나 보 kamu ingin 어

Table 3: Example of baseline system translation result

4.3 Analysis

As the baseline, we first observe and determine which parallel corpus to use for training and testing. The quality of translation results are evaluated by using BLEU score. After performing the evaluation by using each source of corpus as testing data, we decide not to use Bible as testing data because the nature of words in Bible is so much different than in books and subtitles. Moreover, machine translation is rarely used for translating Bible because Bible itself has already been translated into numerous languages.

The evaluation of baseline system shows that using Bible corpus as training data obtains worse results than using books or subtitles. However, when we combine the Bible corpus with one of the

other corpus, we can obtain slightly better performance for both ID-KR and KR-ID translation. Using books and subtitles as training data increases the BLEU score significantly. It even gives better results than combining all the corpus. Although the nature of Bible words is different than the other corpus, this corpus may increase the BLEU score slightly because adding this corpus reduces out-of-vocabulary (OOV) problem, from 11.8% to 1.08 %. However, because of the number of paired-segments in Bible corpus is approximately 5 times than the other corpus, it contributes much more than the other corpus. Therefore, when translating common phrases, it produces uncommon translation which will make the translation difficult to understand. Table 4 shows the example of this case.

There are several problems which can be found in the baseline system, including non-translated phrases, mistranslation, incorrect phrase orders, and remaining Korean particle(s) in the target language (shown in Table 5). Non-translated phrases can be caused by the phrases are not registered as n-gram model even though the phrase is in the parallel corpus (Sulaeman and Purwarianti, 2015). In addition, the absence of phrases in the parallel corpus (OOV problem) may also lead to the existence of untranslated phrases. Mistranslation problem can be a partial or an entire incorrect phrase translation. This problem can be occurred because there are several possible phrase translation pairs in the translation model.

ID–KR	
Source	kau begitu ingin melawan penjahat
Reference	범죄자 와 싸우 고 싶 어 안달 이 났 나
Hypothesis	그리고 그렇 군요 고 penjahat 싶 은데 하나님 을 대적
KR–ID	
Source	약국 에서 약 을 샀 어요
Reference	saya membeli obat di apotek
Hypothesis	apotek dari hadapan orang israel obat tadi nya kamu membeli apakah kamu

Table 4: Example of SMT result which use bB as training data

The following problem is incorrect phrase orders. The structure of Indonesian and Korean languages which are very different as we explained in section 3 can lead to this problem. Unlike Korean language, Indonesian does not have particle which cause the remaining Korean particle(s) in the KR-ID translation result. In this paper, we conduct some experiments to overcome these issues. These experiments will be explained in the next section.

Non-Translated phrase	
Source	aku tak sabar bertemu orang-orang
Reference	사람 들 을 정말 만나 보 고 싶 어
Hypothesis	나 tak sabar 만나 서 사람 들
Mistranslation	
Source	saya makan mi instan setiap hari dalam seminggu
Reference	1 주일 동안 매일 라면 을 먹 었 어 요
Hypothesis	밥 먹 매일 instan 일주일
Incorrect phrase orders	
Reference	1 주일 동안 매일 라면 을 먹 었 어 요 1　　2　　3
Hypothesis	밥 먹 매일 instan 일 주일 3　2　3　1
Remaining Korean particle(s)	
Source	내일 은 목요일 입니다
Reference	besok hari kamis
Hypothesis	besok adalah 은 목요일

Table 5: Example of translation result with baseline system problems

5 Experiments

There are 5 main techniques that are conducted in this study, i.e. adding POS tag information, POS-based reordering rules, multiple steps translation, additional post-process, and their combinations. The additional POS tag information technique, some additional post-process (lemma translation and particle elimination) are adapted from (Simbolon and Purwarianti, 2013; Sulaeman and Purwarianti, 2015).

5.1 POS Tag Information Addition

Adding POS tag information technique is employed to make the translation phrase more accurate and the POS tag arrangement in the translations more natural. The POS tagger used for Indonesian corpus is the modified Pebahasa library (Wicaksono and Purwarianti, 2010), while for Korean corpus is the Mecab class in KoNLPy (Park and Cho, 2014).

Figure 3 and Figure 4 shows the comparison between baseline system and system with POS tag information addition performance in terms of average BLEU score. From the figure, it can be seen that there is a decrease in BLEU score for both ID-KR and KR-ID translation. This decreasing in the BLEU score indicates that the model with POS tag information does not successfully minimize the

phrase translation error. On the other hand, it added the number of non-translated phrases in the translation results (Table 6).

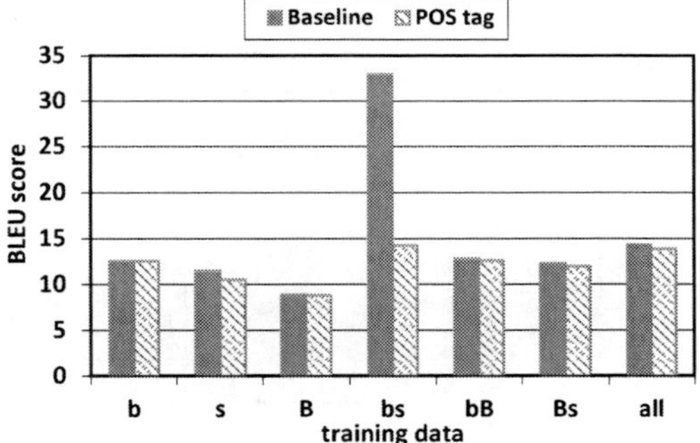

Figure 3: Comparison of baseline system and POS tag information addition system for ID–KR translation

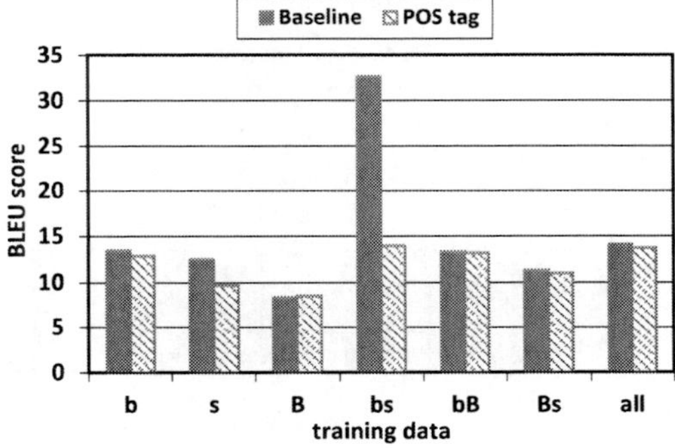

Figure 4: Comparison of baseline system and POS tag information addition system for KR–ID translation

Sumber	할아버지 생신 이 언제 예요
Referensi	kapan ulang tahun kakek
Baseline	kapan ulang tahun kakek
Hipotesis	kakek 생신 yang ini kapan kamu 예 요

Table 6: Example of translation result with POS tag information addition system

5.2 POS-Based Reordering Rules

In this study we do not use the common reordering model, such as syntax-based models (Chiang, 2005) and lexicalized models (Och et al., 2004) because those methods try to solve the common problem which only perform well when the ordering of words does not vary too much (Genzel, 2010). The reordering rule is performed before the source language is translated into the target language. This rule is generated manually based on the POS tag information and the alignment of the segments of source language and target language. This POS tag information is used to define the part that becomes a unity of subject, predicate, object, and adverb. Table 7 shows the example of the reordering rule.

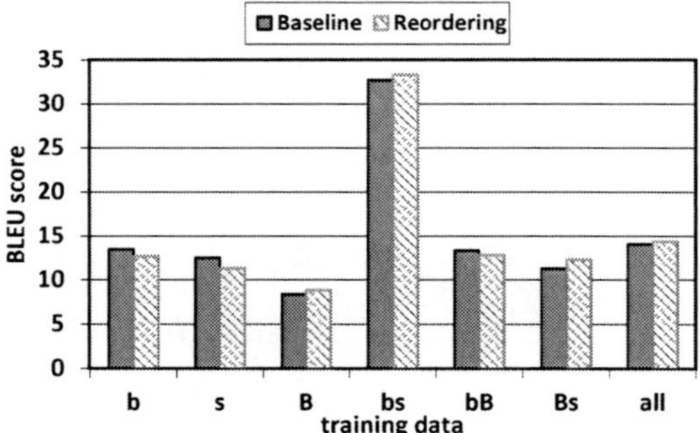

Figure 5: Comparison of baseline system and system with POS-based reordering rule addition for ID–KR translation

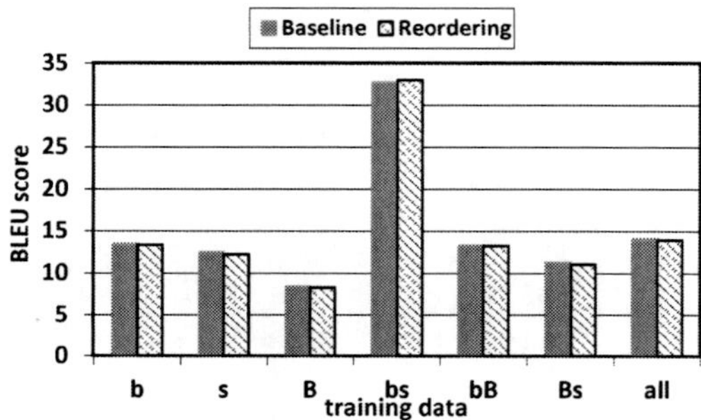

Figure 6: Comparison of baseline system and system with POS-based reordering rule addition for KR–ID translation

lang	segment	POS tag	Rule
ID	bos kami tidak punya banyak uang	NN PRP NEG VBT JJ NN	(1 2) (5 6) (3 4)
KR	약국 에서 약 을 샀 어요	NNG JKB NNG JKO VV+EP EF	(3 4 (5 6)) (1 2)

Table 7: Example of POS-based reordering rule

ID–KR	
Source	jangan berenang
Reference	수영 하 지 마세요
Baseline	지 마세요 수영 을 해요
Hypothesis	수영 을 해요 지 마세요
KR–ID	
Source	약국 에서 약 을 샀 어요
Reference	(saya) membeli obat di apotek
Baseline	obat di apotek saya membeli 어 요 obat
Hypothesis	beli 을 obat ini di apotek

Table 8: Example of the translation result by using POS-based reordering rule

The number of rules which are used in this study is 130 for Indonesian language and 50 for Korean language. Figure 5 and Figure 6 shows the comparison of baseline system and system with POS-based reordering rule addition for ID-KR and KR-ID translation respectively. We can see that even though there is only a small number of rules, this technique can improve the quality of ID-KR translation. Table 8 shows the example of the translation result by using this reordering rules.

5.3 Multiple Steps Translation

ID–KR	
Source	saya ingin memberikan sepatu sebagai hadiah kepada pacar saya tapi saya tidak yakin
Reference	남자 친구 에게 신발 을 선물 하 고 싶 은데 고민 이 에요
bs	saya ingin memberikan 신발 을 선물 kepada pacar saya tapi saya tidak yakin
bs-bB	고 싶 은데 여자 친구 memberikan 신발 을 선물 kepada 지만 지 않 아요 yakin
bs-bB-Bs	고 싶 은데 여자 친구 주 었 으며 신발 을 선물 에게 말씀 해 주 셨 지만 지 않 아요 yakin
bs-bB-Bs-all	고 싶 은데 여자 친구 주 었 으며 신발 을 선물 에게 말씀 해 주 셨 지만 지 않 아요 yakin
KR–ID	
Source	오늘 은 저희 학교 졸업식 이 에요
Reference	hari ini adalah hari wisuda sekolah
bs	hari ini 저희 학교 졸업식 이 에요 adalah
bs-bB	hari ini 저희 sekolah wisuda anak manusia juga akan 에 요 adalah
bs-bB-Bs	hari ini 저희 sekolah wisuda anak manusia juga akan rupa nya adalah
bs-bB-Bs-all	hari ini 저희 sekolah wisuda anak manusia juga akan rupa nya adalah

Table 9: Example of the translation result by using bs-bB-Bs-all multiple steps translation

Adding corpus does not necessarily improve the quality of the translation but it is able to reduce the OOV problem. This underlies the multiple steps translations both to improve translation quality as well as to reduce OOV. The multiple steps translation experiments are performed in two ways, i.e. translation with adding b-s-B-all corpus step-by-step and translation with adding bs-bB-Bs-all corpus step by step. Figure 7 shows that multiple steps translation can give a better translation quality, except for bs-bB-Bs-all steps for KR-ID translation. This is caused by Korean morphemes which has no particular meaning, e.g. particles are translated. Table 9 shows the example of multiple steps translation result.

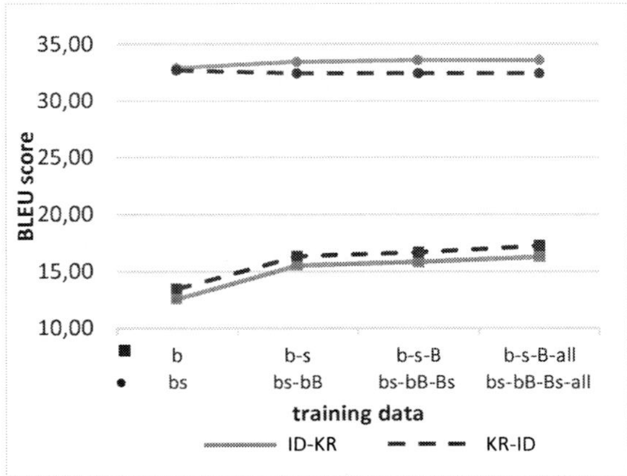

Figure 7: Comparison of baseline system and system with multiple steps translation

5.4 Additional Post-Process

Additional post-processes performed in this study consist of name entity (NE) translation, particle elimination, dictionary translation, lemma translation and basic verb conversion. NE translation process directly translates the word considered as NE from the Indonesian word to the writing of the Korean language and vice versa. The NE is determined by the rules based on its POS tag and lemma. If the NE has high similarity value with vocabulary from training data which is not listed in Kamus Besar Bahasa Indonesia (KBBI) and Son Myun Kwan ID-KR dictionary, the translation of NE is interpreted as that vocabulary.

The following additional process is translating the non-translated phrases by using the ID-KR dictionary help. The contents of this dictionary is not similar to the standard dictionary because it contains examples of sentences and other explanations. Therefore, the translation process is employed by using n-gram matching (from 3-gram to 1-gram). Translation by using dictionary is able to minimize non-translated phrases. However, since

there are many possible translations for a single phrase, the translation obtained from the dictionary is only taken from the first phrase found during the search process. This results in the possibility of generated translations is not commonly used in the target language.

Lemma translation is the development of the dictionary translation. For phrases that still can not be translated in dictionary translation, specifically for ID-KR translation which is conducted by using Indonesian lemma. The following additional process is converting Korean verb to its basic form before dictionary translation. This process is conducted because there are many verbs which can not be translated due to the different form. Figure 8 shows the comparison of baseline system and additional post-process system by using bs corpus as training data.

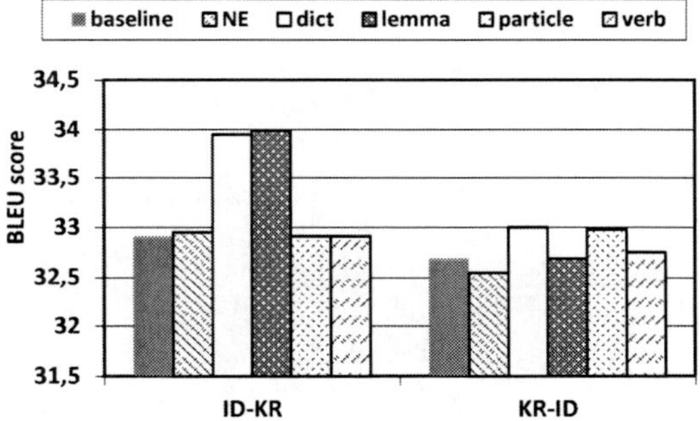

Figure 8: Comparison of baseline system and additional post-process system

5.5 Combination Techniques

Based on the experiment results, we try to combine all the techniques to improve the quality of translations. The combination techniques are performed by not adding the POS tag information since it causes worse result. The experimental combination is divided into two, as follows.
-   1st Combination: Reordering–additional post-processes (particle elimination, dictionary translation, lemma translation, verb conversion, NE translation)–multiple steps translation
-   2nd Combination: Reordering–particle elimination-multiple steps translation-additional post-processes (dictionary translation, lemma translation, verb conversion, NE translation)

Particle elimination is performed first in order to decrease the probability of the Korean particles which usually do not have particular meaning is being translated as some phrases in Indonesian language. 1st combination and 2nd combination is used to determine whether multiple steps translation or additional post-processes is needed to be performed first. Figure 9 shows the comparison of baseline system and these combination system. 1st combination gives better results in both ID-KR and KR-ID translation.

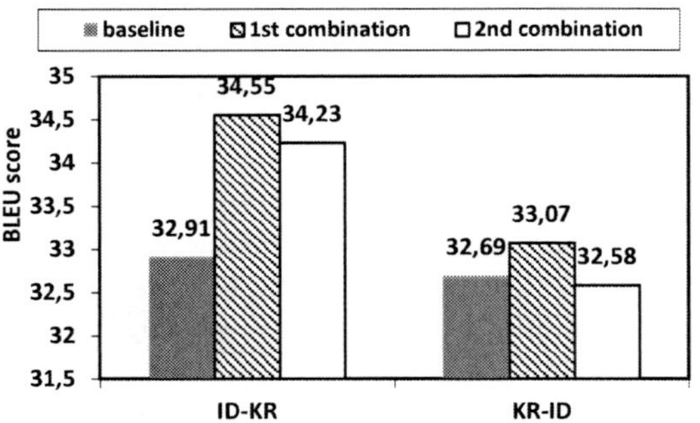

Figure 9: Comparison of baseline system and additional post-process system

ID–KR	
Source	saya ingin memberikan sepatu sebagai hadiah kepada pacar saya tapi saya tidak yakin
Reference	남자 친구 에게 신발 을 선물 하 고 싶 은데 고민 이 에요
Baseline	saya ingin memberikan 신발 을 선물 kepada pacar saya tapi saya tidak yakin
1st Combination	나 바라다 주다 신발 을 선물 에게 애인 나 그러나 나 이 아니다 확신하는
2nd Combination	고 싶 은데 여자 친구 주 었 으며 신발 을 선물 에게 말씀 해 주 셨 지만 지 않 아요 확신하는
KR–ID	
Source	텔레비전 보 기 전 에 숙제 해
Reference	kerjakan prmu sebelum nonton tv
Baseline	dulu sebelum nonton tv 에 숙제 해
1st Combination	dulu sebelum nonton tv pekerjaan rumah Syaka
2nd Combination	dulu sebelum nonton tv pr nya untuk

Table 10: Example of translation by using the combination system

As we can see the result of the 1st combination in Table 10, the untranslated phrases is no longer present in the translation. However, there are more mistranslation phrase, such as "해" which is translated as "Syaka". This word is obtained from dictionary translation and is not related with the reference at all. For ID-KR translation, the dictionary translation help to translate the untranslated verb, such as "tidak yakin" as "아니다 확신하는", this translation is incorrect as a phrase. There are rules to form the Korean verb as explained in section 3. Reordering rules which are provided in this system do not affect this sample translation because of the limitation of the number of the rules. In conclusion, although the problems described in section 4.3 are still found in the translation result, these problems have already been reduced.

On the other hand, the result obtained from the 2nd combination is worse than the 1st combination. The multiple steps translation which performed first causes the unrelated phrase, such as "말씀 해 주 셨" found in the translation result. As shown in Table 9, even though this technique gives the better performance than the baseline system, it causes the appearance of the common Bible phrases, such as "anak manusia".

6 Conclusion and Future Work

In this paper we have presented several experiments on constructing Indonesian–Korean SMT. The combination of books and subtitles corpus is the best corpus which can be used both as training and testing data in this study. Our experiments also show that the corpus collected from Bible is better used as training data after using books and subtitles corpus. Most of the additional techniques can increase the quality of translation in terms of BLEU score, except the adding POS tag information technique. The best technique (1st combination) are able to increase the BLEU score up to 4,97% for ID-KR translation and 1,15% for KR-ID translation.

There are still many things to explore in constructing Indonesian–Korean SMT. Automatic approaches of constructing parallel corpus (Caroline et al., 2007) from subtitles can become alternative in the next study. A source-side reordering model which is introduced in (Genzel, 2010) can also be used to develop the reordering method. Another possibility of improvement is using rules to form the Korean verbs for ID-KR translation. In the future we would like to use these proposed methods in order to improve the Indonesian-Korean SMT.

References

Alfan Farizki Wicaksono and Ayu Purwarianti. 2010. HMM Based POS Tagger for Bahasa Indonesia. Proceedings of 4th International MALINDO (Malay and Indonesian Language) Workshop.

Ayushi Dalmia. 2014. Phrase Based Translation Model. India: International Institute of Information Technology.

Bertoldi, N., Cettolo, M., & Federico, M. (2008). IRSTLM: an open source toolkit for handling large scale language models. INTERSPEECH.

Chin-Yew Lin and Franz Josef Och. 2004. Automatic Evaluation of Machine Translation Quality using Longest Common Subsequence and Skip-Bigram Statistics. 42nd Meeting of the Association for Computational Linguistics (ACL'04), Main Volume. Barcelona, Spain. 605-612.

Christos Christodouloupoulos and Mark Steedman. 2015. A massively parallel corpus: the Bible in 100 languages. Language Resources and Evaluation 375–395.

David Chiang. 2005. A Hierarchical Phrase-Based Model for Statistical Machine Translation. Proceedings of the ACL'05. Ann Arbor, Michigan. 263-270.

Dmitriy Genzel. 2010. Automatically Learning Source-side Reordering Rules for Large Scale Machine Translation. Proceeding COLING '10 Proceedings of the 23rd International Conference on Computational Linguistics. Beijing, China. 376-384.

Ethan M. Balk, Mei Chung, M.L. Chen, T.A. Trikalinos, Kong, Win Chang L. 2013. Assessing the Accuracy of Google Translate To Allow Data Extraction From Trials Published in Non-English Language. Agency for Heatlhcare Research and Quality.

Eunjeong L. Park and Sungzoon Cho. 2014. KoNLPy: Korean natural language processing in Python. 26th Annual Conference on Human & Cognitive Language Technology. Chuncheon, South Korea.

Franz Josef Och and Hermann Ney. 2003. A Systematic Comparison of Various Statistical Alignment Models. Association of Computational Linguistics 29: 19-51.

Franz Josef Och, Daniel Gildea, Sanjeev Khudanpur, Anoop Sarkar, Kenji Yamada, Alex Fraser, Shankar Kumar, et al. 2004. A Smorgasbord of Features for Statistical Machine Translation. HLT-NAACL 2004: Main Proceedings. Boston, Massachusetts, USA. 161–168.

Kishore Papineni, Salim Roukos, Todd Ward, and Wei-Jing Zhu. 2002. BLEU: A Method for Automatic Evaluation of Machine Translation. Proceedings of the 40th Annual Meeting of the Association for Computational Linguistics (ACL). Philadelphia. 311-318.

Lavecchia Caroline, Sma'ıli Kamel, and Langlois David. 2007. Building Parallel Corpora from Movies. The 4th International Workshop on Natural Language Processing and Cognitive Science - NLPCS. Funchal, Madeira, Portugal.

Marta R. Costa-jussa, Carlos A. Henriquez, and Rafael E. Banchs. 2013. Evaluating Indirect Strategies fo Chinese-Spanish Statistical Machine Translation: Extended Abstract. Proceedings of the Twenty-Third International Joint Conference on Artificial Intelligence. Beijing, China. 3142-3145.

M.A Sulaeman and Ayu Purwarianti. 2015. Development of Indonesian-Japanese Statistical Machine Translation Using Lemma Translation and Additional Post-Process. The 5th International Conference on Electrical Engineering and Informatics. Bali, Indonesia: IEEE. 54-58.

Philipp Koehn. 2004. Europarl: A Parallel Corpus for Statistical Machine Translation.

Philipp Koehn. 2010. Statistical Machine Translation. New York: Cambridge University Press.

Roger Kim and Mary Dalrymple. 2013. Porting Grammar between Typologically Similar Languages: Japanese to Korean. Pacific Asia Conference on Language, Information and Computation 2013. Taipei. 98-105.

Sakriani Sakti, Michael Paul, Andrew Finch, Shinsuke Sakai, Thang Tat Vu, Noriyuki Kimura, Chiori Hori, Eiichiro Sumita, Satoshi Nakamura, and Jun Park. 2011. A-STAR: Toward Translating Asian Spoken Languages. Computer Speech & Language Vol. 27, Issue 2, Feb 2013 509-527.

Seon Jung Kim, Kyung Mo Min, Sung Tae Park, and Yong Heo. 2015. EPS-TOPIK untuk Orang Indonesia Panduan Belajar Mandiri Bahasa Korea. Ulsan, South Korea: HRD Korea.

Simon Simbolon and Ayu Purwarianti. 2013. Experiment on Indonesian-Japanese Statistical Machine Translation. IEEE Cyberneticscom 2013 80-84.

Sentence Complexity Estimation for Chinese-speaking
Learners of Japanese

Jun Liu
Graduate School of Information Science
Nara Institute of Science and Technology
8916-5 Takayama, Ikoma, Nara 630-0192, Japan
`liu.jun.lc3@is.naist.jp`

Yuji Matsumoto
Graduate School of Information Science
Nara Institute of Science and Technology
8916-5 Takayama, Ikoma, Nara 630-0192, Japan
`matsu@is.naist.jp`

Abstract

It is fairly challenging for a foreign language learner to read and understand Japanese texts containing words of high difficulty level or low frequency and complicated linguistic structures. Because a large number of Chinese characters (kanji in Japanese) are commonly used both in Chinese and Japanese, the more confusing problem for Japanese language learners from kanji background countries is the acquisition of various complex Japanese functional expressions. In this study, we propose a method utilizing Japanese kanji characters, particularly Japanese–Chinese homographs with identical or similar meanings, as a critical feature of sentence-complexity estimation for Chinese-speaking learners of Japanese language. Experimental results have partially demonstrated the effectiveness of our method in enhancing the accuracy of sentence-complexity estimation.

1 Introduction

Enhancing reading capability is one of the important purposes in second language teaching and learning. There are various factors that impact learners' reading comprehension. A few of these factors involve the learners' vocabulary knowledge, grammar knowledge, reading strategies, interest, attitude, and motivation (Koda, 2007; Han and

Song, 2011; Horiba, 2012; Gilakjani and Sabouri, 2016). Reading comprehension is also influenced by the complexity of the reading material. Texts containing highly demanding vocabularies and highly complex sentence structures are likely to disturb the learners' reading comprehension. Learners of Japanese language from kanji background countries benefit substantially from kanji characters commonly used in both Japanese and Chinese when they read Japanese sentences or documents. However, it is more challenging for them to read and learn various Japanese functional expressions with varied meanings and usages.

The selection of appropriate reading material matching the learners' individual capabilities is highly likely to enable language learners to read in a more focused and selective manner. To support learners in gathering useful information from texts more effectively, certain online public Japanese reading-assistance systems such as Reading Tutor[1], Asunaro[2], Rikai[3], and WWWJDIC[4] are highly effective. These systems are adequately constructed for providing an internet learning environment where learners can make complete use of information from the internet for their Japanese language study, and a few of them are specifically designed to enable language learners to understand Japanese texts by offering words with their corresponding difficulty level information or translation (Toyoda 2016). However, these systems

---

[1] http://language.tiu.ac.jp/
[2] https://hinoki-project.org/asunaro/
[3] http://www.rikai.com/perl/Home.pl
[4] http://nihongo.monash.edu/cgi-bin/wwwjdic?9T

do not take the learners' native language background into account. Moreover, these systems provide learners with limited information on the grammatical difficulty of all the various types of Japanese functional expressions, which learners actually intend to learn as a part of the procedure for learning Japanese.

In Section 2 of this paper, we introduce some previous works. In Section 3, we describe our method for ranking example sentences of Japanese functional expressions by utilizing Japanese–Chinese homographs with identical or similar meanings, as a critical feature. Section 4 describes the several experiments conducted to examine the effectiveness of our method. Finally, in Section 5, we conclude and describe future work.

2   Previous Research

Text difficulty or text readability evaluation is one of the challenges in natural language processing (NLP) owing to the linguistic complexity generated from both vocabulary and grammar. Researchers have been actively exploring methods to evaluate text difficulty (Gonzalez-Dios et al., 2014; Hancke, Vajjala, and Meurers, 2012; Vajjala and Meurers, 2012; Xia, Kochmar and Briscoe, 2016).

For English texts, there are numerous popular formulas such as Flesch Reading Ease (Flesch 1948) and Flesch-Kincaid Grade Level, all of which are used for several applications such as compilation of reading materials for language learners. Collins–Thompson and Callan (2004) proposed a language modeling method to estimate the readability of English and French texts.

For Japanese texts, Tateishi, Ono, and Yamada (1988a; 1988b) introduced a formula based on six surface characteristics: average number of characters per sentence, average number of Roman letters and symbols, average number of hiragana characters, average number of kanji characters, average number of katakana characters, and ratio of touten (comma) to kuten (period). Formula-based approaches have also been used or teaching Japanese to young native speakers (Shibasaki and Sawai, 2007; Sato, Matsuyoshi, and Kondoh, 2008; Shibasaki and Tamaoka, 2010). To evaluate text difficulty level for foreign language learners of Japanese, Wang and Andersen (2016) introduced an approach for evaluating Japanese text difficulty

that focuses on grammar and utilizes grammar templates.

In recent years, a few Japanese text difficulty evaluation systems have been developed to support Japanese language learners (Hasebe and Lee, 2015; Lee and Hasebe, 2016). For example, JReadability[5] can analyze input text and estimate its readability to categorize it as belonging to one of six difficulty levels, on the basis of five characteristics: average length of sentence; percentage of kango (words of Chinese origin), percentage of wago (words of Japanese origin), percentage of verbs, and percentage of particles.

However, JReadability too does not sufficiently consider the various types of Japanese functional expressions with varying difficulty levels. The prediction value calculated by this system is more reliable for long texts (approximately 1000 characters) and not for single sentences.

3   General Method

Japanese and Chinese share a large quantity of homographs that use identical kanji characters (both in simplified Chinese and traditional Chinese). Table 1 presents a few examples of Japanese–Chinese homographs. These words play a significant role while reading Japanese or Chinese texts. According to a report by Wang (2001), approximately 80–95% Japanese–Chinese homographs are used to express identical or similar meanings in both the languages. Foreign language learners from kanji background countries can straightforwardly understand the meaning of these words according to kanji characters. This is occasionally more convenient than grammar for foreign language learners from kanji background countries to learn Japanese.

For Japanese language learners, a vital challenge is to master a large number of complex functional expressions. Hence, providing appropriate example sentences for learners based on their individual Japanese language capabilities are highly likely to aid the enhancement of the efficiency of learning various Japanese functional expressions.

In order to achieve this goal, we utilize Japanese–Chinese homographs as a new feature, which is more or less dissimilar from previous research, to estimate sentence difficulty and select

---

[5] http://jreadability.net

the most appropriate example sentences as learning content for Japanese functional expressions.

Japanese	Chinese	Meaning
社会(society)	社会(society)	Identical
技術(technology)	技术(technology)	Identical
東西(east and west)	东西(east and west; thing)	Similar
培養(culture)	培养(culture; train)	Similar
手紙(letters)	手纸(toilet paper)	Dissimilar
勉強(study)	勉强(reluctantly)	Dissimilar

Table 1: Examples of Japanese–Chinese homographs.

3.1 Difficulty Level Evaluation Standard

To estimate the difficulties of example sentences, we follow the standard of the Japanese Language Proficiency Test (JLPT). The JLPT consists of five levels: N1, N2, N3, N4, and N5. The least difficult level is N5, and the most difficult level is N1[6]. Since 2010, the JLPT official lists of vocabulary and grammar have not been published in books, we referenced a few books (Xu and Reika, 2013a; Xu and Reika, 2013b) and online learning websites[7,8], all of which provide lists of the JLPT vocabulary and grammar with difficulty levels ranging from N1–N5. Here, we consider levels N3/SP3 and lower as "easy" level, levels N2/SP2 and above as difficult level. A few examples of vocabulary and grammar in JLPT are presented in Table 2.

3.2 List of Japanese–Chinese Homographs

Japanese language learners from kanji background countries can conveniently read and understand majority of the Japanese words written in kanji. However, in the vocabulary list of JLPT, numerous Japanese–Chinese homographs are classified as difficult levels (N2 and above) without consideration of learners' differing mother tongue background. Consequently, we attempt to construct a list of Japanese–Chinese homographs that is likely to be helpful in estimating complexity of example sentences that include Japanese functional expressions.

Japanese vocabulary	Difficulty level
山岳(mountains) 養う(to cultivate) 忙しない(busy)	N1
前提(Presupposition) 迫る(to press) 勇ましい(brave)	N2
愛情(love) 含める(to include) 巨大(huge)	N3
複雑(complex) 捨てる(to throw away) 挨拶(greeting)	N4
学校(school) 明るい(bright) 始まる(begin)	N5

Japanese grammar	Difficulty level
べからざる(must not) がてら(while doing something) を顧みず(regardless of)	SP1
からといって(just because) に加えて(in addition to) に違いない(without a doubt)	SP2
にとって(to) に比べて(compare) わけがない(it is impossible that)	SP3
かもしれない(maybe) ことができる(can) みたいだ(similar to)	SP4
てから(after) 前に(before) ている(am/is/are doing)	SP5

Table 2: Examples of Japanese vocabulary and grammar in JLPT.

To accomplish this task, we first extracted the Japanese words containing only kanji characters from two dictionaries: IPA (mecab-ipadic-2.7.0-20070801)[9] and UniDic (unidic-mecab 2.1.2)[10]. These two dictionaries are used as the standard

---

[6] http://jlpt.jp/e/about/levelsummary.html
[7] http://www.tanos.co.uk/jlpt/
[8] http://japanesetest4you.com

[9] https://sourceforge.net/projects/mecab/files/mecab-ipadic/2.7.0-20070801/mecab-ipadic-2.7.0-20070801.tar.gz/download
[10] http://osdn.net/project/unidic/

dictionaries for the morphological analyzer MeCab, with appropriate part-of-speech information for each expression. We then extracted the Chinese translation words of these Japanese words from the following online dictionary websites: Wiktionary[11] and Weblio [12]. We compared the character form of the Japanese word with its Chinese translation word to identify whether the Japanese word is a Japanese–Chinese homograph or not. Because Japanese uses both simplified Chinese characters such as "雨 (rain), 木 (tree), and 本 (book)" and traditional Chinese characters such as "車 (car), 頭 (head), and 雲 (cloud)," we replaced all the traditional Chinese characters with the simplified Chinese characters. If the character form of a Japanese word is similar to the character form of the Chinese translation word, the Japanese word is identified as a Japanese–Chinese homograph. Considering unknown words in the above online dictionaries, we also referenced an online Chinese encyclopedia: Baike Baidu [13] and a Japanese dictionary: Kojien fifth Edition (Shinmura, 1998). If a Japanese word and its corresponding Chinese word share an identical or a similar meaning, then, the Japanese word is also identified as a Japanese–Chinese homograph. Finally, we created a list of Japanese–Chinese homographs consisting of approximately 14 000 words.

3.3 Extraction of Japanese Grammar

There are a large number of Japanese functional expressions in Japanese grammar. A problematic feature of Japanese functional expressions is that each functional expression is likely to exhibit numerous surface forms such as "Headword: なければならない (should) and its surface form variations: なければなりません、なければならず、なければならなく、なければならなかっ、なければならぬ...." Based on the grammar list of JLPT, we finally constructed a list of Japanese functional expressions consisting of approximately 680 headwords and 4000 types of their surface form variations, as illustrated in Table 3.

To extract Japanese functional expressions, we use a publicly available morphological analyzer

MeCab [14]. We incorporate the list of Japanese functional expressions into the IPA dictionary considering it likely that the morphological analyzer MeCab extracts the usages of functional expressions automatically. Table 4 demonstrates certain extracted examples of Japanese functional expressions.

Headword	Surface Forms	Difficulty Level
をふまえて (in accord with)	をふまえ をふまえた を踏まえて を踏まえ を踏まえた	SP1
にさいして (on the occasion of)	にさいし にさいしまして に際して に際し に際しまして	SP2
ねばならない (should)	ねばなりません ねばならなかっ ねばならなく ねばならぬ ねばならず ねばならん	SP3
ていけない (must not)	ていけなかっ ていけません でいけない でいかなかっ でいけません	SP4
ではない (am/is/are not)	ではありません じゃありません ではなかっ じゃない じゃなかっ	SP5

Table 3: Examples of Japanese functional expressions and surface form variations.

4 Experiments

Because our purpose is to provide the Japanese language learners with straightforward example sentences such that they can understand the meaning and usage of the Japanese functional

---

[11] http://ja.wictionary.org/wiki/メインページ
[12] http://cjjc.weblio.jp
[13] https://baike.baidu.com

[14] http://taku910.github.io/mecab/

expressions conveniently, it is necessary to solve the problem of displaying the order of the example sentences based on their difficulty. To achieve this goal, we adopt an online machine learning tool, Support Vector Machine for Ranking (SVM^{rank})[15], to estimate the complexity of example sentence.

Input: 彼は学生ではありません。 Output: 彼 **は** 学生 **ではありません** 。 (He is not a student.)
Input: 野菜を食べなければならない。 Output:野菜 **を** 食べ **なければならない** 。 (You must eat vegetables.)
Input: 私は行きたくてたまらない。 Output: 私 **は** 行き **たく** **てたまらない** 。 (I am eager to go.)
Input: 物価は上がる一方だ。 Output: 物価 **は** 上がる **一方だ** 。 (Prices continue to increase.)
Input: 天気いかんにかかわらず来ます。 Output: 天気 **いかんにかかわらず** 来 **ます**。 (Regardless of the weather, I will come.)

Table 4: Extraction of Japanese functional expressions. In the sentences, Japanese functional expressions are in bold and underlined.

4.1 Data Setting

We utilize the Balanced Corpus of Contemporary Written Japanese (BCCWJ) to carry out our experiments:

- BCCWJ [16] is a corpus created for comprehending the breadth of contemporary written Japanese; it contains extensive samples of modern Japanese texts to create as uniquely balanced a corpus as possible. The data comprises 104.3 million words, covering genres including general books and magazines, newspapers, business reports, blogs, internet forums, textbooks, and legal documents.

4.2 Features

Based on the standardization of difficulty level evaluation in JLPT described in Section 3.1, we employ the following 12 features as the baseline readability feature set:

- Number of N0–N5 Japanese words in a sentence (Here, N0 implies unknown words in the vocabulary list of JLPT.)

- Number of SP1–SP5 Japanese functional expressions in a sentence

- Length of a sentence

As a departure from the standardization of difficulty level evaluation in JLPT, we identify the Japanese words in the list of Japanese–Chinese homographs mentioned in Section 3.2 as belonging to the easy level labeled as NJ–C. We assume that if an example sentence contains a higher number of N3–N5 words, SP3–SP5 Japanese functional expressions, and Japanese–Chinese homographs, this example sentence will be more straightforward to read and understand for Chinese-speaking learners. Therefore, we utilize Japanese–Chinese homographs as a new feature in our experiments.

- Number of NJ–C Japanese words in a sentence

Finally, we combine this new feature with the baseline readability features (all 13 features) as we wish to examine whether this new feature will actually help enhance example-sentence-difficulty estimation.

4.3 Example-Sentence-Difficulty Estimation

We first collected 5000 example sentences from the BCCWJ and divided them into 2500 pairs. Then, we invited 15 native Chinese-speaking learners of Japanese language, all of whom have been learning Japanese for ~1 y, to read two example sentences in one pair and select the one that is more straightforward to read and understand. Considering the feasibility of a learner's decision on a particular pair to vary from that of the other learners, we asked every three learners to compare a particular pair. The final decision was made by majority vote. We finally utilized a set of fivefold cross-validations with each combination of 4000 sentences as the training data and 1000 sentences as the test data.

Experimental results using baseline features and our method are presented in Tables 5 and 6, respectively.

---

[15] https://www.cs.cornell.edu/people/tj/svm_light/ svm_rank.html

[16] http://pj.ninjal.ac.jp/corpus_center/bccwj/en/

Features	Cross-validations	Accuracy
Baseline Features	1	82.4%
	2	82.8%
	3	81.8%
	4	80.8%
	5	81.4%
Average		**81.84%**

Table 5: Experimental results using baseline features.

Features	Cross-validations	Accuracy
Our Method	1	84.4%
	2	86.8%
	3	84.8%
	4	82.8%
	5	83.2%
Average		**84.4%**

Table 6: Experimental results using our method.

According to the experimental results in Tables 5 and 6, our method of incorporating Japanese–Chinese homograph features to baseline readability features effectively estimates the difficulty level of example sentences of Japanese functional expressions, with an average accuracy of 84.4%. In comparison with the experimental results using baseline features, our method enhances the accuracy by 2.56%, partially demonstrating the effectiveness of our method.

5 Conclusion and Future Work

We proposed a method that integrates vocabulary knowledge of Japanese–Chinese homographs that Chinese-speaking learners of Japanese are capable of understanding straightforwardly, with the aim of estimating complexity of example sentences that include Japanese functional expressions. The experimental results demonstrated that this method enhanced the accuracy of estimation of the difficulty levels of example sentences.

However, we did not evaluate the learning effect of using the example sentences of Japanese functional expressions generated by our method. In our future work, we plan to consider other features such as word types and number of verbs to enhance example-sentence-complexity estimation for Chinese-speaking learners of Japanese. Finally, we intend to develop a Computer-aided Language Learning (CALL) system that can recommend learning content to individual learners at appropriate difficulty levels.

Acknowledgments

We wish to thank all those who allocated their time to complete our online survey and the anonymous reviewers for their detailed comments and advice.

References

Abbas Pourhosein Gilakjani and Narjes Banou Sabou. 2016. A Study of Factors Affecting EFL Learners' Reading Comprehension Skill and the Strategies for Improvement. International Journal of English Linguistics, 6(5): pp. 180–187.

Itziar Gonzalez-Dios, María Jesús Aranzabe, Arantza Díaz de Ilarraza, and Haritz Salaberri. 2014. Simple or complex? assessing the readability of basque texts. In Proceedings of COLING 2014: Technical Papers, pp. 334–344, Dublin, Ireland, August.

Fudolf Flesch. 1948. A new readability yardstick. Journal of Applied Psychology, 32(3): pp. 221–233.

Dongli Han, and Xin Song. 2011. Japanese Sentence Pattern Learning with the Use of Illustrative Examples Extracted from the Web. IEEJ Transactions on Electrical and Electronic Engineering, 6(5): pp. 490–496.

Julia Hancke, Sowmya Vajjala, and Detmar Meurers. 2012. Readability classification for German using lexical, syntactic, and morphological features. In Proceedings of COLING 2012, pp. 1063–1080, Mumbai, India, December.

Yoichiro Hasebe and Jae-Ho Lee. 2015. Introducing a Readability Evaluation System for Japanese Language Education. In Proceedings of the 6th International Conference on Computer Assisted Systems for Teaching & Learning Japanese, pp. 19–22.

Yukie Horiba. 2012. Word knowledge and its relation to text comprehension: a comparative study of Chinese -and Korean-speaking L2 learners and L1 speakers of Japanese. The Modern Language Journal, 96(1): pp. 108–121.

Keiko Koda. 2007. Reading Language Learning: Cross-Linguistic Constraints on Second Language Reading Development. Language Learning, 57(1), pp. 11–44.

Takahiro Ohno, Zyunitiro Edani, Ayato Inoue, and Dongli Han. 2013. A Japanese Learning Support

System Matching Individual Abilities. In Proceeding of the PACLIC 27 Workshop on Computer-Assisted Language Learning, pp. 556–562.

Satoshi Sato, Suguru Matsuyoshi, and Yohsuke Kondoh. 2008. Automatic Assessment of Japanese Text Readability Based on a Textbook Corpus. In Proceedings of the Sixth International Language Resources and Evaluation, pp. 654–660, Marrakech, Morocco.

Hideko Shibasaki and Yasutaka Sawai. 2007. Study for constructing a readability formula of Japanese texts using a corpus of language school textbooks. IEICE Technical Report NCL2007-32, pp. 19–24.

Hideko Shibasaki and Katsuo Tamaoka. 2010. Constructing a Formula to Predict School Grades 1-9 based on Japanese Language School Textbooks. Japan Journal of Educational Technology 33(4), pp. 449–458.

Izuru Shinmura (Ed. In chief). 1998. Kojien 5th Editon (in Japanese). Tokyo: Iwanani Press.

Yuka Tateisi, Yoshihiko Ono, and Hisao Yamada. 1988a. A computer readability formula of Japanese texts for ma-chine scoring. In Proceedings of the 12th Conference on Computational Linguistics, volume 2, pp. 649–654.

Yuka Tateisi, Yoshihiko Ono, and Hisao Yamada. 1988b. Derivation of readability formula of Japanese texts. IPSJSIG Note 88-DPHI-18-4, Information Processing Society of Japan.

Kevyn Collins-Thompson and Jamie Callan. 2004. A lan-guage modeling approach to predicting reading difficulty. In Proceedings of the HLT/NAACL 2004 Conference, pp. 193–200.

Etsuko Toyoda. 2016. Evaluation of computerised reading-assistance systems for reading Japanese texts – from a linguistic point of view. Australasian Journal of Educational Technology, 32(5). pp. 94–107.

Sowmya Vajjala and Detmar Meurers. 2012. On improving the accuracy of readability classification using in-sights from second language acquisition. In Proceedings of the Seventh Workshop on Building Educational Applications Using NLP, pages 163–173.

Shuhan Wang, Erik Andersen. 2016. Grammatical Templates: Improving Text Difficulty Evaluation for Language Learners. In Proceedings of COLING 2016, the 26th International Conference on Computational Linguistics: Technical Papers, pp. 1692–1702, Osaka, Japan, December.

Shuyu Wang. 2001. A comparative study of vocabulary in Chinese and Japanese, Sichuan Literature and Art Press.

Menglin Xia, Ekaterina Kochmar, and Ted Briscoe. 2016. Text readability assessment for second language learners. In Proceedings of the 11th Workshop on Innovative Use of NLP for Building Educational Applications, pp. 12–22.

Xiaoming Xu and Reika. 2013a, Detailed introduction of the New JLPT N1-N5 grammar. East China University of Science and Technology Press.

Xiaoming Xu and Reika. 2013b, Detailed introduction of the New JLPT N1-N5 vocabulary. East China University of Science and Technology Press.

Conceptualizing EDUCATION in Hong Kong and China (1984-2014)

Kathleen Ahrens
The Hong Kong Polytechnic University
11 Yuk Choi Road, Hung Hom,
Kowloon, Hong Kong
kathleen.ahrens@polyu.edu.hk

Huiheng Zeng
The Hong Kong Polytechnic University
11 Yuk Choi Road, Hung Hom,
Kowloon, Hong Kong
huiheng.zeng@connect.polyu.hk

Abstract

This study aims to provide an account of metaphor usage in Chinese political rhetoric regarding education over the past thirty years and shed light as to how lexical choices underline and reflect underlying conceptual patterns. Our study shows that the degree of metaphorization of "education" is similar among PRC Premiers while it varies among Hong Kong Governors and Chief Executives. Also, the concept of education in policy addresses in China often relies on the domain of BUILDING, with a focus on 'structure' and 'foundation' and a secondary focus on the concept of education as ENTERPRISE that can be 'invested' in. In contrast, Hong Kong Policy Addresses conceptualize education as a PRODUCT that can be 'advertised' or whose 'quality' and 'quantity' can be 'improved'. In sum, analyzing metaphor variations in political speeches may reveal how politicians with different backgrounds and from different regions use language to present implicit ideologies.

1 Introduction

The last decade has witnessed a growth of research on conceptual metaphors in political discourse (Ahrens, 2009; Ahrens and Lee 2009; Ahrens, 2011; Lu and Ahrens, 2008; Charteris-Black, 2005, 2006, 2009; 2013; Lakoff, 1996, 2004; Musolff, 2004, 2010, 2016). This work may be categorized in terms of authors of the texts and types of source/ target domains being used for analysis. For example, Lu and Ahrens (2008) studied conceptual metaphors with one particular source domain (BUILDING) from Taiwanese presidents, while Charteris-Black (2005) looked at a range of conceptual metaphors from particular British prime ministers and American presidents. In contrast with these examples, this study provides an analysis of the target domain concept of 'EDUCATION' in Chinese to see how a target domain is structured by different political leaders at different points in time. To fulfill this goal, two Mandarin Chinese political corpora will be examined in terms of Chinese metaphors related to the target domain of 教育 *jiaoyu* 'EDUCATION'.

This question of how EDUCATION is conceptualized will be examined by contrasting the keyword-in-context data for 'education/jiao-yu' as found in two corpora: the Hong Kong Governor's Addresses, the Hong Kong (HKSAR) Chief Executive's Policy Addresses, and the Reports on the Work of the Government by Premiers of the PRC. As Hong Kong has been both a colony of Britain (prior to 1997) and a Special Administrative region of China (since 1997), it has had different education systems. The British system only made education compulsory for those up to the age of 15. While the HKSAR originally followed this scheme, more recently it has moved to make education mandatory until the age of 18, while China continues to make education compulsory for students up until the age of 15. Both the British system and the Chinese system are exam-based beyond the age of 15; that is, students can only continue if they perform well on their exams. The HKSAR has continued with a modified form of this system; however, recent structural changes mean that most students will be able to complete a full 18 years of study. Of note for the purposes of this study is that education is taken seriously by the society in both Hong Kong and China as it is seen as a way for people to advance and better their economic situation. Having an educated workforce is also seen as a desirable social and political goal. Thus, issues related to education are discussed in Hong Kong policy addresses and in speeches by Chinese premiers, which allows us to examine metaphorical uses of the concept of 'education' with an eye to further understanding how education is viewed in these societies.

In this study, we will examine the instances of conceptual metaphor use for the keyword 'education'. Conceptual Metaphor Theory (Lakoff, 1993; Lakoff and Johnson, 1980) and associated work within Critical Metaphor Analysis (Lu and Ahrens, 2008; Ahrens, 2009; Ahrens and Lee, 2009; Charteris-Black, 2004, 2005, 2006; Musolff, 2004, 2010, 2016) take as a starting point that more abstract conceptual domains (called target domains) use relatively more concrete conceptual domains (called source domains) in order to get across a particular idea about the target domain. For example, people might say "I spent a lot of time on this project" to indicate that TIME (the target domain) is being understood in terms of MONEY (the source domains). Ahrens (2010) goes on to demonstrate that target domains select source domains for a particular reason; these reasons are known as mapping principles. For example, TIME IS UNDERSTOOD IN TERMS OF MONEY in that MONEY is viewed as a valuable, limited resource and TIME is also viewed as valuable and limited. This is the mapping principle that drives this particular relationship between the source and target domain.

Recent studies have provided insight into how political leaders have used conceptual metaphors, and particularly invoked source domains, to reflect and strengthen their ideological viewpoints. For example, Charteris-Black (2005) argued that Martin Luther King's used conceptual metaphors derived primarily from source domains related to LANDSCAPE and JOURNEY to argue for civil rights, while Winston Churchill focused on source domains relating to LIGHT and DARKNESS as well as JOURNEY to help British citizens boost morale among British citizens in the Second World War.

Lu and Ahrens (2008), in another example of presidential speech analysis, found that Kuomintang (KMT) Presidents used BUILDING metaphors to instil a Chinese ideology, while the president from the Democratic Progressive Party (DPP) preferred not to use BUILDING metaphors, and instead used FARMING metaphors to emphasize Taiwan's agricultural background and political independence. In addition, KMT Presidents used BUILDING metaphors in ways that differ from U.S Presidents, with the KMT Presidents using retrospective BUILDING metaphors to emphasize the history of China, and U.S. Presidents using BUILDING metaphors to emphasize creating a particular type of structure (i.e., economic, educational, and political) for future generations.

In a more recent study, the emphasis was on how the same viewpoint (the viewpoint of the government of the PRC) is shared with different audiences (Jing-Schmidt & Peng, 2017). The authors ran a keyword-in-context search for 'corruption' in both the People's Daily and the English version of the People's Daily, which are the Chinese and English versions of the media mouthpiece of the PRC government. They found a systematic difference in the conceptual metaphors used Chinese and English newspapers and argued that it is the knowledge base within an epistemic community that invokes particular conceptual domains; in this case, corruption is compared to HARM (DISEASE, VERMIN, WEED, SLOVENRY) in Chinese and to WAR in English.

Hypotheses and Research Questions
The hypotheses under study are: 1) Hong Kong Governors will conceptualize "education" differently from Hong Kong Chief Executives; 2) Hong Kong Chief Executives will conceptualize 'education' more in line with Chinese Premiers, as the Chief Executives are overseeing the Special Administrative Region of Hong Kong for China. Three research questions are involved in this study: 1) What types of source domains are used to understand the target domain concept of 教育 *jiaoyu* 'EDUCATION' in Chinese? 2) Do the metaphor source domains used vary by political group and/or by person or by time period? And 3) What underlying reasons can be postulated regarding the variations of source domain patterns by political group and/or by person? (i.e. Mapping Principles – Ahrens, 2010)

2   Methodology

2.1   Corpus Creation

In order to examine these issues, two independently compiled Chinese corpora of political speeches were created by: 1) downloading speeches of Chinese premiers (Corpus of Report on the Work of the Government by Premiers of the People's Republic of China) from 1984 to 2013 with a total of 590,022 words; 2) downloading the policy addresses of Hong Kong Governors (for the period during 1984-1996 when Hong Kong was a British colony) with a total of 298,572 words and Hong Kong Chief Executives (for the period during 1997-2014 when Hong Kong is a Special Administrative Region of the People's Republic of China) with a total of 367,939 words. We have made these two corpora available on the website of Corpus of Political Speech at http://digital.lib.hkbu.edu.hk/corpus/chnsearch-sc.php for the PRC Corpus and at http://digital.lib.hkbu.edu.hk/corpus/chnsearch.php#ui-tabs-2 for the Hong Kong Corpus. Table 1 and Table 2 present the details of the PRC corpus and Hong Kong Corpus respectively.

Table 1. PRC Corpus of Premier Speeches (from the Report on the Work of the Government) (Pre and Post-1999)

Name	Year	Word Count
Zhao Ziyang	1984-1988	82,046
Li Peng	1988-1998	226,253
Pre-1999	**1984-1998**	**308,299**
Zhu Rongji	1999-2003	85,981
Wen Jiabao	2004-2013	195,742
Post-1999	**1999-2013**	**281,723**
Total	**1984-2013**	**590,022**

Source: http://www.gov.cn/test/2006-02/16/Content_200719.htm

Table 2. Hong Kong Corpus of Policy Addresses by Governors (Pre-1997) and Chief Executives (Post-1997) in Chinese

Name	Year	Word Count
Sir Edward Youde	1984-1986	54,147
Sir David Wilson	1987-1991	110,753
Sir Chris Patten	1992-1996	133,672
Pre-1997	**1984-1996**	**298,572**
Tung Chee-hwa	1997-2005	169,654
Donald Tsang Yam-Kuen	2006-2012	144,965
Leung Chung-ying	2013-2014	53,320
Post-1997	**1997-2014**	**367,939**
Total	**1984-2014**	**666,511**

Source: http://www.policyaddress.gov.hk/2017/chi/archives.html

After compiling all the speeches as text files, Natural Language Processing Software (Stanford Word Segmenter 3.7 and Stanford POS Tagger 3.7) (SNLPG, 2015) were operated for Chinese words segmentation and part-of-speech tagging.

In order to build a list of expressions in the target domain of EDUCATION, key-word-in-context searches were run using tools on the websites mentioned above. All the instances with the lexeme '教育 *jiaoyu* education' were extracted and downloaded into excel files for further analyses on both metaphorical tokens and types.

2.2   Metaphor Identification and Source Domain Determination

In this study, we first read through all the instances extracted to determine if 'education' was used metaphorically, literally or as a proper noun. If it was hypothesized to be used metaphorically, we then identified the keyword that drove this decision (i.e. a word such as '投资 *touzi* invest'). We then checked Chinese WordNet to see if this keyword had a meaning unrelated to education as determined by the definition in Sinica Bow at http://bow.ling.sinica.edu.tw/ (Chung & Ahrens, 2006). This is similar to step 3 in MIP (Pragglejaz Group, 2007) and step 2 to 4 in MIPVU (Steen, 2010) in which they checked for the possibility of a cross-domain mapping. Next, we verified the source domain of the keyword by checking the categories and definitions of the keywords provided in WordNet-SUMO (Suggested Upper Merged Ontology) as facilitated by the Sinica Bow interface. WordNet is a large lexical database of English with words being interlinked by means of conceptual-sematic and lexical relations and SUMO is the only formal ontology that has been mapped to all of the WordNet lexicon. Collocation searches of the keywords by using Chinese Sketch Engine (Kilgarriff, Huang, Rychly et al., 2005) at http://wordsketch.ling.sinica.edu.tw/ were also used as a complementary method to WordNet-SUMO method (Gong, Ahrens & Huang, 2008).

For instance, following the procedures below, '投資 touzi invest' is ascertained to be a metaphorical keyword under the source domain of '事業 shiye ENTERPRISE' metaphor: First, by searching definitions of '投資 touzi invest' in WordNet-SUMO in Sinica Bow using the Chinese-English look-up search engine, we locate a list of senses of the word and the concrete sense 'enterprise' is chosen as the suggested source domain for '投資 touzi invest'. Table 3 is the selected sense information from WordNet-SUMO definition.

Table 3. WordNet-SUMO definition of "投資 touzi invest"

Metaphorical Keywords	WordNet Explanations	SUMO nodes
投資 touzi 'invest'	the act of investing; laying out money or capital in an **enterprise** with the expectation of profit	Financial Transaction

Second, to further confirm the suggested source domain ENTERPRISE, we searched collocations of '投資 touzi invest' to check if '事業 shiye ENTERPRISE' is frequently collocated with '投資 touzi invest' by using Chinese Sketch Engine which is based on the Chinese Gigaword corpus. Figure 1 shows the frequency of '投資 touzi invest' is 355,182. The second column is the frequency of the collocate at a grammatical relation to the keyword searched. The third column is the saliency value for that collocation pair. Referring to the saliency values, '事業 shiye

ENTERPRISE' is verified as one of the top collocations of the keyword '投資 touzi invest'.

Figure 1. Collocation Search of '投資 touzi invest'

Chinese_giga_trd freg = 355,182

PP 於	1096	7.2	Object	196827	4.2
資源	60	27.53	報酬率	2062	70.04
有價證券	12	23.26	金額	6992	58.99
股票	30	22.16	意願	4542	56.18
股市	38	20.31	業務處	519	55.98
金額	26	20.04	環境	9713	54.52
製造業	13	18.8	標的	976	52.23
基金	26	17.86	總額	2706	51.11
總額	14	17.23	洽談會	486	48.6
房地產	11	16.41	台股案	76	45.01
公債	10	16.18	保護法	734	44.94
產業	25	16.13	項目	3392	44.41
總金額	6	16.1	抵減率	116	44.15
國債	5	14.82	說明會	1420	43.89
市場	35	14.33	風險	1648	43.61
事業 ←	16	14.19	上限	986	43.49
債券	8	13.81	回報率	124	41.25
企業	22	13.76	業別	149	41.22
建設	22	13.68	規模	1885	41.17
上市公司	6	13.6	組合	594	40.36
研究	20	13.43	比重	926	39.57
項目	13	13.0	基金法	74	39.31
比例	11	12.8	事業 ←	2743	39.12
農業	13	11.96	考察團	513	38.77
資金	13	11.81	件數	397	38.76
未來	14	10.75	年增率	470	38.63

Based on results from WordNet-SUMO and collocation, we ascertain that the source domain of '投資 touzi invest' is suggested to be under the source domain of '事業 shiye ENTERPRISE'.

The following step is the quantification and comparison of relative frequencies (number of metaphorical instances/corpus size multiplied by

100,000) of metaphors with different types or tokens in different regions and/or speakers.

3　Methodology

3.1　Metaphorical Use and Literal Use Analysis

Our analyses show that a relatively similar ratio of metaphorization of 'education' can be found between PRC premiers in pre-1999 and post-1999 (see Table 4).

Table 4. Relative Frequency of Metaphorical Use & Literal Use of EDUCATION by PRC Speakers in Pre-1999 and Post-1999

Name	Literal Use	Metaphorical Use
Pre-1999	60.01	90.82
Post-1999	78.09	105.78

By contrast, it is clear the metaphorization ratio varies significantly between Hong Kong Governors and Chief Executives with Chief Executive conceptualizing 'education' metaphorically more frequently than Governors (see Table 5).

Table 5. Relative Frequency of Metaphorical Use & Literal Use of EDUCATION by Hong Kong Speakers in Pre-1997 and Post-1997

Name	Literal Use	Metaphorical Use
Pre-1997	69.33	34.16
Post-1997	88.06	95.67

3.2　Source Domains Analysis

Analysis of the metaphor source domains patterns shows that in PRC corpus, the target domain concept of 'education' primarily involves the source domain of BUILDING, secondarily focuses on the concept of education as ENTERPRISE, following with the use of SYSTEM, OBJECT and PRODUCT source domains (see Table 6).

Table 6. Top 7 Source Domains Applied to the Target Domain of EDUCATION in PRC Premier Speeches between Pre-1999 and Post-1999

Source Domains	Pre 99	Post 99
BUILDING	27.25	33.37
ENTERPRISE	20.11	21.30
SYSTEM	19.46	12.42
OBJECT	11.35	13.13
PRODUCT	10.38	15.62
JOURNEY	5.84	3.90
VEHICLE	0.65	11.36

From Table 7 we find that Hong Kong corpus applies primarily the source domain of PRODUCT and secondarily conceptualizes education as BUILDING, following with applying source domains of OBJECT, ENTERPRISE and SYSTEM.

Table 7. Top 7 Source Domains Applied to the Target Domain of EDUCATION in Hong Kong Policy Addresses between Pre-1997 and Post-1997

Source Domains	Pre 97	Post 97
PRODUCT	14.74	26.09
BUILDING	8.37	20.11
OBJECT	5.02	10.60
ENTERPRISE	0.67	20.66
SYSTEM	1.34	8.97
PERSON	2.34	2.17
JOURNEY	0.33	2.99

Source domain variations can also be found between different speakers. For example, PRC premiers use SDs consistently among themselves while Hong Kong Chief Executives have conceptualized education more as an BUSINESS ENTERPRISE and SYSTEM in comparison with Hong Kong Governors.

Results in Table 8 show that CEs not only have a similar degree of metaphorization with Premiers who also are consistent within themselves (See Table 6) but also CEs and Premiers share the same top five source domains (BUILDING, ENTERPRISE, PRODUCT, OBJECT & SYSTEM) in the conceptualization of the target domain of EDUCATION.

Table 8. Comparisons on the Source Domains Applied by PRC Premiers in Post 1999 and HK CEs

Source Domains	PRC Premiers - Post 99	HK CE - Post 97
BUILDING	33.37	20.11
ENTERPRISE	21.30	20.66
PRODUCT	15.62	26.09
OBJECT	13.13	10.60
SYSTEM	12.42	8.97
JOURNEY	3.90	2.99

3.3 Metaphorical Keywords Analysis

After discussing and comparing the source domain categories among different speakers in different regions, we looked further into specific metaphorical keywords they applied under different source domains. As we can see in Table 6 & 7, in both PRC corpus and Hong Kong corpus, 'education' primarily involves the source domain of PRODUCT, BUILDING, ENTERPRISE, OBJECT, SYSTEM and JOURNEY. Analysis of the top 3 frequently applied metaphorical keywords to the six source domains shows that, in general, the BUILDING source domain underlines the '结构 *jiegou* structure' and '基礎 *jichu* foundation' of education which should be '加强 *jiaqiang* strengthened', '擴展 *kuozhan* expand' and '支持 *zhichi* supported', e.g. '加强教育基础能力建设 *jiaqiang jiaoyu jichu nengli jianshe* strengthen the construction of education foundational ability'; the source domain of ENTERPRISE emphasizes education as a business that can be '投入/投资 *touru/touzi* invested' and has '效益 *xiaoyi* benefits', e.g. '投資教育事業 *touzi jiaoyu shiye* invest education enterprise'; the source domain of PRODUCT focuses on the '质量/質素 *zhiliang/suzhi* quality', '水準 *shuizhun* standard' and '数量 *shuliang* quantity' of education with the concept that education can be '改进 *gaijin* improved' or '宣传 *xuanchuan* advertised', e.g. '改良教育質素 *gailiang jiaoyu zhisu* improve education quality' (see Table 9 & 10).

Table 9. Top 3 Frequent Metaphorical Keywords in PRC Premier Speeches

	BUILDING	ENTERPRISE	PRODUCT
PRC-Pre 1999	加强 *jiaqiang* strengthen (NR=11.68)	事业 *shiye* enterprise (NR=18.4)	质量 *zhiliang* quality (NR=3.57)
	结构 *jiegou* Structure (NR=6.49)	投入 *touru* invest (NR=3.24)	宣传 *xuanchuan* advertise (NR=3.57)
	建设 *jianshe* build (NR=2.59)	效益 *xiaoyi* benefit (NR=1.30)	改进 *gaijin* improve (NR=0.65)
PRC-Post 1999	加强 *jiaqiang* strengthen (NR=17.75)	事业 *shiye* enterprise (NR=11.36)	质量 *zhiliang* quality (NR=6.74)
	建设 *jianshe* build (NR=4.26)	投入 *touru* invest (NR=5.68)	免费 *mianfei* free (NR=3.90)
	支持 *zhichi* support (NR=3.55)	支出 *zhichu* expenditure (NR=2.48)	优质 *youzhi* good quality (NR=1.42)

Table 10. Top 3 Frequent Metaphorical Keywords in Hong Kong Policy Addresses

	BUILDING	ENTERPRISE	PRODUCT
Hong Kong -Pre 1997	擴展 *kuozhan* expand (NR=3.01)	投資 *touzi* invest (NR=0.67)	質素 *zhisu* quality (NR=6.03)
	基礎 *jichu* foundation (NR=1.34)		水準 *shuizhui* standard (NR=2.34)
	建立 *jianli* strengthen (NR=0.33)		優質 *youzhi* good quality (NR=1.67)
Hong Kong-Post 1997	加强 *jiaqiang* strengthen (NR=6.79)	投資 *touzi* invest (NR=8.97)	質素 *zhisu* quality (NR=4.35)
	擴展 *kuozhan* extend (NR=1.90)	支援 *zhiyuan* support (NR=4.08)	優質 *youzhi* good quality (NR=3.26)
	支持 *zhichi* support (NR=1.36)	事業 *shiye* enterprise (NR=2.99)	免费 *mianfei* free (NR=2.99)

The OBJECT source domain interprets education as a physical object that can be '推动 *tuidong* pushed', '提升 *tisheng* lifted' or '推进 *tuijin* carried forward', e.g. '推进义务教育 *tuijin yiwu jiaoyu* carry forward compulsory education'; the source domain of SYSTEM highlights a concept that education can be '普及 *puji* popularized', '施行 *shixing* implemented' and '改革 *gaige* reformed', e.g. '实施教育改革 *shishi jiaoyu gaige* implement education reform'; the JOURNEY source domain conceptualizes education as a journey with reference to the keywords of '定位 *dingwei* location', '方向 *fangxiang* direction', and '步伐 *bufa* pace', e.g. '教育改革迈出新的步伐 *jiaoyu gaige maichu xin de bufa* education reform makes new steps' (see Table 11 & 12).

Table 11. Top 3 Frequent Metaphorical Keywords in PRC Premier Speeches between Pre-1999 and Post 1999

	OBJECT	SYSTEM	JOURNEY
PRC-Pre 1999	提高 *tigao* raise (NR=3.24)	普及 *puji* popularize (NR=5.51)	步伐 *bufa* pace (NR=1.30)
	放 *fang* put (NR=2.59)	改革 *gaige* reform (NR=4.54)	稳步 *wenbu* steady step (NR=1.30)
	抓 *zhu* grab (NR=2.59)	体系 *tixi* system (NR=2.27)	探索 *tansuo* explore (NR=1.30)
PRC-Post 1999	推进 *tuijin* carry forward (NR=6.74)	普及 *puji* popularize (NR=5.32)	步伐 *bufa* pace (NR=0.71)
	推动 *tuidong* push (NR=1.42)	改革 *gaige* reform (NR=4.26)	稳步 *wenbu* steady step (NR=0.71)
	提高 *tigao* raise (NR=1.42)	体系 *tixi* system (NR=2.84)	里程碑 *lichengbei* milestone (NR=0.71)

Table 12. Top 3 Frequent Metaphorical Keywords in Hong Kong Policy Addresses between Pre-1997 and Post 1997

	OBJECT	SYSTEM	JOURNEY
Hong Kong -Pre 1997	推行 *tuixing* carry out (NR=3.68)	普及 *puji* popularize (NR=1.00)	方向 *fangxiang* direction (NR=0.33)
	放 *fang* put (NR=0.67)	施行 *shixing* implement (NR=0.33)	
	提升 *tisheng* lift (NR=0.33)		
Hong Kong -Post 1997	推行 *tuixing* carry out (NR=4.89)	改革 *gaige* reform (NR=10.87)	定位 *dingwei* location (NR=1.09)
	推動 *tuidong* push (NR=4.89)	普及 *puji* popularize (NR=1.63)	方向 *fangxiang* direction (NR=0.82)
	提升 *tisheng* lift (NR=1.09)	系統 *xitong* system (NR=0.82)	稳步 *wenbu* steady step (NR=0.54)

Results of the use of metaphorical words by PRC Premiers in comparison with Hong Kong Chief Executives show variations on keywords under BUILDING and JOURNEY source domains. We found that when talking about education as a BUILDING, both PRC premiers and Hong Kong Chief Executives highlight the concepts of 'strengthening' and 'supporting' education while Chief Executives have added the concept of 'extending' education in Hong Kong, e.g. '擴展高等教育 *kuozhan gaodeng jiaoyu* extend higher education'. Also, keyword patterns applied from the JOURNEY source domain show that PRC Premiers emphasize more on the 'pace' of education development, with an emphasis on the 'steady' development of PRC education, e.g. '教育稳步发展 *jiaoyu wenbu fazhan* education develops with steady steps', while Hong Kong Chief Executive referring more to the 'direction' and 'location' of the education development, e.g. '香港高等教育的定位和發展方向 *xianggang gaodeng jiaoyu de dingwei he fazhan fangxiang* the location and development direction of Hong Kong higher education'. These subtle differences are interesting in that they retain aspects of the main mapping principle associated with the Source-Target domain pairing, and also show that there can be variation among different groups of speakers within the broader mapping principles. This may be similar in some respects to the notion of sense and meaning facets as discussed in (Ahrens et al., 2003).

3.4 Modifiers of Education Analysis

By categorizing the modifiers of metaphorical education ('education' used as 'head nouns') in Hong Kong and PRC corpora, we found variations on the conceptualizations of education in certain fields between the Hong Kong corpus and PRC corpus.

The top five frequent education fields mentioned in Hong Kong policy addresses from 1984 to 2014 are categorized as '优质 *youzhi* good quality' education (NR=10.69) which is primarily conceptualized as PRODUCT; '高等 *gaodeng* higher' education (NR=10.48) which is mainly understood as BUILDING; 国民 *guomin* national' education (NR=8.22) which is mostly with the source domain of OBJECT; '小学 *xiaoxue* primary' education (NR=7.15) and '学前 *xueqian* pre-school' education (NR=6.44) which both are conceptualized as PRODUCT. By comparison, in the PRC corpus, '义务 *yiwu* compulsory' education (NR=19.17), '职业 *zhiye* vocational' education (NR=13.77), '高等 *gaodeng* higher' education (NR=13.49), '农村 *nongcun* rural' education (NR=11.5) and '思想品德 *sixiang pinde* moral' & '政治 *zhengzhi* political' education (NR=8.00) are found being the top five education fields discussed in speeches of PRC premiers in the past thirty years. Apart from the concept of compulsory education which is mainly interpreted with the source domain of SYSTEM, the other four types of education (vocational/higher/rural/moral education) are all conceptualized with the concept of BUILDING.

Results of the modifier categorizations also show that six education fields (moral education, '农村 *nongcun* rural' education, '劳动 *laodong* labor' education, '民族 *minzu* ethnic' education, '民办 *minban* private' education and '素质 *sushi* quality' education) have been metaphorically discussed in PRC corpus but are not mentioned in Hong Kong corpus. Also, another seven education fields ('校本 *xiaoben* school-based' education, '特殊 *teshu* special' education, '禁毒 *jindu* drug enforcement' education, '環境 *huanjing* environmental' education, '家庭 *jiating* family' education, '健康 *jiankang* health' education and' 區域 *quyu* regional' education) haven't been used metaphorically in PRC speeches but have been discussed metaphorically in Hong Kong policy addresses.

The underlying reasons for these variations may be able to be traced back to the influence in the history of Hong Kong and PRC's educational development, the backgrounds of different speakers and the interplay of political, economic and social factors in these two regions. Metaphor analyses may thus reveal certain viewpoints of political or social issues by political speakers from different areas.

4 Conclusion

In conclusion, this paper provides empirical data and applies a corpus-based approach to analyze metaphor patterns in political speeches by PRC Premiers and Hong Kong Governors and Chief Executives in the past thirty years. The results present different degrees for the metaphorization of 'education' in the PRC and Hong Kong corpora. PRC Premiers in both Pre-1999 and Post-1999 use similar metaphors consistently while Hong Kong Chief Executives applied more metaphors than Governors when conceptualizing the concept of education. In addition, source domains and metaphorical keyword patterns have been examined, revealing the mapping principles underlying the metaphor usage. PRC premiers primarily apply the BUILDING source domain with a focus on 'structure' and 'foundation' and secondarily focus on the concept of education as ENTERPRISE that can be 'invested' in. In contrast, Hong Kong politicians emphasize education as a PRODUCT that can be 'advertised' and its 'quality' and 'quantity' should be 'improved'. Hence, the results discussed show that examinations on metaphor variations in empirical corpus can contribute to revealing the ways lexical choices underline and reflect underlying conceptual patterns and associated ideologies.

Acknowledgements

This paper was funded in part by the General Research Fund (Project No.: 12400014) from the Hong Kong University Grants Committee to the first author.

References

Ahrens, Kathleen. (Ed.). 2009. *Politics, gender and conceptual metaphors.* Basingstoke and New York, Palgrave-MacMillan.

Ahrens, Kathleen. 2010. Mapping principles for conceptual metaphors. In Cameron Lynne, Alice Deignan, Graham Low & Zazie Todd (Eds.), *Researching and applying metaphor in the real world,* pp. 185-207. Amsterdam: John Benjamins.

Ahrens, Kathleen. 2011. Examining conceptual metaphor models through lexical frequency patterns: A case study of US presidential speeches. In Hans-Joerg Schmid (Ed.). *Windows to the mind. Series: Applications of Cognitive Linguistics,* pp 167-184. Mouton De Gruyter, Berlin.

Ahrens, Kathleen, Huang Huang, and Yuan-hsun Chung. 2003. Sense and meaning facets in verbal semantics: A MARVS perspective. *Language and Linguistics,* 4(3): 468-484.

Ahrens, Kathleen and Sophia Lee. 2009. Gender versus politics: When conceptual models collide in the U.S. Senate. In Ahrens, Kathleen (Ed.), *Politics, gender, and conceptual metaphors,* pp. 62-82. Palgrave-MacMillan, Basingstoke and New York.

Charteris-Black, Jonathan. 2004. *Corpus approaches to critical metaphor analysis.* Macmillan, London.

Charteris-Black, Jonathan. 2005. *Politicians and rhetoric: The persuasive power of metaphor.* Palgrave-MacMillan, Basingstoke and New York.

Charteris-Black, Jonathan. 2006. Britain as a container: immigration metaphors in the 2005 election campaign. *Discourse & Society,* 17(5): 563-581.

Charteris-Black, Jonathan. 2009. Metaphor and gender in British parliamentary debates. In A. Kathleen (Ed.), *Politics, gender and conceptual metaphors,* pp. 139-165. Palgrave-MacMillan, Basingstoke and New York.

Charteris-Black, Jonathan. 2013. *Analysing political speeches: Rhetoric, discourse and metaphor.* Palgrave Macmillan, Basingstoke and New York.

Chung, Siaw-Fong and Kathleen Ahrens. 2006. Source Domain Determination: WordNet-SUMO and Collocation. In *Proceedings of the 2nd International Conference of the German Cognitive Linguistics Association,* pp. 1-4. Munich, 5-7 October 2006.

Gong, Shu-Ping, Kathleen Ahrens, and Chu-Ren Huang. 2008. Chinese word sketch and mapping principles: A corpus-based study of conceptual metaphors using the building source domain. *International Journal of Computer Processing of Languages,* 21(01): 3-17.

Jing-Schmidt, Zhuo and Peng, Xinjia. 2017. Winds and tigers: metaphor choice in China's anti-corruption discourse. *Lingua Sinica,* 3(1):1-26.

Kilgarriff, Adam, Chu-Ren Huang, Pavel Rychly, Simon Smith, David Tugwell. 2005. Chinese word sketches. In the *Proceedings of Asialex,* Singapore.

Lakoff, George. 1993. The Contemporary Theory of Metaphor. In A. Ortony (Ed.), *Metaphor and Thought,* pp 202-251. Cambridge University Press, New York.

Lakoff, George. 1996. *Moral politics: How liberals and conservatives think.* The University of Chicago Press, Chicago.

Lakoff, George. 2004. *Don't think of an elephant, know your values and frame the debate.* Chelsea Green Publishing, Vermo.

Lakff, George and Mark Johnson. 1980. Metaphors We Live By. University of Chicago Press, Chicago.

Lu, L. Wei-Lun and Kathleen Ahrens. 2008. Ideological influences on BUILDING metaphors in Taiwanese presidential speeches. *Discourse and Society, 19*(3): 383-408.

Musolff, Andreas. 2004. *Metaphor and political discourse: Analogical reasoning in debates about Europe.* Palgrave Macmillan, Basingstoke and New York.

Musolff, Andreas. 2010. *Metaphor, nation and the Holocaust: The concept of the body politic.* Routledge, London.

Musolff, Andreas. 2016. *Political Metaphor Analysis: Discourse and Scenarios.* Bloomsbury Publishing, New York.

Pragglejaz Group. 2007. MIP: A method for identifying metaphorically used words in discourse. *Metaphor and Symbol, 22*(1): 1-39.

The Stanford Natural Language Processing Group. 2015. Stanford Log-linear Part-Of-Speech Tagger (Version3.6.0) [Software]. Available from http://nlp.stanford.edu/software/tagger.html

Steen, Gerard. J., Aletta G. Dorst, J. Berenike, Herrmann, Anna Kaal, Tina Krennmayr, and Pasma, Trijntje. 2010. *A method for linguistic metaphor identification: From MIP to MIPVU* (Vol. 14). John Benjamins Publishing, Amsterdam and Philadelphia.

Multi-dimensional Meanings of Subjective Adverbs

- Case Study of Mandarin Chinese Adverb Pianpian

Mi Zhou
Department of Chinese and
Bilingual Studies, The Hong
Kong Polytechnic University
mimi.zhou@connect.polyu.hk

Yao Yao
Department of Chinese and
Bilingual Studies, The Hong
Kong Polytechnic University
ctyaoyao@polyu.edu.hk

Chu-Ren Huang
Department of Chinese and
Bilingual Studies, The Hong
Kong Polytechnic University
churenhuang@polyu.edu.hk

Abstract

The combination of strict scalar and exclusive components of focus particles has been considered to be exceptional and rare in the literature. In this study, we identify and analyze a frequently used multi-dimensional focus particle *pianpian* 偏偏 in Mandarin Chinese and claim that it is a strictly scalar exclusive focus particle (which accordingly show evaluative properties). The analysis is based on data from CCL corpus. Different from English only, the scalar feature of pianpian is non-optional and does not depend on the lexical specification of the focus. Furthermore, the negation of the more expected/positive alternatives by *pianpian* gives rise to interesting interactions with surprisal, modality and speaker-orientedness.

1 Introduction

Cross-linguistically, focus can be broadly defined as information in a sentence which introduces alternative(s) of elements associated with meaning interpretation (Rooth, 1992; Krifka, 1999; Spalek, 2014). Focus particles, like other kinds of focus-sensitive expressions, mark the focus of a sentence (König, 1991; Gast, 2006).

Usually, focus particles can be categorized along two dimensions, each with two levels, i.e. whether a focus particle is exclusive (restrictive) or additive (inclusive) and whether it is scalar and/or non-scalar. Exclusive means that the alternative(s) of the focus are not possible variables for interpreting the sentence, on the other hand, the additive indicates that the truth condition of the proposition remains true when alternative(s) are substituted for focus. Within the group of exclusives, often discussed examples include English only, merely and only-like expressions. The additive category is best exemplified by English also, even, and their counterparts in other languages. The component of scalar and/or non-scalar uses measures a kind of ordering property of alternative(s) and focus elements in the perspective of the related event in the context, with scalar reading having such an order and non-scalar use lacking it respectively (König, 1991; Gast, 2006 etc.). Among additives, even and even-like operators are usually utilized in the literature to exemplify scalar interpretation (Karttunen and Karttunen, 1977; Kay 1990; König, 1991; Gast and van der Auwera, 2011; see Giannakidou and Yoon, 2016 for non-scalar use of even) (See (1) – (2) for examples of scalar and non-scalar uses of additives).

(1)   Even John came.
a. $\exists x[(x{=}John)$ & came$(x)]$

b.∃x[(x≠John) & came(x)]
c.(∀y)[(y ≠ John & came (y) →
exceeds(unlikelihood(came(John),unlikelihood(ca
me (y))]

(2)   John also came.
a.∃x[(x=John) & came(x)]
b.∃x[(x≠John) & came(x)]
Note that (1c) has the scalar reading of John being less likely to come than other people; while there is no possible scalar reading for (2).
For exclusives, only and its counterparts are the most frequently mentioned particles supporting scalar use. (See (3) for instance of scalar use of only) However, "only sentences" do not constantly express scalar meaning as the scale is derived from the context - both the existence of the scale and parameter of the dimension of the scale (See (4) as the example of non-scalar use of only) (König, 1991; Horn, 1996; Gast, 2012).

(3)   John only ate three apples.
a.∃=3x[apple(x) & John_ate(x)]
b.¬∃>3x[apple(x) & John_ate(x)]
c.(∀>3y)[apple(y)   &   John_ate(y)   →
exceeds(cardinal   number(John_ate(more   than
three(y))), cardinal number(three (y))]

(4)   Only John came.
a.∃x[(x=John) & came(x)]
b.¬∃x[(x≠John) & came(x)]

Note that in (3), the numbers of apple is a scalar concept triggered by the numeral three in the con-text; while scalar meaning is not triggered in (4). Theoretically and logically it is possible for focus particles to integrate components of exclusive and scalar use. To our best knowledge, jupu in Gurindji is the only particle typologically reported to have both exclusive use and scalar use, without possilbe no non-scalar use. _Jupu_ is an invariant sentence adverb,   which may   often   be   translated_just_or_only (on the S-adverb sense).   It modifies expectations about the whole sentence, the predicate or verb, but is never used in the sense of _only_qualifying an NP (McConvell, 1983:14). This paper presents an analysis of the Chinese adverb *pianpian* 偏偏 as a strictly scalar and exclusive focus particle.

2   Current Study

This study focuses on Mandarin focus marker *pianpian*. Literature from perspectives of both Mandarin focus particles and evaluative adverbs pay no or little attention to focus particle function of *pianpian* (see for instance Lü, 1980; Hou (ed.), 1998; Paris, 1998; Hole, 2004). Liu (2008) and Zhang (2014) labeled *pianpian* as focus particle though without further analysis. We propose *pianpian* to be an exclusively scalar exclusive focus particle, which means: (i) it disallows the alternative(s) (explicit or implicit) to be possible answers for the open sentence (what the speaker takes as the Current Question) in the scope of the particle and displays only scalar reading of the sentence unlike only-like exclusive particles. (ii) The scale pianpian induces to the understanding of the sentence is constant in the direction of ordering and complex as to the parameter of dimension - ranking focus element at higher level of ordering with the scale of expectation disconfirmation or negativity (unfortunateness).

3   Corpus Data Analysis

The hypothesis of this research is as follows:
a.   *Pianpian* is an exclusive focus particle. (i.e. The proposition with focus is true and the proposition with focus substituted by alternative(s) is false.)
b.   *Pianpian* is a strictly scalar focus particle. The scales *pianpian* triggers are of unexpectedness and negativity. And the proposition with focus is evaluated as more unexpected and negative than the proposition with focus substituted by alternative(s).
We retrieved 3740 *pianpian* sentences from the CCL contemporary Chinese corpus (This corpus contains 581,794,456 Chinese characters), among which we extracted 500 random sample sentences with context. We then precluded 68 sentences either because *pianpian* in those sentences mean intentionally or context information is missing. In total, we annotated 432 sentences for this study.
    The annotation criteria are as follows:
-The focus in the *pianpian* sentence (*Pianpian* is very frequently left-adjoined to its scope within which focus can be identified. And focus is

the phrase which has explicit or inferred alternative(s));

-Syntactic components of focus in *pianpian* sentence (subject, object, verb predicate, adjective predicate, adverbial, modifier of NP);

-Alternative(s) of the focus;

-Whether alternative is explicitly excluded in the context;

-Whether unexpectedness is explicitly marked in the context;

-Whether negativity is explicitly marked in the context.

Based on our annotation, in the following two graphs we show the syntactic position of foci pianpian associates (in Graph 1) and whether alternatives are marked or not marked (in Graph 2).

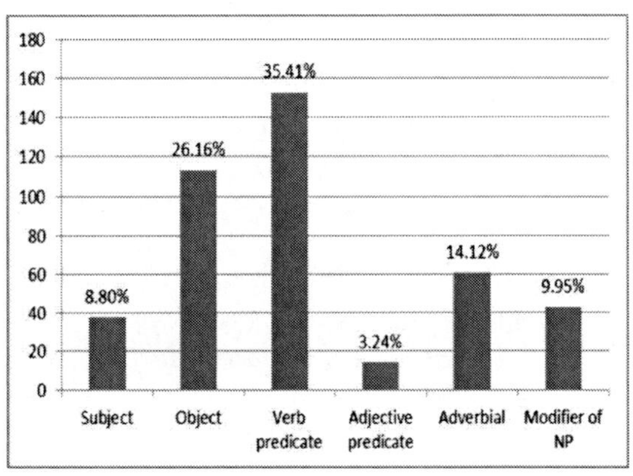

Graph 1: Syntactic positions of foci *pianpian* associates

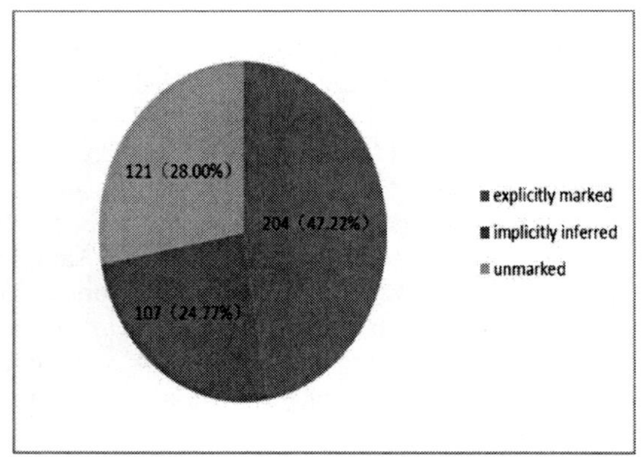

Graph 2: Alternative(s) marked or unmarked

From the Graph 1 we can see that the foci which *pianpian* associates with function mainly as

predicate (35.41% as verb predicate and 3.24% as adjective predicate) and object (26.16%), while only 8.80% of the foci appear in the subject position.

And Graph 2 shows that about half (47.22%) of the alternatives are explicitly marked, and among the rest, about half (24.77%) of the alternatives are implicitly inferred.

3.1　Exclusive Component of Pianpian

Among the 204 sentences where alternatives are explicitly marked, 94 examples (48.04%) explicitly show that the proposition with the focus substituted by alternative(s) is false.

(5)算你们运气，人家也当兵，一茬一茬的复员了，都没有赶上打仗，偏偏让［你们这一茬的］F[1]赶上了。

suan_nimen_yunqi,renjia_ye_dangbing,yichayicha de_fuyuan_le,dou_meiyou_ganshang_dazhang,pia npian_rang_nimen_zheyichade_ganshang_le

count_you_luck,others_also_being　soldier_,year by　　　　　　　year_demobilized_TAM, all_not_encouter_war,pianpian_let_you_encouter

It is so unlucky of you. Other people also served in the army. Year after year, they have all been demobilized and have not encountered any war; you have to participant in the war.

a.(∃x)[(x=you) & participant_in _war(x)]

b.¬(∃x)[(x≠you) & participant_in _war (x)]

(6)她恨自己为什么能护理好医院的每一个病人，偏偏就护理不好［自己的母亲］F。

Ta_hen_ziji_weishenmo_neng_huli_hao_yiyuande _mei_yige_bingren,pianpian_jiu_huli_bu_hao_ziji de_muqin

She blames herself for not having taken good care of her mother while she can take good care of every other patient in the hospital

a.(∃x)[(x=mother)　　　　　　　　& I_did_not_take_good_care_of(x)]

b.¬(∃x)[(x≠mother)　　　　　　　& I_did_not_take_good_care_of (x)]

In those sentences where alternatives are not explicitly excluded, we can inter the exclusiveness from the contrary relation of focus and

---

[1] F stands for the focus of the sentence.

alternative(s). Even though alternative(s) are not excluded, it does not mean that they are included.

(7)晋武帝和他祖父、伯父、父亲都是善于玩弄权术的人，可是他的儿子——太子司马衷偏偏是一个[什么也不懂的低能儿]F。
jinwudi_he_tade_zufu_bofu_fuqin_dou_shi_shanyu_wannong_quanshu_de_ren,keshi_tade_erzi_taizi_simazhong_pianpian_shi_yige_shenmo_ye_bu_dong_de_dinenger
Emperor Jinwu and_his grandfather, his grandfather's brother and his father_all_are_good at_play_political_tricks_person,but_hisson_prince_simazhong_pianpian_is_a_what_also_not_understand_ imbecile
Emperor Jinwu and his grandfather, his grandfather's brother and his father are all skillful in playing political tricks, but his son – Prince Sima Zhong is an imbecile who knows nothing.
a.(∃x)[(x=Sima Zhong) & being_an_imbecile(x)]

b.¬(∃x)[(y≠Sima Zhong) & being_an_imbecile(x)]

(8)团领导几次调他到驻在某城市的机关任职，可他偏偏离不开[梦魂萦绕的导弹竖井]F。
tuan_lingdao_ji_ci_diao_ta_dao_zhuzai_mouchengshi_de_jiguan_renzhi,ke_ta_pianpian_libukai_hunqianmengraode_daodanshujing
The official from the League has tried to transfer him to an organization in the city, but he would not like to leave missile silos which he cares a lot.
a.(∃x)[(x= missile silos) & he_would_not_leave(x)]

b.¬(∃x)[(x≠missile silos) & he_would_not_leave(x)]

(9)眼看该上班了，可老天偏偏[下起了雪]F。
yankan_gai_shangban_le, ke laotian_pianpian_xiaqi_le_xue
It is time to go to work, but, it has started to snow.
a.snow
b.¬[¬snow]

3.2 Scale of Unexpectedness Component of Pianpian

Based on the corpus data, we can see that the events pianpian evaluates are unexpected: 377 tokens (87.27%)
Markers for unexpectedness: strong to weak

unexpectedly, out of one's expectation:
meixiangdao 没想到，
meicengxiangdao 谁曾想到，
shichuyiwai 事出意外，
buliaoxiang 不料想，
jingran 竟（然），
juran 居然…
it is supposed to…,however…:
anlishuo……keshi/danshi……按理说……可是/但是……，
benlaiyinggai…keshi/danshi……本来应该……可是/但是……
but,however:
keshi 可是，
danshi 但是，
que 却…
it is unbelievable…:
lingrenbujiede 令人不解的，
lingrenfeijiede 令人费解的，
guaishi 怪事…

(10)那么多人参加比赛，偏偏我得了一等奖。
namo_duo_ren_canjia_bisai,pianpian_wo_de_le_yidengjiang
so_many_people_participate_competition,pianpian_I_got_TAM_first award
'I, of all the people who participated in the competition, won the first prize.'
a.(∃x)[(x=me) & got_first_place(x)]
b.¬(∃x)[(x≠me) & got_first_place(x)]
c.(∀y)[(y≠me) & participated_in_compitition(y) & got_first_place(y) →
exceeds(surprise(got_first_place(me), surprise(got_first_place(y))]
Pianpian marks 我 wo'I' as the focus as well as the maximal level of expectation disconfirma-tion of the fact that the speaker won. It renders the alternatives (a person other than me winning) ranked as more likely (or less improbable). This is a case showing only-unexpectedness-dimension scale.

3.3 Scale of Negativity Component of Pianpian

The events pianpian evaluates are negative: 236 tokens (54.63%) :
Markers for negativity:
negative emotion words:
taiyihanle 太遗憾了 regretful，
buxingde 不幸的 miserable，
kebeide 可悲的 pathetic，
zhenkexi 真可惜 unfortunate，
daomeide 倒霉的 unlucky
…
nouns with negative meaning：
beiju 悲剧 tragic，
sunshi 损失 loss，
weihai 危害 harm，
mafan 麻烦 trouble
…
negative events：
shengbing 生病 being sick，
chushi 出事 something terrible happens，
shiqujihui 失去机会 losing a chance，
niangchengzhezhongjieju 酿成这种结局 rendering into such a negative consequence
Most of the pianpian sentences show both unexpectedness and negativity evaluations. This is consistent with the frequent co-occurrence of surprise and negativity in the studies of language and emotion (Gendolla& Koller(2001)，Lin, J., & Yao, Y. (2016).

(11)不早不晚，电脑偏偏这时候坏了。
bu_zao_bu_wan,diannao_pianpian_zhe_shihou_hu
ai_TAM
not_early_not_late,computer_pianpian_this_time_
bad_TAM
'Neither one minute earlier, nor one minute later, the computer broke now right at this (critical) moment'.
a.(∃ x)[computer(x) & (break(x))(now)]
b.¬(∃ x)[computer(y) & break(x)(at t) & t≠now]
c.(∀ y)[computer(y)&break(y)(at t)&t ≠ now] →
exceeds(negativity(break(y)(now)),
negativity(break(y)(at t)(t≠now))

Pianpian in this example is associated with the focus 这时候 zheshihou 'this (critical) moment'

. The sentence asserts the fact that the computer broke now and also implies that it did not break at any other time points. And the scale pianpian induces in this sentence is only of negativity as the computer is equally likely to break at any time points, however the speaker finds it very unfortunate that the computer stopped working now. The scalar expectation here is that this particular time point is the worst time for the computer to breakdown (compared with all the possible time points).

(12)这么重要的面试,他偏偏搞砸了。
zhemo_zhongyao_De_mianshi,ta_pianpian_gao_z
a_TAM
so_important_De_interview,ta_pianpian_do_bad_
TAM
'Of all the interviews, s/he blew this most important one.'.
a.(∃ x)[interview(x) & important(x) & he_mishandled(x)]
b. ¬ (∃ x)[interview(x) & important (x) & ¬(he_mishandled(x))]
c.(∀ y)[interview(y) & important (y) & ¬(he_mishandled(y))] →
exceeds(unexpectedness(interview(y) & important (y) & (he_mishandled(y))),
unexpectedness(interview(y) & important (y) & ¬(he_mishandled(y))) &
exceeds(negativity(interview(y) & important (y) & (he_mishandled(y))), negativity(interview(y) & important (y) & ¬(he_mishandled(y)))

Sentence (12) exemplifies the focus being the predicate and the scalar reading being of both unexpec-tation and negativity. To be specific, 搞砸了 gaozale 'blow/mishandle (something)' is the focus element in this sentence. The related alternatives are "did great (in the interview)" etc. Not doing well in a very important interview is evaluated as negative and unexpected by the speaker. It is also important to note that the scalar reading is also possible from 这么重要的面试 'such an important interview'. That is, the expectation being that this interview is the one that the subject (he) can least affords to fail. And with a slightly different focus (and background information), the expectation can also be on the subject 他 he. That is, if the subject is sent by a bidding team

316

to represent them at the important final interview (instead of other team members). Then this he is considered to be the least likely to fail, yet did fail. Of all possible readings, it is important to note that the focus must go hand-in-hand with a contextually specified scalar expectation.

3.4 Subjective (Evaluative) Adverb Component of Pianpian

The unexpectedness and negativity meanings of pianpian renders it as an evaluative adverb[2] which behaves like normal subjective adverbs – positioning before modals, negations, time adverbs, degree adverbs etc., e.g. pianpianneng 偏偏能，pianpianmeiyou 偏偏没有，pianpianxian 偏偏先，pianpianhen 偏偏有些.

(13) "天上掉馅饼"的事情少之又少。不过对于在德国高校求学的大学生而言,就偏偏能碰上这种好事——因为那里不收学费。
It is so rare to see pennies from heaven, however, for college students studying in Germany, pianpian this kind of things could happen since they are not charged by tuition fee.

(14) 今年 5 月,10 余个国家的登山健儿吹响了征服珠穆朗玛峰的号角。其中有为庆祝中国与斯洛伐克建交 5 周年而组建的中斯联合登山队。然而,连日来涌向峰顶的人群中,偏偏没有公认为实力最强的中国队员的身影。
In May this year, mountain climbers from more than ten countries have started to climb Mount Qomolangma. One of the teams was China Slovak Joint Mountaineering Expedition, which was set up to celebrate the 5th anniversary of establishment of the diplomatic relationship between China and Slovak. For days, pianpian no Chinese was found in the mountain climbers who were thought as the strongest.

(15)在国内学了 4 年的马来语,本以为语言上该不会有什么问题,可问题却偏偏先出在了语言上。
He has been learning Malay for four years before going to Malaysia and has thought language would

not be a problem, pianpian, the problem comes first from the aspect of language.

(16)王蝶喜暖,只有在阳光灿烂的时候才频繁活动。当天却偏偏有些多云,我不免有些担心。
Monarch butterfly prefers warmth and only frequently moves around when the sun is shining. Pianpian, that day was a little cloudy, about which I was worried to some extent.

Different form some subjective adverbs, pianpian is not limited to occur in veridical/realis sentences, it can occur in some interrogatives and conditionals – weishenmo pianpian 为什么偏偏……, if…pianpian…如果……，偏偏……。

(17) 既然别人能够回去与家人团聚,为什么偏偏他无法享受这份权利呢?
All the others can get together with their family, why pianpian he doesn't have this right?

(18)如果你是一位营销人员，偏偏性格又很内向，那就迫使自己每天主动与业务单位进行联系、沟通。
If you are a salesperson, pianpian you are controverted, then you need to force yourself to contact and communicate with the cooperating company.

4 Conclusion

According to our data, the majority of examples express the scale formed by both dimensions of expectation reversing and negativity. The phenomenon that unexpectedness is usually found occurring with negativity (unfortunateness) is also supported by previous studies on emotion and language (see Gendolla and Koller, 2001 and Lin and Yao, 2016 for instance). To summarize, different from English only, the scalar property of *pianpian* is non-optional and does not depend on the lexical specification of the focus, but must be associated with the contextually stipulated scale. Furthermore, the negation of the more expected/positive alternatives by *pianpian* gives rise to interesting interactions with the contrary to expectation modality and speaker-orientedness. This study provides evidence for the exclusive and strict scalar focus particle category

---

2 Evaluative adverbs concern with the speaker's evaluative comment/judgment of a proposition (Bonami, 2008).

and shows one possible way of how subjective adverbs could have multi-dimensional meanings.

References

Olivier Bonami. and Godard Danièle. 2008. "Lexical semantics and pragmatics of evaluative adverbs." Adverbs and adjectives: Syntax, semantics, and discourse : 274-304.

Volker Gast. 2006. Focus Particles. In Brown, K. (ed.), The Encyclopedia of Language and Linguistics, Vol. 4 (2nd ed.), 518-519. Oxford: Elsevier.

Volker Gast. and Johan Van der Auwera. 2011. Scalar Additive Operators in the Languages of Europe. Lan-guage 87.1: 1–53.

Volker Gast. 2012. At Least, Wenigstens, and Company: Negated Universal Quantification and the Typology of Focus Quantifiers. Strategies of Quantification. Oxford: OUP, forthc.

Guido HE Gendolla and Michael Koller. 2001. Surprise and Motivation of Causal Search: How are They Af-fected by Outcome Valence and Importance?. Motivation and Emotion, 25(4), 327-349.

Anastasia Giannakidou and Suwon Yoon. 2016. Scalar Marking without Scalar Meaning: Nonscalar, Nonexhaustive Even-marked NPIs in Greek and Korean. Language, 92(3), 522-556.

Daniel Hole. 2004. Focus and Background Marking in Mandarin Chinese. System and Theory behind cái, jiù, dōu and yě. (Asian Linguistics 5.) London & New York: RoutledgeCurzon. Laurence R.Horn. 1996. Exclusive Company: Only and the Dynamics of Vertical Inference. Journal of Semantics 13: 11–40.

Xuechao Hou(侯学超). (ed.)1998. Dictionary of Function Words in Contemporary Chinese (现代汉语虚词词典).Beijing: Peking University Press.

Paul Kay. 1990. Even. Linguistics and Philosophy, 13(1), 59-111.

Ekkehard König. 1991. The Meaning of Focus Particles: A Comparative Perspective. London: Routledge.

Frances Karttunen and Lauri Karttunen. 1977. Even questions. North East Linguistic Society (NELS) 7: 115–34.

Manfred Krifka. 1999. At Least Some Determiners aren't Determiners. In Turner, K. (ed.), The Seman-tics/Pragmatics Interface From Different Points of View, 257-291. Oxford: Elsevier Science B.V.

Jingxia Lin and Yao Yao. 2016. Encoding Emotion in Chinese: a Database of Chinese Emotion Words with Information of Emotion Type, Intensity, and Valence.Lingua Sinica, 2(1), 6.

Tanzhou Liu(刘探宙). 2008. Constructions Containing Multiple Strong Foci in Chinese (多重强式焦点共现句式). Zhongguo Yuwen 3: 259-269.

Shuxiang Lü(吕叔湘). 1980. 800 Words in Modern Chinese (现代汉语八百词).The Commercial Press.

Marie-Claude Paris. 1998. Focus operators and types of predication in Mandarin. Cahiers de Linguistique-Asie Orientale 27, 2: 139-159.

Patrick McConvell. 1983. 'Only' and related concepts in Gurindji. Manuscript, NorthernTerritory University, Darwin.

Mats Rooth. 1992. A theory of focus interpretation. Natural Language Semantics 1: 75-116.

Katharina Spalek, Nicole Gotzner and Isabell Wartenburger. 2014. Not only the apples: Focus sensitive particles improve memory for information-structural alternatives. Journal of Memory and Language, 70, 68-84.

Yisheng, Zhang(张谊生). 2014. Study on Mandarin adverbs (现代汉语副词研究). Beijing: The Commercial Press.

Websites

北京大学中国语言学研究中心现代汉语语料库" CCL Contemporary Chinese Corpus". (n.d.). Retrieved November 1, 2016, from Center for Chinese linguistics PKU: http://ccl.pku.edu.cn/#

A Morphosyntactic Analysis of the Pronominal System of *Southern Alta*

Marvin M. Abreu
De La Salle University
marvinabreu01@gmail.com

Abstract

Pronouns are one of the universal components of language and they provide information on the morphosyntactic characteristics of any languages such as Philippine languages. Past researches show various analyses on the morphosyntax of PLs, a recent typological study claims that Philippine languages (PLs) are ergative. Another study shows a similar claim; however, this study utilizes the pronominal systems of major Philippine languages and uses an ergative-absolutive framework. This research examines the pronouns of *Southern Alta language*. It aims to contribute in the typological studies of pronominal systems of Negrito and Non-negrito languages. This study employs an ergative-absolutive framework. The initial result shows that the pronominal systems of the Southern Alta language consist of absolutive, ergative, oblique, and genitive pronouns. The ergative-absolutive framework unravels the morphosyntax of the pronominal system of Southern Alta. The framework helps describe the functions and characteristic of the different sets of pronouns. The study also reveals linguistic phenomena such as inclusivity/exclusivity, first person dual pronouns, homomorphy, cliticization, hierarchy, person–deixis interface and portmanteau pronouns. In conclusion, the ergative-absolutive framework fits the morphosyntactic analysis of the Southern Alta language. This study also suggests to examine the clausal construction including the noun phrases (NPs) of Southern Alta.

1 Introduction

The Philippines has over 150 languages (Reid, 2013, pp. 330-331). This large inventory excludes the Sama varieties spoken in the Sulu Archipelago and the South Mindanao languages. Although these varieties are spoken within the Republic of the Philippines; they differ morphosyntactically from other Philippine languages and are generally not included in generalizations about Philippine languages (Himmelmann, 2005, p. 111). However, Reid (2013) made a distinction between the original settlers and migrants of pre-colonial Philippines. They are the Negritos and non-Negritos, respectively. Although both groups spoke Austronesian languages, the former was non-Austronesian not until the first Austronesian immigrant the Negritos came in contact 5,000 years ago while the latter groups are the Austronesian-speaking peoples in the Philippines.

Reid and Liao (2004, p. 435) conducted a typological study of the syntax of most Philippine languages and claim that Philippine languages are ergative. In support to the previous claim, Dita (2011) conducted a typological study anchored on ergative-absolutive framework by examining the pronominal systems of most of the major languages of the Philippines.

Dita (Dita, 2011, p. 1) explains that pronominals are a universal component of human languages and are considered basic vocabulary of any given language. In additon, she explains that personal pronouns are generally closed-class and are unaffected by borrowing or code-switching (Dita, 2011). Pronouns exist together with other closed-class words such as prepositions, articles and conjunctions. Unlike open-class categories (e.g. verbs and nouns), pronouns do not change over time, and

31st Pacific Asia Conference on Language, Information and Computation (PACLIC 31), pages 319–328
Cebu City, Philippines, November 16-18, 2017

they signal grammatical relationships between the verb and the subject or object of a clause. The pronominal system of a language is one of the key components to uncover the morphosyntactic structure and properties of the languages, not to mention other linguistic features that may come along with the analysis. She also explains that this new analysis will provide ample understanding on the mophosyntax of many languages in the Philippines (Dita, 2010).

Past studies on the pronominal systems of Negrito and non-Negrito languages focus on reconstructions such as word lists and phonologies (Reid, 1971), Northern Cordilleran subgroup (Tharp, 1974), Arta (Reid, 1989), Alta languages (Reid, 1991), Central Cagayan Agta (Liao, 2005) and Umiray Dumaget (Lobel, 2013). Other topics include deictics (MacFarland, 2006), reference grammar (Headland & Healey, 1974), supplementary texts (Miller & Miller, 1991). This study aims to contribute in the typological study of the pronominal system of Negrito and Non-negrito languages in the Philippines.

1.1 Previous analysis

Dita (2011) explains that early studies on Tagalog language (Bloomfield, 1917) utilized the nominative-accusative distinction and has then dominated the literature on PL for many years. She further explains other analyses have emerged such as active-stative analysis (Drossard, 1994); the fluid voice analysis (Shibatani, 1999); the hybrid analysis (Machlachlan 1996), and the precategorial symmetrical voice analysis (Foley, 1998). But many of the mophosyntactic analysis of Philippine languages remain unclear. However, ergative-absolutive analysis that came about in the 1980s with the works of Payne (1982) and Starosa (1986) and, Gerdts (1988) show viable results.

One of the studies that introduces ergative-absolutive framework is the study of Dixon (1972) on Dyirbal language. This framework is a departure from the nominative-accusative framework that has dominated the early studies of world's languages such as the Indo-European languages. It is, thus congruent to the fact that about a quarter of the world's languages have this unique case-marking. Dita (2011) compares the nominative-accusative and ergative-absolutive analyses. She illustrates the analysis labeled as Figure 1.

Figure 1 – Ergative-absolutive alignment and nominative-accusative alignment

Figure 1 shows two analysis, the one in the left is the ergative-absolutive alignment and on the right is the nominative-accusative alignment. The first row is labeled as A (agent) and O (patient), and they are core arguments of a canonical transitive agent (A) and object (O). The second row with only one argument is marked as S (subject). The object of the transitive clause (or the patient) and the sole argument of an intransitive clause (or the subject) in second row are treated alike, that is, they both receive absolutive case-marks. While on the right shows that the agent of a transitive clause and the subject of an intransitive clause are treated alike, thereby receiving the same case-marks. Dita (2010) simplifies, "if S=A, then the language belongs to the nominative-accusative type, and if S=O, it belongs to the ergative- absolutive type".

Below are examples in Tagalog language (1), (2), and (3) (Dita, 2010).

(1) Bibili ako   ng mangga.
    will.buy ABS.1S DET mango
    'I will buy a mango (or some mangoes).'

(2) Binili ko   ang mangga.
    bought ERG.1S DET mango
    'I bought the mango.'

(3) Nakita nila ako
    saw   ERG. ABS.1S
    'They saw me.'

The absolutive is the actor in an intransitive clause, as in (1); and the ergative is the agent in a transitive clause, as in sentences (2), (3)

1.1 Background of the Study

The *Southern Alta language* is one of the Alta languages, a single branch subgroup of the Meso-Cordilleran languages, an Austronesian language spoken by a group of Negritos in the Philippines.

The Southern Alta language with ISO 639-3 and a three-letter code agy is also known as *Kabuloan Dumagat* in the literature. They live primarily in the Sierra Madre of Eastern Nueva Ecija and the adjacent coastal areas of Quezon Province (north of Umiray Dumaget), Bulacan towns of San Miguel, Norzagaray (Reid, 1991; 2013), and also in Sitio Bato, Baranggay Sapang Bulac, Dona Remedios Trinidad, Bulacan (Abreu, 2014). They are also present in the areas of Luzon, coastal areas of Quezon and Aurora Province, east Nueva Ecija, Sierra Madre (Reid, 1991; 2013). The language status of Southern Alta, according to the Ethnologue, is 'vigorous' (Lewis, Simon, & Fenning, 2015). However, Headland (2010) and Reid (pers. comm., 2016) consider Southern Alta as a "highly endangered" Philippine Negrito language.

2 Methodology

Data includes oral and written forms. Oral data came from the fieldwork of the researcher last year while the written data came from the books or commentaries of the New Testament (Bible). The transcripts consist of elicitations and oral traditions of *Dumagat* elders while the commentaries of the New Testament are being used in Southern Alta communities in Nueva Ecija[1]. The list of abbreviations used is in the footnote.[2]

3 The pronouns and their grammatical functions

The pronouns of Southern Alta consist of absolutive (3.1), ergative (3.2), oblique (3.3), and genitive pronouns (3.4). Each will be dealt separately including the subsets[3]: free and enclitic. The absolutive consists of the free (3.1.1), and enclitics (3.1.2). Similarly, ergative (3.2) consists of free and enclitics (3.2.1). They are followed by the oblique and genitive pronouns respectively.

Person	Absolutive		Ergative		Oblique	Genitive
	Free	Enclitic	Free	Enclitic		
1S	tiyak	=(y)ak	ko	=k	diyak	ko
2S	tikaw	ka	mo	=m	dikaw	mo
3S	siya	siya	na	na	dikana	na
1D	tikita	kita	ta	Ta	dikita	ta
1PE	tikami	kami	me	Me	dikame	me
2P	tikayo	kayo	yo	yo	dikayo	yo

[1] Because of lengthy the sentences in all my written data, readers may email the researcher for a complete interlinear gloss.

[2] List of Abbreviations: AF(Actor Focus), DEG degree, DET determiner, GF(Goal Focus), LIG ligature, OBL oblique, PART particle, PERF perfective, PN proper noun, TL topic linker

[3] The subsets are labeled 'Free' and 'Enclitic'. The former is a morphological terms which means free morpheme in contrast to the latter, 'Enclitic' or bound morpheme.

3P	side	sid	de	de	dikade	de
1PI	tikitam	kitam	tam	tam	dikitam	tam

Table 1- Pronoun System of Southern Alta Negritos

A summary of Southern Alta pronouns is labeled as Table 1. Pronouns in Southern Alta encode person, number, case, and respect[4]. The columns show person, number, and categories. Below the categories specify the subsets. Person refers to the speaker or 1st person, addressee or 2nd person, and the 3rd person 'is some person or thing which is neither speaker nor addressee' (Dixon, 2010, p. 190) while number consists of uppercase S (singular), P (plural), and D (dual). Like other pronominal systems of Philippine languages such as Ilocano, Ibanag or Tagalog, the first person singular has exclusive (does not include the addressee) and inclusive (includes the addressee) forms. They are labeled above as 1PE for first person exclusive and 1PI for first person inclusive. The case system consists of four. They are *absolutives (ABS), ergatives (ERG), obliques (OBL),* and *genitives(GEN)*[5].

Absolutive and genitive have two subsets: free and enclitic. All cases show no distinction on gender unlike English third person singular pronouns (he, she, or it). Neuter forms (e.g. English pronoun *it*) referring to animate or inanimate common nouns (e.g. such boar or arrow) are absent in the pronominal system of Southern Alta. Honorifics and respect in Southern Alta pronouns are shown in the second and third persons plural (see Table 1).

Table 1 shows that the ergative (free) and genitive cases are similar in both respect. They are phonologically and morphologically identical, but they differ in their function and distribution.

This study follows the ergative-absolutive framework of Dita (2007; 2011). The author explains that ergative is used to refer to the agent in a transitive construction while the term genitive is used to refer to the possessor in an NP. She also explains that if a pronoun precedes a verb, it is ergative, and if pronoun precedes a noun, it is geni-

[4] The initial letter of some pronouns that may refer to God or any Supreme Being is capitalized, and the translation is italicized.

[5] Like other pronominal systems of Philippine languages such as Ilocano, Ibanag or Tagalog, the first person singular has exclusive (E) and inclusive (I) forms, they are labeled above as 1PE for exclusive and 1PI as inclusive.

tive. The former is labeled **ERG** as agent of a transitive clause while the latter is labeled **GEN** as the possessor of a possessive construction.

(4) ...*iatod **ko** dikayo at*
   <i>atod ERG.1S OBL.2P TL
   GF-give I   to you   TL
     nu pala lahi   yo."
   DET PL   lahi   GEN.2P
   DET PL   descendant your
...I will give this to you, this one place in Canaan, and to all your descendants.

(5) ...*"Lawin **mo**   yi   gewang **ko**.*"
   lawin   ERG.2S DET gewa<ng> GEN.1S
   see   you   DET to do   my
..."Witness what I can do".

Sentence 4 shows that first person *ko* and second person *yo* pronouns. First person pronoun *ko* precedes a verb while the second person *yo* precedes a noun. The first pronoun functions as a subject and as agent of the transitive clause while the second pronoun *yo* functions as genitive. The genitive *yo* modifies the possessum, *lahi*; this distinguishes second pronoun *yo* as having a possessor-possessum relationship. A similar case in Sentence (5), second person *mo* also precedes a verb while first person *ko* precedes a verbal inflection or a nominal. Both sentences are deemed to provide ample evidence of an ergative-absolutive framework.

3.1 Absolutive pronouns

Absolutive pronouns have first person singular exclusive (1PE) and inclusive (1PI) both in free and bound forms. The singular first person *siya* has no gender distinction.

3.1.1 Free Absolutives

Person	Long	Gloss	Description
1S	tiyak	I	1st person sing
2S	tikaw	you (singular)	2nd person sing
3S	siya	he or she	3rd person sing
1D	tikita	I and you	1st person dual
1PE	tikami	we (excluding 'you')	1st person excl
2P	tikayo	you (plural)	2nd person plural
3P	side	they	3rd person plural
1PI	tikitam	we (meaning 'all')	1st person incl

Table 2 - Free absolutive pronouns

Free absolutive pronouns may stand alone in an utterance. They are usually a response to a ques-

tion or it can be a form of self-referencing from previous utterances. The functions of absolutives are as follows:

(i)   As a subject, a response from a previous inquiry, or as vocative. They are clause-initial. Example (6) is a transcript of an interview. Below the respondent uses absolutive, genitive, and oblique pronouns. All pronouns are first person singular. Pronouns in (7) and (8) are used as a subject, while (9) is vocative.

(6)   "**Tiyak** ti Sonny.
      ABS.1S   PN Sonny
      I   PN Sonny
   *Pangawi **diyak** na pamilya **ko**,   Yayo.*
   nickname   OBL1S DET family   GEN.1S Yayo
   *Asawa **ko**   ay ti Ema.*
   wife   GEN.1S TL PN Ema
   *Yi panganay **me**,   ti Latdok, at*
   PN eldest   GEN. 1PE PN Latdok   TL
   ti Lagyu ti   pangaduwa.
   PN Lagyu   OBL second
   Ti Salon duman ay pangsangay...
   PN Salon EXP   TL third
   ***Tiyak** a tatlongpu at   pito.*"
   ABS.1S LIG thirty   and   three
   I   LIG thirty   and   three
I am Sonny. My family calls me *Yayo*. My wife('s name) is Ema. My eldest son('s name) is *Latdok*, and the second is *Lagyu*. *Salon* is the third. I am thirty-seven years old.'

(7)   ***Tikitam** i   pala anak **Na**.*
      ABS.1PI   DET PL   anak GEN.3S
      We(all)   DET PL   child His
   We (including you) are His children.

(8)   ***Side**   I   umawit.*
      ABS.3P DET <um>awit
      they   DET PERF.sang
   They are the ones who sang.

(9)   '*Tiatin i   ki   adi tu sundang?*' '***Tiyak**.*'
      Q   DET EXIST adi DET dagger   ABS. 1S
   'Who owns the dagger?' 'I am (*or* I own it).'

(ii)   Serves as predicates of identificational constructions such as (10) and (11)

(10) "***Tikaw** linaway **ko**   nuapon.*"
      ABS.2S l<in>way ERG.2S TIME
      you   PERF-saw I   yesterday
   You are the one I saw yesterday.

(11) ...*"**Tikaw** mismo tu petang **ko***
      ABS.1S PART   DET <peta>ng GEN.1S
      you   PART   DET choice my
   a   tu   alta a   mamahala nu iddi."

LIG DET alta LIG   <ma>mahala DET DEM

…"You are the one, my chosen person, who will take care of these.

(iii) As appositive in (12)

(12) ***Tikami*** *a   pala Dumaget*
    ABS.1P LIG PL   Dumaget
    we   LIG PL   Dumagat

*ay mondongol **kami**   na lutu."*
    TL listen   ABS.1P DET lutu
    TL listen   we   DET lutu

We, the Dumagats, (we) listen to the sounds made by the bird *lutu*.

(iv) As a form of respect or honorific. A singular addressee (13) is addressed in the plural form, such as God or any Supreme Being in (15). Sentence (16) is a reference to the elders.

(13) ***Tikayo*** *amo yi isa=y   mongnol,*
    ABS.2P amo yi NUMBER know,
    you   PART DET one   know

Ta uwannak ki   magewa,
    Ta uwan=(n)yak ki   magewa,
    CONJ NEG=ABS.1S EXIST <ma>gewa
    and NEG.I   EXIST can do

*labes tai nu kabudiyan **yo***
    ADV DEM DET <ka>budi<yan> GEN. 2S
    ADV this DET goodness   your

You are the only one who knows everything and I can't give much of it unlike the goodness you do for all us.

(14) ...***Side*** *tu monudu,*
    ABS.3P DET <mon><t>udu
    they   DET teach

*at **side** tu mogdisisyon na...*
    TL ABS.3P DET <mog>disisyon PART
    TL they   DET decide   PART

Taking care of the council is the responsibility of the elders in the council. They should teach and do the decisions on any matters that need to be done in the council.

3.1.2 Enclitic absolutives

Table 3 - Enclitic absolutive pronouns

The 'short' forms in Table 3 show the absolutive enclitics. Although some can stand alone, a few needs a host to complete its syntactic function. The functions are:

(i) as subject in an intransitive clause (15), (16), (17), and (18) or as a sole argument or experiencer in an intransitive clause (19).

(15) *Nakakannak din.*

<naka>kan=(n)yak din.
already.eat=ABS.1S
eat=I   already

I have already eaten, too. (lit. Already ate I)

(15) ...*sinabi ni Lot, a "Umakang **kitam**."*
    s<in>abi PN Lot   LIG <um>akang ABS.1PI
    PERF-said PN Lot   LIG AF-walk   we

…Lot said, "Let's walk."

(16) Ta=din kita.
    let go   1D.ABS
    let go   I and you

    Come, let's go. (lit. I and you go.)

(17) *Mun i budi kita.*
    like   1D.ABS
    like   I and you

    We like one another. (lit. I and you like.)

(19) ...*molamang modognin **siya**.*
    PART   <mo>dognin ABS.3S
    probably   feel.cold   he and she

… probably, he feels very cold.

(ii) As a subject of a monadic intransitive clause,

(20) *Sumubli   kayo.*
    s<um>ubli   ABS.2P
    AF.come back you-P

    Come back, all of you.

(iii) As subject in a dyadic intransitive clause:

(21) *Linumukdes   **siya**   ti   gebunay.*
    l<inum>ukdes   ABS. 3S OBL gebunay
    AF-descended down he   on   earth

    He descended down on earth.

(iv) As object in a dyadic transitive clause

(22) *Sinabi **na**   dut a   apostol **siya**.*
    s<in>abi 3S.ERG PART LG apostle   3S.ABS
    PERF-said   PART LG apostle   he

    He also said that he is an apostle.

Person	Short	Gloss	Description
1S	yak=(y)ak	I	1st person sing
2S	ka	you (singular)	2nd person sing
3S	siya	he or she	3rd person sing
1D	kita	I and you	1st person dual
1PE	kami	we (excluding 'you')	1st person excl
2P	kayo	you (plural)	2nd person plural
3P	sid	They	3rd person plural
1PI	kitam	we (meaning 'all')	1st person incl

(23) *Inabuyanan **de**   **siya***
    <in>abuyanan ERG. 3P ABS.3S
    PERF-knew   they   he

They knew him.

(v) As object in a triadic transitive clause
(24) *Olagean* **Na** **sid** *mopatud*
   <o>alage<an> ERG.3S ABS.3P <mo>patud
   GF-took care of he   they   male siblings
He took care of them, the brothers.

(vi) As respect to God (24) and to the elders
(14). Example (14) and (24) also shows that absolutive free and clitic pronouns co-exist in a clause.
(25) ... *"Dingol **ta=kayo***   *a*
     hear   ERG.1D=ABS.2P DET
     hear   I.she=you
monakang,   *kanya nonsuksuk **kami***
DET PROG-walk PART PST-hide   ABS.1P
DET PROG-walk PART PST-hide   we
*ta   motakottak   dehil **tiyak** ay obe."*
PART <mo>takot=(t)yak   PART ABS.1S TL obe
PART <mo>takot=ABS.1S PART ABS.1S TL obe
PART fear=   I   PART I   TL obe
Adam said, we heard *You* walking towards us,
so we hid ourselves and I was scared (of You) be-
cause I am nude.

3.2   Ergative pronouns

Dita (2011) explains that genitives are morphologically identical with ergatives. It is with this
morphological synonymity that prompted some
Philippinists to use the label GEN to both ergative
and genitive pronouns. She argues that these items
should not receive similar treatment. Again to distinguish the two, PL genitives are generally post-
nominals whereas ergatives are postverbals (Dita,
2011). Table 4 is a summary of the ergative (free
and enclitic) pronouns.

Person	Ergative	Gloss	Description
1S	ko=k	I	1st person sing
2S	mo=m	you (singular)	2nd person sing
3S	na	he or she	3rd person sing
1D	ta	I and you	1st person dual
1PE	me	we (excluding 'you')	1st person excl
2P	yo	you (plural)	2nd person plural
3P	de	they	3rd person plural
1PI	tam	we (meaning 'all')	1st person incl

Table 4 – Ergative (Free and Enclitic) Pronouns

(i) As subject of a transitive clause, either dyadic (26) and triadic (27) and (28).
(26) ... *iatod **ko** dikayo at*
    <i>atod ERG.1S OBL.2P CONJ
    GF-give I   to you and
nu pala lahi   yo."

DET PL   decendant GEN.2P
DET PL   decendant your
God said, I will give this (place) to you to all
your descendants.

(27) *Inotos*   **Na**   **sid**
   <in>otos   ERG.3S ABS.3P.
   GF-ordered he   they
   a   mampakaadu
   LIG to become many
He orders them to multiply.

(28) ... *"Lapditon **mo**   tu detnap*
    lapdit<on> ERG.2S DET detnap
    GF-hit   you   DET stone
*nu salokod **mo**."*
DET salokod GEN.2S
DET cane   your
Then it happened, God said to Moises, (You)
Strike the stone with your cane.

(ii) Ergative and genitive constructions co-
exist in a clause
(29) ... *"Dehil nu   ginawam=mo,*
    CONJ DET   g<in>awa=ERG.2S
    CONJ DET   GF.do =you
*ialagang **mo** i   tiyan **mo***
<i>alaga<ng> ERG.2S DET tiyan GEN.2S
GF-take care   you   DET belly your
ti dupit umpisa   niedut."
OBL dupit <um><p><isa> TIME
OBL soil   PERF.starting now
Then, God said to the snake, "Because of what
you've done, you will carry your belly on the
ground from this day onward.

3.3   Oblique pronouns

Person	Oblique	Gloss	Description
1S	diyak	'to me'	1st person sing
2S	dikaw	'to you' (singular)	2nd person sing
3S	dikana	'to him/ her'	3rd person sing
1D	dikita	'to me and you'	1st person dual
1PE	dikame	to both of us	1st person excl
2P	dikayo	'to you' (plural)	2nd person plural
3P	dikade	'to them'	3rd person plural
1PI	dikitam	'to us'	1st person incl

Table 5 - Oblique pronouns

Dita (2010) explains that oblique pronouns are
used to express direction towards a person or persons, or the transmission of an object towards the
entity or party specified by the oblique pronoun.
They are formed by adding pronouns to the stem
di-. Table 5 shows the oblique pronouns. Their
functions are the following:

(i)   as semantic role of 'source' (29).

(30) *Opodin **tam**   tu   Makidepat*
    <o>podin ERG.1PI DET Makidepat
    praise   we(all)   DET Makidepat

*pagmogpasalamat   **kitam dikana**,*
<pag><mog><pa>salamat ABS.1PI OBL.3S
to give thanks   we(all)   to him

*ta   ipalaway   **tam dikana***
CONJ <ipa>laway   ERG.1PI OBL.3S
CONJ to see   we(all)   to him

nu pamamagitan nu   paagpasalamat
DET pa<mama>gitan   DET <paag><pa>salamat
DET act of   DET to give thanks

***tam   dikana**, a Siya*
ERG.1PI OBL3S   LIG ABS.3S
we(all)   to him   LIG he

tu ki   kapangyadihan at ki   gewa
DET EXIST kapangyadihan   CONJ EXIST gewa
DET EXIST greatness   and   EXIST creation

na lahat, bala lahat a
DET PART   PART PART   LIG
of all   before all   LIG

*mopeya ay unalang **dikana**.*
<mo>peya TL una<lang>   OBL.3S
goodness TL came from   him

Let us praise and give thanks to Him, and let us show Him our gratitude by glorifying His greatness and His creations. Because all things before us are good, and that all things came from Him.

(ii)   As a semantic role of 'goal' in (31)

(31) *I ginawa   nu Makidepat, ay impanol **Na***
DET g<in>awa DET Makidepat   TL inform   ERG.3S
DET GF-make DET Makidepat   TL inform   he

***dikade** tu   kailangan de*
OBL.3P   DET kailangan   GEN.3P
to them   DET kailangan   their

God made sure that what He informs them is what they should write about.

(iii)   Third, obliques can also function as benefactives (Dita, 2010)

(32) *Namate ti   Hesus pade **dikitam**.*
<na>mate PN Hesus   PART OBL.3P
AF-die   PN Jesus   for   all of us
Jesus gave his life for us.

(iv)   obliques express possession when they co-occur with existentials.

(33) *Ki katahimekang kitam   **dikana**.*
exist peacefulness   ABS.1PI OBL.3S
exist peacefulness   we (all)   (to) him
We have peacefulness in Him.

(v)   as a deictic pronoun in place of a personal pronoun

(34) *Yie magkalake   tu   pinakaminona **tam***
this <mag><ka>lake DET <pinaka>minona   GEN.1PI
this adult man-P   DET DEG.old   our

*a   lahat, kanya matotkakaylang   **kitam***
LIG PART   PART   <matot>kakaylang   ABS.1PI
LIG all   PART   DEG.close relative   we

a   lahat ti gebunay.
LIG PART   OBL earth

These men, the oldest of all, are our ancestors, so we are all relatives on earth.

(35) *Yie   lahat a   alta   ay kausil*
    PROX/SP PART LIG alta   TL companion
    this   all   LIG person TL companion

ni Pablo de   idi...
PN
of Paul   before there
Long ago, these people are companions of Paul there.

In (33), the proximal spatial demonstrative *Yie* (this) can be replaced with third person plural *side* (we) such as (34) and (35).

(36) *Side a magkalake tu   pinakaminona **tam***
    ABS.3P LIG men   DET DEGREE.old   GEN.1PI
    they   DET men   DET DEGREE.old   our

a   lahat, kanya...
LIG PART, PART
They, the old men, are our ancestors, so...

(37) ***Side** a   lahat a   alta   ay*
    ABS.3P LIG PART LIG alta   TL
    they   PART all   DET person TL

kausil   ni Pablo de   idi...
companion PN   Paul   before there
Long ago, they, all the people there, are companions of Paul.

3.4   Genitive pronouns

Genitive pronouns encode possession. The noun (possessum) follows the pronoun (the possessor) which is opposite to the phrase structure like English language (e.g. my book, possessor-possessum) (Payne, 1997).   Table 6 shows the genitive pronouns. Besides possessive phrases (36) and (37), many other examples are shown in sentence (6).

(38) *tu   anak   **de***
DET anak-S GEN.3P
their child

(39) *tu*   *bele*   ***na***
        DET   house GEN.1S
        his/ her house

Person	Genitive	Gloss	Description
1S	ko	my	1st person sing
2S	mo	your (singular)	2nd person sing
3S	na	his or her	3rd person sing
1D	ta	our (mine and yours)	1st person dual
1PE	me	ours (excluding 'you')	1st person excl
2P	yo	your (plural)	2nd person plural
3P	de	their	3rd person plural
1PI	tam	our (meaning 'all')	1st person incl

Table 6 - Genitive Pronouns

3.5 Other linguistic phenomena

This study uncovers other linguistic phenomena, similar to the results found in Dita (2010). These are homomorphy (3.5.1), cliticization (3.5.2), hierarchy (3.5.3), and person-deixis interface (3.5.4).

3.5.1 Homomorphy

Dita (2010) explains that ergatives and genitives are spelled and pronounced the same but they differ in their distributional properties. Consider the sentences (23) and (24), and compare them with sentences (38) and (39). The third person plural *de* is labeled ERG (23) while GEN in (38). And also the first person singular *na* is labelled ERG (24) while GEN (39). Consider also sentence (29), second person singular ERG and GEN co-exist in the clause.

3.5.2 Cliticization

Clitics are grammatical words that are unable to stand on their own phonologically, but must instead lean on another adjacent word. They must be incorporated into the prosodic structure of another word. Dita (2010) explains that pronominal clitics exhibit various characteristic. Examine Table 1 above. Absolutives and genitives have enclitics and they enclitizes with the preceding word such as sentence (13), (15), (25) and (29), and they all enclitize with the predicate.

3.5.3 Hierarchy

Another note-worthy observation is the study of Schachter (1973) on Tagalog language (in Dita, 2010). According to him, monosyllabic pronouns always precede disyllabic. Consider the sentences (4), (23), (25), (30), (31), and (33).

3.5.4 Person-deixis interface

Another note-worthy study is done by MacFarland (2006) on Tagalog language (in Dita, 2010). He explains that it is quite common in PL to use a deictic pronoun in place of a personal pronoun. Consider the sentences (34) and (35) and the revised sentences (36) and (37). The revised sentences are replaced with third person plural pronouns, and yet the contextual meanings of the clauses are the same.

3.5.5 Portmanteau

Dita (2011) explains that portmanteau pronouns exist in Philippine languages. These portmanteau pronouns is a combination of ERG.1s and ABS.2s, where the former is the agent and the latter the patient in a clause. Data shows that it is also present in Southern Alta language. Interlinear gloss and symbols use **1D** instead of **1s** in Dita (2011) such as (40). In addition, the absolutive pronoun in (25) encodes ABS.1D+ERG.2P as a form of respect to a Supreme Being.

(40) *Besan **taka.***
       read   ta=ka.
       read   ERG.1D+ABS.2S
       Let us read this biblical passage.

4 Summary and Recommendation

This initial analysis shows that the pronominal systems of the Southern Alta language consist of absolutive, ergative, oblique and genitive pronouns. The ergative-absolutive framework unravels the morphosyntax of the pronominal systems of Southern Alta. The framework help describe the functions and characteristic of the different sets of pronouns. Other linguistic phenomena are revealed such as inclusivity/exclusivity, first person dual pronouns, homomorphy, cliticization, hierarchy, person–deixis interface and portmanteau. In conclusion, the ergative-absolutive framework fits the morphosyntactic analysis of the Southern Alta language. In conclusion, the ergative-absolutive framework fits the morphosyntactic analysis of the Southern Alta language. This study also suggests to examine the clausal construction including the noun phrases (NPs) of Southern Alta.

Acknowledgments

My sincerest thanks to my all-time adviser, Dr. Shirley Dita, for the inspiring words and wisdom to pursue this study. I am also very thankful to Dr. Lawrence Reid, who never forgets the helpful tips and keen suggestions despite his busy trips and schedules. I am thankful to our Dean Dr. Crisol Bruza and his associates at the CAS for their unwavering support. Thank you also for the time, words, and wisdom to all of my *Kabuloan Dumagat* respondents and friends, Rogelio Del Monte, Sonny Del Monte, Johny Bote, Ruping Ramos, and their families.

References

Abreu, M. (2014). *The Dumaget language.* An unpublished short paper on AgraPhil, Manila.

Adelaar, A. (2005). The Austronesian languages of the Asia and Madagascar: A historical perspective. In A. Adelaar, & N. Himmelmann (Eds.), *The Austronesian languages of the Asia and Madagascar* (pp. 1-42). New York, USA: Routledge.

Blust, R. (2013). *The Austronesian languages.* The Australian National University, Research School of Pacific and Asian Studies. Canberra: Asian-Pacific Linguistics.

Dita, S. (2007). *A Reference Grammar of Ibanag.* De La Salle University, DEAL. Manila: De La Salle University.

Dita, S. (2011). A morphosyntactic analysis of pronominal system of Philippine languages. *Proceedings of the 24th Pacific Asia Conference on Language, Information and Computation* (pp. 45-59). Institute of Digital Enhancement of Cognitive Processing, Waseda University.

Dixon, R. (2010). *Basic Lingusitic Theory* (Vol. 2). Oxford: Oxford University Press.

Headland, T. (2003). Thirty endangered languages in the Philippines. *Work Papers of the Summer Institute of Linguistics, 47,* 1-12.

Headland, T. (2010). Why the Philippine Negrito languages are endangered. In Florey, M., *Endangered Languages of Austronesia* (pp. 110-120). Oxford: Oxford University Press.

Headland, T., & Healey, A. (1974). Grammatical sketch of Dumagat (Casiguran). *Pacific Linguistics,* 1-54.

Himmelmann, N. (2005). The Austronesian languages of Asia and Madagascar: Typological characteristics. In A. Adelaar, & N. Himmelmann, *The Austronesian languages of Asia and Madagascar* (pp. 110-181). New York: Routledge.

Lewis, P., Simon, G., & Fenning, C. (Eds.). (2015). *Ethnologue: Languages of the World* (18th ed.). Dallas, Texas, USA: SIL-International.

Liao, H. (2005). Pronominal forms in Central Cagayan Agta. In H. Liao, & C. Rubino, *Current Issues in Philippine Linguistics and Anthropology: Parangal kay Lawrence A. Reid* (pp. 346-363). Manila: LSP: SIL-Philippines.

Lobel, J. (2013). *Philippine and North Bornean languages: Issues in description, subgrouping, and reconstruction.* University of Hawai'i, Graduate Division. Manoa: University of Hawai'i.

Miller, H., & Miller, J. (1991). *Mamanwa Texts.* Quezon City: LSP and SIL.

Payne, T. (1997). *Describing morphosyntax: A guide for field liguists.* Cambridge, UK: Cambridge University Press.

Reid, L. (1971). Philippine minor languages: Word lists and phonologies. *Oceanic Linguistics Special Publications,* 1-241.

Reid, L. (1989). Arta, another Philippine negrito language. *Oceanic Linguistic,* 47-74.

Reid, L. (1991). The Alta languages of the Philippines. In R. Harlow (Ed.), *Fifth International Conference on Austronesian Linguistics* (pp. 265-297). Auckland: Linguistic Society of New Zealand.

Reid, L. (2006). On reconstructing the morphosyntax of
Proto-Northern Luzon. *Paper presented at
Tenth International Conference on
Austronesian Linguistics* (pp. 1-73). Palawan:
SIL-International.

Reid, L. (2013). Who are the Philippine Negritos?:
Evidence from language. *Human Biology,
85*(1), 1-32.

Reid, L., & Liao, H. (2004). A brief syntactic typology
of Philippine languages. *Language and
Linguistics, 5*(2), 433-490.

Tharp, J. (1974). *The Northern Cordilleran subgroup pf
Philippine languages.* University of Hawai'i,
Department of Linguistics. University of
Hawai'i.

Wh-island Effects in Korean Scrambling Constructions

Juyeon Cho
Seoul National University
juyeoncho@snu.ac.kr

Abstract

This study examines the wh-island effects in Korean. Since wh-in-situ languages like Korean allow wh-scrambling, the absence of wh-island constraints is accepted. However, it is controversial whether wh-clauses can take a matrix scope or not. In order to clarify the issue of wh-islands in Korean, the current paper designed an off-line experiment with three factors: island or non-island, scrambling or non-scrambling, and embedded scope or matrix scope. The following acceptability judgment task revealed that wh-PF-island does not exist but wh-LF-island plays a role in Korean. Among results of wh-LF-island, it was observed that a majority of speakers prefer the matrix scope reading.

1   Introduction

It has been widely assumed that gap position cannot occur inside the island structures due to island constraints. In terms of filler-gap dependencies, there exists a gap position, which is the argument of an embedded verb, and an antecedent (or filler), which indicates the sentence-initial wh-phrase in (1).

(1) *What do you wonder [whether John bought
    __]?

As one of islands in English, whether-island constraints do not allow any phrases to be out of whether-clause, the sentence in (1) becomes ungrammatical. However, wh-in-situ languages, such as Korean, do not exhibit such island effects as in (2).

(2) Mwues-ul ne-nun [John-i ___ sa-ss-nunci]
    What-Acc you-Top J-Nom   buy-Past-Q
    a-ni?
    Know-Q

Thus, the wh-phrase can be placed in the gap position without degrading grammaticality. However, it is controversial to interpret the sentences with wh-phrase which can undergo the LF-movement, as shown in (3).

(3) ?Nani-o$_i$ John-ga   [$_{WH-ISL}$ Taroo-ga   t$_i$
    What-Acc John-Nom   Taro-Nom
    katta   ka   siritagatteiru.
    buy-Past   Q   want-to-know
    'John wants to know what Taro bought.'

The sentence in (3) contains the wh-word extracted from overt wh-island. Although the wh-word is extracted, it seems to take the scope in its original embedded position. Saito (1989) claimed that question marker such as –ka in Japanese indicates the scope of wh-phrases, so that the proper scope for the extracted wh-word in (3) is the question-marked embedded phrase. Since the movement of the wh-phrase is semantically vacuous regardless of its surface position, Saito considered that this kind of scrambling can be undone or undergoes reconstruction into the indirect question at LF level.

On the other hand, Miyagawa (2005) analyzed the same sentence as grammatical showing that it does not violate the wh-island effects in either at overt syntax or at LF. According to him, the wh-word in the original position can moves through the specifier of CP, which is an empty position in Japanese. This employment of the Spec of CP as an escape hatch makes the sentence circumvent the Subjacency Condition as well as the wh-island constraints.

Considering that wh-movement can occur overtly and covertly, this paper investigates the wh-island effects in Korean, especially in scrambling structures. To clarify whether wh-island effect does exist in Korean, I separate the wh-island effect based on where it occurs. The island effect which is caused by the overt movement out of wh-phrase (or scrambling) is called *wh-PF-island effect*, whereas the effect which bans the wide-scope reading for a wh-phrase is called *wh-LF-island effect*.

In section 2, previous studies toward wh-scrambling in Korean data will be reviewed. The following section 3 presents the experimental design of this paper and the results of the experiment. In section 4, I will discuss the results and proceeds to conclusion suggesting the further direction of this study in section 5.

2   Wh-island effects in Korean

Given that wh-movement is free in wh-in-situ languages, it is still controversial whether the wh-word in so-called wh-island is compatible with wide-scope reading over the entire sentence or not. First, for the wh-in-situ condition, some researchers asserted that it cannot take a matrix scope out of wh-islands (Nishigauchi, 1990; Han, 1992; Watanabe, 1992).

(4) (?) John-wa [Mary-ga   nani-o   katta
        John-Top Mary-Nom   what-Acc buy-Past
        ka dooka]   siritagatte iru no?
        whether   know-want-Q
        'What does John want to know whether Mary bought?

They assumed that there exists a phonetically invisible movement so that it is affected by wh-island effect at LF, which assimilates the Subjacency Condition in the overt syntax. However, they admitted that the degree of acceptability can vary among speakers. Likewise,

Takahashi (1993: 657) presented that such sentences can yield ambiguous interpretation due to the fact that the question marker –*ka* has the ambiguous status between a scope-marker for a wh-phrase and complementizer, similar to English whether. If it is used as a former, then sentence (4) should be read as 'Does John want to know what Mary bought?' If it functions as a complementizer, on the other hand, the wh-word can have a matrix scope to be interpreted as a direct wh-question.

Furthermore, the ambiguity in scope interpretation is also observed for the wh-scrambled condition. Aoshima et al (2003) suggested a questionnaire study showing that Japanese speakers permit the interpretation of yes/no question as well as that of wh-question. This supports that wh-scrambling is a true scrambling and it results in ambiguous scope reading for wh-phrase. However, they posited the context which was in favor of the embedded scope reading, although the results revealed that context does not affect the biased scope toward an embedded reading.

As for Korean, Yoon (2013) conducted an acceptability judgment test for wh-island effect of scrambling. The results demonstrated that native Korean speakers prefer embedded scope reading to matrix scope reading. Although her study proved the existence of wh-island, the preference to yes/no-reading would not be accepted as reliable if participants considered the tested sentences as unacceptable. It is unreliable to rate the acceptability of ungrammatical sentences which are assumed to violate the wh-island constraints.

Unlike Aoshima et al and Yoon, Takahashi (1993) treated certain type of wh-scrambling as syntactic wh-movement. He suggested that when the wh-phrase moves to the initial position headed by [+WH] Comp, it does not move further in LF. If the idea of Takahashi is right, the sentence such as (5) should allow only a wide-scope reading.

(5) Nani$_i$-o John-wa [CP Mary-ga t$_i$ tabeta ka]
        siritagatteiru no?
        'What does John want to know whether Mary ate?

There also exist some studies which treat the wh-scrambling with reference to prosodic structures, suggesting that ambiguous scope reading is possible in specific prosody patterns

(Ishihara, 2002; Kitagawa and Hirose, 2013 among others). Therefore, in order to complement the former studies, this paper examines whether Korean native speakers have different intuition towards wh-PF-island effect and wh-LF-island effect.

3 Experiments

3.1 Research Questions and Hypotheses

To ascertain whether wh-island effect does exist in Korean, I attempt to distinguish the wh-island based on where it occurs. For violation of the overt movement out of wh-phrase, I call this wh-PF-island effect. For the effect that bans the wide-scope reading for the wh-phrase, I call it wh-LF-island effect. Given that two wh-island effects are detected at different level, this paper provides empirical evidence toward existence of each wh-island effect in Korean.

The research questions are as follows:

(6) a. Does Korean show wh-PF-island effect?
b. Does Korean show wh-LF-island effect?

For the research questions, the hypotheses are made.

(7) a. If overt wh-movement in Korean would be accepted without causing acceptability, wh-PF-island effect will be regarded as non-island constraint.
b. If non-scrambled wh-island sentence does not allow matrix scope reading, there will be wh-LF-island effect. Still, both scope reading can be compatible even if the preference over one reading varies among speakers.

3.2 Method

To examine the wh-island effects in Korean, this paper follows the factorial definition of Sprouse et al (2016) with slight modifications. Also, answer type was designed following Kim and Goodall (2016). Therefore, the current experiment was conducted under a 2 x 2 x 2 factorial design, with three factors: Structure (non-island/island), Wh-position (non-scrambling/scrambling) and Answer type (yes/no-answer/wh-answer).

The target sentences are represented in (8) and (9)[1].

(8) Questions

a. Non-island | non-scrambling
Ne-nun [Yeji-ka nwuku-ul manna-ss-ta-ko]
You-Top Y-Nom who-Acc meet-Past-Decl
tul-ess-ni?
hear-Past-Q

b. Non-island | scrambling
Nwuku-ul ne-nun [Yeji-ka __ manna-ss-ta-ko]
Who-Acc you-Top Y-Nom   meet-Past-Decl
tul-ess-ni?
hear-Past-Q

c. Island | non-scrambling
Ne-nun [Yeji-ka nwuku-ul manna-ss-nunci]
You-Top Y-Nom who-Acc meet-Past-Q
tul-ess-ni?
hear-Past-Q

d. Island | scrambling
Nwuku-ul ne-nun [Yeji-ka __ manna-ss-nunci]
Who-Acc you-Top Y-Nom   meet-Past-Q
tul-ess-ni?
hear-Past-Q

(9) Answers
a. Yes/no answer
Ung,   tul-ess-e.
Yes,   hear-Past-Decl
b. Wh-answer
Minsu(-lul manna-ss-ta-ko / nunci tul-ess-e).
M-Acc   meet-Past-Decl / -Q   hear-Past-D

Thirty-two items (4 tokens for each condition) were used in the experiment. Each item consists of Question-Answer pair. All the questions are bi-clausal sentences, which contain either a declarative phrase or an interrogative phrase as a complement. The matrix verbs used were *tutta* 'hear,' *malhata* 'say,' while the embedded verbs include *mannata* 'meet,' *ttaylita* 'hit,'

---

[1] Note that wh-words in Korean can be interpreted as indefinite pronouns. In addition to the interpretation as true interrogative, the question in (8a), for example, can deliver the meaning that 'Did you know whether Yeji met someone?' This interpretation would be only compatible with yes/no answer, identical to the case where a true wh-word takes scope over the embedded scope.

chingchanhata 'compliment,' *paysinhata* 'betray.' For the consistent interpretation, a single wh-word *nwukwu* 'who' was used. The experiment contains forty-eight filler items, leading to a 1.5:1 ratio of fillers to target items.

Twenty participants were asked to check the acceptability of the answers, with a 7-point Likert scale task (1 at the lowest and 7 at the highest of acceptability). As noted in Kim and Goodall (2016), the felicity of question-answer pairs were measured to avoid the biased reading toward one particular scope reading and only to test the speakers' interpretation of sentences.

3.3 Results

The basic descriptive results are presented in Table 1 and illustrated in Figure 1.

		Wh-answer	Y/N-answer	Total
Island	Non-scrambling	4.70 (1.93)	5.70 (1.50)	5.20 (1.79)
	Scrambling	4.24 (2.06)	3.58 (1.83)	3.91 (1.97)
	Total	4.47 (2.00)	4.64 (1.98)	4.55 (1.99)
Non-island	Non-scrambling	5.81 (1.33)	4.29 (2.03)	5.05 (1.87)
	Scrambling	4.80 (1.93)	2.65 (1.57)	3.73 (2.06)
	Total	5.31 (1.73)	3.47 (1.98)	4.39 (2.07)

Table 1. Descriptive results of the data

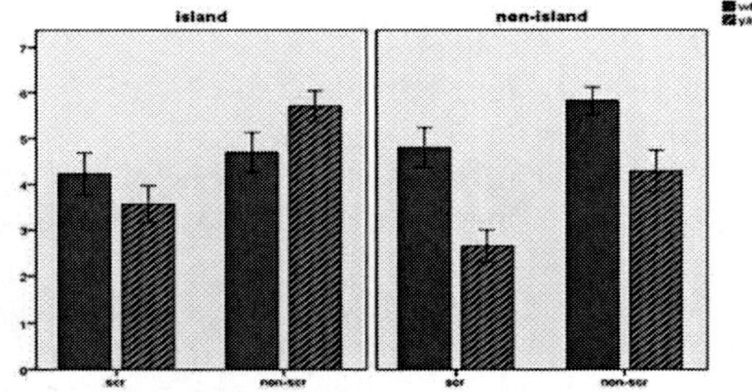

Figure 1. Ratings of acceptability judgment task

Although the results need to be statistically verified, there show little differences between Structures (island/non-island). As for Wh-position, scrambled questions were rated slightly lower than non-scrambled questions, which means that scrambling might affect the acceptability of sentences. For Answer type, participants generally preferred wh-answer reading which indicates that they considered the question as a direct wh-question. Only the non-scrambled island condition exhibits a reverse pattern of preference. This can

be suggestive for existence of wh-LF-island effect in Korean, following the hypothesis above.

First, based on the transformed z-scores, two-way ANOVA was conducted in order to examine wh-PF-island in Korean. The transformation into z-scores can eliminate the biases of scales among participants because it makes each rating into a standardized one. An interaction between Structure and Wh-location were calculated by differences-in-differences (DD) scores for each participant (Sprouse et al, 2016): DD = D1 (non-island/non-scrambling – island/non-scrambling) – D2 (non-island/scrambling – island/scrambling). The results are plotted in Figure 2.

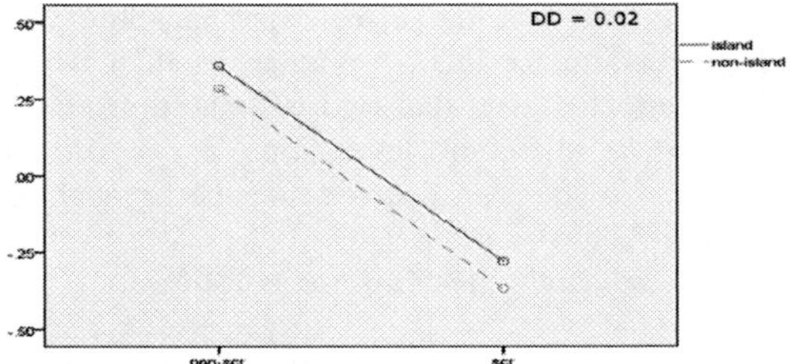

Figure 2. Interaction plot for wh-PF-island

For wh-PF-island, the results revealed nearly perfect linear additivity (DD score of .02). This sub-additive wh-island effect is detected regardless of Answer types (a *p*-value of .21 and a DD score of −.24 for y/n answer; a *p*-value of .18 and a DD score of −.27 for wh-answer), as in Figure 3.

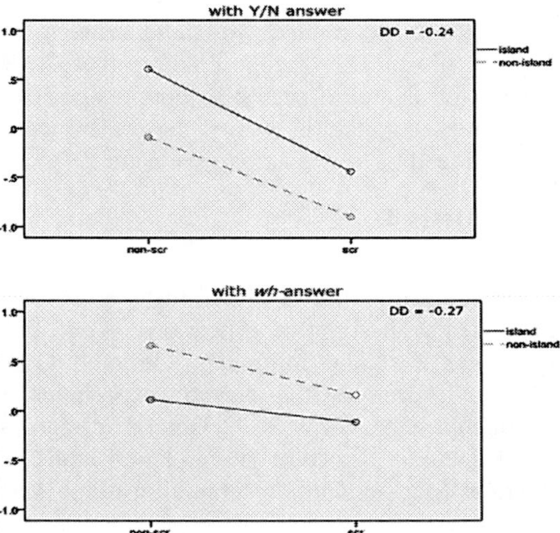

Figure 3. Interaction plot for wh-PF-island by Answer type

Secondly, I compare the acceptability of wh-in-situ sentences and wh-scrambled sentences, both of which contain wh-islands, marked with question marker *–(nun)ci*. It was tested to see if there is any island effect at LF level. Two-way ANOVA was run for Wh-location in each Answer type, which is displayed with the effect plot in Figure 4. The DD scores for their interaction are also given.

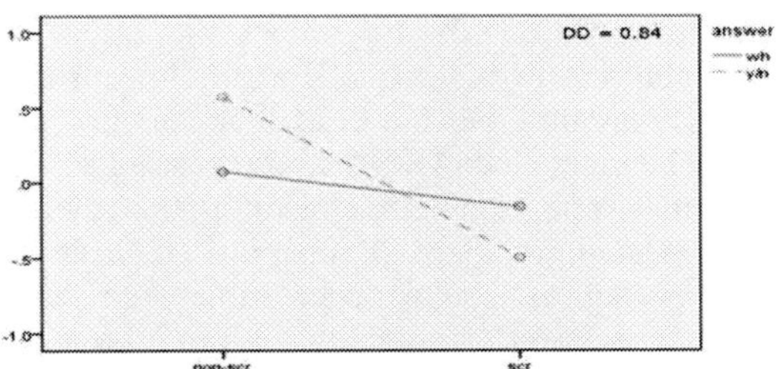

Figure 4. Interaction plot for wh-LF-island

Compared to the effect plot for wh-PF-island (Figure 2), the effect plot for wh-LF-island in Figure 4 has the two non-parallel lines. Accordingly, the DD score showed interaction with the score of .84. Moreover, the gap between Wh-location is much bigger in yes/no answers than in wh-answers. This provides that an embedded scope reading is more affected by the location of wh-phrases: even though the sentence was inclined to be read as an indirect question in non-scrambled condition, the same reading was not chosen when the wh-word is scrambled to the initial of the sentence.

4 Discussion

Supporting the hypothesis, Korean native speakers are not sensitive to wh-PF-movement since the presence of overt wh-movement does not affect the acceptability of the sentences. Whether the sentence has wh-island or not, the differences in acceptability come from the location of wh-phrase. Reflecting the sub-additive results, I can see wh-clauses do not behave like islands, indicating the absence of wh-PF-island in Korean.

When it comes to wh-LF-phrase, however, a closer look is needed. In a non-scrambled island condition, there showed a preference of yes/no reading (z-score = .58) over wh-reading (z-score = .07). What it means is that when wh-words occur in wh-island, it is more associated with embedded clause. Then, we can assume that even though the overt movement is allowed, the LF movement is somewhat disallowed to be interpreted out of the island.

In a scrambled island condition, the preference of answer type shows a reverse pattern: wh-reading (z-score = -.15) is more acceptable compared to yes/no scope reading (z-score = -.49). The results seem to be consistent with Takahashi (1993) in that matrix scope is preferred; however, both scope reading is still possible.

Overall, the results of island construction are consistent with Aoshima et al (2003): wh-reading is preferred for both scrambled structure, whereas yes/no reading is preferred for non-scrambled structure. However, as for non-island construction, the results of the current study are leant toward wh-reading, which are inconsistent with Aoshima et al (2003) showing yes/no-reading preference. Though it is not the main focus of this paper, these reverse results for non-island structure can be easily illustrated. Following Saito (1989), the scope for wh-words is the entire sentence in non-island sentences. Thus, wh-words can freely take scope in matrix clause.

Concerning the individual variations, Figure 5 displayed a pattern for each subjects to see how individual participant interpreted the sentences with wh-island.

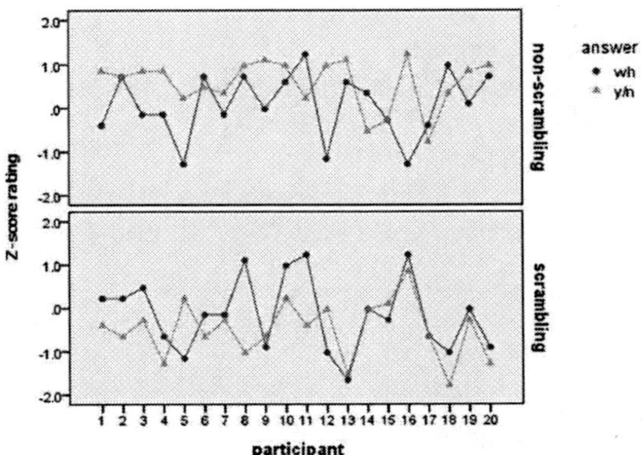

Figure 5. Individual scope preference

The general pattern for the subjects follows the results mentioned above. Still, there are some individual variations. Four out of twenty subjects exhibits a preference over an embedded scope reading but three of them show a preference over a matrix scope reading, regardless of Structure and Wh-location condition.

Last thing to note is about one type of filler items of the experiment, the wh-island structures with specifier position of CP filled. Though it is not the main target of the current study, it is to identify whether the specifier position of CP can function as an escape hatch (Miyagawa, 2005; Han, 2015). If the sentences with Spec CP filled are not compatible with wide scope reading, then their argument can be supported. The filler sentences used are as shown in (10) for questions and (11) for answers. The results of interpreting those sentences are illustrated in Figure 6.

(10) Questions
    a. Spec CP island | non-scrambling
    Ne-nun [encey [Yoonseo-ka   nwuku-lul
    You-Top when   Y-Nom   who-Acc
    honnae-ss-nunci] tul-ess-ni?
    scold-Past-Q   hear-Past-Q
    b. Spec CP island | scrambling
    Nwuku-lul ne-nun [encey [Yoonseo-ka
    Who-Acc you-Top when   Y-Nom
    ___ honnae-ss-nunci]   tul-ess-ni?
       scold-Past-Q   hear-Past-Q

(11) Answers
    a. Yes/no answer
    Ung,   tul-ess-e.
    Yes,   hear-Past-Decl
    b. Wh-answer
    Seongho(-lul honnae-ss-nunci tul-ess-e).
    S-Acc   scold-Past-Q   hear-Past-D
    c. Wh2-answer
    Ecey   (honnae-ss-nunci tul-ess-e).
    Yesterday scold-Past-Q   hear-Past-D

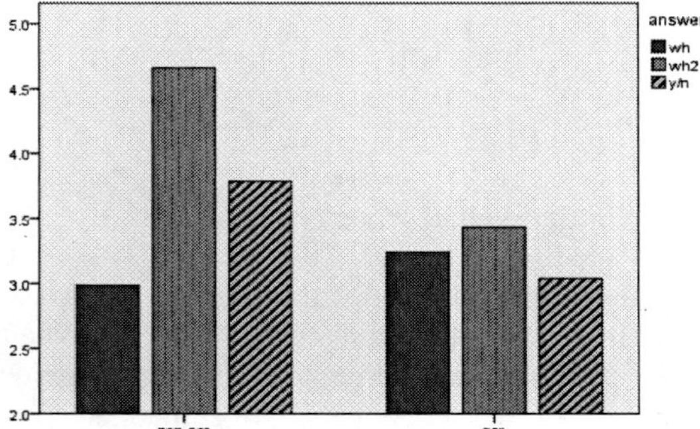

Figure 6. Ratings for Spec CP-filled condition

Unlike Miyagawa (2005) and Han (2015) assumed, the sentence whose Spec CP position is filled can be interpreted as a direct wh-questions, although the matrix reading is not highly preferred. If the Spec CP position was regarded as a real escape hatch, the wh-word in the embedded clause cannot move through the filled Spec CP. However, the results demonstrated that whether that position is lexically specified or not, wh-word can have the widest scope above entire sentence. Hence, the specifier position of CP does not affect the acceptability of wh-island in Korean. It needs to be closely examined but the brief look for their idea cannot be maintained with the current results.

Besides, one unexpected result is that the wh-word located in Spec CP position (indicated as Wh2 in Figure) is most compatible with matrix scope for both conditions. The issue of understanding islands which has the Spec CP filled would be accounted for by comparing the sentences without such islands.

5   Conclusion

This study is to investigate the existence of wh-island constraints in Korean scrambling constructions. By separating wh-PF-island and wh-LF-island, the ambiguous definition for island effects in Korean can be divided. The current experiment suggested the lack of island effect with wh-PF-island, but the presence of effect with wh-LF-island.

For wh-LF-island, the results vary between scrambled and non-scrambled structures. When the wh-words is placed in-situ, embedded scope reading received higher acceptability scores than matrix scope reading. This indicates that the speaker obeys the wh-LF-movement to ban the embedded wh-word to have a matrix scope. The reverse results were exhibited from scrambled structures, contrary to Yoon (2013)'s generalization that embedded scope reading is more accepted.

The results displayed the consistent preference pattern with Takahashi (1993) in terms of high preference for interpretation as a direct question. However, since it is not limited to wh-movement, it seems to follow the Saito (1989) arguing that wh-scrambling can be undone at LF.

There remain some issues toward how to illustrate the wh-reading preference in overall condition. It can be clarified with consideration of other syntactic and semantic properties of wh-movement and scrambling. Further study with more controlled experiment stimuli is needed to contribute to clarifying ambiguous interpretation of wh-scrambling constructions.

References

Aoshima, S., Phillips, C., & Weinberg, A. (2003). Processing of Japanese wh-scrambling constructions. Japanese/Korean Linguistics, 12, 179-191.

Han, H. S. (1992). Notes on reflexive movement. Journal of East Asian Linguistics, 1(2), 215-218.

Han, H. R. (2015). Scrambling Out of a Wh-Island: Types and Acceptability. The journal of studies in language, 31(1), 157-177

Ishihara, S. (2002). Invisible but audible wh-scope marking: Wh-constructions and deaccenting in Japanese. In Proceedings of WCCFL (Vol. 21, pp. 180-193).

Kim, B., & Goodall, G. (2016). Islands and Non-islands in Native and Heritage Korean. Frontiers in psychology, 7.

Kitagawa, Y., & Hirose, Y. (2012). Appeals to prosody in Japanese Wh-interrogatives—Speakers' versus listeners' strategies. Lingua, 122(6), 608-641.

Miyagawa, S. (2005). EPP and semantically vacuous scrambling. The free word order phenomenon: Its syntactic sources and diversity, 181-220.

Nishigauchi, Taisuke (1990) Quantification in the Theory of Grammar, Dordrecht: Kluwer.

Saito, M. (1989). Scrambling as semantically vacuous A'-movement. Alternative conceptions of phrase structure, 182-200.

Sprouse, J., Caponigro, I., Greco, C., & Cecchetto, C. (2016). Experimental syntax and the variation of island effects in English and Italian. Natural Language & Linguistic Theory, 34(1), 307-344.

Takahashi, D. (1993). Movement of wh-phrases in Japanese. Natural Language & Linguistic Theory, 11(4), 655-678.

Watanabe, A. (1992). Subjacency and S-structure movement of wh-in-situ. Journal of East Asian Linguistics, 1(3), 255-291.

Yoon, J. M. (2013). Undoing and wh-island effects of scrambling in Korean. Studies in Generative Grammar, 23(1), 41-63.

A Crowdsourcing Approach for Annotating Causal Relation Instances in Wikipedia

Kazuaki Hanawa, Akira Sasaki, Naoaki Okazaki, Kentaro Inui
Tohoku University
{hanawa, aki-s, okazaki, inui}@ecei.tohoku.ac.jp

Abstract

This paper presents a crowdsourcing approach for annotating causal relation instances to Wikipedia. Because an annotation task cannot be decomposed into multiple-choice problems, we integrate a crowdsourcing service and brat, a popular on-line annotation tool, to provide an easy-to-use interface and quality control for annotation work. We design simple micro-tasks that involve annotating textual spans with causal relations. We issued the micro-tasks to crowd workers, and collected 95,008 annotations of causal relation instances among 8,745 summary sentences in 1,494 Wikipedia articles. The annotated corpus not only provides supervision data for automatic recognition of causal relation instances, but also reveals valuable facts for improving the annotation process of this task.

1 Introduction

Commonsense knowledge such as entities and events, and their causal relationships, are indispensable in various natural language processing (NLP) applications, including question answering (Oh et al., 2013; Oh et al., 2016; Sharp et al., 2016), hypothesis generation (Radinsky et al., 2012; Hashimoto et al., 2015), stance detection (Sasaki et al., 2016), and literature curation for systems biology (Pyysalo et al., 2015; Rinaldi et al., 2016).

In many previous researches, corpora for acquiring causal relations were built by annotating two text spans (e.g., entities) and their relations in the text (Doddington et al., 2004; Hendrickx et al., 2010; Pyysalo et al., 2015; Rinaldi et al., 2016; Dunietz et al., 2017; Rehbein and Ruppenhofer, 2017). However, this approach is extremely work intensive. It involves choosing a target domain, designing an ontology (semantic classes) of entities, building a corpus for named entity recognition, designing an annotation guideline for relations, and annotating the relations between entities. Building such a corpus also requires the annotation efforts of experts. For these reasons, this approach is almost non-scalable to various domains or genres of text although the knowledge of the causal relations is highly target-specific.

This paper presents an approach for harnessing causal relation instances to Wikipedia articles via crowdsourcing. Wikipedia is the central infrastructure for knowledge curation, as exemplified by Freebase (Bollacker et al., 2008) and Wikification (Mihalcea and Csomai, 2007). Therefore, we base Wikipedia articles for building a corpus with causal relation instances. This work represents a first step toward organizing the causal knowledge in Wikipedia articles covering various topics.

Recently, researchers have recognized the value of crowdsourcing services in constructing wide-ranging language resources at low cost (Brew et al., 2010; Finin et al., 2010; Gormley et al., 2010; Jha et al., 2010; Fort et al., 2011; Kawahara et al., 2014; Lawson et al., 2010; Hovy et al., 2014; Takase et al., 2016). Unfortunately, causal relations cannot be directly annotated by crowdsourcing. For this purpose, non-expert workers on crowdsourcing services require a clear and simple micro-task. A crowdsourcing service only provides a standardized interface for workers. The micro-tasks on this interface

31st Pacific Asia Conference on Language, Information and Computation (PACLIC 31), pages 336–345
Cebu City, Philippines, November 16-18, 2017

are often limited to multiple choice questions or free descriptions.

This study also explores the potential of crowdsourcing for collecting annotations about causal relation instances. To this end, we tailor a simple micro-task in which crowd workers annotate textual spans with causal relations to the title of a Wikipedia article. We also develop an annotation system that cooperates with a crowdsourcing service. By virtue of the widely used annotation tool brat[1] (Stenetorp et al., 2012), the system is easy to use and extendible to other annotation tasks.

We collected 95,008 annotations of causal relation instances for 8,745 summary sentences[2] in 1,494 Wikipedia articles. By analyzing the annotation results, we provide valuable hints for improving the annotation process in terms of the number of crowd workers necessary for an article, the number of agreements necessary for improving the quality of causal relation instances, syntactic profiles of annotated spans (e.g., noun and verb phrases), and common confusions of annotations.

The annotation results are also useful for mining expressions inverting polarity of causality (promotion and suppression) and provide supervision data for automatic extraction of causal relation instances from Wikipedia articles. We have released the annotation system, annotated corpus, and the automatic extraction tool on a dedicated website[3]. Although the corpus was built for Japanese Wikipedia articles, we here use English translations for illustrative purposes.

2 Related work

NLP researchers have built corpora for various NLP tasks through crowdsourcing. These tasks include part-of-speech tagging (Hovy et al., 2014), PP attachment (Jha et al., 2010), named entity recognition (Finin et al., 2010; Lawson et al., 2010), sentiment classification (Brew et al., 2010), relation extraction (Gormley et al., 2010), semantic modeling of relation patterns (Takase et al., 2016), and discourse parsing (Kawahara et al., 2014). In most of these tasks, the micro-tasks are designed

---

[1] http://brat.nlplab.org/

[2] The lead paragraph of a Wikipedia article containing a quick summary of the most important points of the article.

[3] http://www.cl.ecei.tohoku.ac.jp/

on the way to Tomales Bay for a BBQ w/ friends. discussing pc tuned!

Word	Person	Place	Organization	None	???
on	○	○	○	◉	☐
the	○	○	○	◉	☐
way	○	○	○	◉	☐
to	○	○	○	◉	☐
Tomales	○	○	○	◉	☐
Bay	○	○	○	◉	☐
for	○	○	○	◉	☐
a	○	○	○	◉	☐
BBQ	○	○	○	◉	☐
w/	○	○	○	◉	☐

Figure 1: Named entity annotation by the multiple-choice method (Finin et al., 2010).

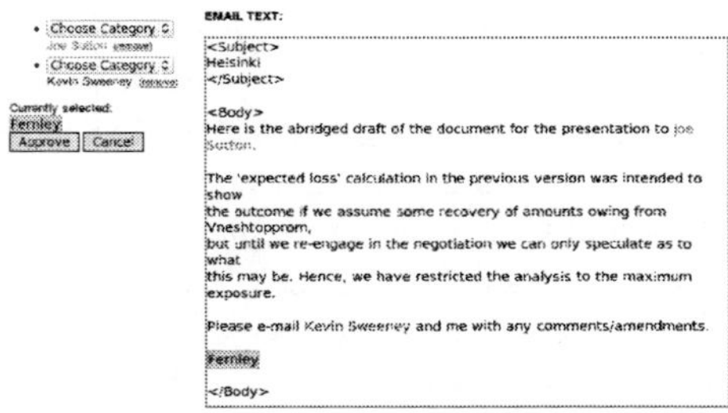

Figure 2: A custom interface for annotating named entities via crowdsourcing (Lawson et al., 2010).

as multiple-choice problems. For example, Brew et al. (2010) annotated sentiment polarity in a micro-task where workers labeled an article as positive, negative, or irrelevant. When the target task cannot be broken into micro-tasks of multiple-choice problems, a special approach is needed. Labeling of text spans falls into this category.

Notwithstanding, corpora with span annotations built by crowdsourcing have been reported in several studies. Finin et al. (2010) annotated the boundaries and semantic classes of named entities by converting the annotation task into a micro-task of multiple-choice problems. They applied the standard interface of Amazon Mechanical Turk (see Figure 1). In this interface, the worker selected a label (PERSON, PLACE, ORGANIZATION, or NONE) from a row of radio buttons placed beside every word in a sentence. This interface not only reduces the readability of the sentence but also requires many selections of radio buttons. The closest work to ours is Lawson et al. (2010). They implemented a custom interface in which workers selected arbitrary spans of text and attached a label to each span (see Figure 2). However, their interface is specific to named entity recognition, and is not generalizable to other annotation tasks. In addition, their annotation tool has not been released to the public.

In contrast, we combine a crowdsourcing service with brat, a popular open-source annotation tool, to provide an easy-to-use interface and quality control for the annotation work. This approach is not limited to causal relations but can be adapted to any brat-supported tasks (e.g., part-of-speech tagging and information extraction). We also present a quality control mechanism that is applicable to any crowdsourcing services accepting free text for a micro-task.

Several studies have dedicated to identify causal relations mentioned in text. For instance, Dunietz et al. (2017) present the version 2.0 of Bank of Effects and Causes Stated Explicitly (BECauSE). The corpus includes annotations of causes and effects as well as seven semantic relations that are frequently associated with causation. Rehbein and Ruppenhofer (2017) use the similar annotation scheme for building a German corpus with some changes in the label set and the scope of causality. Built on top of well-established linguistic theories, these studies focus more on "causal language" (expressions of causation) than real-world causation. In contrast, our ultimate goal is acquisition of real-world causal knowledge by exploting Wikipedia as an encyclopedia. We thus design a curation process with crowdworkers involved in, focussing on how humans 'read' Wikipedia articles for causal knowledge.

3 Annotating promotion/suppression relations in Wikipedia articles

3.1 Labels of causal relations

This study annotates promotion/suppression relations (Hashimoto et al., 2012; Fluck et al., 2015) in Wikipedia articles. Here, "X promotes Y" means that Y is activated when X is activated. Analogously, "X suppresses Y" means that Y is inactivated when X is activated.

Many corpora for acquiring relational knowledge are created by annotating two entities and the relation between the pair of entities in a sentence (Doddington et al., 2004). However, this approach is too difficult for crowd workers be-cause it requires locating the entities and considering the promotion/suppression relations for all possible pairs of entities. Moreover, to create a valuable corpus, it is important to annotate the promotion/suppression relations involving the article title (a variable T, hereafter), because the article is naturally intended to provide knowledge about T. Therefore, we force T to participate in an argument of a promotion/suppression relation. In other words, the annotation task is accomplished by labeling PRO ("T promotes Y"), SUP ("T suppresses Y"), PRO_BY ("X promotes T"), or SUP_BY ("X suppresses T") for text spans (denoted by Y for PRO and SUP, and denoted by X for PRO_BY and SUP_BY) in the article.

We randomly selected 1,494 articles belonging to nine categories and to the subcategories/sub-subcategories: "Social issues", "Disasters", "Diseases and disorders", "Innovation", "Policy", "Finance", "Energy technology", "Biomolecules" and "Nutrients". It is hoped that articles in these categories contain many promotion/suppression relations.

3.2 Annotation policy

The units to be annotated must also be defined in the annotation design. In this research, we examined two kinds of units: noun phrases and verb phrases. However, neither of these units were satisfactory for annotating promotion/suppression relations.

For example, consider the following sentences in the Wikipedia article "Nyctalopia"[4].

> Nyctalopia, also called night-blindness, is a condition making it difficult to see in relatively low light. Nyctalopia may exist from birth, or be caused by injury or severe malnutrition.

Among these sentences, we seek an instance of ⟨SUP, nyctalopia, see in relatively low light⟩. However, when we limited the annotation unit to noun phrases, we could not annotate the phrase "see in relatively low light". Similarly, when we limited the annotation unit to verb phrases, we failed to obtain ⟨PRO_BY, nyctalopia, injury⟩.

Furthermore, whether adopting noun phrases or verb phrases, the segmentation problem of

---

[4] `https://en.wikipedia.org/wiki/Nyctalopia`

noun/verb phrases remained. For example, both of "severe malnutrition" and "malnutrition" can be interpreted as causes of nyctalopia. When multiple overlapping spans are plausible, we need a criterion that prioritizes one span over the others. However, such a criterion is difficult to define. Instead of defining strict guidelines for annotation spans, we collect multiple annotations within an article and explore the best set of guidelines for crowd workers. A side product of this approach is the varying degree of confidence for each span in the corpus. Thus, this corpus provides useful hints for further improving the annotation process for causal relations.

3.3 Using brat in crowdsourcing

Quality control is a major concern in language resources built by crowdsourcing. In most crowdsourcing services, the quality of an annotation and the worker can be judged by inserting test questions with the correct annotations provided by the task designer.

Although test questions and verifications are essential for quality control, they are inapplicable to the annotation policy described in Section 3.2, because they measure annotation quality by exact match. In contrast, our approach allows multiple spans for arguments of causal relations. If such annotations are judged by exact match, almost all of them will be assessed as incorrect. Therefore, we incorporate the verification process of the test questions in brat, and feedback the annotation quality of a worker to the crowdsourcing service.

Figure 3 is an overview of the proposed system. The annotation procedure is described below:

1. Workers click the link to the modified version of brat (for working on an external website) from a virtual task in the crowdsourcing service.

2. Workers perform the annotation tasks on brat.

3. When a worker complete the set of micro-tasks, we measure the worker's performance against the test questions hidden in the set. As the performance measure, we adopted the character-level F1 score between the worker's annotations and the gold standard.

	PRO	SUP	PRO_BY	SUP_BY
Exact	0.192	0.192	0.132	0.197
Partial	0.448	0.325	0.379	0.380
Character	0.332	0.282	0.309	0.317

Table 1: Inter-annotator agreement of each relation (micro F1 score)

4. The worker is requested to return to the crowdsourcing service and enter the password issued on brat. If the F1 score of a worker's annotation exceed a specified threshold (0.3), the worker is issued a correct password and could claim rewards. If the F1 score is below this threshold, the worker is issued an incorrect password (with no rewards).

4 Annotation results

Using the system described in the previous section and the Yahoo! crowdsourcing service[5], we collected ten annotations per article. We offered an independent task for each promotion/suppression relation PRO, SUP, PRO_BY and SUP_BY. Besides simplifying the annotation task, this assignment ensures that a worker collecting the annotation results is unaware of other relations. Figure 4 shows an example of "Leukemia" annotations. As shown in this fugure, each span has a varying degree of confidence. Most annotators judged that leukemia causes "abnormal white blood cells", followed by "high numbers of abnormal white blood cells". In addition, we observe a nested structure in which leukemia promotes "abnormal white blood cells" but also suppresses the subsequence "white blood cells". Nested structures in annotations can reveal patterns (e.g., "abnormal X") that reverse the polarity of causal relations, for example, from promotion to suppression (see Section 4.5).

4.1 Inter-annotator agreement

How is the quality of the causal relation corpus constructed in this study? Table 1 shows the average inter-annotator agreements for each relation. The agreement between two annotations was measured by the F1 scores of the exact match, partial match and character-level match. The agreement of annotations for an article was obtained by micro-

[5]https://crowdsourcing.yahoo.co.jp/

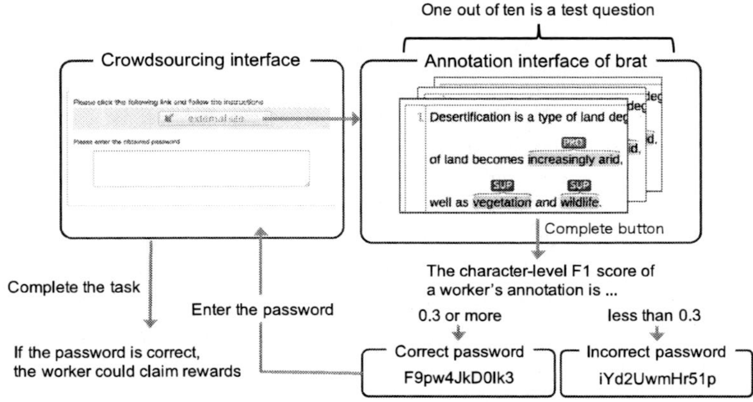

Figure 3: Overview of the annotation system integrating Yahoo! crowdsourcing and brat

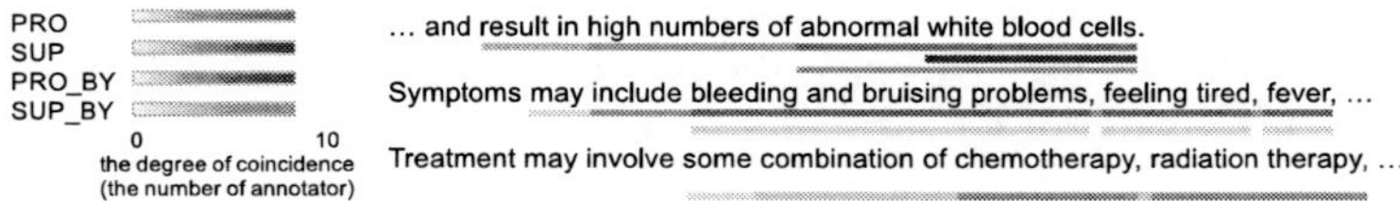

Figure 4: An excerpt of annotation results for "Leukemia" Wikipedia articles. The color at the bottom of the text indicates the relation label, and the color intensity indicates the degree of agreement between the workers.

PRO annotations	7,624
SUP annotations	2,923
PRO_BY annotations	5,387
SUP_BY annotations	1,127

Table 2: Number of annotations in the data created by 2-match aggregation.

averaging the agreements of all ($_{10}C_2 = 45$) pairs of workers. The exact match F1 score regards two annotations as matched when the start and the end of the segments are the same. The partial match F1 score regards two annotations as matched when they have an overlapping region. Although the inter-annotator agreements reported in Table 1 appear low, the results are reasonable considering the difficulty of the task.

4.2 Recommended number of annotations

The consistency of the annotations can be improved by adopting only spans with n or more exactly matched annotations. We call this treatment n-*match aggregation*. Figure 5 shows the micro-averages of the agreements between the raw annotations and those obtained by n-match aggregation.

As shown in the figure, the highest consistency was achieved in 2-match aggregation. In other words, spans should be aggregated when two or more annotations are exactly matched. Therefore, the data created by 2-match aggregation were used in subsequent experiments. Table 2 shows the number of spans for each relation in the dataset.

Can we reduce the number of annotators per article without degrading the annotation quality? In this experiment, we extracted $_{10}C_m$ combinations of m annotations and calculated the micro-average of the agreements between the gold standard data (reference annotations used in the check questions) and n-match aggregations. The F1 score for each m and n is presented in Figure 6.

As shown in this figure, increasing the number of annotators improves the result; the more annotators (m) we use, the higher agreement we obtain from the n-match aggregations. Interestingly, the 2-match aggregation obtains high agreement in five annotations ($m = 5, n = 2$). Considering the tradeoff between number of annotations and cost, five annotations per article may be sufficient to achieve a satisfactory cost–performance balance.

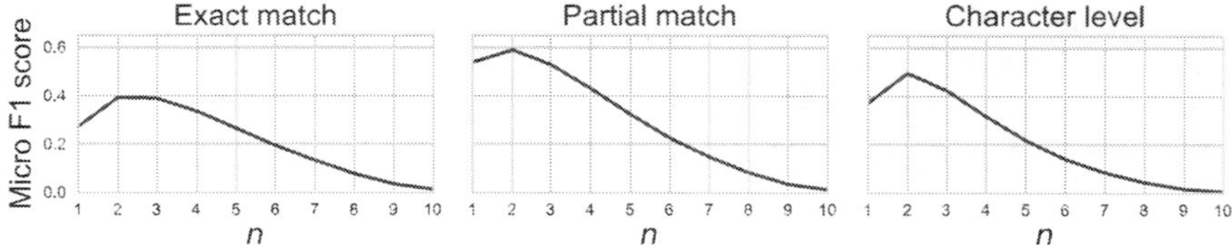

Figure 5: Agreement between the raw annotations and those obtained by n-match aggregation.

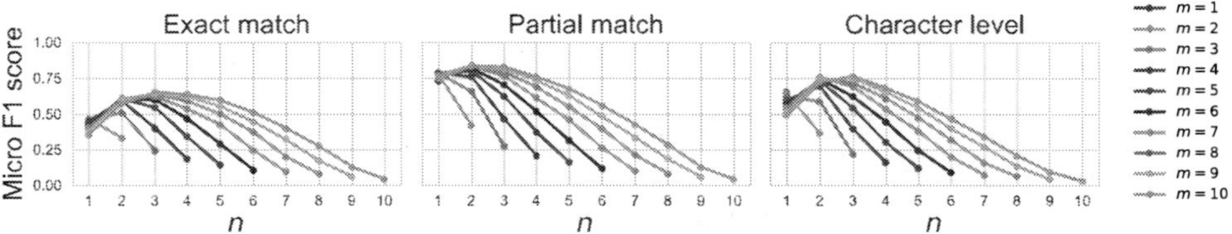

Figure 6: Agreement between the gold standard data and n-match aggregations from m annotations.

Part-of-speech	PRO	SUP	PRO_BY	SUP_BY	Average
Noun	85.99	97.66	90.06	90.76	90.17
Verb	9.53	0.60	4.24	4.79	5.76
Auxiliary verb	1.52	0	1.30	1.22	1.09
Adjective	0.59	0.04	0.45	0.22	0.41
Mark	2.15	1.61	0.35	2.56	2.27
Particle	0.19	0.04	0.40	0.45	0.27
Adverb	0.03	0.04	0.02	0	0.02
Prefix	0	0	0.04	0	0.01

Table 3: Percentage of part-of-speeches of head words of annotated spans.

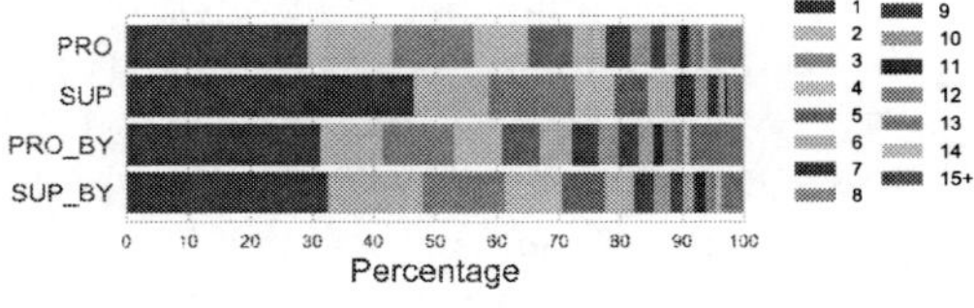

Figure 7: Distribution of word numbers in an annotated span.

4.3 Improving the annotation guidelines

In Section 3.2, we explained the conflict between defining noun phrases and verb phrases as the units of annotation spans. To which part-of-speech did the crowd workers tend to annotate causal relations? The ratios of part-of-speeches labeled during the annotations are listed in Table 3. Here, we focused on the part-of-speech of the last word of the annotated phrases[6]. As shown in Table 3, noun phrases constitute approximately 90.2% of the annotated spans, distantly followed by verb phrases (5.7%).

Further investigations revealed that noun phrases can be annotated within the verb phrases annotated by the workers. For example, when a worker annotates the verb phrase "increases the risk" with PRO, the noun phrase "the risk" can be annotated with

the same relation. To estimate the number of such instances, we manually analyzed 300 randomly selected verb phrases from the annotations. We found that 53.0% of verb phrases were re-annotatable as noun phrases. Therefore, it may be sufficient to limit annotation spans to noun phrases in the guideline.

Figures 7 and 8 depict the distributions of the numbers of words and bunsetsu chunks[7], respectively, in an annotated span. Naturally, we observe that shorter phrases occupy most of the annotations. Unfortunately, the length of the spans to be annotated cannot be clarified. Therefore, determining the noun phrases prior to an annotation work may be unreasonable, but allowing crowd workers to choose their segment boundaries might be necessary.

---

[6]In Japanese, both noun and verb phrases are head final.

[7]The smallest meaningful sequence consisting of content word(s) attached with function word(s).

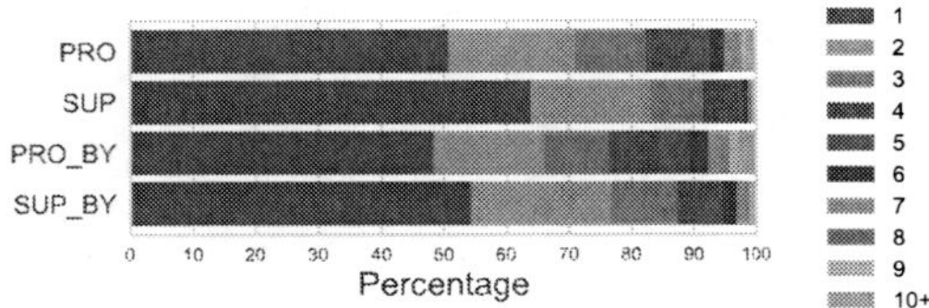

Figure 8: Distribution of numbers of bunsetsu chunks in an annotated span.

4.4 Annotation confusions

How do the crowd workers make erroneous annotations, and what relations are likely to be confused? To answer these questions, we analyzed the tendency of annotation confusions by comparing the data created by the 2-match aggregation and individual annotation data. Here, we define that a confusion occurs when the label assigned to a span differs from that allocated in the 2-match aggregation.

We analyze annotation confusions by the following method. Suppose that causal labels PRO, SUP, PRO_BY, and SUP_BY are annotated 4000, 3000, 2000, and 1000 times in a corpus, respectively. In other words, the annotation ratios of the PRO, SUP, PRO_BY, and SUP_BY labels are 40%, 30%, 20%, and 10%, respectively. In addition, suppose that some spans that should be labeled PRO are incorrectly labeled with SUP, PRO_BY, and SUP_BY. Let the number of incorrect labels be 200, 300, and 100, respectively.

Assuming that labeling errors follow the same probability distribution as the individual labels, the expectation of incorrectly labeling PRO as SUP is given by

$$(200 + 300 + 100) \times \frac{30}{30 + 20 + 10} = 300. \quad (1)$$

The peculiarity of the confusions PRO $\to$ SUP can be measured by the deviation between the number of incorrect annotations and the above expectation. Here, we adopt a modified chi-squared test (in which the numerator is not squared):

$$\frac{\text{observation} - \text{expectation}}{\text{expectation}} = \frac{\text{observation}}{\text{expectation}} - 1. \quad (2)$$

For PRO $\to$ SUP confusions, Equation 2 gives $200/300 - 1 = -0.333$, indicating that the annotation errors were 33.3% fewer than expected.

		incorrect			
		PRO	SUP	PRO_BY	SUP_BY
correct	PRO	-	-0.510	0.425	0.019
	SUP	-0.612	-	-0.405	1.037
	PRO_BY	0.556	-0.198	-	-0.567
	SUP_BY	-0.222	0.969	-0.670	-

Table 4: Deviations (ratios) from expected numbers of annotation errors.

Table 4 shows the results of Equation 2 for all kinds of confusions. According to this table, few workers confused the polarity of a causal relation, e.g., PRO and SUP. Most of the confusions were caused by the direction of a causal relation such as PRO and PRO_BY. Such confusions might be reduced by decomposing the annotation task into two steps. In the first step, workers could annotate the polarity of a causal relation regardless of its direction (i.e., by equating PRO and PRO_BY). The direction of the causal relations, e.g., PRO and PRO_BY, could then be classified in the next step.

4.5 Nested structure of promotion and suppression

Figure 4 shows an interesting example of nested spans of promotion and suppression. To examine patterns that reverse the polarity of causal relations, we extract regions containing overlapping regions of PRO and SUP annotations. The overlapping regions can be divided into four types: (PRO = SUP) the regions of PRO and SUP are identical; (PRO $\supset$ SUP) the region of PRO contains that of SUP; (PRO $\subset$ SUP) the region of SUP contains that of PRO; and (OTHER) the regions of PRO and SUP have overlaps but no inclusion relation.

Table 5 gives an example and lists the number of instances of each type. The majority of nested spans occur when PRO completely contains SUP (PRO $\supset$ SUP). This means that suppression relations are often described by polarity inversion patterns such as "decrease in X", "prevent X", and "reject X". In cases of two polarity inversion patterns, e.g., "fail to prevent unintentional results", we find opposite inversions in which SUP completely contains PRO (PRO $\subset$ SUP). The type PRO = SUP simply denotes annotation errors (confusions between PRO and SUP).

Table 6 lists some polarity inversion patterns mined by this analysis. Some of these patterns

Type	Number	Example		
		A part of a sentence	PRO	SUP
PRO = SUP	154	paralysis of the limb occurs	paralysis of the limb	paralysis of the limb
PRO ⊃ SUP	1,850	exhibits a decrease in platelets	a decrease in platelets	platelets
PRO ⊂ SUP	54	fail to prevent unintentional results	unintentional results	prevent unintentional results
OTHER	85	can control smoke caused by fire	control smoke	smoke caused by fire

Table 5: Examples and numbers of PRO and SUP overlaps.

Japanese	English	Number
X 障害	X disorder	53
X の低下	decline in X	25
X 異常	X abnormality	12
X 減少	decrease in X	9
X を阻害	inhibition of X	7
X の治療	treatment of X	7
X が障害される	X is impaired	6
抗 X	anti-X	6
X を防ぐ	prevent X	5
X の制御	control of X	5
X 被害	X damage	4
X 汚染	X pollution	4
X を拒否	reject X	3
X の代替	alternative to X	3

Table 6: Examples of polarity inversion patterns.

are easily crafted by humans, e.g., "decline in X" and "prevent X". However, this analysis also mines novel patterns within noun phrases, e.g., "X damage (health damage)" and within words, e.g., "anti-X (antidepressant)".

4.6 Automatic recognition of causal relations

How do the data created in this research contribute to acquiring causal relation instances from Wikipedia articles? We formalize this task as a sequential labeling problem of predicting labels of promotion/suppression for words in a sentence. We use the data built by 2-match aggregation as a training data. Because the dataset includes spans with multiple relation labels (as explained in Section 4.5), we build a model for each relation.

The sequential labeling was performed by a one-layer bi-directional LSTM. The dimension of the input word vectors and the hidden layer was 300. In addition, word vectors were initialized with ones trained on Japanese Wikipedia articles. The IOB2 notation was applied to the causal relations, such as B-PRO, I-PRO, B-SUP, I-SUP. All occurrences of the title phrase in the article text were replaced with __TITLE__. With this replacement, the model can learn the textual clues between the title phrase and an argument of a relation. We also deleted expressions in parentheses, which often describe pronunciations.

The F1 scores of PRO, SUP, PRO_BY and SUP_BY were 0.365, 0.282, 0.315 and 0.167, respectively. Although the F1 scores are relatively low, the prediction performance is reasonable because the F1 score of the annotator agreement was approximately 0.5.

5 Conclusion

We presented a crowdsourcing-based approach for annotating causal relation instances to Wikipedia articles. For this purpose, we designed a simple micro-task in which crowd workers annotated textual spans having causal relations with the title of a Wikipedia article. To provide an easy-to-use interface with sufficient quality control, we integrated the crowdsourcing service with the brat interface. The annotated corpus not only provides supervision data for automatic recognition of causal relation instances, but also reveals valuable facts for improving the annotation process.

In the imminent future, we consider refining the annotation process as suggested in Section 4, and increase the size and variety of the corpus. We will also extend target articles to other languages (e.g., English) because the approach in this paper is not language-specific. In addition to the intrinsic evaluation (automatic recognition of causal relations), we plan to extrinsically evaluate the corpus; for example, by applying the model trained on the corpus to a downstream task such as question answering and stance detection

Acknowledgments

This work was supported by JSPS KAKENHI Grant Number 15H01702 and 15H05318 and JST CREST.

References

Kurt Bollacker, Colin Evans, Praveen Paritosh, Tim Sturge, and Jamie Taylor. 2008. Freebase: a collaboratively created graph database for structuring human knowledge. In *Proc. of SIGMOD 2008*, pages 1247–1250.

Anthony Brew, Derek Greene, and Pádraig Cunningham. 2010. Using crowdsourcing and active learning to track sentiment in online media. In *Proc. of ECAI 2010*, pages 145–150.

George R Doddington, Alexis Mitchell, Mark A Przybocki, Lance A Ramshaw, Stephanie Strassel, and Ralph M Weischedel. 2004. The automatic content extraction (ACE) program-tasks, data, and evaluation. In *Proc. of LREC 2004*, pages 837–840.

Jesse Dunietz, Lori Levin, and Jaime Carbonell. 2017. The BECauSE corpus 2.0: Annotating causality and overlapping relations. In *Proc. of the 11th Linguistic Annotation Workshop*, pages 95–104.

Tim Finin, William Murnane, Anand Karandikar, Nicholas Keller, Justin Martineau, and Mark Dredze. 2010. Annotating named entities in Twitter data with crowdsourcing. In *Proc. of NAACL-HLT 2010 Workshop on Creating Speech and Language Data with Amazon's Mechanical Turk*, pages 80–88.

Juliane Fluck, Sumit Madan, Tilia Renate Ellendorff, Theo Mevissen, Simon Clematide, Adrian van der Lek, and Fabio Rinaldi. 2015. Track 4 overview: Extraction of causal network information in biological expression language (BEL). In *Proc. of the Fifth BioCreative Challenge Evaluation Workshop*, pages 333–346.

Karën Fort, Gilles Adda, and K. Bretonnel Cohen. 2011. Amazon Mechanical Turk: Gold mine or coal mine? *Computational Linguistics*, 37(2):413–420.

Matthew R. Gormley, Adam Gerber, Mary Harper, and Mark Dredze. 2010. Non-expert correction of automatically generated relation annotations. In *Proc. of NAACL-HLT 2010 Workshop on Creating Speech and Language Data with Amazon's Mechanical Turk*, pages 204–207.

Chikara Hashimoto, Kentaro Torisawa, Stijn De Saeger, Jong-Hoon Oh, and Jun'ichi Kazama. 2012. Excitatory or inhibitory: a new semantic orientation extracts contradiction and causality from the web. In *Proc. of EMNLP-CoNLL 2012*, pages 619–630.

Chikara Hashimoto, Kentaro Torisawa, Julien Kloetzer, and Jong-Hoon Oh. 2015. Generating event causality hypotheses through semantic relations. In *Proc. of AAAI 2015*, pages 2396–2403.

Iris Hendrickx, Su Nam Kim, Zornitsa Kozareva, Preslav Nakov, Diarmuid Ó Séaghdha, Sebastian Padó, Marco Pennacchiotti, Lorenza Romano, and Stan Szpakowicz. 2010. SemEval-2010 Task 8: Multi-way classification of semantic relations between pairs of nominals. In *Proc. of the 5th International Workshop on Semantic Evaluation*, pages 33–38.

Dirk Hovy, Barbara Plank, and Anders Søgaard. 2014. Experiments with crowdsourced re-annotation of a POS tagging data set. In *Proc. of ACL 2014*, pages 377–382.

Mukund Jha, Jacob Andreas, Kapil Thadani, Sara Rosenthal, and Kathleen McKeown. 2010. Corpus creation for new genres: A crowdsourced approach to PP attachment. In *Proc. of NAACL-HLT 2010 Workshop on Creating Speech and Language Data with Amazon's Mechanical Turk*, pages 13–20.

Daisuke Kawahara, Yuichiro Machida, Tomohide Shibata, Sadao Kurohashi, Hayato Kobayashi, and Manabu Sassano. 2014. Rapid development of a corpus with discourse annotations using two-stage crowdsourcing. In *Proc. of COLING 2014*, pages 269–278.

Nolan Lawson, Kevin Eustice, Mike Perkowitz, and Meliha Yetisgen-Yildiz. 2010. Annotating large email datasets for named entity recognition with mechanical turk. In *Proc. of NAACL-HLT 2010 Workshop on Creating Speech and Language Data with Amazon's Mechanical Turk*, pages 71–79.

Rada Mihalcea and Andras Csomai. 2007. Wikify!: Linking documents to encyclopedic knowledge. In *Proc. of CIKM 2007*, pages 233–242.

Jong-Hoon Oh, Kentaro Torisawa, Chikara Hashimoto, Motoki Sano, Stijn De Saeger, and Kiyonori Ohtake. 2013. Why-question answering using intra- and inter-sentential causal relations. In *Proc. of ACL 2013*, pages 1733–1743.

Jong-Hoon Oh, Kentaro Torisawa, Chikara Hashimoto, Ryu Iida, Masahiro Tanaka, and Julien Kloetzer. 2016. A semi-supervised learning approach to why-question answering. In *Proc. of AAAI-16*, pages 3022–3029.

Sampo Pyysalo, Tomoko Ohta, Rafal Rak, Andrew Rowley, Hong-Woo Chun, Sung-Jae Jung, Sung-Pil Choi, Jun'ichi Tsujii, and Sophia Ananiadou. 2015. Overview of the cancer genetics and pathway curation tasks of BioNLP shared task 2013. *BMC Bioinformatics*, 16(10):S2.

Kira Radinsky, Sagie Davidovich, and Shaul Markovitch. 2012. Learning causality for news events prediction. In *Proc. of WWW 2012*, pages 909–918.

Ines Rehbein and Josef Ruppenhofer. 2017. Catching the common cause: Extraction and annotation of causal relations and their participants. In *Proc. of the 11th Linguistic Annotation Workshop*, pages 105–114.

Fabio Rinaldi, Tilia Renate Ellendorff, Sumit Madan, Simon Clematide, Adrian van der Lek, Theo Mevissen,

and Juliane Fluck. 2016. BioCreative V track 4: a
shared task for the extraction of causal network information using the Biological Expression Language.
*Database: The Journal of Biological Databases and
Curation*, page baw067.

Akira Sasaki, Junta Mizuno, Naoaki Okazaki, and Kentaro Inui. 2016. Stance classification by recognizing related events about targets. In *Proc. of WI 2016*,
pages 582–587.

Rebecca Sharp, Mihai Surdeanu, Peter Jansen, Peter
Clark, and Michael Hammond. 2016. Creating causal
embeddings for question answering with minimal supervision. In *Proc. of EMNLP 2016*, pages 138–148.

Pontus Stenetorp, Sampo Pyysalo, Goran Topić, Tomoko
Ohta, Sophia Ananiadou, and Jun'ichi Tsujii. 2012.
brat: a web-based tool for NLP-assisted text annotation. In *Proc. of EACL 2012 (demonstrations)*, pages
102–107.

Sho Takase, Naoaki Okazaki, and Kentaro Inui. 2016.
Composing distributed representations of relational
patterns. In *Proc. of ACL 2016*, pages 2276–2286.

Automatic Categorization of Tagalog Documents Using Support Vector Machines

April Dae C. Bation

Department of Computer Science
University of the Philippines Cebu
Cebu City, Philippines 6000
acbation@up.edu.ph

Erlyn Q. Manguilimotan

AI Innovation Center
Weather News, Inc.
Chiba, Japan 261-0023
erlynqm@gmail.com

Aileen Joan O. Vicente

Department of Computer Science
University of the Philippines Cebu
Cebu City, Philippines 6000
aovicente@up.edu.ph

Abstract

Automatic document classification is now a growing research topic in Natural Language Processing. Several techniques were incorporated to build a classifier that can categorize documents written in specific languages into their designated categories. This study builds an automatic document classifier using machine learning which is suited for Tagalog documents. The documents used were news articles scraped from Tagalog news portals. These documents were manually annotated into different categories and later on, underwent preprocessing techniques such as stemming and removal of stopwords. Different document representations were also used to explore which representation performed best with the classifiers. The SVM classifier using the stemmed dataset which was represented using TF-IDF values yielded an F-score of 91.99% and an overall accuracy of 92%. It outperformed all other combinations of document representations and classifiers.

1 Introduction

Due to the explosive growth of documents in digital form, automatic text categorization has become an important area of research. It is the task of assigning documents, based solely on its contents, to predefined classes or categories.

Through time, approaches to this field of study evolved from knowledge engineering to machine learning. In the machine learning approach, the defining characteristics of each document are learned by the model from a set of annotated documents used as "training" data. Such includes Naïve Bayes and Support Vector Machine classifiers.

Different standard machine learning techniques treat text categorization as a standard classification problem, and thereby reducing the learning process into two steps — feature selection and classification learning over the feature space (Peng et. al., 2003). Of these two steps, feature selection is more critical since identifying the right features will guarantee any reasonable machine learning technique or classifier to perform well (Scott & Matwin, 1999). However, feature selection is language-dependent. Several preprocessing methods such as stopword removal, lemmatization and root-word extraction require domain knowledge of the language used (Peng et. al., 2003).

Methodologies used in researches concerning automatic document categorization are unique from language to language, depending on the structure and morphological rules of the specific language. Although automatic text categorization is becoming a great area of research in most languages aside from English such as Chinese and Arabic, researchers have paid little to no attention

31st Pacific Asia Conference on Language, Information and Computation (PACLIC 31), pages 346–353
Cebu City, Philippines, November 16-18, 2017
Copyright ©2017 April Dae Bation, Aileen Joan Vicente and Erlyn Manguilimotan

in categorizing Tagalog documents. Tagalog exhibits morphological phenomena that makes it a little different than the English language. Thus, this study aims to investigate the factors and explore on different methods that will affect the process of building a Tagalog document classifier. Specifically, this study intends to:

- Collect Tagalog news articles and label them according to their category
- Represent and extract features from documents using NLP techniques
- Build an SVM Classifier
- Evaluate classification performance and present results

2   Related Studies

2.1   Document Categorization and Machine Learning

Different researchers have already explored on automatic document categorization to help manage documents efficiently. Over the years, many approaches have already been adopted to such research problem — from data mining techniques to machine learning models.

Although many approaches have been proposed, text categorization is still a major area of interest since these classifiers have been devoted and focused on English documents and can still be improved.

Several studies used different machine learning models in document categorization. McCallum and Niggam (1998) compared two different types of naïve bayes which assumes that all attributes of the examples are independent of each other. Eyheramendy et. al (2003) used multinomial naïve bayes but found out that it is often outperformed by support vector machines. The use of decision trees for multi-class categorization was explored by Weiss et. al (1999). K-Nearest Neighbors algorithm is also applied in text categorization such as that in a study by Soucy and Mineau (2001) where the model performed better with only few features. Zhang and Zhou (2006) experimented on the use of neural networks for multilabel categorization.

Although there were several researches on document categorization, none had replaced Support Vector Machines as the state-of-the-art method in this research area. A study by Joachims (1998) showed that Support Vector Machines are suited for text categorization, and has consistently showed good performance in all experiments. Yang and Liu (1999) conducted a controlled study and re-examined five of machine learning text categorization methods where SVM outperformed all other methods.

2.2   Support Vector Machines

This type of classifier, proposed by Vladimir Vapnik and Alexey Chervonenkis, began to establish as the state-of-the-art method for text categorization in 1992. Figure 1 shows the framework for SVM on text categorization.

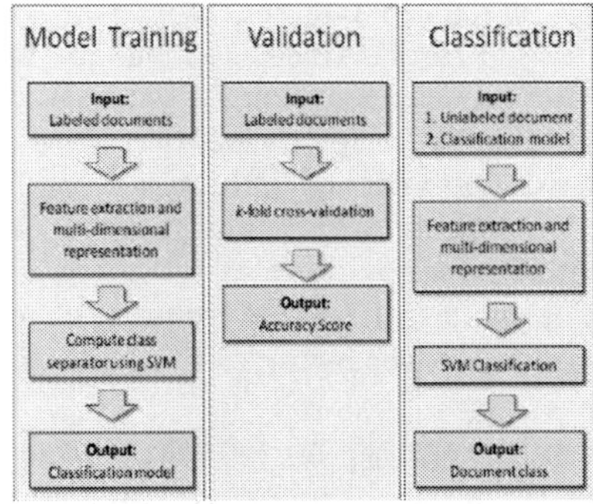

Figure 1. Classification Infrastructure of SVM on Text Categorization (Mertsalov and McCreary, 2009)

Joachims (1998) concluded that SVM will work well for text categorization since (1) it uses overfitting protection which gives it the potential to handle large feature spaces, especially that learning text classifiers deal with more than 10000 features, (2) document vectors are sparse which means that only few entries in it have non-zero values.

2.3   Existing Classifiers in Other Languages

Since feature extraction is language-dependent and requires language-specific knowledge, building a classifier for documents in different languages will introduce different challenges.

In an automatic Arabic document categorizer by Kourdi et. al. (2004), the word morphology was considered. A root extraction technique suited for the non-concatenative nature of Arabic and the challenge of their plural and hollow verbs was used.

In Chinese document categorization, word segmentation became a challenging issue since the language does not have a natural delimiter between words, unlike English and other Indo-European languages. He et. al. (2003) adopted a word-class bigram model to segment each training document into a feature vector.

With regards to Indian languages, Nidhi (2012) stated that using only statistical approaches to classify Punjabi documents won't provide good classification results since the language has a very rich inflectional morphology compared to the English language. This means that there is a need of linguistic approaches and a good understanding of the language's morphology for the selection of the features that will increase efficiency. Nidhi (2012) used a rule-based approach to extract language-dependent features.

Concerning Tagalog, no work has been done to classify Tagalog documents. Although recently, there are morphological analysis tools for the Tagalog language such as the Two-level Engine for Tagalog Morphology (Nelson, 2004), the Tagalog Stemming Algorithm (TagSA) (Bonus, 2012), different proposed POS taggers including the works of Cheng (n.d.) and Reyes et al., (2014), none of which are being applied in the automatic categorization of Tagalog documents.

3   Methodology

This study follows the basic framework for document categorization which is divided into three, namely: data preparation and preprocessing, feature extraction and selection, and the building of classifier.

3.1   Preprocessing of Data

In the preprocessing of data, the first step was removing the whitespaces and punctuations. The documents were also transformed into lowercase.

In the next step, stopwords were removed. This includes words such as *ang, mga, si, dahil,* etc. These are frequent occurring words in Tagalog language which do not offer information about the category of the document.

Lastly, stemming was done. This is used to reduce the words in the documents into its canonical form. Words with the same canonical form is counted as one. For example, *maaga, pinakamaaga,* and *umaga,* will be counted as one since they all have the same canonical form, *aga.*

In Tagalog, there are four types of affixation: (1) prefixation, (2) infixation, (3) suffixation, and (4) circumfixation. Prefixation is when the bound morpheme is attached before the root word, infixation is when it is attached within the root word, and suffixation is when it is attached at the end. Circumfixation is when the bound morpheme can occur as prefix, infix, or suffix. Reduplication of these affixes is also common in the language. The stemmer created by the researcher was meant to remove the affixes, including the reduplicated parts, and retrieve the root word only

The stemmer retrieves the canonical form by removing all affixes that can occur as prefix, infix, and suffix. Affixes in Tagalog include *um, ma,* and *in.* Words with these affixes include *k(um)ain, (ma)bilis, s(in)abi.* After stemming these words, *kain, bilis* and *sabi* will be retrieved respectively.

The stemmer also removes reduplicated parts. In the word *pupunta,* the morpheme *pu-* was reduplicated; hence it will be removed. After stemming, its canonical form, *punta,* will be retrieved.

On the other hand, Non-Tagalog words were considered foreign words. -

3.2 Document Representation and Feature Extraction

After the preprocessing method, a Bag-of-Words model, containing all words in the documents, was created. This is used as the basis for extracting features.

3.3 Feature Vectorization

Typically, the feature space consists of an $m \times n$ matrix where m is equal to the number of documents and n is equal to the number of tokens in the Bag-of-Words.

In this study, three schemes in numerical representation were used, namely: Binary Representation, Word Counts, and the TF-IDF.
–

3.4 Classification of Documents

After vectorizing the documents into different numerical representations, they were then shuffled and divided into two: the training set and testing set. 80% of the dataset went to the training set while the remaining 20% went to the testing set. Sklearn's train_test_split was used.

In this study, two classifiers were experimented, namely: Naïve Bayes and Support Vector Machines. Both were implemented using Python's sklearn.

Support Vector Machines
In this study, a linear kernel and a one-vs-all strategy were used where a single classifier per class is trained, with the samples of that class as positive samples and all other samples as negatives The OneVsRestClassifier, together with the LinearSVC of sklearn were utilized.

Multinomial Naïve Bayes
For the second classifier in this study, a Multinomial Naive-Bayes, which estimates probabilities of a given document to belong to a specific category, was used. The MultinomialNB of sklearn was used in this study.

4. Results and Discussions

Several experiment setups with the different document representations and machine learning

classifiers were conducted. Out of the 2,121 news articles, 1,696 news articles (80%) went to the training set. The remaining 425 news articles (20%) went to the testing set.

4.1 Dataset

The dataset is comprised of Tagalog news articles retrieved from Philippine news websites from August 2016 to January 2017 using scrapy (https://scrapy.org/). The collected data comprised of 2,121 manually annotated news articles. Table 1 summarizes the distribution of data for each category.

Categories	Number of Articles
Crime	295
Disaster	347
Entertainment	330
Economic	234
Health	106
Political	364
Sports	299
Terrorism	146

Table 1. Distribution of Pre-defined Categories

4.2 Document Representation

In this study, three document representations were used for the experiments that were conducted — Binary Feature Representation, Word Count Representation, TF-IDF Representation. From the training set, 22,824 total terms/words were retrieved and stored in the Bag-of-Words.

Some words included in the Bag-of-Words are not part of the Tagalog vocabulary. These includes frequently occurring foreign words and proper nouns such as are *city* and *duterte*. Some proper nouns were also stemmed such as *philippe* which is originally *philippine* but -in- was removed because the stemmer thought it is an infix.

4.3 Core Experiment

For the core experiment, an SVM classifier is used together with the TF-IDF representation for all documents. The overall accuracy of this classifier is 92%. Table 2 summarizes the performance metrics of the classifier.

Category	Precision	Recall	F-Score
Crime	93.65%	92.18%	92.91%
Disaster	91.30%	95.45%	93.33%
Entertainment	98.63%	100%	99.31%
Economic	90.24%	77.08%	83.14%
Health	100%	83.33%	90.9%
Political	81.01%	90.14%	85.33%
Sports	100%	98.43%	99.2%
Terrorism	76.47%	81.25%	78.78%
Overall	*91.41%*	*89.73%*	*91.99%*

Table 2. SVM Classifier Performance

Based on Table 2, the classifier was able to yield relatively high F-Scores, except that of Terrorism which yielded an F-Score of only 78.78%. This was expected since the amount of news articles that belong to this category was relatively low compared to that of other categories. On another note, it can be seen in the table that the Entertainment category got a recall of 100%, Health and Sports categories both got a precision of 100%. Also, Economic and Political categories both got an F-score below 90%. This could stem from the nature of the two categories — both talk about the government or the status of the country, which makes it hard for the classifier to distinguish the difference between the two.

4.4   Validation and Evaluation

Based on the core experiment, the performance measure of the classifier is already acceptable. To ascertain the contribution of Tagalog language processing in the classification of Tagalog document, the following experiments were conducted:-

Effect of Stemmer

To show the contribution of stemming to the whole process of building the classifier, an unstemmed dataset was fed to the SVM classifier.

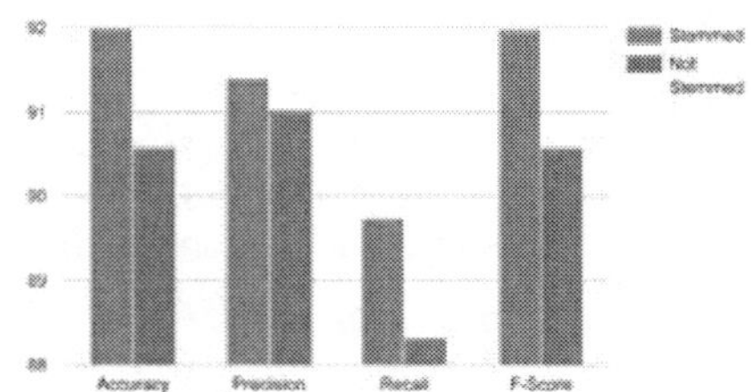

Figure 2. Comparison of Performance Measures for Stemmed and Unstemmed Data

As seen in Figure 2, the classifier with the stemmed data performed better than that with unstemmed data. Although the stemmer wasn't perfect, the process of reducing words to their word stems has helped significantly in improving the performance of classifier.

A Multinomial Naïve Bayes (MultiNB) classifier was tested to see if stemming data still achieves high performance, like in the SVM classifier. Both datasets were fed to the MultiNB classifier. Using TF-IDF, the classifier with the stemmed data yielded an F-Score of 83.55% while the other yielded only 81.41%.

Effect of Document Representation

Based on the previous experiments, it can be seen that TF-IDF representation yielded impressive performance measures for the SVM classifier. For comparison purposes, two other document representation were used — Binary Representation and Word Count.

Feature	Precision	Recall	F-Score
Binary	89.01%	87.58%	88.17%
Word Count	90.3%	88.8%	89.47%
TF-IDF	91.41%	89.73%	91.99%

Table 3. SVM Classifier Performance Measure for Different Document Representations

Table 3 summarizes the performance measures of the SVM classifier for the three different document representations where TF-IDF resulted to the highest F-Score of 91.99%.

For the sake of comparison, all three document representation were fed to the MultiNB classifier.

Feature	Precision	Recall	F-Score
Binary	91.02%	84.56%	89.50%
Word Count	92.4%	88.72%	91.41%
TF-IDF	88.11%	74.37%	83.55%

Table 4. Naïve Bayes Classifier Performance Measure for Different Document Representations

Table 4 shows the performance measures for the MultiNB classifier. It can be seen that, unlike in SVM, TF-IDF yielded the lowest F-Score of 83.55% while Word Count yielded 91.41%. The Multinomial Naive Bayes implements the Naive Bayes algorithm for multinomially distributed data, which means that it models the data based on probability counts. Since multinomial distribution normally requires integer feature counts, TF-IDF representation is likely to produce poor results.

Furthermore, TF-IDF with SVM yields a higher F-score compared to that of Word Count with Naïve Bayes, and it in fact outperformed all other combinations of document representation with the classifiers.

Cross-Validation

A 10-fold cross validation scheme was used to validate the performance of the multinomial SVM classifier. Training and testing were repeated 10 times on stratified folds for the whole dataset. Table 5 summarizes the result of the performance of all categories averaged at each fold.

k-fold	Accuracy
1st	91.95%
2nd	91.86%
3rd	89.47%
4th	89.41%
5th	90%
6th	91.12%
7th	89.29%
8th	91.67%
9th	91.01%
10th	92.22%

Table 5. Ten-Fold Cross Validation

The ten-fold cross validated classifier yielded an average accuracy of 90.8%. The test shows that although randomness was introduced to the experiment by means of the folds, the performance is generally the same.

5 Conclusion and Recommendations

5.1 Conclusion

Tagalog document categorization, like in other languages, is affected by many factors. Such includes the size of the corpus, the classifier type, the feature selection and feature reduction method, and the weighting scheme. In this study, stemming each document, representing it with TF-IDF values and using it to train an SVM classifier yielded the highest F-Score of 91.99% among all other combination of methods and experiment setups.

Although the stemming process wasn't perfect, it still served the purpose of conflating and integrating different word forms into their common canonical form; therefore, reducing the number of terms in the whole corpus. This method in computational linguistic can result to either poor or good performance, depending on some cases. In this study, it was shown that stemming, which performs iterative affix removal, is effective in Tagalog documents and that it has contributed to the high performance of the machine learning classifier which automatically classifies documents into categories.

In this study, it was also proven that an SVM classifier performs well in categorizing text data. More than 10000 features were used in this study and each document vector was sparse; however, the SVM classifier was able to handle the large feature space.

5.2   Recommendations for Future Work

Although high performance measures were achieved in building a machine learning classifier that can automatically categorize text documents, it would be better to use a larger dataset with a more even distribution for each class. Future researches could also experiment on more complicated feature representations such as the use of POS tags or N-grams to explore more on their performance on Tagalog documents. Also, researches could try on the use of lemmatization instead of just stemming the Tagalog words. In this research, Tagalog words that weren't stemmed properly by the stemmer, such as *nam* and *sabg,* were included. While stemming only chops off morphemes in words to remove the derivational affixes, lemmatization refers to the use of a vocabulary and morphological analysis of words to be able to do return the correct base or dictionary form of a word. More categories can also be incorporated; for example, Sports can be divided into more specific categories such as Basketball, Volleyball, etc. Lastly, Future researches should also be able to build a classifier that can label the Tagalog documents with more than one category (multi-labeled instead of just multiclass).

References

Dumais, S., Platt, J., Heckerman, D., & Sahami, M. (1998). Inductive learning algorithms and representations for text categorization. In *Proceedings of the seventh international conference on Information and knowledge management -* CIKM '98. doi:10.1145/288627.288651

Eyheramendy, S., Lewis, D. D., & Madigan, D. (2003). On the naive bayes model for text categorization.

He, J., Tan, A., & Tan, C. (2003). On Machine Learning Methods for Chinese Document Categorization. Applied Intelligence, 18, 311-322. Retrieved from https://www.comp.nus.edu.sg/~tancl/publications/j2003/he03apin.pdf

Joachims, T. (1998, April). Text categorization with support vector machines: Learning with many relevant features. In European conference on machine learning (pp. 137-142). Springer Berlin Heidelberg.

Kourdi, M. E., Bensaid, A., & Rachidi, T. (2004). Automatic Arabic document categorization based on the Naïve Bayes algorithm. *Proceedings of the Workshop on Computational Approaches to Arabic Script-based Languages* -Semitic '04. doi:10.3115/1621804.1621819

Lewis, D. (1992). Feature selection and feature extraction for text categorization. In *Proceedings of a Workshop on Speech and Natural Language Processing,* (pp. 212-217). San Mateo, CA: Morgan Kaufmann.

McCallum, A., & Nigam, K. (1998, July). A comparison of event models for naive bayes text classification. In AAAI-98 workshop on learning for text categorization (Vol. 752, pp. 41-48).

Nelson, Hans J., "A Two-level Engine for Tagalog Morphology and a Structured XML Output for PC-Kimmo" (2004). All Theses and Dissertations. Paper 133. Retrieved from http://scholarsarchive.byu.edu/cgi/viewcontent.cgi?article=1132&context=etd

Nidhi, V. G. (2012). Domain Based Classification of Punjabi Text Documents using Ontology and Hybrid Based Approach. *Proceedings of the 3rd Workshop on South and Southeast Asian Natural Language Processing* (SANLP) (pp. 109-122). Retrieved from http://www.aclweb.org/anthology/W12-5009

Peng, F., Schuurmans, D., & Wang, S. (2003). Language and task independent text categorization with simple language models. *Proceedings of the 2003 Conference of the North American Chapter of the Association for Computational Linguistics on Human Language Technology* - NAACL '03. doi:10.3115/1073445.1073470

Roxas, R. (1997). Machine Translation from English to Filipino: A Prototype. *International Symposium of Multilingual Information Technology (MLIT '97)*, Singapore.

Scott, S., & Matwin, S. (1999). Feature Engineering for Text Classification. In Proceedings of the Sixteenth International Conference on Machine Learning (ICML '99), pp. 379- 388.

Soucy, P., & Mineau, G. W. (2001). A simple KNN algorithm for text categorization. In Data Mining, 2001. ICDM 2001, Proceedings IEEE International Conference on (pp. 647- 648). IEEE.

Weiss, S. M., Apte, S., Damerau, F., Johnson, D. E., Oles, F. J., Goetz, T., and Hampp, T. (1999). Maximizing Text-Mining Performance. IEEE Intelligent Systems, 14, 63-69.

Yang, Y., & Liu, X. (1999). A Re-examination of Text Categorization Methods. Carnegie Mellon University. Retrieved from http://www2.hawaii.edu/~chin/702/sigir99.pdf

Zhang, M., & Zhou, Z. (2006). Multilabel Neural Networks with Applications to Functional Genomics and Text Categorization. IEEE Transactions on Knowledge and Data Engineering, 18(10), 1338-1351. doi:10.1109/tkde.2006.162

Lexicalization, Separation and transitivity:
A comparative study of Mandarin VO compound Variations

Menghan Jiang and Chu-Ren Huang
Department of CBS, The Hong Kong Polytechnic University
menghan.jiang@connect.polyu.hk;
churen.huang@polyu.edu.hk

Abstract

Our study takes a comparable corpus-based statistical approach, to empirically examine the correlation between transitivity and separation ability for VO compound in Mandarin Chinese. The results of the two studies show that inseparable VOs are more likely to be used in a transitive way, compared to separable ones. In addition, there is a statistical negative correlation between transitivity and separation ability, i.e. the more a VO sequence is lexicalized, the less likely it can take an object. Our paper further empirically proves that the grammatical variations of VO compound are to a large extent depend on the degree of lexicalization. The differences in separation and transitivity between Mainland and Taiwan actually indicate the different stages that Mainland and Taiwan VO compounds are located in the continuum of lexicalization.

1   Introduction

In Modern Chinese, there is an increasing number of disyllabic VO compounds which gradually changed from intransitive to transitive verbs. The transitive VO compounds can take another constituent (e.g., a word, a phrase or a sentence) as their objects, and yield the configuration of $[VO_1+O_2]$, such as 投资 房地产 *touzi fnagdichan* throw_money_real-estate 'invest in real estate', 进军 美国 市场 *jinjun meiguo shichang* march_towards_American_market 'march towards American market'. This phenomenon has attracted the interests of numbers of scholars in Chinese linguistics (e.g., Liu, 1998a, 1998b; Gao, 1998 among others). One research question that often being addressed is the transition requirement of VO compounds (i.e. what kind of VO is easier to be transferred from intransitive to transitive). Numbers of researches claim that for a VO compound, the ability of taking the object is closely related to its lexical status. The higher degree of lexical status, the more possibility it can take the object and be used transitively (e.g., Liu, 1998a; Luo, 1998; Gao, 1998). Actually, this is in accordance with Brinton and Traugott (2005) which claims that lexicalization is to use a syntactic construction or word formation as a new form, which cannot be completely derivable or predictable from the constituents of the construction or the word formation pattern.

It is also well known that the degree of lexicalization can be tested through separation test (e.g., Her, 1997; Liu, 1998a). The easier it can be separated, the higher degree of its lexicalization. In fact, this is related to the 'Lexical Integrity Hypothesis' proposed by Huang (1984: 60): no phrase-level rule may affect a proper sub-part of a word. Since a VO compound as a word is thus a lexical unit whose internal structure is of a V+O (Her, 1997), and an important feature that distinguishes a lexical units from a phrase is the lexical integrity.

Therefore based on the previous discussions, it has become a common belief among linguistic researchers that there is a strong correlation between the transitivity of VO and whether the VO is separable (the lexical status), i.e. the VO which cannot be separated is much more likely to be used as a transitive verb, and vice versa. For example, Gao (1998) has classified VO into three types according to their separation ability: VO can be separated without constraints (e.g., 着急 *zhaoji* 'worry', 放心 *fangxin* 'reassure', 发愁 *fachou* 'be anxious'), VO can be separated with constraints (e.g., 毕业 *biye* 'graduate', 担心 *danxin* 'anxious', 留心 *liuxin* 'be careful', 害怕 *haipa* 'be scare') and VO cannot be separated (e.g., 出版 *chuban* 'publish', 当心 *dangxin* 'take care', 动员 *dongyuan* 'mobilize'). After investigating some of the VO in the corpus, he then concludes that all the VOs that cannot be separated are used as a transitive verb (e.g., 动员 群众 *dongyuan qunzhong* 'mobilize the masses') while the VOs which can be separated without constraints are usually cannot be used transitively (e.g., *放心 他 的 能 力 *fangxin ta de nengli* put_heart_he_DE [1] _ability 'rest assured his ability'). For the VOs that can be separated with constraints, they usually have transitive usages in the corpus (e.g., 担心 工程 的 进度 *danxin gongcheng de jindu* worry_about_project_DE_progress 'worry about the progress of the project'), but some of the words are still under the process of changing (e.g., ?过目 这 份 文件 *guomu zhefen wenjian* look over_this_CL [2] _document 'look over this document').

One thing should be noted is although the correlation between transitivity and separation for a VO has been well recognized by linguists, in literature we can barely find empirical study using real data to verify this common belief. For the very few studies (e.g., the study of Gao (1998) we mentioned above) that are conducted based on empirical data, their data size is relatively small and the statistical methods they are using are also quite simple (often just percentage or pure numbers). Although the numbers and percentages can reveal the difference, they cannot tell whether there is significance or not.

Therefore it is important for us to investigate this issue in a more empirical and quantitative way, with the assistance of large-scale corpus as well as the statistical tool. In that sense, the correlation between transitivity and lexical status can be verified systematically and comprehensively.

Another point often ignored by previous researches is that, although there are numbers of researches discussing the transitivity and separation ability of VO compounds, the variation difference between different variants of the same language are lack of studied. There are a very few study using relatively small set of data to point out that Taiwan and Singapore VO compounds have higher transitivity frequency (e.g., Wang, 1997; Diao, 1998) and Mainland words tend to have more separation usages than Taiwan (Diao, 2016). But the relationship of transitivity and separation

between language variations has not been examined. Then we would also like to ask questions: are there any transitivity differences between Mainland and Taiwan Mandarin? If the variation difference in transitivity exists, is this variation dependent on the degree of lexicalization? In other words, whether the variation differences in transitivity indicate the different stages that VO compounds from different variants are located in the continuum/process of lexicalization?

2   Data collection and calculation

2.1   Measurement of separation ability

Therefore, our first aim is to examine the relationship between transitivity frequency and lexical status of VO sequences, with the assistance of large-scale comparable corpus. It should be noted that previous studies usually examine both separation status and transitivity issue in a dichotomy way. In other words, the VO is classified as separable vs. inseparable, transitive vs. intransitive (e.g., Gao, 1998; Her, 1996 among others). But we argue that the issues of both separation and transitivity are not simply binary dichotomy, it is more about tendency/frequency difference. For example, both 把关 *baguan* guard_pass 'guarantee' and 插 手 *chashou* 'intervene' are separable (e.g., 把了关 *ba le guan* insert_hand 'guaranteed'; 插过手 *cha guo shou* 'have intervened'), but the frequency of separation usages are very different (把关 *baguan* 'guarantee a pass' is much more frequently to be used separately than 插手 *chashou* 'intervene'). In addition, the grammatical elements which can be inserted also vary a lot for these two words. Plenty of elements can be inserted into 把关 *baguan* (把 产 品 质 量 关 *ba chanpin zhiliang guan* guard_product_quality_pass 'guarantee the quality of products'; 把 好 了 进出 口 检验 关 *ba hao le jinchukou jianyan guan* guard_good_LE [3] import_export_inspect_pass 'have guaranteed the inspection of import and export') while only aspectual marker can insert into 插手 *chashou* 'intervene' (插过手/插了手 *cha guo shou/cha le*

---

[1] 的 DE: particle which appears between the modifier and the head noun
[2] CL: classifier.

[3] 了 LE: perfective marker.

shou 'have intervened/intervened'). In terms of transitivity of VO compound, the transitivity degree also varies a lot. For example, although both 驰名 *chiming* 'famous' and 约会 *yuehui* 'date' can be used transitively, the frequency of using as a transitive verb for 驰名 *chiming* (e.g., 驰名中外 *chiming zhongwai* 'renowned both inside and outside the country') is much higher than that of 约会 *yuehui* (e.g., 约会拜金女 *yuehui baijinnü* 'date material girl'). In that sense, we argue in our paper that examining the transitivity and separation issue in a continuous way would reflect the real situation of language more objectively.

In this study, we use frequency/percentage of separation usages to measure the separation degree.

relative frequency=separated usages/all the usages (e.g., Ren and Wang, 2005)

Example: separation frequency for 操心 *caoxin* 'worry about' = the number of 操....心 usages (10 tokens)/all the usages of 操心 *caoxin* (287 tokens) + Separation usages (10 tokens) = 3.367%

2.2 Measurement of transitivity degree

The transitivity of VOs is measured by frequency also: **transitivity frequency=transitive tokens/all the tokens.** For example, transitivity frequency of 签约 *qianyue* 'sign a contract' =number of transitive usages of 签约 *qianyue* (13 tokens)/all the tokens of 签约 *qianyue* (1000 tokens) = 1.3%. The VO word list we use in this study is the same as we have used in the previous section: the 109 VO compounds which we have collected from previous researches (e.g., Qian, 2011; Luo, 1998). But in this study, we exclude 13 words that do not show significant variation difference in both transitivity frequency and Chi-square test: 登场 *dengchang* 'show'、操心 *caoxin* 'worry about'、致信 *zhixin* 'write letter to'、出土 *chutu* 'be unearthed' 、参演 *canyan* 'act in'、更名 *gengming* 'rename'、涉嫌 *shexian* 'be sespected' 、领军 *lingjun* 'play a leading role'、揭秘 *jiemi* 'expose'、解码 *jiema* 'decoding'、启航 *qihang* 'set sail'、失信 *shixin* 'break promise'、移情 *yiqing* 'love someone else'. For all the 96 words in our wordlist, we calculate their separation and

transitivity frequency in both Mainland and Taiwan.

3 Data analysis and result

3.1 Study 1: Comparison between separable words and inseparable words

The 96 words in the wordlist are divided into two categories according to their separation frequency: the VOs that have separable usages (separation frequency >0) in the corpus (here we call it "separable VO compound") and the VOs that do not have any separate usages (separation frequency =0) in the corpus ("inseparable VO compounds")[4]. Based on their separation status, we ask the first research question: is there a significant difference in transitivity frequency between these two groups (Empirically and statistically, is it true that the inseparable VOs are more likely to be used in a transitive way, and vice versa)? The data distribution of separable and inseparable words in both Mainland and Taiwan varieties is shown in table 1.

	Taiwan	Mainland
Separable VO	39	37
Inseparable VO	57	59

Table 1. Number of separable/inseparable VO

As we can see from the table, the numbers of separable VO and inseparable VO are close and the distributions in Mainland and Taiwan are also very similar, which make the comparison more reasonable.

A Mann-Whitney U test was run to determine if there were differences in transitivity frequency between separable and inseparable VO compounds in each variety. Mann-Whitney U test is often presented as the non-parametric alternative to independent-sample t-test, as it does not require the normality of the data, it is very suitable for our current study. The statistical tool we use is IBM SPSS V.22.

The result of Mann Whitney U test for Taiwan data is shown in Table2. It displays that the median value of transitivity frequency for inseparable VO compounds (0.3607142857) is significantly higher

---

[4] For the 'inseparable VO', we are not claiming that separation is impossible under any context. But since Gigaword corpus is very large, if no separation usages are detected in the corpus, the separation frequency should be very low.

than that for separable VO compounds (median value is 0.1378091873), U=801.000, Z=-2.316, P=0.021.

Hypothesis Test Summary

Null Hypothesis	Test	Sig.	Decision
The distribution of TW transitivity is the same across categories of separation type	Independent-Samples Mann-Whitney U Test	0.021	Reject the null hypothesis

Asymptotic significances are displayed. The significance level is .05

Total N	96
Mann-Whitney U	801.000
Wilcoxon W	1581.000
Test Statistic	801.000
Standard Error	134.049
Standardized Test Statistic	-2.316
Asymptotic Sig. (2-sided test)	.021

Table 2. Mann Whitney U test for TW data

Mainland data presents the same result, table 3 shows that median value of transitivity frequency for inseparable compounds in Mainland is 0.278, which is statistically significant higher than that of separable VO compounds (0.076), U=761.500, Z=-2.485, P=0.013.

Hypothesis Test Summary

Null Hypothesis	Test	Sig.	Decision
The distribution of ML transitivity is the same across categories of separation type	Independent-Samples Mann-Whitney U Test	0.013	Reject the null hypothesis

Asymptotic significances are displayed. The significance level is .05

Total N	96
Mann-Whitney U	761.500
Wilcoxon W	1464.500
Test Statistic	761.500
Standard Error	132.811
Standardized Test Statistic	-2.485
Asymptotic Sig. (2-sided test)	.013

Table 3. Mann Whitney U test for Mainland data

Summary for study 1: The results of Mann Whitney U test in both Mainland and Taiwan Mandarin show that the transitivity frequencies between separable and inseparable VO compounds are significantly different in both varieties. In other words, in both Mainland and Taiwan Mandarin, we can observe empirically that inseparable VOs are much more likely to be used in a transitive way.

3.2 Study 2: Correlation between separation ability and transitivity

In the first study, we have shown that compared to separable VO compounds, the inseparable ones are more likely to be used as a transitive verb. But as we have mentioned in the first section, the separation frequencies vary a lot among separable VO compounds. Therefore, what would be the case if we consider the separation frequency: Is there a significant statistical correlation between the separation frequency and the transitivity frequency of the VOs? (i.e. is it empirically true that the more frequently it is used separately, the less frequent it can be used transitively?)

In this study, the separation frequency (separation frequency=separated usages/all the usages) is included as a variable for statistical analysis. We use the Spearman's rank-order correlation to assess the relationship between transitivity frequency and separation frequency in both Taiwan and Mainland Mandarin. The result of Taiwan data is shown in the table.

Correlations

			TW separation fre	TW Transitivity
Spearman' rho	TW separation fre	Correlation coefficient	1.000	-.221*
		Sig. (2-tailed)	.	0.030
		N	96	96
	TW transitivity	Correlation coefficient	-.221*	1.000
		Sig. (2-tailed)	0.030	.
		N	96	96

*.Correlation is significant at the 0.05 level (2-tailed).

Table 4. Spearman's correlation for TW data

The result indicates that there exist a negative correlation between transitivity frequency and separation frequency in Mainland Mandarin, the correlation is statistically significant, r=-0.221, P=0.03.

We have the similar result for Mainland data, as shown below. There is a significant negative correlation between transitivity frequency and separation frequency in Taiwan Mandarin: r=-0.237; P=0.02.

Correlations

			ML separation fre	ML Transitivity
Spearman' rho	ML separation fre	Correlation coefficient	1.000	-.237*
		Sig. (2-tailed)	.	0.020
		N	96	96
	ML transitivity	Correlation coefficient	-.221*	1.000
		Sig. (2-tailed)	0.030	.
		N	96	96

*.Correlation is significant at the 0.05 level (2-tailed).

Table 5. Spearman's correlation for Mainland data

The results of spearman's correlation in both Taiwan and Mainland show that for a VO compound, the more frequently it is used separately, the less likely it can be used as a transitive verb. In other words, for a VO compound, the more it is lexicalized, the more likely it is used in a transitive way.

Summary for study 2, based on the result of the two empirical studies we have conducted, the tendency can be observed is that, compared to separable VO compounds, inseparable ones are more likely to be used in a transitive way. And also, for a VO compound, the less frequently it is used separately, the more likely it is used as a transitive verb. In other words, if a VO sequence is less lexicalized, its probability of being transitive is higher. The tendency is in accordance with what has been presented in the previous papers and is true for both Mainland and Taiwan data.

But it should also be noted that although the result of our second study show that there is a significant negative correlation between transitivity and separation, the correlation coefficients in both Mainland and Taiwan are to some extent low, which indicates that the negative correlation is relatively weak in both varieties. This can be explained because although the lexical status of a VO compound does affect the transitivity, it is not the only factor. In the real language, there are varieties of factors which are influencing the transitivity apart from the lexical status. The factors include not only some internal linguistic factors (e.g., word frequency; the degree of freedom for each morpheme; event type of the verb), but also some external social factors (e.g., the influence of social media or other languages/dialects).

4   Grammatical   Variation   and Lexicalization

As we discussed in the above section, the transitivity of a VO compound is statistically significant correlated with separation ability (which is measured by separation frequency) in both Mainland and Taiwan Mandarin. Then one question needed to be asked is: are there any variation differences in transitivity between Mainland and Taiwan Mandarin? If the answer is yes, does this transitivity difference is depend on the process of lexicalization of these VO compounds? In other words, do the differences of transitivity and separation between Taiwan and Mainland Mandarin indicate the different stages that Mainland and Taiwan VO compounds are located in the continuum/process of lexicalization?

In order to have a general picture of the data distribution, first we start from the comparison between average transitivity and separation frequency in Mainland and Taiwan Mandarin. As the table below displays, the average transitivity frequency of Taiwan VO compounds (0.3538) is higher than that of Mainland Mandarin (0.2919) whereas the separation frequency of Taiwan VO compounds (0.00707) is obviously lower than that of Mainland VO compounds.

	Taiwan VO	Mainland VO
Average transitivity fre	0.3538	0.2919
Average separation fre	0.007068073	0.019565008

Table 6. Average transitivity and separation

The first impression is that in general, the Taiwan VO compounds are more likely to have transitive usages while their Mainland counterparts have more probabilities to be used separately. But the average can only give us a general tendency about data distribution, and more statistical tests (e.g., Z-test, likelihood ratio test) are still needed to carefully examine the variation difference in transitivity frequency and separation frequency. We will illustrate the statistical analysis in detail in the following section.

In terms of the transitivity frequency, Z-test is conducted to investigate whether the transitivity frequencies between these two varieties have significant differences. According to the result of

Z-test (shown in the figure below), among all the 96 words we include in our study, 76 VO compounds show significant differences in transitivity frequency between the two varieties while 20 words are not significant different. Among the 76 words, 53 Taiwan VO compounds show significant higher transitivity frequency than their Mainland counterparts and 23 VOs have significantly higher transitivity frequency in Mainland than in Taiwan usages. In this sense, we can see the clear tendency that Taiwan VO compounds tend to be more likely to have higher transitivity usages.

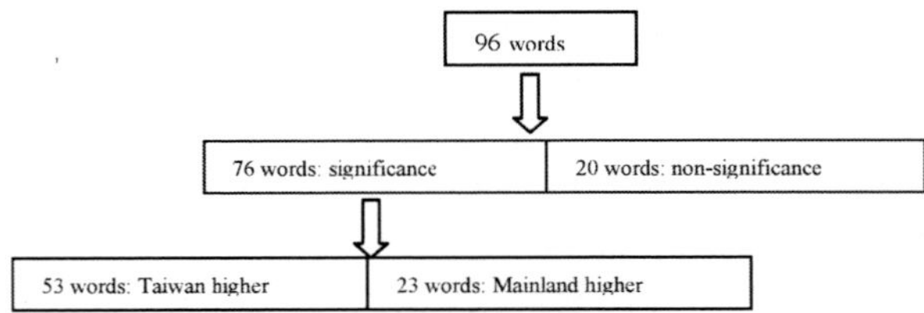

Figure 1. The result of Z-test

The VO compounds can be categorized into three types according to the Z-test result: the VO whose transitivity frequency in Taiwan is significantly higher than in Mainland (Taiwan transitivity higher); the VO whose transitivity frequency in Mainland is significantly higher than in Taiwan (Mainland transitivity higher); and there is no significant difference in transitivity frequency between Mainland and Taiwan (no transitivity difference). Based on this classification, we found that for the compounds in "Taiwan transitivity higher" group, their separation frequencies in Taiwan are much lower. For the other two groups ("Mainland transitivity higher" and "no transitivity difference"), the differences in separation frequency between varieties are not very obvious.

Transitivity frequency	Mainland separation frequency	TW separation frequency
TW transitivity higher	0.0579	0.015
ML transitivity higher	0.0251	0.019
No significance	0.008	0.002

Table 7. separation difference based on Z-test

So far, the general tendency is clear: the transitivity of Taiwan VO compound is

significantly higher, especially for the words whose Taiwan transitivity is significantly higher than their Mainland counterparts. But ones thing should be noted is that the P value cannot tell us everything. In other words, among the 76 words which show significant difference in transitivity frequency between Mainland and Taiwan, their degree of difference varies. For example (as shown in table 8), the transitivity frequencies of both 过境 *guojing* 'transit boarder' and 借道 *jiedao* 'channeled through' have significant difference between Mainland and Taiwan at P<0.01 level, but for 借道 *jiedao*, its transitivity frequencies in Taiwan and Mainland are quite close (0.871383/0.689655) whereas the transitivity of 过境 *guojing* in two varieties actually have much bigger difference (0.341/0.033). To solve the problem, likelihood ratio test is also used in our study to measure the degree of variation difference. The formulation is shown below: likelihood ratio = higher frequency/lower frequency. For 过境 *guojing*, the likelihood ratio of Taiwan to Mainland is 10.33 (=0.341/0.033), meaning that Taiwan 过境 *guojing* is about 10 times more likely to be used as a transitive verb than the Mainland counterpart while for 借道 *jiedao*, the likelihood ratio of Taiwan to Mainland is only 1.26, which is much lower than the one of 过境 *guojing*. And this actually indicates that the transitivity difference of 借道 *jiedao* between Mainland and Taiwan is not as obvious as that of 过境 *guojing*.

	P value for Z-test	TW Transitivity	Transitivity in Mainland	Likelihood ratio
过境	<0.01	0.341	0.033	10.33
借道	<0.01	0.871	0.690	1.26

Table 8. Comparison between Z-test and likelihood

We calculate the likelihood ratio variation for all the 76 words which show significance in Z-test. Based on the result of likelihood ratio test, the tendency difference between Mainland and Taiwan becomes clearer. When the likelihood ratio is larger than 10 (ratio >=10), we consider the two varieties to have prominent significant differences in transitivity frequency. And we found for the 8 words which belong to this group, all of them have higher transitivity in Taiwan, in other words, our data shows that Taiwan VO compounds have significantly higher transitivity, especially when the difference is prominent. And when the transitivity of Taiwan VO compounds is prominent higher than that of Mainland VO, the separation frequency between the two varieties are also observed to have prominent difference: but this time, the separation frequency of Mainland is significantly higher than Taiwan.

For example, the transitivity frequency of 把关 in Taiwan (24.5%) is significantly higher than in Mainland (0.71%).

	TW	ML
Separation usages	**43** types, **59** tokens	**906** types, **1808** tokens
Separation frequency	1.19%	45.75%
Transitivity frequency	24.5%	0.71%
Examples	把 好 质 量 关 *bahao zhiliang guan* guard_good_quality_pass 'guarantee the quality'	天津市 严 **把** 进津 企业 资质 审验 **关** *tianjinshi yanba jinjin qite zizhi shenyan guan* Tianjin_strict_guard _enter_Tianjin_enter prise_qualification_v erification_pass 'Tianjin strictly guarantee the enterprise qualification' 把 好 建设 前期 工作 质量 关 *bahao jianshe qianqi gongzuo zhiliang guan* guard_good_constru ction_preparatory_w ork_quality_pass 'guarantee the quality of preparatory work of construction' 把 了/过关 *ba le/guo guan* guard_LE/GUO[5]_pas s 'guaranteed/have guaranteed'

Table 9. separation comparison of 把关

The differences in separation usages between Mainland and Taiwan are also very obvious (not only in separation frequency, but also in the grammatical elements can be inserted). The separation frequency of Mainland 把关 *baguan* (45.74%) is significantly higher than that of Taiwan counterpart (1.19%), with a likelihood ratio of 38.437, indicating that 把关 *baguan* is about 38 times more likely to be used separately in Mainland than in Taiwan. Furthermore, the corpus data shows that very few grammatical elements can be inserted into Taiwan 把 关 *baguan* (examples like 严把质量关 *yan ba zhiliang* guan 'strictly check the quality' is frequently appeared in Taiwan corpus) while varieties of elements can be inserted into 把关 *baguan* in Mainland Mandarin (e.g., aspectual marker 把了/过 关 *ba le/guo guan* 'checked/have checked'; classifier 把 好几道关 *ba haojidao guan* 'carefully check for several times'; the object 把质量关 *ba zhiliang guan* 'guarantee the quanlity'; and even the object with modifier 把好进津企业资质审验关 *ba hao jin jin qiye zizhi shenyan guan* 'Tianjin strictly guarantee the enterprise qualification' , etc.).

Moreover, the words which have prominent significant variation differences in transitivity frequency are also observed to have contrast differences in separation frequency[6] (i.e. separation usages can only be detected in Mainland corpus). Examples are shown below:

VO	ML examples	TW
撤军 *chejun* 'withdraw troop'	从约旦河**撤了军** *cong yuedanhe che le jun* from_Jordan_River_Withdra wal_LE_troops 'pull troops out of the River Jordan'	Not detected
联手 *lianshou* 'join hands'	需要香港和内地**联起手** *xuyao xianggang he neidi lianqishou* need_Hong Kong_and_Mainland_join_up _hand 'need the alliance between Hong Kong and Mainland'	Not detected
献计	为改革发展**献一计** *wei*	Not detected

---

[5]过 GUO: experiential marker.

---

[6] Although no separation example was found in the corpus, we are not claiming that there is no separation usage in other context. But we argue that since the Gigaword corpus is very large (contains more than 1.1 billion characters), if no separation example was detected in the corpus, the separation frequency should be very low.

xianji 'offer advice'	*gaige fazhan xianyiji* for_reformation_development _offer_one_advice 'offer advice to reformation development'	
移民 yimin 'immigrate'	**移了民** *yi le min* move_LE_nationality 'have immigrated'	Not detected

Table 10. Contrast difference between ML and TW

To summarize what we have found so far, the separation frequencies of Mainland VO compounds are obviously higher than that of Taiwan VO compounds. For the VOs whose transitivity frequencies in Taiwan are significant higher than in Mainland, their separation frequencies in Taiwan are significantly lower, especially when two varieties have prominent significant differences in transitivity frequency, their differences in separation frequency are also prominent, sometimes even have contrast difference (separation usages can only be detected in Mainland corpus).

Therefore it is possible for us to argue that the differences in transitivity frequency and separation frequency between Mainland and Taiwan Mandarin actually indicate the different stages that Mainland and Taiwan VO compounds are located in the continuum/process of lexicalization. In particular, if the status of lexicalization is considered as a continuum from phrase to word, then compared to Mainland VO compounds, Taiwan VOs behave more like words instead of phrases, therefore it is more likely for the Taiwan VO sequences to be used in a transitive way.

But as we have pointed in section 3, the lexical status is not the only factor which can affect the transitivity of VO compound. A Variety of factors (both internal linguistic factor and external social factor) are also influencing the degree of transitivity. Therefore the variation difference between transitivity and lexical status is not absolute. Exceptions always exist. For example, 感恩 *ganen* 'be thankful' in Mainland has a relatively high separation frequency (0.067797) while in Taiwan the separation frequency is 0.005. Mainland 感恩 *ganen* is about 380 times more likely to have separate usages than its Taiwan counterpart. But the transitivity difference between the two varieties for 感恩 *ganen* is not significant.

It may imply that other factors are actually influencing both transitivity and separation ability. Therefore what we report here is a general tendency of two variants, and the significance of statistical results indicates that the tendency we have proposed is reliable and convincing.

5 Conclusion

In our study, we take a large corpus-based statistical approach to examine the correlation between separation and transitivity of VO compound. The results prove that empirically compared to separable VO compounds, inseparable ones are more likely to be used in a transitive way. And also, for a VO compound, the less frequently it is used separately, the more likely it is used as a transitive verb. In other words, if a VO sequence is less lexicalized, its probability of taking an object is higher. But it should be noted that separation ability is not the only factor that is affecting the transitivity of a VO compound, therefore the correlation coefficient of statistical analysis is not very high. In terms of grammatical variation between Taiwan and Mainland Mandarin, our paper further compare the transitivity of VO compound between the two varieties and argue that the differences in separation and transitivity between Mainland and Taiwan actually indicate the different stages that Mainland and Taiwan VO compounds are located in the continuum of lexicalization.

References

Brinton, L. J., & Traugott, E. C. (2005). *Lexicalization and language change.* Cambridge University Press.

Her, O. S. (1997). *Interaction and variation in the Chinese VO construction.* Crane Publishing Company.

Huang, C. T. J. (1984). Phrase structure, lexical integrity, and Chinese compounds. *Journal of the Chinese Language Teachers Association*, 19(2), 53-78.

Diao, Y. B. (1998). Study on VO+O construction.也谈 "动宾式动词+ 宾语"

形式. *Chinese Construction. 语文建设*, (6), 39-41.

Diao, Y. B. (2016). The comparisons of separable words usages cross-strait. *海峡两岸离合词使用情况对比考察*. Education of overseas Chinese, *海外华文教育*, (4), 435-446.

Gao, G. (1998). Collation rules of VO+O. "动宾式动词+ 宾语" 的搭配规律. *Chinese Construction. 语文建设*, (6), 36-38.

Liu, D. W. (1998a) Thoughts on VO+O construction (1). 关于动宾带宾现象的一些思考 (上). *Chinese Construction. 语文建设*, (1), 22-26.

Liu, D. W. (1998b). Thoughts on VO+O construction (2). 关于动宾带宾现象的一些思考 (下). *Chinese Construction. 语文建设*, (3), 28-29.

Luo, X. R. (1998). Exploration on VO+O. *Chinese Construction. 语文建设*, (5), 27-30.

Qian, C. Y. (2011). *Analysis on VO+O construction in Modern Chinese. 现代汉语 "动宾式复合词带宾语" 结构分析*. MA thesis. Fudan University.

H. D. Wang. (1997). What is the rule/pattern for VO+O? "动宾式动词+ 宾语" 规律何在?. *语文建设*, (8), 30-31.

Extracting Important Tweets for News Writers using Recurrent Neural Network with Attention Mechanism and Multi-task Learning

Taro Miyazaki, Yuka Takei, Ichiro Yamada, Jun Goto
NHK Science & Technology Research Laboratories
1-10-11 Kinuta, Setagaya-ku, Tokyo, Japan
`{miyazaki.t-jw, takei.y-ek,`
`yamada.i-hy, goto.j-fw}@nhk.or.jp`

Shin Toriumi
Tokyo City University
3-3-2 Ushikubo-Nishi, Tsuzuki-ku
Yokohama, Kanagawa, Japan
`g1683108@tcu.ac.jp`

Abstract

Social media is an important source for news writers. However, extracting useful information for news writers from the vast amount of social media information is laborious. Therefore, services that enable news writers to extract important information are desired. In this paper, we describe a method to extract tweets that include useful information for news writers. Our method uses a Recurrent Neural Network (RNN) with an attention mechanism and multi-task learning that processes each character in the tweet to estimate whether the tweet includes important information. In our experiment, we compared two types of attention mechanism and compared their types with/without multi-task learning. By our proposed method, we obtained an F-measure of 0.627, which is 0.037 higher than that of baseline method.

1 Introduction

Social media information is now an important source for news writers. People who encounter an incident can post what is happening before his/her eyes using photos and videos. These posts are important primary information, so news writers want to gather them. However, extracting useful information from the vast amount of social media information is laborious. For this reason, services that enable news writers to extract information that can be used as a news source are desired. In fact, some services such as Spectee[1] and FASTALERT[2] have been launched

in Japan. These services gather much information from social media and extract information that can be used as news sources.

Information that news writers want to extract from social media includes many different topics such as fires, accidents, and other incidents. Therefore, extracting information from social media by filtering with keywords is difficult. Assuming the words "delay" and "train" are included in the keywords, the tweet "xxx line is delayed by accident," which can be used as a news source, can be extracted. However, the tweet "I hope the train is delayed because I haven't studied for today's exam," which cannot be used as a news source, is also extracted. To extract tweets that include important information, filtering by keyword is not enough because the output may include tweets that cannot be used as news sources.

For this reason, we have been studying automatic extraction of useful information from social media. Our purposes are to reduce the amount of laborious work and extract information that cannot be extracted by using queries. In this paper, we describe a method to extract tweets that include useful information for news writers. Generally, social media posts are often written in colloquial style and often include abbreviations, slang and emojis. This makes word segmentation difficult. Therefore, our method is character-based approach, not a word-based one. Our method analyzes each character in a tweet by using a Recurrent Neural Network (RNN) and then decides whether the tweet includes important information. We adopted an attention mechanism and multi-task learning in our method and confirmed the effectiveness of our method. Our contribution is to

---

[1] http://www.spectee.com
[2] https://fa.xwire.jp

31st Pacific Asia Conference on Language, Information and Computation (PACLIC 31), pages 363–369
Cebu City, Philippines, November 16-18, 2017

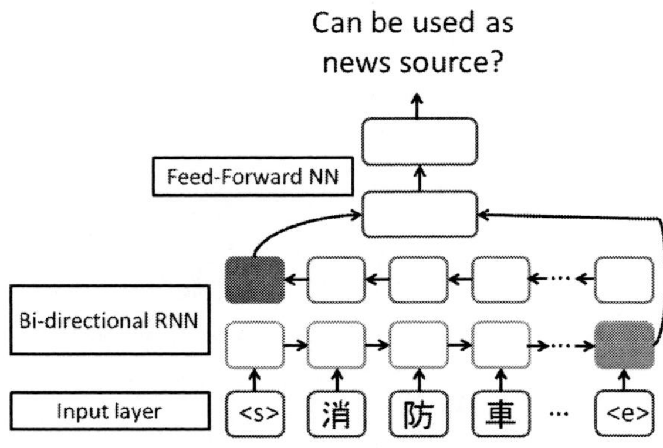

Figure 1: Architecture of our basic system.

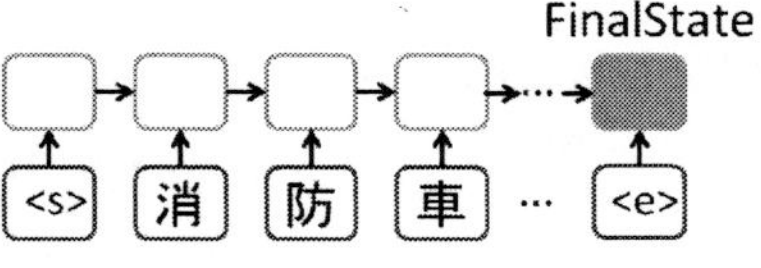

(a) FinalState Attention

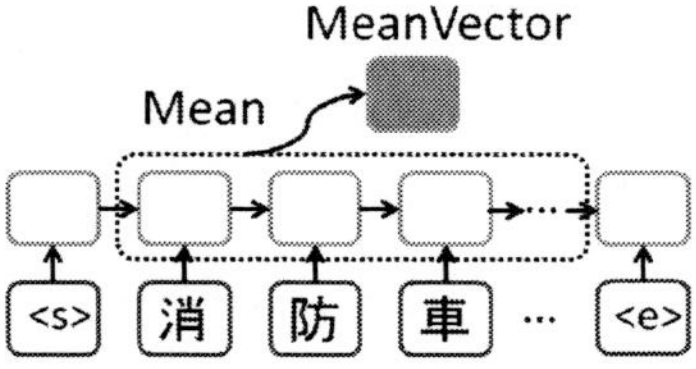

(b) MeanVector Attention

Figure 2: Two types of attention.

reveal that the combination of attention mechanism and multi-task learning is effective for character-based approaches.

2 Methods for extracting important tweets

In this section, we describe our method for extracting important tweets for news writers. We use a Recurrent Neural Network (RNN)-based model as the basic method. And, we add the attention mechanism and multi-task learning.

2.1 Basic model (RNN-based model)

As we mentioned, sentences in social media are often written in colloquial style and often include abbreviations, slang and emojis. This makes it difficult to use state-of-the-art word segmentation or other natural language processing (NLP) tools. Japanese, our target language, is written without word separation, so the accuracy of the word segmentation directly affects the performance of word-based NLP tasks. Actually, according to Ling et al. (2015) and Dhingra et al. (2016), the character-based approach outperformed the word-based one in the social media analysis task. For these reasons, we chose characters, not words, as the input of our models.

Our basic method uses bi-directional RNN (biRNN) for obtaining vector representations of the input tweet. Each character in a tweet is sequentially inputted for both the forward and backward directions. When all characters are inputted, the final

hidden states of the biRNN are used as vector representations. Then, our method classifies the tweet according to whether it is important by using a two-layer Feed-Forward Neural Network (FFNN). Figure 1 shows the architecture of our basic model.

2.2 Attention-based model

The attention mechanism has been used in many NLP tasks, such as machine translation (Bahdanau et al., 2015; Luong et al., 2015a) and image captioning (Xu et al., 2015), and can give weights to each input data taking into account the importance. In this paper, for comparison, we prepare two types of attention mechanism: "FinalState" and "MeanVector."

2.2.1 FinalState attention

FinalState attention is the conventional method. In this method, we calculate the attention weight using the final hidden state of biRNN (Figure 2-(a)). Here, we explain using the example of forward RNN: actually, we use both forward and backward RNNs.

The score for the t-th character $score_t$ is calculated as follows:

$$score_t = h_f^T \bar{h}_t$$

Here $\bar{h}_t$ is the hidden state of RNN, in which the t-th character of the input tweet has been inputted, and h_f is the hidden state of RNN, in which the final character of the tweet has been processed.

By using the score, the weight for the t-th character W_t is as follows:

$$W_t = \frac{\exp(score_t)}{\sum_{t'} \exp(score_{t'})}$$

Here, t' means the set of all characters in the tweet.

By using the weight and hidden state of the character, the FinalState attention a_f can be given:

$$a_f = \sum_{t'} W_t h_t$$

Our method uses the sum of a_f and h_f as a feature, and judges whether the tweet can be used as a news sources. The architecture of the FFNN consists of two layers as shown in Figure 1.

This method can give high weight to the characters that strongly affect the vector representation of the whole tweet because the higher the similarity between the t-th character's vector h_t and the tweet's vector h_f, the higher the weight W_t is.

2.2.2 MeanVector attention

MeanVector attention is our proposed method. In this method, we calculate the attention weight using the mean vector of the hidden state of biRNN for every character in the tweet (Figure 2-(b)). Similar to section 2.2.1, we explain using the example of the forward RNN.

The score for the t-th character $score_t$ is calculated as follows:

$$score_t = h_m^T \bar{h}_t$$

$$h_m = \frac{\sum_{t'} \bar{h}_t}{t'}$$

By using $score_t$, we can calculate the weight W_t and MeanVector attention a_m in a similar way to that in section 2.2.1.

$$W_t = \frac{\exp(score_t)}{\sum_{t'} \exp(score_{t'})}$$

$$a_m = \sum_{t'} W_t h_t$$

We use the sum of a_m and h_f as the input of the two-layer FFNN, and judge the tweet according to whether it can be used as a news source.

MeanVector attention can also give high weight to the characters that strongly affect the meaning of the

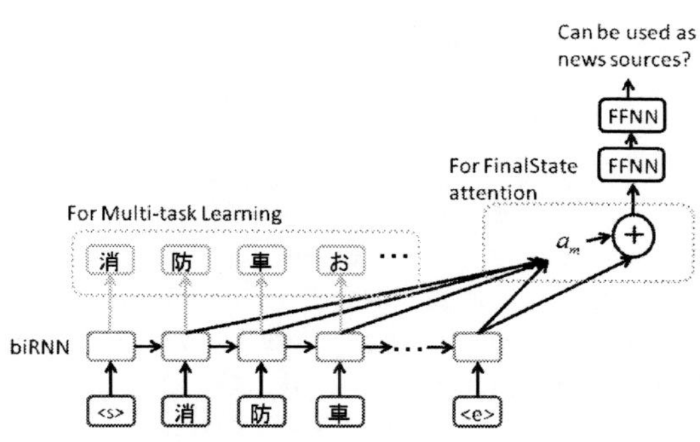

Figure 3: Overall structure using FinalState attention and multi-task learning.

whole tweet. However, compared with FinalState attention, the effect of the position of the character appeared to be reduced.

2.3 Multi-task learning

In some studies using a neural network, models are trained with multiple tasks. This technique is called "multi-task learning." It has been reported that by using multi-task learning, the model can be generic and accurate (Luong et al., 2015b; Søgaard et al., 2016). Therefore we also use multi-task learning so that our model is more accurate.

In addition to our target task, by judging whether the tweet can be used as a news sources, we prepare the task that involves estimating the next character of the input character as another task. This task is the same as "neural language model learning." We do not need to prepare training data for this task; we can use the same dataset as that of the target task without new annotated data.

We designed our architecture as sharing input and a biRNN layer with these two tasks and prepared two output layers for each task. To train this model, first we start to train with the neural language model learning. After finishing this task, we start to train for the target task using the results of the first training as the initial model of the target task.

Figure 3 illustrates the overall structure of our method using FinalState attention and multi-task learning.

3 Experiment

3.1 Dataset

For training data, we gathered tweets that can be used as actual news sources as positive samples and randomly sampled tweets as negative samples. NHK's social listening team gathered positive samples. About 20 people work for the team. The team members have been working every day for about three years as professionals, so they are well trained and highly reliable. Negative samples were randomly sampled, so some positive samples are included in the data. However, there are not that many positive samples[3], so we regarded that their effect is limited.

For evaluation data, we prepared two datasets. One was gathered in a similar way to that of gathering the training data. The ratio of positive to negative samples are adjusted to be almost the same as that of the actual tweets to reflect actual usage of our method in the news reporting section. This dataset is named "all the data" in this paper.

The other was gathered from 2,000 tweets by using a combination of queries, which include about 180 words connected with "and" / "or" / "not"[4]. These tweets are annotated according to whether they can be used as news sources by one evaluator. This dataset is designed to consider actual use by a news reporting section of a broadcasting company. Compared to the task of the other dataset, this is a more difficult task because all the data in this dataset includes some news-related words. This data is named "filtered data" in this paper.

The size of each dataset is given in Table 1. The hashtags, user names, HTML tags, and URLs are removed from all tweets in the datasets. The ratio of positive / negative samples in the training data does not reflect real-world distribution because of the training cost.

3.2 Implementation

We use Chainer (Tokui et al., 2015) to implement our models.

---

[3]We gathered 8 million tweets every day, and the number of positive samples is less than 8,000. Therefore, the positive / negative rate is about 0.1%.

[4]These queries are used by a social media analysis team in a broadcast company in Japan.

Table 1: Size of each dataset

Dataset		Amount
Training data	Positive sample	19,962
	Negative sample	1,524,155
All the data	Positive sample	2,582
	Negative sample	190,011
Filtered data	Positive sample	426
	Negative sample	1,574

Table 2: Results of evaluation using all the data

Method	Recall	Precision	F-measure
Without attention	0.887	0.872	0.880
+ multi-task	0.945	0.765	0.846
FinalState	0.861	0.922	0.890
+ multi-task	0.860	0.932	0.894
MeanVector	0.912	0.871	0.891
+ multi-task	0.906	0.875	0.890
Query filtering	0.495	0.893	0.637

For the middle layer, we use Long Short-Term Memory (LSTM) for each model of biRNN with 200 hidden states, and FFNN with a unit size of 200 and 100 from the near side of the input layer. The number of epochs is set to 10 for the target task and 3 for the neural language model learning (for multi-task learning). The mini-batch size is set to 200. We use Adam (Kingma and Ba, 2014) to optimize the parameters and Exponential Linear Units (ELUs) (Clevert et al., 2015) to activate function.

3.3 Evaluation results

3.3.1 Evaluation using all the data

The results of the evaluation experiment using all the data are given in Table 2. "Query filtering" uses the combination of queries mentioned in section 3.1 and is shown for reference.

This table indicates that all methods outperformed query filtering, but the differences between each method are small. Therefore, we try another evaluation to find out the differences.

3.3.2 Evaluation using filtered data

The results of the evaluation experiment using filtered data are given in Table 3. The accuracy of each method is lower than that shown in Table 2 because this task is far more difficult than the task in the other

Table 3: Results of evaluation using filtered data

Method	Recall	Precision	F-measure
Without attention	0.615	0.567	0.590
+ multi-task	0.552	0.622	0.585
FinalState	0.580	0.572	0.576
+ multi-task	0.674	0.573	0.619
MeanVector	0.650	0.535	0.587
+ multi-task	0.650	0.606	0.627
Query filtering	1.000	0.213	0.351

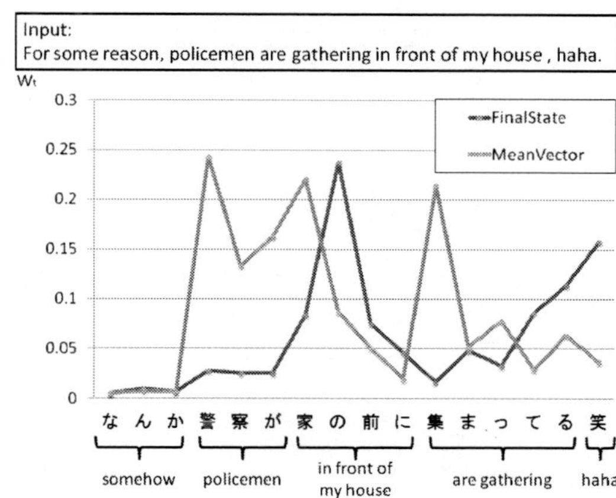

Figure 4: Comparing two attention methods.

experiment.

In total, the method using MeanVector attention with multi-task learning, which is our proposed method, obtained the highest F-measure, which is 0.037 higher than that of the basic method without attention and multi-task learning.

The result of the MeanVector attention method is rather good compared to those of the two attention mechanisms. Both attention methods cannot increase the accuracy from basic method without multi-task learning, but using multi-task learning increased the F-measures of both attention methods.

We can say that MeanVector attention is better, and multi-task learning is necessary for this task.

3.4 Discussion

MeanVector attention outperforms FinalState attention. Figure 4 shows the comparison of the attention weight for each character between the two attention methods. The input tweet is "For some reason, policemen are gathering in front of my house, haha." This tweet can be a news source because "policemen are gathering" may mean an incident has occurred near the place where the post was written. In the example in Figure 4, the FinalState attention method gives high weight to the character "笑" (haha). In this way, the FinalState attention method tends to give high weight to the characters that appear at the end of the tweet. On the other hand, MeanVector attention gives weight without being affected much by the position of the character in the tweet. Therefore, MeanVector attention gives high weight to "警察" (policemen) and "集まる" (gathering). This is the reason MeanVector attention outperforms the other attention method in this task.

In our experiment, which is described in section 3.3.2, the methods with attention mechanism without multi-task learning did not increase the accuracy; however, using multi-task learning increased the accuracy. Calculating the attention weight uses the hidden states of biRNN for each input character. We assume that the methods using attention without multi-task learning cannot learn the hidden state precisely, and multi-task learning allows the models to learn the hidden state for each input character more precisely. For more details, losses for the model update are calculated only once per mini-batch in our "target task" training. This means that only one loss covers the RNN of each input character. On the other hand, in our "neural language model" training, losses are calculated for each input character, and these losses are much more than those of "target task" training. Therefore "neural language model" training can help the model to learn more precisely for each input character. By using the "neural language model" trained model as the initial model of the "target task," we can obtain the hidden states of biRNN that are used for calculating attention more precisely. As a result, the attention weight for each character can be calculated more precisely by using multi-task learning, so the attention mechanism works well. Figure 5 shows the effect of using multi-task learning from the viewpoint of the attention weight for each character. The input tweet is "Awful, Sakai-gawa river may overflow." This can be used as a news source because we can find out from the tweet that a river is now dangerous. The method without multi-task learning gives almost constant at-

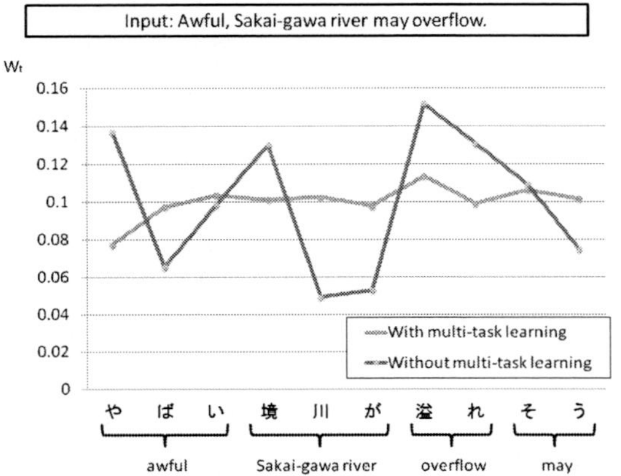

Figure 5: Effect of using multi-task learning.

tention weight. On the other hand, the method with multi-task learning gives high attention weight to " 溢れ" (overflow). For this reason, using multi-task learning made the accuracy high.

The ratio of positive / negative samples in our training data is quite imbalanced, and our methods did not includes any special features to manage the imbalanced. However our methods can perform with rather high accuracy. Therefore, we can say that our neural network can overcome the imbalanced training data.

4 Related work

Large-scale social media analysis systems named "DISAANA," and "D-SUMM" are now in operation (Mizuno et al., 2016). These systems analyze tweets as information sources and extract useful information to assess the damage caused by large-scale disasters.

There are many studies on extracting information that can be used as a news source (Vosecky et al., 2013; Hayashi et al., 2015). They used the bag-of-words approach and obtained good results. However, as we mentioned, tweets are often written in colloquial style, so word segmentation is difficult. Moreover, generally, tweets include too many words to handle, so we avoid using bag-of-words approach.

To do this, there are some studies that use a character-based approach to handle tweets (Vosoughi et al., 2016; Dhingra et al., 2016; Vakulenko et al., 2017). By using these approaches,

word segmentation is not necessary, and the vocabulary to be handled is reduced; however, there are few studies that use the attention mechanism in character-based approaches. We used a similar architecture to that of the Tweet2Vec model (Dhingra et al., 2016). We expanded this model by using the attention mechanism and multi-task learning.

We referred to some studies for our future work. Dredze et al. (2016) estimated the geolocation of the tweet. They used the time the tweet was written and obtained good results. Chi et al. (2016) used textual features selected based on a frequency-based feature selection strategy. Kanouchi st al. (2015) classified each tweet according to the people who was mentioned in the tweet, such as the person who posted the tweet of himself/herself, his/her family or people around him/her. These studies are useful to detect where and who is the subject of the tweet, which is important to news writers, who are our target users.

5 Conclusion

We presented a method to extract tweets that can be used as news sources using a recurrent neural network with attention and multi-task learning. In this paper, we confirmed the effect of the attention mechanism and multi-task learning in our task. Comparing the two methods of attention mechanism, FinalState and MeanVector, we showed that the MeanVector method is better in our task. Overall, our method (MeanVector attention with multi-task learning) achieved an F-measure of 0.627 in F-measure, which is 0.037 higher than baseline method. In our experiment, the attention mechanism is effective only when used with multi-task learning.

Our future work is adding new features according to the task, multi-class classifying to detect which kind of incident is mentioned in the tweet, and extracting more information such as geolocation and the subject person of the tweet.

References

Dzmitry Bahdanau, Kyunghun Cho and Yoshua Bengio. 2014. Neural Machine Translation by Jointly Learning to Align and Translation. *arXiv: 1409.0473*.

Lianhua Chi, Kwan Hui Lim, Nebula Alam and Christopher K. Butler. 2016. Geolocation Prediction in Twitter Using Location Indicative Words and Textual Features. *In proceedings of the 2nd Workshop on Noisy User-generated Text: 227–234.*

Djork-Arné Clevert, Thomas Unterthiner and Sepp Hochreiter. 2015. Fast and Accurate Deep Network Learning by Exponential Linear Units (ELUs). *arXiv: 1511.07289.*

Bhuwan Dhingra, Zhong Zhou, Dylan Fitzpatrick, Michael Muehl and William W. Cohen. 2016. Tweet2Vec: Character-Based Distributed Representations for Social Media. *In Proceeding of the 54th Annual Meeting of the Association for Computational Linguistics (ACL): 269–274.*

Mark Dredze, Miless Osborne and Prabhanjan Kambadur. 2016. Geolocation for Twitter: Timing Matters. *In proceedings of NAACL-HLT: 1064–1069.*

Kohei Hayashi, Takanori Maehara, Masashi Toyoda and Ken-ichi Kawarabayashi. 2015. Real-Time Top-R Topic Detection on Twitter with Topic Hijack Filtering. *In proceedings of the 21st International Conference on Knowledge Discovery and Data Mining (ACM SIGKDD): 417–426*

Shin Kanouchi, Mamoru Komachi, Naoaki Okazaki, Eiji Aramaki and Hiroshi Ishikawa 2015. Who caught a clod? – Identifying the subject of a symptom. *In proceedings of the 53rd Annual Meeting of the Association for Computational Linguistic (ACL): 1660-1670.*

Diederik Kingma and Jimmy Ba. 2014. Adam: A Method for Stochastic Optimization. *arXiv: 1412.6980.*

Wang Ling, Tiago Luís, Luís Marujo, Ramón F. Astudillo, Silvio Amir, Chris Dyer, Alan W. Black and Isabel Trancoso. 2015. Finding Function in Form: Compositional Character Models for Open Vocabulary Word Representation. *arXiv: 1508.02096.*

Minh-Thang Luong, Hieu Pham and Christopher D. Manning. 2015a. Effective Approaches to Attention-based Neural Machine Translation. *arXiv: 1508.04025.*

Minh-Thang Luong, Quoc V. Le, Ilya Sutskever, Oriol Vinyals and Lukasz Kaiser. 2015b. Multi-task Sequence to Sequence Learning. *arXiv: 1511.06114.*

Junta Mizuno, Masahiro Tanaka, Kiyonori Ohtake, Jong-Hoon Oh, Julien Kloetzer, Chikara Hashimoto and Kentaro Torisawa 2016. WISDOM X, DISAANA and D-SUMM: Large-scale NLP Systems for Analyzing Textual Big Data. *In proceedings of the 26th International Conference on Computational Linguistics (COLING): 263–267*

Seiya Tokui, Kenta Oono, Shohei Hido and Justin Clayton. 2015. Chainer: a Next-generation Open Source Framework for Deep Learning. *In proceedings of NIPS15 Worksyop on LearningSys.*

Anders Søgaard and Yoav Goldberg. 2016. Deep Multitask Learning with Low Level Tasks Supervised at Lower Layers. *In proceedings of 54th Annual Meeting of the Association for Computational Linguistics (ACL): 231-235.*

Svitlana Vakulenko, Lyndon Nixon and Mihai Lupo. 2017. Character-based Neural Embedding for Tweet Clustering. *In proceedings of the Fifth International Workshop on Natural Language Processing for Social Media: 36-44.*

Soroush Vosoughi, Prashanth Vijayaraghavan and Deb Roy 2016. Tweet2Vec: Learning Tweet Embeddings using Character-level CNN-LSTM Encoder-Decoder. *In proceedings of the 39th International conference on Research and Development in Information Retrieval (ACM SIGIR): 1041–1044.*

Jan Vosecky, Di Jiang, Kenneth Wai-Ting Leung and Wilfred Ng. 2013. Dynamic Multi-Faceted Topic Discovery in Twitter. *In proceedings of International Conference on Information and Knowledge Management (CIKM): 879–884.*

Kelvin Xu, Jimmy Lei Ba, Ryan Kiros, Kyunghyun Cho, Aaron Courville, Ruslan Salakhutdinov, Richard S. Zemel and Yoshua Bengio. 2015. Show, Attend and Tell: Neural Image Caption Generation with Visual Attention. *In proceedings of the 32nd International Conference on Machine Learning (ICML): 77–81.*

Tweet Extraction for News Production Considering Unreality

Yuka Takei, Taro Miyazaki, Ichiro Yamada, Jun Goto
NHK Science & Technology Research Laboratories
1-10-11 Kinuta, Setagaya-ku, Tokyo, Japan
`{takei.y-ek, miyazaki.t-jw, yamada.i-hy, goto.j-fw}@nhk.or.jp`

Abstract

Acquiring information on incidents and accidents from social media can be useful for broadcasters to report news faster. However, many tweets including words related to incidents and accidents are actually irrelevant to real events, for example, "Backdraft's explosion scene was impressive!!!" Social media contains many comments on events in unreal worlds such as movies, animations and dramas, and it is time-consuming to discriminate these tweets manually. This work presents a method for automatically extracting useful tweets for news reports by focusing on "unreal" information. We first prepare unreal tweets as learning data and use a distributed representation and features that can determine if a tweet is real or unreal. By adding the features of a neural network, we generate a learning model that can effectively discriminate whether a tweet includes information on actual incidents or accidents. Results of evaluations revealed that the proposed method achieved a 3.8-point higher F-measure than the baseline method.

1. Introduction

Social networking services (SNSs) enable us to easily transmit information anywhere in real-time. The large amount of information transmitted on SNS, known as "Social Big Data," is a valuable information source for grasping newsworthy occurrence (Vieweg et al., 2010; Kanouchi et al., 2015), and broadcasters monitor social media such as Twitter to collect information about incidents and accidents. By obtaining information directly from witnesses of such events, broadcasters can report news more quickly and effectively. They use various tools to manually search for tweets that have potential news value, using keywords to find tweets indicating incidents and accidents. However, a lot of effort is required to find valuable information from among the large number of tweets sent every day.

Methods have been reported for automatically extracting tweets with potential news value by using machine learning (Freitas et al., 2016; Mizuno et al., 2016; Doggett et al., 2016). However, many tweets irrelevant to actual incidents or accidents include relevant words, which worsen the extraction results. Examples include tweets about events in current animations and TV programs, such as "ドラえもん「のび太の家火事になる・前編」 (Doraemon - Nobita's House Fire・Part 1)." Many viewers tweet while watching TV to share their opinions with other people. Therefore, many tweets include names of animations (which we call "virtual proper nouns") and TV programs. In addition, words in Japanese idioms could also suggest incidents or accidents, such as "火の無いところに煙は立たない (Where there's smoke, there's fire)." Furthermore, there are tweets that include hypothetical expressions that assume an incident or accident occurring, such as "火事になったら、どこに逃げるべきだろう (If a fire occurs, where should I escape to?)."

All three tweets include the word "fire" but do not indicate the occurrence of a real fire. The conventional method extracts information from tweets that include words related to incidents and accidents, regardless of whether one has actually occurred. Therefore, to utilize the extracted tweet as a news source, more work is required to determine

31st Pacific Asia Conference on Language, Information and Computation (PACLIC 31), pages 370–375
Cebu City, Philippines, November 16-18, 2017

whether it is a "real event" or "unreal event." In this paper, virtual proper nouns (movies and animations), TV program titles, and idiomatic phrases are defined as "characteristic phrases." In addition, phrases including expressions of hypothesized situations are defined as "hypothesis expressions." By adding the presence or absence of "characteristic phrases" and "hypothesis expressions" to the input of a neural network as features, we generate a learning model that can efficiently discriminate whether a tweet includes information on actual incidents or accidents. Extending the input dimension like this, improved the F-measure by 3.8 points, revealing the effectiveness of the proposed method.

2. Related Work

During large-scale disasters, such as the 2011 Great East Japan Earthquake, SNSs such as Twitter are effective for transmitting information (Aida et al., 2012). On the basis of information on SNSs, public officials and emergency workers can grasp what is happening in the disaster area in real-time. However, on Twitter, unreliable and unnecessary information is also diffused excessively, requiring more effort to discriminate relevant information.

To extract relevant information during a disaster, Neubig et al. developed a semiautomatic information extraction method (Neubig et al., 2011, 2013) that efficiently filters information by using active learning. In the process of active learning, an annotator labels each tweet presented by the system as positive or negative. Conventional active learning labels sequentially from the tweets near the boundary of positive and negative samples. On the other hand, their method presents tweets that have the highest possibility of being positive samples, making it possible to minimize the number of negative samples labeled by annotators and improving work efficiency. However, when large-scale incidents or accidents occur, secondary tweets such as retweets often occur, so the absolute number of tweets judged to be positive samples increases. Continually presenting tweets with high scores as positive samples will increase the accuracy, but less information will be covered, causing tweets judged to be positive samples to be overlooked.

Broadcasters must acquire a wide variety of information, not only information about large-scale disasters. By limiting negative samples to the minimum, we aim to improve information gathering efficiency, and by maintaining the diversity of the positive samples, we reduce the risk of information being missed.

3. Methodology

In this section, we describe a method for extracting tweets for news reporting. In the proposed method, we generate a model that learns by focusing on unreal negative samples. We use a feed forward neural network as a learning algorithm to automatically extract tweets that have potential news value. The input to the neural network uses the distributed representation of tweets. By adding a feature of whether a characteristic phrase or hypothesis expression is included in a tweet, learning models are generated. The configuration of the neural network is shown in Figure. 1.

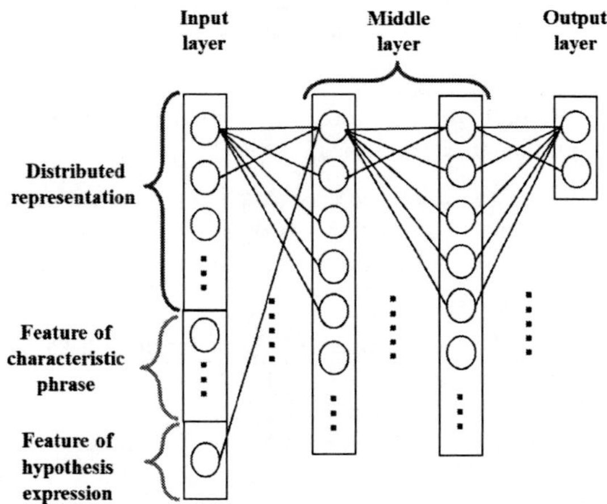

Figure 1. Configuration of neural network

In this paper, our target for news production is to extract tweets related to "fire," which is the most frequently occurring topic in Japanese news.

3.1 Features based on Distributed Representation

First, a tweeted sentence is divided into morpheme units using the morphological analyzer MeCab (Kudo et al., 2004). Then, by using Word2Vec (Mikolov et al., 2013), each unit is converted into a 200-dimensional distributed representation. The average of all vectors for words included in a sentence is regarded as the sentence vector and is used for an input for a neural network. We used the Wikipedia dump data of September 2016 to generate distributed expressions using Word2Vec.

3.2 Features of Characteristic Phrases

As described in the introduction, information about broadcast content such as dramas and animations is often sent to SNSs, and some tweets includes idiomatic phrases. We prepared three kinds of characteristic phrases: TV program names, virtual proper nouns, and idiomatic phrases. If a tweet includes them, we put "1" in the corresponding dimension of the phrase and "0" if not.

TV program names
We gathered 9,473 titles, mainly of dramas, using the program guide application programming interface (API) of broadcasting stations and Wikipedia.

Virtual proper nouns
12,310 proper nouns such as animation, movie, and video game titles were gathered from Wikipedia.

Idiomatic phrases
We gathered 32 phrases that contained "fire" from published dictionaries[1].

In characteristic phrases, we exclude titles that contained common verbs or adjectives such as "生きる (live)" and single-character titles such as "江 (Gou)."

Table 1. Examples of characteristic phrases

Feature type	Example
TV program names	ひよっこ (Hiyokko), べっぴんさん (Beppinnsann), あさイチ(Asaichi)
Virtual proper nouns	スーパーマン (Superman), マリオパーティ (Mario-Party), スラムダンク (Slam-Dunk)
Idiomatic phrases	対岸の火事 (taiganno-kazi), 火事場の馬鹿力 (kajibano-bakadikara)

The features of characteristic phrases are set as follows. The example sentence "海外の事例を対岸の火事と楽観視できない (Foreign cases cannot be optimistic about the fire on the other side,)" includes the Japanese idiomatic phrase "対岸の火事 (the fire on the other side)." The idiomatic phrases dimension corresponding to it is "1." Since the sentence does not include any TV program names or virtual proper nouns, their values are set to "0."

3.3 Features of Hypothesis Expressions

Due to the effect of recent news of terrorism overseas, tweets expressing worries about terrorism have been posted such as "近くで爆発が起きたら怖いな (If an explosion occurs nearby, I'll be scared)" We extract this kind of assumption from a sentence and use it as a feature for tweet extraction. We analyze the relationship between words that include expressions related to fire such as "爆発 (explosion)" and include assumptions such as "たら (if)." A tweeted sentence is divided into clauses by using the parser CaboCha (Kudo and Matsumoto, 2002). If the tweet includes (1) or (2), it is determined to include a "hypothesis expression."

(1) A dependency relationship between an expression related to fire and an assumption

(2) An Expression related to fire and an assumption in the same clause

In the above example, since "if" has a dependency relationship with "explosion," the feature of the "hypothesis expressions" is set to "1." Specific examples are shown in Figure. 2.

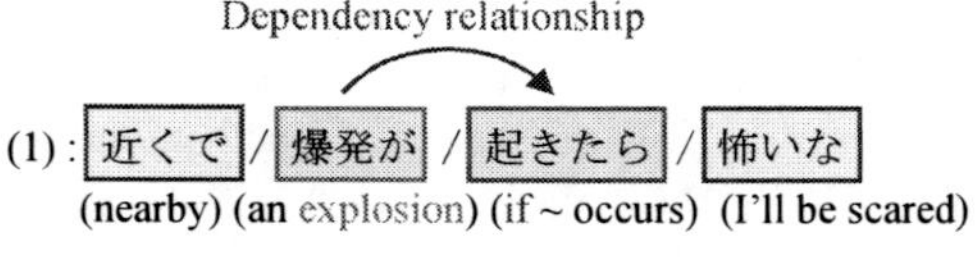

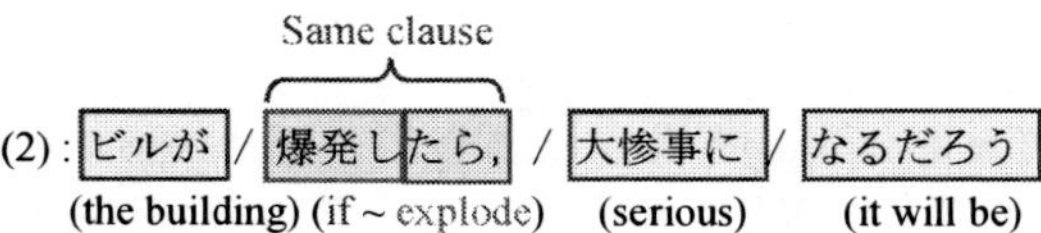

Figure 2. Examples of hypothesis expressions

4. Evaluation Experiment

We conducted two experiments to evaluate the effectiveness of our method. The first was to evaluate the effect of learning data using tweets that include "characteristic phrases." The second is to evaluate the effect of the features including "characteristic phrases" and "hypothesis expressions."

---

[1] http://www.jlogos.com/

4.1 Experimental Settings

Dataset
For the training data, we gathered 5,065 tweets used in actual news reports as positive samples, which included information related to "fire" from March 2014 to August 2015. For comparison, we prepared two kinds of negative samples.

(A) A random sample of 5,065 tweets randomly selected from all tweets in September 2016. This random sample did not include news source.

(B) A mixed sample of 5,065 tweets randomly selected from a dataset that mixed tweets in (A) and tweets including characteristic phrases.

The evaluation data were narrowed down to 8,154 tweets from about 7,700,000 from October 23rd, 2016. These were selected by keyword matching concerning fire-based events. The keywords are devised by the news production section of our broadcasting station[2]. There are 61 keywords related to fire, and broadcasters combine them to search for newsworthy information. Then a positive sample label was given to tweets with content related to actual fires or explosions, and a negative sample label was given to tweets with content not related to fire. For example, if a fire is happening in an unreal world or someone's imagination, this tweet is a negative sample. All the tweets are annotated by one annotator.

Implementation
We use Chainer (Tokui et al., 2015) to implement our method. The input layer uses 204 dimensions (1 to 200 dimensions indicate the distributed representation and 201 to 204 dimensions respectively indicate presence or absence of TV program names / virtual proper nouns / idiomatic phrases / hypothesis expressions). The output layer is two-dimensional, and the middle layer has two layers. The middle layers contain 500 nodes and 250 nodes from the nearest to the input layer. In addition, exponential linear units (ELUs) (Clevert et al., 2015) were used as an activation function, and batch normalization was performed in each layer. The number of learning sessions was set to 30.

[2]NHK (Japan Broadcasting Corporation) has a social media analysis team, that looks for news on the internet.

4.2 Experimental Results

Comparison of training data
The experimental results of the training data are shown in Table 2. The random sample uses negative samples (A) of the learning data as the baseline. The mixed sample uses negative samples (B) of the learning data.

Table 2. Experimental results
for each training dataset

Method	Recall	Precision	F-measure
Random sample	84.1	79.7	81.9
Mixed sample (MS)	85.4	83.4	84.4

Comparing the training data, the mixed sample including the characteristic phrases performs better than the random sample. Therefore, we used the mixed sample as training data in the next experiment and experimental results with various features.

Effects of features
Table 3 shows the experimental results for using each feature. Mixed sample (MS) is the method that learned only distributed representation as described in Section 3.1. We added the features of TV program names, virtual proper nouns, and idiomatic phrases described in Section 3.2. Characteristic (1d) indicates the results of summarizing three features expressing characteristic phrases into one dimension, and Characteristic (3d) indicates the results of simultaneously adding three features to different dimensions. Furthermore, as a result of adding hypothesis expressions described in Section 3.3 as a feature to the MS method, the results obtained by adding all the features are shown.

Table 3. Experimental results for each method

Method	Recall	Precision	F-measure
Mixed sample (MS)	85.4	83.4	84.4
MS + TV program names	84.5	84.6	84.6
MS + Virtual proper nouns	89.7	80.1	84.7
MS + idiomatic phrases	83.9	**85.2**	84.5
MS + Characteristic (1d)	82.7	83.7	83.2
MS + Characteristic (3d)	88.9	82.8	**85.7**
MS + Hypothesis Expression (HE)	82.5	84.4	83.4
MS + All feature (3d+HE)	83.5	84.4	84.0

Among the three types of features of characteristic phrases, using virtual proper nouns achieves the highest F-measure. Performance was improved more by dividing each feature into three dimensions rather than putting each feature together. In addition, even when the features of hypothesis expressions were added, the F-measure did not improve.

4.3 Discussion

Training data
As a negative sample of the training data, the mixed sample that included characteristic phrases performed better than the random sample. By including these mixed tweets, our method can learn negative samples including news-related words precisely. It can also learn combinations of news-related words and other words. Therefore, a characteristic phrase is a clue to select effective training data from among a large number of tweets.

Effects of features
The results of adding features of characteristic phrases to different dimensions (3d) is better than those of other methods. The proposed method has a 1.3-point higher F-measure and 3.5-point higher recall than the MS method. This result shows that we can acquire many positive samples as well as excluding tweets about unreal worlds. Examples of improvements by the proposed method are shown in case-A and case-B.

┌─ Case-A ─────────────────────────────
MS method: Positive → proposed method: Negative

「火の鳥」の最終回が炎上
(The last round of "Fire Bird" is flaming.)
└──────────────────────────────────────

┌─ Case-B ─────────────────────────────
MS method: Negative → proposed method: Positive

せっかく特急乗ったのに, 沿線火災で電車が
止まっている
(Even though I got on a limited express, the train
stopped due to a fire along the railroad.)
└──────────────────────────────────────

In Case-A, words related to fires such as "fire" and "flame" were included, so the MS method judged it as a positive. However, "Fire Bird" is the name of Japanese animation. Therefore, by adding proposed features, the proposed method can judge it as negative.

The MS method sometimes judged tweets including words related to fire as negative such as Case-B, because the method learned mixed sample including characteristic phrase without adding proposed features. For example, the method learned tweet including phrases related to fire like a "対岸の火事 (the fire on the other side)" as a negative example. Thus, words related to fire are included in negative examples as well as positive examples. When the features were added, the positive and negative criteria were clarified. Therefore, our proposed method can maintain the diversity of the positive samples. In addition, features of characteristic phrases were improved more by dividing each feature into three dimensions rather than using each feature as one dimensions. By dividing TV program names, virtual proper nouns, and idiomatic phrases into features, the proposed method can learn patterns of notation when phrases appear in sentences.

The features of hypothesis expressions could not improve the F-measure because recall decreased. From results of error analysis, our method judged positive samples in the evaluation data as negative. For example, the negative results included tweets attributing causality to fire such as "たくさんの煙が見える, 火事だったらこまるなぁ (There is a lot of smoke over there, I'm in trouble if it's a fire)". In order not to miss such a tweet expressing the possibility of an incident or accident, a detailed analysis method needs to be developed to analyze causality.

5. Conclusion

In this paper, we presented a method to automatically extract tweets with potential news value by adding new features focusing on "unreal" events to a neural network. The proposed method achieved a highest F-measure of 85.7, a 3.5-point increase over the baseline method, by focusing on "characteristic phrases" (TV program names, virtual proper nouns, and idiomatic phrases). This method is expected to reduce the workload of broadcasters who acquire information from social media.

In the future, we aim to further improve the performance by acquiring more characteristic phrases such as "cast of a TV program" and "TV program-related information" from real-time data.

References

Shin Aida, Yasutaka Shindoh, and Masao Utiyama. 2013. Rescue Activity for the Great East Japan Earthquake Based on a Website that Extracts Rescue Requests from the Net. *Proceedings of the Workshop on Language Processing and Crisis Information 2013*, pages 19-25.

Djork-Arné Clevert, Thomas Unterthiner, and Sepp Ochreiter. 2015. Fast and Accurate Deep Network Learning by Exponential Linear Units (ELUs). arXiv:1511.07289.

Erika Doggett and Alejandro Cantarero. 2016. Identifying Eyewitness News-Worthy Events on Twitter. *Proceedings of The Fourth International Workshop on Natural Language Processing for Social Media*, pages 7-13.

Jesse Freitas and Heng Ji, 2016. Identifying News from Tweets. *Proceedings of 2016 EMNLP Workshop on Natural Language Processing and Computational Social Science*, pages 11-16.

Shin Kanouchi, Mamoru Komachi, Naoaki Okazaki, Eiji Aramaki, and Hiroshi Ishikawa. 2015. Who caught a cold? — Identifying the subject of a symptom. *Proceedings of the 53rd Annual Meeting of the Association for Computational Linguistics and the 7th International Joint Conference on Natural Language Processing*, pages 1660-1670.

Taku Kudo and Yuji Matsumoto. 2002. Japanese dependency analysis using cascaded chunking. *In Proceedings of the 6th Conference on Natural Language Learning 2002*, pages 1-7.

Taku Kudo, Kaoru Yamamoto, and Yuji Matsumoto. 2004. Applying Conditional Random Fields to Japanese Morphological Analysis. *In Proceedings of the Conference on Empirical Methods in Natural Language Processing*, pages 230-237.

Tomas Mikolov, Kai Chen, Greg Corradoet, and Jeffrey Dean. 2013. Efficient estimation of word representations in vector space. *arXiv*:1301.3781.

Junta Mizuno, Masahiro Tanaka, Kiyonori Ohtake, Jong-Hoon Oh, Julien Kloetzer, Chikara Hashimoto, and Kentaro Torisawa. 2016. WISDOM X, DISAANA and D-SUMM: Large-scale NLP Systems for Analyzing Textual Big Data. *In proceedings of the 26th International Conference on Computational Linguistics, pages 263–267.*

Graham Neubig, Yuichiroh Matsubayashi, Masato Hagiwara, and Koji Murakami. 2011. Safety information mining - what can NLP do in a disaster -. *Proceedings of the 5th International Joint Conference on Natural Language Processing*, pages 965-973.

Graham Neubig, Shinsuke Mori, and Masahiro Mizukami. 2013. A Framework and Tool for Collaborative Extraction of Reliable Information. *In Proceedings of the Workshop on Language Processing and Crisis Information*, pages 26-35.

Seiya Tokui, Kenta Oono, Shohei Hido, and Justin Clayton. 2015. Chainer: a next-generation open source framework for deep learning. *In Proceedings of Workshop on Machine Learning Systems (LearningSys) in The Twenty-Ninth Annual Conference on Neural Information Processing Systems.*

Sarah Vieweg, Amanda L Hughes, Kate Starbird, and Leysia Palen. 2010. Microblogging during two natural hazards events: what Twitter may contribute to situational awareness. *In Proceedings of the SIGCHI conference on human factors in computing systems*, pages 1079-1088.

Discovering Conversation Spaces in the Public Discourse of Gender Violence: a Comparative Between Two Different Contexts

Meliza M. De La Paz
Ateneo de Manila University
Katipunan Ave., Quezon City
Philippines, 1108
azidelapaz@gmail.com

Ma. Regina E. Estuar
Ateneo de Manila University
Katipunan Ave., Quezon City
Philippines, 1108
restuar@ateneo.edu

John Noel C. Victorino
Ateneo de Manila University
Katipunan Ave., Quezon City
Philippines, 1108
jvictorino@ateneo.edu

Abstract

A huge factor in gender-based violence is perception and stigma, revealed by public discourse. Topic modelling is useful for discourse analysis and reveals prevalent topics and actors. This study aims to find and compare examples of collectivist and individualist conversation spaces of gendered violence by applying Principal Component Analysis, N-Gram analysis and word association in two gender violence cases which occured in the different contexts of the Philippines and the United States. The data from the Philippines consist of 2010-2011 articles on the 1991 Vizconde Massacre and the data from the United States consist of 2016-2017 articles from the 2015 Stanford Rape Case. Results show that in both cases' conversation space there is a focus on institutions involved in the cases that does not really change over time, and a time-dependent conversation space for victims. Even in two different contexts of gender violence, patterns in conversation space appear similar.

1 Introduction

In 2010, around 20 people in the United States were being physically abused by a partner every minute (Black, Basile, Breiding, et al, 2011). Gender-based violence is a prevalent problem, even until today: 1 in 3 women have experienced some form of physical or sexual violence worldwide(World Health Organization, 2016). The emphasis on gender points to the context that this violence happens because of unequal power relations between women and men. Gendered expectations and structures of power are passed down and learned through interactions and discussions - discourse datasets are a potential source to analyze for this (Butler, 1988).

This study uses principal component analysis, word frequency counts, word associations, and N-gram analysis to compare two different public discourses on gender violence, specifically articles written about the Stanford rape case and the Vizconde massacre. This is done between two sets of discourse that happens in an individualist society(U.S.) and a collectivist society(Philippines). It aims to analyze a conversation space to see what aspect of gender violence discourse appears to be the primary focus - victims, perpetrators, institutions or society as an initial diagnosis of how gender violence is framed in such discourses.

People v. Brock Allen Turner(the official name of the legal case of the Stanford rape) began on January 18, 2015 when a college student athlete named Brock Turner was indicted for charges of rape and sexual assault. Turner was convicted on March 30, 2016 for charges of sexual assault. On June 2, 2016, he was sentenced to 6 months of jail. This case raised controversy because of the constant defense of the Turner family, claiming their son's reputation would be ruined, as well as the short amount of time given to Brock Turner for his crime.

On the other hand, the Vizconde massacre in June 30, 1991 was a homicide case where one of the victims was raped before being killed. Several men were involved as suspects in the case, including Hubert Webb, Joey Filart, Artemio Ventura, Michael Gatchalian, Hospicio Fernandez and Anto-

31st Pacific Asia Conference on Language, Information and Computation (PACLIC 31), pages 376–383
Cebu City, Philippines, November 16-18, 2017
Copyright ©2017 Meliza De La Paz, Maria Regina Estuar and John Noel Victorino

nio Lejano II. All of them were convicted in regional court as well as the court of appeals. However, the Supreme Court chose to reverse this decision and acquit the men on December 14, 2010. Recent discussion on the memory of the case emerged once more during Lauro Vizconde's death on February 13, 2016.

The study is limited to the data of articles about the Stanford rape case starting from when its decision was released on June 2, 2016, until 2 weeks afterward, as well as articles written 6-7 months afterwards. The articles chosen for the Vizconde massacre are the ones written after the announcement of the Supreme Court's reversal and acquittal on December 14, 2010 up to two weeks afterward, as well as articles written 6-7 months afterwards.

2   Related Literature

Discussions on rape frame how it is understood by readers. It is thought that whoever's story is believed is the story that gets to determine the definition of what rape is (Kaiser, 2002). This is aggravated by several rape myth acceptance factors that exist in society today - things which can shift responsibility from victims to perpetrators, or only accept certain kinds of events as 'real rape' (Frese, 2004). Individualist and collectivist societies have displayed differences in gender violence perception due to different notions of responsibility (Lo, So and Zhang, 2010; Yamawaki, 2007).

Several feminist scholars have talked about concepts such as masculine aggressiveness and feminine weakness(MacKinnon, 1989), constant victim narratives for women (Sjoberg, 2010; Maeda, 2011), entitlement over female bodies and promiscuity as invitation(MacKinnon, 1989; Maeda, 2011). There has also been analysis that incidents of gender violence talk about perpetrators as outliers(du Toit, 2010; Murphy, 2007). Several of these play into how victims of violence are perceived (Menaker and Franklin, 2015; Olwan, 2013), and how this violence is potrayed in artworks (Nixon, Rodier and Meagher, 2012; Yarbro-Bejarano, 2013).

Other studies have also looked at various institutions and how they affect gender violence perception (Joyce-Wojitas and Keenan, 2016; Hudson, 2002; Morrison, Ellsberg and Bott, 2007).

What these various literature show are different aspects at play when rape narratives are framed - for the purpose of this study, these can be summarized into four entities: victims, perpetrators, institutions, and society/culture.

3   Methodology

Two datasets are used in this study. The first is the set of articles on the Stanford rape committed by Brock Turner starting from June 2, 2016 on the day Brock Turner's sentence was given. The second is the set of articles on the Vizconde murders starting from December 14, 2010 when the suspects of the case were acquitted by the Supreme Court. These articles were gathered from various media sources. To account for different media biases, a single source was never to exceed a fourth of the total dataset. Data for each event was divided into two sets: one dataset of articles starting from the day of acquittal or sentence for up to two weeks afterward. The second dataset would be for articles occuring six months after the event.

3.1   Pre-Processing

Stop words, filler words and punctuation are removed from articles, and documents converted to lowercase. Aside from the standard dictionary of English stopwords, profanities are also removed from the data because of the vague emotions often associated with their use. Names of individuals involved in the cases are also removed for most processing steps. These are retained for bigram frequency count to see which actors in the discourse are more mentioned than others.

3.2   Word Frequency, Bi-Gram Frequency, and Word Association

Document-term matrices are generated for both unigrams and bigrams and collapsed into a word-frequency and bi-gram-frequency tables, arranged in descending order. Word association is done for the top fifteen unigrams and top five bigrams, using a minimum correlation value of 0.5.

3.3   Principal Component Analysis on Unigrams and Bi-Grams

Using document-term matrices generated for unigramas and bi-grams, principal component analysis is applied for each. Generated document-term matrices had sparse terms removed, allowing for 85% to 90% maximum sparsity. Topics are located using PCA results, using all words in the first and second dimensions with a correlation value of 0.5 and above.

Principal component analaysis is applied three times to the Stanford Rape and Vizconde Massacre datasets. Once for the set immediately after the chosen events, once for the set six months afterward, and one for the datasets as a whole.

3.4 Comparison

Lastly, the results of the two datasets are compared by looking into similarities and differences in key topics and actors in the conversation space. First, comparisons are drawn by looking into any changes over time for both events. Secondly, comparisons are drawn by looking at any similarities and differences between the two cultures. These are contextualized and analyzed by looking at cultural differences between the Philippines and United States as collectivist and individualist states.

4 Results and Discussion

Results are analyzed with the overall goal of finding out (a) if there are changes in the conversation space for the same gender violence event over a period of six months (b) what particular aspect of gender violence discourse appears to be the focal point of a particular set (victim, perpetrator, institution, or society), and (c) if there are similarities between two different contexts of gender violence(between the Philippines and the United States) even if the events occur in different times and societies.

4.1 Frequency Count and Associations

Frequency counts for words and bi-grams in the Stanford dataset can be found in table 1. Some things are worthy of note. First of all, words such as "victim" and "woman" disappear from the top 10 frequently mentioned words six months afterwards. "Campus", most possibly referring to the Stanford Rape, disappears as well. "Judge" appears to be a consistent entity mentioned even six months afterward.

This trend continues even with bi-gram analysis, in table 1. The closest bi-gram which could refer to

Table 1: Stanford Rape: Frequency Words and Bi-Grams

After Sentencing	
victim	197
sentence	137
woman	130
judge	121
time	114
statement	112
campus	99
night	98
life	96
unconscious	91
After 6 Months	
judge	76
commission	62
sentence	43
judicial	40
recall	39
probation	29
campaign	28
misconduct	28
months	28
jail	26
After Sentencing	
brock turner	65
stanford university	42
santa clara	29
county jail	28
aaron persky	25
probation officer	25
clara county	24
minutes action	23
unconscious woman	22
pine needles	20
After 6 Months	
judge persky	49
brock turner	19
commission judicial	15
santa clara	15
clara county	14
judicial performance	14
recall campaign	13
stanford university	13
evidence bias	10
former stanford	10

the victim in this case is "unconscious woman", not even "Emily Doe" as she used a pseudonym. "Aaron Persky", "Brock Turner", and "Stanford University" appear more consistent.

Table 2: Stanford Rape: Word Associations for 'Victim'

confirmed	0.71
crime	0.7
actions	0.65
serious	0.64
caused	0.63
remembered	0.63
county	0.62
attempt	0.61
lives	0.61
meet	0.61
conversations	0.6
lines	0.6
remorse	0.6
request	0.6
genuine	0.59
letter	0.59
punishment	0.59
tried	0.59
legal	0.58
leniency	0.58

What this is presenting so far is a discourse that inconsistently talks about victims. An analysis of some words associated with "victim" that can be found in table 2 in the Stanford Rape dataset reveal that many words that are associated with "victim" are still in reference to legal institutions - words such as "legal", "leniency", "crime" and "punishment" which are more tied to the legal aspect of the cases. However, one set of word association results shows a break from this - when looking at associated words for "sentence" in table 3, there does appear to be a sudden association with the victim 6 months afterward with words such as "emily" and "victim" which were not present earlier.

The emerging trend of a more institution-centric discourse is consistent with findings in the Vizconde Massacre dataset, presented in table 4. Top words are "court" and "nbi", referring to the Supreme Court of the Philippines and the Bureau of Investigations in the top words without any words that could be attributed to victims, and "Supreme Court"

Table 3: Stanford Rape: Word Associations for 'Sentence'

Immediately After	
law	0.7
county	0.68
felony	0.67
minutes	0.66
hours	0.64
clara	0.61
leniency	0.61
probation	0.61
santa	0.61
send	0.61
viral	0.61
urged	0.6
dedicated	0.59
pages	0.59
superior	0.59
action	0.58
convicted	0.58
california	0.57
class	0.57
court	0.57
6 Months After	
prison	0.89
jail	0.82
judicial	0.82
recommended	0.81
defense	0.8
excuses	0.8
independent	0.8
looked	0.8
assessment	0.78
decision	0.77
critics	0.75
probation	0.75
national	0.74
prosecutors	0.74
emily	0.73
offender	0.73
performance	0.73
victim	0.72
clara	0.66
defendant	0.66

and "de Lima"(the head of the Department of Justice) being the top bi-grams. Bi-gram analysis for the Vizconde Massacre dataset does, however, have "Lauro Vizconde" as a more consistent bi-gram immediately after the events and even 6 months afterwards. "Carmela Jennifer" appears in the case six months afteward, referring to two of the victims who were murdered in the case, Carmela and Jennifer Vizconde.

4.2 Principal Component Analysis

Principal component analysis results for the Stanford Rape case are in tables 5 and 6.The topics continue to show more of a focus towards institutional aspects of the case, with a topic on cultural discussion that emerged in the dataset six months after. A topic that would be close to the victim is the rape event itself which she herself narrated in the letter that she had written - a topic which can no longer be found in the later set's PCA results. However, when PCA is applied to the overall dataset, the topic of the "victim" does emerge.

Meanwhile, in the case of the Vizconde Massacre in tables 7 and 8, the victims of the case, the Vizconde Family, emerge as a topic only six months afterwards. It is possible that this is a response to their family announcing things such as their remembrance masses and 20th anniversary of the deaths of the victims. The institution of the Supreme Court appears prominent throughout time, as "failure of prosecution" is still being talked about six months afterwards. Running PCA for the overall dataset reveals the topic "perceived injustice".

5 Conclusion

In both datasets from the United States and the Philippines, discourse appears to be primarily institution-centric, though it could possibly be argued that there is a very prominent space for the perpetrator as well. This is based on the consistency of their prominence even across a change of 6 months - with topics such and words such as 'court' 'judge', 'nbi' and topics such as 'court decision', 'judge persky' and the like. Victims, however, do not appear to have a very consistent space in the conversation as conversations seem likelier to change focus over time. Instead, victims are promi-

Table 4: Vizconde Massacre Frequency Words and Bi-Grams

After Acquittal	
court	306
justice	129
accused	110
decision	108
supreme	94
crime	92
family	82
witness	81
evidence	72
nbi	72

After 6 Months	
nbi	54
investigation	41
evidence	40
witnesses	40
crime	38
court	36
justice	33
time	29
country	22
doj	22

After Acquittal	
supreme court	92
hubert webb	55
jessica alfaro	39
lauro vizconde	37
trial court	31
court appeals	30
reasonable doubt	30
beyond reasonable	28
co accused	28
associate justices	24

After 6 Months	
de lima	45
hubert webb	24
supreme court	22
lauro vizconde	15
bureau investigation	11
carmela jennifer	10
national bureau	10
leila de	9
crime scene	8
double jeopardy	8

Table 5: Stanford Rape: PCA Dimensions Immediately After

Rape as Crime

santa clara	0.8620547
clara county	0.8562122
minutes action	0.6171062
intent commit	0.5957213
intoxicated person	0.5732411
former stanford	0.5321426
county jail	0.5047081

Rape Event

night	0.9308822
time	0.9091522
body	0.9084846
life	0.8999215
family	0.8937538
told	0.8856298
drinking	0.8837296
party	0.8835866
happened	0.8788474
consent	0.8695934
attorney	0.8629541
dumpster	0.851985
unconscious	0.8511993
naked	0.8508088

Turner's Sentence

clara	0.7986594
santa	0.7986594
county	0.6862388
sentence	0.6565878
law	0.6543873
california	0.6096214
sentencing	0.5948697
media	0.5923465
report	0.5858502
felony	0.5478694
prison	0.5177417
court	0.5151062
national	0.5084797
judge	0.5053399

Table 6: Stanford Rape: PCA Dimensions 6 Months After

Cultural Discussion

discipline	0.893028
social	0.8883636
bias	0.8625273
conclude	0.8556272
convincing	0.8556272
warranting	0.8556272
published	0.8554577
thousands	0.8258422
party	0.8134658
online	0.790534
authority	0.7841988
california	0.7760179
prosecutors	0.7727551
media	0.7695833
engaged	0.7258757
received	0.7150418
misconduct	0.7033931
passed	0.6973579
ignited	0.6958733
concluded	0.6665783
system	0.6654961

Judge Persky

judicial performance	0.7815202
commission judicial	0.7355416
judicial misconduct	0.6994272
california commission	0.696224
turner months	0.5849886
law professor	0.5161074
stanford law	0.5145941

Table 7: Vizconde Massacre: PCA Dimensions Immediately After

Court Decision

court	0.868481
prosecution	0.808735
accused	0.777947
evidence	0.76032
associate	0.758914
testimony	0.736475
trial	0.716811
crime	0.697268
justices	0.69006
paranaque	0.680054
inconsistencies	0.643145
appeals	0.607427
sister	0.599042
ruling	0.591526
dna	0.581791
midas	0.560098
released	0.551964
decision	0.547805
prove	0.54019
witness	0.53984

Hubert Webb

senator	0.744941
father	0.652629
son	0.615067
home	0.602323
prison	0.582448
family	0.546761
day	0.531314
former	0.50988

Jessica Alfaro

positive identification	0.786539
credible witness	0.726663
court court	0.709272
court appeals	0.678953
substitute witness	0.648001
lower court	0.589628
defense alibi	0.587118
witness nbi	0.559133
nbi asset	0.557574
trial court	0.548972
alfaros testimony	0.506208
physical evidence	0.503106

Table 8: Vizconde Massacre: 6 Months After

Crime Investigation

national	0.768269
investigation	0.725393
secretary	0.676848
bureau	0.668087
period	0.651219
suspects	0.610525
country	0.589908
crime	0.577354
reinvestigation	0.565068
nbi	0.544061
evidence	0.512984
file	0.502901

Vizconde Family

friends	0.750561
people	0.746146
family	0.66433
wife	0.660527
paraaque	0.630516
involved	0.621915
homes	0.618088
told	0.607636
supposed	0.596577
murders	0.525381
witness	0.511999
daughters	0.502754

Failure of Prosecution

co accused	0.715868
corroborated testimony	0.697234
period apply	0.697234
testimony witness	0.697234
national police	0.6949
defense alibi	0.66142
time crime	0.66142
charges filed	0.630004
crime happened	0.630004
failed establish	0.630004
police pnp	0.630004
prescriptive period	0.615335
prove guilt	0.592484
based testimony	0.53435
acquitted supreme	0.520877
crime evidence	0.520877
file charges	0.520877

nent when there is a particularly striking occurence within the case events - such as Emily Doe's letter in the Stanford rape case leading to the topic "rape event" and the words "victim", "woman" and "unconscious woman" being more prominent in the discourse; while the Vizconde Family's remembrance mass in the Vizconde massacre case lead to people discussing the topic "Vizconde family". Thus, it can be said that victims have a time-dependent role in the conversation space. Societal discussions, on the other hand, appear inconsistent as well - with topics such as "cultural discussion" or "perceived injustice" not being as prominent.

Even in two different contexts- in two different cultures and two different times -patterns in gender violence discourse appear to be similar - both focusing on institutions and perpetrators more than on victims and society. This opens up further questions still in terms of how much more understanding or progress still needs to be made in terms of how cases such as these are discussed, and if these kinds of attitudes towards discussions on gender violence exist across various cultures. In any case, for both events that were studied for this research, it appears that media discourse remains somewhat silent when it comes to analyzing societal culture; as a result, victims may still find themselves in the background of their own injustice.

References

Michele Black, Kathleen Basile, Matthew Breiding, and Sharon Smith. National intimate partner and sexual violence survey: 2010 summary report, November 2011. (Accessed on 07/10/2016).

Judith Butler. Performative acts and gender constitution: An essay in phenomenology and feminist theory. *Theatre Journal*, 40(4):519–531, 1988.

Louise du Toit. 5 how not to give rape political significance. *Confronting Global Gender Justice: Womens Lives, Human Rights*, page 85, 2010.

Bettina Frese, Miguel Moya, and Jesús L. Megías. Social perception of rape. *Journal of Interpersonal Violence*, 19(2):143–161, feb 2004.

Barbara Hudson. Restorative justice and gendered violence: Diversion or effective justice? *The British Journal of Criminology*, 42(3):616–634, 2002.

Niamh Joyce-Wojtas and Marie Keenan. Is restorative justice for sexual crime compatible with various criminal justice systems? *Contemporary Justice Review*, 19(1):43–68, 2016.

Daniel H. Kaiser. He said, she said: Rape and gender discourse in early modern russia. *Kritika: Explorations in Russian and Eurasian History*, 3(2):197–216, 2002.

Ven hwei Lo, Clement Y.K. So, and Guoliang Zhang. The influence of individualism and collectivism on internet pornography exposure, sexual attitudes, and sexual behavior among college students. *Chinese Journal of Communication*, 3(1):10–27, mar 2010.

Randelle Nixon Kristin Rodier, Michelle Meagher. Cultivating a critical classroom for viewing gendered violence in music video. *Feminist Teacher*, 23(1):63–70, 2012.

Catherine A MacKinnon. Sexuality, pornography, and method:" pleasure under patriarchy. *Ethics*, 99(2):314–346, 1989.

Donna Maeda. Transforming the representable: Asian women in anti-trafficking discourse. 2011.

Tasha A. Menaker and Cortney A. Franklin. Gendered violence and victim blame: subject perceptions of blame and the appropriateness of services for survivors of domestic sex trafficking, sexual assault, and intimate partner violence. *Journal of Crime and Justice*, 38(3):395–413, jan 2015.

A. Morrison, M. Ellsberg, and S. Bott. Addressing gender-based violence: A critical review of interventions. *The World Bank Research Observer*, 22(1):25–51, feb 2007.

Sara Murphy. Traumatizing feminism: Prevention discourse and the subject of sexual violence. *Traumatizing Theory: The Cultural Politics of Affect in and beyond Psychoanalysis*, 2007.

Dana M. Olwan. Gendered violence, cultural otherness, and honour crimes in canadian national logics. *The Canadian Journal of Sociology / Cahiers canadiens de sociologie*, 38(4):533–556, 2013.

Laura Sjoberg. Women and the genocidal rape of women. *Confronting Global Gender Justice: Womens lives, human rights*, page 21, 2010.

World Health Organization. Who — violence against women, January 2016. (Accessed on 07/10/2016).

Niwako Yamawaki. Differences between japanese and american college students in giving advice about help seeking to rape victims. *The Journal of Social Psychology*, 147(5):511–530, oct 2007.

Yvonne Yarbro-Bejarano. Diane gamboa's invasion of the snatch the politics and aesthetics of representing gendered violence. *Cultural Critique*, 85:61–83, 2013.

Investigating Phrase-Based and Neural-Based Machine Translation on Low-Resource Settings

Hai-Long Trieu, Duc-Vu Tran, Le-Minh Nguyen
Japan Advanced Institute of Science and Technology
`{trieulh,vu.tran,nguyenml}@jaist.ac.jp`

Abstract

Neural-based and phrase-based methods have shown the effectiveness and promising results in the development of current machine translation. The two methods are compared on some European languages, which show the advantages of the neural machine translation. Nevertheless, there are few work of comparing the two methods on low-resource languages, which there are only small bilingual corpora. The problem of unavailable large bilingual corpora causes a bottleneck for machine translation for such language pairs. In this paper, we present a comparison of the phrase-based and neural-based machine translation methods on several Asian language pairs: Japanese-English, Indonesian-Vietnamese, and English-Vietnamese. Additionally, we extracted a bilingual corpus from Wikipedia to enhance machine translation performance. Experimental results showed that when using the extracted corpus to enlarge the training data, neural machine translation models achieved the higher improvement and outperformed the phrase-based models. This work can be useful as a basis for further development of machine translation on the low-resource languages.

1 Introduction

Recent approaches have shown the promising results in the development of machine translation. During a long period from statistical models (Brown et al., 1990; Brown et al., 1993) to phrase-based models (Och et al., 1999; Koehn et al., 2003; Chiang, 2005) to recent neural-based methods (Sutskever et al., 2014; Cho et al., 2014), the phrase-based and neural-based become dominant methods in current machine translation. Statistical machine translation (SMT) systems achieve a high performance in many typologically diverse language pairs (Bojar et al., 2013). SMT can be applied to any pair of languages with minimal engineering effort (Bisazza and Federico, 2016). Meanwhile, neural machine translation (NMT) has obtained the state-of-the-art performance in machine translation for several languages including Czech-English, German-English, English-Romanian (Sennrich et al., 2016a). NMT has been proposed recently as a promising framework for machine translation, which learns sequence-to-sequence mapping based on two recurrent neural networks (Sutskever et al., 2014; Cho et al., 2014), called encoder-decoder networks. In a basic encoder-decoder network, the dimension of the context vector in the encoder is fixed, which leads to a low performance when translating for long sentences. In order to overcome the problem, (Bahdanau et al., 2015) proposed a method called attention mechanism, in which the model encodes the most relevant information in an input sentence rather than a whole input sentence into the fixed length context vector. NMT models with the attention mechanism have achieved significantly improvement in many language pairs (Jean et al., 2015; Gulcehre et al., 2015; Luong et al., 2015).

SMT and NMT models have shown successfully in language pairs in which large bilingual corpora are available such as English-German, English-French, Chinese-English, and English-Arabic. There are some work that evaluated the phrase-based versus neural-based methods such as

31st Pacific Asia Conference on Language, Information and Computation (PACLIC 31), pages 384–391
Cebu City, Philippines, November 16-18, 2017

the comparison of the two methods on English-German (Bentivogli et al., 2016), the comparison on 30 translation directions on the United Nations Parallel Corpus (Junczys-Dowmunt et al., 2016). Nevertheless, for low-resource settings like Asian language pairs which contain only small bilingual corpora, there are few work of the comparison of the two methods on such language pairs. Additionally, the problem of unavailable large bilingual corpora causes a bottleneck for machine translation on such languages.

In this work, we compared the SMT and NMT methods on several low-resource language pairs. The standard phrase-based SMT was used based on the work of (Koehn et al., 2007). The NMT model was used based on the state-of-the-art model (Sennrich et al., 2016a) in the WMT 2016,[1] which used encoder-decoder networks with attention mechanism and open-vocabulary translation. Experiments were conducted on Asian language pairs: Japanese-English, Indonesian-Vietnamese, and English-Vietnamese with only small bilingual corpora. Furthermore, in order to overcome the problem of unavailable large bilingual corpora, we extracted a bilingual corpus from Wikipedia to enhance machine translation on both SMT and NMT models. Moreover, we aim to evaluate the effects of enlarging training data to the two different machine translation methods and to the overall performance. Experimental results showed meaningful findings in the comparison of the two machine translation methods on the low-resource settings. This work can be useful as a basis for further development of NMT as well as machine translation in general on the low-resource languages. The scripts, corpora, and trained models used in this research can be found at the repository.[2]

2 Approaches

In this section, we discuss the two powerful approaches in machine translation currently: SMT and NMT. Additionally, we discuss one of the main factors that affects translation quality using both of the two machine translation approaches: bilingual corpora. For most language pairs in the world,

large bilingual corpora are unavailable (Wang et al., 2016), which causes a bottleneck for machine translation on such language pairs. We extracted a parallel corpus from comparable data to enhance machine translation.

2.1 Phrase-based Machine Translation

In phrase-based SMT models (Koehn et al., 2003; Och and Ney, 2004), phrases are used as atomic units for translation. An input sentence is separated into phrases. Then, each phrase is translated to target phrases, which can be reordered to produce the translation output.

Given a source sentence s, the goal is to find the best translation t, which maximizes both the adequacy and fluency. Assume that the source sentence s can be segmented into a sequence of phrases $s_1^I = s_1 s_2 ... s_I$, which can be decoded into a sequence of target phrases $t_1^J = t_1 t_2 ... t_J$. The best translation $\hat{t}$ can be modeled as follows.

$$\hat{t}_1^J = argmax \, P(t_1^J | s_1^I) \tag{1}$$

The translation probability $P(t_1^J | s_1^I)$ can be computed using the Bayes theorem.

$$P(t_1^J | s_1^I) = \frac{P(s_1^I | t_1^J) P(t_1^J)}{P(s_1^I)} \tag{2}$$

Since the objective is to find the best translation $\hat{t}$, it can be computed based on the two components as follows.

$$\hat{t}_1^J = argmax \, P(s_1^I | t_1^J) P(t_1^J) \tag{3}$$

Where: the component $P(s_1^I | t_1^J)$ is called *translation model*; $P(t_1^J)$ is called *language model*.

2.2 Neural Machine Translation

For neural machine translation, one of the basis frameworks is the encoder-decoder (Cho et al., 2014; Sutskever et al., 2014). The basis framework can be improved by several components such as attention mechanism, open-vocabulary. We discuss the basis framework and the components in this section.

NMT Models Given a source sentence $s = (s_1, ..., s_m)$, and a target sentence $t = (t_1, ..., t_n)$, the goal of a NMT is to model the conditional probability $p(t|s)$. This process bases on the encoder-decoder framework as proposed in (Cho et al., 2014; Sutskever et al., 2014).

$$logp(t|s) = \sum_{j=1}^{n} logp(t_i|\{t_1, ..., t_{i-1}\}, s, c) \quad (4)$$

in which, the source sentence s is represented by the context vector c using the encoder. For each time, a target word is translated based on the context vector using the decoder.

For the decoding, the probability of each target word t_i can be computed as follows.

$$p(t_i|\{t_1, ..., t_{i-1}\}, s, c) = softmax(h_i) \quad (5)$$

where h_i is the current target hidden state as in Equation 6.

$$h_i = f(h_{i-1}, t_{i-1}, c) \quad (6)$$

Finally, for the bilingual corpus B, the training objective is computed as in Equation 7.

$$I = \sum_{(s,t) \in B} -logp(t|s) \quad (7)$$

Attention Mechanism As shown in (Bahdanau et al., 2015), the translation performance decreases when translating long sentences. Instead of encoding entire the input sentence into the context vector, the most relevant information of the input sentence is encoded into the single, fixed-length vector. The representation c for the source sentences is set as follows.

$$c = [\bar{h_1}, ..., \bar{h_m}] \quad (8)$$

There are two stages in the function f in Equation 6: attention context and extended recurrent neural network (RNN). In the attention context, an alignment vector a_i is learned by comparing the previous hidden h_{i-1} with individual source hidden states in the context vector c; then the model derives a weighted average (c_i) of the source hidden states based on the alignment vector a_i. For the second stage, extended RNN, the RNN unit is expanded for the context vector c_i in addition to the previous hidden state h_{i-1} and the current input t_{i-1} to compute the next hidden state h_i.

Byte-pair Encoding In order to overcome the problem of out-of-vocabulary, (Sennrich et al., 2016b) proposed a method for open-vocabulary translation by encoding rare and unknown words as sequences of subword units. This is because various word classes can be translated by smaller units like compositional translation for compounds, phonological and morphological transformations for cognates and loanwords. In order to do that, words are segmented using byte-pair encoding that originally devised as a compression algorithm (Gage, 1994).

2.3 Bilingual Corpus: An Essential Resource in Machine Translation

Current Status Both of the two approaches: SMT and NMT require large bilingual corpora to train machine translation models. There are several large bilingual corpora which contain up to millions of parallel sentences such as European languages (Europarl corpus (Koehn, 2005), JRC-Acquis corpus (Steinberger et al., 2006)), English-French (the Canadian Hansard[3], the Giga-FrEn corpus[4]), and English-Chinese (the UM-Corpus (Tian et al., 2014)). Nevertheless, such large bilingual corpora are unavailable for most language pairs in the world (Irvine, 2013; Wang et al., 2016), which causes a bottleneck for both of the SMT and NMT machine translation methods. We extracted a bilingual corpus from comparable data in order to: i) investigate how the extracted bilingual corpus affects the two SMT and NMT approaches, and ii) enhance machine translation using SMT and NMT methods.

Extracting Bilingual Sentences from Wikipedia We extracted a bilingual corpus from Wikipedia, a large comparable data that contains a number of articles in the same domain in many languages. First, we extracted parallel titles of Wikipedia's articles based on the Wikipedia database dumps.[5] For a

---

[3]http://www.isi.edu/naturallanguage/download/hansard/
[4]http://www.statmt.org/wmt14/translation-task.html
[5]https://dumps.wikimedia.org/backup-index.html

language pair, the two resources were used to extract the parallel titles: the articles' titles and IDs in a particular language (ending with *-page.sql.gz*) and the interlanguage link records (file ends with *-langlinks.sql.gz*). Then, the title pairs were used to collect parallel articles using a crawler that we implemented on Java. After article pairs were collected, we preprocessed the data including: removing noisy characters, splitting sentences from paragraphs, word tokenization using the Moses scripts.[6] Finally, for each parallel article pair, sentences were aligned using the Microsoft sentence aligner (Moore, 2002), a powerful sentence alignment algorithm. The extracted bilingual corpus was used to improve SMT and NMT models.

3 Experiments

We conducted experiments on Asian language pairs: Japanese-English, Indonesian-Vietnamese, and English-Vietnamese using the two machine translation methods: SMT and NMT. Additionally, we extracted a bilingual corpus from Wikipedia to enhance the machine translation on both of the two methods.

3.1 Setup

For SMT models, we used the Moses toolkit (Koehn et al., 2007). The word alignment was trained using GIZA++ (Och and Ney, 2003) with the configuration *grow-diag-final-and*. A 5-gram language model of the target language was trained using KenLM (Heafield, 2011). For tuning, we used the batch MIRA (Cherry and Foster, 2012). For evaluation, we used the BLEU scores (Papineni et al., 2002).

For NMT models, we adapted the attentional encoder-decoder networks combined with byte-pair encoding (Sennrich et al., 2016a). In our experiments, we set the word embedding size 500, and hidden layers size of 1024. Sentences are filtered with the maximum length of 50 words. The minibatches size is set to 60. The models were trained with the optimizer Adadelta (Zeiler, 2012). The models were validated each 3000 minibatches based on the BLEU scores on development sets. We saved the models for each 6000 minibatches. For decoding, we used

---

[6]https://github.com/moses-smt/mosesdecoder/tree/master/scripts/tokenizer

beam search with the beam size of 12. We trained NMT models on an Nvidia GRID K520 GPU.

3.2 SMT vs. NMT on Low-Resource Settings

Experiments on Japanese-English We conducted experiments on Japanese-English using the Kyoto bilingual corpora (Neubig, 2011). The training data includes 329,882 parallel sentences. For the development and the test data, there are 1,235 parallel sentences in the development set and 1,160 parallel sentences in the test set (see Table 1 for the data sets).

	Train	Dev	Test
Sentences	329,882	1,235	1,160
ja Words	6,085,131	34,403	28,501
en Words	5,911,486	30,822	26,734
ja Vocabs	114,284	4,909	4,574
en Vocabs	161,655	5,470	4,912

Table 1: Bilingual data set of Japanese-English of the training set (Train), development set (Dev), and test set (Test), (ja: Japanese, en: English).

Experimental results of Japanese-English translation are showed in Table 2. The NMT model obtained 11.91 BLEU point on the development set. For the test set, the model achieved 14.91 BLEU point after training 20 epochs. Meanwhile, the SMT model obtained the higher performance: +1.18 BLEU point on the development set, and +2.86 BLEU point on the test set. The experimental results indicated that for a small bilingual corpus (329k parallel sentences of the Japanese-English Kyoto corpus), the SMT model showed the higher performance than the NMT model.

Model	Dev	Test
SMT	13.09	17.75
NMT	11.91	14.91

Table 2: Experimental results in Japanese-English translation (BLEU)

Experiments on Indonesian-Vietnamese We conducted experiments on the Indonesian-Vietnamese language pairs, which has yet investigated on machine translation to our best knowledge.

For training data, we used two resources: TED data (Cettolo et al., 2012) and the ALT corpus (Asian Language Treebank Parallel Corpus) (Thu et al., 2016). We extracted Indonesian-Vietnamese parallel sentences from the TED data. For the ALT corpus, we dived the Indonesian-Vietnamese bilingual corpus into three parts: 16,000 sentences for training, 1,000 sentences for the development set, and 1,084 sentences for the test set. We combined the Indonesian-Vietnamese TED data with the training set extracted from the ALT corpus to create 226,239 training sentence pairs. The data sets are described in Table 3.

	Train	Dev	Test
Sentences	226,239	1,000	1,084
id Words	1,932,460	22,736	25,423
vi Words	2,822,894	32,891	36,026
id Vocabs	52,935	4,974	5,425
vi Vocabs	29,896	3,517	3,751

Table 3: Bilingual data sets of Indonesian-Vietnamese translations (id:Indonesian, vi: Vietnamese).

We showed the experimental results of the Indonesian-Vietnamese translations in Table 4. The NMT model achieved 14.48 BLEU point on the development set and 14.98 BLEU point on the test set after training 22 epochs. Meanwhile, the SMT model obtained the much higher performance: 27.37 BLEU point on the development set and 30.17 BLEU point on the test set.

Model	Dev	Test
SMT	27.37	30.17
NMT	14.48	14.98

Table 4: Experimental results on Indonesian-Vietnamese translation (BLEU)

Experiments on English-Vietnamese We conducted experiments on English-Vietnamese using the data sets of the IWSLT 2015 machine translation shared task (Cettolo et al., 2015). The *constrained* training data contained 130k parallel sentences from the TED talks.[7] We used the *tst2012* for the devel-

opment set, *tst2013* and *tst2015* for the test sets. The data set are presented in Table 5.

Data	Sent.	Src Vocab.	Trg Vocab.
constr	131,019	50,118	54,565
unconstr	456,350	114,161	124,846
tst2012	1,581	3,713	3,958
tst2013	1,304	3,918	4,316
tst2015	1,080	3,175	3,528

Table 5: Data sets on the IWSLT 2015 experiments; **constr, unconstr**: the constrained, unconstrained training data set; **Src Vocab. (Trg Vocab.)**: the vocabulary size in the source (target) side of the corpus

In addition, we used two other data sets to enlarge the training data from the two resources: the corpus of National project VLSP (Vietnamese Language and Speech Processing)[8] and the EVBCorpus (Ngo et al., 2013). The two data sets were merged with the *constrained* data to create a large training data called *unconstrained* data. This aims to investigate how the large training data affects the SMT and NMT models.

System	tst2013	tst2015
constr (SMT)	26.54	24.42
constr (NMT)	23.59	17.27
unconstr(SMT)	27.19	25.41
unconstr(NMT)	26.71	22.30

Table 6: Experimental results English-Vietnamese translations (BLEU); **constr (SMT)**: the model trained on the constrained data using SMT; **unconstr (NMT)**: the model trained on the unconstrained data using NMT

Experimental results of English-Vietnamese are presented in Table 6. In overall, the SMT model obtained the higher performance than the NMT model (26.54 vs. 23.59 BLEU points on the *tst2013* using the *constrained* data, 25.41 vs. 22.30 BLEU points on the *tst2015* using the *unconstrained* data). Another point is the effect of enlarging the training data using the *unconstrained* data set. Enlarging the training data (increasing from 130k to 456k parallel sentences) improved both SMT and NMT models. Specifically, the SMT model achived +0.65

BLEU point on the *tst2013* and +0.99 BLEU point on the *tst2015*. The interesting point is that the NMT model showed the higher improvement than the SMT model when using the *unconstrained* data: +3.12 BLEU point on the *tst2013* and +5.03 BLEU point on the *tst2015*.

3.3 Improving SMT and NMT Using Comparable Data

Building An English-Vietnamese Bilingual Corpus from Wikipedia As presented in Section 2.3, we used the Wikpedia database dumps to extract parallel titles, which were updated on *2017-01-20*. After collecting, processing, and aligning sentences in parallel articles using the Microsoft sentence aligner (Moore, 2002), we obtained 408,552 parallel sentences for English-Vietnamese. The extracted corpus are available at the repository of this work.

Improving SMT and NMT models We evaluated the extracted bilingual corpus in improving SMT and NMT models. Experimental results are shown in Table 7. There are several interesting findings from this experiment. First, although using only the Wikipedia corpus to train SMT and NMT models, we obtained promising results: 20.34 BLEU point using SMT and 17.58 BLEU point using NMT on the *tst2015*. Second, when the Wikipedia corpus was merged with the *unconstrained* for the training data, both SMT and NMT models achieved the improvement. For the SMT model, the improvement was +0.09 BLEU point on the *tst2013* and +0.95 BLEU point on the *tst2015*. Meanwhile, the NMT model showed the higher improvement with +2.22 BLEU point on the *tst2013* and up to +4.51 BLEU point on the *tst2015*. The next interesting point is that when using the large training data (more than 800k parallel sentences of merging 456k sentences the *unconstrained* with 408k sentences of the Wikipedia corpus), the NMT model outperformed the SMT model: 28.93 BLEU point vs. 27.28 BLEU point on the *tst2013*, 26.81 BLEU point vs. 26.36 BLEU point on the *tst2015*.

4   Conclusion

Recent methods of phrase-based and neural-based have showed the promising directions in the development of machine translation. Neural ma-

System	tst2013	tst2015
wiki (SMT)	22.06	20.34
wiki (NMT)	18.43	17.58
unconstr(SMT)	27.19	25.41
unconstr(NMT)	26.71	22.30
unconstr+wiki(SMT)	27.28	26.36
unconstr+wiki(NMT)	28.93	26.81

Table 7: Experimental results of English-Vietnamese using the corpus extracted from Wikipedia (BLEU); **wiki (NMT)**: the model trained on the extracted corpus from Wikipedia using NMT models; **unconstr+wiki**: the unconstrained data was merged with the Wikipedia corpus for the training data

chine translation models have been applied successfully on several language pairs with large bilingual corpora available. The phrase-based and neural-based methods are also compared and evaluated on some European language pairs. Nevertheless, there is still a bottleneck in SMT and NMT on low-resource language pairs when large bilingual corpora are unavailable. In this work, we conducted a comparison of SMT and NMT methods on several Asian language pairs which contain small bilingual corpora: Japanese-English, Indonesian-Vietnamese, and English-Vietnamese. In addition, a bilingual corpus was extracted from Wikipedia to enhance the machine translation performance and investigate the effects of the extracted corpus on the two machine translation methods. Experimental results showed meaningful findings. For a small bilingual corpus, SMT models showed the better performance than NMT models. Nevertheless, when enlarging the training data with the extracted corpus, both SMT and NMT models were improved, in which NMT models showed the higher improvement and outperformed the SMT models. This work can be useful for further improvement for machine translation on the low-resource languages.

References

Dzmitry Bahdanau, Kyunghyun Cho, and Yoshua Bengio. 2015. Neural machine translation by jointly learning to align and translate. In *Proceedings of the International Conference on Learning Representations (ICLR)*.

Luisa Bentivogli, Arianna Bisazza, Mauro Cettolo, and Marcello Federico. 2016. Neural versus phrase-based machine translation quality: a case study. *arXiv preprint arXiv:1608.04631*.

Arianna Bisazza and Marcello Federico. 2016. A survey of word reordering in statistical machine translation: computational models and language phenomena. *Computational Linguistics*, 42(2):163–205, June.

Ondřej Bojar, Christian Buck, Chris Callison-Burch, Christian Federmann, Barry Haddow, Philipp Koehn, Christof Monz, Matt Post, Radu Soricut, and Lucia Specia. 2013. Findings of the 2013 Workshop on Statistical Machine Translation. In *Proceedings of the Eighth Workshop on Statistical Machine Translation*, pages 1–44. Association for Computational Linguistics, August.

Peter F Brown, John Cocke, Stephen A Della Pietra, Vincent J Della Pietra, Fredrick Jelinek, John D Lafferty, Robert L Mercer, and Paul S Roossin. 1990. A statistical approach to machine translation. *Computational linguistics*, 16(2):79–85.

Peter F Brown, Vincent J Della Pietra, Stephen A Della Pietra, and Robert L Mercer. 1993. The mathematics of statistical machine translation: Parameter estimation. *Computational linguistics*, 19(2):263–311.

Mauro Cettolo, Christian Girardi, and Marcello Federico. 2012. Wit3: Web inventory of transcribed and translated talks. In *Proceedings of the 16th Conference of the European Association for Machine Translation (EAMT)*, pages 261–268.

Mauro Cettolo, Jan Niehues, Sebastian Stüker, Luisa Bentivogli, Roldano Cattoni, and Marcello Federico. 2015. The iwslt 2015 evaluation campaign. *Proceedings of the International Workshop on Spoken Language Translation (IWSLT)*.

Colin Cherry and George Foster. 2012. Batch tuning strategies for statistical machine translation. In *Proceedings of HLT/NAACL*, pages 427–436. Association for Computational Linguistics.

David Chiang. 2005. A hierarchical phrase-based model for statistical machine translation. In *Proceedings of the 43rd Annual Meeting on Association for Computational Linguistics*, pages 263–270. Association for Computational Linguistics.

Kyunghyun Cho, Bart Van Merriënboer, Caglar Gulcehre, Dzmitry Bahdanau, Fethi Bougares, Holger Schwenk, and Yoshua Bengio. 2014. Learning phrase representations using rnn encoder-decoder for statistical machine translation. In *Proceedings of the Conference on Empirical Methods in Natural Language Processing (EMNLP)*.

Philip Gage. 1994. A new algorithm for data compression. *The C Users Journal*, 12(2):23–38.

Caglar Gulcehre, Orhan Firat, Kelvin Xu, Kyunghyun Cho, Loic Barrault, Huei-Chi Lin, Fethi Bougares, Holger Schwenk, and Yoshua Bengio. 2015. On using monolingual corpora in neural machine translation. In *CoRR 2015*.

Kenneth Heafield. 2011. Kenlm: Faster and smaller language model queries. In *Proceedings of the Sixth Workshop on Statistical Machine Translation*, pages 187–197. Association for Computational Linguistics.

Ann Irvine. 2013. Statistical machine translation in low resource settings. In *Proceedings of HLT/NAACL*, pages 54–61. Association for Computational Linguistics.

Sébastien Jean, Orhan Firat, Kyunghyun Cho, Roland Memisevic, and Yoshua Bengio. 2015. Montreal neural machine translation systems for wmt15. In *Proceedings of the Tenth Workshop on Statistical Machine Translation (WMT)*, pages 134–140.

Marcin Junczys-Dowmunt, Tomasz Dwojak, and Hieu Hoang. 2016. Is neural machine translation ready for deployment? a case study on 30 translation directions. *arXiv preprint arXiv:1610.01108*.

Philipp Koehn, Franz Josef Och, and Daniel Marcu. 2003. Statistical phrase-based translation. In *Proceedings of the 2003 Conference of the North American Chapter of the Association for Computational Linguistics on Human Language Technology-Volume 1*, pages 48–54. Association for Computational Linguistics.

Philipp Koehn, Hieu Hoang, Alexandra Birch, Chris Callison-Burch, Marcello Federico, Nicola Bertoldi, Brooke Cowan, Wade Shen, Christine Moran, Richard Zens, et al. 2007. Moses: Open source toolkit for statistical machine translation. In *Proceedings of ACL*, pages 177–180. Association for Computational Linguistics.

Philipp Koehn. 2005. Europarl: A parallel corpus for statistical machine translation. In *MT summit*, volume 5, pages 79–86. Citeseer.

Minh-Thang Luong, Hieu Pham, and Christopher D. Manning. 2015. Effective approaches to attention-based neural machine translation. In *Proceedings of the Conference on Empirical Methods in Natural Language Processing (EMNLP)*, pages 1412–1421.

Robert C Moore. 2002. *Fast and accurate sentence alignment of bilingual corpora*. Springer.

Graham Neubig. 2011. The Kyoto free translation task. http://www.phontron.com/kftt.

Quoc Hung Ngo, Werner Winiwarter, and Bartholomäus Wloka. 2013. Evbcorpus-a multi-layer english-vietnamese bilingual corpus for studying tasks in comparative linguistics. In *Proceedings of the 11th Workshop on Asian Language Resources (11th ALR within the IJCNLP2013)*, pages 1–9.

Franz Josef Och and Hermann Ney. 2003. A systematic comparison of various statistical alignment models. *Computational Linguistics*, 29(1):19–51.

Franz Josef Och and Hermann Ney. 2004. The alignment template approach to statistical machine translation. *Computational linguistics*, 30(4):417–449.

Franz Josef Och, Christoph Tillmann, Hermann Ney, et al. 1999. Improved alignment models for statistical machine translation. In *Proc. of the Joint SIGDAT Conf. on Empirical Methods in Natural Language Processing and Very Large Corpora*, pages 20–28.

Kishore Papineni, Salim Roukos, Todd Ward, and Wei-Jing Zhu. 2002. Bleu: a method for automatic evaluation of machine translation. In *Proceedings of ACL*, pages 311–318. Association for Computational Linguistics.

Rico Sennrich, Barry Haddow, and Alexandra Birch. 2016a. Edinburgh neural machine translation systems for wmt 16. In *Proceedings of the First Conference on Machine Translation (WMT)*.

Rico Sennrich, Barry Haddow, and Alexandra Birch. 2016b. Neural machine translation of rare words with subword units. In *Proceedings of the 54th Annual Meeting of the Association for Computational Linguistics (ACL)*.

Ralf Steinberger, Bruno Pouliquen, Anna Widiger, Camelia Ignat, Tomaz Erjavec, Dan Tufis, and Dániel Varga. 2006. The jrc-acquis: A multilingual aligned parallel corpus with 20+ languages. *arXiv preprint cs/0609058*.

Ilya Sutskever, Oriol Vinyals, and Quoc V Le. 2014. Sequence to sequence learning with neural networks. In *Advances in neural information processing systems (NIPS)*, pages 3104–3112.

Ye Kyaw Thu, Win Pa Pa, Masao Utiyama, Andrew Finch, and Eiichiro Sumita. 2016. Introducing the asian language treebank (alt). In *Proceedings of the Tenth International Conference on Language Resources and Evaluation (LREC)*, pages 1574–1578.

Liang Tian, Derek F Wong, Lidia S Chao, Paulo Quaresma, Francisco Oliveira, and Lu Yi. 2014. Um-corpus: A large english-chinese parallel corpus for statistical machine translation. In *LREC*, pages 1837–1842.

Pidong Wang, Preslav Nakov, and Hwee Tou Ng. 2016. Source language adaptation approaches for resource-poor machine translation. *Computational Linguistics*.

Matthew D Zeiler. 2012. Adadelta: an adaptive learning rate method. *CoRR*.

Japanese all-words WSD system using the Kyoto Text Analysis ToolKit

Hiroyuki Shinnou   Kanako Komiya   Minoru Sasaki   Shinsuke Mori
Ibaraki University, Department of Computer and Information Sciences
4-12-1 Nakanarusawa, Hitachi, Ibaraki 316–8511, Japan
hiroyuki.shinnou.0828@vc.ibaraki.ac.jp
{kanako.komiya.nlp, minoru.sasaki.01}@vc.ibaraki.ac.jp
Kyoto University, Yoshida Honcho, Sakyouku, Kyoto 606–8501, Japan
mori.shinsuke.8u@kyoto-u.ac.jp

Abstract

In this paper, we discuss Japanese all-words word sense disambiguation (WSD) and propose a new system KyWSD to achieve it. KyWSD uses the Kyoto Text Analysis ToolKit, a learning system building a Japanese morphological analysis model. It accepts plain Japanese text, segments it into words, and assigns a sense to each segmented word. KyWSD is open source software that can serve as the baseline system for a Japanese all-words WSD system. Therefore, it can be useful for several Japanese semantic analysis systems and is an advancement in all-words WSD technology. Furthermore, we show that Japanese all-words WSD involves a peculiar problem different from those of general WSD and that KyWSD is adaptable and highly precise.

1 Introduction

Word-sense disambiguation (WSD) is a basic procedure of semantic analysis, but it has not been widely used in practice. This is because current WSD systems adopt a supervised learning approach, limiting WSD target words. WSD for all words called "all-words WSD" has been studied for a long time (Navigli, 2009). However, a sense in many all-words WSD systems is defined as a concept, resulting in coarse granularity. Furthermore, the target language is generally English. Japanese all-words WSD has not been achieved, preventing easy access to it. Given this background, we created a Japanese all-words WSD system called *KyWSD*[1]. KyWSD is

useful for several Japanese semantic analysis systems. Using it, we can add sense features when we use a learning method to solve various NLP tasks, thereby improving precision.

The substance of KyWSD is a model built using the Kyoto Text Analysis ToolKit (KyTea)[2], a learning system. By executing KyTea using this model, KyWSD accepts plain Japanese text, segments it into words, and assigns a sense to each segmented word (Neubig et al., 2011). Briefly KyTea is a system learning a morphological analysis model. We build KyWSD using KyTea because all-words WSD can be regarded as a kind of morphological analysis. Therefore, KyTea contains a mechanism for learning a model to adapt to a target domain. The ability to use this mechanism provides KyWSD with high adaptability. For example, adding training data to KyWSD, senses to all words, but a target sense. Thus, KyWSD is an appropriate system for domain adaptation. As seen above, KyWSD provides great value as new use of KyTea.

We evaluated KyWSD using a Japanese dictionary task in Senseval-2 (Kiyoaki Shirai, 2001). Adding training data of this task to its original training data enabled KyWSD to perform better than a general supervised support vector machine (SVM) based learning method. This evaluation revealed a peculiar problem of Japanese all-words WSD through which it differs from general WSD.

---

[1] KyTea for WSD.

[2] http://www.phontron.com/kytea/

31st Pacific Asia Conference on Language, Information and Computation (PACLIC 31), pages 392–399
Cebu City, Philippines, November 16-18, 2017

2   Related Work

The availability of a supervised learning method for all-words WSD typically requires specifying the domain. Some systems using a supervised learning method have used all-words WSD tasks of SemEval-07 (Navigli et al., 2007), but these systems have a problem with scalability.

All-words WSD methods not using a supervised learning method are divided into two types: knowledge based methods and unsupervised learning methods (Kulkarni et al., 2010).

Lesk's method (Lesk, 1986), a well known classical knowledge based method uses a dictionary in which each sense of every word is provided with definition sentences. Lesk's method counts the overlapping words that are between the words used in the definition sentence and words that are surrounding the target word in the test sentence. Finally, the sense with the largest overlapping is selected. However, a knowledge based method generally cannot make use of the distribution of senses, resulting in low precision.

There are various unsupervised learning methods (Yarowsky, 1995; Izquierdo-Beviá et al., 2006; Zhong and Ng, 2009). Recently, methods using a generative model have been studied (Boyd-Graber et al., 2007; Tanigaki et al., 2013; Tanigaki et al., 2015; Komiya et al., 2015). These methods have higher precision than knowledge based methods, in general, and can be expected to improve in the future. However, current unsupervised learning methods have the problem that the sense assigned to a word is a concept, because such a method essentially uses the following heuristic: "If the context surrounding the sense a is similar to the context surrounding the sense b, then a is similar to b." In general, a and b are ambiguous, so we must measure the distance between a and b to use this heuristic. In the case which a and b are concepts, we can measure that distance. However, if a and b are senses defined in a dictionary, we cannot. This is the problem of sense granularity. In general, a sense defined in a dictionary is finer than a concept. Therefore, it is more difficult to assign a sense defined in a dictionary to a word than to assign a concept. KyWSD does the former using "Iwanami Kokugo Jiten[3]."

Furthermore, we must note that the input-output for an all-words WSD system using an unsupervised learning method is different from that of a general WSD system. The input of the former is a corpus, and the output is the same corpus, in which all words are assigned senses. When we input a sentence including a WSD target word to the system, it cannot assign a sense to the target word. This means that we cannot use these all-words WSD systems as general WSD systems.

Recently, methods for using the distributed representation of a word sense for all-words WSD have been studied (Chen et al., 2014)(Neelakantan et al., 2014). Here, we denote the distributed representation of the ith sense of the word w as s_i, and the distributed representation of the context of w as v. By measuring the similarity between s_i and v, we choose the s_i with the greatest similarity as the sense of w. This method is knowledge based and therefore has low precision. In general, such knowledge based methods lack the precision of a most frequent sense (MFS) method. A method for estimating MFS using the distributed representation of a word has been studied for this reason (Bhingardive et al., 2015).

KyWSD was constructed using a supervised method. Moreover, a sense in KyWSD is not a concept, but a sense in a dictionary.

Hatori et al. uses a similar supervised approach as KyWSD by treating the all-word WSD task as a sequence labelling problem (Hatori et al., 2008). They also regarded all-words WSD as a sequential labeling problem. To solve it, they used a conditional random field (CRF), but KyWSD uses pointwise prediction. This is the essential difference. Assigning a sense defined in a dictionary to a word, the sense s of a word w is not assigned to any word other than w. For this reason, we need not look fully sequentially for all-words WSD to assign a sense defined in a dictionary. Pointwise prediction is all that is required.

3   KyTea

All-words WSD is a same problem as part of speech tagging. For example, we do all-words WSD for following word segmented Japanese sentece:

／ 国民／ の／ 声／ を／ 聞く／

---

[3] "岩波国語辞典 (Iwanami Kokugo Jiten)" is used as a standard dictionary for Japanese WSD task.

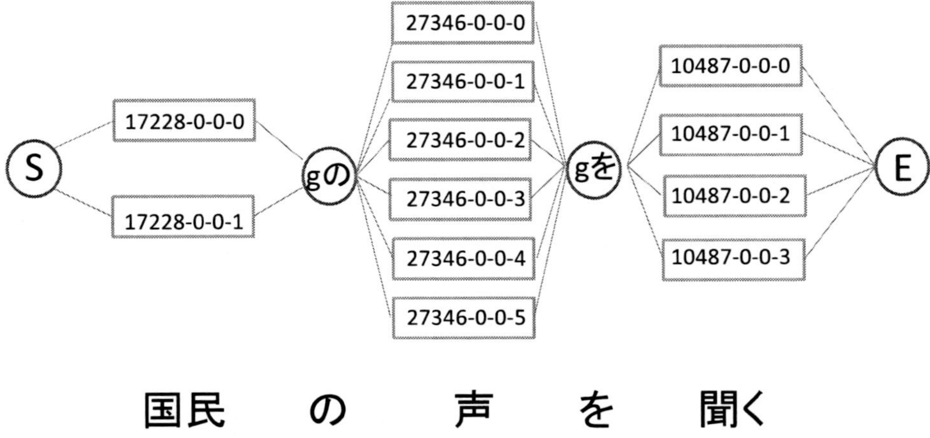

Figure 1: Directed graph for all-words WSD

The word "国民", "声", and "聞く" in the sentence has multi senses. Concretely, the sense IDs are '17228-0-0-0' and '17228-0-0-1' for the word "国民", '27346-0-0-0','27346-0-0-1', · · ·, '27346-0-0-5' for the word "声", and '10487-0-0-0','10487-0-0-1' and '10487-0-0-3' for the word "聞く". The problem of all-words WSD is the estimate of the correct combination of these sense IDs. Regarding the sense ID as the part of speech, all-words WSD is a same problem as part of speech tagging. That is, to solve all-words WSD, we make a directed graph like Figure 1, and then estimate the optimum path from the start node 'S' to the end node 'E'. To do this effectively, we uses KyTea.

KyTea is essentially a system for building a model of a word segmentation system. In general, a word segmentation problem can be modeled as a sequential labeling problem. However, KyTea models such a problem as a binary classification problem that judges whether each two characters are segmented or not. In learning, KyTea uses only n-grams surrounding the target place using a linear SVM or logistic regression. The training data of KyTea are very simple, just a word-segmented text. Hence, it is easy to scale the model up and adapt the model to another target domain.

We can create a tagger system using KyTea. When a tag is given to a segmented word in the train-ing data, KyTea learns the model for assigning the tag to each segmented word. If the tag is the part of speech, KyTea learns a general morphological analysis model. The tag can be used for far more than the part of speech. For example, the pronunciation and BIO tags for a name recognition task have been used (Neubig and Mori, 2010)(Sasada et al., 2015).

In this study, we set the sense of the word as the tag. Using this setting, we can build an all-words WSD system based on a sense-tagged corpus and KyTea.

4   KyWSD

4.1   System Overview

KyWSD is a Japanese all-words WSD system, and we can try it on the following demonstration site:

```
http://nlp.dse.ibaraki.ac.jp/
~shinnou/cgi-bin/demo.html
```

The Figure 2 shows a demonstration of KyWSD. Input a Japanese sentence in the text field, and push the 'KyWSD' button. The analysis result by KyWSD will be shown. In this demonstration site, the given sentence is segmented into words, and the part of speech and the sense ID for each segmented word are assigned.

Note that this demonstration site is just built in order to get the picture of KyWSD. When we use

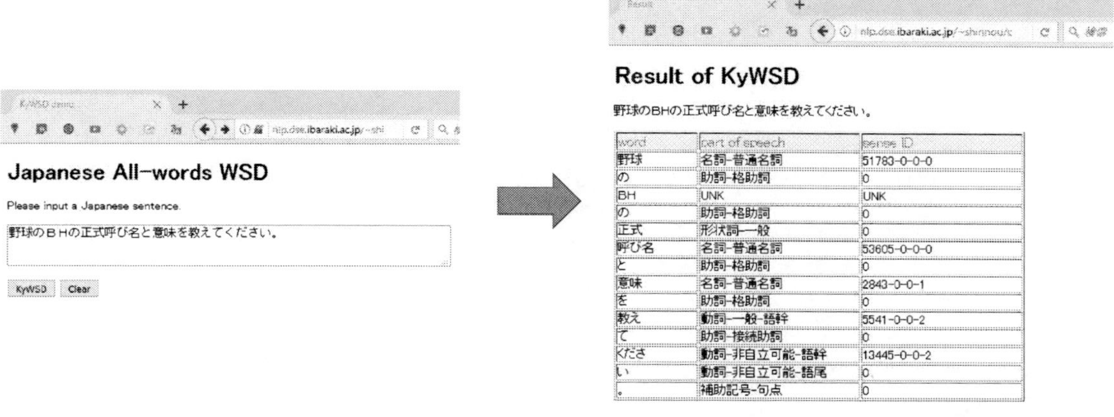

Figure 2: Demonstration of KyWSD

KyWSD for real, commands are used in the character terminal, that is CUI interface. We can get a set of KyWSD from the following:

```
http://nlp.dse.ibaraki.ac.jp/
     ~shinnou/wsd/kywsd.zip
```

KyWSD is essentially a model of KyTea. Therefore, KyWSD works under the operating system supported by KyTea, Linux, Windows, and Mac OS.

We show an example of KyWSD execution in Figure 2. The `wsd.mod` is the model learned by KyTea. The input is the plain Japanese text file (`sample.txt`), and the output is that shown in Figure 1, i.e., the input texts are segmented into words, and the part of speech and the sense are assigned to each segmented word. However, a sense is assigned for content words, including nouns and verb or adjective, stems, but for other kinds of words the sense s set to "0." The "UNK" in Figure 1 means that the word "ＢＨ" appears in neither the training data nor the dictionary.

KyWSD can omit the first tags, i.e., the POS tags with the option `-notag 1`. In addition, it can output the confidence degree with the option `-out conf`. The confidence degree is the probability when option wsd.mod is used because logistic regression is used for the estimation. For example, KyWSD outputs the word senses for the word "意味" (meaning) as follows.

```
意味/2843-0-0-1&2843-0-0-2&2843-0-0-3
```

This shows that the senses of "意味" are three, i.e., 2843-0-0-1, 2843-0-0-2, and 2843-0-0-3. The confidence degree of the word sense of "意味" is as follows.

```
0.807761&0.108979&0.0807573
```

This shows that the probabilities of the word senses 2843-0-0-1,2843-0-0-2, and 2843-0-0-3 are 0.807761, 0.108979, and 0.0807573, respectively. This degree enables KyWSD to use active learning easily.

4.2 Building of KyWSD

KyWSD is built by providing a sense-tagged corpus to KyTea as training data. As the sense-tagged corpus, we used a corpus developed by Okumura Laboratory at Tokyo Institute of Technology. This corpus consists of core data of the Balanced Corpus of Contemporary Written Japanese (BCCWJ) (Maekawa, 2007). It contains 1,980 documents of six genres, and all multisense words in them are assigned a sense defined in the dictionary "Iwanami Kokugo Jiten." There are 114,696 assigned senses and 4,916 types of senses.

It is easy to translate the above corpus into training data for KyTea, but there is a problem, Japanese inflection. A Japanese verb and adjective consist of

```
> cat sample.txt
野球のＢＨの正式呼び名と意味を教えてください。

> kytea -model wsd.mod < sample.txt
野球/名詞-普通名詞/51783-0-0-0 の/助詞-格助詞/0 ＢＨ/UNK/UNK の/助詞-格助詞/0
正式/形状詞-一般/0 呼び名/名詞-普通名詞/53605-0-0-0 と/助詞-格助詞/0
意味/名詞-普通名詞/2843-0-0-1 を/助詞-格助詞/0 教え/動詞-一般-語幹/5541-0-0-2
て/助詞-接続助詞/0 くださ/動詞-非自立可能-語幹/13445-0-0-2 い/動詞-非自立可能-語尾/0
。/補助記号-句点/0

>kytea -model wsd.mod -notag 1 -out conf < sample.txt
野球/51783-0-0-0 の/0&39930-0-1-3&40065-0-0-0 ＢＨ/UNK
の/0&39930-0-1-3&39930-0-1-1 正式/0 呼び名/53605-0-0-0
と/0&37713-0-0-1&37446-0-0-2 意味/2843-0-0-1&2843-0-0-2&2843-0-0-3
を/0 教え/5541-0-0-2&5541-0-0-1&5541-0-0-3 て/0&35369-0-0-0
くださ/13445-0-0-2&0 い/0&1707-0-0-2&52935-0-0-3 。/0

    ・・・ (omit) ・・・

1 0.999999&7.94354e-07&1.23533e-07 1 1&6.47248e-08&3.92486e-08 1 1
1&1.8927e-09&1.8105e-09 0.807761&0.108979&0.0807573 1
0.863406&0.135187&0.0012201 1&4.35077e-09 0.999236&0.00076433
0.999999&1.22639e-07&8.67671e-08 1
```

Figure 3: Example of KyWSD execution

a stem and a desinence, and the desinence changes depending on modality and tense. In general, a Japanese word segmentation system regards the combined stem and desinence as one word, sometimes resulting in a word having different character sequences. KyTea recognizes these words as different words. For example, the word "書く (write)" changes to "書か (write)" + "ない (not)" when the word is used in the negative form. The word "書く (write)" and "書か (write)" are essentially the same, but have different character sequences. To overcome this problem, we define the stem as the word, i.e. all verbs and adjectives in the corpus are separated into the stem and the desinence. Note that the SA-row irregular verb "する" is an exception, because its stem is not fixed. However, the KA-row irregular verb "来る" is not an exception, because the sound of its stem is not fixed, but its character is fixed as "来".

KyTea can use dictionaries in learning. A sense of the word not appearing in the training data is assigned by the dictionary. By registering MFS for a word in the dictionary, KyWSD can output MFS as the default sense. KyWSD registers the first sense of a word in "Iwanami Kokugo Jiten."

5 Evaluation

5.1 Precision

We evaluated the precision of KyWSD, but it is difficult to measure the precision of an all-words WSD system. Here, we investigate the precision of KyWSD using test data of a Japanese dictionary task in Senseval-2 (Kiyoaki Shirai, 2001). This task has 100 WSD target words (50 nouns and 50 verbs). For each target word, 100 test instances are provided for a total of 10,000 test instances.

First, we investigate the precision of a standard method, a supervised learning method using an SVM. For each target word, 175 training instances are provided on average. Using these training data and the following six features (e1 to e6) for WSD,

[4] we build the SVM classifier for each target word.

e1: the word w_{i-1}
e2: the word w_{i+1}
e3: two content words in front of w_i
e4: two content words behind w_i
e5: thesaurus ID number of e3
e6: thesaurus ID number of e4

In 10,000 test instances, 7,244 instances were identified correctly using the above SVM classifiers. This means that the precision (i.e., F-value) of a standard supervised method is 0.7244.

Next, we translate test data to plain text and input it to KyWSD. As a result, every words in the text is assigned its sense. If the target word in a test instance is correctly segmented, and the correct sense is assigned to the word, then we judge it to be a correct answer. Among 10,000 test instances, Ky-WSD correctly segmented 9,935 target words, and correctly assigned 6,258 senses to them. That is, the precision is 0.6571, the recall is 0.6528, and the F-value is 0.6549.

The F-value of KyWSD is lower than that of an SVM. One reason is that the problem setting of all-words WSD is more difficult than that of general WSD. In general WSD, the sense list L_w of the target word w is given in advance, requiring us to select only one sense in L_w. In contrast, L_w is not given in all-words WSD. In Japanese, there are many words with the same character sequence. Therefore, the real sense list L'_w of the target word w in all-words WSD is larger than the L_w in general WSD.

For example, the Japanese word "間" has six types of pronunciation: "あい (21)", "あいだ (105)", "あわい (1432)", "かん (9518)", "けん (15147)" and "ま (48408)" [5]. Each of these six words is listed in "Iwanami Kokugo Jiten" as one word. The word "間" is one of the target words in the Japanese dictionary task in Senseval-2, but the sense listed for this word is that of the word "あいだ (105)" only. This problem has been ignored in conventional Japanese WSD. However, it is a serious problem in Japanese

all-words WSD, and we must take measures to address it.

In the above experiment, KyWSD output 1,372 incorrect senses because KyWSD selected a sense not belonging to L_w. If KyWSD does not select such senses, the number of evaluation target instances changes to 8,563, and the correct answers for them number 6,258. Therefore, the precision of KyWSD is 0.7623 and the F-value is 0.7076.

5.2 Adaptability

The principal advantage of KyWSD is its ease of adaptation. The new adapted model can be learned as a consequence of adding training data to the current model. In this section, we show this using the above experimental data. In the above experiment, KyWSD did not use the training data provided by that task. Here, we adapt the model of KyWSD by using it for that task. Note that only senses of target words are included in the training data.

As a result, among 10,000 test instances, the new KyWSD correctly segmented 9,938 target words, and assigned 6,986 correct senses for them. That is, the precision is 0.7030, the recall is 0.6986, and the F-value is 0.7008. Moreover, as explained above, ignoring senses not in the sense list provided by that task, there are 6,986 correct senses for 8,953 answered instances. Therefore, the precision is 0.7803, and the F-value is improved to 0.7395. This value is better than that of a supervised learning method using an SVM.

5.3 Use for document classification

In this section, we apply KyWSD to document classification.

In document classification, a document is translated to a vector using a bag-of-words model. That is, the learning feature is each word. A word is given a sense using KyWSD. Thus, the sense is added to the learning features.

We downloaded 316 documents from the netnews site:http://news.goo.ne.jp/. This document set has five categories: politics, economics, national, society and sports. The classifier is learned using naive Bayes method. We evaluated it using leave-one-out cross validation. Using words as the learning feature, the number of correct classifica-

---

[4]Suppose that the target word is w_i which is the i-th word in the sentence.

[5]The number in a parenthesis means the word ID in "Iwanami Kokugo Jiten."

tions was 246. Using words and senses as the learning feature, the number was 247.

This improvement is only slight, but it is very easy to add a sense to the learning features using KyWSD. Therefore, KyWSD can be used for far more than document classification.

6 Conclusion

In this paper, we introduced the Japanese all-words WSD system called KyWSD, which we produced and launched. KyWSD uses KyTea, a learning system for building a Japanese morphological analysis model. KyWSD provides great value as new use of KyTea. KyWSD estimates senses using pointwise prediction. It is simple, and adapting the model to another domain is easy. Through experiments, we showed that the precision of KyWSD is comparable to that of a supervised learning method, and that Japanese all-words WSD has a peculiar problem different from those of general WSD.

KyWSD is useful for many Japanese semantic analysis systems, and can add senses to the learning features of various NLP learning systems. It clearly deserves further attention.

Acknowledgments

The work reported in this article was supported by the NINJAL collaborative research project ' Development of all-words WSD systems and construction of a correspondence table between WLSP and IJD by these systems.'

References

Sudha Bhingardive, Dhirendra Singh, V Redkar Murthy, Hanumant Redkar, and Pushpak Bhattacharyya. 2015. Unsupervised Most Frequent Sense Detection using Word Embeddings. In *HLT-NAACL-2015*, pages 1238–1243.

Jordan L Boyd-Graber, David M Blei, and Xiaojin Zhu. 2007. A topic model for word sense disambiguation. In *EMNLP-CoNLL-2007*, pages 1024–1033.

Xinxiong Chen, Zhiyuan Liu, and Maosong Sun. 2014. A Unified Model for Word Sense Representation and Disambiguation. In *EMNLP-2014*, pages 1025–1035.

Jun Hatori, Yusuke Miyao, and Jun'ichi Tsujii. 2008. Word Sense Disambiguation for All Words using Tree-Structured Conditional Random Fields. In *COLING-2008*, pages 43–46.

Rubén Izquierdo-Beviá, Lorenza Moreno-Monteagudo, Borja Navarro, and Armando Suárez. 2006. Spanish all-words semantic class disambiguation using Cast3LB corpus. In *MICAI 2006: Advances in Artificial Intelligence*, pages 879–888.

Kiyoaki Shirai. 2001. SENSEVAL-2 Japanese Dictionary Task. In *SENSEVAL-2*, pages 33–36.

Kanako Komiya, Yuto Sasaki, Hajime Morita, Hiroyuki Shinnou, Minoru Sasaki, and Yoshiyuki Kotani. 2015. Surrounding Word Sense Model for Japanese All-words Word Sense Disambiguation. In *PACLIC-29*, pages 35–43.

Anup Kulkarni, Mitesh M Khapra, Saurabh Sohoney, and Pushpak Bhattacharyya. 2010. CFILT: Resource conscious approaches for all-words domain specific WSD. In *SemEval-2010*, pages 421–426.

Michael Lesk. 1986. Automatic sense disambiguation using machine readable dictionaries: how to tell a pine cone from an ice cream cone. In *the 5th annual international conference on Systems documentation*, pages 24–26.

Kikuo Maekawa. 2007. Design of a Balanced Corpus of Contemporary Written Japanese. In *Symposium on Large-Scale Knowledge Resources (LKR2007)*, pages 55–58.

Roberto Navigli, Kenneth C. Litkowski, and Orin Hargraves. 2007. SemEval-2007 Task 07: Coarse-grained English All-words Task. In *SemEval-2007*, pages 30–35.

Roberto Navigli. 2009. Word sense disambiguation: A survey. *ACM Computing Surveys (CSUR)*, 41(2):10.

Arvind Neelakantan, Jeevan Shankar, Alexandre Passos, and Andrew McCallum. 2014. Efficient Non-parametric Estimation of Multiple Embeddings per Word in Vector Space. In *EMNLP-2014*, pages 1059–1069.

Graham Neubig and Shinsuke Mori. 2010. Word-based Partial Annotation for Efficient Corpus Construction. In *LREC-2010*.

Graham Neubig, Yosuke Nakata, and Shinsuke Mori. 2011. Pointwise Prediction for Robust, Adaptable Japanese Morphological Analysis. In *ACL-HLT-2011*, pages 529–533.

Tetsuro Sasada, Shinsuke Mori, Tatsuya Kawahara, and Yoko Yamakata. 2015. Named Entity Recognizer Trainable from Partially Annotated Data. In *PACLING-2015*.

Koichi Tanigaki, Mitsuteru Shiba, Tatsuji Munaka, and Yoshinori Sagisaka. 2013. Density maximization in context-sense metric space for all-words wsd. In *ACL-2013*, pages 884–893.

Koichi Tanigaki, Shuichi Tokumoto, Tatsuji Munaka, and Yoshinori Sagisaka. 2015. Hierarchical bayesian word sense disambiguation for mapping context space to sense space (in japanese). In *IPSJ SIG on NLP*, pages NL–220–5.

David Yarowsky. 1995. Unsupervised word sense disambiguation rivaling supervised methods. In *ACL-95*, pages 189–196.

Zhi Zhong and Hwee Tou Ng. 2009. Word sense disambiguation for all words without hard labor. In *IJCAI-2009*, pages 1616–1622.

Revisiting Tones in Twic East Dinka

Yu-Leng Lin

Hong Kong Polytechnic University /
Department of Chinese and Bilingual Studies,
Hung Hom, Hong Kong

Abstract

This work is based on data elicited from a native speaker of the Twic East variety of Dinka. It focuses on tones, and shows that tones in Dinka can alter syntactic categories and word meaning, mark direct objects, indicate whether objects are viewable/present and distinguish plurality.

1. Introduction

This paper investigates tones in Twic East Dinka (a variety of Dinka), a Western Nilotic language spoken in South Sudan. Some literature reports that Luanyjang (Remijsen and Ladd 2008), Nyarweng (Remijsen 2010) Dinka have four contrastive tones and that Agar Dinka has three (Andersen 1992-1994). I am not aware of any literature touching on the tonal system of Twic East Dinka or the interface between tone and other phonological phenomena, morphology, syntax and semantics, except for one study on Twic East Dinka syntax (Yuan 2013). Three research questions have motivated this study: (1) how many surface contrastive tones does Twic East Dinka have; (2) What functions do tones have in phonology, morphology, syntax and semantics and (3) What are the contexts of tone sandhi in Twic East Dinka?

In general, tone is unlike accent and intonation. Tone can distinguish words lexically or grammatically, and tonal information is present as part of lexical representation. Accent can distinguish words, and typically two components, 'tone' and 'no tone', form a lexical contrast. For instance, in certain languages, H tone (accented) is active in phonological systems, and L (unaccented and treated as 'no tone') is supplied to the rest of toneless syllables or vice versa. Intonation cannot distinguish words lexically or grammatically, but it can be used in phrasal level. For instance, it can express emphasis or make a distinction between interrogative sentences (i.e., yes-no questions) and declarative sentences (see more discussion about tone, intonation and accent in Inkelas and Zec 1988, and Yip, 2002).

The paper is organized as follows. Section 2 presents background information about the language consultant. Section 3 shows five contrastive tone groups with corresponding vocabulary and pitch values for each tone group. Section 4 introduces the five functions of tones in Twic East Dinka phonology, morphology, syntax or semantics. Section 5 explores the contexts of tone sandhi. Section 6 concludes this paper.

400

31st Pacific Asia Conference on Language, Information and Computation (PACLIC 31), pages 400–406
Cebu City, Philippines, November 16-18, 2017

2. Language consultant

The language consultant was born and raised in Southern Sudan, speaking the Twic East dialect of Dinka.

He came to Canada to obtain his bachelor's degree at the University of Toronto. He was 21 years old, a fourth-year undergraduate student, when the elicitation sessions were conducted September-December, 2011.

3. Five Surface Contrastive Tones

In Twic East Dinka, the writing system does not encode tones as tonal languages like Mandarin do. With this concern, careful elicitation is necessary in order to investigate the exact number of tone values in Twic East Dinka. Currently five citation tones have been found, as presented in Table 1.

(ˆ) (tone 21) (Figure 1)	(ˉ) (tone 1) (Figure 2)	(ˉ) (tone 2) (Figure 3)	(ˉ) (tone 3) (Figure 4)	(ˉ) (tone 4) (Figure 5)
(1) [die:r²¹] 'below the knee'	(7) [ɣam¹] 'thigh'	(13) [tuɔŋ²] 'egg'	(19) [nɔk³] 'feather'	(25) [piu⁴] 'water'
(2) [ruɔn²¹] 'year'	(8) [die:r¹] 'worry'	(14) [ʈʊk²] 'end'	(20) [wɪn³] 'cow'	(26) [ɲi:l⁴] 'python'
(3) [mɪɛm²¹] 'hair'	(9) [kɔ:r¹] 'elbow, tornado'	(15) [piɔ²] 'heart'	(21) [ca³] 'milk'	(27) [tɕɔl⁴] 'rock'
(4) [ʈi:m²¹] 'trees'	(10) [ri:ɔ:c¹] 'fear'	(16) [ku:r²] 'stone'	(22) [diek³] 'three'	(28)[tɕa⁴] 'milk'
(5) [wa:r²¹] 'shoe'	(11) [ra:n¹] 'person'	(17) [cɔk²] 'leg'	(23) [ɣɔɣ³] 'cows'	(29) [tul⁴] 'hole'
(6) [kuin²¹] 'food'	(12) [kar] 'run'	(18) [da:r²] 'tiredness'	(24) [gʌc³] 'people'	(30) [ʈin⁴] 'see'

Table 1: Five citation tones

In order to determine the exact tone values of the five tones and to check whether the five tones are falling, level, rising, or contour, this paper examines five different words with these five tones by using Praat (see Figure 1-5).

Specially, the starting pitch value of Tone 21 is 125 Hz, the highest pitch value of Tone 21 is 150, and the ending pitch value of Tone 21 is 104, all of which show a falling curve. The average pitch values for Tone 2, Tone 3, and Tone 4 individually are: 124, 141, 163 and 173. After looking at the exact tonal values of these five tones, we know that only one tone is falling (ˆ), and the others are all level (ˉ) (see Yip (2002) and Hyman (2010) for the convention of tones). Based on the phonetic facts, this paper treats the five tones as Tone 21 (ˆ), Tone 1 (ˉ), Tone 2 (ˉ), Tone 3 (ˉ) and Tone 4 (ˉ) throughout. Interestingly, the number of vowels in the Tone 21 group is always greater than one.

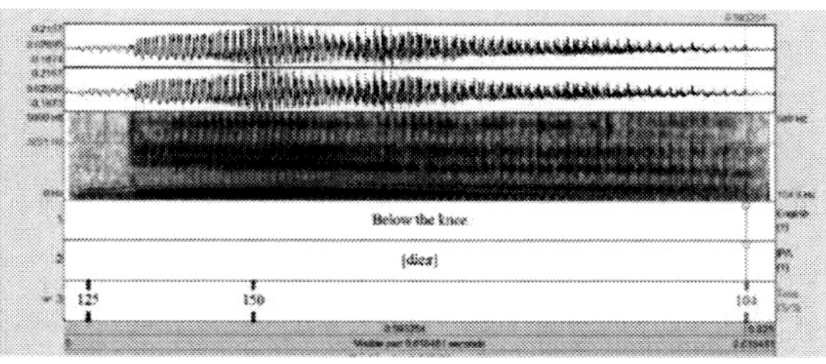

Figure 1 (Tone 21: beginning point = 125; highest point = 150 and end point = 104)

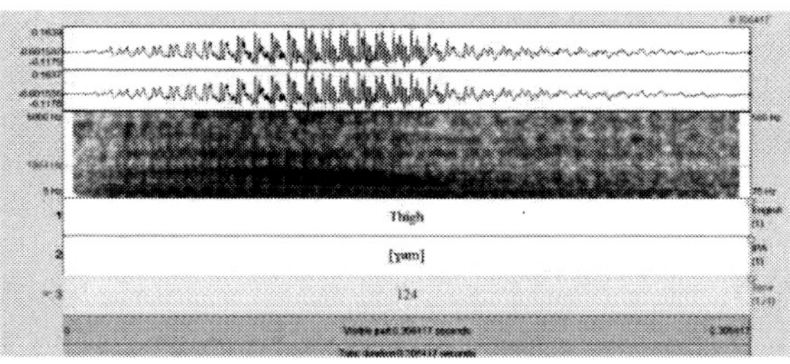

Figure 2 (Tone 1: average pitch value = 124)

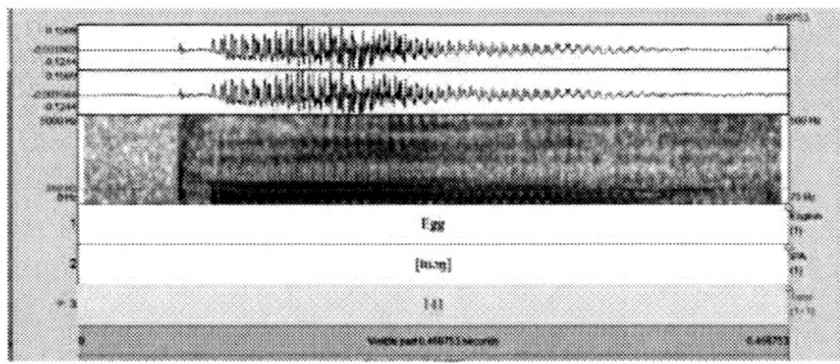

Figure 3 (Tone 2: average pitch value = 141)

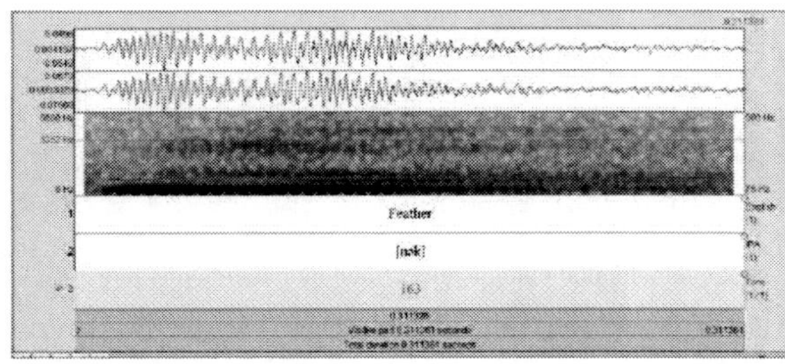

Figure 4 (Tone 3: average pitch value = 163)

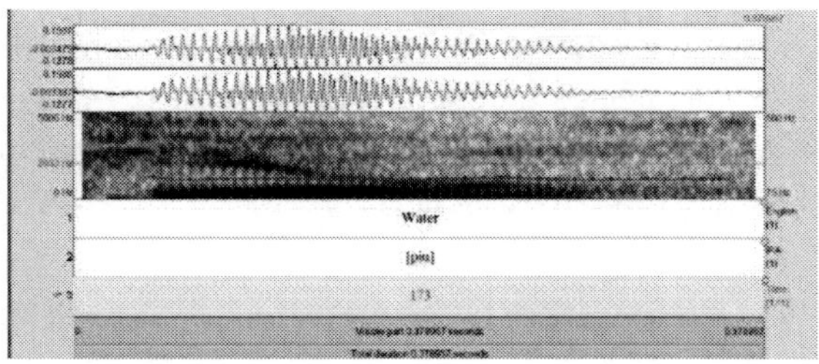

Figure 5 (Tone 4: average pitch value = 173)

In addition to the above discussion, two remaining issues need to be clarified. The first issue is that the language consultant said that sometimes it is harder to distinguish Tone 3 from Tone 4, because they sound very similar. It is also confirmed in my phonetic spectrograms that the tonal difference between Tone 3 'feather' (see Figure 4) and Tone 4 'water' (see Figure 5) is only 10 and that both of them are level instead of falling. Furthermore, it seems that we cannot distinguish or predict the contexts of Tone 3 and Tone 4. That is, words with these two tones individually could occur in syllables with short or long nuclei (i.e., one or two vowels). Therefore, if the tones are not perceptually distinct and their contexts of occurrence are quite similar, is it possible that Tone 3 and Tone 4 are actually one tone rather than two separate tones?

The other remaining issue is that someone may ask why Tone 21 and Tone 1 are not classified into the same contrast since the beginning pitch value of Tone 21 is roughly the same as the average pitch value of Tone 1 (125 vs. 124). However, I treat them as two different tone contrasts in terms of two reasons. First, in phonetic spectrograms, Tone 21 shows a falling curve, but Tone 1 shows a horizontal line. Second, in my current data, the contexts in which each tone occurs is not the same. Specifically, words with Tone 21 always have at least two vowels in the syllable, while the words with Tone 1 could have one, two, three or even four vowels in the syllable.

4. Five Functions of Tones in Phonology, Morphology and Syntax

In this section, the bulk of data will be presented and will show that Twic East Dinka tones bear five functions in phonology, morphology, syntax or semantics. First, tones can distinguish words lexically (see Table 2). For examples, (31) [akɔɬ²] means 'sun', but if speakers pronounce this word with tone 1 (i.e., (32) [akɔɬ¹]) instead of tone 2, then the meaning will be 'day, afternoon'.

Tone 21 vs. Tone 1	Tone 2 vs. Tone 1	Tone 1 vs. Tone 4	Tone 4 vs. Tone 2
(1) [die:r²¹] 'below the knee' (8) [die:r¹] 'worry'	(31) [akɔɬ²] 'sun' (32) [akɔɬ¹] 'day, afternoon'	(35) [ki:r¹] 'Nile' (36) [ki:r⁴] 'star'	(39) [ʈɔn⁴] 'thought' (40) [ʈɔn²] 'bull'
	(33) [cam⁴] 'eat' (V) (34) [cam¹] 'left (side)'	(37) [tɕʊm¹] 'special type of tree' (38) [tɕʊm³] 'planting'	(41) [liep⁴] 'tongue' (42) [liep2] 'tongues'

Table 2 Minimal pairs

Second, tones can distinguish singulars from plurals grammatically (See Table 3). That is, singulars are different from plurals only in tone values (cf. (43)-(52)). Moreover, plurals can be distinguished from singulars in two other ways: (i) the singular-plural contrast can be expressed by means of consonant or vowel mutation (in addition to potential tonal shift) (cf. (53)-(62)). Second, singular and plural can be distinguished by suppletion ((11) [ra:n¹] 'person' vs. (24) [gʌc³] 'people').

Changing tones only	Changing tones and certain segments
(43) [kin⁴] 'hand' [SG] (44) [kin¹] 'hands' [PL]	(53) [jɪt⁴] 'ear' [SG] (54) [jɪh¹] 'ears' [PL]
(45) [ŋɪŋ¹] 'eye' [SG] (46) [ŋɪŋ²] 'eyes' [PL]	(55) [ɣum¹] 'nose' [SG] (56) [ɰum²] 'noses' [PL]
(47) [θɔk²] 'mouth' [SG] (48) [θɔk¹] 'mouths' [PL]	(57) [riuö²] 'nail' [SG] (58) [riuːp¹] 'nails' [PL]
(49) [liep⁴] 'tongue' [SG] (50) [liep²] 'tongues' [PL]	(59) [a²mal¹] 'sheep' [SG] (60)[a²mel²]
(51) [njul¹] 'knee' [SG] (52) [njul⁴] 'knees' [PL]	(61) [bu²ro¹] 'cat' [SG] (62) [bu¹ra¹] 'cats' [PL]

Table 3 Singular vs. plural

Third, words can change their syntactic category by alternating tonal values or segments (see Table 4). In Twic East Dinka, all verbs and adjectives should be inserted in sentences (cf. (70)-(76)). If you want to present these lexicon without putting into the sentences/phrases, they have to be presented in the form of nouns (cf. (63)-(69)).

Standing alone	In phrases or sentences
(63) [dɪr⁴] 'bigness' [N]	(70) [dɪt¹] 'big' [Adj]
(64) [dɪ²el¹] 'red' [N]	(71) [dɪl²] 'red' [Adj]
(65) [lɔ²¹] 'go' [N]	(72) [lɔ⁴] 'go' [V]
(66) [caɫ¹] 'walk' [N]	(73)[caɫ²] 'walk' [V]
(67) [bar⁴] 'come' [N]	(74) [bar¹] 'come' [V]
(68) [biṳːk¹] 'herd' [N]	(75) [biṳːk²] 'herd' [V]
(69) [pɪŋ⁴] 'hear, listen' [N]	(76) [pɪŋ¹] 'hear' [V]

Table 4 Changing syntactic category

Fourth, tones seem to be able to encode the presence of a direct object (see Table 5). Specifically, when a direct object becomes explicit, the tonal value of the main verb changes and all breathy segments become non-breathy.

Implicit direct object	Explicit direct object
(77) duɔ²nɛ¹　　cam¹ 　NEG.2SG　　2SG.eat 'Don't eat' (2rd sg)	(79) duɔ²nɛ¹　　cam⁴ 　NEG.2SG.it　2SG.eat.**it** Don't eat it (2rd sg)
(78) duɔ²kɛ¹　　cam¹ 　NEG.2PL　　2PL.eat Don't eat (2rd pl)	(80) duɔ²kɛ¹　　cam⁴ 　NEG.2PL.it　2PL.eat.**it** Don't eat it (2rd pl)

Table 5 Direct object

Fifth, a suffix [ɛ] with two kinds of tones indicates whether objects are visible and can be pointed at (i.e., deixis, distance information) (see (81)-(84)). When a suffix -ɛ with Tone 1 is attached to an object noun, it means that people are able to point at this object (equal to the usage of 'this' in English) and that this object is visible (cf. (81) and (82)). However, when a suffix -ɛ with Tone 4 is attached to an object noun, it either means that people could point at that object or that the object is too far away to be pointed at (the general usage of 'that' in Dinka, cf. (83) and (84)). That is, the suffix -ɛ with Tone 4 is unspecified for proximal/distal, while the suffix -ɛ with Tone 1 is explicitly proximal. In addition to the suffix -ɛ, the demonstrative ti can be used to denote that object can be pointed at (specific usage of 'that' in Dinka) (cf. (85) and (86)).

-ɛ: this (pointing)	-ɛ: that (pointing & unseen)	ti: that (pointing)
(81) jɛ θɔn.ɛ¹ DEM. bull.this-proximal 'this bull'	(83)) jɛ θɔn.ɛ⁴ DEM. bull.that-proximal-or-distal 'that bull'	(85) jɛ θɔn ti DEM. bull that-proximal 'that bull'
(82) jɛ a²mal.ɛ¹ DEM. sheep.this-proximal 'this sheep'	(84) jɛ a²mal.ɛ⁴ DEM. sheep.proximal-or-distal 'that sheep'	(86) jɛ a²mal ti DEM. sheep that-proximal 'that sheep'

Table 6 Demonstratives

5. The Contexts of Tone Sandhi

According to my current data, tone sandhi is a mystery that needs further study. Here I present my observation rather than concrete explanation. One tone sandhi rule seems to be found in Twic East Dinka: Tone 4 will become Tone 3 when it precedes another Tone 4, as in (87). For example, when (88) [cɛ⁴] 'past' and (25) [piu⁴] 'water' are combined together in a sentence (as in 89), [cɛ⁴] will become [cɛ³]. This tone sandhi rule could also be applied to (91) (cɛ⁴ + tɔŋ⁴ → cɛ³ + tɔŋ⁴). However, if Tone 4 precedes Tone 2, no tone sandhi will occur (cf. (90)). That is, that this tone sandhi rule would apply in (91) if it were not blocked by a following Tone 2. Given this, perhaps Twic East Dinka exhibits an OCP constraint (Obligatory Contour Principle) that prohibits two identical tones adjacent to each other (see OCP in Leben 1973, Goldsmith 1976, Kager 1999). Nevertheless, one caveat is warranted: (88)-(91) are all examples of one specific structure (PST + N). Therefore further studies should investigate other structures to see if the tone sandhi rule (87) applies throughout the phonology.

In fact, I did find one exception in an imperative structure as in (92). No tone sandhi happens even though two Tone 4 (i.e., dɪt⁴ + gʌc⁴) syllables are put together. In my further studies, I will also look at whether other imperative sentences also exhibit this kind of phenomena.

(87) Tone 4→ Tone 3/ __ + Tone 4

(88) [cɛ⁴] 'past', [jɔr³] 'find' [N] (25) [piu⁴] 'water'

(89) ɣɛn² cɛ³ piu⁴ jɔr¹
I   PST water find
'I have found water'

(90) [tɔŋ⁴] 'eggs' [PL]   (13) [tꭐɔŋ²] 'egg' [SG]

(90) ɣɛn² cɛ⁴ tꭐɔŋ² ɣa:c
I   PST egg   buy
'I have bought an egg'

(91) ɣɛn² cɛ³ tɔŋ⁴ ɣa:c
I   PST eggs buy
'I have bought eggs'

(92) dɪt⁴ gʌc⁴
     wait people
'Wait for people' (imperative)

In (93)-(97) are shown examples of the same tonal value for the main verb (i.e., Tone 1), but different tonal values of the direct objects from Tone 21 to Tone 4. However, no tone sandhi occurs, which implies that these five combinations, (Tone 1 + Tone 21), (Tone 1 + Tone 1), (Tone 1 + Tone 2), (Tone 1 + Tone 3), and (Tone 1 + Tone 4), do not induce tone sandhi.

Crucially, it seems that the OCP does not constrain and affect (Tone 1 + Tone 1) like (Tone 4 + Tone 4)[1]. It might be interesting to examine the other three combinations (Tone 21 + Tone 21), (Tone 2 + Tone 2), and (Tone 3 + Tone 3) to see whether the OCP could be applied to these three combinations.

(93) ɣɛn² tar¹ kuin²¹ I cook.PST prepared.food 'I am cooking the prepared food'	(96) ɣɛn² tar¹ wɪn³ I cook.PST cow 'I am cooking a cow'
(94) ɣɛn² tar¹ mɪl¹ I cook.PST general food 'I am cooking the general food'	(97) ɣɛn² tar¹ dɪt⁴ I cook.PST bird 'I am cooking a bird'
(95) ɣɛn² tar¹ tuɔŋ² I cook.PST egg 'I am cooking an egg'	

I also found a complex tonal change in one specific structure, N1 of N2— possessive structure. In (104), Tone 4 ([dɪt⁴] 'bird') will become Tone 21 when following a word starting with Tone 1 ([dɛ¹] 'of') (i.e., Tone 4→ Tone 21/ Tone 1+ __). It looks like Twic East Dinka will try to decrease the perceptual difference of tones when two adjacent

---

[1] Yip (2002) said that in African languages, sometimes OCP can be violated to satisfy other higher ranked OT constraints.

tones sound distinct (Tone 1 + Tone 4: Tone 2 and Tone 3 lies between them). It might be worthy to see whether the combinations of (Tone 21 + Tone 4) or (Tone 2 + Tone 4) also induce any tone sandhi that could make the tonal values of two adjacent tones become closer to each other.

In (105), Tone 3 ([nar¹] 'fathers') becomes Tone 2 when *preceding* Tone 2 (i.e., Tone 3→ Tone 2/ __ + Tone 2). In (112), Tone 3 (gʌc³) becomes Tone 2 when *following* Tone 2 (i.e., Tone 3→ Tone 2/ Tone 2 + __). Surprisingly, both tone sandhi phenomena will make two adjacent tones identical, which contradicts what the OCP proposes. More data like (105) and (112) need to be collected to figure out this puzzle.

In (110), Tone 1 ([ra:n¹] 'person') becomes Tone 3 when following a word starting with Tone 1 ([dɛ¹] 'of') (i.e., Tone 1→ Tone 3/ Tone 1 __). However, in (111), Tone 1 does not become Tone 3, even though it follows another Tone 1. Is this tone sandhi random or predicable? If it is predicable, perhaps it is possible that this tone sandhi rule interacts with plurality. That is, this tone sandhi happens only when both N1 and N2 are singular. If either N is plural (i.e., [kɛ²] 'of' gets involved), then no tone sandhi will happen. In order to figure out whether this tone sandhi is predicable, any further study should look at more tonal examples about 'N1 of N2' like (110) and (111).

(98) [dɪt⁴] 'bird'   (99) [dier¹] 'birds'
(19) [nɔk³] 'feather'   (100) [nar¹] 'fathers'
(101) [bu²ro¹] 'cat'   (102) [bu¹ra¹] 'cats'
(53) [jɪt⁴] 'ear'   (54) [jɪh¹] 'ears'
(11) [ra:n¹] 'person'   (24) [gʌc³] 'people'
(7) [ɣam¹] 'thigh'   (103) [rɔ:m¹] 'thighs'

(104) nɔn³   dɛ¹ dɪt²¹   (105) nar²   kɛ² dɪt⁴
      feather of   bird   feathers of   bird
      'bird's feather'   'bird's feathers'

(106) nar¹   kɛ² dier¹
      feathers of birds
      'birds' feathers'

(107) jɪn⁴ dɛ¹ bu²ro¹   (108) jɪh¹ kɛ² bu²ro¹
      ear of cat   ears of cat
      'cat's ear'   'cat's ears'

(109) jɪh¹ kɛ² bu¹ra¹
      ears of   cats
      'cats' ears'

(110) ɣam¹ dɛ¹ ra:n³   (111) rɔ:m¹ gɛ¹ ra:n¹
      thigh of   person   thighs of person
      'person's thigh'   'person's thighs'

(112) rɔ:m¹ kɛ² gʌc²
      thighs of people
      'people's thighs'

In addition to tone sandhi, I also found an interesting phenomenon regarding nasalization. Regarding (104), (107) and (110), it is possible that a floating feature [nasal] is on an initial consonant [d] of the word ([dɛ¹]). When word A precedes [d] of [dɛ¹], that floating feature [nasal] will be specified and linked to that final oral consonant of word A. If that final consonant of the word is a nasal, then no nasalization will occur. Note that this could not be explained by [+anterior] assimilation. If this is [+anterior] assimilation, a final consonant [m] of [ɣam] in (110) should become [n], since [n] shares a feature [+anterior] with [d] of [dɛ¹]. However, in (110), [m] of [ɣam] does not change into [n].

This nasalization also occurs in another structure as shown in (113). In (113), when (98) [dɪt⁴] 'bird' and (57) [dɪt¹] 'big' are combined together, [dɪt⁴] 'bird' will change into [dɪn⁴]. Interestingly, even if a phrase (115) 'big singing' is made up, nasalization still occurs.

(98) [dɪt⁴] 'bird' [N]   (63) [dɪr⁴] 'bigness'

(113) dɪn⁴] dɪt¹]
      bird big
      'big bird'

(114) [kɛt⁴] 'singing' [N]

(115) kɛn⁴   dɪt¹
      singing big
      'big singing'

6. Conclusion

Twic East Dinka, a tonal language, has abundant morphophonological alterations and complex tone sandhi. My current study tried to answer three research questions, namely (1) how many surface contrastive tones does Twic East Dinka have; (2) What functions do tones have in phonology, morphology, syntax or semantics and (3) What are the contexts of tone sandhi in Twic East Dinka? For question (1), I propose that there are five tones: Tone 21, Tone 1, Tone 2, Tone 3 and Tone 4. Note that these five tones are named after their contours, and not named in sequence like Mandarin tones are. For question (2), five functions of tones are found: (a) tones can distinguish words lexically; (b) tones can distinguish plurality grammatically; (c) tones can alter syntactic categories; (d) tones can mark the presence of a direct object and (e) tones can offer information whether objects are visible to present observers. For question (3), the tone sandhi phenomena are too complex to get a clear picture. Sometimes tone sandhi makes two adjacent identical tones become different, sometimes tone sandhi make two adjacent different tones become the same, and sometimes tone sandhi makes two adjacent different tonal values become closer. For the moment, only one clear tone sandhi rule is found in Twic East Dinka: Tone 4→ Tone 3/ __ + Tone 4. However, this rule might be exclusive to one specific structure (PST + N). More data need to be collected in order to figure out when and where tone sandhi will occur, and what kinds of tone sandhi there are.

References

Andersen, Torben. 1992-1994. Morphological stratification in Dinka: On the alternations of voice quality, vowel length and tone in the morphology of transitive, verbal roots in a monosyllabic language. Studies in African Linguistics, 23, 1-63.

Goldsmith, John. 1976. Autosegmental Phonology. PhD Dissertation, MIT (Published 1979, New York: Garland).

Hyman, Larry. 2010. How to Study a Tone Language, with Exemplification from Oku (Grassfields Bantu, Cameroon). UC Berkeley Phonology Lab Annual Report.

Inkelas, Sharon and Draga Zec. 1988. Serbo-Croatian pitch accent: the interaction of tone, stress, and intonation, Language, Vol. 64(, No. 2), 227-248.

Kager, René. 1999. Optimality Theory. Cambridge: Cambridge University Press.

Leben, William. 1973. Suprasegmental Phonology. PhD Dissertation, MIT.

Proceedings of the 2013 annual conference of the Canadian Linguistic Association.

Remijsen, Bert and Robert Ladd. 2008. The tone system of Luanyjang Dinka. Journal of African Languages and Linguistics, 29(2), 149-189.

Remijsen, Bert. 2010. Tone systems of Dinka dialects. Paper presented at the Fourth European Conference on Tone and Intonation (TIE4), Stockholm University, September 9-11, 2010.

Yip, Moira. 2002. Tone. Cambridge: Cambridge University Press.

Yuan, Michelle. 2013. Ā-fronting in Dinka (Twic East): Evidence for a left-peripheral domain below CP.

Author Index